SEPs, SSOs and FRAND

This book is a very useful reference guide on how de jure and de facto standards are being developed and how these standards compete against each other. The book also looks at how fair, reasonable, and non-discriminatory (FRAND) commitments made to the standard setting organizations (SSOs) are being determined across countries, how these disputes have played out, especially in Asia, and how they can be better dealt with in future globally.

The book gives a broad overview of the business model of dominant standard essential patent (SEP) patentees and analyzes some standards for FRAND licensing of SEPs which are converging in major Asian jurisdictions. It highlights the need for ex ante regulation in the FRAND licensing of SEPs and suggests how we can reconcile conflicts which may arise from different legal standards.

This book provides detailed and comprehensive analysis of recent SEP cases with an emphasis on Asia and will interest anyone who wishes to have more insight into the legal, policy, industrial and economic implications of such issues.

Kung-Chung Liu is Lee Kong Chian Professor of Law (Practice), Director of the Applied Research Centre for Intellectual Assets and the Law in Asia (ARCIALA) at Singapore Management University and also Professor at Renmin University of China.

Reto M. Hilty is Professor and Director of Max Planck Institute for Innovation and Competition, Germany.

Routledge Research in Intellectual Property

Available:

Protecting Intellectual Property in the Arabian Peninsula
The GCC States, Jordan and Yemen
David Price and Alhanoof AlDebasi

Biodiversity, Genetic Resources and Intellectual Property
Developments in Access and Benefit Sharing
Edited by Kamalesh Adhikari and Charles Lawson

Pharmaceutical Patent Protection and World Trade Law
The Unresolved Problem of Access to Medicines
Jae Sundaram

Patent Pools, Competition Law and Biotechnology
Devdatta Malshe

Copyright Law and Derivative Works
Regulating Creativity
Omri Rachum-Twaig

The Patentability of Software
Software as Mathematics
Anton Hughes

Annotated Leading Trademark Cases in Major Asian Jurisdictions
Edited by Kung-Chung Liu

SEPs, SSOs and FRAND
Asian and Global Perspectives on Fostering Innovation in Interconnectivity
Edited by Kung-Chung Liu and Reto M. Hilty

For more information about this series, please visit www.routledge.com/Routledge-Research-in-Intellectual-Property/book-series/INTELLPROP

SEPs, SSOs and FRAND

Asian and Global Perspectives on Fostering Innovation in Interconnectivity

Edited by Kung-Chung Liu and Reto M. Hilty

Routledge
Taylor & Francis Group
LONDON AND NEW YORK

First published 2020
by Routledge
2 Park Square, Milton Park, Abingdon, Oxon OX14 4RN

and by Routledge
52 Vanderbilt Avenue, New York, NY 10017

Routledge is an imprint of the Taylor & Francis Group, an informa business

First issued in paperback 2021

British Library Cataloguing-in-Publication Data
A catalogue record for this book is available from the British Library

Library of Congress Cataloging-in-Publication Data
Names: Liu, Kongzhong, 1961– editor. | Hilty, Reto M., 1958–, editor.
Title: SEPs, SSOs and FRAND : Asian and global perspectives on fostering innovation in interconnectivity / edited by Kung-Chung Liu and Reto M. Hilty.
Other titles: Standard-Essential Patents, Standard Setting Organizations and Fair, Reasonable, and Non-Discriminatory
Description: New York : Routledge, 2019. | Series: Routledge research in intellectual property | Includes bibliographical references and index.
Identifiers: LCCN 2019037222 (print) | LCCN 2019037223 (ebook) | ISBN 9780367429379 (hardback) | ISBN 9781003000259 (ebook)
Subjects: LCSH: Foreign licensing agreements. | Patent licenses. | Standardization—Law and legislation. | Patents (International law)
Classification: LCC K1530 .S47 2019 (print) | LCC K1530 (ebook) | DDC 346.04/86—dc23
LC record available at https://lccn.loc.gov/2019037222
LC ebook record available at https://lccn.loc.gov/2019037223

ISBN: 978-0-367-42937-9 (hbk)
ISBN: 978-1-03-208329-2 (pbk)
ISBN: 978-1-003-00025-9 (ebk)

Typeset in Galliard
by Apex CoVantage, LLC

Contents

Illustrations

Figures

Tables

Contributors

Feroz Ali, Department of Industry Policy and Promotion, Ministry of Commerce and Industry Chair on Intellectual Property Rights, Indian Institute of Technology, Madras, India.

Felix Conde, PhD candidate, Institute for Intellectual Property Management, School of Management, Zhejiang University, China.

Peter Damerell, Partner, Powell Gilbert LLP.

Biswajit Dhar, Professor, Centre for Economic Studies and Planning, School of Social Sciences, Jawaharlal Nehru University, India.

Liyang Hou, Associate Professor, KoGuan Law School, Shanghai Jiao Tong University, China.

Shengtao Hu, Director, IPR Policy, Ericsson.

Can Huang, Professor, Co-Director of Institute for Intellectual Property Management, Head of Department of Innovation, Entrepreneurship and Strategy, School of Management, Zhejiang University, China.

William Hubbard, Professor, School of Law, University of Baltimore, USA.

Sang Jo Jong, Professor of Intellectual Property Law, Seoul National University, South Korea.

Reji K. Joseph, Associate Professor, Institute for Studies in Industrial Development, India.

Jinyul Ju, Professor, Pusan National University School of Law, Korea.

Jyh-An Lee, Associate Professor, Assistant Dean for Undergraduate Studies, Director of the LLB Programme, City University of Hong Kong.

Matthias Leistner, Professor, Ludwig Maximilians University of Munich, Germany.

Lanhua Li, PhD candidate, Institute for Intellectual Property Management, School of Management, Zhejiang University, China.

Kung-Chung Liu, Lee Kong Chian Professor of Law, Director, Applied Research Centre for Intellectual Assets and the Law in Asia, Singapore Management University; Renmin University of China; National Chenchi University (Taiwan).

Burton Ong, Associate Professor, Faculty of Law, National University of Singapore.

Masabumi Suzuki, Professor, Nagoya University Graduate School of Law, Japan.

Prashant Reddy Thikkavarapu, Assistant Professor, National Academy of Legal Studies & Research (NALSAR) University of Law, Hyderabad, India.

Mengchi Tian, Doctoral Candidate, KoGuan Law School, Shanghai Jiao Tong University, China.

Tess Waldron, Senior Associate, Powell Gilbert LPP.

Haoran Zhang, Renmin University of China.

Jiyu Zhang, Associate Professor, Dean Assistant of the Law School, Executive Director of the Law and Technology Institute, Renmin University of China.

1 Introduction

As a matter of standard for Asia and beyond?

Kung-Chung Liu

1 A hot topic that will be even hotter in major Asian economies

The licensing of standard essential patents (SEP) on fair, reasonable and non-discriminatory (FRAND) terms has been a thorny issue for major Asian economies for at least two decades. However, these economies, as beneficiaries of global value chains, are without exception standard-takers rather than standard setters, not the least in the information and communications (ICT) sector.[1] They are strong in manufacturing, management of factories and cutting costs and highly dependent on following the standards and applying related SEPs. Therefore, ICT SEPs owners generated more revenues from these major Asian countries than the rest of the world combined. Taking the world's number one SEP patentee in ICT, Qualcomm, for example, its annual reports show that from the People's Republic of China (PRC, including Hong Kong), South Korea and Taiwan, it has generated 68% (32%, 19% and 17%, respectively) of its revenues in 2011, 78% (42%, 22% and 14%, respectively) in 2012 and 2013, 80% (49%, 20% and 11%, respectively) in 2014 (in the PRC alone USD 13.2 billion), 81.98% (52.75%, 16.23% and 13%) in 2015 (PRC alone USD 13.33 billion), and 86% (57%, 16.63% and 12%) in 2016 (PRC alone USD 13.5 billion).[2]

The same goes for InterDigital, the second-largest SEP patentee in ICT. Its annual reports reveal that the absolute majority of its revenue was derived from Taiwan, South Korea and Japan: 72.15% (27.88%, 34.72% and 12.55%, respectively) in 2014 and 90.6% (63%, 15.6% and 12%, respectively) in 2015.

1 Major standard setting organizations (SSOs) in the ICT sector are all registered in non-Asian countries. Telecommunications Industry Association (TIA), the Alliance for Telecommunications Industry Solutions (ATIS) and Electrical and Electronics Engineers Inc. (IEEE) are registered in the U.S. The European Telecommunication Standard Institute (ETSI) is registered in France.

2 Qualcomm suffered a decrease in revenue of about 11%, from USD 26,487 million in 2014 to USD 23,554 million in 2016. See QUALCOMM Incorporated, 2011–2016 Annual Reports, available at https://investor.qualcomm.com/annual-reports.

InterDigital generated 61.48% of its revenue from Taiwan, China and South Korea (27.88%, 23.24% and 10.36%, respectively) in 2016.[3]

Unfortunately, the Asian manufacturing business generally has a single-digit profit margin of around 5%,[4] and any disputes over FRAND-compliant terms could mean double marginalization and even business life or death. With the rise of the fourth industrial revolution, driven by the internet of things (IoT), 5G, driverless vehicles and artificial intelligence (AI), which relies even more on interconnectivity,[5] more and more new standards and SEPs will emerge, making the issue of FRAND licensing of SEPs even hotter. Another indicator attesting to our observation is that years after antitrust cases have occurred in Japan, Korea, the PRC, Taiwan, India, Germany and the European Union, the U.S. is now also grappling with the issue of FRAND licensing of SEPs, as the U.S. Fair Trade Commission (FTC) and the tech giant Apple separately brought antitrust suits against Qualcomm on January 17 and 20, 2017, in the District Court for the Northern District[6] and Southern District of California.[7]

3 InterDigital enjoyed an increase of revenue of 32% during this period, from USD 403 million in 2014 to USD 432 million in 2015, USD 655 million in 2016, and USD 512 million in 2017. See InterDigital, 2014–2017 Annual Report, available at http://ir.interdigital.com/FinancialDocs.

4 For example in the PRC, the average profit margin in the smartphone industry was 4.8% in 2014, 5.8% in 2015 and 4.7% in 2016. See Ministry of Industry and Information Technology of PRC, China ICT Comprehensive Development Index Research Report, available at http://m.c114.com.cn/w186-1028011.html.

5 See Klaus Schwab, The Fourth Industrial Revolution, World Economic Forum, 2016: 28–30, available at https://luminariaz.files.wordpress.com/2017/11/the-fourth-industrial-revolution-2016-21.pdf.

6 Judge Lucy Koh found in May 2019 that Qualcomm did illegally monopolize markets for the CDMA and 4G LTE modem chips used in premium smartphones, see *FTC v. Qualcomm*, Case 5:17-cv-00220-LHK Document 1490 Filed 05/21/19, available at www.courtlistener.com/recap/gov.uscourts.cand.306945/gov.uscourts.cand.306945.1490.0.pdf.

7 Apple sought declarations with respect to several of Qualcomm's patents and alleged that Qualcomm breached certain agreements and violated federal antitrust laws. Apple also sought declaratory judgments of non-infringement by Apple of nine of Qualcomm's patents, or in the alternative, a declaration of royalties Apple must pay for the patents. Apple further sought a declaration that Qualcomm's sale of baseband chipsets exhausts Qualcomm's patent rights for patents embodied in those chipsets. Separately, Apple sought to enjoin Qualcomm from seeking excessive royalties from Apple and to disgorge royalties paid by Apple's contract manufacturers that the court finds were not FRAND. Apple also claimed that Qualcomm's refusal to make certain payments to Apple under a business cooperation and patent agreement constitutes a breach of contract in violation of California law and sought damages in the amount of the unpaid payments, alleged to be approximately USD 1 billion. In addition, Apple claimed that Qualcomm has refused to deal with competitors in contravention of Qualcomm's agreements with applicable SSOs, has used its market position to impose contractual obligations on Apple that prevented Apple from challenging Qualcomm's licensing practices, has tied the purchase of Qualcomm's CDMA-enabled and "premium" LTE-enabled chipsets to licensing certain of Qualcomm's patents and has required Apple to purchase baseband chipsets exclusively from Qualcomm as a condition of Qualcomm's payment to Apple of certain rebates, in violation of section 2 of the Sherman Act. Apple sought injunctive relief with

Yet there seems to be no ex ante and systematic way of managing this issue, as people still rely on litigation and alternative dispute resolution mechanisms such as settlement and arbitration. Litigation is time-consuming and expensive, whereas settlement and arbitration lack positive externality (there is no disclosure of decisions). The industry is left without clear guidance.

The present book strives to provide some guidance on how de jure and de facto standards are being developed, how standards compete against each other, how FRAND commitments have been determined substantively and procedurally on a global scale, how these disputes have played out, especially in Asia, and how they can be better dealt with in the future. In the following, we will give a broad overview of the business model of dominant SEP patentees (section 2); analyze some standards for FRAND licensing of SEPs which are converging in major Asian jurisdictions (section 3); argue that the FRAND licensing of SEPs needs ex ante regulation, at least in Asia (section 4); and ask how to reconcile conflicts between different legal standards (section 5). This chapter will end with a critical review of a statement made by the leading supporter for strong protection of SEPs.

2 The business model of dominant SEP patentees in the ICT sector

The technological complexity of ICT standards, and also the companies' attempts to systematically file patents in order to license them or obtain freedom to operate through cross-licensing agreements, have resulted in one of the key features of SEPs in the ICT sector, namely its high volume, as the 2017 Science for Policy report "Licensing Terms of Standard Essential Patents" by the Joint Research Centre (JRC), the European Commission's (EC) science and knowledge service, shows in the following.[8]

As of September 2018, one source indicates that Qualcomm has a total of 46,489 granted patents and 106,500 patent applications distributed into 28,730 patent families.[9] As of December 31, 2017, Huawei held a total of 74,326

respect to these claims and a judgment awarding its expenses, costs and attorneys' fees; see Case 3.17-cv-00108-GPC-NLS Document 1 Filed 01/20/17 PageIP.2. However, Apple and Qualcomm settled this dispute on April 16, 2019. As Daniel Ives commented, "Ultimately, Apple realized this was more about two kids fighting in the sandbox and they have bigger issues ahead with 5G and iPhone softness versus battling Qualcomm in court", see http://time.com/5572162/apple-qualcomm-dispute-iphone/.

8 Chryssoula Pentheroudakis & Justus Baron, Licensing Terms of Standard Essential Patents, Joint Research Centre (JRC) Science for Policy report, 2017, available at https://ec.europa.eu/jrc/en/publication/eur-scientific-and-technical-research-reports/licensing-terms-standard-essential-patents-comprehensive-analysis-cases, at 31.

9 See www.patsnap.com/resources/innovation/qualcomm. According to Qualcomm's website, it has 130,000+ patents and patent applications worldwide, see www.qualcomm.com/news/media-center/quick-facts.

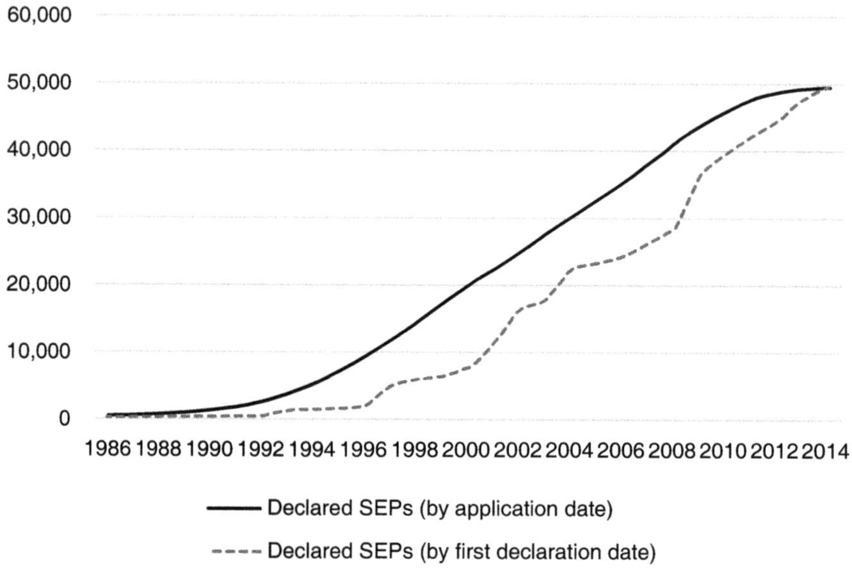

Figure 1.1 Cumulative number of declared SEPs by application and first declaration date

patents,[10] and InterDigital held a patent portfolio of approximately 19,000 patents and patent applications.[11]

To manage patent portfolios of such volume, SEP patentees tend to set up a 100% owned subsidiary to hold all their patents, which include SEPs. Qualcomm and InterDigital are the two commonly known instances, and MediaTek (a Taiwanese company) less so.[12] The patent portfolios are licensed in a package, bundling the SEPs with non-SEPs, and the licensees can only either take the whole package or leave it. Licensing of individual patents based on individual licensing negotiation is simply not feasible. As any patent portfolio, the patents of these SEP holders' patent bundles are in flux, as some older ones will expire and new ones will flow in. This leads to a point of conflict between SEP patentees and licensees, where the latter could complain about having to pay for patents that they do not really need or use or that are no longer valid.

In addition, based on Apple's complaint against Qualcomm, Qualcomm's business model is summarized in Figure 1.2:

10 See www.gizmochina.com/2018/04/26/world-intellectual-property-day-huawei-reveals-it-has-74397-patents-as-at-dec-2017/.

11 See www.uspto.gov/sites/default/files/documents/comment-interdigital.pdf.

12 MediaTek has set up such a patent holding company in Singapore in 2004 – obviously also for tax reasons.

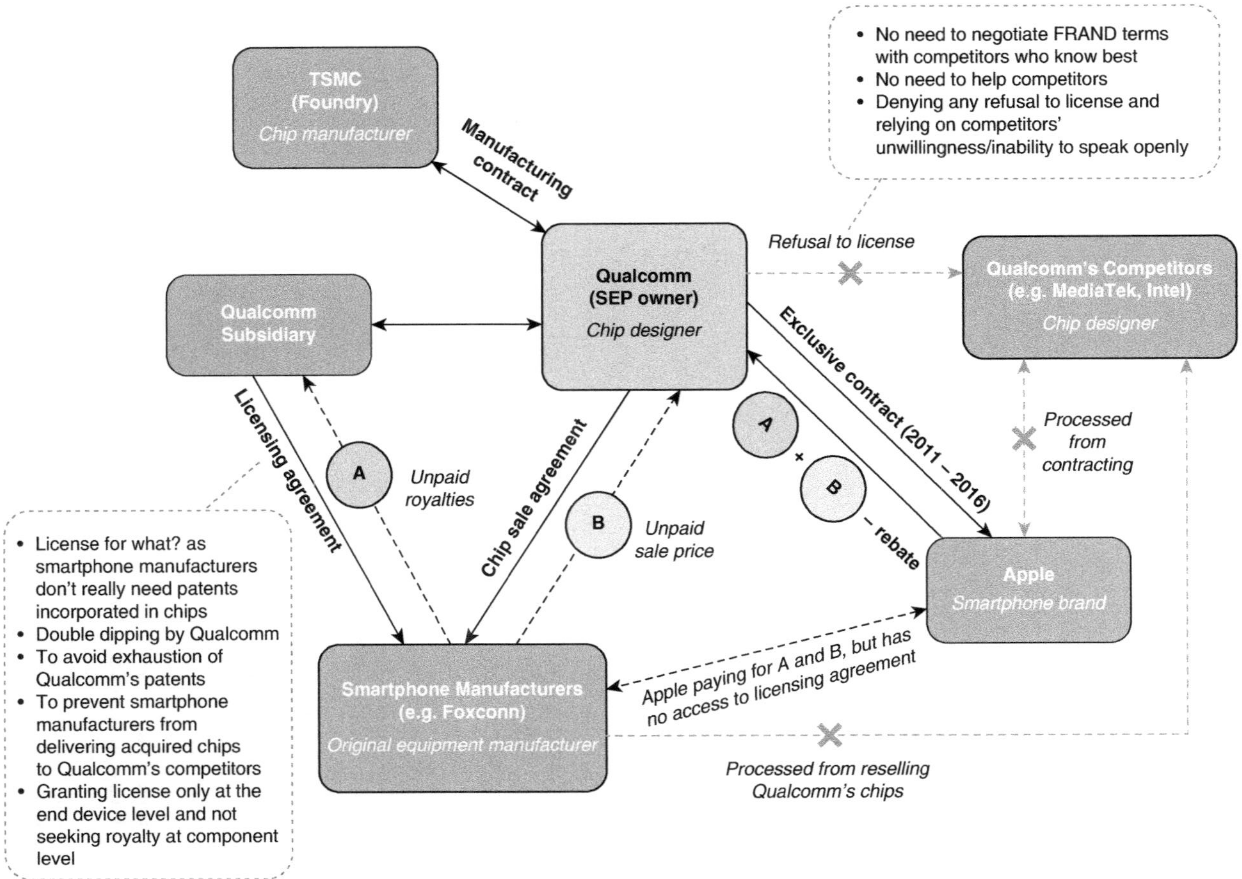

Figure 1.2 Qualcomm's business model

Although Qualcomm has made FRAND licensing commitments to SSOs, it has consistently refused to license its SEPs to competing chip designers,[13] such as Intel and MediaTek, which eliminated the possibility of a FRAND rate with Qualcomm being negotiated by its competitors, who are best placed to do so because they know the technology and are immune from a threatened chipset supply disruption. By refusing to license its competitors, Qualcomm made them work around its SEPs, which is very costly and would delay their competition. In addition, Qualcomm has disputes with its licensees over the interpretation of the FRAND-compliant terms.[14]

But as far as mobile phone manufacturers are concerned, all they want from Qualcomm is to buy its chips, which actually incorporated all of Qualcomm's SEPs, and they are not interested in getting SEP licenses to work the technology of the SEPs. Since the patents are now being held by a separate subsidiary company and licensed out by the company, Qualcomm maintains a "no license, no chips" policy, asking OEM mobile phone manufacturers supplying brand names such as Apple to sign a patent package licensing agreement with its licensing subsidiary, or there will be no supply of chips.

Once the patent portfolio licensing agreement is signed, Qualcomm's chips are delivered as part of the licensing agreement and not a sale per se, which Qualcomm hopes will not exhaust its patent rights. The licensing agreement, not the sales agreement, prohibits its licensees from reselling the thus acquired chips to Qualcomm's competitors and also contains a non-disclosure agreement (NDA). However, OEM mobile phone manufacturers, after paying royalties to Qualcomm, will be reimbursed by Apple. This is why, when Apple sued Qualcomm for antitrust violation and ceased to reimburse its contract manufacturers, the latter ceased to pay royalties to Qualcomm and were immediately sued by Qualcomm.[15] That is also why Qualcomm has signed an exclusive business cooperation and patent agreement with Apple from 2011 to 2016,[16] which prevents

13 Qualcomm denies it has refused to license, but Intel and MediaTek have never been able to secure a licensing agreement from Qualcomm. In *FTC v. Qualcomm*, Judge Koh asked Qualcomm to license its SEPs to competing suppliers of modem chips on FRAND terms. Case 5:17-cv-00220-LHK Document 1490 Filed 05/21/19, 229.

14 For the many legal proceedings on this issue with Qualcomm's Taiwanese licensees, see Kung-Chung Liu, Chapter 8 of the present book.

15 On May 17, 2017, Qualcomm filed a complaint in the U.S. District Court for the Southern District of California against FIH Mobile Ltd. and Hon Hai Precision Industry Co., Ltd. (together known as Foxconn), Pegatron Corporation, Wistron Corporation and Compal Electronics, Inc. – the four manufacturers of all Apple iPhones and iPads – for breaching their license agreements and other commitments with Qualcomm and refusing to pay for use of Qualcomm's licensed technologies. See *Qualcomm Inc. v. Compal Electronics Inc., FIH Mobile Ltd., Hon Hai Precision Industry Co., Ltd., Pegatron Corp. and Wistron Corp.*, U.S. District Court for the Southern District of California, Case No. 3:17-cv-01010-GPC-MDD. The case was later dropped as a result of settlement between Apple and Qualcomm.

16 The business cooperation and patent agreement that Apple has signed with Qualcomm is not understandable since Apple's contract manufacturers have already signed a patent licensing agreement with Qualcomm, unless there is some arrangement in the business cooperation and patent agreement that asks or allows Apple to pay or absorb the royalty of its contract manufacturers. It would not make economic sense for Apple's contract manufacturers to

Apple from buying chips from Qualcomm's competitors, as engagement with Apple helps modem-chip suppliers improve the quality of their products and provides Apple with rebate in return. Apple sued Qualcomm almost immediately after the business cooperation and patent agreement expired.

3 Standards for FRAND licensing of SEPs in the ICT sector: from Asia to the world?

To some extent, some standards for FRAND licensing of SEPs are converging in major Asian jurisdictions such as Japan, Korea, the PRC, Taiwan and India. Worth reflecting on is whether these standards for FRAND licensing of SEPs can be extended to reach beyond Asia.

3.1 Standards on FRAND licensing of SEPs in Asia: 3 Nos and 1 Yes

3.1.1 No to bundling non-SEPs with SEPs

Competition authorities in Korea (Qualcomm II case),[17] the PRC (*NDRC v. Qualcomm*),[18] Japan,[19] and Taiwan[20] blacklist "the compelling of the licensing to purchase, accept or use patents or technical know-how that he does not need". Specifically, these economies make it illegal per se to bundle licenses of SEPs with those of non-SEPs by SEP holders which have dominant market power.

3.1.2 No to continual payment of royalty after the expiration of SEPs

A natural consequence of the standard listed in subsection 3.1.1 is that once patents (whether SEPs or non-SEPs) expire, the licensees should not be required to continue to pay royalty for them. Competition authority in Korea (Qualcomm case I),[21] the PRC (*NDRC v. Qualcomm*)[22] and Taiwan (Philips CD-R case) indeed take this stance.

---

have agreed to first pay royalty to Qualcomm out of their own pockets and get reimbursed later, as they operate on a small profit margin and such payment would be too big a financial burden. On the other hand, Qualcomm would prefer to be paid not by the OEM mobile phone manufacturers either but rather directly by the brand names they are supplying, as only in this way can Qualcomm charge royalty by the price of the whole device and not by the very meagre price of stand-alone chips.

17 For more details, see Jinyul Ju, Chapter 10 of the present book.

18 For more details, see Liyang Hou and Mengchi Tian, Chapter 11 of the present book.

19 The Japanese Fair Trade Commission (JFTC), Guidelines for the Use of Intellectual Property under the Antimonopoly Act (2016 last amended), Part 4(5)(iv).

20 The TFTC Guidelines on Technology Licensing Agreements (last amended in 2016), 6.6.

21 See Byungil Kim, Anti-competitive Licensing Practice: Qualcomm's Abuse of Market Dominance, in Kung-Chung Liu (ed.), *Annotated Leading Patent Cases in Major Asian Jurisdictions* (City University of HK Press, 2017), 188.

22 Li Jing & Lin Xiuqin, Anti-monopoly Case Against Qualcomm's Patent Licensing Practice, in Kung-Chung Liu (ed.), *Annotated Leading Patent Cases in Major Asian Jurisdictions* (City University of HK Press, 2017), 219.

3.1.3 No to royalty-free cross-licensing

Competition authorities in Japan (Qualcomm case),[23] Korea (Microsoft/Nokia case, Qualcomm II case) and the PRC (*NDRC v. Qualcomm*) have clearly responded no to royalty-free cross-licensing.

3.1.4 Yes to provisioning of patent lists

Competition authorities in Korea,[24] the PRC (*NDRC v. Qualcomm*) and Taiwan (Philips CD-R case) demand that SEP holders provide a patent list when negotiating licensing agreements with willing licensees.

3.2 The 3 Nos resemble the *per se* rule under the Nine No-Nos of the U.S. (1970–1995)

The 3 Nos discussed in subsection 3.1 follow the per se illegal approach and might look too rigid. However, they mirror or resemble the "Nine No-Nos" that reigned in the U.S. from 1970 to 1995.[25] From 1995 onward, the "Nine No-Nos" have been replaced by the Antitrust Guidelines for the Licensing of Intellectual Property, which no longer views certain patent licensing agreements as automatically unlawful but subjects them to the rule of reason on a case-by-case basis. The Asian 3 Nos should therefore be treated with equal tolerance, as they might evolve according to changing conditions and mindset.

23 The JFTC issued a cease and desist order against Qualcomm's unfair trade practices on September 30, 2009, relating to Qualcomm's license agreements with Japanese manufacturers. Qualcomm appealed to Tokyo High Court, which on February 12, 2010, stayed the enforcement of the order. The stay will remain in effect throughout the JFTC's full evidentiary hearing on the merits of the order and until the JFTC issues its final decision following the hearing. The JFTC has held hearings on 37 different dates. No further hearing is currently scheduled according to the Qualcomm 2017 Annual Report, available at https://investor.qualcomm.com/static-files/3bee5a52-757b-4ac6-9468-b0102bdc4418, at F31.

24 KFTC, Review Guidelines on the Unfair Exercise of IPRs (2014 amended), 5A(2) provides: "unreasonably failing to disclose information of patents applied for or registered to increase the possibility of those technologies being designated as the standard technologies or to avoid prior negotiation on licensing conditions."

25 Bruce Wilson, former Deputy Assistant Attorney General of the DOJ, Remarks before the Fourth New England Antitrust Conference, Patent and Know-How License Agreements: Field of Use, Territorial, Price and Quantity Restrictions (November 6, 1970), which summarized the Nine No-Nos as (1) tying the purchase of unpatented materials as a condition of the license; (2) requiring the licensee to assign back subsequent patents; (3) restricting the right of the purchaser of the product in the resale of the product; (4) restricting the licensee's ability to deal in products outside the scope of the patent; (5) a licensor's agreement not to grant further licenses (exclusive licensing); (6) mandatory package licenses; (7) royalty provisions not reasonably related to the licensee's sales; (8) restrictions on a licensee's use of a product made by a patented process; and (9) minimum resale price provisions for the licensed products.

3.3 Divergence among Asian jurisdictions

There is also divergence among major Asian jurisdictions on four issues: the legality of FRAND-encumbered SEP owners seeking injunction, the court's role in determining royalty rate, no-challenge clause and charging royalties based on the whole devices. While Korean, Indian and Chinese (Shenzhen) courts issue injunction as a matter of course, Japan's Tokyo IP High Court is of the opinion that this would amount to abuse of right in the context of FRAND commitment.[26] Moreover, courts in Japan (Tokyo IP High Court setting 5% royalty rate in aggregate), the PRC (Shenzhen People's Intermediate Court setting 0.019% royalty rate)[27] and India (*Dolby v. Oppo and Vivo*)[28] follow their counterparts in the U.S. and UK and do not shy away from determining FRAND-compliant terms, whereas Korean and Taiwanese courts have not yet ventured into the business of determining royalty rates for FRAND commitment. Regarding a no-challenge clause, in line with Article 5(1)(b) EU Commission Regulation (EU) No 316/2014 of March 21, 2014, on the application of Article 101(3) of the Treaty on the Functioning of the European Union to categories of technology transfer agreements, the TFTC prohibits no-challenge or no-contest outright (Philips CD-R), as does KFTC.[29] In contrast, JFTC takes a conditional prohibition approach,[30] and the

26 Noteworthy is that Communication from the EU Commission to the European Parliament Setting out the EU approach to Standard Essential Patents (November 29, 2017, COM (2017) 712 final), points out in 3.2. PROPORTIONALITY CONSIDERATIONS: "When assessing the availability of injunctive relief, courts are bound by Article 3(2) of the IPR Enforcement Directive, and notably the requirement to ensure that injunctive relief is effective, proportionate and dissuasive. Given the broad impact an injunction may have on businesses, consumers and on the public interest, particularly in the context of the digitalised economy, the proportionality assessment needs to be done carefully on a case-by-case basis. The Commission feels that considerations need to be given to the relative relevance of the disputed technology for the application in question and the potential spill-over effects of an injunction on third parties."

27 For more also see Jyh-An Lee, The Determination of FRAND Rate for SEPs: *Huawei v. InterDigital*, in Kung-Chung Liu (ed.), *Annotated Leading Patent Cases in Major Asian Jurisdictions* (City University of HK Press, 2017), 203.

28 See Biswajit Dhar and Reji K. Joseph, Chapter 12 of the present book.

29 KFTC, Review Guidelines on Unfair Exercise of Intellectual Property Rights (2014 last amended), 3D(6).

30 JFTC, Guidelines for the Use of Intellectual Property under the Antimonopoly Act (2016 last amended), Part 4(4)(vii) is about no-contest obligation. It states that "Imposing an obligation by a licensor on its licensees not to contest the validity of rights for licensed technology (Note 14) is recognized to have aspects to promote competition by facilitating technology transactions and is unlikely to reduce competition directly. However, it may constitute an unfair trade practice when it is found to tend to impede fair competition by continuing rights that should be invalidated and by restricting the use of the technology associated with the said rights. In principle, stipulating termination right of the agreement for the technology with any licensee that challenges the validity of rights may not constitute unfair trade practices."

2017 consultation draft "Guidelines on Abuse of IPRs" by the Antimonopoly Committee of State Council PRC takes a rule of reason approach.[31]

On the issue of charging royalties for SEPs based on the whole devices or the smallest saleable patent practicing unit (SSPPU), competition authorities in the PRC, Korea and Taiwan do not require that the calculation of FRAND-compliant royalties be based on SSPPU. For example, the TFTC concluded in its decision to impose fine on Qualcomm for its alleged abuse of dominant power: "However, since the legitimacy and reasonableness of such clauses (royalty based on the whole devices and free cross-licensing) are full of controversy, they should be left to the equal negotiation (of the parties) or third-party arbitration or court litigation, to ensure the equality of contract negotiation". The Competition Commission of India held in the Ericsson cases that charging "two different license fees per unit phone for use of the same technology prima facie is discriminatory and also reflects excessive pricing vis-à-vis high-cost phones".[32]

3.4 *From Asian to world de facto standards due to commitments made to Asian competition authorities*

The many concrete undertakings that Qualcomm and InterDigital have made to the Chinese competition authorities, the National Development and Reform Commission (NDRC) in China, have the potential of spreading from China and becoming binding on a worldwide scale, as these conglomerates are operating and licensing globally. Legally speaking, these commitments that SEP owners have made should not be limited to any specific jurisdiction and should be applicable irrespective of the location where the licensees are registered. If SEP owners are allowed to apply their undertakings to a certain national competition authority only to that particular jurisdiction and refuse to apply them elsewhere, it can hardly be "non-discriminatory".

4 The FRAND licensing of SEPs needs ex ante regulation, at least in Asia

4.1 *What justifies ex ante regulation?*

4.1.1 *Global litigation as a strong indicator of massive market failure*

The many litigated and pending cases in Asia (between Samsung and Huawei),[33] the EU (*SLC v. Vodafone, Sisvel v. Haier, Huawei v. ZTE*, etc.), the UK (*Unwired*

31 Available at http://fldj.mofcom.gov.cn/article/zcfb/201703/20170302539418.shtml.

32 For more details, see Feroz Ali, Chapter 13 of the present book.

33 The two companies are embroiled in over 40 litigations globally since 2016 and settled all of them in May 2019 under the mediation of Guangdong People's High Court, according to Guangdong Court Net (www.gdcourts.gov.cn/index.php), available at http://210.76.68.2/index.php?v=show&cid=173&id=53683.

Planet v. Huawei, Conversant v. Huawei and ZTE, TQ Delta, LLC v. Zyxel Communications) and the U.S. (*FTC v. Qualcomm, Apple v. Qualcomm* (later settled)) are a strong indicator of massive market failure caused by the imbalance of market power between manufacturers and SEP owners. Such a market failure is indeed very troubling and even debilitating for Asian manufacturers, as they normally operate with extremely low profit margins. Such a market failure will further lead to the lessening of competition and innovation and welfare loss of consumers. Ex post intervention by way of competition law is generally costly and time-consuming, and therefore it might not be adequate. The need for and importance of collective management of patents must be taken seriously. SSO could play a more active role.

4.1.2 SEPs equal monopoly or joint monopoly and justifying ex ante intervention

SSOs, such as ETSI, normally require members to declare during the process of standard setting if they have SEPs and are willing to license those SEPs on FRAND terms before incorporating them into standards. Patent owners will principally declare their SEPs as early as possible. In addition, to avoid any possible antitrust liability for not having declared beforehand, patent owners tend to declare broadly that their patents are SEPs. In reality, not every declared SEP is necessarily technologically or commercially essential. However, the essentiality of those declared SEPs will not be checked by any institution. Even licensees will not verify this issue, for two reasons: there is no need to challenge it, as those patents are already part of the standard; and verifying the essentiality of all SEPs would be simply infeasible due to prohibitive expenditure on time and resources and possibly the lack of technical capability. As a result, SEPs would become irreplaceable for licensees, and SEP owners would acquire market power nearing monopoly or joint monopoly. What Fairfield Resources International, Inc., the Association of Radio Industries and Businesses of Japan and the Telecommunications Technology Association of South Korea did in 2008 is a rare exception, namely conducting an evaluation about the essentiality of the 1,889 declared SEP families within the 3GPP and finding only some 529 genuine SEPs.[34]

4.1.3 De facto standards overtaking de jure standards

With globalization and worldwide interconnection, SSOs from the private sector are replacing sovereign states in the development and adoption of new standards. De jure standards need to work hard to catch up with the progress of de facto standards. In the mobile internet era, de facto standards have overtaken de jure

34 See Tokyo IP High Court, 2013 (Ne) 10043 (May 16, 2014), available at www.ip.courts.go.jp/eng/vcms_lf/25ne10043full.pdf, at 132.

standards. Market forces transcend national borders, which makes the measured ex ante intervention necessary.

4.2 General intervention

4.2.1 To qualify the FRAND commitment by the SEP owner as contract with third-party beneficiary

Common law jurisdictions such as the U.S. and UK treat FRAND commitment between the SEP owner and an SSO as a contract with a third-party beneficiary. This third-party beneficiary is not a party to the contract itself, but once the contract is fulfilled, the third party stands to realize a benefit, here the signing of a licensing agreement for SEPs. Under certain circumstances, the third party is legally entitled to enforce the contract or share in its proceeds.[35] In contrast, civil law jurisdictions typically treat the FRAND commitment as a self-imposed unilateral obligation by the SEP owner, not a contract with a third-party beneficiary (Vertrag zu Gunsten Dritter), and any third party does not yet enjoy any right to use SEPs. The German Civil Code (Bürgerlichen Gesetzbuch) does not recognize contract with a third-party beneficiary that is of property (in rem, or 'dinglich' in German) nature, but only the ones that are of obligation (in personam) nature, as it follows the principle of certainty (Bestimmtheitsgrundsatz). The principle of certainty requires that an act of disposition, which is of "property" nature, is only allowable when the scope of such undertaking is certain or at least sufficiently ascertainable. The purpose of the principle of certainty is to protect the debtor's interest in being able to estimate the scope of the obligation towards the third party. Therefore, it prohibits contract with a third-party beneficiary with property effect when the third party is not certain or at least not sufficiently ascertainable. Patent licensing is considered to be a property act in addition to a "written surrender"[36] with the "property effects" that can universally exclude the patentee from exercising his patent right when infringed upon.

However, this traditional view does not match the intangible nature of patent as IP right. What is required of a patentee when he commits to issue license to any third party (willing licensee) is that he tolerates the latter's use of his patent rights, with financial returns (patent licensing) or without financial returns (de facto partial surrender), and will not impose an unforeseeable duty or overburden the patentee.[37] Therefore, even under civil law, FRAND commitment by the SEP

35 *Microsoft Corp. v. Motorola, Inc.*, 696 F.3d 872 (9th Cir. 2012); *Apple Inc. v. Motorola, Inc.*, No. 2012-1548 (Fed. Cir. April 25, 2014).

36 Article 20 of the German Patent Act stipulates: "The patent shall lapse if 1. the proprietor of the patent surrenders it by written declaration to the German Patent and Trade Mark Office, or 2. the annual renewal fee or the difference is not paid in due time."

37 German scholars are now beginning to advocate that the FRAND commitment by the SEP owner could qualify as contract with a third-party beneficiary, depending on the agreement between SEP holders and the respective SSO; see Reto Hilty & Peter Slowinski,

owner should also qualify as a contract with a third-party beneficiary with the SSO. The commitment alone does yet not bestow upon third parties any right with "property effect" to use SEPs, but equips willing licensees (third-party beneficiaries) with a right to concluding a licensing agreement and immunity from injunctive relief. Although the terms and conditions still need to be worked out between parties, they remain ascertainable. SEP owners will not be entangled in unforeseeable risks. Without recognizing contractual relations between SEP holders, SSOs, and implementers, the courts would need to apply a general legal provision or doctrine to parties.[38] In contrast, with a smoothly functioning contract with a third-party beneficiary, the utility of SEPs will be maximized and the purpose of SSOs fulfilled.[39]

4.2.2 To reexamine Georgia-Pacific factors for determining reasonable royalty

In the U.S., the so-called *Georgia-Pacific* factors are widely used by courts in their determination of reasonable royalty. The 15 factors are:

1. Royalties patentee receives for licensing the patent in suit.
2. Rates licensee pays for use of other patents comparable to the patent in suit.
3. Nature and scope of license in terms of exclusivity and territory/customer restrictions.
4. Licensor's established policy and marketing program to maintain patent monopoly by not licensing others to use the invention.
5. Commercial relationship between licensor and licensee, such as whether they are competitors or inventor and promoter.
6. Effect of selling the patented specialty in promoting sales of other products of the licensee; the existing value of the invention to the licensor as a generator of sales of his non-patented items; and the extent of such derivative or convoyed sales.
7. Duration of patent and term of license.
8. Established profitability of the products made under the patent, its commercial success and its current popularity.
9. Utility and advantages of patent property over old modes and devices.
10. The nature of the patented invention; the character of the commercial embodiment of it as owned and produced by the licensor; and the benefit of those who have used the invention.

Standardessentielle Patente – Perspektiven außerhalb des Kartellrechts, *GRUR Int.* 788 (2015).

38 Chinese, Japanese and Korean courts have done so. For more, see Jyh-An Lee and Sang Jo Jong, Chapter 6 of the present book.

39 Reto Hilty & Peter Slowinski, Standardessentielle Patente – Perspektiven außerhalb des Kartellrechts, *GRUR Int.* 788 (2015).

11 The extent to which the infringer has made use of the invention and the value of such use.
12 The portion of profit or selling price customarily allowed for the use of the invention.
13 The portion of realizable profit attributable to the invention as distinguished from non-patented elements, significant features or improvements added by the infringer, the manufacturing process or business risks.
14 Opinion testimony of qualified experts.
15 Outcome from hypothetical arm's-length negotiation at the time infringement began.[40]

These 15 factors are generally useful for the consideration of reasonable royalty. However, the huge number of licensed patents, the non-exclusiveness of the SEP license, the mandate of equal treatment of licensees and the ex ante nature of the SEP license mean that the following should no longer be applicable: the consideration of ex post factors such as effects of selling the patented specialty in promoting the sales of other products of the licensee, established profitability of the products made under the patent, the character of the commercial embodiment of patented invention as owned and produced by the licensor and the proportion of realizable profit attributable to the invention and so forth. As a result, factors 3, 4, 5, 6, 8, 10 and 13 should be excluded or limited.[41]

4.2.3 To adopt "lump-sum" or "top-down" approach unavoidable

When determining FRAND-compliant terms, a lump-sum or top-down approach seems unavoidable.[42] The approach of adding every patent up (counting every SEP approach) is simply infeasible, and can furthermore lead to royalty stacking and over-patenting by the SEP owners. The lump-sum or top-down approach must factor in all other relevant SEPs.[43] In other words, all relevant SEPs must be taken into consideration as a whole. Ideally, licensees need to pay only one reasonable lump-sum royalty for all the SEPs they require, and SEP owners share this royalty among themselves according to their respective technical contribution. That would greatly enhance the efficiency of SEP licensing and maintain the incentive for innovation. Actually, Tokyo IP High Court in the *Apple v. Samsung*

40 *Georgia-Pacific Corp. v. U.S. Plywood Corp.*, 318 F. Supp. 1116, 1119–2 (S.D.N.Y. 1970), modified and aff'd, 446 F.2d 295 (2d Cir.); *Unisplay, S.A. v. American Electronic Sign Co., Inc.*, 69 F.3d 512, 517 n.7 (Fed. Cir. 1995).

41 See, e.g., *Microsoft Corp. v Motorola, Inc.*, No. C10-1823JLR, 2013 WL 2111217, at *54–65 (W.D. Wash. April 25, 2013); *Ericsson, Inc., et al. v. D-Link Systems, Inc.*, 773 F.3d 1201 (Fed. Cir. 2014).

42 *Unwired Planet International Ltd. v. Huawei Technologies Co.*, UK High Court, Decision of July 21, 2015, [2015] EWHC 2097 (Pat).

43 Mark A. Lemley & Carl Shapiro, A Simple Approach to Setting Reasonable Royalties for Standard-Essential Patents, 28 *Berkeley Tech. L.J.* 1150–1151 (2013).

case (2013 (Ne) 10043) set a 5% royalty cap by referring to the consensus of both parties, Nokia's statement that "the industry-wide aggregate royalty rates for the IPRs for the WCDMA should not exceed 5%", and the practices by the UMTS (Universal Mobile Telecommunications System) related SEP owners as well as the WCDMA patent platform, a patent pool by the UMTS SEP owners, which stipulates in the standard license agreement: standard royalty rate of 0.1% of the ex-factory price for each of the essential patents, and a maximum aggregate royalty rate of 5% for the essential patents. If this aggregate royalty rate exceeds 5%, the standard royalty rate is recalculated so that the aggregate royalty does not exceed 5%. The figure coincides with the estimate of cumulative royalties for smartphones of around 5% globally.

4.3 De lege ferenda suggestion for patent law

4.3.1 To expressly qualify FRAND commitment as contract with third-party beneficiary

There remains substantial uncertainty over whether FRAND commitment can qualify as a contract with a third-party beneficiary, as SSOs might adopt very different practices. Legal certainty can only be achieved based on a special legislative provision, especially when the SSO does not even require its members to make FRAND commitment, as there will not be any contractual limitation on SEP holders' freedom of whether to issue license (and eventually under what terms and conditions), and only at best limitation from competition law. It is therefore conceivable to intervene through positive law by taking two steps. One is to provide a legal fiction that makes every FRAND commitment, no matter how it is formulated or worded, a contract for the third-party beneficiary, namely any willing license seeker. The other is to require SSOs to set standards only against SEP holders' FRAND commitment. The two steps combined can give the willing license seeker the right to the granting of a license.[44]

4.3.2 To expressly allow compulsory licensing in a failed voluntary FRAND licensing of SEPs

Patent law should perhaps deal with SEP-related issues. To leave the licensing of SEPs entirely to individual negotiations between SEP owners and potential licensees can lead to daunting transaction costs and even holdup or holdout, hampering the working of patents, the promotion and implementation of new technology, and standards and market competition. To prevent SEPs from being abused or not sufficiently used, it seems justifiable to explicitly provide for compulsory licensing if voluntary licensing negotiation has proven to be in vain.

44 Reto Hilty & Peter Slowinski, Standardessentielle Patente – Perspektiven außerhalb des Kartellrechts, *GRUR Int.* 790–791 (2015).

To make such compulsory licensing workable in the SEP context, it is worthwhile to explore the desirability of inducing SEP owners to speed up the voluntary licensing negotiation by shortening the "reasonable period" and allowing interim use of SEPs by potential licensees upon deposit of a fair royalty, which is commonly practiced on the market, provided that the actual royalty is subject to later decision by the competent authority.

4.3.3 To mandate the disclosure of FRAND-compliant royalties by SEP owners

It is worth considering the imposition of a duty on SEP owners to disclose the FRAND-compliant royalties that they have charged other licensees. In order to ascertain whether the royalties that the SEP owners are charging are fair and free of discrimination, comparison must be made between the royalties they have charged for the same SEPs, even between royalties they have charged for different SEPs. First, the royalties can hardly be trade secrets, as they are part of the FRAND commitment that would inevitably be subject to examination. Second, even trade secrets are not entirely immune from disclosure, at least to some trustworthy third parties, such as SSOs, courts, competition authorities, and arbitrators, when higher or public interest is at stake. Third, the disclosure of this information will lead to its accumulation, which will in turn enhance the transparency, which is the hallmark of fairness, of the licensing markets for SEPs. With FRAND royalties hidden in the dark, no creditable academic research or oversight from the Fourth Estate is possible, which will encourage patent abuse and trolls.

4.4 De lege ferenda suggestion for antitrust law

4.4.1 To delete special treatment of the exercise of IPRs

Japan, South Korea, Taiwan, the PRC and India are distinct in their ways of dealing with the interface between the exercise of IPRs and antitrust law.[45] They

45 Article 21 of the Japanese Anti-monopolization Act stipulates "The provisions of this Act shall not apply to such acts recognizable as the exercise of rights under the Copyright Act, Patent Act, Utility Model Act, Design Act or Trademark Act." Article 59 (Exercise of Right to Intangible Property) of the Monopoly Regulation and Fair Trade Act of South Korea follows: "The provisions of this Act shall not apply to any act deemed to be a justifiable exercise of rights under the Copyright Act, Patent Act, Utility Models Act, Design Act, or Trademark Act." Article 45 of Taiwan's Fair Trade Act provides conditional immunity: "No provision of this Act shall apply to any proper conduct in connection with the exercise of rights pursuant to the provisions of the Copyright Act, Trademark Act, or Patent Act." Section 3(5) of the Indian Competition Act (2002) follows: "Nothing contained in this section shall restrict – (i) the right of any person to restrain any infringement of, or to impose reasonable conditions, as may be necessary for protecting any of his rights which have been or may be conferred upon him under – (a) the Copyright Act; (b) the Patents Act; (c) the Trade and Merchandise Marks Act, or the Trade Marks Act; (d) the Geographical Indications of Goods

provide various degrees of "special" treatment to the exercise of IPRs, which are unconditionally (in the case of Japan and Korea) or conditionally (in the case of Taiwan, India and the PRC) immune from the scrutiny of antitrust law. This approach is rarely found elsewhere other than Asia. As a matter of fact, IP law as part of the broader competition law is only to be applied in ways that are compatible with competition law. Therefore, the exercise of IPRs is always subject to the check of antitrust law. The unconditional exemption regime is clearly incorrect, and the conditional exemption regime is nothing but an express repetition of what is self-evident, which can only lead to misconception and confusion. These jurisdictions are advised to delete the said special treatment provision from their respective antitrust law.

4.4.2 Competition authorities to actively claim jurisdiction over FRAND licensing of SEPs

SSOs are mostly registered in Europe and the U.S. SSOs' patent or IPR policy often foresees the country where they are registered as the jurisdiction and its law as applicable law when FRAND-related controversies arise. As ETSI is registered in France and it demands that French law be the applicable law, Seoul Central District Court, Korea, applied French law, and the Tokyo IP High Court in case 2013 (Ne) 10043 applied French Civil Law in the determination of the nature of FRAND commitment. The Taiwan IP Court applied Dutch law to determine the royalty and interest rate for delayed payment of royalty.[46] Obviously, there are problems associated with this practice. First, application by IP court judges of foreign law in which they have no expertise contradicts the professionalism that justifies the establishment of IP courts. SEP licensees are forced into agreeing to the application of foreign law of which they are totally ignorant, which can pose unpredictable risks. Furthermore, there is the risk of hollowing out the patent policy of the country where SEP licensees are headquartered. Patent law is powerless to intervene due to the territoriality principle. The need for intervention by antitrust law is evident. Competition authorities are advised to actively claim jurisdiction over FRAND licensing of SEP cases that impact the domestic market, especially when SEP licensees' civil lawsuits against SEP holders for violation of antitrust law have been withdrawn due to arbitration based on a forced arbitration clause or settlement.[47]

(Registration and Protection) Act; (e) the Designs Act; (f) the Semi-conductor Integrated Circuits Layout-Design Act." Article 55 of China's Antimonopoly Act articulates further: "This Law does not govern the conduct of business operators to exercise their intellectual property rights under laws and relevant administrative regulations on intellectual property rights; however, business operators' conduct to eliminate or restrict market competition by abusing their intellectual property rights shall be governed by this Law."

46 Kung-Chung Liu (ed.), *Annotated Leading Patent Cases in Major Asian Jurisdictions* (Hong Kong: City University of HK Press, 2017), pp. 427–438.

47 For more on this see Kung-Chung Liu, Chapter 8 of the present book.

4.4.3 Competition authorities to demand SEP licensors revise arbitration clause

Even if SEP licensees were right in all their antitrust complaints, they would probably not get to the stage where competition authorities or courts can render substantive decisions, as SEP patentees routinely implant an arbitration clause in the PLAs, which will compel licensees to arbitrate rather than to litigate. The result of such arbitration tends to take a formalistic and pure contract law approach to the interpretation of PLA and ignore the dominant market power possessed by SEP licensors and its abuse, as arbitrators will not wish to upset these SEP patentees, who are an important source of income for them.[48]

Also often neglected is the fact that there is no room for equal negotiation for SEP implementers not to agree to an arbitration clause dictated by SEP holders, which would inevitably favor the latter. Therefore, competition authorities are advised to act via promulgating some guidelines to demand that SEP licensors revise the arbitration clause to limit its application scope to pure contractual disputes and exclude antitrust-related ones from arbitration.

4.4.4 To adopt regulated self-regulation: SSOs should play a more important role

It is stunning to see how courts, which are most remote from business reality, in the U.S. and UK dove into the calculation of FRAND-compliant terms. However, in reality no other institutions are better positioned than SSOs to come up with FRAND terms. The WCDMA patent platform did stipulate a standard license agreement for its SEPs. The professional knowledge of SSOs should be put to more use. The other role that SSOs could play would be to provide arbitration service to SEP owners and implementers. At the beginning stage, disputing parties could go through the "baseball-style" or final offer arbitration under the auspices of SSOs, in which each of the parties can make one final offer and the arbitrator can only choose one from the two offers and may not make a decision of his own. To expand the chance of its offer being taken by the arbitrator, each party will do its best to collect and analyze existent FRAND terms, easing the work for arbitrators. SSOs would also do their own collection and analysis of relevant data to empower arbitrators. If in the future SSOs can be the depository for FRAND-compliant royalties by SEP owners as Chapter 17 (3.2) suggested,

48 For example, ICDR issued a final award on April 17, 2013, in a proceeding InterDigital initiated to resolve a dispute surrounding its 2008 PLA with Pegatron and required Pegatron to pay Qualcomm USD 29.9 million, including USD 23.5 million for past patent royalties and USD 6.2 million in interest, and additional amounts for certain arbitration costs and expenses. ICDR further issued a final award on May 13, 2014, in a dispute between Arima and InterDigital regarding Arima's PLA with InterDigital and awarded InterDigital unpaid patent license fees of USD 14.5 million plus USD 9.1 million in interest and related fees and costs.

then SSOs can even more competently provide such service. In addition, SSOs should take the need for collective management of SEPs seriously. They can learn from the examples of the extended collective management of copyright,[49] to form umbrella organizations or arrangements that provide one-stop clearance for both SEP owners and implementers.

In the area of mobile internet standards, SSOs have already taken over the role of nation states and should therefore be subject to a certain degree of oversight and regulation. We suggest the light touch approach, allowing self-regulation to reign first and foremost and initiating intervention from the public sector as the last resort (for more discussion see sections 3 and 4 of Chapter 17).

5 How to reconcile conflicts between different legal standards?

There is some divergence between major Asian jurisdictions and the U.S. and UK. For one thing, major Asian jurisdictions have treated FRAND licensing of SEP as an antitrust issue, and the U.S. and UK have thus far treated this as a pure contract issue.[50] For another, while major Asian jurisdictions have treated the bundling of SEPs with non-SEPs in the licensing of SEPs as per se anticompetitive, the U.S. and UK take it for granted.[51] The conflicts between different legal standards can be solved not by preferring one set of standard over the other but at best through empathy for the differences as to where they are coming from and leading to, and mutual respect for nation states' choice about the path and standard that best suits their developmental need and paradigm system. These differences need not be "harmonized", as they represent diverse values and are the source for inspiration. Dialogue and mutual persuasion is the only reconciliation. In that spirit, the following will address two differences and argue for one standard that allegedly has more merits over the other.

5.1 To bundle SEPs with non-SEPs or not to bundle?

The two seemingly justifiable reasons for SEP owners to bundle SEPs with non-SEPs and license them together are the ease of portfolio management and the guarantee of comprehensive coverage for the licensees. However, "ease of portfolio management" is a faulty one, as SEPs are declared by their owners and they

49 M. Schaefer & C. Czychowski, Wer bestimmt, was FRAND ist? Ein Blick über den patentrechtlichen Tellerrand, *GRUR* 582 (2018).

50 As Justice Birss has said, "it is not necessary to rely on competition law to enforce the FRAND undertaking." See *Unwired Planet International Ltd. v. Huawei Technologies Co.*, UK High Court, Decision of July 21, 2015, [2015] EWHC 2097 (Pat), para. 806(2).

51 In *Unwired Planet v. Huawei*, Justice Birss stated that "Unwired Planet did not abuse their dominant position . . . by bundling SEPs and non-SEPs". See *Unwired Planet International Ltd. v. Huawei Technologies Co.*, UK High Court, Decision of July 21, 2015, [2015] EWHC 2097 (Pat), para. 807(17).

therefore clearly know that these SEPs are separated and different from non-SEPs. With regards to the extent of coverage that the licensees desire, it should be their choice alone. If SEPs owners impose non-SEPs on licensees, the latter would be compelled to accept, leading to an issue of abuse of dominance. Consequently, it is more justified not to bundle SEPs with non-SEPs when licensing the SEPs.

The "unbundled" requirement of the U.S. Telecommunications Act of 1996 could provide a supporting footnote to our advocacy. The law intended to eliminate the monopolies enjoyed by the inheritors of AT&T's local franchises. Therefore, when an entering competitor chooses to lease certain of an incumbent's "network elements", the incumbent cannot refuse, and has in addition a duty to provide them "on an unbundled basis" at terms that are "just, reasonable, and nondiscriminatory".[52]

5.2 *To issue anti-suit injunction or not to?*

Anti-suit injunction is another point of contention between SEP owners who are used to applying for this injunction and licensees who would be compelled to drop their litigation in other jurisdictions and litigate in the jurisdiction where such injunction is issued, rather than their home turf or where the working of SEPs and sale of SEP-protected products is actually taking place. This injunction is enforced by contempt of court order and therefore rare in the Asian jurisdictions we discussed. It is used in the U.S. For example, on May 26, 2015, InterDigital received a civil complaint filed by Pegatron with Taiwan IP Court, alleging that InterDigital abused its market power by improperly setting, maintaining or changing the royalties that Pegatron is required to pay and engaging in unreasonable discriminatory treatment and other unfair competition activities. InterDigital filed a complaint in the Northern District Court of California, seeking injunction against Pegatron prohibiting Pegatron from prosecuting Pegatron's action in Taiwan. On June 29, 2015, the court granted InterDigital's motion for a temporary restraining order and preliminary injunction requiring Pegatron to take immediate steps to dismiss the action in Taiwan. On July 1, 2015, InterDigital was informed that Pegatron had withdrawn its complaint from the TIPC.[53] On April 13, 2018, Judge William Orrick of the Northern District Court of

52 Section 251(c)(3), U.S. Telecommunications Act of 1996.

53 See Kung-Chung Liu, Chapter 8 of the present book. Noteworthy is that Qualcomm's anti-suit injunction against Apple, seeking to temporarily halt 11 separate lawsuits against Qualcomm and its subsidiaries in the UK, Japan, China and Taiwan over many of the same pricing and practices issues as the U.S. case, was rejected on September 9, 2017, by Judge Gonzalo Curiel: "Apple's declarations make evident that it has sought to challenge Qualcomm's patent licensing practices and anticompetitive conduct territory by territory. While Qualcomm may object to this litigation strategy as duplicative, the Court will not conclude that Apple's exercise of its rights under foreign laws is vexatious." See www.reuters.com/article/us-apple-qualcomm/apple-lawsuits-against-qualcomm-can-proceed-u-s-judge-rules-idUSKCN1BJ29V.

California in *Huawei v. Samsung* again issued an order that enjoins Huawei from enforcing an injunction on Chinese SEPs entered by the Chinese People's Court of Shenzhen.[54]

Anti-suit injunction is often used as a means to prevent forum shopping. However, in recent years many jurisdictions have placed a high standard to obtain an injunction, such as where the proceedings are "oppressive or vexatious".[55] We are basically confident that the proceedings in the major Asian jurisdictions discussed here are not "oppressive or vexatious", and these jurisdictions have set up specialized IP courts. The anti-suit injunction should as a matter of principle be no longer made available by courts outside of Asia, especially U.S. courts, against litigation in the said Asian jurisdictions.

6 To debunk "debunking myths at the intersection between intellectual property and competition laws"

Despite efforts by academics and courts around the global to strike a balance between the holdup and holdout problem, advocacy for no government intervention is being drummed up, especially from the U.S., where the most powerful SEP owners originate. For example, in March 2016 David Kappos, the former director of the U.S. PTO, warned that in Taiwan, where the storm of an antitrust investigation against Qualcomm was gathering, "the promise of a remarkable future brought about by the fourth industrial revolution is at risk. Governments and technology users are taking aim at patent-based innovation incentives associated with standards. The very same standards that have been such huge successes are being questioned as if the facts were precisely opposite of what they are". He suggests that "We should comprehend, confront, and dispel key myths surrounding the drivers of innovation in the digital era: SEPs".[56] In the same vein, since November 2017, the U.S. Assistant Attorney General of the Justice Department (DOJ) Makan Delrahim has moved DOJ in a direction that allows SEP owners more freedom to use the exclusionary potential of those patents. DOJ also has redirected its focus toward the conduct of licensees and the SSOs. On December 7, 2018, Delrahim took another step and withdrew DOJ's assent to the more balanced 2013 Joint DOJ-USPTO "Policy Statement on Remedies for

54 Available at https://law.justia.com/cases/federal/district-courts/california/candce/3:2016cv02787/299039/310.

55 In the U.S., under the framework set by the Ninth Circuit in *E.&J. Gallo Winery v. Andina Licores S.A.*, any of four factors can justify an anti-suit injunction, including whether the foreign litigation would "(1) frustrate a policy of the forum issuing the injunction; (2) be vexatious or oppressive; (3) threaten the issuing court's in rem or quasi in rem jurisdiction; or (4) prejudice other equitable considerations." See *E.&J. Gallo Winery v. Andina Licores S.A.*, 446 F.3d 984, 990 (9th Cir. 2006).

56 David Kappos, The *Real* Innovation Economy – Debunking Myths at the Intersection Between Intellectual Property and Competition Laws, available at www.ipleadership.org/articles/real-innovation-economy-debunking-myths-intersection-between-intellectual-property-and.

Standards-Essential Patents Subject to Voluntary F/RAND Commitments".[57] To conclude this chapter, it seems opportune to examine six of the seven myths that Kappos has identified as threats to "our individual and collective growth as countries and trading partners" and the corresponding truths he has professed.

Myth number 1: SEPs lead to licensing holdup. Truth: There have been no documented cases of SEP holders demanding excessive royalties to keep entrants out of a market.[58] We counter that SEPs have been used by certain SEP owners as strategic weapons to block or suppress competition. For example, a document shows that Qualcomm has refused to issue its SEPs license to its archcompetitor MediaTek and Intel despite having made commitment to licensing SEPs on FRAND terms, and extracted an exclusive deal with Apple to keep Qualcomm's competitors away from accessing Apple to test and grow their chips.

Myth number 2: FRAND is broken. Truth: FRAND policies maintain balanced royalty rates that serve the interests of both innovators and implementers.[59] We counter that what constitutes FRAND remains unclear and controversial; comparable terms that would help demystify FRAND have been hidden behind NDA and the pretext of trade secrets, which leads to litigation and needs fixing.

Myth number 3: Royalties stack and impede implementation of standards. Truth: For 20 years there has been no sign of royalty stacking in the mobile telecommunications industry. Instead, cellphone and smartphone prices have declined even as average gross margins of SEP holders were constant.[60] We counter with the question: how can SEP holders maintain the gross margins at a constant 5% despite the price drops of smartphones, if not due to their exploitive SEP licensing practice?

Myth number 4: Patent thickets obstruct innovation. Truth: The history of technology innovation, from sewing machines and airplanes to DVDs and smartphones shows this to be false.[61] We counter that there are now some 10 million valid invention patents globally and 250,000 patents on smartphones. Both innovators and implementers have no overview of this patent thicket, which directly leads to the rise of patent trolls.[62]

57 In particular, the Policy Statement on Remedies for Standards-Essential Patents Subject to Voluntary F/RAND Commitments states: "In some circumstances, the remedy of an injunction or exclusion order may be inconsistent with the public interest. This concern is particularly acute in cases where an exclusion order based on a F/RAND-encumbered patent appears to be incompatible with the terms of a patent holder's existing F/RAND licensing commitment to an SDO", available at: www.justice.gov/atr/page/file/1118381/download, at 5.

58 Chinese translation, 210 IP Monthly by Taiwan IP Office (June 2016) at 80.

59 *Id.* at 83.

60 *Id.* at 86–87.

61 *Id.* at 87–88.

62 Mark Lemley & Douglas Melamed, Missing the Forest for the Trolls, 113 *Columbia L. Rev.* 2117–2189 (2013) (footnote 60).

Myth number 5: In the world of damages calculations, the SSPPU is king.[63] Truth: This theory of basing SEP royalties on small components instead of devices made possible by the SEPs is rooted not in law but in implementers' desire to free ride on the toil of others. We counter one fact and one question. In Asia only one competition commission, that of India, has demanded the adoption of SSPPU. How have the chip SEP owners toiled except in the designing of chips, which are SSPPU? It is the OEMs, such as Foxconn, which have made great contribution in aggregating all components under extremely low profit margins, and smartphone brand names' marketing magic that make the smartphones appealing even at high prices.[64]

Myth number 7: Patents stifle growth. Truth: Again, the history of technological innovation from the first industrial revolution through the digital age shows how wrong this is. We counter that excessive (unlimited, absolute) protection of patents does stifle growth. To mitigate this problem, we have edited the book *Compulsory Licensing—Practical Experiences and Ways Forward.*[65] We can have more innovation with more social justice and at lower costs to developing countries[66] and SEP implementing economies.

63 Chinese translation, 210 IP Monthly by Taiwan IP Office (June 2016) at 90.

64 Myth number 6 is really about criticizing IEEE's change of its IPR policy in 2015, which advocates the adoption of SSPPU and disallows SEP holders who have made FRAND commitment to file for injunctive relief. We have already offered different thoughts and therefore will skip this here.

65 Kung-Chung Liu & Reto Hilty (eds.), *Compulsory Licensing—Practical Experiences and Ways Forward*, Max Planck Asian Intellectual Property Law Series (Springer, 2015).

66 As Joseph Stiglitz advocates (*Globalization and Its Discontents Revisited*, W. W. Norton & Company, New York, 2018, xlii), "The global economy is not a zero-sum game, with their gains [referring to emerging markets – added by the authors] at the expense of the U.S. or Europe. Rather, if others prosper, demand for the goods and services of the advanced countries overall can increase, and so too their GDP."

Part I

The formation of standards and some economic observations

2 De facto standards

Jiyu Zhang[1]

1 Introduction

The importance of technological standards has been increasing tremendously in many modern industries for the past few decades. It has been commonly accepted that standards generally benefit developers, manufacturers and consumers. First, the setting and promotion of industry standards will be very beneficial to improving the interoperability and compatibility between products of different manufacturers and facilitating the expansion of product utility, thus ensuring that as many developers and manufacturers as possible can supply compatible products, maintaining market competition, reducing costs and prices of products, offering a wider range of choices to consumers and promoting social public interest.

For the manufacturers and developers in a certain industry field, the setting and promotion of industry standards will make access to and use of technology information easier. Companies can choose to focus on incremental innovations and supply only supporting products, plug-ins or some products which can interoperate with popular products or platforms according to their own technology and funding situations.

On the national and international levels, standards also play an important role. Modern society relies heavily on mass production and ICT systems and has become vulnerable to public risks. Standards and standardization can contribute to enhanced safety. Standards can also help enhance international cooperation and communication. For example, nowadays people are using their mobile phones to reach out to people in many foreign countries. International standards also help break down trade barriers and further world trade and globalization.

In the past two decades, we have been seeing many disputes and litigations on standard essential patents (SEPs) all over the world. Although most of the litigation has been about the standards made by standard setting organizations (SSOs), there are still many standards that are not set or approved by SSOs but have become de facto standards, as they are being more and more widely adopted

1 Associate Professor, Law and Technology Institute, Law School, Renmin University of China.

in the market. De facto standards may involve patented technologies, which brings to us the following questions:

1 How are de facto standards formed, and how do the SEPs affect the interests of the standard implementers and consumers?
2 Should there be any limitations to or regulations on the exercise of these SEP rights?

This chapter is a fact-finding exercise, searching for examples and typical issues relating to de facto standards, and is organized as follows: in section 2 we will introduce the basic concepts of de jure standards and de facto standards, and discuss the impact of interoperability and network effects. Section 3 will provide examples of de facto standards in the information and communication technologies (ICT) sector and discuss their impact on competition and consumer welfare. Section 4 will discuss the main competition law issues of de facto standards, and section 5 will give a brief conclusion.

2 Standards and network effects

2.1 De jure standards and de facto standards

Standards are ubiquitous in human society. In order to better communicate and cooperate with each other in ancient times, human beings in different parts of the world developed their separate standardized ways of telling time, languages, scripts and so on. The industrial revolution changed the way people produce goods. With the introduction of new technologies and machines, products have become better and cheaper. The rise of assembly lines has led to the extensive use of standardized, interchangeable components. These ultimately made possible the success of mass production in modern society, which in turn increases the importance of and demand for standardization.

When human society entered the electrical age, the role of standardization became even more prominent. Electricity and ICT have grown rapidly. As stated by the International Electrotechnical Commission (IEC), millions of devices that contain electronics, and use or produce electricity, rely on standards to perform, fit and work safely together.[2] A common example is electronic devices connected to electronic networks via standardized electrical sockets with standardized plugs. ICT products made by different manufacturers also need standards to be able to exchange information and operate.[3] Computers connect to the internet via

2 The IEC is the "world's leading organization for the preparation and publication of International Standards for all electrical, electronic and related technologies. These are known collectively as 'electrotechnology' ". See www.iec.ch/about/.

3 Just as the EU Computer Programs Directive states: "The function of a computer program is to communicate and work together with other components of a computer system and with users and, for this purpose, a logical and, where appropriate, physical interconnection and

standardized network protocols and technologies, such as TCP/IP. Browsers correctly translate the 0s and 1s into web pages according to standardized protocols, such as http. Software runs on an operating system (OS) and calls its functions via the required application programming interfaces (APIs).[4] A modern laptop computer implements around 251 interoperability standards,[5] when we only look at the standards set by SSOs. We can hardly imagine how chaotic our modern lives could be without such standards.

A standard sets out requirements for a specific item, material, component, system or service, or describes in detail a particular method or procedure.[6] A technical standard usually provides a design specification that either has been or is intended to be commonly adopted for a product or a process.

Standards can be divided into three main categories according to their forms of organization: government-set standards, private-SSO-set standards and de facto standards. Governments organize the setting of national or local standards. Nowadays most international standards are set by private SSOs. These two kinds of standards are usually collectively referred to as "formal standards", or de jure standards. The International Organization for Standardization (ISO)[7] and the IEC define such a formal standard as a

> document, established by consensus and approved by a recognized body, that provides, for common and repeated use, rules, guidelines or characteristics for activities or their results, aimed at the achievement of the optimum degree of order in a given context (Note: Standards should be based on the

---

interaction is required to permit all elements of software and hardware to work with other software and hardware and with users in all the ways in which they are intended to function. The parts of the program which provide for such interconnection and interaction between elements of software and hardware are generally known as 'interfaces'. This functional interconnection and interaction is generally known as 'interoperability'; such interoperability can be defined as the ability to exchange information and mutually to use the information which has been exchanged." See Directive 2009/24/EC of the European Parliament and of the Council of April 23, 2009, on the legal protection of computer programs.

4 In computer programming, an API is "a set of subroutine definitions, communication protocols, and tools for building software. In general terms, it is a set of clearly defined methods of communication among various components. A good API makes it easier to develop a computer program by providing all the building blocks, which are then put together by the programmer. An API may be for a web-based system, operating system, database system, computer hardware, or software library. An API specification can take many forms, but often includes specifications for routines, data structures, object classes, variables, or remote calls. POSIX, Windows API and ASPI are examples of different forms of APIs. Documentation for the API usually is provided to facilitate usage and implementation." See https://en.wikipedia.org/wiki/Application_programming_interface.

5 See www.standardslaw.org/How_Many_Standards.pdf.

6 Competition Directorate-General of the European Commission, Standard-Essential Patents, Competition Policy Brief, Issue 8, June 2014. Also see www.cencenelec.eu/standards/DefEN/Pages/default.aspx.

7 www.iso.org/.

consolidated results of science, technology and experience, and aimed at the promotion of optimum community benefits).[8]

In this chapter, we will focus on the third kind of standards, that is de facto standards. Unlike formal standards, de facto standards are generally the result of market success. When a product developed by a company becomes successful in the marketplace and many other companies determine to manufacture products compatible or interoperable with it, the interface design of the former product becomes a de facto standard. Some de facto standards are later adopted as formal standards by government bodies or SSOs. For example, the Portable Document Format (PDF)[9] developed by Adobe eventually became one of the most commonly used formats and the de facto standard for fixed-format electronic documents. In 2018 it was formally adopted as an ISO international standard, ISO32000–1.[10] Some other de facto standards, although never adopted as formal standards, may have enjoyed popularity and market influence no less than many formal standards set by SSOs or government bodies in other market sectors. Microsoft's Windows operating systems are a typical example. The series of Windows and Windows APIs have been the de facto standard for the desktop operating system and APIs for decades. No SSO formally adopted Windows or Windows API as a standard, but the market did. Application software developers will continue to use Windows API, since Windows still occupies more than 88% of the market.[11] Thus, unlike formal standards, whose market shares might differ a lot, the de facto standards usually imply a certain degree of market dominance.[12]

Economists have had many discussions over the different economic impacts of the formal standards and the de facto standards. Generally speaking, formal standards are usually preferred for the reason that they are developed through agreed, open and transparent procedures based on consensus among all interested parties.

8 ISO/IEC Guide 2: "Standardization and Related Activities – General Vocabulary", 8th ed., 2004, p. 12, available at www.iso.org/iso/iso_iec_guide_2_2004.pdf.

9 PDF is a file format developed by Adobe, aiming to present and share documents independent of the computer hardware and operating systems, and to materialize the idea of paperless offices.

10 See Laurens Leurs, *The History of PDF*, available at www.prepressure.com/pdf/basics/history. Also see https://en.wikipedia.org/wiki/History_of_the_Portable_Document_Format_(PDF).

11 See Operating System Market Share, available at www.netmarketshare.com/operating-system-market-share.aspx.

12 When defining the concept of de facto standards, people usually pay more attention to emphasizing that they are chosen by the market, only implying their market dominance. For example, the U.S. DOJ and FTC have stated "standards also may be set in the marketplace where firms vigorously compete in a winner-take-all standards war to establish their own technology as the de facto standard", U.S. Department of Justice & Federal Trade Commission, Antitrust Enforcement and Intellectual Property Rights: Promoting Innovation and Competition, 34 (2007). Prof. Gifford also stated that "A standard is mandatory in a de facto sense when the market demands compliance"; see Daniel J. Gifford, Developing Models for a Coherent Treatment of Standard-Setting Issues under the Patent, Copyright, and Antitrust Laws, 43 *IDEA* 331, 335 (2003).

However, if a certain technical field is changing fast and the market shows urgent need for and clear benefits of standardization, the pace of reaching formal standards would be too slow compared to the emergence of de facto standards. [13]

2.2 De facto standards and network effects

De facto standards are particularly likely to appear in markets characterized by strong network effects because of the large benefits associated with everyone adopting the same product and/or service.[14] "Network effects" refer to the fact that "there are many products for which the utility that a user derives from consumption of the good increases with the number of other agents consuming the good".[15]

The ICT sector usually shows strong network effects, including both direct and indirect ones. Communication systems, such as telephones, mobile phones and instant messagers, are typical examples of direct network effects. If only one person in the world uses a phone, the phone is useless to that user; if there is one more person in the world using a phone, then each user can use a phone to communicate with the other. Thus, the phone has some utility to its users because of the presence of the other user. When the number of people using phones increases, the utility that a user derives from the phone increases, as the user can use the phone to communicate with more people.

Computer operating systems (OSs) and other kinds of platforms show indirect network effects.[16] The utility that a user derives from an operating system will not directly increase with the number of people using the same operating system. However, the number of users of an operating system can often influence the decision of the application software developers, who will be more interested in developing application software for an operating system with many users. Thus an operating system with more users generally will attract more applications to be developed on that operating system, and this indirectly increases the utility to the users. In other words, operating systems and similar platforms are typical two-sided markets.[17]

13 See Paul Belleflamme, Coordination on Formal vs. De Facto Standards: A Dynamic Approach, 18 *Eur. J. Polit. Econ.* 153–176, 154 (2002).

14 Mark A. Lemley, Intellectual Property Rights and Standard-Setting Organizations, 90 *Cal. L. Rev.* 1889, 1894 (2002).

15 Michael L. Katz & Carl Shapiro, Network Externalities, Competition, and Compatibility, 75 *Am. Econ. Rev.* 424 (1985). See also Mark A. Lemley and David McGowan, Legal Implications of Network Economic Effects, 86 *Cal. L. Rev.* 479, 481 (1998).

16 See Katz and Shapiro (n 15) 424, 424. Katz and Shapiro use "virtual networks" instead of "indirect network effects" in a later paper. See Michael L. Katz & Carl Shapiro, Systems Competition and Network Effects, 8 *J. Econ. Persp.* 93, 95 (1994).

17 "There are many examples of markets involving two groups of agents who need to interact via platforms, and where one group's benefit from joining a platform depends on the number of agents from the other group who join the same platform." Mark Armstrong, "Competition in Two-Sided Markets", first presented at the ESEM meeting in Venice, August 2002, revised in 2005.

The theory of network effects predicts that the value of a given technology standard increases when it is adopted more widely. Network effects markets will be attractive targets for firms who can position their own proprietary technology as the technical standard in that market.[18] In the next section, we will present several examples of de facto standards in the ICT sector to better understand the formation of these de facto standards and their potential impacts on innovation and competition.

3 Examples of de facto standards in ICT sector

In the development of the computer industry, there are many examples of de facto standards. A computer system is composed of hardware and software, including an operating system and many applications. Inside the computer system, the application software interoperates with the operating system, and the operating system interoperates with hardware. The whole computer system communicates or interoperates with human users and/or other computer systems. The network effects in the ICT industry tend to tip the market toward concentration, which is oftentimes not mainly due to the intrinsic innovation or advantage of some players but rather their early entrance into the market.

3.1 IBM PC architecture

Perhaps one of the most famous de facto standards in the early age was the IBM PC architecture in the 1980s. IBM was one of the leading companies in the early generation of computers starting in the 1940s. At that time, computers were huge in size and mainly used for scientific computing in research and certain businesses such as weather forecast.[19] Thomas Watson, who was the president of IBM, once famously said in 1943 that "I think there is a world market for maybe five computers". Ken Olsen, the founder of Digital Equipment Corporation, said in 1977 that "there is no reason anyone would want a computer in their home".[20]

However, computer technology began evolving rapidly in the late 1970s, and computers became much smaller and easier to operate. IBM began to sell low-cost single-user personal computers (PCs) in the 1980s as a quick response to Apple's success in the microcomputer market.[21] IBM PCs used an open architecture and soon became so successful that many software programs were developed targeting IBM PCs. Hardware component manufactures also aimed to be compatible with IBM PC architecture[22] so as to use the same software and support the same expansion cards and other kinds of external devices.

18 Janice M. Mueller, Patent Misuse through the Capture of Industry Standards, 17 *Berkeley Tech. L.J.* 623, 634 (2002).

19 See www.historyofcomputer.org.

20 See www.pcworld.com/article/155984/worst_tech_predictions.html.

21 See https://en.wikipedia.org/wiki/IBM_Personal_Computer.

22 Michael J. Miller once commented "that decision led to the market for add-in boards, for large numbers of third party applications, and eventually to a large number of competitors

When technologies develop exponentially, there might be no way for anyone, not even the industry leaders, to exactly predict future market changes or the next generation of products. As a result, companies may see sudden swings in market demand and potential. In such areas, formal standards might not be established in time. Leading companies which quickly seize on market demand will have an advantage to provide a commonly adopted design specification, and de facto standards might arise from this process.

Over time, IBM has changed its policy regarding the interfaces, which were de facto standards. However, IBM later refused to disclose new interfaces, claiming them as secret,[23] although licensing interface information did facilitate the development of IBM-compatible technologies. IBM upset many of its licensees by making frequent changes to its interfaces, which caused the licensees' previously compatible technologies to be less compatible or wholly incompatible. The European Commission (EC) charged IBM with abusing its dominant position by, among other things, changing interfaces in a manner that rendered IBM-compatible peripherals inoperable. IBM settled the lawsuit by agreeing to pre-disclose changes to its interfaces to aid other firms in adapting their products in a timely manner.[24]

3.2 Computer instruction set architecture

A computer instruction set architecture (ISA) is an abstract model of a central processing unit (CPU). It defines, among other things, the instructions that a CPU contains, and it is the interface between software and hardware. The binary code of a software program consists of instruction sequences and data. Thus, a software program running on a certain CPU is not able to run on another CPU with a different ISA.

The CPU sector is usually considered to have relatively high barriers to entry. This is not only because of the high level of technology needed and the high startup cost but also because the success of a CPU requires a good software ecosystem for its ISA. ISAs can be considered de facto standards, since all the system software and complex application software will need to be compatible with a certain ISA. Intel's x86 ISAs are dominant in the desktop market, and ARM CPUs are dominant in mobile computing devices nowadays.[25]

---

all creating 'IBM-compatible' machines." See Michael J. Miller, Why the IBM PC Had an Open Architecture, August 8, 2011, available at https://forwardthinking.pcmag.com/pc-hardware/286065-why-the-ibm-pc-had-an-open-architecture.

23 Maria Lilla Montagnani, Predatory and Exclusionary Innovation: Which Legal Standard for Software Integration in the Context of the Competition versus Intellectual Property Rights Clash? 37 *Int'l Rev. Intell. Prop. Competition L.* 304, 310 n. 17 (2006).

24 See Pamela Samuelson, Are Patents on Interfaces Impeding Interoperability? 93 *Minn. L. Rev.* 1943, 1988 (2009).

25 For example, according to Prof. Prabhaker Mateti, Characteristics of Mobile Computing, ARM CPUs are dominant in the mobile electronics market, where low power consumption

Information of ISAs is usually open and free in order to attract more software developers. CPU design companies usually use patents and trademarks to occupy an advantageous position in the market. One example is that sometimes CPU companies will patent all the possible implementations of one or a few instruction in the ISA. If other CPU manufacturers want to implement CPUs with the same ISA, they will have to implement all the instructions and will definitely use at least one of the patents. Before those patents expire, CPU designers may sometimes extend the ISA by introducing some new instructions to the architecture. They will usually patent the implementations of some of the new instructions. The compilation toolchains will support and use the new instructions, and software developers are free and even encouraged to use the new instructions, too. Thus the software ecosystem will use the extended instruction sets eventually, which will make the implementation of all the extended new instructions quite necessary for the manufacturing of compatible CPU. Therefore, other manufacturers will need to get licenses to implement the new instructions in order to provide compatible CPUs.

3.3 Operating systems

As mentioned in subsection 1.2, OSs are platforms with indirect network effects. For an OS, market success usually means that there are a large number of software applications, printer drivers, and other devices for that OS. So generally speaking, OS developers will tend to open the APIs and encourage independent application software developers to use the APIs and develop more applications for the OS.

However, there may be some exceptions. For example, Windows has been the dominant OS in the desktop OS market for decades. Many Windows APIs are open to everyone. Independent software developers can use them to write software that can run on Windows. However, there is some interface information that Microsoft did not open, so that other OSs for servers cannot work with Windows OS for PCs as well as Microsoft's Windows NT servers. Some software developers want to have the information of those interfaces to build more functions and achieve better performance. One of the leading IT companies, Sun Microsystems, found that its UNIX-based OS for servers was not fully compatible with Microsoft's Windows OS for PCs. The EC found that Microsoft had a dominant position in the PC OS market, and the information that Sun had sought from Microsoft was indispensable to Sun's ability to remain a viable competitor in the Working Group Server (WGS) OS market. Microsoft's refusal to supply this information threatened to eliminate competition in the WGS OS market because of powerful network effects that were tipping this market toward

---

is a critical design goal. The ARM family accounts for approximately 75% of all embedded 32-bit RISC CPUs today. See http://cecs.wright.edu/people/faculty/pmateti/Courses/3900/Lectures/Sensors/Mobile-Sys-Characteristics.pdf.

Microsoft's products. Microsoft believed it had designed the interfaces creatively, and got some patents on the protocols and interfaces, which justified the refusal to license interface information to Sun Microsystems and others.

The EC did not accept this opinion and ordered Microsoft to prepare sufficiently detailed specifications of its communications protocols to enable Sun and other makers of WGS OS systems to achieve interoperability with Microsoft's Windows-based technologies, to provide the specifications to Sun and others on reasonable and nondiscriminatory (RAND) terms and to update the information promptly as its protocols changed. Microsoft was also ordered to establish an evaluation mechanism to ensure compliance with the Commission's order.[26] Microsoft appealed the Commission's order to the European Court of First Instance (CFI), which affirmed the Commission's order in 2007.[27] Microsoft then disclosed large amounts of interface information under the Commission's order. However, the Commission didn't think Microsoft provided sufficiently detailed interoperability information, and fined Microsoft EUR 899 million. Microsoft lodged an appeal with the CFI. On June 27, 2012, the CFI upheld the decision but reduced the fine from EUR 899 million to EUR 860 million due to a "miscalculation" by the EC.[28]

A more recent example of OS is Google's mobile phone OS, Android, which it chose to develop based on a modified version of the Linux kernel and other open-source software, and welcomed all the mobile device manufacturers to use and modify Android for free, so that they could concentrate more on the hardware device development. Many phone developers chose to use Android, which in turn attracted numerous software developers to write software for this platform. As of 2018, Android OS occupied more than 85% of the global mobile OS market.[29]

However, Google's open and free policies regarding Android might also change over time. First, Google developed its own code of the Java Standard Edition libraries in Android. However, Oracle claimed copyright and patent rights over Java API and sued Google for infringement in 2010 in the District Court for the Northern District of California. The jury found no patent infringement, and Judge William Alsup found that the APIs were not copyrightable in the first place. The case was appealed to the Federal Circuit, which ruled in favor of Oracle in the Java copyright case and remanded it to the District Court for a second trial, to consider whether Google's use was fair use. In 2016, the jury found Android does not infringe Oracle-owned copyrights because its re-implementation of 37 Java APIs was protected by fair use. However, CAFC found no fair use. Google filed a petition for writ of certiorari with the U.S. Supreme Court in January 2019

26 See Case T-201/04, *Microsoft Corp. v. Comm'n*, 2007 E.C.R. II-03601 pp. 2–20.

27 Press Release, Microsoft Corp., Microsoft Statement on Compliance with European Commission 2004 Decision (October 22, 2007), www.microsoft.com/Presspass/press/2007/oct07/10- 22MSStatement.mspx.

28 See Case T-167/08, *Microsoft Corp. v. Comm'n*, ECLI:EU:T:2012:323.

29 See www.statista.com/statistics/266136/global-market-share-held-by-smartphone-operating-systems/.

and centered its case on whether copyright extends to a software interface like an API, and whether the use of the Java API by Google fell within fair use.[30] If ultimately, the case leads to Oracle charging copyright license fee from Google and other Android phone manufacturers in the U.S. for Java API, Google's open and free policies regarding Android will have to change.

In addition, after the EC's decision to fine Google EUR 4.34 billion for using Android as a vehicle to cement the dominance of its search engine and thereby breaching EU antitrust rules in 2018,[31] Google's CEO Sundar Pichai responded in a blog:

> So far, the Android business model has meant that we haven't had to charge phone makers for our technology, or depend on a tightly controlled distribution model. . . . But we are concerned that today's decision will upset the careful balance that we have struck with Android, and that it sends a troubling signal in favor of proprietary systems over open platforms.[32]

Many considered this blog a signal or warning that Google might change its policy and start to charge a license fee at some point in the future.

3.4 Formats

When we talk about various file formats created and used in the ICT industry, people will always think of the seemingly endless "format wars". A format war is indeed a standard war. Unlike the CPU or OP, where companies generally need a large R&D team and investment, developing file formats seems to require less people and money. Whichever format wins, it becomes a de facto standard.

30 See *Oracle America, Inc. v. Google LLC*, https://en.wikipedia.org/wiki/Oracle_America,_Inc._v._Google,_Inc.

31 European Commission, Press release, http://europa.eu/rapid/press-release_IP-18-4581_en.htm. Commissioner Margrethe Vestager said: "Today, mobile internet makes up more than half of global internet traffic. It has changed the lives of millions of Europeans. Our case is about three types of restrictions that Google has imposed on Android device manufacturers and network operators to ensure that traffic on Android devices goes to the Google search engine. In this way, Google has used Android as a vehicle to cement the dominance of its search engine. These practices have denied rivals the chance to innovate and compete on the merits. They have denied European consumers the benefits of effective competition in the important mobile sphere. This is illegal under EU antitrust rules." "In particular, Google: 1) has required manufacturers to pre-install the Google Search app and browser app (Chrome), as a condition for licensing Google's app store (the Play Store); 2) made payments to certain large manufacturers and mobile network operators on condition that they exclusively pre-installed the Google Search app on their devices; and 3) has prevented manufacturers wishing to pre-install Google apps from selling even a single smart mobile device running on alternative versions of Android that were not approved by Google (so-called 'Android forks')."

32 www.blog.google/around-the-globe/google-europe/android-has-created-more-choice-not-less/.

Software or hardware intending to be compatible with certain file formats may also require licenses of related patents. For example, TIFF (Tagged Image File Format) and GIF (Graphics Interchange Format) are both very popular image file formats, which can be seen as de facto standards.[33] Most of the image file formats include compression methods to reduce the file sizes.[34] Compression algorithms can be divided into two categories: lossless compression and lossy compression. The former allows the original data to be perfectly reconstructed from the compressed data, while the latter permits reconstruction only of an approximation of the original data, though usually with improved compression rates (and therefore reduced file sizes).[35] TIFF was created in 1980s and offered the option of several lossless compression methods, including LZW.[36] GIF was released by CompuServe as a free and open specification in 1987. GIF uses the lossless compression method of LZW. If an image reader software wants to be fully compatible with either TIFF or GIF formats, it needs to implement LZW. The earliest article describing LZW was published in the June 1984 issue of *IEEE Computer Magazine*. However, the article did not mention that one company, Unisys, was holding a patent on LZW.[37] It seems that the designers of either TIFF or GIFF had no idea about the patent and simply assumed that the LZW compression method was in the public domain. Perhaps among computer science researchers and developers, only Unisys itself knew that LZW was patented by Unisys and that LZW developers might need to get patent licenses and pay royalties.

One popular article, "The GIF Controversy: A Software Developer's Perspective", described the situation:

> GIF soon became a world standard, and also played an important role in the internet community. It was well supported by CompuServe's Information Service, and many developers wrote (or acquired under license) software supporting GIF without even needing to know that a company named

33 There are other popular image file formats. See http://preservationtutorial.library.cornell.edu/presentation/table7-1.html.

34 There are usually many pixels with the same colors and many recurring patterns. If you think about the famous painting "Composition II in Red, Blue, and Yellow" by the Dutch artist Piet Mondrian, it will be very easy to understand that we can describe the picture in a more streamlined way, instead of presenting its colors pixel by pixel.

35 See https://en.wikipedia.org/wiki/Lossless_compression.

36 The baseline TIFF readers must handle the following three compression schemes: No compression, CCITT Group 3 1-Dimensional Modified Huffman RLE, and PackBits compression.

37 The patent "High Speed Data Compression and Decompression Apparatus and Method" (U.S. patent No. 4,558,302) was granted to Sperry Corporation on December 10, 1985. Sperry merged with Burroughs Corporation in 1986 to form Unisys Corporation. Unisys retained all of Sperry's patents, including LZW until it expired in 2003. See "LZW Compression & GIF", https://cs.stanford.edu/people/eroberts/cs181/projects/software-patents/lzw.html.

> CompuServe existed. GIF was relatively simple, and very well documented in books, articles and text files. . . . It is likely that the success of LZW and its thousands of implementations, especially among small developers, caught Unisys unprepared. Otherwise, it would be difficult to understand how Unisys could first allow a very large number of small and big developers to use LZW for years, and then, after the establishment of various standards based on LZW, change its attitude.[38]

In 1994, CompuServe and Unisys announced plans to charge a license fee from the public. On January 27, 1995, Unisys announced new licensing policies, which would require software companies selling products which made use of the GIF format to pay Unisys 0.45% of the selling price of GIF/LZW products (with a 10 cent minimum and 10 dollar maximum). However, no payment of any royalty to CompuServe was required. In addition, Unisys stirred up a furious response in early 1999 when it demanded that some operators of noncommercial websites containing GIF images pay the company a one-time license fee of $5,000, whether or not the images had been created with licensed software. Unisys demanded even larger payment from some commercial sites. In the case of AccuWeather, Inc., operator of Accuweather.com, Unisys demanded a license fee of USD 3.8 million. AccuWeather refused to agree and subsequently switched to another file format.[39] New formats such as PNG (Portable Network Graphics) have been developed, but they are not as widespread as GIF.

When GIF was created, its developer, CompuServe, clearly had various alternatives to the LZW compression method. However, because it mistakenly assuming that the LZW compression method was patent-free, CompuServe chose to use LZW in GIF without compelling reasons and opened GIF for free. Many other independent software developers chose to use GIF, assuming it would be free. For some reason, Unisys did not send out notices of patent infringement until GIF was very popular. The LZW patent expired in 2003 in the U.S. and in 2004 globally, and GIF has been free for more than a decade. However, this example illustrates that lack of information on patents when developing and using a certain standard may provide the patent owner a clear negotiating advantage, which oftentimes is not largely due to its technological superiority.

3.5 Human-machine interfaces

De facto standards may also arise in the human-machine interaction part. As the EU Software Directive states, "the function of a computer program is to communicate and work together with other components of a computer system and

38 The GIF Controversy: A Software Developer's Perspective, available at https://mike.pub/19950127-gif-lzw.

39 https://cs.stanford.edu/people/eroberts/cs181/projects/software-patents/lzw.html.

with users".[40] People usually need to spend some time and energy to learn the user interfaces. Once they are used to certain user interfaces, people will tend to stick with devices with similar user interfaces. Thus, the user interface of a popular device may become a de facto standard.

The QWERTY keyboard is an example often mentioned. This keyboard layout is based on a layout created for the Sholes and Glidden typewriter and sold to Remington in 1873. It became popular with the success of the Remington No. 2 of 1878, remains in widespread use and still dominates the market today.[41] QWERTY may not be the best typewriter or computer keyboard layout. However, most people have learned to type rapidly on the QWERTY keyboard layout and generally prefer keyboards with the same layout. "A path-dependent sequence of economic changes is one of which important influences upon the eventual outcome can be exerted by temporally remote events, including happenings dominated by chance elements rather than systematic forces", Paul A. David wrote, "[while people are] perfectly 'free to choose', their behavior, nevertheless, is held fast in the grip of events long forgotten and shaped by circumstances in which neither they nor their interests figured".[42]

The menu commands hierarchy of Lotus 1–2–3 can be considered another example of de facto standards of user interfaces. Perhaps nobody uses Lotus 1–2–3 nowadays, but it was one of the most successful spreadsheet programs in the early 1990s. It also allows users to write "macros" to "designate a series of command choices with a single macro keystroke". Lotus competitor Borland released a spreadsheet product, Quattro Pro, that had a compatibility mode in which its menu imitated that of Lotus 1–2–3. While none of the source code or machine code that generated the menus was copied, the names of the commands and the organization of those commands into a hierarchy were virtually identical. Lotus filed suit in the District Court for the District of Massachusetts on July 2, 1990, claiming that the structure of the menus was copyrighted by Lotus and infringed. The district court ruled that Borland had infringed Lotus's copyright. The U.S. Court of Appeals for the First Circuit reversed the district court's decision, agreeing with Borland's legal theory that considered the menu hierarchy a "method of operation".[43] Judge Boudin said in his concurring opinion,

> Requests for the protection of computer menus present the concern with fencing off access to the commons in an acute form. A new menu may be a

40 See Directive 2009/24/EC of the European Parliament and of the Council of April 23, 2009, on the legal protection of computer programs.

41 See https://en.wikipedia.org/wiki/QWERTY.

42 Paul A. David, CLIO and the Economics of QWERTY, 75 *Am. Econ. Rev.* 332, 332–333 (1985).

43 Due to the recusal of one justice, the Supreme Court decided the case with an eight-member bench that split evenly, leaving the lower court's decision affirmed but setting no national precedent, *Lotus Dev. Corp. v. Borland Int'l, Inc.*, 516 U.S. 233 (1996), see https://en.wikipedia.org/wiki/Lotus_Dev._Corp._v._Borland_Int%27l,_Inc.

> creative work, but over time its importance may come to reside more in the investment that has been made by users in learning the menu and in building their own mini-programs – macros – in reliance upon the menu.[44]

The pioneer of touchscreen smartphone manufacturers, Apple, came up with many innovative ideas about the human-machine interaction part, such as its multi-touch command pinch-to-zoom, slide-to-unlock and so forth, and also secured patents on them. In a letter to the U.S. Senate Judiciary Committee, Google counsel Kent Walker said some of these proprietary innovations have become de facto standards. He wrote:

> While collaborative Standards Setting Organizations (SSOs) play an important part in the overall standard setting system, and are particularly prominent in industries such as telecommunications, they are not the only source of standards. . . . Because proprietary or de facto standards can have just as important effects on consumer welfare, the Committee's concern regarding the abuse of SEPs should encompass them as well.

Of course, Apple general counsel Bruce Sewell disagreed and argued that just because "a proprietary technology becomes quite popular does not transform it into a 'standard' subject to the same legal constraints as true standards".[45]

4 Issues of de facto standards and SEPs

De facto standards also lead to competition issues as de jure standards do, such as abuse of dominance and holdup problem, by other IP holders and the setters of de facto standards alike.

4.1 The issue of abuse of dominance

The examples described in section 2 show the typical issues and problems regarding de facto standards and de facto SEPs. Although de facto standards are usually formed by market choice, their owners may take advantage of the standards to eliminate or restrict competition, and inflict negative effects on technical development and consumer welfare. The owner of a de facto standard might exclude or restrict competition in a secondary market via refusal to license standard essential IPs or to give access to the interoperability information, or changing the interfaces abruptly without pre-disclosing the changes. The IBM PC architecture and Microsoft OSs described in subsections 2.1 and 2.3 are examples in point. Since the dominant position of the owner of a de facto standard can be inferred, such as IBM and Microsoft, the issue of abuse of dominance will arise

44 *Lotus Dev. Corp. v. Borland Int'l, Inc.*, 49 F.3d 807, 819 (1st Cir. 1995).

45 See www.techradar.com/news/phone-and-communications/mobile-phones/google-thinks-iphone-patents-should-be-considered-industry-standards-1089798.

for competition authorities to deal with, as the EC has with regards to IBM and Microsoft. Another example of abuse of dominance by de facto standard setters is the CD-R cases in Taiwan, where the Taiwanese Fair Trade Commission has successfully found Philips, Sony and Taiyo Yuden to be abusing their joint monopoly market power.[46]

4.2 The issue of holdup by other essential IP rights owners

The owner of a de facto standard and its implementers may face the holdup problem. Some standard essential IP rights may be owned by entities other than the owner of a de facto standard, such as Oracle's possible copyright over the Java API described in subsection 2.3 and the LZW compression method described in subsection 2.4. Oftentimes, the owner of the de facto standard might not notice the existence of these IP rights. To avoid holdup issues, owners of these IP rights should be required to charge only FRAND-like license fees.

4.3 The issue of holdup due to "self-reinforcing" effect

De facto standards are often set by one or a few entities, due to the success of the corresponding products. Consumers tend to build a strong connection between a de facto standard and its setters, and have greater trust in the technological compatibility and advancement of the latter. This leads more vendors to try to be fully compatible with products of the de facto standard setters, and further strengthens the latter's control of the de facto standard. The "self-reinforcing" effect of de facto standards may continue between product generations.[47] A possible situation is that the owner or the major leader of a de facto standard may combine the standard and patents in its business strategies. By carefully planning the extension of the standard and continuously applying for patents related to the standard, the leader of the de facto standard may be able to control the implementation of the standard for a much longer time than the duration of the initial related patents. The computer ISA described in subsection 2.2 is an example. In the subsequent development of the de facto standard, the self-reinforcing effect will lead the market to choose the original developer's latest version out of many possible evolutions, not necessarily because of the inventiveness of its technology or design. The standard implementers will be continuously locked in the control of the de facto standard owners.

5 Conclusion

This chapter introduces the concept of de facto standards and describes several examples in the ICT sector. There have been various disputes and concerns

46 For more details, see Kung-Chung Liu, Chapter 8 of the present book.

47 Mark A. Lemley, Antitrust and the Internet Standardization Problem, 28 *Conn. L. Rev.* 1041, 1057 (1996).

regarding the de facto standards and de facto SEPs. In view of the aforementioned problems in the de facto standards and SEPs, we cannot ignore the regulation of related behaviors. On the one hand, since de facto standards often imply market domination, antitrust law should continue to be an important regulating tool for de facto standards. On the other hand, de facto standards often exist in fields with strong network effects, which implies that standard implementers and consumers will be locked into de facto standards. Therefore, if an IP rights owner initially showed an open attitude towards the licensing of its SEPs, attracted a lot of standard implementers and consumers to adopt its design or platform, acquired some market power, and was eventually able to set the next generation of standards due to a "self-reinforcing" effect, then it should not be allowed to stop free or fair licensing of the IP rights over de facto standards without justifiable reasons, as it would be contravening the principle of good faith.

3 De jure standard setting in the telecom industry – its evolution and the developing country case for reform

*Prashant Reddy Thikkavarapu**

1 Introduction

Standards play a crucial role in the development of any new technology or industry and can be classified into different categories such as reference standards, safety standards and interoperability standards.[1] Each of these standards meet different requirements of the economy and the interface between different standards with intellectual property (IP) law is different. For instance, 'reference standards' provide an industry with the means to measure or evaluate certain products, thereby facilitating checking the quality of particular goods traded in an industry.[2] Pharmacopeias are a good example of 'reference standards' which provide the pharmaceutical industry the means to test products for purity and quality thereby facilitating trade. These same pharmacopeias also allow drug regulators to test the quality of drugs produced by different manufacturers.[3] Similarly, 'safety standards' such as building codes are prescribed by governments to ensure that all contractors follow safe practices while designing and constructing new buildings. Both reference standards and safety standards can be protected under copyright law to differing degrees, although even this proposition is currently being litigated in multiple jurisdictions by activists who argue that the mandatory standards that are prescribed by the law should be made freely available to everybody.[4]

The third category of standards, which are interoperability standards, are very important in the telecommunication industry. These standards allow the equipment produced by one manufacturer to 'speak' to the equipment of other manufacturers.[5] For example, the LTE standard, which is a commonly referred to as

* Vidhi Centre for Legal Policy.

1 P.A. David & S. Greenstein, The Economics of Compatibility Standards- An Introduction to Recent Research, 1 *Econ. Innov. New Techn.* 3–41 (1990) at p. 4.

2 *Id.* at 4.

3 World Health Organization, *Pharmacopoeial Standards*, WHO Drug Information Vol. 28, No. 4, 2014.

4 State of Georgia v. Public.Resources.Org Inc., No. 17-11589 (11th Cir. 2018) before the U.S. Court of Appeals.

5 David & Greenstein (n 1) 1–2.

'True 4G', is a technological standard that facilitates high-speed wireless communications for mobile devices and data terminals. Interoperability standards are particularly important in the telecom industry because products and devices manufactured by different companies have to be compatible in order to communicate with each other.

IP law, especially patent law, is an important issue in the field of interoperability standards because the company that owns the patents for these standards can effectively decide who enters the market for products incorporating the standard; depending on the technology, this same patent owner may be able to influence downstream competition and innovation.[6] Given the importance of these standards to the telecommunications industry and the impact of IP, it is imperative to understand how certain technologies get selected as industry standards and the commitments imposed on those who own the patents over those standards.

The process of standard setting can be broadly classified into two categories: de facto and de jure standard setting.[7] De facto standard setting takes place when the market chooses certain technologies through uncoordinated activity. For example, Windows is almost the market standard for desktop operating systems in many jurisdictions. De jure standard setting, on the other hand, involves the selection of standards through coordinated activities by standard developments organizations, where both developers and implementers of technologies come together to select technologies as standards to be adopted by the entire industry.[8]

At the national level, the control of standards development organizations can be either with non-government organizations consisting of industry professionals or private companies, or it can lie with the government. In the U.S., for example, there are several private standard development organizations which function without any interference of the government but whose standards are often adopted by the government as being legally binding on others.[9] In other countries like India, for example, a statutory body called the Bureau of Indian Standards (BIS) selects all standards for the country, with the exception of telecom standards.[10] The key difference between non-governmental standards development organizations and governmental ones is that the former can only make recommendations and hope for the industry to adopt the same,

6 J. Farell, J. Hayes, C. Shapiro & T. Sullivan, Standard Setting, Patents, and Hold-up, 74 *Antitrust L.J.* 603–670 (2007).

7 David & Greenstein (n 1) 4. Please also refer to Chapter 1 of the present book.

8 *Id.*

9 D. Ernst, America's Voluntary Standards System – A Best Practice Model for Innovation Policy? East-West Center Working Paper No. 128, (2012); American National Standards Institute, 'United States Standards Strategy' (2015) https://share.ansi.org/shared%20documents/Standards%20Activities/NSSC/USSS_Third_edition/ANSI_USSS_2015.pdf.

10 The Bureau of Indian Standards Act, 2016; Telecom standards are set by the Telecommunication Engineering Centre.

while the latter can make them mandatory through legal decrees. Even though non-governmental standards development organizations cannot force industry to accept their standards, the industry is more likely to adopt their standards because they are involved in the process of selecting standards and also because the standard development organizations play an important role in promoting the adoption of technologies selected by them.[11]

At the international level, standard development organizations can be either non-governmental or specialized bodies within the United Nations framework, where each country has voting rights. In the telecommunications sector, for example, there are international standards development organizations like the Institute of Electrical and Electronics Engineers (IEEE), which is a professional non-governmental body, while the International Telecommunications Union (ITU) is an international organization that works within the framework of the United Nations and has both states and private organizations as its members. There are also regional standard development organizations backed by national governments in a region, like the European Telecommunications Standards Institute (ETSI), which was set up in 1988 by the European Conference of Postal and Telecommunications Administrations (CEPT) and recognized by the European Commission.[12]

The development of standards in the telecommunications industry prior to the large-scale adoption of wireless cellular technologies was a relatively mundane affair because most telecommunication service providers were monopolies and the nature of the fixed line services did not give rise to concerns such as roaming which was a significant problem in the context of the wireless industry. Interoperability between different manufacturers or services therefore was not a major concern.

However, rapid technological innovations coupled with globalization of trade and IP law, under the World Trade Organization (WTO) Agreement, has contributed to the creation of a fast expanding telecommunications industry across jurisdictions in a span of 30 years. India is a prime example of how these various factors have converged to exponentially boost tele-density in a country where it was normal to wait a few years to get a new connection. Urban tele-density in India rose from 10.37% in 2001 to 145.46% in 2014 while rural tele-density grew from 0.93% to 44% in the same duration.[13] These are phenomenal growth rates for any technology in any country.

In this backdrop, the setting of technological standards for the telecommunications industry is no longer a mundane issue. It is a high stakes game for private players who stand to earn billions of dollars in revenue if their proprietary

11 M. Rysman & T. Simcoe, Patents and the Performance of Voluntary Standard-Setting Organizations, 54(11) *Mgmt. Sci.* 1920–1934 (2008).

12 S. Besen, The European Telecommunications Standards Institute: A Preliminary Analysis, 14(6) *Telecommun. Policy* 521–530 (1990).

13 Year-wise tele-density percentage from 2001 to 2014, available at https://visualize.data.gov.in/?inst=f19fc673-a53f-45ae-9328-0a9e18fc76ce&vid=4763#.

technologies are selected as global standards. Given the monopolistic powers that vest in the owners of these standards, most standard development organizations will try to impose conditions on the owners of standards during the de jure standard setting process. The conditions include the requirement of disclosures as well as imposition of licensing conditions and are meant to be used as tool for ex post regulation of standards through courts and competition agencies.

While developed countries have the institutional capability to effectively regulate standards using these ex post measures, it is doubtful whether most developing countries have the means to use the same regulatory tools given their weak judicial and competition agencies. Does the solution then lie in developing the tools for developing countries to have a greater say in the de-jure standard development process so as to ensure that their concerns of providing more affordable telecommunication and internet services are taken into consideration? This is one of the issues sought to be addressed in this chapter.

The structure adopted by this chapter will be as follows. Section 2 will provide a brief history of the standard development organizations in the context of the telecommunications industry, focusing on the demise of both the ITU and the monopolies in the telecommunication industry. Section 3 will explain how the global IP landscape has changed post the Agreement on Trade Related Intellectual Property Rights (TRIPS) and its impact on the standard debates from the perspective of developing countries. Section 4 will focus on the manner in which the de jure standard development process works and the commonly raised issues in this regard. Section 5 will examine the challenges faced by developing countries in ex post regulation of these standards. Section 6 will reflect on the lessons learnt and propose the manner in which developing countries may try regulating their standards.

2 Standards in the telecommunication industry – the declining relevance of the ITU and the new age of standard setting

The birth of the telecommunications industry can be traced back to the invention of the telephone by Alexander Graham Bell in 1876. Bell owned the patent for the telephone and founded the first telecom company, in the U.S., the Bell Telephone company which evolved over the years into the American Telephone and Telegraph (AT&T) Company which remained a private monopoly (albeit heavily regulated) till it was broken up under antitrust law into nine smaller companies that would compete against each other.[14] With the end of the cold war and the increasing global influence of neo-liberal economic policies, governments around the world opened their markets to private players allowing them to invest in the

14 R. Lucky & J. Eisenberg, *Renewing U.S. Telecommunications Research* (Washington D.C.: National Research Council of the National Academies, 2006) at p. 13.

telecommunication industry and purchase spectrum from governments to provide wireless cellular services.

When telecom operators were primarily owned by governments or monopolists like in the U.S., standards were less of an issue because of the relatively primitive nature of the technology, the lack of interconnection and the fact that national system evolved independently with little interconnection or exchange of equipment.[15] In these early days of the telecommunication industry, standards were primarily set by industry leaders who developed new technologies which then became de facto industry standards.[16] Marconi for example was the leader in developing radio technology, which then became the de facto standard for the industry.[17] At the time, the de jure standard setting process was spearheaded by state-run telecommunication service providers because they were the only players in the field. On the international stage, the ITU set standards for wireline and spectrum technology.[18] As is expected of any institution working within the UN system, the setting of standards through these fora was a significantly complicated and took several years to complete because it involved coordination amongst a large number of countries. Telecom experts correctly predicted that the ITU would be irrelevant in the face of rapid technological development because private players would want to adopt quicker, more efficient standard development processes.[19]

With time, as the telecommunications networks grew due to more private investment and better technologies on offer in the market, there was a need to develop better standards in order to maintain interoperability.[20] The development of the microprocessor industry and the accompanying technology revolution gradually transformed the nature of the telecommunication industry, not only because voice and data services started converging, but because there were also new devices and services that had to be interoperable at the same time.[21] What was originally an industry dependent on fixed landlines, slowly evolved into an industry propelled by wireless communications starting in the 80s that required the installation of towers across cities as opposed to laying cables. The ITU's influence over the standard setting process began to wane over time as the private and regional standard development organization began to play a more active role

15 K. Jayakar, Globalization and the Legitimacy of International Telecommunications Standard-Setting Organizations, 2(5) *Indiana J. Global Legal Studies* 711–738 (1998).

16 *Id.*

17 *Id.*

18 F. Lyall, Communications Regulation: The Role of the International Telecommunications Union, 3 *J. Info. L. Tech.* (1997), available at https://warwick.ac.uk/fac/soc/law/elj/jilt/1997_3/lyall/, G.A. Codding, The International Telecommunications Union: 130 Years of Telecommunications Regulation, 23 *Denver J. Intl. Policy* 501–512 (1995).

19 M. Besen & J. Farrell, The Role of the ITU in Standardisation: Pre-eminence, Impotence or Rubber Stamp, 15(4) *Telecommun. Policy* 311–321 (1991).

20 Jayakar (n 15) 722.

21 *Id.*

in standard setting, primarily because technology evolved rapidly and the ITU processes were time consuming.[22]

In a span of approximately 30 years, the wireless telecommunications saw huge technological leaps over 4 generations of technologies. With each new generation of technology, the state's involvement in standard setting appears to have progressively reduced with the balance of power shifting to private players who wielded increasing influence over the process.[23]

For instance, 1G standards were introduced in 1980 in the U.S., Japan, Europe and China and fixed by regulators like the Federal Communications Commission (FCC) or by state-run telecom corporations. This was not surprising because the telecom industry in these countries consisted of either private or state-run monopolies.[24]

Within the EU, Nordic countries like Iceland, Norway, Sweden, Finland and Denmark got together to establish a standard known as the Nordic Mobile Telecommunication (NMT) standard, replaced by the NMT 450 standard in 1981.[25] These countries are presumably one of the first to understand that adopting common regional standards for a group of countries would lead to benefits such as roaming and economies of scale.[26] The early development of standards by the Nordic region is also considered as one of the reasons for the development of Ericsson and Nokia as two of the largest players in this field. The Nordic governments and industry also took these learnings in cooperative standard setting to the European stage when different European countries decided on a unified approach to standards for 2G technology. This approach is said to have benefitted Ericsson and Nokia who had made investments in that technology.[27] The process in itself was being mediated by the ETSI, which brought together European governments, manufacturers and operators on one platform to select GSM as the 2G standard.[28]

By the time 3G standards were commercially launched in 1998, the telecommunications industry was globalized and privatized with multiple players. In jurisdictions like Europe, it was government-backed standard development organizations like ETSI that took the lead in deciding standards.[29] Only in some jurisdictions, like China for example, the state actively intervened to create a

22 *Id.* at 735.

23 G.V.D. Kaa & M.J. Greeven, Mobile Telecommunication Standardization in Japan, China, the United States, and Europe: A Comparison of Regulatory and Industrial Regimes, 65 *Telecommun. Syst.* 181–192 (2017).

24 *Id.* at 187–188.

25 J. Rice & M. Shadur, The Mobile Telephone Cluster in the Nordic Countries: Policies to Foster Innovation and Success through Provider Competition and Knowledge Alliance Development, 28th Annual Telecommunications Policy Research Conference, Alexandria (VA), September 23–25 (2000).

26 *Id.*

27 *Id.*

28 Besen (n. 12).

29 Kaa & Greeven (n 23) 187.

new standard called TD-SCDMA for 3G technology which never caught on anywhere in the world and was gradually phased out even in China since both consumers and service providers upgraded to 4G technology.[30] The development of this technological standard by China is likely a result of its 'techno-nationalism' policy.[31]

In Japan, the Japanese government traditionally influences the process of standard development through standard development organizations like the Japan Industrial Standard Committee (JISC), which has membership from industry, academia and consumer groups.[32] However, in the context of telecommunications standards the government involvement progressively reduced until the government withdrew entirely from the setting of standards for 3G and 4G technology leaving the standard development process to industry bodies.[33]

In the U.S., the national regulator FCC selected the 1G technology developed by AT&T and Motorola, as the standards for the American market. Thereafter the private industry, especially companies like Qualcomm, Motorola, Lucent and Northern Telecom led the way in deciding standards with the government playing no role.[34]

Thus, the main levers of power in the *de jure* standard setting process are no longer with national regulators or international governmental organizations like the ITU, but rather with regional or non-governmental standard development organizations, like ETSI or IEEE, both of which have limited representation from developing countries. There is a theoretical argument to be made that if the ITU was involved in defining standards, developing countries would have a greater say in the process because they have voting rights in the ITU process. In reality, as admitted by the ITU in a report published in 2012, developing countries do not play an active role in discussions over technological standards.[35] In this report, which assessed the role played by developing countries in development of standards, the ITU concluded as follows:

> Developing countries are typically involved in regulatory and administrative aspects of standards, such as country code assignments and accounting rates to terminate calls, but are less active in non-regulatory, more technical standardization work.[36]

30 M. Ogasawara, Standardization Trend of the Communications Field in China, 8(12) *NTT Rev.* 1–5 (2010). Kaa & Greeven (n 23) 186.

31 Y. Zhou, State and Commercial Enterprises in China's Technical Standard Strategies, 6(1) *China Rev.* 37–65 (2006).

32 T. Sugura, Who Participates in the De Jure Standard Setting in Japan? *RIETI Policy* (2013) Discussion Paper Series 13-P-018, available at www.rieti.go.jp/jp/publications/pdp/13p018.pdf.

33 Kaa & Greeven (n 23) 185.

34 *Id.* at 187.

35 Venkatesh Mauree, International Telecommunications Union (2012) ICT Standardization Capabilities of Developing Countries- Bridging the Standardization Gapm, available at www.itu.int/dms_pub/itu-t/oth/0B/1F/T0B1F0000013301PDFE.pdf.

36 *Id.*

The three reasons attributed for the low participation of developing countries were listed as the following by the ITU: low availability of human resources and low levels of private sector involvement, low priority attached to standardization activities by governments and the lack of sufficient funds to support ICT standardization activities.[37]

These low levels of participation of developing countries in standard development organizations are also reflected in international non-governmental standard development organizations.[38] The only exception to the general trend of developing countries having little say or ability to influence technological standards, is China, which has increased its participation at these fora.[39] This is because China is a major manufacturer and exporter of telecommunication equipment and cellular phones and it has significant commercial interests in the global telecommunication industry.[40]

For most developing countries, the lack of ability to influence the setting of standards becomes all the more complicated when viewed through the perspective of international IP law because the international IP framework restricts the ability of developing countries to regulate standards. The issue of standard setting on the international stage then is not merely one of trade and market dynamics, but also of equity and development concerns of countries that view increased digital inclusion of their citizenry as a key development goal.

3 TRIPS and its implications for the de jure standard setting

A key event in global IP history took place on April 15, 1994, when a total of 124 countries came together to form the WTO to bring down trade barriers and facilitate free trade amongst all members of the WTO. An important component of the WTO Agreement was the TRIPS Agreement. Until TRIPS, international efforts to harmonize patent law across the world were relatively muted in the sense that developing countries had significant leeway in shaping their domestic patent law. The TRIPS Agreement altered that position by imposing significant obligations on developing countries and controlling their ability to tailor their domestic patent law to meet their development agenda.[41]

37 *Id.*

38 J.L. Contreras, National Disparities and Standard Essential Patents, in A. Bharadwaj, V. Devaiah and I. Gupta (eds.), *Complications and Quandaries in the ICT Sector – Standard Essential Patents and Competition Issues* (Singapore: Springer, 2018), pp. 1–19.

39 K. Jacobs, The Future Role of China in ICT Standardisation – A European Perspective, 38(10) *Telecommun. Policy* 863–877 (2014).

40 S. Kennedy, The Political Economy of Standards Coalitions: Explaining China's Involvement in High-Tech Standards Wars, 2 *Asia Policy* 41–62 (2006).

41 J. Watal & A. Taubman (eds.), *The Making of the TRIPS Agreement: Personal Insights from the Uruguay Round Negotiations* (Geneva: World Trade Organization, 2016).

One of the most important provisions of TRIPS is Article 27, which prevents members from discriminating against different technologies under their national patent laws.[42] This meant that countries which earlier prohibited the grant of patents for certain technologies would now have to grant patents for all technologies without discrimination. Since TRIPS was linked to trading rights, any country that failed to comply with Article 27 could be sanctioned under the WTO Agreement. Therefore, countries like India which until then prohibited the grant of patents for a range of technologies such as pharmaceuticals, chemicals, alloys etc. in order to protect domestic industry could no longer do so.[43] The larger problem with TRIPS, from a developing country perspective, is that TRIPS also reduces the space available to governments in these countries to deal with proprietary technologies selected as standards. This is because TRIPS sharply limited the power of states to interfere with patent rights. The Agreement does provide for certain limitations and exceptions under Article 30 and 31 but those are limited in nature.

As per Article 30 of TRIPS, members may provide only certain limited exceptions to the monopoly rights enjoyed by the patentee provided the exceptions did not unreasonably conflict with the normal exploitation of the patent, does not unreasonably prejudice the legitimate interests of the patent owner and it takes into count the legitimate interest of third parties. Such an exception would basically allow countries to provide for exceptions such as the experimental use and Bolar style regulatory exceptions.[44]

Article 31 allows governments or third parties authorized by the government to use patents without the authorization of the patentee provided certain conditions are met. This would include cases of anti-competitive conduct where a patentee is found to be abusing its market position or cases of non-commercial use. However, there are certain stringent procedural requirements imposed by Article 31 of TRIPS that limit the manner in which developing countries may use these provisions. For instance, Article 31 requires that all such authorizations need to be considered on individual merits and that the right-holder shall be paid adequate remuneration taking into count the economic value of authorization.[45] These restrictions prevent WTO members from using remedies like the erstwhile 'license of rights' used in India pre-2002 where a class of process patents could be mandatorily licensed to anybody at a fixed rate of 4% of the net ex-factory sale price in bulk of the patented article, after an initial period of 3 years of exclusivity expired.[46] The advantage of a 'license of right' type solution was the fact that

42 J. Watal, *Intellectual Property Rights in the WTO and Developing Countries* (New Delhi: Oxford University Press, 2001) at pp. 108–109.

43 P. Reddy & S. Chandrashekharan, *Create, Copy, Disrupt: India's Intellectual Property Dilemmas* (New Delhi: Oxford University Press, 2017) at chapter 1.

44 S. Basheer & P. Reddy, The 'Experimental Use' Exception Through a Development Lens, 50(4) *IDEA: The Intell. Prop. L. Rev.* 831–873 (2010).

45 Watal (n 42) 314–322.

46 Sections 86, 87 and 88 of the Patents Act, 1970 prior to its amendment in 2002.

it saved India from the time, resources and litigation associated with hearing each case on the merits in order to determine remuneration and other license conditions.[47]

These restrictions under TRIPS meant that developing countries, which anyway had little influence on the de-jure standard setting process, have little room for ex post regulation of proprietary standards.

The permitted exceptions under TRIPS lie under competition law regimes or injunction jurisprudence. Both these forms of regulations are not easy to administer for developing countries. As will be explained later in this chapter, most developing countries have enacted competition law only in the last two decades and are struggling to learn the ropes of this complex area of law and economics. Similarly, the judicial systems of most developing countries are only now learning to deal with patent infringement lawsuits and it will take time for them to attain the levels of sophistication that we see in the developed world.

In a world without TRIPS, developing countries would have significantly more flexibility in regulating standards including the option of simply not recognizing patents for certain technologies if they felt the same was helping with their development agenda. The fact that they no longer have this option is an important point that should be factored into the policy calculus while debating the equity of the de jure standard setting process for proprietary technologies.

4 Ex ante regulation of standards through the de jure standard setting process

The process of selecting new technologies as a standard is a long-drawn process. It involves several hours of negotiations between different stakeholders. As explained earlier, inter-operability standards in the context of the telecommunications industry bestow extraordinary power in the hands of the patentee because once selected as a standard it theoretically vests in the patentee the market power to deny entry to new entrants. If the patentee who owns a standard essential patent (SEPs), refuses to license the SEPs to new entrants (holdup situation), then it effectively means that new players cannot enter the market for certain products and this influences the competition in that segment.[48] Innovators owning these SEPs are also aware that once a particular standard has been selected the costs of switching the entire industry to a new technological standard is prohibitively high. The 'lock-in' effect of such standards offers these patentees enormous market power and the ability to decide who enters the market.[49] With this power in their

47 Reddy & Chandrashekharan (n 43) 15.

48 C. Chien, Holding Up and Holding Out, 21(1) *Michigan Tech. L. Rev.* (2014).

49 J. S. Miller, Standard Setting, Patents, and Access Lock-In: RAND Licensing and the Theory of the Firm, 40 *Indiana L. Rev.* 351–395 (2006).

hands, SEP patentees can charge royalties that far exceed the royalties, payable in a perfect market where there are substitutes for the proprietary technology.[50]

Keeping in mind this extraordinary power being vested in the hands of these patentees who own proprietary standards, most standard development organizations have an IPR policy requiring all participants to adhere to some basic rules during the standard setting process.[51] This includes making extensive disclosures and commitments related to licensing practices post the selection of their proprietary technologies as standards.

4.1 Disclosure practices

Most standard development organizations require members to disclose ownership of any patents over the technologies that are being discussed as potential standards. Such disclosures have not always been the norm in the standard setting process,[52] but have become part of the rules of most standard development organizations as patents became more important in the standard setting process.[53] These disclosures are crucial in order to ensure transparency in the standard setting process because the number of patents covering a technology may influence the final decision of the standard development organizations to choose a particular technology as a standard. The failure to make such disclosures prior to the selection of standards can result in 'patent ambush'.[54]

Simply put, a patent ambush takes place when a member who owns patents over a technology does not disclose it at the time of the standard setting process, but begins to make assertions at a later stage once the standard has been adopted and that it is not possible anymore for companies implementing the standard to switch to other technologies. The implementers of standards therefore will have to negotiate with the patentees who hold the upper hand in such negotiations and the patentee can demand patent royalties that are wildly disproportionate to the actual value of the technology in question. This is but one manifestation of the holdup problem mentioned earlier. Such patent ambush may also upset the calculations involved in selecting a particular technology as a standard and is generally considered to be anti-competitive conduct.[55]

50 M. Lemley & C. Shapiro, Patent Holdup and Royalty Stacking, 85 *Texas L. Rev.* 1991–2049 (2007).
51 J. L. Contreras, Technical Standards, Standards-Setting Organizations and Intellectual Property: A Survey of the Literature (with an Emphasis on Empirical Approaches), 11 *Utah L. Fac. Sch.* 1–62 (2017).
52 T. S. Simcoe, Explaining the Increase in Intellectual Property Disclosure. Working Paper (2005), available at https://papers.ssrn.com/sol3/papers.cfm?abstract_id=1396332.
53 Lemley (n 14) 1889–1980.
54 B. D. Abramson, The Patent Ambush: Misuse or Caveat Emptor? 51(1) *IDEA – The Intell. Prop. L. Rev.* 71–109 (2011).
55 Lemley (n 53) 1943.

The pattern and extent of disclosure of patent related information varies across different standard development organizations. A study in 2005 demonstrated that participants in the standard development process were making more disclosures related to their patents over the technologies that were being considered. However, the specificity of the disclosure reportedly varied significantly.[56] The study in 2005 found that at least half of the disclosures provided a reference to patents or patent applications. Of these, 18% of the disclosures referred to unpublished patent applications. The remaining 33% provided no information that could be used to identify the IP in question. Depending on the IP policy, patentees may also have to declare whether their patents are essential to the standard being decided by the standard development organizations.[57] The same study from 2005 states that the disclosure requirement does not extend to pricing. Only 8% of the IP disclosures gave specific pricing terms.[58] The reluctance to disclose pricing is understandable since it gives the patentees a superior position in negotiations with implementers across the world.

A failure to make adequate disclosures before the standard development organization may work against patentees in some jurisdictions if the defendant invokes the doctrine of equitable estoppel. This doctrine applies when a patentee through its misleading conduct leads the infringer to reasonably infer that the patentee does not intend to enforce its patent.[59]

In the U.S., the Federal Trade Commission (FTC) initiated action under American antitrust law in at least two cases where Dell Computers[60] and Rambus[61] tried to enforce patents that had not been disclosed to the standard development organizations during the standard setting process. In the Dell case, a consent decree was entered into between the parties that required Dell to grant royalty free licenses for the patents, while in the case of Rambus, FTC placed royalty caps on the undisclosed patents.[62] There have been other cases in the U.S. involving private actions where defendants in patent infringement actions have argued that patentees failed to disclose their patents during the standard setting process. The disputes in these cases revolve around the issue of whether the standard development organization's IP policy mandatorily required disclosure of all patents.[63]

56 Simcoe (n 52) 3.
57 Contreras (n 51) 26–27.
58 Simcoe (n 52) 4.
59 Lemley (n 53) 1918.
60 FTC Docket No. C-3658.
61 FTC Docket No. 9302.
62 M. Rysman & T. Simcoe, Patents and the Performance of Voluntary Standard-Setting Organizations, 54(11) *Mgmt. Sci.* 1920–1934 (2008).
63 Contreras (n 51) 26–27.

4.2 Licensing practices

The other important role played by standard development organizations is the formulation of licensing practices for patents that cover standards. This is an important function because as explained earlier owners of patents covering standards will have considerable market power and a set of fair licensing practices can help check against a possible market abuse of power by these patentees. A seemingly obvious ex ante solution to this problem is for standard development organizations to fix the patent royalty after consulting all stakeholders. This however does not happen in reality because of the danger that such coordinated activity with regard to pricing may invite adverse scrutiny from competition authorities.[64] Thus, rather than fixing royalties, most standard development organizations will limit themselves to requiring a commitment from all patentees to license their patents on a fair, reasonable and non-discriminatory basis (FRAND).[65]

The FRAND terms of conduct are meant to create a level playing field and curtail the ability of the owners of the patents over standards to abuse their powers to deny a license or favour one implementer over the other.[66] But the reality is slightly more complicated. There is a serious question of law as to whether a FRAND commitment made by a patentee to an international standard development organization can be enforced as an implied license or a contract before national courts by third parties who may or may not have been members of the same standard development organizations.[67] In most common law countries, for a contract to come into effect there is a requirement for adequate consideration to be exchanged between both parties. Going by this requirement, a simple FRAND commitment made to a standard development organization may not be considered a binding contractual obligation.

There are several other problems with effectively enforcing a FRAND obligation. For example, most patentees require potential licensees to sign non-disclosure agreements (NDAs) preventing the disclosure of the terms of the license for the patents covering the standards. Once the licensing terms for one licensee have been subject to confidentiality, there is no way for other potential licensees to determine whether the patentee is indulging in discriminatory behaviour.[68]

Regardless of whether potential licensees are aware of the terms of licensing, experience has shown that they are unlikely to agree, with standard owning

64 J. G. Sidak, Patent Holdup and Oligopsonistic Collusion in Standard-Setting Organisation, 5(1) *J. Comp. L. Econ.* 123–188 (2009).

65 D. Litman, Understanding the RAND Commitment, 47 *Houston L. Rev.* 1023 (2010).

66 *Id.*

67 Lemley (n 52) 1909–1923.

68 V. Kathuria & J. C. Lai, Validity of Non-Disclosure Agreements in SEP Licensing, 40(6) *Euro. Intell. Prop. Rev.* 358–368 (2018).

patentees, on what exactly is a reasonable royalty or non-discriminatory conduct.[69] For example, can a patentee link the licensing rate to the value of final product, which may have several hundred components contributing to its value or should they charge a fee not linked to the value of the final product? When the patentee demands a royalty that is unreasonable in the view of the implementer, the latter faces a 'holdup' problem wherein it has to negotiate with the patentee under a constant threat of a lawsuit for an injunction restraining patent infringement. In a perfectly competitive market, even patented technologies would have substitutes but some technological standards by their nature cannot be substituted. There are no clear-cut answers to any of these situations and very often the answer will depend on who is trying to provide the answers.

In most jurisdictions, the disagreements between owners of patents over standards and implementers have either ended up before a court of law or before competition authorities on the grounds of either patent infringement or anti-competitive conduct. In some Asian jurisdictions like China and South Korea, competition authorities have imposed huge penalties on Qualcomm, which is one of the largest owners of patents over telecom standards, for its anti-competitive conduct.[70] In the U.S., the federal courts have decided disputes over FRAND licensing by deciding the 'reasonable royalty' that was payable to the patentee.[71] In India, while the courts granted ex parte interim injunctions in patent infringement lawsuits filed by patentees who owned standards, the country's competition commission, initiated investigation against the same patent on the ground that there was a prima facie abuse of dominant position due to its patent licensing practices.[72] Despite high decibel litigation in multiple jurisdictions over royalties for SEPs and their reasonableness, there remain commentators who vehemently argue that patent 'holdups' do not occur in the context of standards.[73]

Thus, although developing countries do not have much of an opportunity to influence the standard setting process at international standard development organizations, these countries theoretically speaking, can influence either through the judicial system or the competition framework, the manner in which these standards are enforced in their respective jurisdictions. In other words, these developing countries have had to sacrifice ex ante regulation of standards in

69 M.A. Carrier, A Roadmap to the Smartphone Patent Wars and FRAND Licensing, 2 *CPI Antitrust Chronicle* 2–7 (2012).

70 G. Kim, D. Koo & K.Y. Lee, The Competition Law Regulation of Standard Essential Patents in South Korea, 62(3) *The Anti-Trust Bull.* 465–482 (2017); J. Deng, Antitrust Treatment of Standard Essential Patent Abuse: China's Experience and Lessons, 8(2) *Jindal Global L. Rev.* 203–219 (2017).

71 *Microsoft Corp. v. Motorola Inc.*, 104 U.S.P.Q.2d 2000.

72 A. Bharadwaj & T. Yoshioka-Kobayashi, Regulating Standard Essential Patents in Implementer-Oriented Countries: Insights from India and Japan, in A. Bharadwaj, V. Devaiah and I. Gupta (eds.), *Multi-dimensional Approaches Towards New Technology: Insights on Innovation, Patents and Competition* (Singapore: Springer, 2018), pp. 183–211.

73 K. Gupta, Technology Standards and Competition in the Mobile Wireless Industry, 22(4) *George Mason L. Rev.* 865–869 (2015).

favour of ex post regulation of standards. The problem with this form of ex post regulation is that most developing countries are still in the process of building the institutional competencies in the area of competition law and IP law. The next section will explain some of these challenges in more detail.

5 The challenges for developing countries in ex post regulation of standards set through a de jure process

As explained earlier in this chapter, developing countries have had little influence in the process of international standard setting for the telecommunications industry.[74] With the advent of internet of things (IoT) and 5G technology, the issue of patents over standards is going to become all the more important for even developing countries that have so far paid little attention to the de-jure standard setting process. The only option then for these countries is to try and influence these standards through an ex post mechanism. The relevant question in this backdrop, as explained earlier, is whether developing countries have the institutional capability to adopt the same ex post mode of regulating these standards as followed in advanced countries?

The prima facie answer to this question appears to be that most developing countries lack the judicial capacity to adjudicate in an efficient manner, commercial disputes involving complicated technologies. The delays in adjudication in developing countries can be attributed to lack of funding, judges and of course the larger political debate on judicial independence and separation of powers between the judiciary and the executive.[75] While efforts have been afoot for some time to expedite judicial reforms in developing countries, these efforts are not succeeding in equal measure across jurisdictions.

Even a country like India, which is a stable democracy with a remarkably independent judiciary by developing country standards, has faced some extraordinarily embarrassing situations where foreign courts have assumed jurisdiction in some cases on the ground that backlog before Indian courts meant that litigants could not expect justice in a time bound manner in India.[76] In the context of international arbitration under a Bilateral Investment Treaty, an arbitral panel held that the Republic of India had violated its treaty obligations to provide effective legal remedies because of severe delays before Indian courts. The arbitral panel thus ordered the Indian government to compensate the Australian company that had sued it under the treaty.[77] Even with regard to enforcement of contracts, India is ranked at 164 out of 190 economies in the World Bank's annual ranking on the

74 Contreras (n 38) 4.

75 R. J. Daniels & M. J. Trebilcock, The Political Economy of Rule of Law Reform in Developing Countries, *Michigan J. Int'l L.* 99–140.

76 Law Commission of India, 188th Report on Proposals for Constitution of Hi-Tech Fast-Track Commercial Divisions in High Court (2003).

77 Arbitration Award under BIPA & CECA, Press Information Bureau, Government of India, February 5, 2014.

ease of enforcement of contracts.[78] Adjudicating patent infringement lawsuits is significantly more complicated than the enforcement of contracts and will take much longer to conclude in developing countries like India.

In the context of IP enforcement, the developed world is well aware of the challenges of enforcement of IP rights in the developing world. It is for this reason that the TRIPS Agreement contains specific clauses that require all members to provide for 'effective' and 'expeditious remedies' for enforcement actions to enforce IP actions.[79] Recent treaty negotiations, whether at CPTPP or RCEP have explored options to allow for international enforcement actions before arbitral tribunals as a means to compensate for judicial delays in national legal systems.[80]

Similar, if not more complicated, issues arise in context of competition law enforcement in developing countries. For competition law to be enforced efficiently, a country need to have a strong rule of law regime with a well-resourced competition agency. Most developing countries reportedly have a shortage of skilled human resources in their competition agencies and judiciaries. This lack of personnel with expertise in competition law can cause delays and also severely hamper the development of competition law.[81] A second problem identified in developing countries is the lack of political support for strong enforcement of competition law. Most of these countries which are making a transition from state-controlled economies to the free market face opposition from opponents of markets or crony capitalists. Such political opposition will usually act as a deterrent to the development of a culture of market competition.[82]

An illustrative example of the difficulties faced by developing countries in ex post regulation of standards fixed through injunctions or competition law is India. In 2013, Ericsson filed patent infringement lawsuits against Indian phone manufacturers before the Delhi High Court over patents that were supposedly essential and it claimed INR 1 billion in damages and managed to secure interim injunctions early in the litigation and gained the upper hand.[83] The court did not evaluate the possibility of a 'holdout' and whether 'irreparable injury' was caused before granting an interim injunction. On the other hand, when the Indian manufacturers responded by complaining to the Competition Commission of India (CCI), the agency found a prima facie case of competition law violation

78 Brief Note on World Bank Report on Doing Business 2018: Enforcing Contracts, Department of Justice, Law Ministry, Government of India, available at http://doj.gov.in/page/brief-note-world-bank-report-doing-business-2018-enforcing-contracts-0

79 Article 41 of the Agreement on Trade Related Intellectual Property Rights (TRIPS).

80 J. Gathii & C. Ho, Regime Shifting of IP Lawmaking and Enforcement from the WTO to the International Investment Regime, 18(2) *Minnesota J.L. Sci. Tech.* 427–515 (2017).

81 U. Adyin & T. Buthe, Competition Law & Policy in Developing Countries: Explaining Variations in Outcomes, Exploring Possibilities and Limits. 79(4) *L. Contemporary Problems* 1–36 (2016).

82 *Id.*

83 Bharadwaj & Yoshioka-Kobayashi (n 72) 185–187; *Telefonaktiebolaget LM Ericsson (Publ) v. Micromax CS(OS)* 442 of 2013 before the High Court of Delhi.

by Ericsson and initiated an investigation.[84] Five years later, the trial before the High Court kept dragging on, while the CCI's investigation was embroiled in litigation before the same High Court on the issue of whether the CCI even had the jurisdiction to investigate the issue.[85] At least one of the lawsuits ended with a settlement between Ericsson after 5 years, while the rest remain pending.[86] In a different case involving patents over DVD standards, the Delhi High Court took 9 years to complete trial and deliver a judgment. The patents in question had expired by the time.[87]

The Indian experience with ex post regulation of standards is a reminder of how regulatory models developed in the west may not be suitable for developing countries which lack competition or judicial institutions of similar expertise. The question then is how should developing countries regulate proprietary standards?

6 De jure standard setting and developing countries – what should be the way forward?

As explained in this chapter, developing countries are in the unfortunate position of not having much influence in the de-jure standard setting process while at the same time being subject to restrictions under TRIPS on the manner in which the patents covering standards can be regulated.

The options before developing countries are three-fold.

The *first* option is to influence the de-jure standard setting process by participating in the process. China is already an active participant and countries like India are trying to participate in the 5G standard setting process. Unlike China which has considerably increased its investments in R&D and has built up a portfolio, India still lags in R&D in the telecom sector. In fact, a recent study showed that almost 100% of patents granted by the Indian Patent Office in the telecom sector are owned by foreign companies.[88] Countries like India which lack companies with a significant patent portfolio are unlikely to be able to influence the standard setting process in different standard development organizations. In this backdrop, the best way forward maybe for developing countries to press for the creation of a new international treaty to regulate the standard setting process for patented technologies. The aim of such a treaty should be to streamline the

84 *Micromax Informatics Ltd. v. Telefonaktiebolaget LM Ericsson (Publ)* Case No. 50/2013 before the Competition Commission of India.

85 *Telefonaktiebolaget LM Ericsson (Publ) v. Competition Commission of India* W.P.(C) 464/2014 before the High Court of Delhi.

86 G. Aulakh, Micromax to Take Global Patent License from Ericsson, *The Economic Times*, March 14, 2018, available at https://economictimes.indiatimes.com/news/company/corporate-trends/micromax-to-take-global-patent-licence-from-ericsson/articleshow/63293517.cms.

87 *Koninklijke Philips Electronics N.V. v. Rajesh Bansal* CS(OS) No. 1034/2009 & CS(OS) No. 1082/2009 before the Delhi High Court.

88 J.L. Contreras & R. Lakshane, Patents and Mobile Devices in India: An Empirical Survey, 50(1) *Vanderbilt J. Transn'l L.* 1–44 (2017).

standard setting process to prevent patent ambushes by ensuring that patentees who fail to disclose their patents during the standard setting process are penalized when they seek to enforce the patents in question. Similarly, the treaty should aim to lend binding force to the FRAND licensing terms that are agreed upon by members of a standard development organization in all member countries of the treaty. There should also be an attempt to iron out the licensing terms in a manner that restricts the ability of powerful patentees to impose unfair licensing terms.

The *second* option for developing countries is to amend their domestic legislation to make it easier to regulate standards developed through a de jure process. One simple solution is to introduce more transparency into the FRAND process. For example, in India, a provision in its national patent law has a clause that requires patentees to disclose the extent to which they have worked their patented inventions in Indian territory every year.[89] Theoretically, this requirement injects transparency into the negotiation of royalties by FRAND owners, but in reality, most patentees do not comply with this requirement, on the grounds that they license portfolios of patents and not individual patents. Provisions like this, if introduced into national law, may at the very least force owners of patents over standards to provide more information on their pricing. Disclosure of such information will help in understanding whether these patentees are indeed fair, reasonable and non-discriminatory in their dealings with patentees. The other option, within the national patent law framework, is to provide for broad compulsory licenses and a simple process by which those licenses can be issued.

A *third* option is to provide for a 'safe harbor' under national competition laws, to allow for standard development organizations to allow their members to fix the royalties payable, in advance, for different standards in different jurisdictions without the risk of being penalized for violation of competition laws.[90] Alternatively, standard development organizations could allow members to fix royalty caps.[91] Such conduct where all parties sit together and fix prices may be considered as anti-competitive in most countries. Creating a 'safe harbor' under the competition law would make it possible for different players in a standard development organization to co-ordinate pricing as part of the standard development organization. Such an approach would likely give implementers of standards in developing countries the opportunity to have greater negotiating leverage in the process of developing standard, especially if the implementers create their own buyer's cartels to negotiate with patentees. The more significant benefit of having royalties determined at the same time as fixing standards is that it will relieve the industry of the uncertainty and litigation that now define the landscape in

89 Section 146, Patents Act, 1970; S. Basheer, Making Patent Work: of IP Duties and Deficient Disclosures, 7(1) *Queen Mary J. Intell. Prop.* 3–24 (2017).

90 T. Simcoe, Open Standards and Intellectual Property Rights, in H.W. Chesbrough, & W. Vanhaverbeke (eds.), *West J. Open Innovation: Researching a New Paradigm* (Oxford: Oxford University Press, 2008), pp. 161–183.

91 Contreras (n 51) 34–38.

the telecommunications industry. This is a proposal that obviously needs to be thought through in much more detail before going ahead but is one that needs to be considered by the governments of developing countries.

7 Conclusion

Technological standards are going to be of increasing importance in a globalized world where new generations of technology are being developed at a breath-taking speed. The current process of setting these standards through standard developing organizations is not in favour of developing countries mostly because they lack the technology, skills or markets to influence the process in its current format. If this continues, it will have a long-term impact on the widening gulf between the developed and developing world and will cause an increasing out-flow of royalties from developing countries to developed countries. While no single developed country has the capability to influence the standard development process by itself, through collective bargaining this process can be influenced. Developing countries have succeeded in challenging international copyright norms in 1967 during the Stockholm Diplomatic Conference on the Berne Convention and then again during the negotiations leading up to the TRIPS Agreement. Any future international efforts on harmonizing patent law should link the patent reform agenda to the de jure standard development process in a manner that evens the scales for developing countries.

4 Standard setting organizations, standard essential patents and FRAND terms

An economic observation

Felix Conde, Lanhua Li and Can Huang[1]

1 Introduction

Standards are an essential part of our society, and generate broad-ranging benefits. For companies, the benefits of standardization include (but are not limited to) reduced costs of R&D and production, the provision of a wider range of supplies with the same quality level, and reduced risks of liability (DIN, 2000). From a macroeconomic perspective, standards have a positive impact on a country's economic growth (Temple et al., 2005; Haimowitz and Warren, 2007; CIE, 2007) through many channels, such as boosting trade, facilitating efficient technology diffusion and enhancing international competitiveness (DIN, 2000). For example, it is estimated that the economic benefit of standardization is approximately EUR 16.77 billion per year for Germany, accounting for approximately 0.72% of its GDP (Knut et al., 2011).

In general, there are different types of standards, defined by their different functionalities, such as ensuring interoperability and compatibility, providing guidance for quality control, and optimizing production processes based on best practices (Hatto, 2010). In this chapter, we only study technology standards, for which intellectual property rights (IPRs) are more critical than for other types of standards. Technology standards represent the uniform technical specifications adopted by an industry to ensure interoperability between multiple devices and systems. These technical specifications are either generated by dominant actors and become the "de facto standards", or mostly by industry consortia which serve as standard setting platforms or standard setting organizations (SSOs) (Baron and Gupta, 2018).

Firms that participate in a standard setting process are obliged to declare their patents which might be essential to the implementation of the standard to SSOs. These patents are thus called standard essential patents (SEPs). The time

1 Institute for Intellectual Property Management, School of Management, Zhejiang University, Hangzhou, Zhejiang Province 310058, China. Corresponding author's e-mail address: canhuang@zju.edu.cn.

to declare a patent as essential for a standard and the meaning of essentiality differ among SSOs (Baron and Spulber, 2018). SSOs usually require members to disclose IPRs that might be essential for a standard before the standard is settled. Apart from patents, some SSOs also recognize know-how, copyrights, and trade secrets as essential for a standard. After the standard is set, these SEP owners can profit from licensing and other commercial activities. To prevent SEP owners from abusing excessive market power, SSOs commonly request that their members license their SEPs on fair, reasonable and nondiscriminatory (FRAND) terms.

This chapter discusses the legal and economic literature on SSOs, SEPs and FRAND terms. We used the following keywords to retrieve 66 highly relevant papers, reports or articles from the economic, management and policy journals: SSOs, SEPs, FRAND, patent pool, consortia, royalty stacking, holdup, holdout and essentiality. We present the literature review in two sections. First, we introduce relevant SSOs and their policies, and firms' participation in the standardization activities. Second, we summarize the literature on SEPs and FRAND terms, regarding the economic returns of SEPs, the essentiality of SEPs, licensing practices based on FRAND terms, and royalty calculation methods. Lastly, we summarize the main conclusions in each area, considering the debate among scholars and the challenges for future research.

2 Standard setting organizations (SSOs)

The primary purpose of an SSO is to set technical standards, which requires the processes of development, promotion, amendment and reissue of standards. SSOs also play a crucial role in defining the policies on disclosure and the licensing of relevant IPRs that could affect the future development and adoption of standards. From the late 1980s, the focus of industrial debates on standardization shifted from the underlying technologies to intellectual property issues (Bekkers et al., 2002). Following this trend, the topics of academic studies in the standardization field also moved from network effects and collaboration to SSOs and their IPR policies. The existing literature offers a variety of theoretical arguments, while empirical research has been limited in number due to the short supply of relevant data.

The studies that we analyze in this chapter mainly focus on the information and communication technology (ICT) industries, since standardization plays a vital role in promoting the development of technologies in these industries. Hence, to offer a context for discussion, we first introduce some of the most representative SSOs releasing standards in the ICT industries and their IPR policies.

2.1 Relevant SSOs

2.1.1 Institute of Electrical and Electronics Engineers (IEEE)

In 1884, a small group of prominent electrical professionals formed the American Institute of Electrical Engineers (AIEE) in the U.S. Later, in 1912, along with the advancement of radio communication technologies, wireless practitioners created the Institute of Radio Engineers (IRE). In 1963, the AIEE and the IRE merged to form the Institute of Electrical and Electronics Engineers (IEEE). Today, IEEE has more than 423,000 members in more than 160 countries. It has set up a portfolio of more than 1,300 standards, and more than 600 standards are currently under development.

In 2015, the IEEE amended its IPR policy and proposed determining royalty rates based on "the Smallest Salable Patent-Practicing Unit (SSPPU)" (Kappos and Michel, 2018; IEEE, 2018). According to the policy, a reasonable royalty should reflect "the value that the functionality of the claimed invention or inventive feature within the Essential Patent Claim contributes to the value of the relevant functionality of the smallest saleable Compliant Implementation". The compliant implementation can be a component, subassembly or end product that practices the standard. The new policy also states that, for IEEE members, reasonable royalty rates shall mean "appropriate compensation to the patent holder for the implementation of an Essential Patent Claim excluding the value, if any, resulting from the inclusion of that Essential Patent Claim's technology in the IEEE Standard". Apart from the new methodology on royalty calculation, the policy also diminishes the availability of injunctive relief. It says that an SEP holder must waive the seeking of injunctions unless it has successfully litigated against the infringers in the court of appeals, and the implementers have failed to participate in or to comply with the outcome of an adjudication. Although some patent owners have claimed that their interests were not considered during the formulation of the new policy, the policy received a positive business review letter from the U.S. Department of Justice (DOJ, 2015), encouraging the IEEE Board to approve the changes. The review letter concluded that the new policy promotes competition among technologies, facilitates licensing negotiations, and mitigates the hazards of patent holdup (when a patent owner demands higher royalties or other more costly or burdensome licensing terms after the standard is implemented than could have been obtained before the standard was chosen (FTC, 2011)) and royalty stacking (situations in which a single product potentially infringes on many patents and thus bears multiple royalty burdens (Lemley and Shapiro, 2006)), thus benefiting consumers. The new IPR policy came into effect in March 2015.

2.1.2 European Telecommunications Standards Institute (ETSI)

The European Telecommunications Standards Institute (ETSI) was founded in 1988 by the European Conference of Postal and Telecommunications Administrations (CEPT). Since its establishment, ETSI has produced more than 30,000 standards, with the joint efforts of more than 800 members from more than 60 countries. ETSI is also a major partner in the Third-Generation Partnership Project (3GPP). The GSM cell phone system, 3G and 4G are some of the most recognized standards set by the organization.

Bekkers and West (2009) reviewed the evolution of ETSI's IPR policy and discussed the potential direction for reforming the current IPR policy. Considering the IPR conflicts emerging in GSM standard setting processes, ETSI developed its own IPR policy in 1994, which was later referred to as the (F)RAND model (ETSI, 2019),[2] and it has been followed by many other SSOs (Bekkers and West, 2009). However, ETSI members criticized this policy for being insufficient to resolve issues such as deferred IPR declarations, the absence of a definition of commercial terms in the FRAND model, royalty stacking and the lack of IPR transparency. Thus, to address these concerns, in 2005, ETSI established an ad hoc IPR review group to discuss and provide advice on its existing IPR rules. This work only brought minor changes, since it is rather challenging for ETSI to coordinate the heterogeneous interests of its members and achieve consensus.

2.1.3 Alliance for the Telecommunications Industry (ATIS) and the World Wide Web Consortium (W3C)

The Alliance for Telecommunications Industry (ATIS) was established in 1983 under the name of the Exchange Carriers Standards Association (ECSA). Its IPR Policy claims that

> a license will be made available without compensation to the applicants desiring to utilize the license for the purpose of implementing the standard; or a license will be made available to applicants under reasonable terms and conditions that are demonstrably free of any unfair discrimination.
>
> (ATIS, 2018a)[3]

This policy indicates that participants in the organization should choose between FRAND licensing and royalty-free licensing. In addition to ATIS, the World Wide Web Consortium (W3C), created in 1994 with the purpose of developing web standards, has a royalty-free licensing requirement applied to all SEP holders (W3C, 2004; ATIS, 2011; ATIS, 2018b).

2.1.4 VMEbus International Trade Association (VITA)

The VMEbus International Trade Association (VITA) was established in 1982 by a group of VMEbus manufacturers aiming to develop and promote open technology standards. To address the threat of patent holdup, in 2006 VITA required its members to declare the ex ante maximum royalty rates that they would demand for a FRAND license through a letter of assurance (LOA). LOA states the submitter's position regarding the ownership, enforcement or licensing of essential

2 These principles remain in the ETSI Rules of Procedures as published in April 2019.

3 These principles remain in the ATIS Operating Procedures for ATIS Forums and Committees (version 5.5) as published in August 2018.

patents (claims) for a specifically referenced standard. Requiring LOAs from members is a common practice in the SSOs, though the required declaration content might vary across different organizations (IEEE, 2015; VITA, 2015).[4] The organization has been a frequently cited reference when discussing ex ante declarations. This policy change, as in the case of IEEE, also received a favorable review letter from the U.S. (DOJ, 2006), which stated that it could bring important procompetitive benefits.

2.1.5 Digital Video Broadcasting Project (DVB)

The Digital Video Broadcasting Project (DVB), which evolved from the European Launching Group (ELG) in 1993, mainly focuses on the development of digital television broadcasting and multimedia broadcasting standards. DVB introduced several novel elements into its IPR policy, including "negative disclosure", which refers to a notice of refusal to license IPR on FRAND terms (Eltzroth, 2008). Thus, all members must grant licenses by default unless they provide notice of the unavailability of their IPRs. This rule contrasts with the more common policies in other SSOs (e.g. IEEE, ESTI), which require members to disclose their IPRs relevant to the standards and confirm the availability of the IPR on FRAND terms. In addition to this rule, DVB also introduces arbitration to resolve disputes arising from licensing negotiations among members and encourages the fostering of patent pools (DVB, 2014, 2018).[5]

2.1.6 The 3rd Generation Partnership Project (3GPP)

The 3rd Generation Partnership Project (3GPP) is an SSO formed in 1998 as a strategic initiative between Nortel Networks and AT&T Wireless. It evolved to become one of the most relevant partners for many SSOs in the telecommunications industry, defining the third-generation (3G) and fourth-generation (4G) wireless cellular standards. Currently, 3GPP attracts organizational partners worldwide, from regions such as the U.S., Europe, India, Japan, China and the Republic of Korea. Since 3GPP agglomerates a group of SSOs, the individual members are bound by the IPR policies of the respective SSOs they participate in. Generally, they should opportunely declare any IPRs which could be essential, or potentially essential, to any work ongoing within 3GPP. The organization also encourages members to grant licenses under FRAND terms (3GPP, 2016).

4 These principles remain in the VITA Policies and Procedures as published in September 2015.

5 These elements remain in the DVB Memorandum of Understanding, further amended and restated for the development of harmonized digital video broadcasting (DVB) services based on European specifications as published in January 2014.

2.2 SSOs' IPR policy changes and their impacts

In the past years, as presented earlier, a number of important SSOs have modified their IPR policies. As a trend, most SSOs shifted toward more stringent policies on SEP disclosure and licensing (Baron and Spulber, 2018) to avoid threats, such as patent holdup and royalty stacking. In particular, most of the policy changes, such as introducing FRAND licensing commitments, aimed to address patent holdup issues.[6]

Lerner and Tirole (2015) argued that imposing stringent licensing policies, such as structured price commitments, preserves competition by curbing the monopoly power of SEP holders and, under certain circumstances, increases social welfare. However, strict policies, especially on SEP licensing activities, can weaken firms' incentives to join an SSO. Lerner and Tirole (2006) argued that SSOs differ in their level of IPR disclosure and licensing requirements. They found that although firms' preferences for SSOs vary considerably across technologies, according to a theoretical model of forum shopping, firms with more valuable patents tend to select SSOs with less strict licensing regulations. Schmalensee (2009), through a model of patent licensing, concluded that antitrust authorities should not encourage or allow collective negotiation of ex ante royalties, since it is not workable in practice and could slow the pace of technical progress.

Furthermore, Chiao et al. (2007) developed and tested a mathematical model to empirically investigate the relationship between disclosure policies and license pricing, with the data from 59 SSOs, 80% of them in the "information technology and offices machines" category. They found that, if an SSO is more oriented toward technology sponsors (i.e. IP holders), sponsors will make fewer concessions. For instance, IP holders are less likely to agree to royalty-free licensing. The sponsors of an attractive technology can afford to choose a friendly SSO to make a few concessions to potential technology implementers. In addition, Layne-Farrar et al. (2014) found that a requirement by an SSO for a firm to provide a licensing cap reduces the probability of the firm joining the SSO and investing in relevant technologies, resulting in less innovation generated.

In particular, IPR policy changes in some SSOs have been highly controversial in both industrial and academic discussions since they could potentially discourage the participation of SEP holders. For example, the IEEE policy amendment in 2015 received widespread attention from IP scholars. Pohlmann (2017) analyzed the impact of the 2015 IEEE policy change on its standardization activities. The study showed that, although the number of LOAs decreased, it was still in line with historical fluctuations and could be attributed to IEEE workflow

6 Although patent holdup is usually considered by SSOs when designing their IPR licensing policies, and scholars have published a considerable number of theoretical studies on patent holdup, there is a lack of empirical studies showing patent holdup to be a common problem in practice (B. Heiden & N. Petit, Patent "Trespass" and the Royalty Gap: Exploring the Nature and Impact of Patent Holdout, *Santa Clara High Tech L.J.* (2017).

issues rather than the change in its IPR policy. In addition, the number of standards completed and published, and the technical influence of these standards and the number of new project authorization requests (PARs) have continued to grow steadily. Thus, Pohlmann concluded that standardization work at IEEE has continued to move forward as usual since the new IPR policy adoption in 2015. However, more recently, Gupta and Effraimidis (2018) also empirically examined the impact of the IEEE patent policy revision, and held different views from Pohlmann (2017) arguments. The analysis focused on the IEEE 802 LAN/MAN standards, which are characterized by a large number of associated SEPs, and other standards that would not be affected by the new IPR policy were eliminated from the study. Their results showed that the policy significantly affected the LOA submissions from 2015 to 2016. The number of positive LOA submissions decreased by 91%, from 31 to 3, while the number of negative LOA submissions reached a historic high, rising from 0 in 2015 to 7 in 2016.[7] Additionally, Gupta and Effraimidis (2018) pointed out a significant delay in the approval of 802.11 standards after the policy change. Finally, they called on SSOs to strike a proper balance between protecting the rights of innovators and implementers while designing IPR policies.

Furthermore, an industry survey conducted by Heiden and Petit (2017) showed that the 2015 IEEE policy change worsened patent holdout issues. They renamed patent holdout as patent trespass, which they considered more suitable to explain this conduct and more in conformity with mainstream economic theory. As the opposite of patent holdup, patent trespass is defined as the situation in which "a SEP holder's licensing revenue decreases, because some (or all) technology implementers avert, either temporarily or permanently, the conclusion of a licensing agreement on terms that correspond to recognized industry practices". According to their statistics, SEP holders experienced considerable reductions in licensing revenue due to payment delay of SEP implementers or nonpayment. Respondents in the survey reported that the 2015 IEEE policy change caused a negative impact on SEP royalty rates and time to license and, as a result, worsened patent trespass issues. Thus, Heiden and Petit (2017) suggested that patent trespass issues should be considered by SSO policy revision in the future.

Other than the preceding advice, researchers have offered a variety of suggestions to SSOs to improve their regulation. Farrell and Simcoe (2012) argued that policies that limit vested interests, such as starting the standard setting process early, before firms engage in developing particular technologies or endorsing incomplete standards that allow firms to differentiate their products, can be effective instruments in expediting the consensus-building process and enhancing firms' incentives to improve technical proposals. Otherwise, firms often hold strong vested interests in specific technologies and are unwilling to compromise

7 A positive LOA is a letter in which a patent owner agrees to license its SEPs under a current IPR policy, while a negative LOA is a letter in which the SEP holder explicitly declines giving any assurance regarding its licensing intentions.

to reach consensus. Kokoulina (2015) highlighted the potential benefits of cooperation between SSOs and patent offices. Possible collaboration, such as sharing SSOs' working documents with patent offices, can increase efficiency and transparency of standard setting activities, as well as improving the quality of patent examination. To address the royalty-stacking issue, Contreras (2013) proposed a pseudo-pool approach, which attempts to determine royalty caps and the allocation of these royalties through joint negotiation. Using this approach, SEP holders and potential standard implementers in an SSO working group could establish an aggregate royalty rate for the standard, and then patent holders could jointly negotiate and determine the distribution of the agreed aggregate royalty rate prior to market adoption of the standard.

However, few SSOs have modified their policies following academic recommendations due to antitrust concerns, lack of practicality and other considerations. For example, Contreras (2017a) analyzed why his proposed pseudo-pool approach has rarely been adopted in practice and concluded that, due to the perceived risk of antitrust liability, SSOs and their member companies have avoided this joint negotiating and pricing mechanism.

2.3 *Firms' participation in standardization*

2.3.1 *Through SSOs*

Members of SSOs do not equally contribute to the formulation of standards. Baron and Gupta (2018) studied firms' participation in the 3GPP and found that the distribution of contributions submitted by firms is highly skewed. More precisely, the top 2% of firms are responsible for submitting 60% of all contributions. In addition, nearly one-third of participants (161 of 500 members) did not submit any technical contributions to 3GPP during the period 2005–2013. In addition, Blind and Thumm (2004) concluded that firms with higher patenting intensity are less likely to join standardization processes since they have alternatives with lower opportunity costs to market their products.

SSOs can play a role in guaranteeing firms' involvement and efficient collaboration among members and eventually forming standards that fulfill the manufacturers' and market expectations. Some SSOs have introduced a variety of structural changes and in-house processes to serve this purpose. For example, ETSI organized industry specification groups and specialist task forces, which offer technical support and expedite the technical specification process.

2.3.2 *Through consortia*

In addition to the aforementioned formal alternatives to facilitate collaboration during the standard setting process, firms have formed industry consortia. Thus, this subsection addresses firms' participation in consortia, emphasizing how consortia benefit formal standard setting processes. An industry consortium refers to a cooperation system among a group of firms that seek a common goal through joint efforts, usually within a certain industry. In the standardization process, consortia facilitate coordination among participants, support the generation of technical specifications and work as a platform for firms to build business communities (Hawkins, 1999). There are some examples of consortia that have successfully worked in the development and promotion of standards, including the DVD Forum, RosettaNet and the Video Electronics Standards Association.

Baron and Pohlmann (2013) found that firms formed standard consortia especially when there is fragmented ownership of IPPs and a high degree of technological overlap among firms. In such a circumstance, coordination in standard setting is difficult to accomplish. Standards consortia serve as an informal means to solve coordination failures and reduce conflicts of interest emerging in the formal standardization process. The study also concluded that firms with substitutable rather than complementary patents are more likely to be members of the same consortium, which can reduce the risk of R&D duplication and the costs of standard development. In addition, from a strategic point of view, firms with similar technologies in a consortium can strengthen their positions against outside competitors.

Additionally, Blind and Gauch (2008) examined the relationship between standardization activities in formal standardization bodies (i.e. SSOs) and in informal standardization bodies (i.e. standard consortia). Their findings showed that the technical content of activities in these two organizations is complementary rather than substitutive, indicating that most technical issues are discussed in both SSOs and standard consortia. They proposed that synergies might exist between standardization activities in the two types of organizations. For example, the specifications developed in consortia can be utilized as input for formal standardization processes.

Delcamp and Leiponen (2014) found that industry consortia can expedite standardization by facilitating the negotiation of technical features, as well as mobilizing the bandwagon effect to achieve the widespread adoption of standards. However, consortia appear to lack transparency and openness, impeding the participation of latecomers or small firms. Thus, the authors called on policy makers to promote open membership, publicly available meetings and decision documents and public disclosure of decision-making rules to improve the image of industry consortia.

As mentioned earlier, some consortia have also developed consortia standards, which are less formal than those developed by formal SSOs. Farrell and Saloner (1988) compared the advantages and disadvantages of both types of standards. They found that informal standards are defined faster but are of lower quality than formal standards, usually with slow formulation processes but superior quality. The study also concluded that, if the two standard setting processes are run at the same time, they would benefit from each other and both improve.

Consortia not only facilitate the standardization process as a whole but also benefit the individual firms that participate in it. Focusing on the development of 3GPP standards, Leiponen (2008) found that, if firms participate in consortia, especially when firms can interact with other 3GPP members, their contributions and influence in the standard setting process increase. However, small firms benefit less from the cooperation networks in consortia since extensive human, technological and financial resources are required. The results suggest that resource-constrained firms can increase their influence in 3GPP by joining large consortia with formal relationships with 3GPP, since this type of consortium can engender more legitimacy for the firms, thus enhancing their ability to influence standards. Participation in consortia has also been found beneficial for firms' innovation output. Baron et al. (2014) concluded that firms enjoy an increase in innovation after joining a consortium.

Regarding consortia per se, Pohlmann (2014) studied the evolution of 435 standard consortia in the ICT industries. The results of survival analyses revealed that the type of membership (flat, tiered, revenue based and so on), size and scope of the standard projects were factors determining a consortium's longevity. For example, standards consortia with a broader focus in their standards projects survived longer than narrowly focused consortia. In other words, the consortia formed to solve particular problems might not survive over a long period of time unless they can extend their focus to other standard projects. In addition, Kamps et al. (2017) empirically studied 69 standard consortia in the information technology, consumer electronics, telecommunications and home automation industries. They found that openness to new members at the highest organizational level of a consortium increases its likelihood of survival. Their study also showed that internal competition among members of consortia has a negative impact on the survival time of consortia because high internal competition could lead to opportunistic behaviors that undermine inter-firm trust.

2.3.3 Patent pools

Another type of organization associated with standardization is patent pools, which can be considered a one-stop shop where patents are licensed by two or more parties under certain terms, as well as a platform for different types of firms to collaborate and develop sound solutions for implementers. Since standardization increasingly involves joint development of complex technologies by groups of different firms (Simcoe et al., 2007), fragmentation of patent ownership emerges naturally. The widely distributed essential patents associated with standards increase the costs of negotiation, the probability of possible future litigation, and other transaction costs, ultimately impeding the widespread adoption of technology standards. Patent pools can improve the efficiency of technology diffusion and generate procompetitive benefits by reducing transaction costs, integrating complementary technologies, clearing blocking positions and avoiding costly infringement litigation (DOJ, 2017). Therefore, some SSOs, such as the DVB, have encouraged the formation of patent pools after standards were set.

Royalty stacking gives rise to the excessive amount of royalties that producers must pay due to the large number of patents involved in one or multiple standards and the lack of coordination among patent holders. As a vexing issue in the licensing of SEPs, royalty stacking can be overcome by patent pooling. The issue has gained much attention and received suggestions from academia. For example, Contreras (2013) proposed a pseudo pool in which SEP holders and manufacturers come together to negotiate and define a reasonable royalty rate based on the expected overall market for standardized products and other factors. Tirole (2015) also praised patent pools as a tool that benefits licensors and technology users through the aggregation of complementary patents and the reduction of overall royalties.

A more recent study by Merges and Mattioli (2017) measured the costs and benefits of patent pools. They found that patent pools substantially reduce transaction costs. For example, the MEPG audio patent pool and HEVC pool reduced patent transaction costs by USD 600 million and almost USD 400 million, respectively, while the cost of establishing each patent pool was less than USD 8 million. Vakili (2016) showed that the establishment of patent pools leads to an increase in the rate of follow-on innovations, despite the concern that patent pools could decrease subsequent investment in innovation activities due to the pressure induced by grant-back provisions and the cannibalization risks, which result from follow-on innovations that could replace the established standard. Using data from seven major patent pools created during the period 1997–2004, he found that, on average, the annual citation rate increased by 14% for patents included in a pool.

In terms of patent pool regulations, they are contingent on whether they have in majority complementary or substitutive patents in the pool. Lerner et al. (2007) examined the rules of 63 patent pools and found that pools comprising complementary patents are more likely to adopt independent licensing rules, allowing patent holders to independently license their pooled patents, as well as follow-up patents based on the pooled patents. In addition, pools with complementary patents are more likely to implement grant-back provision, which requires follow-on innovations based on the pooled patents to be licensed to the pool members at no fee or under fair and reasonable terms.

After a patent pool is formed, firms decide whether to contribute their patents to the pool. The factors that affect the firms' participation in patent pools have been discussed in a number of studies. Pure R&D firms, which mainly profit from licensing rather than manufacturing and selling products, might prefer their patents to be licensed outside of the pool, where they can seek higher royalties, and thus are less likely to join a patent pool (Dequiedt and Versaevel, 2013; Han, 2015). Layne-Farrar and Lerner (2011) demonstrated with empirical research that vertically integrated firms that maintain a licensing business model as an upstream technology provider and sell products as a downstream manufacturer are more likely to join patent pools since they can enjoy lower costs from cross-licensing and earn royalties through widespread licensing. In addition to firms' characteristics, studies have also found that royalty allocation rules enacted in patent pools have an impact on firms' participation. For example, if the proportion of royalties that each firm can attain merely depends on the number of patents that the firm has contributed to the pool, namely the numeric proportional sharing rule, firms with valuable patents would be less likely to join this type of pool and would choose pools in which the value of each patent is considered (Layne-Farrar and Lerner, 2011).

Baron and Delcamp (2015) investigated the strategies of seven patent pools on including patents and concluded that the founding members who hold major patents usually continue to file and include incremental and less cited patents in the pool, taking advantage of their experience and bargaining power. Therefore, after the patent pool is launched, the number of patents included in the pool grows remarkably, while the width and technological significance of patents measured by the number of claims and the number of forward citations respectively, decrease over time. Further, Delcamp (2016) compared the value of pooled patents with non-pooled patents, which have characteristics similar to the pooled patents. He found that patents with a larger number of forward citations are more likely to be included in a pool, and these patents also received more forward citations after being included in the patent pool. Thus he concluded that patents selected to be included in a pool are generally more valuable than similar patents not included.

Since patent pools appear to be highly beneficial for the development of product markets, their widespread use would be a natural expectation. However, in a report for the European Commission, Pohlmann and Blind (2016) found that 91% of worldwide declared SEPs are directly licensed by SEP holders, rather than through patent pools. According to their analysis, the failures of many patent pool initiatives are mainly caused by the difficulty in integrating the various interests of multiple participants. In addition, some patent pools require participants to agree on a maximum licensing royalty and prohibit higher licensing prices outside the pool, which can dissuade SEP holders during negotiations and cross-licensing.

3 SEPs and FRAND terms

Firms which develop technologies can obtain economic profits from SEPs, which incentivize them to further invest in R&D. For example, if a patented innovation of a firm is included in the standards, it will generate additional licensing demand for this patent, thus leading to more royalty revenue for the firm. However, SSOs' IPR policies often require SEP owners to license their patents on FRAND terms, which prevent them from charging exorbitant royalties and from blocking market entry of competitors. In this vein, studies on SEPs and FRAND terms can be divided into two streams. One stream of the literature argues that owning SEPs increases firms' financial returns, which in turn motivates firms to participate in R&D and standard setting processes. The other stream argues that the SSO's IPR policies, such as licensing under FRAND terms, will eventually limit the royalties that SEP holders can obtain.

3.1 The effects of SEPs and firms' filing strategies

Pohlmann et al. (2016) have tested the effects of owning SEPs on firms' financial performance. Their results showed a curvilinear (inverted U-shaped) relationship between the number of declared SEPs and a firm's return on assets (ROA). They also confirmed that the impact of owning SEPs on firms' financial performance depends on the size of the whole patent portfolio and the types of SSOs that firms join. Therefore, firms should think strategically about which patents are to be incorporated into technology standards to build a balanced patent portfolio with essential and nonessential patents. In addition, they should consider the types of SSOs that can offer a better platform for their essential patents, allowing the firms to realize their financial potential.

Hussinger and Schwiebacher (2015) adopted a market value approach to investigate the effects of SEPs on firm performance, and concluded that the number of declared SEPs is positively correlated with a firm's market value, even after controlling for the size of patent portfolios in general. However, this relationship does not apply for blanket disclosure, in which firms state that they are willing to grant licenses on the terms required by the SSO such as FRAND terms. However, without disclosing information on the IP that they hold, they create uncertainty for market valuation of these SEPs. Overall, the remuneration of SEPs appears to be attractive, even though most SEP licenses must comply with FRAND terms.

In terms of patent citations, empirical analysis has found that the number of patent citations increases substantially after a patent is declared essential to a standard, indicating an increase in the use of the patented invention due to its inclusion in the standard (Simcoe et al., 2007; Rysman and Simcoe, 2008). As confirmed by Simcoe et al. (2007), the litigation rate also increases after a firm has declared a patent to be essential to a standard. In particular, small firms are more likely to file a lawsuit after declaring their patents to be essential, because they face a bigger challenge capturing rents in complementary markets than large incumbents and have to defend their SEPs more aggressively as an alternative way to grab value from their IP.

SEPs also have a positive impact on future standard development. Baron et al. (2014) argued that the characteristics of standards determine whether the economic returns generated by SEPs can provide incentives for further R&D investment. They also concluded that R&D coordination among firms can mitigate two types of inefficiency (i.e. excessive or insufficient incentives for R&D investment). Moreover, Baron et al. (2016b) found that existing essential patents play a significant role in the subsequent development of standards. Their analyses showed that standards subject to SEPs change more frequently than otherwise. Specifically, the inclusion of SEPs has a strong positive effect on the rate of standard upgrades and a negative impact on standard replacement. However, the results show that, when the SEP ownership is more fragmented, the positive effects of SEPs on the rate of technological progress diminish.

Realizing the importance of SEPs, firms adopt different strategies to build SEP portfolios. Berger et al. (2012) documented the patent filing behaviors of firms participating in standard development and found that SEPs have a higher number of claims than nonessential patents, which could help firms to gain greater bargaining power in negotiations with competitors and higher royalty payments as a result. They also demonstrated that the claims of essential patents are amended approximately 25% more often than those of nonessential patents, and the applications of essential patents have longer periods of pendency than those of nonessential patents. By amending the claims, firms can keep filings and make claims in line with the standards under development. Overall, firms' motivation to achieve broad patent claims and attain strong protection is magnified in the standardization context.

Another type of firm strategy related to SEPs is called just-in-time patenting (Kang and Bekkers, 2015). These authors analyzed firms' patent filing and SEP disclosure behavior during the development of the W-CDMA and LTE standards, and the results showed that seven days preceding the standardization meeting appears to be a peak time for patent filings among participants. Although standards are supposed to include patents with significant technical value, those just-in-time patents which mainly come from vertically integrated firms were found to have significantly fewer citations but were more likely to be declared essential. These authors suggest that the inclusion of just-in-time patents could undermine competition and increase the end-product price. It might also unnecessarily complicate the standards and slow down the standard setting process. However, current SSOs' IPR policies have not undertaken measures to control these opportunistic behaviors.

3.2 Essentiality of SEPs

In the standardization context, a patent is defined as essential when there is no technical or commercial alternative for implementing the standard without using the patent. In other words, if a firm cannot obtain a license for using the essential patents, it is unable to implement the standard without infringing on those essential patents.

Bekkers and Updegrove (2012) studied the policies with regard to essentiality in 10 SSOs and found that the subject of essentiality differs substantially among SSOs. For example, some SSOs include contributions, such as copyrights, utility model patents, know-how and trade secrets, as essential components for a standard, while others explicitly exclude them. Moreover, SSOs usually use two different definitions of essentiality, namely commercial and technical essentiality. Commercial essentiality refers to a patented technology being the only commercially feasible way in which the standard can be implemented given factors such as manufacturing cost, efficiency, reliability, manufacturability and so on. In this case other optional technologies that exceed the expected cost of the standard implementation will not be considered (Contreras, 2017b). For example, the IEEE and VITA have included a commercial essentiality consideration for essential patents, while other SSOs only consider technical essentiality, viewing patent claims essential to the standard merely as technical or engineering matters, irrespective of their economic costs. The U.S. DOJ reviewed the DVD patent pool proposal, the essentiality policy of which includes economic essentiality, and the MPEG-2 pool proposal, which only considers technical essentiality, and approved both pooling proposals (DOJ, 2017).

In addition to the issues that could arise from different definitions of essentiality among SSOs, the lack of essentiality evaluations of the patents declared as essential to standards has also raised concerns among scholars and practitioners. By declaring a large number of essential patents, firms could fall into a practice known as over-declaration, resulting in the inclusion of patents not necessarily essential to the standard implementation. Goodman and Myers (2005) reviewed 887 patent families declared essential to 3GPP and 3GPP2 projects and found that only approximately 21% of declared SEPs are actually essential.

Similarly, the Cyber Creative Institute (2011), after evaluating a total of 1,147 patents declared according to the LTE standard, found that only 55.4% of them were truly essential patents, while 30.8% of them partially matched the standard and the remaining 13.8% did not match it at all. Moreover, the report calculated the essentiality ratio of each company as the number of truly essential patents of a company divided by all of the patents declared by the same company, and found that the ratios varied across companies. The essentiality ratios of the firms such as ZTE, NTT DOCOMO and Nokia Siemens were greater than 80%. However, for Motorola and Samsung, truly essential patents only accounted for 36.2% and 48.4% of their total patent portfolios, respectively. A possible reason related to over-declaration could be the firms' opportunistic patenting and SEP declaration behaviors, such as just-in-time patenting, as analyzed by Kang and Bekkers (2015).

Bekkers et al. (2011a) studied the determinants of essential patents in compatibility standards using SEP data. They found that both the intrinsic technological value of patents and the active involvement of patent holders in the standard setting process increased the patents' likelihood of being declared essential to a standard. Moreover, their results showed that the involvement of patent holders in the standardization process has a stronger impact on the likelihood of the patents being included in standards than on the technical value of the patents.

Finally, in terms of essentiality evaluation, a report by Régibeau et al. (2016) for the European Commission investigated the economic benefits and costs of checking the essentiality of patents in the standard setting process. The report concluded that the adoption of essentiality checks could save litigation costs of EUR 6.66 million, assuming that the average cost of a patent litigation is EUR 3.33 million, and the existence of essentiality checks would reduce the litigation probability from 0.1 to 0.05. In addition, to reduce the implementation cost of essentiality checks, Régibeau et al. (2016) proposed a random essentiality test of patents declared essential. In this test, they first evaluated a random sampling of the patents declared by a company and ascertained an essentiality ratio of the sample. Then, by multiplying this ratio by the total number of the firm's declared patents, the total number of patents truly essential for a standard in the firm's portfolio can be estimated. According to the analysis, the essentiality ratio of each company obtained from the random test could be used as the quality weight for a firm's patent portfolio in other contexts, such as royalty allocation in patent pools.

3.3 FRAND terms

As a widely adopted licensing policy by many SSOs, FRAND terms can be traced back to the early 1940s (Contreras, 2015). During World War II, the U.S. federal courts ordered patent holders to license their patents to others on "reasonable" terms, similar to the current FRAND terms. In Europe, ETSI has been recognized as a pioneer in the invention of FRAND terms. In 1994, it introduced a (F)RAND model into its newly formulated IPR policy. Since then, the inclusion of FRAND terms in its IPR policy has remained unchanged over the decades and has been followed by a number of SSOs worldwide.

FRAND terms require firms to license their essential patents under a nondiscriminatory principle and offer fair and reasonable royalties. Based on theoretical modeling, Stryszowska (2014) argued that, on the one hand, the adoption of standards can generate network externalities, which in turn increase the number of product users. Thus upstream technology providers expect to collect a larger amount of royalties and are willing to promote standard setting. On the other hand, if a standard is adopted without FRAND licensing terms, the holders of patents included in the standard can abuse their market power by charging excessive royalties, which would deter the market entry of downstream manufacturers. Consequently, upstream firms might receive less royalty income and might prefer to support several incompatible technologies. If the positive effect of network externalities outweighs the negative effect of market deterrence, upstream patent holders will prefer to set a compatible standard, instead of supporting two incompatible technologies, to maximize their royalties and vice versa. Therefore, the author concluded that the overall outcome of standard development and adoption hinges on the degree of network externality when FRAND terms are not applied.

However, many scholars have argued FRAND commitments are ambiguous (Bekkers et al., 2011b; Tirole, 2015; Padilla and Wong-Ervin, 2017). For example, Bekkers and West (2009) showed that ETSI members were concerned about the insufficiency of FRAND terms in the UMTS standardization process since it is difficult for them to evaluate whether royalties are fair, reasonable and nondiscriminatory based on a vague definition.

Moreover, Dewatripont and Legros (2013) analyzed the consequences of FRAND agreements, focusing on fairness and nondiscrimination, and suggested that, under FRAND principles, upstream firms tend to overinvest in R&D and include more patents (even some inessential) in standards to increase their profits. They argued that, although fair and reasonable in FRAND terms means that royalty rates should not be excessive, such a requirement does not prevent firms with more patents from asking for a higher aggregate royalty rate. Therefore, current FRAND settings could lead to opportunistic behaviors, such as over-declaration, and could affect the quality of the patents that firms contribute to standards. However, Baron et al. (2016a) held a different view and argued that FRAND itself does not represent any problem, but reflects the dynamics and complexity of the market, in which disputes are inevitable among different stakeholders.

3.3.1 Licensing FRAND-incumbent patents

Layne-Farrar and Salinger (2018)'s study of bundling patents with FRAND and non-FRAND commitments showed that, to comply with its obligation and at the same time attain higher licensing revenues, patent holders can license separately the FRAND-incumbent patent and the non-FRAND-incumbent patent. Furthermore, this study suggests that, when it is required to set licensing fees during the standard setting process (such as ex ante declaration of licensing fees), the higher the value that a patent can generate outside the standard, the less likely the patent holder will be to agree to a low royalty rate (even royalty free) in the standard setting negotiation, as the patent holder has the option of reaping value from its patents outside the standard and does not have to aggressively compete with other patent holders by setting lower royalty rates to win the standard competition.

Since firms would strategically license to firms which produce components or final products, identifying appropriate licensee companies in the value chain is another important but unsettled issue, which was partially addressed in Padilla and Wong-Ervin's (2017) research. Their research focused on SEP holders' licensing decisions regarding nondiscriminatory commitment. They found that in practice, SEP holders usually choose not to assert their patents at the component level but seek to license at the end product level, and that factors such as costs, monitoring sales, and patent exhaustion doctrine can explain this strategy.

3.3.2 Royalty calculation under FRAND terms

Although some SSOs, such as IEEE and W3C, have defined FRAND royalties, debates have still arisen from conflicting interests among different parties, and the calculation of royalties for SEPs under FRAND commitments remains unstandardized. Here we mainly discuss two common calculation methods (i.e. the bottom-up approach and the top-down approach) as well as relevant decisions in courts.

The bottom-up approach is used to determine the proportion of contribution of an SEP and its royalties independently of one another, often by referencing a comparable license, such as the license of other patents owned by the same SEP holder and those owned by others with the same or similar standards. There are many factors to be considered when determining whether a license is comparable. In *Lucent v. Gateway* (Cassiman et al., 2009), the court stated that whether the license is exclusive or not should be one of the considerations when determining the royalty rate. Other factors include whether the license applies to similar territories and whether the license is achieved through a court settlement or through normal negotiations (JPO, 2018).

The top-down approach refers to the determination of royalties proportionally allocated to individual SEPs, considering the total royalties of all SEPs in a standard that should be payable. Today, the top-down approach is widely adopted in many court cases; for example, in the case of *TCL v. Ericsson* (2017), the court set the cumulative royalty rate at 5% for 2G/3G and between 6% and 10% for 4G. Judge Robart also employed a top-down method to determine a FRAND royalty rate in the case of *Microsoft v. Motorola*. The method states that, in a hypothetical negotiation, the parties should evaluate the importance of SEPs, first, relative to the standard and, second, relative to the importance of the standard to the products when determining a reasonable royalty rate. Moreover, this reasonable royalty should be restricted to the value of the patented technology, apart from the value associated with incorporation of patents into the standard. In addition, due to uncertainty regarding the essentiality of Motorola's SEPs, the rate was adjusted. The calculation resulted in a royalty range with an upper bound of 16.389 cents and a lower bound of 0.555 cents per unit for the H.264 Standard (Maldonado, 2014).

In the case of *Innovatio IP Ventures v. LLC Patent Litigation* (N.D. Ill. 2013), two parties agreed to apply Judge Robart's methodology with some modifications. Judge Holderman, who presided over the case, determined a single FRAND rate, instead of a range, and argued that there was no need to adjust the rate, since the essentiality of Innovatio's SEPs had already been judicially confirmed by the court, in which all the 168 claims under examination were determined to be essential for the standard. The court used the smallest saleable unit as the royalty base to implement the 802.11 standard. Finally, using a top-down approach, the court determined the value of the chip attributable to the 802.11 standard was 151 cents per chip, multiplied by the ratio of the contribution of Innovatio's SEPs to the 802.11 standard to attain the final royalty rate, which was 9.56 cents per Wi-Fi chip.

Scholars have also provided some suggestions for FRAND royalty calculation. Hytönen et al. (2012) proposed that, to comply with FRAND terms, the royalty calculation should be conducted at two levels. One is based on the contribution of a specific technology to the end product and the other is according to the value of each patent owner's portfolio added to this technology. Employing the system dynamics simulation method, these authors identified the royalty rates through the preceding two-level royalty calculation model and analyzed the effect of licensing cost on product and technology markets. The conclusion shows that the implementation of this model could benefit all types of companies so that healthy product markets and sustainable technology development can be maintained. Additionally, Layne-Farrar and Salinger (2016) suggested that patents under FRAND commitments should set their royalties either by the net value that the patented technology contributes to the end product or the manufacturer's investment cost in inventing the technology multiplied by its odds of success. Moreover, Contreras (2017a) argued that joint negotiation of FRAND royalties, in which SSO participants discuss together and define royalties, can serve as one of the most promising means for determining aggregate royalty levels.

4 Conclusion

In this chapter, we offered an overview of economics and management studies on SSOs, SEPs and FRAND terms. SSOs have modified their IPR policies in the last decades toward more stringent regulation on IPR disclosure and licensing. The discussion in the literature focuses on SSOs' policy changes and how firms' participation in the standard setting process has been affected by these changes. Although some scholars have argued that imposing stricter policies can preserve competition, other studies have demonstrated that it could discourage firms from joining SSOs. In particular, the IEEE policy change in 2015 has been deemed controversial in the academic discussions.

We also discussed firms' participation in consortia and patent pools, which are two highly relevant organizations in the context of standardization. The literature focuses on their functions in facilitating collaboration among firms and licensing transaction. With regard to consortia, it has been established that they can expedite standardization by facilitating consensus-building processes, as well as reducing the cost of standard development by coordinating R&D activities among firms. Participation in consortia can help firms to increase their influence and contribute to the standard process, also increasing their innovation output. Regarding patent pools, it has been found that they can substantially reduce transaction costs and increase the rate of follow-on innovations.

In addition to reviewing the studies on SSOs, we summarized studies on SEPs and FRAND. Scholars have found that SEPs can generate considerable economic returns for firms, and owning a number of SEPs can promote firms' financial performance. Perceiving the value of SEPs, firms adopt different filing strategies to enlarge and enhance their SEP portfolios, such as filing patents immediately before standardization meetings and later amending claims frequently. However, the essentiality that underpins SEPs remains unclearly defined. Currently, some SSOs adopt commercial essentiality, and the others choose technical essentiality. Moreover, there is a lack of essentiality checks on declared essential patents, which can cause the over-declaration problem and heighten litigation costs. According to some estimates, a considerable number of SEPs are not truly essential. Given the substantial benefits that essentiality evaluation can possibly generate, some scholars have attempted to design methods, such as random essentiality testing, to render it workable in practice and to reduce the implementation cost.

In terms of FRAND commitment, its definition and application have been widely discussed in the standardization literature. Scholars have expressed concerns about the ambiguity of its definition. Although some SSOs have defined FRAND terms, their definitions remain inconsistent among different organizations, and the calculation methods of the royalties for SEPs under FRAND commitments remain unstandardized. Today, a number of courts have adopted a top-down approach to calculate the royalty rates of FRAND-committed patents. Given the importance of SSO, SEP and FRAND to modern technologies and industries and the controversies surrounding them currently, more studies on these topics are needed in the future to guide firms' strategy-making and to provide policy recommendations to governments and SSOs alike.

Acknowledgements

The authors acknowledge the financial support provided by the National Natural Science Foundation of China through grant Nos. 71874152 and 71732008, by Zhejiang Provincial Soft Science Research Program through grant No. 2019C25038 and by the Fundamental Research Funds for the Central Universities.

References

2017. TCL v Ericsson. U.S. District Court, Central District of California.

3GPP. 2016. 3GPP Working Procedures, Article 55. Intellectual Property Rights (IPR) Policy.

ATIS. 2011. *ATIS Response to NIST RFI* [Online]. Available at: www.nist.gov/sites/default/files/documents/standardsgov/ATIS.pdf [Accessed on 4 September 2018].

ATIS. 2018a. Operating Procedures for ATIS Forums and Committees, 10. Intellectual Property Rights Policy.

ATIS. 2018b. *Patent Policy* [Online]. Available at: www.atis.org/01_legal/patent-policy/ [Accessed on 4 September 2018].

Baron, J. & Delcamp, H. 2015. The strategies of patent introduction into patent pools. *Economics of Innovation and New Technology*, 24, 776–800.

Baron, J. & Gupta, K. 2018. Unpacking 3GPP standards. *Journal of Economics & Management Strategy*, 27(3), 433–461.

Baron, J., Ménière, Y. & Pohlmann, T. 2014. Standards, consortia, and innovation. *International Journal of Industrial Organization*, 36, 22–35.

Baron, J., Pentheroudakis, C. & Thumm, N. 2016a. FRAND Licensing in theory and in practice: proposal for a common framework. *Antitrust Chronicle*, 3.

Baron, J. & Pohlmann, T. 2013. Who cooperates in standards consortia – rivals or complementors. *Journal of Competition Law & Economics*, 9, 905–929.

Baron, J., Pohlmann, T. & Blind, K. 2016b. Essential patents and standard dynamics. *Research Policy*, 45, 1762–1773.

Baron, J. & Spulber, D.F. 2018. Technology standards and standard setting organizations: an introduction to the Searle Center Database. *Journal of Economics & Management Strategy*, 27, 462–503.

Bekkers, R., Bongard, R. & Nuvolari, A. 2011a. An empirical study on the determinants of essential patent claims in compatibility standards. *Research Policy*, 40, 1001–1015.

Bekkers, R., Iversen, E. & Blind, K. 2011b. Emerging ways to address the reemerging conflict between patenting and technological standardization. *Industrial and Corporate Change*, 21, 901–931.

Bekkers, R. & Updegrove, A.S. 2012. A study of IPR policies and practices of a representative group of standards setting organizations worldwide.

Bekkers, R., Verspagen, B. & Smits, J. 2002. Intellectual property rights and standardization: the case of GSM. *Telecommunications Policy*, 26, 171–188.

Bekkers, R. & West, J. 2009. The limits to IPR standardization policies as evidenced by strategic patenting in UMTS. *Telecommunications Policy*, 33, 80–97.

Berger, F., Blind, K. & Thumm, N. 2012. Filing behaviour regarding essential patents in industry standards. *Research Policy*, 41, 216–225.

Blind, K. & Gauch, S. 2008. Trends in ICT standards: the relationship between European standardisation bodies and standards consortia. *Telecommunications Policy*, 32, 503–513.

Blind, K. & Thumm, N. 2004. Interrelation between patenting and standardisation strategies: empirical evidence and policy implications. *Research Policy*, 33, 1583–1598.

Cassiman, B., Di Guardo, M.C. & Valentini, G. 2009. Organising R&D projects to profit from innovation: insights from co-opetition. *Long Range Planning*, 42, 216–233.

CCI. 2011. *Evaluation of LTE Essential Patents Declared to ETSI.* Cyber Creative Institute.

Chiao, B., Lerner, J. & Tirole, J. 2007. The rules of standard-setting organizations: an empirical analysis. *RAND Journal of Economics*, 38, 905–930.

CIE. 2007. Standards, innovation and the Australian economy. *Standards Australia.* Centre for International Economics.

Contreras, J.L. 2013. Fixing FRAND: a pseudo-pool approach to standards-based patent licensing. *Antitrust Law Journal*, 79, 47–97.

Contreras, J.L. 2015. A brief history of FRAND: analyzing current debates in standard setting and antitrust through a historical lens. *Antitrust Law Journal*, 80, 39–120.

Contreras, J.L. 2017a. Aggregated royalties for top-down FRAND determinations: revisiting "joint negotiation". *The Antitrust Bulletin*, 62, 690–709.

Contreras, J.L. 2017b. Chapter 13. Essentiality and standard-essential patents, in *The Cambridge Handbook of Technical Standardization Law: Competition, Antitrust, and Patents.* Cambridge University Press, New York.

Delcamp, H. 2016. The value of patents in pools and its implications for competition. *The Criterion Journal on Innovation*, 1, 161–178.

Delcamp, H. & Leiponen, A. 2014. Innovating standards through informal consortia: the case of wireless telecommunications. *International Journal of Industrial Organization*, 36, 36–47.

Dequiedt, V. & Versaevel, B. 2013. Patent pools and dynamic R&D incentives. *International Review of Law and Economics*, 36, 59–69.

Dewatripont, M. & Legros, P. 2013. 'Essential' patents, FRAND royalties and technological standards. *The Journal of Industrial Economics*, 61, 913–937.

DIN. 2000. *Economic Benefits of Standardization Summary of Results* [Online]. Available at: www.iec.ch/about/globalreach/academia/pdf/academia_governments/economic_benefits_standardization.pdf [Accessed on 13 September 2018].

DOJ. 2006. *Response to VMEBus International Trade Association (VITA)'s Request for Business Review Letter* [Online]. Available at: www.justice.gov/atr/response-vmebus-international-trade-association-vitas-request-business-review-letter [Accessed on 4 September 2018].

DOJ. 2015. *Response to Institute of Electrical and Electronics Engineers, Incorporated* [Online]. Available at: www.justice.gov/atr/response-institute-electrical-and-electronics-engineers-incorporated_ftn3 [Accessed on 4 September 2018].

DOJ. 2017. Antitrust Guidelines for the Licensing of Intellectual Property.

DVB. 2014. *Memorandum of Understanding Further Amended and Restated for the Development of Harmonised Digital Video Broadcasting (DVB) Services Based on European Specifications* [Online]. Available at: www.dvb.org/resources/public/documents_site/dvb_mou.pdf [Accessed on 4 September 2018].

DVB. 2018. *History of DVB* [Online]. Available at: www.dvb.org/about/history [Accessed on 4 September 2018].

Eltzroth, C. 2008. IPR Policy of the DVB project: negative disclosure, FR&ND arbitration unless pool rules OK, Part 2. *International Journal of IT Standards and Standardization Research (IJITSR)*, 7(2), 1–22.

ETSI. 2019. *ETSI Intellectual Property Rights Policy, Annex 6 of ETSI Rules of Procedure, European Telecommunications Standards Institute, Sophia Antipolis, France, April 2019* [Online]. Available at: https://portal.etsi.org/directives/40_directives_apr_2019.pdf [Accessed on 23 October 2019].

Farrell, J. & Saloner, G. 1988. Coordination through committees and markets. *The RAND Journal of Economics*, 235–252.

Farrell, J. & Simcoe, T. 2012. Choosing the rules for consensus standardization. *The RAND Journal of Economics*, 43, 235–252.

FTC. 2011. *FTC to Host Public Forum on Competition Issues in Standard-Setting* [Online]. Available at: www.ftc.gov/news-events/press-releases/2011/05/ftc-host-public-forum-competition-issues-standard-setting [Accessed on 4 September 2018].

Goodman, D.J. & Myers, R.A. 2005. 3G cellular standards and patents. *Wireless Networks, Communications and Mobile Computing, 2005 International Conference*. IEEE, 415–420.

Gupta, K. & Effraimidis, G. 2018. IEEE patent policy revisions: an empirical examination of impact. *Working Paper*.

Haimowitz, J. & Warren, J. 2007. Economic value of standardization. Standards Council of Canada.

Han, Y-J. 2015. Analysis of essential patent portfolios via bibliometric mapping: an illustration of leading firms in the 4G era. *Technology Analysis & Strategic Management*, 27, 809–839.

Hatto, P. 2010. *Standards and Standardization Handbook*. European Commission, European Research Area, Industrial Technologies.

Hawkins, R. 1999. The rise of consortia in the information and communication technology industries: emerging implications for policy. *Telecommunications Policy*, 23, 159–173.

Heiden, B. & Petit, N. 2017. Patent "Trespass" and the royalty gap: exploring the nature and impact of patent holdout. *Santa Clara High tech Law Journal*. 34, 179–249.

Hussinger, K. & Schwiebacher, F. 2015. The market value of technology disclosures to standard setting organizations. *Industry and Innovation*, 22, 321–344.

Hytönen, H., Jarimo, T., Salo, A. & Yli-Juuti, E. 2012. Markets for standardized technologies: patent licensing with principle of proportionality. *Technovation*, 32, 523–535.

IEEE. 2015. *Letter of Assurance for Essential Patent Claims* [Online]. Available at: https://development.standards.ieee.org/myproject/Public//mytools/mob/loa.pdf [Accessed on 4 September 2018].

IEEE. 2018. IEEE-SA Standards Board Bylaws, 6. Patents.

JPO. 2018. Guide to licensing negotiations involving standard essential patents.

Kamps, X., Vries, H.D. & Kaa, G.V.D. 2017. Exploring standards consortium survival in high tech industries: the effects of commitment and internal competition *Computer Standards & Interfaces*, 52, 105–113.

Kang, B. & Bekkers, R. 2015. Just-in-time patents and the development of standards. *Research Policy*, 44, 1948–1961.

Kappos, D. & Michel, P.R. 2018. The smallest salable patent-practicing unit: observations on its origins, development, and future. *Berkeley Technology Law Journal*, 32, 1433.

Knut, B., Jungmittag, A. & Mangelsdorf, A. 2011. The economic benefits of standardization. An update of the study carried out by DIN in 2000.

Kokoulina, O. 2015. Standardization in the ICT: towards ever closer union between SSOs and patent offices? *Standardization and Innovation in Information Technology (SIIT), 2015 IEEE 9th International Conference*. IEEE, 1–8.

Layne-Farrar, A. & Lerner, J. 2011. To join or not to join: examining patent pool participation and rent sharing rules. *International Journal of Industrial Organization*, 29, 294–303.

Layne-Farrar, A., Llobet, G. & Padilla, J. 2014. Payments and participation: the incentives to join cooperative standard setting efforts. *Journal of Economics & Management Strategy*, 23(1), 24–49.

Layne-Farrar, A. & Salinger, M.A. 2016. Bundling of RAND-committed patents. *Research Policy*, 45, 1155–1164.

Layne-Farrar, A. & Salinger, M.A. 2018. The policy implications of licensing standard essential FRAND-committed patents in bundles. *Complications and Quandaries in the ICT Sector*. Springer, Singapore.

Leiponen, A.E. 2008. Competing through cooperation: the organization of standard setting in wireless telecommunications. *Management Science*, 54, 1904–1919.

Lemley, M.A. & Shapiro, C. 2006. Patent holdup and royalty stacking. *Texas Law Review*, 85, 1991–2050.

Lerner, J., Strojwas, M. & Tirole, J. 2007. The design of patent pools: the determinants of licensing rules. *The RAND Journal of Economics*, 38, 610–625.

Lerner, J. & Tirole, J. 2006. A model of forum shopping. *American Economic Review*, 96, 1091–1113.

Lerner, J. & Tirole, J. 2015. Standard-essential patents. *Journal of Political Economy*, 123, 547–586.

Maldonado, K. 2014. Breaching RAND and reaching for reasonable: Microsoft v. Motorola and standard-essential patent litigation. *Berkeley Technology Law Journal*, 29, 419–464.

Merges, R.P. & Mattioli, M. 2017. Measuring the costs and benefits of patent pools. *Ohio State Law Journal*, 78, 281–347.

Padilla, J. & Wong-Ervin, K.W. 2017. Portfolio licensing to makers of downstream end-user devices: analyzing refusals to license FRAND-assured standard-essential patents at the component level. *The Antitrust Bulletin*, 62, 494–513.

Pohlmann, T. 2014. The evolution of ICT standards consortia. *Communications & Strategies*, 95, 17–40.

Pohlmann, T. 2017. Empirical study on patenting and standardization activities at IEEE. *IPlytics*.

Pohlmann, T. & Blind, K. 2016. Landscaping study on Standard Essential Patents (SEPs). *IP Lytics EU Report*.

Pohlmann, T., Neuhäusler, P. & Blind, K. 2016. Standard essential patents to boost financial returns. *R&D Management*, 46, 612–630.

Régibeau, P., De Coninck, R. & Zenger, H. 2016. Transparency, predictability, and efficiency of SSO-based standardization and SEP licensing. *A Report for the European Commission*.

Rysman, M. & Simcoe, T. 2008. Patents and the performance of voluntary standard-setting organizations. *Management science*, 54, 1920–1934.

Schmalensee, R. 2009. Standard-setting, innovation specialists and competition policy. *The Journal of Industrial Economics*, 57, 526–552.

Simcoe, T.S., Graham, S.J. & Feldman, M. 2007. Competing on standards? Entrepreneurship, intellectual property and the platform paradox. *National Bureau of Economic Research Working Paper.*

Stryszowska, M.A. 2014. Fair, reasonable, and non-discriminatory terms and technology adoption: standard setting vs. incompatible technologies. *Economics of Innovation and New Technology*, 23(8), 717–738.

Temple, P., Witt, R., Spencer, C., Blind, K., Jungmittag, A. & Peter, S. 2005. The empirical economics of standards. *DTI Economics Paper No. 12.* DTI.

Tirole, J. 2015. Market failures and public policy. *American Economic Review*, 105, 1665–1682.

Vakili, K. 2016. Collaborative promotion of technology standards and the impact on innovation, industry structure, and organizational capabilities: evidence from modern patent pools. *Organization Science*, 27, 1504–1524.

VITA. 2015. VSO Policies and Procedures, 10. Patent Policy.

W3C. 2004. *W3C Patent Policy* [Online]. Available at: www.w3.org/Consortium/Patent-Policy-20040205/-sec-Requirements [Accessed on 4 September 2018].

Part II

Beneficiaries and enforcement of FRAND declarations/commitment

5 U.S. perspectives

William Hubbard[1]

1 Introduction

Interoperability standards allow products manufactured by different companies to interface, and are extremely important in some industries, particularly those related to ICT (information and communication technology) products. For example, standards allow smartphones from different companies to work on the same high-speed wireless data networks and computer parts from different manufacturers to be assembled in diverse configurations, expanding the range of products available to end consumers. Standards thus can increase consumer demand and at the same time enhance competition among manufacturers. Consumers also benefit when standards incorporate innovative technologies, thus providing improved product functionality.

The incorporation of advanced technologies into standards also introduces new complexities, in that innovative features of a standard may be covered by patents. These standards essential patents (SEPs) provide patent owners with substantial economic power because all companies seeking to make standards-compliant products must use the patented technology. As a result, SEPs threaten to produce two economic problems that limit the social utility of standards. First, a SEP owner may be able to engage in patent "holdup", that is, to demand onerous licensing terms from a manufacturer who has already implemented a standard. Given the essential nature of a SEP, such a manufacturer often cannot redesign its products to avoid infringement. Even if it is possible to revise the standard to exclude the patented technology, redesigning products and retooling related manufacturing processes may be enormously expensive. To avoid these switching costs, the manufacturer instead might agree to royalties that far exceed the technical value of the patented invention.[2] The second economic problem that may arise with SEPs is known as "royalty stacking", which occurs when a product utilizes numerous patented technologies, all of which must be licensed to manufacture the product. If manufacturers must pay substantial royalties for

1 Professor of Law at the University of Baltimore School of Law and Senior Counsel at Womble Bond Dickinson.

2 Strategic considerations may also dissuade some manufacturers from pursuing revisions to the standard if that manufacturer is able to obtain a cheaper license than its competitors.

each of these patents, then the royalties will "stack" one on top of another so that the total amount of royalties exceeds a commercially viable threshold. Concerns of royalty stacking are especially likely to arise with standards and SEPs because some standards incorporate hundreds if not thousands of patented inventions.

To address licensing problems related to SEPs, standard setting organizations (SSOs) often require that their members identify publicly their SEPs and agree to license them on "fair, reasonable, and non-discriminatory" (FRAND) terms.[3] Despite the use of FRAND declarations for decades, SSOs have provided little guidance regarding the legal effects of such statements, leading litigants in U.S. courts to dispute the legal meaning of FRAND in various respects. As these fights have percolated through the U.S. courts, the legal landscape of FRAND has begun to come into focus. Most importantly, courts in the U.S. have held that FRAND commitments carry important legal consequences, ranging from comparatively modest limitations on patent infringement remedies to supporting affirmative antitrust claims brought by manufacturers against SEP owners.

Moreover, the impact of these decisions extends beyond the geographic borders of the U.S. in at least three respects, and therefore should be considered by many Asian companies and policymakers. First, companies headquartered outside of the U.S. today acquire U.S. patents in record numbers. Indeed, the percentage of U.S. patents issued to foreign inventors has steadily increased for decades, reaching an all-time high in 2015 of 52.8%, when the U.S. Patent and Trademark Office issued 157,483 patents to non-U.S. inventors.[4] Indeed, each year Asian companies regularly rank among top recipients of U.S. patents.[5] For the same reasons, many Asian companies today own U.S. SEPs. The second international facet of U.S. FRAND law stems from the value of the U.S. market. Though the economies of many countries have grown in recent years, U.S. markets remain important in many industries. The U.S. represents about a quarter of global GDP and is home to more than 300 million people. With a U.S. trade deficit of half a trillion dollars, many of the products purchased by U.S. consumers come from abroad, and many products in U.S. markets are manufactured by U.S. subsidiaries of non-U.S. companies.[6] U.S. SEPs may be

3 Some SSOs require declarations to license SEPs on terms that are "fair, reasonable and non-discriminatory" (FRAND), while other SSOs require declarations on terms that are simply "reasonable and non-discriminatory" (RAND). U.S. courts have not distinguished between FRAND and RAND, and this chapter likewise draws no such distinction.

4 Patent Tech. Monitoring Team, *U.S. Patent Statistics, Calendar Years 1963–2015*, U.S. Patent & Trademark Office, available at www.uspto.gov/web/offices/ac/ido/oeip/taf/us_stat.htm.

5 Patent Tech. Monitoring Team, *Patenting by Geographic Region (State and Country), Breakout by Organization: Count of 2011–2015 Utility Patent Grants, By Calendar Year of Grant*, U.S. Patent & Trademark Office, available at www.uspto.gov/web/offices/ac/ido/oeip/taf/stcasg/all_stcorg.htm.

6 The U.S. trade deficit in 2017 was USD 556 billion. Lucia Mutikani & David Lawder, U.S. Trade Deficit Rises to Nine-Year High on Robust Imports, *Reuters*, February 6, 2018, available at www.reuters.com/article/us-usa-economy-trade/u-s-trade-deficit-rises-to-nine-year-high-on-robust-imports-idUSKBN1FQ1XG.

asserted against the many manufacturers of standards-compliant products in the U.S., regardless of where those manufacturers are headquartered. Indeed, as demonstrated by the many high-profile cases against Samsung Electronics Co., Asian manufacturers may find themselves embroiled in U.S. litigation related to SEPs. These lawsuits give rise to a third international dimension to the U.S. FRAND law: some U.S. FRAND disputes have the potential to determine global FRAND terms, thereby resolving disputes in both the U.S. and other countries. Some Asian SEP owners and implementers may find the prospect of global patent peace conceptually appealing. But to evaluate whether such global resolution under the direction of U.S. courts would be advantageous, those companies must grapple with the still-solidifying details of U.S. FRAND law.

This chapter therefore endeavors to provide an overview of the legal effects of FRAND declarations under U.S. law and to explore how these issues of U.S. law impact Asian interests. To do so, the chapter proceeds in five sections following this introduction. Section 2 begins to explore the legal nature of FRAND declarations by examining the consequences under U.S. law of failing to adhere to SSO policies, which require members to declare SEPs and provide FRAND commitments. These legal consequences provide powerful incentives for SSO members to provide FRAND declarations. This section also begins to lay the groundwork for exploring the ramifications of FRAND declarations under U.S. law in the sense that, if the failure to make FRAND declarations has legal consequence, then making FRAND declarations likewise should have legal effect. Section 3 describes the first of three types of legal effect for FRAND declarations in U.S. patent infringement disputes, where U.S. courts have found that FRAND commitments limit the remedies available to SEP owners and in some cases prohibit injunctive relief altogether. Section 4 evaluates the legal consequences of FRAND declarations under U.S. contract law. Courts in the U.S. have held that FRAND declarations create binding contracts that can be asserted by potential licensees and that a SEP owner's contractual obligations include both a commitment to license on FRAND terms and to negotiate for a FRAND license in good faith. U.S. courts have thus held that SEP owners may breach their FRAND commitments by taking actions inconsistent with good faith negotiations, including by filing patent infringement suits seeking to enjoin infringement. Finding breach, U.S. courts have issued powerful remedies in favor of potential licensees, going so far as to enjoin patent disputes in countries beyond the U.S. borders. Along the way, these U.S. courts have undertaken detailed economic analyses to establish FRAND terms. Section 5 examines the antitrust implications of FRAND rates, which potentially offer the most powerful remedies to potential FRAND licensees, including treble damages. However, U.S. courts have ruled that SEP owners may be liable for antitrust violations related to FRAND declarations only in the limited case where SEP owners provided intentionally false declarations to SSOs. Finally, the chapter concludes in section 6 by examining how these features of U.S. law apply to Asian businesses, both from the perspective of Asian SEP owners and manufacturers.

2 Failure to make FRAND declarations under U.S. law

A threshold issue in evaluating the legal effect of FRAND declarations under U.S. law is determining whether they are legally binding statements or whether they are simply precatory marketplace statements. As discussed throughout in this chapter, U.S. courts uniformly consider FRAND declarations to be legally binding commitments in various respects. In fact, SEP owners in U.S. courts generally do not dispute that FRAND declarations are binding commitments.[7] SEP owners take this position for many reasons, including to maintain their memberships in various SSOs. Another important reason SEP owners concede that FRAND declarations are legally binding – and an important consideration in determining the nature of that legal effect – is that U.S. courts have held a SEP owner's failure to make FRAND declarations entails legal consequences in patent, fraud, and antitrust disputes.

Importantly, U.S. courts have ruled that by failing to submit FRAND declarations, SEP owners may waive their rights to enforce those patents. While the clearest examples of waiver under U.S. patent law arise when a patent owner knowingly and intentionally disclaims rights to an invention, waiver may also be implied when a patent owner engages in conduct that is inconsistent with an intent to enforce the patent.[8] As a result, though waiver might not be found when SEP nondisclosure stems from negligence or oversight, U.S. courts have found that intentional nondisclosure may imply waiver, preventing a patent owner from being able to enforce a SEP against standards-compliant products.[9] In fact, waiver can even arise under U.S. law when an undisclosed patent or application would be essential to a proposed standard but the SSO does not adopt that standard.[10] Threat of waiver thus serves as a strong incentive for SEP owners to submit to SSOs patent declarations, including FRAND commitments where SSO rules require them.[11] Even though a SEP owner may be limited to FRAND rates for declared SEPs (as described later), a patent owner receives no royalties whatsoever when there is a finding of waiver.

Intentional failure to disclose SEPs may also violate U.S. antitrust laws, thereby subjecting a SEP owner to powerful remedies including treble damages and automatic fee shifting.[12] Section 2 of the Sherman Antitrust Act prohibits the unlawful acquisition or maintenance of a monopoly, and U.S. courts recognize

7 *See, e.g.*, *Ericsson, Inc. v. D-Link Sys., Inc.*, 773 F.3d 1201, 1209 (Fed. Cir. 2014).

8 *See Qualcomm Inc. v. Broadcom Corp.*, 548 F.3d 1004, 1020 (Fed. Cir. 2008).

9 *Id.* at 1022. Importantly, a showing of implied waiver does not require detrimental reliance by an accused infringer. *Id.* at 1021.

10 In such a situation, waiver would arise only if the patent owner either engages in "egregious conduct" or obtains some benefit from non-disclosure. *Core Wireless Licensing S.A.R.L. v. Apple Inc.*, No. 2017-2102, 2018 WL 3893122, at *10 (Fed. Cir. August 16, 2018).

11 In fact, U.S. courts have held that waiver may apply when a patent owner intentionally fails to disclose patents that "reasonably *might* be necessary" to a standard. *Id.* at 1018 (emphasis added). As a result, waiver might even apply to some patents that are not actually essential.

12 15 U.S.C. § 15(a). Under U.S. law, each party typically bears its own legal expenses.

that SEPs may provide monopoly power in the market for standards-compliant technology.[13] Non-infringing technological alternatives cannot compete in this market once a standard has already been widely adopted and market participants face high switching costs.[14] If a patent owner intentionally fails to disclose a SEP, a would-be licensee may be able to show that the failure to disclose was an unlawful acquisition or maintenance of a monopoly.[15] To do so, however, an antitrust claimant may need to prove that had the patent owner disclosed the SEP, then the SSO would not have incorporated the patented technology into the standard.[16] For example, an antitrust claimant might have to show that equivalent technological alternatives were available at the time of standardization and that the particular SSO involved has a policy of avoiding patented technology.

It is less clear, however, whether an antitrust violation occurs under U.S. law when an SSO would still have selected a patented technology had the patent owner disclosed the SEP, perhaps because the patented invention was technologically superior to other options available at the time. If there had been disclosure, the SEP owner might have been asked to provide a FRAND commitment. But U.S. courts are divided as to whether the failure to make a FRAND declaration constitutes an antitrust violation. To some U.S. courts, § 2 of the Sherman Act prevents only the acquisition of monopoly power and is not violated when a party that lawfully obtains monopoly power abuses that power to obtain greater profits.[17] In contrast, other U.S. courts note that interoperability standards often enhance competition, but that these competitive benefits are undermined if a SEP owner has not made and is therefore not bound by a FRAND commitment.[18] The latter approach also addresses the inherent difficultly that antitrust claimants face in seeking to demonstrate the availability of technological alternatives. Had the SEP owner explicitly refused to commit to FRAND licensing, technological alternatives might have been identified or developed. By intentionally

13 *Id.* § 2.

14 *Broadcom Corp. v. Qualcomm Inc.*, 501 F.3d 297, 315 (3d Cir. 2007).

15 *Rambus Inc. v. F.T.C.*, 522 F.3d 456, 463 (D.C. Cir. 2008). This case arose in the context of an investigation by the Federal Trade Commission, a U.S. administrative agency tasked with laws protecting consumers and promoting competition, often through administrative investigations. *See* 15 U.S.C. § 45(a).

16 *See id.* at 463 (describing the F.T.C.'s decision); *see also Matter of Dell Computer Corp.*, 121 F.T.C. 616, 621–624 (1996) (issuing a consent decree prohibiting enforcement of a SEP against standards-compliant technologies and asserting that there was evidence that the SSO would have implemented a different non-proprietary design had it been informed of the SEP).

17 *Id.* at 465 (holding that "an otherwise lawful monopolist's use of deception simply to obtain higher prices normally has no particular tendency to exclude rivals and thus to diminish competition); *see also NYNEX Corp. v. Discon, Inc.*, 525 U.S. 128 (1998). Effectively, these courts hold that section 2 is designed only to prevent unlawful monopolies from arising, and not to limit the harmful effects of otherwise lawful monopolies.

18 *Broadcom Corp.*, 501 F.3d at 314; *see infra* section 5 (discussing in more detail the effects on competition).

failing to disclose its patent, the SEP owner has prevented the SSO from pursing alternatives.

Another potential consequence under U.S. law of SSO members failing to disclose SEPs and therefore to commit to licensing on FRAND terms is that such conduct might constitute fraud, in which case a successful claimant would be able to obtain both compensatory and punitive damages. However, proving fraud based a patent owner's failure to disclose a SEP can be difficult in U.S. courts, even if there is evidence demonstrating that the SEP owner concealed the SEP in bad faith. Fraud is a state-law claim, and state law varies among the 50 U.S. states. Nevertheless, the elements of fraud are largely the same from state to state, requiring (1) a false representation or omission in the face of a duty to disclose, (2) of a material fact, (3) made intentionally and knowingly, (4) with the intent to mislead, (5) with reasonable reliance by the misled party and (6) resulting in damages to that party.[19] When a patent owner intentionally chooses not to disclose a SEP, the owner has likely satisfied many of the elements of fraud. The timing of this failure to disclose and the particular terms of the intellectual property rights policy (IPR policy) of the SSO in question, however, may prevent a finding of fraud under U.S. law. For example, if the SSO's IPR policy requires only the disclosure of patents with claims that read on the standard, and the claims of an undisclosed SEP are not written until after the standard is established, then a SEP owner may not have engaged in fraud even if the specification for the SEP was written before the standard was finalized.[20] Nevertheless, if a SEP is obtained before standardization or if the SSO's IPR policy requires disclosure of a broader group of patents, such as those that could become essential through claim amendments, an intentional failure to disclose a SEP might support a claim of fraud.

U.S. courts have thus held that patent owners take great risks by failing to disclose SEPs. At best, a non-disclosing patent owner may waive its rights to any concealed SEPs, and at worst the SEP owner might incur massive financial liability under U.S. antitrust and tort law. SEP owners therefore face powerful incentives to declare their patents and applications during standard setting. Moreover, because that disclosure protects SEP owners from these liabilities, patent owners in U.S. courts are reluctant to later claim that these declarations have no legal effect. Similarly, because many SSOs require that such SEP disclosures include commitments to license on FRAND terms, these patent owners are likewise less likely to argue in U.S. courts that FRAND commitments are merely precatory. Instead, SEP owners often concede in U.S. cases that FRAND declarations are binding. As explored in the following sections, however, SEP owners and potential licensees often differ significantly regarding the legal effects of these commitments under U.S. law.

19 *Rambus v. Infineon Techs. AG*, 318 F.3d 1081, 1096 (Fed. Cir. 2003) (describing fraud under Virginia law).

20 *Id.* at 1104.

3 FRAND in U.S. patent infringement disputes

One of the most common types of U.S. cases in which FRAND issues arise are patent infringement lawsuits, where FRAND commitments are seen as limitations on the remedies available to SEP owners. When a SEP is infringed, U.S. courts have held that FRAND declarations limit both the availability of injunctions and the amount of damages.

3.1 Injunctions

U.S. courts eschew bright-line rules regarding the availability of injunctions. Instead, U.S. courts determine whether to award injunctive relief by weighing four factors:

1 Any irreparable harm to the patent owner from the infringement
2 The adequacy of other legal remedies, such as monetary damages
3 The balance of hardships between the patent owner from infringement and the infringer if an injunction issues
4 The impact of an injunction on the public interest.[21]

Moreover, U.S. courts weigh these factors equitably in individual cases, avoiding the development of rules requiring or prohibiting injunctions in broad categories of cases.[22] As a practical matter, however, cases with similar facts produce similar results, at times giving the appearance of categorical results.

U.S. courts have held that injunctions are less likely to issue when a SEP owner has made a FRAND declaration because the patent owner may be unable to establish irreparable harm. By committing to licensing on FRAND terms, the patent owner has promised to license the patent to anyone willing to acquire a license on FRAND terms.[23] Having embraced widespread use of its invention, even by direct competitors, a SEP owner typically cannot establish that allowing continued use of the invention by an infringer would produce an irreparable form of harm. Nevertheless, U.S. courts have noted that in appropriate cases a patent owner may be able to obtain injunctive relief despite having made a FRAND commitment, such as if a competitor refuses to take a FRAND license, unreasonably delays FRAND negotiations, or is incapable of paying FRAND rates.[24] This point should not be overstated, as some U.S. judges have expressed reluctance to award an injunction even when an infringer refuses to accept a FRAND license.[25] Under U.S. law infringers who negotiate in good faith but have not concluded

21 *eBay v. MerkExchange*, 547 U.S. 388, 391 (2006).
22 *Id.*
23 *Apple Inc. v. Motorola, Inc.*, 757 F.3d 1286, 1332 (Fed. Cir. 2014), *overruled on other grounds by Williamson v. Citrix Online, LLC*, 792 F.3d 1339 (Fed. Cir. 2015).
24 *Id.*; *Realtek Semiconductor Corp. v. LSI Corp.*, 946 F. Supp. 2d 998, 1007 (N.D. Cal. 2013).
25 *Apple Inc.*, 757 F.3d at 1342 (J. Prost concurring in part and dissenting in part).

licenses are thus unlikely to face injunctions for infringing SEPs subject to a FRAND declaration.

3.2 Damages

U.S. courts have also found that FRAND declarations often limit damages for patent infringement. Under U.S. law, following a finding of infringement, patent owners are entitled to recover "damages adequate to compensate for the infringement".[26] These compensatory damages may include the profits lost due to infringement. But to obtain this form of damages patent owners must prove that, absent the infringement, the patent owner would have obtained greater profits through the sale of goods or services.[27] Nevertheless, even patent owners who cannot make this counterfactual showing are entitled to recover for patent infringement, as U.S. patent law provides that patent owners are entitled to recover, at the very minimum, a "reasonable royalty" for an infringer's use of a patented invention.[28] In fact, reasonable royalties are, by far, the most common form of damages awarded by U.S. courts for patent infringement. For instance, because lost profits may only be recovered by a patent owner that participates in the marketplace, reasonable royalties are typically the only form of compensatory damages available to non-practicing entities.[29] Even for patent owners that make goods or offer services, reasonable royalties are the predominant form of damages in U.S. courts. By one estimation, 81% of damage awards to practicing entities between 2008 and 2017 included reasonable royalties.[30]

26 35 U.S.C. § 284. In patent disputes in the U.S. damages are usually set by a jury. *Festo Corp. v. Shoketsu Kinzoku Kogyo Kabushiki Co.*, 72 F.3d 857, 866 (Fed. Cir. 1995) ("The assessment of damages is a question of fact, and is decided by the jury when trial is to a jury."). The jury must, however, be properly instructed on the law related to patent damages. Moreover, parties may waive the right to a determination of damages by a jury, in which case the judge will assess damages. 35 U.S.C. § 284.

27 *Georgetown Rail Equip. Co. v. Holland L.P.*, 867 F.3d 1229, 1241 (Fed. Cir. 2017). Patent owners may also be able to obtain an infringer's profits under a theory of unjust enrichment. *See Medisim Ltd. v. BestMed, LLC*, 758 F.3d 1352, 1358 (Fed. Cir. 2014).

28 35 U.S.C. § 284. Damages may be enhanced beyond a reasonable royalty if the infringement was willful. *Id.* However, U.S. courts have not yet ruled on whether a FRAND declaration impacts the availability of enhanced damages. A SEP owner's commitment to accepting "fair and reasonable" compensation might be construed as a waiver of any entitlement to enhanced damages.

29 *See Georgetown Rail Equip. Co.*, 867 F.3d at 1241 (holding that to obtain lost profits the patent owner must demonstrate the "manufacturing and marketing capability to exploit the demand" for the patented invention).

30 PWC, 2018 Patent Litigation Study: Change on the Horizon? May 2018, available at www.pwc.com/us/en/forensic-services/publications/assets/2018-pwc-patent-litigation-study.pdf (reporting that 60% of infringement awards to practicing entities are only reasonable royalties and another 21% of infringement awards include both reasonable royalties and lost profits).

U.S. law grants courts substantial flexibility regarding the methodology for assessing reasonable royalties, and by far the most common approach frames the inquiry as determining the rate that the parties would have agreed upon in a hypothetical negotiation taking place just before infringement began.[31] This analytical framework is grounded on the assumption that the parties could have negotiated mutually acceptable terms had they had the opportunity, information, and motivation to negotiate effectively. This analysis is inherently counterfactual, and the parties often have drastically different views on the results of a hypothetical negotiation. Indeed, in many cases the parties actually tried to negotiate licenses before or during litigation but failed to agree on a royalty rate.

To address these difficulties, U.S. courts rely on a complicated body of law to provide structure to this hypothetical negotiation. Importantly, this same legal framework requires that reasonable royalties be adjusted – typically reduced – in the contexts of SEPs and FRAND commitments.

3.2.1 The entire market value rule

A critical limitation on reasonable royalties in patent disputes in the U.S. is known as the entire market value rule (EMVR). This complex rule has two dimensions.

First, the EMVR impacts substantive U.S. patent law by requiring, in cases involving multi-component products, that "the ultimate combination of royalty base and royalty rate reflect the value attributable to infringing features of the product, and no more".[32] In many cases, a product includes numerous patented and unpatented features, and U.S. courts therefore must apportion patent damages to separate the value added by a patent from the value stemming from other sources, including other patented inventions. This feature of the EMVR is consequently known as "apportionment".[33] The only context in which apportionment is not required for a multi-feature product – and damages therefore may be based on the entire value of the product – is when the patented feature provides the "basis" for customer demand.[34]

Issues of proportionality and the EMVR are likely to arise with many SEPs for at least a couple of reasons. To start, standards are often used with complex products that utilize many innovations, such as consumer electronics.[35] Moreover, technological improvement in these areas frequently proceeds incrementally, so that both early patents and improvement patents may simultaneously be SEPs practiced by products. Under the EMVR, the reasonable royalty for a SEP in

31 *Lucent Techs., Inc. v. Gateway, Inc.*, 580 F.3d 1301, 1324 (Fed. Cir. 2009) ("The second, more common approach, called the hypothetical negotiation or the "willing licensor–willing licensee" approach, attempts to ascertain the royalty upon which the parties would have agreed had they successfully negotiated an agreement just before infringement began.").

32 *Ericsson, Inc.*, 773 F.3d at 1226.

33 *Id.*

34 *LaserDynamics, Inc. v. Quanta Computer, Inc.*, 694 F.3d 51, 67 (Fed. Cir. 2012).

35 *Id.* at 66.

these industries must be limited to reflect only the value of the part of the product that infringes the patent, that is, the part of the product that implements the portion of the standard for which the patent is essential.[36] Concerns of proportionality are additionally important with SEPs because U.S. courts have held that royalties for such patents must be limited to the technical value of the invention itself and not include "any value added by the standard's adoption of the patented technology".[37] However, distinguishing the isolated value of an invention from its value once incorporated into a standard may be factually difficult. On the one hand, the inclusion of a patented technology in a standard may be an arbitrary choice among technically equal alternatives, and a substantial portion of the value of a SEP is therefore attributable to standardization and should be excluded under the EMVR from a determination of a reasonable royalty for the use of the SEP.[38] On the other hand, a technology may be included in a standard because that technology is superior to alternatives, and standardization thus may not substantially impact value even under the EMVR.[39]

The difficulties inherent in proportionality determinations are addressed at least in part by the second dimension to the EMVR, which is evidentiary in nature. Specifically, in a case involving a multi-component product, a patent owner generally may not introduce evidence of the total revenue for the product unless the patented feature is the basis for consumer demand for the product.[40] Instead, U.S. courts generally "insist on a more realistic starting point" regarding multi-component products in such patent disputes, typically by using a royalty base defined by the "smallest saleable unit".[41] For example, in a case in which a laptop computer sold by Company A contains a disk drive manufactured by Company B, and that disk drive infringes a patent, the owner of that patent typically cannot introduce evidence of the total revenues to Company A for the laptops and instead must argue for a reasonable royalty rate based on the revenues to Company B stemming from the sales of the disk drives.

From one perspective, this requirement under U.S. law is somewhat surprising given that mathematically equivalent royalties can be calculated using a royalty base defined by either the smallest saleable unit or the entire multi-component product. Achieving such equivalence requires only that a smaller royalty rate be applied to the larger royalty base and vice versa.[42] However, juries are often

36 *Ericsson, Inc.*, 773 F.3d at 1232–1233.

37 *Id.* This proportionality limit for royalties regarding SEPs does not require a FRAND declaration.

38 *Id.* at 1233.

39 *Apple Inc.*, 757 F.3d at 1333 (J. Rader, dissenting in part).

40 *LaserDynamics, Inc.*, 694 F.3d at 68.

41 *Ericsson, Inc.*, 773 F.3d at 1227; *LaserDynamics, Inc.*, 694 F.3d at 67–68. However, in setting FRAND *contract* terms (in contrast to patent infringement damages for a SEP subject to a FRAND declaration) at least one court has held that FRAND terms do not need to be based on the smallest saleable unit. *HTC Corp. v. Telefonaktiebolaget LM Ericsson*, No. 6:18-CV-00243-JRG, 2019 WL 126980, at *5 (E.D. Tex. January 7, 2019).

42 *Ericsson, Inc.*, 773 F.3d at 1226.

involved in setting royalties, and U.S. courts have expressed concern that a lay-person jury asked to determine a reasonable royalty may be misled by evidence of the value of the product as a whole.[43] Specifically, a jury may consider an unreasonably high royalty calculation nevertheless to be modest when compared to the total revenues for the entire product.[44] U.S. courts protect jury verdicts from this potential error by insulating the jury from information regarding the total revenues for the infringing products, which requires that royalties be calculated using components as a royalty base.

Indeed, this concern regarding the misunderstanding of evidence extends to a jury's consideration of existing patent licenses in some cases. Normally, U.S. courts consider the royalty rates in existing licenses are one of the best measures of "reasonable royalties".[45] However, the negotiation of private licenses is not subject to the strictures of the EMVR and may reflect the total value of a multi-component product rather than the smallest saleable unit. In such a situation, U.S. courts enjoy discretion to decide whether the probative value of a license based on the total value of a multi-component product exceeds the potential prejudice that may arise to the accused infringer from exposing the jury to this evidence.[46] If a court decides to allow the use of such licenses (and related expert testimony), however, it must instruct the jury regarding the appropriate need for apportionment and the EMVR.[47]

For the same reasons noted earlier regarding proportionality, the evidentiary dimension of the EMVR are likely to arise with jury trials regarding the infringement of SEPs. Oftentimes, SEPs cover only small portions of complex, multi-component products, raising concerns that juries may be misled by evidence regarding the higher prices of end products and by licenses based on those higher values. Moreover, with SEPs, these concerns regarding juries and evidence loom particularly large because, as noted earlier, the EMVR requires that reasonable royalties be limited to the value of the patented innovation and not include any value stemming from the incorporation of the invention into the standard. Both the final prices of multi-component products and patent licenses related to those products could include the value added by compliance with the standard. Thus, at least when juries are involved, the EMVR limits the evidence available to patent owners in disputes regarding reasonable royalties.[48]

43 *Id.*; *LaserDynamics, Inc.*, 694 F.3d at 67 ("Where small elements of multi-component products are accused of infringement, calculating a royalty on the entire product carries a considerable risk that the patentee will be improperly compensated for non-infringing components of that product.").

44 *Id.* at 68.

45 *Monsanto Co. v. McFarling*, 488 F.3d 973, 978 (Fed. Cir. 2007).

46 *Ericsson, Inc.*, 773 F.3d at 1227 [discussing Fed. R. Evid. 403(a)].

47 *Id.* at 1228.

48 Evidentiary shortcomings will not, however, prevent a court from calculating reasonable royalties altogether. After a finding of infringement, U.S. courts must award reasonable royalties even if the evidentiary record does not support either party's particular royalty arguments. *Apple Inc.*, 757 F.3d at 1328.

3.2.2 Modified Georgia-Pacific factors

As noted earlier, U.S. courts typically determine "reasonable royalties" by identifying a rate that the parties would have agreed upon during hypothetical negotiations shortly before infringement began. Predicting the behavior of the parties in such a counterfactual negotiation is difficult, particularly when the parties previously tried but failed to negotiate a voluntary license. By far, the most common approach to analyzing this "hypothetical negotiation" involves the evaluation of 15 factors, known as the *Georgia-Pacific* factors.[49] These factors are:

1. The royalties received by the patentee for the licensing of the patent in suit, proving or tending to prove an established royalty.
2. The rates paid by the licensee for the use of other patents comparable to the patent in suit.
3. The nature and scope of the license, as exclusive or non-exclusive; or as restricted or non-restricted in terms of territory or with respect to whom the manufactured product may be sold.
4. The licensor's established policy and marketing program to maintain his patent monopoly by not licensing others to use the invention or by granting licenses under special conditions designed to preserve that monopoly.
5. The commercial relationship between the licensor and licensee, such as, whether they are competitors in the same territory in the same line of business, or whether they are inventor and promoter.
6. The effect of selling the patented product in promoting sales of other products of the licensee; the value of the invention to the licensor as a generator of sales of its non-patented products.
7. The duration of the patent and the term of the license.
8. The established profitability of the infringing product, its commercial success, and its current popularity.
9. The utility and advantages of the patent over the old modes or devices, if any, that had been used for working out similar results.
10. The nature of the patented invention; the character of the commercial embodiment of it as owned and produced by the licensor; and the benefits to those who have used the invention.
11. The extent to which the infringer has made use of the invention, and any evidence probative of the value of that use.

49 *Georgia-Pac. Corp. v. U.S. Plywood Corp.*, 318 F. Supp. 1116, 1120 (S.D.N.Y. 1970), *modified sub nom. Georgia-Pac. Corp. v. U.S. Plywood-Champion Papers, Inc.*, 446 F.2d 295 (2d Cir. 1971). U.S. law does not require the use of these factors, however, in part because some of the factors are irrelevant in some cases. *Ericsson, Inc.*, 773 F.3d at 1230 (noting that "we have never described the Georgia-Pacific factors as a talisman for royalty rate calculations"). Nevertheless, use of the factors is extremely common in patent disputes in the U.S.

12 The portion of the profit or of the selling price that may be customary in the particular business or in comparable businesses to allow for the use of the invention or analogous inventions.
13 The portion of the realizable profit that should be credited to the invention as distinguished from non-patented elements, the manufacturing process, business risks, or significant features or improvements added by the infringer.
14 The opinion testimony of qualified experts.
15 The amount that a licensor (such as the patentee) and a licensee (such as the infringer) would have agreed upon (at the time the infringement began) if both had been reasonably and voluntarily trying to reach an agreement; that is, the amount which a prudent licensee – who desired, as a business proposition, to obtain a license to manufacture and sell a particular article embodying the patented invention – would have been willing to pay as a royalty and yet be able to make a reasonable profit and which amount would have been acceptable by a prudent patentee who was willing to grant a license.

U.S. courts candidly recognize that the application of these factors is "not an exact science" and that the evidence in a case may support a range of reasonable royalties.[50]

U.S. courts have held application of the *Georgia-Pacific* factors must be adjusted in various respects when a SEP is subject to a FRAND declaration. To start, some of the factors are irrelevant to the hypothetical negotiation of FRAND royalties.[51] For example, Factor 4, which addresses the patent owner's interest in maintaining market exclusivity, should no longer be considered because the SEP owner has committed through the FRAND declaration to license the patent.[52] Similarly, Factor 5, which describes the commercial relationship between patent owner and the accused infringer, such as whether the two parties are competitors, is not relevant to FRAND royalty determinations because the patent owner has committed to licensing the patent on "non-discriminatory" terms.[53] The application of other *Georgia-Pacific* factors to SEPs subject to FRAND commitments must be adjusted as well.[54] For instance, under Factor 8, a court setting a "reasonable royalty" usually may consider the "profitability of the product made under the patent" and its "current popularity". In the case of SEPs, however, the "profitability" and "current popularity" of the invention stem largely from the inclusion of the invention in the standard, and U.S. law regarding proportionality prevents the patent owner from claiming value stemming from standardization.[55]

50 *Apple Inc.*, 757 F.3d at 1315.
51 *Ericsson*, 773 F.3d at 1230–1231.
52 *Id.* at 1230.
53 *Id.* at 1230–1231.
54 *Id.* at 1231.
55 *Id.*; *see also supra* subsection 3.2.1 (discussing proportionality and the EMVR).

Likewise, Factor 9 describes the "utility and advantages of the patent property over the old modes or devices", and with SEPs the "utility and advantages" stem largely from inclusion in the standard, which under the EMVR cannot be included in the determination of FRAND rates.[56] Factor 10 instructs courts to consider any "commercial embodiment" of a patented invention produced by the patent owner. However, because the standard requires use of the invention, the use of that invention by the patent owner carries little weight.[57] Finally, in FRAND determinations, U.S. courts consider an additional 16th factor: the SEP owner's commitment to license on FRAND terms.[58] Thus, FRAND commitments will substantially impact the determination of reasonable royalties following a finding of infringement of a SEP.

Issues of holdup and royalty stacking, however, have not directly modified the application of the *Georgia-Pacific* factors, even when the SEP owner has committed to licensing on FRAND terms. U.S. courts have declined, for instance, to instruct juries regarding the general possibility of holdup or royalty stacking in the absence of evidence of those issues.[59] For instance, evidence of holdup might include an increase in the royalties demanded by a SEP owner after the patented invention was incorporated into a standard.[60] However, under U.S. law, the fact that holdup is conceptually possible does not warrant a jury instruction regarding that concern. Likewise, U.S. courts have declined to instruct juries regarding the royalty stacking simply because thousands of patents have been declared essential to a standard. Particular evidence of royalty stacking is required.[61]

4 FRAND in U.S. contract disputes

Recently, potential licensees have succeeded in arguing in U.S. courts that FRAND declarations create binding contracts that are breached both when SEP owners fail to provide FRAND licenses and when those patent owners fail to negotiate in good faith. Moreover, using this approach to FRAND declarations,

56 *Ericsson, Inc.*, 773 F.3d at 1231.

57 *Id.*

58 *Id.*

59 *Id.* at 1234.

60 *Id.*

61 *Id.* In many cases, a FRAND commitment may also prevent a SEP owner from obtaining enhanced damages for patent infringement. Under the U.S. patent laws, courts may increase the damages awarded to patent owner for willful infringement "up to three times." 35 U.S.C. § 284. Such enhanced damages, however, are only available in "egregious cases of misconduct." *See Halo Elecs., Inc. v. Pulse Elecs., Inc.*, 136 S. Ct. 1923, 1932 (2016). In many cases, a SEP owner and a manufacturer of standards-compliant products may both be willing to enter a FRAND license but nevertheless disagree regarding the particular terms of such a license. If the SEP owner files a suit for patent infringement, a U.S. court may not consider the manufacturer's disagreement regarding FRAND terms to render the infringement "egregious", particularly if the court finds that the rates demanded by the SEP owner were not FRAND.

potential licensees have obtained powerful remedies including injunctions that prevent SEP owners from pursuing certain patent disputes outside of the U.S. Along the way, U.S. courts have undertaken detailed economic analyses to calculate FRAND terms, a result that may be as useful to potential licensees as affirmative breach of contract claims.

4.1 FRAND declarations as binding contracts

Under U.S. law, there are two threshold issues in a contract dispute against a SEP owner based on a FRAND declaration. A potential licensee must establish first that FRAND declarations create binding contracts and second that potential licensees are beneficiaries under those contracts. In the past decade, U.S. courts have routinely found in favor of licensees on both of these issues.[62]

In doing so, U.S. courts must begin by determining which jurisdiction's contract laws to apply to FRAND declarations, and these choice-of-law issues threaten to introduce substantial complexity in FRAND contract disputes. Each of the 50 U.S. states determines its own contract law. Moreover, some FRAND declarations are governed by the law of countries other than the U.S.[63] As a result of the legal diversity among jurisdictions, the contractual implications of FRAND declarations could vary among SSOs or even among different SEP owners within the same SSO. Fortunately, U.S. courts have generally found the relevant contract law among U.S. and foreign jurisdictions to be largely similar (with at least one important exception noted later).

For example, U.S. courts have found that the law regarding contract formation is consistent among U.S. states and most countries, requiring (1) an offer, (2) an acceptance, (3) a mutual exchange of valuable consideration, and (4) an understanding between the parties regarding the essential terms of the agreement, which is often described in the U.S. as "a meeting of the minds".[64] Applying this law, U.S. courts have found that SSOs offer various benefits to their members, including opportunities to participate in standard setting, and that the terms of these offers include the IPR policies of the SSOs, notably those that require FRAND declarations.[65] SSO members accept these terms by joining

62 *See, e.g., Realtek Semiconductor Corp.*, 946 F. Supp. 2d at 1005; *In re Innovatio IP Ventures, LLC Patent Litig.*, 921 F. Supp. 2d 903, 922–923 (N.D. Ill. 2013); *Apple, Inc. v. Motorola Mobility, Inc.*, 886 F. Supp. 2d 1061, 1083–1085 (W.D. Wis. 2012); *Microsoft Corp. v. Motorola, Inc.*, 864 F. Supp. 2d 1023, 1031–1033 (W.D. Wash. 2012).

63 For example, U.S. courts have held that contract claims related to FRAND declarations to the European Telecommunications Standards Institute (ETSI) are governed by French law. *Apple, Inc.*, 886 F. Supp. 2d at 1081. Indeed, the IPR policy of ETSI explicitly states that it is governed by French law. ETSI Intellectual Property Rights Policy, available at www.etsi.org/images/files/IPR/etsi-ipr-policy.pdf (part 12).

64 *Apple, Inc.*, 886 F. Supp. 2d at 1083 (describing contract law under the laws of Illinois, New York, Wisconsin and France); *Microsoft Corp.*, 864 F. Supp. 2d at 1031 (describing the law of the State of Washington).

65 *Apple, Inc.*, 886 F. Supp. 2d at 1083–1084; *Microsoft Corp.*, 864 F. Supp. 2d at 1032.

the SSOs, participating in standard setting, identifying SEPs, and committing to licensing SEPs on FRAND terms.[66] Both SEP owners and SSOs benefit from this exchange.[67] SSO members are able to advocate for their patented technologies to be incorporated into standards. SSOs enjoy the assistance of members in developing technically effective standards. Moreover, SSO members commit to licensing SEPs on FRAND terms, thereby helping SSOs to promote widespread adoption of standards. Finally, the policies of the SSOs demonstrate that SSOs and their members understand the essential terms of this exchange, evincing a detailed meeting of the minds. U.S. courts thus find that contractual relationships exist between SSOs and their members and that FRAND declarations are included in the terms of these contracts.

In fact, SEP owners often concede that FRAND commitments are binding contracts.[68] Numerous strategic considerations encourage SEP owners to take such positions. To start, SEP owners may predict that U.S. courts will find their FRAND declarations to be binding for the reasons already noted and thus decide to avoid making arguments that would ultimately lose. Moreover, SEP owners may worry that an argument that FRAND declarations are not binding could generate other legal problems, such as supporting claims of patent waiver or antitrust claims.[69] SEP owners may also concede that FRAND commitments are contractually binding because the owners wish to continue to be involved with standard setting, and SSOs might sanction members who trivialize SSO policies, including through expulsion. Additionally, many SEP owners manufacture standards-compliant products and therefore need licenses to SEPs owned by other SSO members. As a result, a SEP owner may stand to gain more than to lose from FRAND declarations being treated as contracts.

Even if FRAND declarations are contracts, those contracts exist between SEP owners and SSOs, not potential licensees. Indeed, potential licensees may not even be members of the SSO to which a SEP owner submitted a FRAND declaration. Normally, third parties cannot enforce the terms of a contract. To present a viable contract claim based on FRAND declarations, a potential licensee therefore must establish that it is a third-party beneficiary of the contract between the SSO and the FRAND declarant. As with contract law in general, the law regarding third-party beneficiaries could, at least in theory, vary from jurisdiction to jurisdiction,

66 *Apple, Inc.*, 886 F. Supp. 2d at 1084; *Microsoft Corp.*, 864 F. Supp. 2d at 1032.

67 *Apple, Inc.*, 886 F. Supp. 2d at 1083–1084; *Microsoft Corp.*, 864 F. Supp. 2d at 1032.

68 *See, e.g.*, *In re Innovatio IP Ventures, LLC Patent Litig.*, 921 F. Supp. 2d at 922 ("[The patent owner] does not dispute the general theory that patent holders who make RAND commitments to a standards-setting organization may be liable in contract."); *Research in Motion Ltd. v. Motorola, Inc.*, 644 F. Supp. 2d 788, 797 (N.D. Tex. 2008) (asserting that a contract claim based on a FRAND declaration should be dismissed because it inadequately alleged breach and damages).

69 *See supra* section 2 (discussing patent waiver and antitrust liability as potential consequences of failure to disclose SEPs to SSOs); *see also infra* section 4 (discussing antitrust violations based on a failure to honor FRAND commitments).

requiring a conflict-of-laws analysis. Fortunately, U.S. courts have found the law among the U.S. states regarding third-party beneficiaries to be largely uniform. Specifically, a third party is a beneficiary of a contact if the contract is entered for the "direct benefit" of that third party.[70] Applying this law, U.S. courts have concluded that potential licensees "directly benefit" from FRAND declarations because the primary purpose of these declarations is to protect companies who need to obtain licenses to implement the standard.[71] Moreover, U.S. courts have found that the law of some foreign countries regarding third-party beneficiaries is consistent with U.S. law. Notably, U.S. courts have found that the law of France is consistent with U.S. law on issues related to third-party beneficiaries and that potential FRAND licensees are third-party beneficiaries under declarations to the European Telecommunications Standards Institute (ETSI).[72] In contrast, at least one U.S. court has found that German law does not recognize third-party beneficiaries.[73]

Some SEP owners have argued in U.S. courts that, even if a potential licensee is a third-party beneficiary of contractually binding FRAND declarations, it must request a license from the SEP owner to perfect its contractual rights to a FRAND license.[74] According to these SEP owners, failure to request a license before filing a suit for breach of contract voids the right to a FRAND license. U.S. courts, however, have rejected this argument for at least three reasons. First, analyzing the language of SSO policies, U.S. courts have found that these policies do not require a potential licensee to apply for a FRAND license to avoid losing the right to that license.[75] Second, U.S. courts have found that the filing of a suit by a potential licensee is not a repudiation of the desire for a license, at least when the prospective licensee's breach of contract claim includes an assertion that it is ready and willing to accept a FRAND rate set by the court.[76] U.S. courts have recognized that the filing of suit may be the only way that licensees can obtain FRAND terms. Finally, U.S. courts recognize that SEP owners and potential licensees may disagree regarding the essentiality and validity of certain patents. As a result, a potential licensee may decline to accept licensing terms offered by a patent owner, choosing

70 *In re Innovatio IP Ventures, LLC Patent Litig.*, 921 F. Supp. 2d at 922–923; *Apple, Inc.*, 886 F. Supp. 2d at 1085; *Microsoft Corp.*, 864 F. Supp. 2d at 1032 (applying Washington law); *see also Glass v. U.S.*, 258 F.3d 1349, 1354 (Fed. Cir.), *opinion amended on reh'g*, 273 F.3d 1072 (Fed. Cir. 2001) (citing Restatement (Second) of Contracts § 302 (1981)).

71 *Apple, Inc.*, 886 F. Supp. 2d at 1085.

72 *TCL Commc'n Tech. Holdings, Ltd. v. Telefonaktiebolaget LM Ericsson*, No. CV 15-2370 JVS(DFMX), 2017 WL 6611635, at *5 (C.D. Cal. December 21, 2017), *Apple, Inc.*, 886 F. Supp. 2d at 1085; *Apple Inc.*, 2012 WL 1672493, at *12.

73 *Microsoft Corp. v. Motorola, Inc.*, 696 F.3d 872, 879 (9th Cir. 2012).

74 *Microsoft Corp.*, 864 F. Supp. 2d at 1035.

75 *Id.*

76 *Id.* at 1035–1036.

instead to litigate simultaneously issues of infringement, validity and breach of contract.[77]

4.2 Conduct constituting breach

Because U.S. courts have held that FRAND commitments create binding contracts enforceable by potential licensees, a naked refusal to license SEPs would constitute breach of contract. For instance, U.S. courts have found that a SEP owner breaches a FRAND contract by filing a patent infringement suit for injunctive relief without first attempting to license the SEP on FRAND terms.[78] U.S. courts consider such conduct an attempt to pressure potential licensees to accept license terms more onerous than FRAND.[79]

Typically, however, SEP owners attempt to license those patents, so that FRAND disputes more often arise in the context of contentious license negotiations in which the rates offered by a SEP owner exceed those that the potential licensee considers acceptable. In the midst of these negotiations, it may be difficult to demonstrate that a SEP owner has refused to license on FRAND terms. In fact, because the FRAND commitment relates only to the final terms of a license, U.S. courts have held that a SEP owner does not breach the FRAND commitment simply by offering preliminary terms that are not FRAND.[80] To the contrary, U.S. courts consider FRAND to define a range of rates, and non-FRAND offers may be stepping-stones along a path that ultimately reaches FRAND terms.[81]

Nevertheless, in some instances breach may occur during FRAND negotiations. Under U.S. law, a contract automatically includes an implied covenant of good faith and fair dealing, which requires parties to a contract to fulfill their contractual obligations in good faith.[82] As a result, FRAND declarants commit not only to providing FRAND licenses but also to negotiating FRAND rates in

77 *See TCL Commc'ns Tech. Holdings Ltd*, 2014 WL 12588293, at *4; *Realtek Semiconductor Corp.*, 946 F. Supp. 2d at 1007 (noting that a potential licensee can simultaneously pursue RAND breach of contract claims "while denying infringement or asserting invalidity"). Potential licensees must be careful to express a willingness to license SEPs on FRAND terms to avoid claims that FRAND contract rights have been waived. *See, e.g.*, *HTC Corp. v. Telefonaktiebolaget LM Ericsson*, No. 6:18-CV-00243-JRG, 2018 WL 6617795, at *5 (E.D. Tex. December 17, 2018) (discussing the forfeiture of FRAND rights).

78 *See id.* at 1008. The breaching conduct in *Realtek Semiconductor Corp. v. LSI Corp.* was seeking an exclusion from the U.S. International Trade Commission. This exclusion order is the functional equivalent of an injunction.

79 *Id.*

80 *TCL Commc'ns Tech. Holdings Ltd*, 2014 WL 12588293, at *2; *Microsoft Corp.*, 864 F. Supp. 2d at 1037–1038.

81 *TCL Commc'n Tech. Holdings, Ltd.*, 2017 WL 6611635, at *55; *Microsoft Corp.*, 864 F. Supp. 2d at 1038.

82 *Id.* Whether a similar duty of good faith and fair dealing applies to FRAND declarations made outside of the U.S. depends on conflict of laws issues and the particular details of foreign law. *See Apple Inc. v. Samsung Elecs. Co.*, No. 11-CV-01846, 2012 WL 1672493, at *12

good faith.[83] One context in which U.S. courts have found breach of the covenant of good faith and fair dealing in a FRAND agreement is when a SEP owner only briefly negotiates for a FRAND license and then files an action for patent infringement seeking to enjoin the use of a SEP.[84] A critical component of such a finding of breach is that the SEP declarant sought to use the desired injunction to obtain higher than FRAND rates in violation of the FRAND commitment. To make this determination, a court often must determine a FRAND rate and a FRAND range.[85] If a SEP owner offered FRAND terms but the potential licensee refused to accept them, the subsequent filing of an infringement suit may reflect the desire of the SEP owner to obtain those FRAND terms rather than an effort to obtain higher than FRAND returns.[86] In contrast, if the SEP owner demanded rates much higher than FRAND, then filed suit seeking an injunction, a U.S. judge or jury may conclude that the injunction is intended to support the demands for supra-FRAND rates. In such a situation, the duty of good faith and fair dealing may be breached.

Suits regarding breach of the covenant of good faith and fair dealing thus may allow for speedier resolution of FRAND disputes than suits for breach of the FRAND commitment itself. Under the covenant of good faith and fair dealing, the potential licensee may sue for breach while negotiations are still taking place. In contrast, to sue for breach of the commitment to license on FRAND terms, a potential licensee may need to wait until negotiations have concluded, which may take many years and require substantial investment of resources.

4.3 Determining FRAND terms

For various reasons, a court may need to determine a global FRAND terms. For example, as noted earlier, a court may need to assess whether there has been a breach of the FRAND commitment or the related implied covenant of good

(N.D. Cal. May 14, 2012) (recognizing a claim for breach of good faith negotiations under French law stemming from FRAND declarations to ETSI).

83 *See, e.g.*, *HTC Corp. v. Telefonaktiebolaget LM Ericsson*, No. 6:18-CV-00243-JRG, 2018 WL 6617795, at *6 (E.D. Tex. December 17, 2018) (refusing to dismiss a claim for breach of the covenant of good faith stemming from a FRAND declaration).

84 *Microsoft Corp.*, 864 F. Supp. 2d at 1045. Another context where U.S. courts might find breach of the covenant of good faith and fair dealing is when a SEP owner seeks enhanced damages for patent infringement. U.S. patent laws grants courts discretion to increase damages for willful patent infringement "up to three times." 35 U.S.C. § 284. However, willful infringement is an inherent feature of SEPs in many cases. Given that many SSOs require their members to disclose SEPs publicly, a manufacturer who implements a standard will often infringe a SEP with knowledge of the SEP. *See Halo Elecs., Inc.*, 136 S. Ct. at 1932. SEP owners might be able to use threats of treble damages to force manufacturers to accept license terms more onerous than FRAND.

85 *Microsoft Corp.*, 864 F. Supp. 2d at 1038.

86 U.S. courts certainly have not held that FRAND declarations permit a potential licensee to refuse to license a SEP on FRAND terms by negotiating ad infinitum.

faith and fair dealing.[87] Likewise, to determine whether a patent infringement suit by a SEP owner for an injunction violates a FRAND commitment, a U.S. court may need to first determine whether the SEP owner offered FRAND terms before filing the patent case. Some potential FRAND licensees have also sought declaratory judgments from U.S. courts regarding the particular meaning of a SEP owner's FRAND commitment without alleging any breach.[88] In many respects, U.S. law setting FRAND rates is still in its early development, as only two U.S. courts have actually determined FRAND rates.[89] Nevertheless, these cases provide valuable guidance for future litigants as well as parties negotiating in the shadow of the law.

These U.S. courts recognize that, while SSO policies provide little detail regarding the calculation of FRAND terms, FRAND commitments must reflect the primary goal of SSOs: promoting the adoption of their standards.[90] To do so, however, the FRAND determination must balance a fundamental tension inherent in standard setting. On the one hand, SSOs seek to mitigate the risks of holdup and royalty stacking.[91] On the other hand, SSOs seek to encourage participation of technically adept members in standards development, which may require that holders of valuable patent rights receive sufficient remuneration to remain incentivized to participate in standard setting. In balancing these tensions, U.S. courts have adopted two approaches to determining terms that are "fair and reasonable", using patent pools to construct a new, comparable license and applying a SEP owner's previous statements regarding the appropriate aggregate royalty for all SEPs to construct a FRAND license from the top down. Moreover, U.S. courts have evaluated whether a proposed license is discriminatory by comparing its terms to other licenses of the same SEPs owners. These issues are explored in more detail in the following subsections.

4.3.1 Comparable-license calculations

To account for the policy tensions inherent in FRAND, some U.S. courts have constructed FRAND terms utilizing a modified version of the hypothetical

87 As FRAND licenses may involve other terms, U.S. courts have held that in FRAND breach of contract disputes, U.S. judges or juries may determine all terms "material" to FRAND. *TCL Commc'ns Tech. Holdings Ltd*, 2016 WL 4150033, at *5.

88 *See, e.g.*, *id.* at *2.

89 Other U.S. courts have provided some additional guidance regarding the determination of FRAND rates without actually setting rates. *See, e.g.*, *HTC Corp. v. Telefonaktiebolaget LM Ericsson*, No. 6:18-CV-00243-JRG, 2019 WL 126980, at *5 (E.D. Tex. January 7, 2019) (holding that an IPR policy did not require that FRAND rates be based on the "smallest saleable patent-practicing unit").

90 *TCL Commc'n Tech. Holdings, Ltd.*, 2017 WL 6611635, at *7–*8 (noting that the IPR policy of an SSO does not provide "definitive guidance" in determining FRAND terms); *Microsoft Corp.*, 2013 WL 2111217, at *12.

91 *Microsoft Corp. v. Motorola, Inc.*, 795 F.3d 1024, 1031 (9th Cir. 2015); *TCL Commc'n Tech. Holdings, Ltd.*, 2017 WL 6611635, at *6.

negotiation from the calculation of "reasonable royalties" in typical U.S. patent disputes.[92] Specifically, these courts have determined FRAND ranges and rates by determining the amounts that the parties would have negotiated in a hypothetical negotiation for FRAND terms. In such negotiations, U.S. courts posit that SEP owners and licensees would rely on existing FRAND licenses regarding other SEPs to construct new FRAND licenses for the SEPs in question. This approach thus builds from the well-developed U.S. law regarding reasonable royalties as damages for patent infringement, but this approach to FRAND differs from the normal royalty assessment in at least four respects.[93]

First, in determining reasonable royalties outside of the FRAND context, parties would consider any existing licenses to the relevant patents, but in a hypothetical FRAND negotiation, the parties would only give considerable weight to licenses that are similar to FRAND licenses. As a result, FRAND negotiators would not discuss licenses that are not comparable to FRAND licenses, such as licenses to non-essential patents and licenses taken to end patent lawsuits.[94] In some cases, this approach requires courts to exclude from consideration some existing licenses regarding the SEPs at issue. For example, portfolio licenses that were entered to settle infringement lawsuits regarding patents that are not essential provide little guidance regarding FRAND rates because that litigation provides an additional incentive to license through settlement that would not be included in FRAND negotiations.[95] In theory, portfolio licenses that include both SEPs and non-SEPs might be used in setting FRAND rates, but to do so the royalties first must be apportioned to determine the amounts related only to SEPs. As a practical matter, such apportionment can be prohibitively difficult, and U.S. courts may ignore those licenses altogether.[96]

U.S. courts have considered one category of licenses particularly helpful in determining FRAND rates: SEP pools. SEP pools seek to balance considerations nearly identical to those that lie at the heart of the FRAND determination: setting a royalty rate high enough to encourage participation in the pool yet low enough to encourage broad licensing.[97] Moreover, like FRAND licenses, the rights granted through patent pools are often worldwide, encompassing many SEPs from jurisdictions other than the U.S.[98] U.S. courts therefore have calculated FRAND rates by modeling the royalties that a SEP owner would receive if it and all other "readily identifiable" SEP owners joined an existing SEP patent

92 *Microsoft*, 795 F.3d at 1040–1041; *see supra* subsection 3.2 (discussing the calculations of infringement damages for a SEP subject to a FRAND declaration).

93 *See supra* subsection 3.2.2 (describing the use of hypothetical negotiations by U.S. courts to set royalties).

94 *Microsoft Corp.*, 795 F.3d at 1043; *Microsoft Corp.*, 2013 WL 2111217, at *18, *66.

95 *Id.* at *67–*68.

96 *Microsoft Corp.*, 795 F.3d at 1044.

97 *Microsoft Corp.*, 2013 WL 2111217, at *75.

98 *Id.* at *78.

pool.[99] This calculation is complicated by the fact that in some SEP pools, licensors receive royalty-free access to all of the other SEPs in the pool. As a result, the value to a SEP owner if it were to join such a hypothetical SEP pool would include two components: monetary royalties and the cross-license to SEPs owned by many other SSO members.[100] For example, in a SEP pool where 10 companies each contribute 10 SEPs, a participating company would receive royalties for 10 patents licensed to companies outside of the pool but would also receive a free license to the 90 SEPs. A SEP owner may therefore agree to join a pool that provides for lower monetary royalties to gain access to the other SEPs in the pool. In fact, in some cases, the value of the broad cross license can exceed the value of monetary royalties that the SEP owner would receive as a member of a patent pool.[101] In the hypothetical FRAND negotiation between just two parties, however, SEP owners would not receive broad cross licenses to SEPs owned by other companies. Consequently, to draw realistic comparisons between a hypothetical SEP pool and a FRAND license, U.S. courts have ruled that the monetary royalties paid in the pool should in some cases be increased for the FRAND licensee to account for the lack of royalty-free licenses to SEPs owned by third parties.[102]

U.S. courts nevertheless recognize certain limitations in relying on rates from SEP pools. To start, the rates for patent pools are often lower than those from bilaterally negotiated licenses, so that royalty rates higher than those of SEP pools might still be FRAND.[103] Additionally, determining other "readily identifiable" SEP owners is difficult because SSOs do not evaluate the accuracy of declarations by patent owners that their patents are essential. Consequently, a court's royalty estimate based on an expanded patent pool in many cases may be impacted by erroneous declarations. The use of SEP pools is also imperfect because they often allocate royalties without differentiating SEPs on the basis of their technical importance. As a result, a court may determine that the hypothetical FRAND royalties for patents on technologies central to the standard are the same as for patents on peripheral technologies.[104] Parties to a hypothetical FRAND negotiation, however, likely would agree in some cases to higher royalties for more important patents. Nevertheless, when the particular SEPs at issue in a FRAND contract dispute are not particularly important to the standard, use of a pool rate may be appropriate. Thus, while SEP pools are unlikely to define precisely FRAND, the rates calculated using those pools are likely to provide useful information that parties to a hypothetical FRAND negotiation would consider, particularly as evidence of the lower bound in a FRAND range.[105] Large patent pools with more licensees may provide particularly robust evidence of FRAND rates,

99 *Id.* at *64.
100 *Id.* at *81, *84.
101 *Id.* at *84.
102 *Id.*
103 *Id.* at *79–*80.
104 *Id.* at *80.
105 *Id.* at *83.

but even smaller pools that have been less successful provide some evidence of FRAND rates.[106]

A second difference between the hypothetical negotiation normally used in patent infringement disputes in U.S. courts and the hypothetical FRAND negotiation is that parties to a FRAND negotiation would consider the contribution of particular SEPS to the relevant standard.[107] In particular, SEPs for which there were technical alternatives at the time of standardization, including prior art alternatives, are less valuable, though U.S. courts also consider the extent to which such alternatives might have been less desirable than the invention covered by the SEP.[108] U.S. courts also consider the extent to which the products produced by a potential FRAND licensee implement the parts of the standard covered by the licensor's SEPs, as a licensee would not agree to pay as much in royalties when its products do not use or only seldom use the portion of a standard covered by the SEPs.[109] In short, while all SEPs may be essential to practicing the standard, not all SEPs are equal in FRAND licensing negotiations, and some SEPs will command low rates in FRAND negotiations.

Third, U.S. courts hold that parties to a hypothetical FRAND negotiation would be committed to supporting widespread adoption of the standard by avoiding royalty stacking concerns. Accordingly, negotiating SEP owners and licensees would consider the potential financial implications of royalty demands by all other SEP holders.[110] One way that U.S. courts have evaluated this consideration is by multiplying the proposed rate of an individual SEP owner by the number of SEP declarants.[111] While this calculation provides only an approximation of the effect of royalty stacking, U.S. courts consider such an approach useful in evaluating the reasonableness of a proposed individual FRAND rate, particularly when the aggregate royalties would render the adoption of the standard

106 *Id.* at *83, *89. U.S. courts setting a FRAND term might consider issues of cross licensing between the parties to a FRAND dispute, but only if both parties have presented evidence regarding the FRAND value of their respective SEP portfolios. *Id.* at *72.

107 *Id.* at *28.

108 *Id.* at *19. Of course, as a part of this determination, U.S. courts also examine whether declared SEPs are actually essential to the standard, though this analysis may not be as fulsome as the analyses in a patent infringement dispute. *E.g., id.* at *28, *30. Potential licensees may have little reason to dispute essentiality if those licensees practice the patented invention given that the FRAND commitment may be contingent on a declared patent actually being essential and FRAND rates are likely lower than non-FRAND rates. *E.g., id.* at *28, 30, *56. Because a FRAND case may involve all of the patents declared essential by a patent owner, the technical aspect of FRAND contract cases can grow to be lengthy and complex.

109 *Id.* at *42.

110 *Id.* at *20. In this respect, the hypothetical FRAND negotiation differs from the traditional hypothetical negotiation analysis of U.S. courts in patent infringement disputes. *See supra* subsection 3.2.

111 *Id.* at *73. This estimate is imperfect, as U.S. courts have not evaluated the accuracy of the underlying declarations of essentiality, so that the courts' evaluations of royalty stacking may be impacted by erroneous declaration.

financially infeasible.[112] U.S. courts have also evaluated royalty-stacking issues by comparing the total rates calculated using the rates proposed by an individual SEP owner to the total rates discussed by patent owners involved with the establishment of patent pools.[113] Finally, U.S. courts have considered industry reports regarding royalty stacking as evidence relevant to the FRAND determination.[114] Parties to a FRAND negotiation would consider such reports, though the weight of such evidence may be discounted due to differences between the patents analyzed in a report and the particular SEP portfolio that is subject to hypothetical negotiations.

A fourth and final consideration that parties in a hypothetical FRAND negotiation would consider but that is not part of the typical assessment of royalties in U.S. patent infringement disputes is the importance of maintaining sufficient remuneration for SEP owners to encourage their participation in standards development.[115] Many of the considerations noted earlier militate in favor of lower FRAND rates, but the parties in a hypothetical negotiation would recognize that the development of effective standards often requires the discovery and application of cutting-edge innovations. Inadequate compensation for SEP owners could discourage innovators both from developing the technologies that will be critical to future standards and from participating in standard development. However, while hypothetical FRAND negotiators would recognize the importance of maintaining incentives to support standard setting, U.S. courts have offered little guidance on incorporating this consideration into the FRAND analysis.

Importantly, U.S. courts have also ruled that the hypothetical FRAND negotiation would be subject to some of the qualifications from the traditional "reasonable royalty" analysis for patent infringement.[116] For instance, the EMVR rule would apply so that the parties would focus on the technical contribution of the patented invention and exclude from consideration any value stemming from a SEP's inclusion into the standard.[117] Likewise, some of the *Georgia-Pacific* factors would be irrelevant to the FRAND negotiation, including the SEP owner's policy of maintaining exclusive rights in the market, and the commercial relationship between the SEP owner and the licensee.[118]

4.3.2 Top-down calculations

The second approach used by U.S. courts to determine "fair and reasonable" terms for SEP licenses is a "top-down" approach that begins by first estimating

112 *Id.*

113 *Id.* at *87. To do so, U.S. courts have calculated the percentage of essential patents owned by a particular SEP owner using the number of declared SEPs. *Id.* at *84, *87.

114 *Id.* at *97–*98.

115 *Id.* at *20.

116 *See supra* subsection 3.2.

117 *Microsoft Corp.*, 2013 WL 2111217, at *19.

118 *Id.* at *18–*19.

the total royalties for all patents throughout the world that are essential to a particular standard and then apportioning those royalties to an individual patent owner based on the relative value of its SEP portfolio compared to the value of all SEPs. An advantage of this top-down approach is that it prevents royalty stacking because SEP royalties are determined as a portion of an overall capped rate. As a result, if the total aggregate royalty rate is sufficiently low, the top-down approach also avoids issues of holdup by preventing a SEP owner from charging exorbitant rates.[119]

The first step in a top-down FRAND calculation is to determine the total royalty rate for standards-compliant products. The one and only approach that U.S. courts have used for this assessment is to rely on public statements by SEP owners themselves regarding such rates. U.S. courts consider these statements particularly reliable when they were made around the same time as standardization, as they are likely to reflect extraneous valuation issues like holdup.[120] Additionally, the statements are more likely to be reliable when the SEP owner also planned to implement the standard, so that at the time of the statement the SEP owner was motivated to strike a reasonable balance between (1) providing substantial royalties to *all* SEP owners to encourage participation in standardization and (2) keeping royalties low to promote adoption of the standard.[121] In contrast, statements made well after a standard has been created and by SEP owners who do not implement standards lack these features of credibility and reasonableness. Such a SEP owner might strategically advocate for inflated aggregate royalties in an attempt to increase the value of its portion of the total.

The next step in calculating "fair and reasonable" royalties is to apportion the total aggregate royalties by comparing the value of a particular patent owner's SEP portfolio to the collection of all SEPs. A critical aspect of this apportionment is to identify all of the SEPs for a given standard. This can be a monumental task for many standards. Although standards organizations require patent owners to disclose SEPs, they do not verify the accuracy of these claims of essentiality. Moreover, the legal consequences of failing to disclose SEPs can be severe, and patent owners therefore may err in favor of declaring patents as essential even when essentiality is in question.[122] As a result, identifying all of the SEPs for a standard may require an essentiality analysis for thousands of patent families.[123] By practical necessity, this analysis is not as fulsome as that used in an infringement lawsuit. Streamlined essentiality reviews may nevertheless be sufficient to assist a

119 *TCL Commc'n Tech. Holdings, Ltd.*, 2017 WL 6611635, at *8.

120 *Id.* at *11; *see also* subsection 3.2.1 (discussing the importance of valuing SEPs independent of the value stemming from inclusion in a standard).

121 *TCL Commc'n Tech. Holdings, Ltd.*, 2017 WL 6611635, at *11.

122 *See supra* section 2 (describing the legal consequences of nondisclosure). Some SEP owners may also strategically over-declare to further efforts to license those patents.

123 In the one U.S. case that has applied the top-down approach, the FRAND analysis involved the review of 2,600 patent families. *TCL Commc'n Tech. Holdings, Ltd.*, 2017 WL 6611635, at *16.

U.S. court in determining "fair and reasonable" royalties using the top-down approach.[124] An essentiality analysis of all declared patents will also determine the number of essential patent families owned by individual companies, including the SEP owner in the FRAND suit.[125] Dividing the number of SEPs owned by a company by the total number of SEPs produces a global ratio that could be used to determine the SEP owner's share of the aggregate royalties for the standard.

U.S. courts have declined, however, to use this simple ratio because such an approach ignores the geographic variation in the relative strength of a SEP owner's portfolio. For example, under a license with a single global rate for a portfolio containing many U.S. SEPs but only a few Indian SEPs, substantial royalties would be paid for sales in India despite the relative weakness of the licensor portfolio in that country. A single global FRAND rate thus would skew royalties in favor of companies that intensely patent in only a few jurisdictions and effectively enforce SEPs in countries where those patents have no force.[126] Perhaps an ideal FRAND analysis therefore would consider the relative strength of SEP portfolios owned by a company in each country. However, such a fine-grained approach may be difficult to support with evidence and to administer.[127] U.S. courts engaging in FRAND analyses are particularly reluctant to consider the "technical nuances of patent law in dozens of jurisdictions".[128] Issues of global trade further impact the consideration of geography in the FRAND analysis. Many companies manufacture their products exclusively in China and then distribute those products globally. As a result, even when the FRAND analysis considers geographic variation in SEP portfolio strength, a patent owner's Chinese SEP portfolio effectively creates a global minimum for FRAND licensing.[129] To balance these complex considerations, U.S. courts therefore may determine FRAND rates by region rather than by country. For instance, one U.S. court determined separate FRAND rates for the U.S., for Europe, and for the rest of the world, which reflected in part the rate applicable to China.[130]

In contrast to their willingness to consider geographic variation in SEP portfolios, U.S. courts have been reluctant to adjust FRAND rates to reflect technical differences between SEP portfolios. Certainly, some SEPs are more valuable than others, as some SEPs cover foundational features of a standard while other SEPs are related to relatively minor aspects of the standard. But U.S. courts have rejected arguments that FRAND rates should be increased (or decreased) because

124 *Id.* at *18.

125 The expiration of SEPs, however, introduces additional complexities in this calculation. *Id.* at *20.

126 A single global rate may also lead to a greater portion of royalties being exported from some countries to foreign companies.

127 *Id.* at *25. Indeed, many global patent portfolio licenses use single rates rather than rates that vary geographically. *Id.* at *24.

128 *Id.* at *25.

129 *Id.* at *24–*25.

130 *Id.* at *25.

a particular SEP portfolio is stronger (or weaker) than the average SEP. Such analyses require difficult and potentially error-laden evaluations of SEP importance. Moreover, such value adjustments may conflict with a SEP owner's previous commitment to base FRAND rates on the raw percentage of SEPs owned rather than apportionment weighted for technological importance.[131]

U.S. courts thus may determine "fair and reasonable" rates using a top-down approach. However, effective application of the top-down approach requires special facts that may not be available in some cases, particularly a commitment by the SEP owner to an aggregate royalty rate. Notably, in the absence of statements by a SEP owner regarding the appropriate total aggregate rates for licensing SEPs, U.S. courts have not determined another technique for determining this value.[132] As a practical matter, a top-down analysis may be unavailable in many cases, leaving litigants to rely on a comparable-license approach.

4.3.3 Identifying discriminatory terms

FRAND declarations also require that SEP owners provide licenses on "non-discriminatory" terms. In perhaps the simplest form of discrimination, U.S. courts have found that FRAND commitments prevent SEP owners from refusing to license broad categories of manufacturers involved in standards implementation. For instance, a SEP owner cannot refuse to license the makers of components found within standards-compliant products.[133]

Though harder to detect, U.S. courts have also ruled that SEP owners cannot charge discriminatory rates for FRAND licenses. To identify such discrimination, these courts compare SEP owners' terms to other licenses between SEP owners and "similarly situated" licensees.[134] However, the FRAND commitment does not require that SEP owners offer the same rates to all licensees; some measure of variation is consistent with FRAND.[135]

U.S. courts begin the non-discrimination analysis by identifying firms that are similarly situated to a potential FRAND licensee. These courts recognize at least two types of firms for FRAND analysis: global firms and local kings. A local king is a company that sells most of its products in a single country, while global firms operate in multiple countries.[136] A local king accordingly has little interest in a global license and instead seeks to license only the portion of a SEP owner's

131 *Id.* at *11.

132 *Id.* at *10–*11.

133 *Fed. Trade Comm'n v. Qualcomm Inc.*, No. 17-CV-00220-LHK, 2018 WL 5848999, at *11 (N.D. Cal. November 6, 2018) (holding that Qualcomm's FRAND commitments required the licensing of manufacturers that produced modem chips in competition with Qualcomm).

134 *TCL Commc'n Tech. Holdings, Ltd.*, 2017 WL 6611635, at *57.

135 *Id.* at *55. For instance, U.S. courts have held that FRAND does not require that SEP owners offer licensees "most favored nation" status. *Id.* at *49.

136 *Id.* at *32.

portfolio related to the country where the local king operates.[137] When the SEP owner's portfolio is disproportionately weaker (or stronger) in the local king's country, the rates charged for a FRAND license will be commensurately lower (or higher) compared to a global rate. Global firms are thus similarly situated to each other and not to local kings. However, U.S. courts have declined to distinguish global firms on the basis of sale volume. Although large global firms may have greater bargaining power than smaller firms, U.S. courts have interpreted FRAND to promote competition from emerging firms and have held that allowing discrimination on the basis of sales volume would insulate dominant firms from competition.[138] In contrast, local kings may not be "similarly situated" to each other. For instance, one local king may operate in a country where a patent owner had a strong SEP portfolio, so that the local king needs a license to many SEPS and pays relatively high royalties. Another local king may operate in a different country where the same patent owner has a weak SEP portfolio, and thus would need a license that includes fewer SEPs and relatively lower royalties.

The other step in the non-discrimination analysis is to "unpack" the existing licenses to facilitate comparison between different licenses. This process is often complex, as different licenses may include different cross-licenses, different lump-sum payments, and different royalty rates based on product type, product volume, and geography. Experts play a large role in the unpacking process, though U.S. courts evaluate expert opinions regarding the unpacking process with a measure of skepticism, as the experts are paid by the parties to a FRAND dispute.[139] As a result, the process of "unpacking" existing licenses is imperfect. Nevertheless, at least when existing licenses are "radically divergent" from a proposed FRAND rate, the unpacking analysis may demonstrate that such a rate is discriminatory.[140]

4.4 Remedies: damages, injunctions and anti-suit injunctions

In addition to demonstrating breach of a binding contract, potential licensees must also demonstrate entitlement to some form of relief in order to prevail on a breach of contract claim.[141] One form of relief that a potential FRAND licensee could allege is monetary damages. Some SEP owners have argued that potential licensees suffer no harm even if a FRAND contract is breached because either the SEP owner will not sue for infringement (in which case the licensee pays nothing to the SEP owner) or the SEP owner sues for infringement in a lawsuit where

137 *Id.*
138 *Id.* at *30.
139 *Id.* at *35.
140 *Id.* at *50. As a practical matter, U.S. courts may not perform a separate non-discrimination analysis when FRAND terms are determined using the comparable-license approach, as that method of determining FRAND rates relies heavily on existing licenses to construct new FRAND rates. So long as those licensees are "similarly situated" to the potential licensee, the rate determined by the court generally will be non-discriminatory.
141 *Apple, Inc.*, 886 F. Supp. 2d at 1088.

damages are limited to FRAND terms.[142] U.S. courts are divided on these arguments, with some courts finding that an allegation that a FRAND commitment has been breached sufficiently avers monetary damages to support a claim for breach of contract.[143] Other U.S. courts, however, have taken the opposite view and dismissed breach of contract FRAND cases.[144]

As a result, some potential licensees could find themselves in a difficult position. After a SEP owner offers a license, the potential licensee may doubt whether the terms are FRAND. In some U.S. courts, however, the skeptical licensee might be unable to bring a breach of contract dispute to obtain clarification regarding FRAND rates, forcing the licensee to choose between rejecting terms that might be FRAND or accepting terms that might not be FRAND. As a result, where possible, more particular damages allegations may be useful. For instance, U.S. courts have found that patent infringement suits seeking injunctive relief are inconsistent with FRAND and therefore awarded damages for attorney's fees as a form of contract damages for defending against those suits.[145] Another potential remedy for breach of contract is injunctive relief in the form of specific performance, that is, an order from the court requiring the FRAND declarant to satisfy its FRAND declaration.[146] Furthermore, a potential FRAND licensee might avoid these problems by bringing a declaratory judgment action to request a declaration elucidating FRAND terms rather than damages or injunctive relief.[147]

One of the more powerful remedies that U.S. courts have awarded in FRAND contract disputes is an injunction preventing a patent owner from pursuing parallel patent infringement actions to enforce SEPs in countries other than the U.S. In U.S. parlance, these injunctions are often termed "anti-suit injunctions"

142 *E.g., Research In Motion Ltd.*, 644 F. Supp. 2d at 797.

143 *Id.* (describing as "inherently flawed" the assertion by a SEP owner that a potential licensee suffers no damages when a FRAND declaration is breached); *see also HTC Corp. v. Telefonaktiebolaget LM Ericsson*, No. 6:18-CV-00243-JRG, 2018 WL 6617795, at *5 (E.D. Tex. December 17, 2018) (finding contract damages adequately alleged based on "the time and resources" spent unsuccessfully attempting to negotiate a FRAND license prior to litigation). Additionally, some U.S. courts have noted differences between the assessment of damages in infringement litigation regarding SEPs and the determination of FRAND terms. *See supra* subsection 4.3.

144 *Godo Kaisha IP Bridge 1 v. TCL Commc'n Tech. Holdings Ltd.*, No. CV 15-634-SLR-SRF, 2017 WL 750700 (D. Del. February 27, 2017) (dismissing a breach of contract claim based on a FRAND declaration because the potential licensee failed to "identify the resultant injury from this purported breach").

145 *Microsoft*, 795 F.3d at 1045–1052; *see also Huawei Techs., Co. v. Samsung Elecs. Co.*, No. 3:16-CV-02787-WHO, 2019 WL 655279, at *4 (N.D. Cal. February 17, 2019) (finding that certain litigation costs may be recoverable as contract damages in a case where a FRAND contract was governed by French law). However, in the U.S., each party typically bears its own legal costs, including attorney's fees.

146 *See, e.g., Apple, Inc. v. Motorola Mobility, Inc.*, 886 F. Supp. 2d at 1081 (describing that a potential SEP licensee's request for specific performance of a FRAND obligation).

147 *See, e.g., Huawei Techs., Co. v. Samsung Elecs. Co.*, No. 3:16-CV-02787-WHO, 2019 WL 655279, at *4 (N.D. Cal. February 17, 2019).

because they restrain litigation in another lawsuit, typically in another forum.[148] For example, one U.S. court issued an anti-suit injunction barring a patent owner from continuing patent infringement actions regarding SEPs in six different countries.[149] In general, U.S. courts determine whether to award anti-suit injunctions based on three factors, and although anti-suit injunctions regarding the actions of foreign courts are generally rare, each of these factors is more likely to be satisfied in certain FRAND contract disputes.

First, U.S. courts consider whether the same parties are involved in the dispute in the U.S. and a foreign jurisdiction, as well as the relationship between the issues in those cases.[150] The first part of this element is satisfied when the same parties are involved in both jurisdictions. However, the parties need not be identical and instead need only be "functionally the same", which may occur when the parties to the foreign litigation are subsidiaries or affiliates of the parties in the U.S. litigation.[151] Similarly, the issues in the two cases need not be the same; rather, the issues are sufficiently similar if the dispute in the U.S. will resolve the foreign litigation.[152] With U.S. FRAND contract disputes and foreign patent infringement disputes, the first factor is often satisfied. The parties involved are often multinational corporations or domestic subsidiaries, so that the parties are sufficiently similar in the parallel lawsuits. Moreover, in the course of adjudicating the U.S. FRAND contract claim, the U.S. court will often establish FRAND terms that support the global licensing of SEPs, thereby resolving any SEP patent litigation pending in other countries.[153]

The second factor U.S. courts consider in deciding whether to award an anti-suit injunction is whether the foreign lawsuit would "frustrate a policy" of the U.S. court, which may occur if the foreign litigation is "vexatious or oppressive" or "prejudices equitable considerations".[154] In the context of a U.S. FRAND contract dispute and a foreign patent infringement claim seeking injunctive relief, this factor is likely to be satisfied. If a SEP owner can enforce a foreign SEP

148 Sometimes, the forum targeted by the injunction is in the U.S. For instance, U.S. courts have enjoined SEP owners from obtaining exclusion orders that prevent a manufacturer from importing standards-compliant products into the U.S. *See, e.g.*, *Realtek Semiconductor Corp.*, 946 F. Supp. 2d at 1008.

149 *See TCL Commc'n Tech. Holdings, Ltd. v. Telefonaktiebolaget LM Ericsson*, No. 8:14-CV-00341-JVS-AN, at 11 (C.D. Cal. June 29, 2015). However, the SEP owner in this dispute did not oppose the issuance of the injunction.

150 *Microsoft Corp.*, 696 F.3d at 882.

151 *Huawei Techs., Co. v. Samsung Elecs. Co.*, No. 3:16-CV-02787-WHO, 2018 WL 1784065, at *6 (N.D. Cal. April 13, 2018).

152 *Microsoft Corp.*, 696 F.3d at 882–883. In fact, the issues in a U.S. dispute may be sufficiently similar to those in a foreign patent infringement case to support an anti-suit injunction even if the FRAND issue in the U.S. court is presented as an alternative to a challenge to the validity or essentiality of purported U.S. SEPs. *Huawei Techs., Co.*, 2018 WL 1784065, at *9.

153 *Microsoft Corp.*, 696 F.3d at 884–885.

154 *Id.* at 885–886.

with an injunction, the potential FRAND licensee will be under great pressure to accept a license, even if the terms are not FRAND, and to dismiss its breach of contract claim in the U.S. as part of consummating the non-FRAND license.[155] U.S. courts are likely to find foreign suit to be "vexatious" and inequitable.

Finally, U.S. courts deciding whether to award an anti-suit injunction evaluate the impact on comity, requiring that it be "tolerable". This is a low threshold and is more likely to be satisfied in a contractual dispute between private parties than in cases involving government institutions and claims implicating public law.[156] Additionally, the impact on comity is more likely to be "tolerable" to U.S. courts when the foreign suit to be enjoined was filed after the start of the U.S. dispute.[157] In other words, U.S. courts are more likely to enjoin a foreign suit that was started as an attempt to hamstring existing U.S. litigation. A final consideration is the scope of the requested anti-suit injunction, with broader injunctions being more likely to trigger concerns regarding comity. In the context of FRAND contract disputes in U.S. courts and foreign patent infringement disputes, this final factor is often satisfied, particularly when the FRAND dispute is filed before the foreign patent action and when the anti-suit injunction is narrowly tailored to preventing the patent owner from enforcing foreign injunctions.[158] Additionally, U.S. courts consider patent disputes to be issues of private law, though courts also note that issues of SEPs and FRAND implicate multiple patent owners and multiple licensees.[159] U.S. courts may be less likely to consider the effect on comity "tolerable" when the requested anti-suit injunction prevents a SEP owner from pursuing damages in a foreign jurisdiction and when the foreign lawsuit was filed before the start of the U.S. litigation.[160]

Though anti-suit injunctions may be available in some FRAND disputes, U.S. courts emphasize that they should not be issued "routinely".[161] Indeed, anti-suit injunctions may be less likely to issue when the requesting party is a SEP owner seeking to enjoin a foreign challenge to the validity of a SEP. In such a situation, the party to be enjoined in a foreign jurisdiction (the potential licensee) has made no contractual commitment to resolving the dispute through FRAND negotiations.[162] Moreover, while anti-suit injunctions may ensure that a breach of contract dispute in a U.S. court remains the single forum for the resolution

155 *Id.* at 886; *Huawei Techs., Co.*, 2018 WL 1784065, at *10.

156 *Microsoft Corp.*, 696 F.3d at 887.

157 *Id.*

158 *Id.* at 888.

159 *Apple Inc. v. Qualcomm Inc.*, No. 3:17-cv-00108, 2017 WL 3966944, at *17 (S.D. Cal. September 7, 2017).

160 *Microsoft Corp.*, 696 F.3d at 887.

161 *Id.* at 889.

162 *Apple Inc.*, 2017 WL 3966944, at *10. After a FRAND contract dispute has begun in the U.S., a potential licensee should still plan carefully before initiating lawsuits in other countries, as U.S. courts have suggested that such foreign disputes might demonstrate that the potential licensee is not a "willing licensee" and thus is not entitled to FRAND terms. *Id.* at *10 n.7.

of the issues closely tied to FRAND declarations, issues that are separate from FRAND licensing, such as claims of antitrust and invalidity, may still proceed in foreign jurisdictions. As U.S. courts are poorly equipped to assess the standards essentiality of foreign patents, anti-suit injunctions might not be issued regarding certain foreign patent infringement disputes. Far from undermining a U.S. court's determination regarding a global FRAND rate, foreign proceedings might instead provide helpful information regarding the essentiality and validity of foreign SEPs.[163]

Finally, it is important to recognize a remedy that may be implicitly provided by FRAND breach of contract disputes in U.S. courts. By establishing FRAND ranges and rates, a court may effectively require the parties to enter a FRAND license using those terms even if the court does not order the parties to sign such a license as a form of specific performance. For example, following the conclusion of a FRAND contract dispute, if a potential licensee refuses to enter a FRAND license using the values set by the court, the SEP owner may sue for patent infringement and argue that the infringer has rejected the offer of a license on FRAND terms. Conversely, if a SEP owner demands royalties higher than those identified by a court following a FRAND breach of contract case and subsequently sues for patent infringement, the potential licensee will be able to counterclaim for breach of contract once again, relying on the previous contract dispute to quickly and easily prove breach a second time.

5 FRAND in U.S. antitrust disputes

Potential licensees have also sought to give legal effect to FRAND declarations in the U.S. through antitrust claims.[164] In resolving these suits, U.S. courts have held that in limited situations a SEP owner might violate U.S. antitrust laws by failing to implement a FRAND commitment. Importantly, however, simply enforcing through a patent infringement suit a SEP encumbered by a FRAND commitment is unlikely to violate the U.S. antitrust laws.

U.S. courts have typically evaluated antitrust claims against FRAND declarants under section 2 of the Sherman Antitrust Act, which requires that an antitrust plaintiff show that the defendant willfully acquired or maintained monopoly power through anticompetitive conduct.[165] In the case of SEPs, demonstrating

163 *Id.* at *11–*12.

164 Typically, FRAND antitrust claims are brought by competitors of the FRAND declarant, but these suits may also be filed by government regulators and consumers. *See, e.g.*, *Fed. Trade Comm'n v. Qualcomm Inc.*, No. 17-CV-00220-LHK, 2018 WL 5848999 (N.D. Cal. November 6, 2018) (regarding a suit by the U.S. Federal Trade Commission); *In re Qualcomm Antitrust Litig.*, 292 F. Supp. 3d 948, 973 (N.D. Cal. 2017) (involving a state law antitrust claim for damages brought by consumers).

165 *Broadcom Corp.*, 501 F.3d at 306–308 (discussing 15 U.S.C. § 15). Recently, some antitrust claims have also been brought under state law. *See, e.g.*, *In re Qualcomm Antitrust Litig.*, 292 F. Supp. 3d 948, 973 (N.D. Cal. 2017). However, because these cases have not

that the patent owner possesses monopoly power is often straightforward. Non-infringing technological alternatives cannot compete in the market for standards-compliant technology when the standard has already been widely adopted and market participants face high switching costs.[166] In such a situation, owners of SEPs may be able to "hold up" the industry and "extract supracompetitive royalties".[167]

It is less clear, however, whether a patent owner engages in unlawful anti-competitive conduct when it commits to licensing on FRAND terms but subsequently fails to do so. Many U.S. courts readily acknowledge that FRAND declarations are closely linked to competition. Widely accepted standards can generate substantial network effects and thereby expand the market for standards-compliant products. At the same time, absent implementation barriers, publicly disclosed standards promote competition among manufacturers of products that comply with those standards.[168] SEPs threaten to reduce this competition, reduce network effects and shrink the market for standards-compliant products. U.S. courts therefore recognize that FRAND commitments ameliorate these market harms by preventing SEP owners from obtaining supracompetitive royalties through holdup and are thus "an important factor" to standard setting.[169]

Despite this connection between FRAND declarations and competition, U.S. courts have been reluctant to find SEP owners liable for antitrust violations based on FRAND declarations. For example, SEP owners may not violate U.S. antitrust laws in asserting SEPs subject to FRAND declarations based on the *Noerr-Pennington* doctrine, a form of immunity to U.S. antitrust laws named for a pair of decisions from the U.S. Supreme Court.[170] This doctrine is grounded on the provision of the First Amendment to the U.S. Constitution prohibiting laws that limit rights "to petition the Government for a redress of grievances".[171] Under the *Noerr-Pennington* doctrine, parties that petition the government for redress are generally immune from antitrust liability, including parties that petition the U.S. courts for redress in business disputes against private parties.[172]

---

yet concluded, it is not yet clear whether state antitrust laws can be used to enforce FRAND commitments.

166 *Broadcom Corp.*, 501 F.3d at 315.

167 *Id.* at 310; *see also supra* text accompanying note 2 (discussing holdup).

168 *Broadcom Corp.*, 501 F.3d at 309.

169 *Id.* at 310, 313; *see also Research in Motion Ltd.*, 644 F. Supp. 2d at 795–796 (holding that "FRAND commitments are intended as a 'bulwark' against the unlawful accumulation of monopoly power that antitrust laws are designed to prevent"). FRAND commitments are intended as a 'bulwark' against the unlawful accumulation of monopoly power that antitrust laws are designed to prevent." *Id.*

170 *See Eastern R.R. Presidents Conference v. Noerr Motor Freight, Inc.*, 365 U.S. 127 (1961); *Mine Workers v. Pennington*, 381 U.S. 657 (1965).

171 U.S. Const. amend I.

172 *California Motor Transp. Co. v. Trucking Unlimited*, 404 U.S. 508, 510–511 (1972).

This immunity under the *Noerr-Pennington* doctrine is subject to an exception for objectively groundless "sham" litigation brought with malfeasant intent.[173]

U.S. courts have held that the *Noerr-Pennington* doctrine generally protects patent owners from antitrust claims based on the attempted enforcement of a SEP.[174] Certainly, if a patent is a valid SEP, then an infringement claim against standards-compliant products is not baseless. Moreover, U.S. courts have held inapplicable the exception for sham litigation even if the SEP is subject to a FRAND declaration. These courts recognize that the assertion of a SEP would be baseless if the accused infringer possessed a license to the SEP. However, FRAND declarations are commitments to provide licenses on FRAND terms. As a result, while FRAND declarations may mature into licenses that provide a full defense to suits for infringement, FRAND declarations are not actually licenses.[175] Moreover, while FRAND declarations may limit the remedies available to a SEP owner, the curtailment of remedies does not render infringement cases objectively baseless.[176]

In light of the *Noerr-Pennington* doctrine, U.S. courts have held that SEP owners may be liable for antitrust violations in only two situations. First, a SEP owner will not be protected by the *Noerr-Pennington* doctrine when the owner intentionally submits a false FRAND commitment to an SSO.[177] In such a case, the conduct challenged as anticompetitive is not the assertion of the SEP through the courts but rather the misrepresentation in the context of the SSO. The *Noerr-Pennington* doctrine does not apply to conduct in private organizations like SSOs.[178] Second, the *Noerr-Pennington* doctrine does not apply when a SEP owner provides a FRAND declaration in good faith but later refuses to acknowledge it. In other words, the SEP owner simply refuses to license a company that implements a standard.[179] However, because competitors are generally entitled to "refuse to deal" with one another, a refusal to license a SEP encumbered by a FRAND declaration violates U.S. antitrust laws only if SEP owner is motivated by "anticompetitive malice".[180]

Despite the possibility of FRAND-related antitrust liability, to date no U.S. court has actually found a SEP owner liable for antitrust violations based on FRAND declarations. To start, proving that a SEP owner's FRAND commitments were false at the time they were made or that a SEP owner acted with

173 *Prof'l Real Estate Inv'rs, Inc. v. Columbia Pictures Indus., Inc.*, 508 U.S. 49, 57 (1993).

174 *See, e.g., In re Innovatio IP Ventures, LLC Patent Litigation*, 921 F. Supp. 2d 903 (N.D. Ill. 2013); *Apple, Inc.*, 886 F. Supp. 2d at 1076–1077.

175 *In re Innovatio IP Ventures, LLC Patent Litig.*, 921 F. Supp. 2d at 915–916; *see supra* section 3 (discussing the impact of FRAND declarations on patent remedies in U.S. courts).

176 *In re Innovatio IP Ventures, LLC Patent Litig.*, 921 F. Supp. 2d at 916.

177 *Broadcom Corp.*, 501 F.3d at 315; *Apple Inc.*, 2012 WL 1672493, at *7; *Research in Motion Ltd.*, 644 F. Supp. 2d at 795–796.

178 *Broadcom Corp.*, 501 F.3d at 308.

179 *See, e.g., Fed. Trade Comm'n v. Qualcomm Inc.*, No. 17-CV-00220-LHK, 2017 WL 2774406 (N.D. Cal. June 26, 2017).

180 *Id.* at *22.

"anticompetitive malice" is difficult.[181] Moreover, an antitrust plaintiff may be unable to prove that failure to license on FRAND terms harmed competition because of the impact of FRAND declarations on related legal doctrines. For example, in a patent infringement suit, a SEP owner who has made a FRAND declaration may be unable to obtain injunctive relief and infringement damages may be substantially reduced.[182] These patent law doctrines thus limit the market harms from the violation of a FRAND declaration. Likewise, a potential SEP licensee could bring a breach of contract claim to obtain a FRAND license to obtain a FRAND license, which substantially reduces the harm from a SEP owner's failure to voluntarily offer one.[183] Antitrust plaintiffs thus face numerous obstacles in proving that a SEP owner who makes FRAND promises is liable for antitrust violations.[184]

6 Conclusions for Asian companies

The legal nature of FRAND in the U.S. has evolved into a complex, integrated system that includes aspects of patent law, contract law, antitrust law and even constitutional law. A SEP owner who fails to commit to FRAND licensing may waive its patent rights and potentially incur antitrust liability. On the other hand, by making a FRAND declaration, a SEP owner both accepts limits on remedies for infringement of that patent and enters a binding contract with licensees as third-party beneficiaries. Antitrust law further encourages a SEP owner to honor its FRAND commitment, as a SEP owner may violate U.S. antitrust laws by providing a false FRAND declaration.[185] Of these FRAND-related claims, contract issues are poised to be the most important because they often resolve or moot other claims related to SEPs. In particular, U.S. courts in FRAND contract cases have both determined global FRAND rates and enjoined SEP owners from

181 For example, a potential FRAND licensee may be unable to prove a FRAND declaration was false if the SEP owner offers to submit to a binding process for determining FRAND terms, such as arbitration. *See, e.g.*, *Huawei Techs., Co, Ltd v. Samsung Elecs. Co, Ltd.*, 340 F. Supp. 3d 934, 955 (N.D. Cal. 2018); *see also id.* at 951–953 (finding no "anticompetitive malice").

182 *See supra* section 3.

183 *See supra* section 4.

184 Perhaps for these reasons, some antitrust claimants assert as antitrust harms only litigation costs. However, U.S. courts have been reluctant to consider such costs cognizable antitrust harms. *See, e.g.*, *Huawei Techs., Co, Ltd v. Samsung Elecs. Co, Ltd.*, 340 F. Supp. 3d 934, 956 (N.D. Cal. 2018).

185 In a lawsuit, a potential FRAND licensees may allege that a SEP owner made a knowingly false FRAND declaration in order to force a SEP owner to choose between (1) denying that allegation, in which case the SEP owner must agree the FRAND commitment is binding, thereby supporting a FRAND contract claim, or (2) admitting the allegation is true because the SEP owner had no intention of honoring the FRAND declaration at the time it was made, thereby supporting an antitrust claim. In other words, a SEP owner who submits a FRAND declaration may be forced to choose between breach of contract claims and antitrust claims.

pursuing related patent infringement litigation both inside of and outside of the U.S.[186]

Asian companies operating in the U.S. accordingly must be mindful of the impact of FRAND declarations on their SEP portfolios and their manufacturing and distribution of standards-compliant products.[187] For their part, Asian SEP owners should consider the advantages and disadvantages of FRAND adjudication in the U.S. One noteworthy consideration for Asian companies is the role of the jury in FRAND litigation.[188] Moreover, an Asian SEP owner that seeks to enforce its SEPs through patent litigation – whether in its home country or in the U.S. – may find its plans derailed by an anti-suit injunction issued in a U.S. FRAND contract dispute. Asian SEP owners accordingly should consider laying the foundations for successful FRAND litigation in the U.S.[189] For example, Asian SEP owners might consider supporting SEP pools with favorable rates (to support comparable-license FRAND calculations) or advocating for aggregate royalties on a standard (to support top-down FRAND calculations).[190] Asian SEP owners may also consider funding industry reports on FRAND rates and SEPs for potential use in later U.S. FRAND litigation. Additionally, Asian SEP owners should consider licensing their SEPs separately from non-essential patents, so

186 *See, e.g.*, *TCL Commc'n Tech. Holdings, Ltd.*, 2017 WL 6611635, at *9.

187 Of course, Asian companies should consider the advantages and disadvantageous of U.S. litigation more generally. U.S. litigation is notoriously expensive, and U.S. juries can be unpredictable.

188 Damages for infringement of SEPs subject to FRAND declarations will often be determined by juries. Likewise, juries may be involved in determining FRAND rates in a breach of contract dispute. The interpretation of a contract is typically an issue of law for the court, rather than the jury. *Mays v. U.S. Postal Serv.*, 995 F.2d 1056, 1059 (Fed. Cir. 1993) (holding that "contract . . . interpretation is a matter of law"). Such an issue of law for the court may, however, involve some subsidiary issues of fact, leaving some uncertainty whether the judge or jury should determine the FRAND rate. In some cases, the parties consented to having the court determine FRAND rates without the involvement of the jury. *Microsoft Corp.*, 795 F.3d at 1033. Other cases suggest that a jury must determine FRAND terms. *See TCL Commc'ns Tech. Holdings Ltd*, 2016 WL 4150033, at *2–*3 (stating that the "fact-finder" must determine FRAND terms in some cases). U.S. courts generally agree, however, that whether a contract has been breached is an issue for the jury. *See, e.g.*, *Microsoft Corp.*, 795 F.3d at 1044. As a result, some U.S. courts have held that a jury may determine whether a FRAND commitment has been breached. *Huawei Techs., Co. v. Samsung Elecs. Co.*, No. 3:16-CV-02787-WHO, 2019 WL 655279, at *4 (N.D. Cal. February 17, 2019).

189 Of course, Asian companies must consider U.S. procedural law to ensure that U.S. courts have jurisdiction to hear such disputes. *TCL Commc'ns Tech. Holdings Ltd. v. Telefonaktenbologet LM Ericsson*, No. SACV1400341JVSANX, 2014 WL 12606650, at *4 (C.D. Cal. July 28, 2014); *see Romero v. Int'l Terminal Operation Co.*, 358 U.S. 345, 391 n.1 (1959) (noting that U.S. courts cannot hear certain claims between foreign parties).

190 SEP owners that manufacture standards-compliant products may advocate for lower aggregate royalties in an effort to limit the FRAND royalties that must be paid to other SEP owners. In contrast, SEP owners that seek substantial profits from FRAND royalties may prefer to advocate for higher aggregate royalties to support higher FRAND rates.

that their bilaterally negotiated SEP licenses can be used as evidence of FRAND terms in future FRAND disputes. Naturally, Asian SEP owners should continue to work to obtain SEPs, particularly in jurisdictions critical to global trade, such as China.

For their part, Asian manufacturers should consider the merits of resolving a global patent fight through FRAND litigation in the U.S. In some respects, the FRAND rates set by U.S. courts may appeal to Asian manufacturers, as they heavily rely on the rates from SEP pools and commitments to aggregate royalties, which tend to be lower than the rates from bilaterally negotiated patent licenses. In fact, Asian manufacturers might also consider assisting SEP pools, advocating for lower aggregate royalties for a standard, and commissioning industry reports regarding FRAND rates and essential patents. In some cases, Asian manufacturers who are "local kings" could argue for lower FRAND rates when facing SEP owners with strong SEP portfolios outside of Asia and weak SEP portfolios in Asia.[191] In making these arguments, Asian manufacturers should be aware that U.S. courts to have on some occasions set FRAND rates as a fixed per unit price than as a percentage.[192] For manufacturers that sell products in Asian countries at prices substantially lower than the prices for similar products in the U.S., global FRAND rates based on a fixed price could generate royalty amounts that are a relatively high percentage of the products' prices. In contrast, when FRAND rates are based on percentages, lower prices produce lower royalties. Fortunately, some U.S. courts consider dollar-per-unit royalties to be the exception rather than the rule and instead have determined FRAND royalties using percentages.[193]

In developing their strategies, Asian companies should recognize that U.S. law regarding FRAND is still developing, particularly in the contexts of breach of contract and antitrust claims.[194] Many of the U.S. courts that have ruled on these issues are lower courts, and some of the FRAND decisions by appellate courts are not binding on other courts. Predicting the outcomes in future FRAND cases in the U.S. is difficult because U.S. courts are reluctant to adopt bright-line principles in the context of FRAND. In the words of one court: "The search

191 *See* subsection 4.3.3 (discussing the impact of discriminatory terms on "local kings").

192 *Microsoft Corp.*, 2013 WL 2111217, at *101.

193 *TCL Commc'n Tech. Holdings, Ltd.*, 2017 WL 6611635, at *37.

194 In addition, other legal theories related to FRAND are still being developed under U.S. law. For example, manufacturers in some FRAND disputes in the U.S. have raised issues of promissory estoppel and patent misuse. *E.g.*, *Saint Lawrence Commc'ns LLC v. Motorola Mobility LLC*, No. 2:15-CV-351-JRG, 2018 WL 915125, at *6 (E.D. Tex. February 15, 2018) (discussing cases related to patent misuse); *TCL Commc'ns Tech. Holdings Ltd v. Telefonaktenbologet LM Ericsson*, No. 8:14-CV-00341-JVS-AN, 2014 WL 12588293, at *5 (C.D. Cal. September 30, 2014); *In re Innovatio IP Ventures, LLC Patent Litig.*, 921 F. Supp. 2d at 924; *Microsoft Corp.*, 864 F. Supp. 2d at 1029; *but see Apple Inc.*, 2012 WL 1672493, at *15 (dismissing a promissory estoppel claim related to FRAND declarations because such a claim would not be recognized under French law). However, no U.S. court has held that breach of a FRAND obligation is patent misuse rendering a SEP unenforceable. *Saint Lawrence Commc'ns LLC*, 2018 WL 915125, at *6.

for precision and absolute certainty [regarding FRAND terms] is a doomed undertaking".[195] Indeed, U.S. courts are yet to determine FRAND rates in the absence of (1) SEP patent pools, which can be used to calculate FRAND terms using a comparable-license approach, or (2) statements by SEP owners regarding aggregate standard royalties, which can form the basis of top-down FRAND analyses.

Nevertheless, given the importance of the U.S. market to global trade, in the absence of a FRAND license, litigation in the U.S. often may be unavoidable, and many Asian companies might be well-served by preparing for this possibility. Of course, FRAND litigation in the U.S. will not arise if the parties have already entered a FRAND license. As a result, Asian courts and lawmakers may provide the best mechanism for avoiding U.S. litigation insofar as disputes in Asian countries establish FRAND rates and induce parties to enter licenses with those terms.

195 *TCL Commc'n Tech. Holdings, Ltd.*, 2017 WL 6611635, at *8.

6 Asian perspectives

Jyh-An Lee and Sang Jo Jong

1 Introduction

Implementing a standard sometimes requires employing certain patents when standard implementers cannot design around the patents or cannot choose an alternative technology to replace these patents.[1] These patents are the so-called standard essential patents (SEPs).[2] Most standard setting organizations (SSOs) require their members to declare that they agree to license their SEPs under fair, reasonable, and non-discriminatory (FRAND) terms.[3] This is the so-called FRAND declaration.[4] Different SSOs have different practices regarding the format of FRAND declarations. Some SSOs, such as IEEE, require each member to submit a FRAND declaration letter, whereas in other SSOs, FRAND declarations may be derived from the interpretation of their IPR Policies.[5] Nonetheless, the FRAND declaration does not provide the precise terms of the license,[6] nor does the declaration define what is "fair, reasonable, and non-discriminatory".[7] Therefore, controversies occasionally occur when an implementer fails to reach an agreement regarding FRAND with the SEP holder.[8]

Because most of the issues relating to FRAND-encumbered SEPs arise from the SEP holders' FRAND declaration, it is crucial to explore the legal nature of FRAND declaration and how this nature will affect the application of patent law, contract law and competition law in various FRAND disputes. This chapter first explores the purpose of the FRAND declaration, followed by a comparative study of FRAND's legal characteristics in three major countries in East Asia, namely China, Japan and Korea. While courts in these three civil law countries

1 Schellekens (2015), 234–235.
2 Contreras (2013), 50–51; Ratliff & Rubinfeld (2013), 3; Lemley & Shapiro (2013), 1136.
3 Contreras (2013), 51, 55; Cotter (2014), 312; Kesan & Hayes (2014), 233, 238; Lemley & Shapiro (2013), 1136–1137.
4 The term "FRAND declaration" is sometimes used interchangeably with FRAND commitment, FRAND undertaking or FRAND pledge.
5 Pentheroudakis & Baron (2017), 33.
6 Ko (2014), 212.
7 Lee (2016), 45.
8 *Id.* at 46; Nakayama & Tamura (2015), 285.

all recognize that FRAND declaration does not constitute a license agreement between the SEP holder and the implementer, their approaches to the legal effect of FRAND declaration are subtly different. We also explore the convergence of FRAND declaration's legal effect in these three jurisdictions in terms of good faith negotiation and injunctive relief.

2 Purpose and rationale of FRAND declaration

FRAND declaration is designed to balance the interests of SEP holders and standard implementers by ensuring the former's fair compensation and the latter's access to the standard.[9] On the one hand, the FRAND rate should be high enough so that inventors' incentives to develop new technologies will not be hampered. On the other hand, SEP holders are bound by FRAND declaration so that implementers can legally employ the SEPs without the risk of infringement, being locked in by the SEPs, or losing their standard-specific investments.[10]

It is widely believed that the purpose of FRAND terms is to prevent the "holdup problem", wherein SEP holders withhold a license until an implementer agrees to pay an unduly high royalty rate for the patent.[11] Because implementers will have invested substantially in developing products based on the specific standard, it is quite expensive to opt out of the standard.[12] Consequently, SEP holders enjoy an advantageous position in negotiations associated with licensing the subject patents to other entities due to the SSOs' adoption decision rather than the incremental value of those patents.[13]

FRAND has strong private-ordering nature stemming from collaborations between private parties.[14] FRAND declaration can also be viewed as a consideration provided by the SEP holder in exchange for the inclusion of its patent in the standard during the standard setting process.[15] In other words, patentees volunteer to limit their patent rights and royalties within FRAND terms because they expect their inventions will enjoy considerable market share as a result of standard adoption.[16]

3 The legal characteristics of FRAND declaration

As the implementer ordinarily expects to enforce FRAND declaration against SEP owners, the first question that courts need to deal with is whether FRAND

9 Lim (2014), 41.
10 Contreras (2013), 56–57; Lim (2014), 42.
11 Carlton & Shampine (2013), 534; Contreras (2013), 49–51; Lim (2014), 29; Melamed & Shapiro (2018), 2116.
12 Contreras (2013), 48–49; Lim (2012), 3.
13 Contreras (2013), 50–51.
14 Contreras (2017), 214–16; Kesan & Hayes (2014), 253.
15 Atkins (2019), 953–954; Lemley & Shapiro (2013), 1140; Michaels (2018), 975–976; Richter & Slowinski (2019), 19.
16 Atkins (2019), 954. *See also* Nagakoshi & Tamai (2016), 254.

declaration constitutes a license agreement between these two parties. Courts in China, Japan and Korea are no exception.

3.1 China

Chinese IP scholar Cui Guobin suggests that the SEP holder's FRAND declaration to the SSO should be an offer, and the implementer could accept the offer by notifying the SEP holder of its plan to implement the subject standard.[17] However, this viewpoint is not adopted by the judiciary. In *Huawei v. InterDigital* (I),[18] both the first instance and the second instance courts ruled out the possibility that the implementer Huawei can request a FRAND licensing rate based on its alleged contract with the SEP holder InterDigital.[19] The courts stated that there was no contractual relationship between Huawei and InterDigital, and such a relationship would only be formed after both parties reached a consensus over the license rates and other licensing terms.[20] In other words, there was no contractual basis for Huawei to claim a FRAND licensing rate against InterDigital.

The other option for enforcing FRAND commitment is to define InterDigital's FRAND declaration with the European Telecommunications Standards Institute (ETSI) as a contract with a third-party beneficiary.[21] Put more clearly, this approach suggests that InterDigital entered into a binding contractual commitment with the ETSI, agreeing to license its SEPs on FRAND terms, and Huawei is a third-party beneficiary of this commitment. A contract with a third-party beneficiary has been common practice to cope with FRAND-encumbered SEPs in the U.S.[22] However, it should be noted that China derived its civil law, including contract law, from the German system.[23] Therefore, the way in which German courts and scholars interpret contract law has a significant impact on Chinese contract law.[24] In Germany, courts have made it clear that SEP holders' FRAND commitment is nothing but an invitation for third parties to make offers and does not yet grant other SSO members a right to obtain a license.[25] In *Huawei*, InterDigital also cited a German court decision to dissuade the court from holding that Huawei was a third-party beneficiary to the contract between

17 Cui (2014), 347.

18 For further detailed analysis of this case, *see* Lee (2017), 197–205.

19 Huawei Jishu Youxian Gongsi Su Jiaohu Shuzi Tongxin Youxian Gongsi (华为技术有限公司诉交互数字通信有限公司) [*Huawei Tech. Co. v. InterDigital Communications, Inc.* (*Huawei v. InterDigital* (I))], 2013 Yue Gao Fa Min San Zhong Zi No. 305 (Guangdong High People's Ct. 2013) (China).

20 *Id.*

21 Cui (2014), 349.

22 *See, e.g.*, *Microsoft Corp. v. Motorola, Inc.*, 696 F.3d 872, 878 (9th Cir. 2012); *Research in Motion Ltd. v. Motorola, Inc.*, 644 F. Supp. 2d 788, 797 (N.D. Tex. 2008); *Ericsson, Inc. v. Samsung Elecs. Co.*, No. 2:06-CV-63, 2007 WL 1202728, at *1 (E.D. Tex. April 20, 2007).

23 Lee (2016), 55.

24 Wang (1999), 354–355, 385.

25 Cotter (2014), 318.

InterDigital and ETSI.[26] Although the *Huawei* court did not view Huawei as a third-party beneficiary, it did not explain why.[27] One possible explanation is that under Chinese contract law, contracting parties cannot impose any obligation on a third party, and a third-party beneficiary may only benefit without any obligation. In other words, a third party only receives obligor's performance and is not subject to any contractual obligation.[28] However, in the SEPs scenario, standard implementers are still obliged to pay SEP holders a royalty based on FRAND terms. Therefore, such arrangement cannot be a contract with a third-party beneficiary under Chinese law.[29]

3.2 Japan

In *Samsung v. Apple*, although the Intellectual Property High Court of Tokyo ("IP High Court") acknowledged that the French Civil Code, the governing law of the declaration in the case, does not always require that the amount to be paid be specific for there to be a contract, it still ruled out the possibility that FRAND declaration could be viewed as an offer for potential implementers.[30] The IP High Court explained that because the FRAND declaration did not include terms and conditions that would normally be the required main body of a license, such as royalties, geographical scope and contractual duration, there is no way to determine the scope and effect of the possible contract.[31] The lack of specific terms and conditions was the first ground on which the IP High Court viewed the FRAND declaration as neither a valid contract nor an offer for the potential licensee.[32]

Second, Samsung's FRAND declaration was made in accordance with the IPR Policy of ETSI, which was supplemented by the "ETSI Guide on Intellectual Property Rights" (ETSI Guide). The ETSI Guide indicated that the terms and conditions of licenses were to be negotiated by patentees and potential licensees.[33] According to the ETSI Guide, ETSI expected both its members and non-members to negotiate in good faith for specific FRAND terms to conclude their valid license agreements (Clause 4.4).[34] It was therefore clear to the IP High Court that the SSO in this case would not intervene in the negotiations between

26 Huawei Jishu Youxian Gongsi Su Jiaohu Shuzi Tongxin Youxian Gongsi (华为技术有限公司诉交互数字通信有限公司) [*Huawei Tech. Co. v. InterDigital Communications, Inc.* (*Huawei v. InterDigital* (I))], 2013 Yue Gao Fa Min San Zhong Zi No. 305 (Guangdong High People's Ct. 2013) (China).

27 *Id.*

28 Contract Law of the People's Republic of China (promulgated by Nat'l People's Cong., March 15, 1999), art. 64, 1999 P.R.C. Contract Law.

29 Lee (2016), 56.

30 *Id.*

31 *Id.*

32 For more detailed description of IP Court's viewpoint on this, *see* Suzuki (2017), 247–248; Masabumi Suzuki, Chapter 9 of the present book.

33 Answer 6 of the ETSI IPR Policy FAQs.

34 Suzuki (2017), 248.

patentees and potential licensees with regard to specific terms.[35] That said, the IPR Policy of ETSI appeared to assume that the FRAND declaration did not immediately give rise to a license agreement.[36]

Third, the IP High Court opined that to view a FRAND declaration as an offer for a license would contradict the historical background of ETSI's IPR Policy. When ETSI members discussed the organization's IPR Policy, some members proposed a so-called advance disclosure obligation to set royalty rates in advance and a clause granting implementers "automatic licenses".[37] However, the proposal was not accepted because of the opposition from other members.[38] Therefore, in view of the historical backdrop in which ETSI rejected the proposal of "advance disclosure" or "automatic licenses", FRAND declaration could not be interpreted as an offer for a license agreement.

3.3 Korea

In Korea, during the course of patent litigations between Samsung and Apple and the alleged violation of the Monopoly Regulation and Fair Trade Act (MRA) by Qualcomm, there have been many debates as to whether the FRAND declaration amounts to a license agreement for a third-party implementer. First, in *Samsung v. Apple*, Apple argued that a valid licensing agreement was concluded between ETSI and Samsung for the benefit of third parties, including Apple. And, yet, the Seoul Central District Court disagreed.[39] After hearing expert testimonies on the interpretation of the French contract law, the governing law of the FRAND declaration, the Seoul Central District Court held that the offer and acceptance of a possible contract should include its essential terms and conditions such as royalties and duration and, also, that the terms and conditions should be sufficiently precise and complete. The court ruled that the FRAND declaration in this case had no precise and complete terms and conditions of any possible license and could not be construed as a license agreement for the benefit of a third-party implementer.

Second, the court noticed that the French Intellectual Property Law Code relied on a "written contract" requirement for any contract to transfer or license patent rights,[40] and unless there were written offer and acceptance of license terms and conditions, it could not find any valid contract in the FRAND declaration.

Third, in determining important terms and conditions such as royalty rates, it is reasonable for the parties to go through negotiations and take into account various factors such as the production capability and marketing channels of potential licensees. There is a risk that, if an SSO imposes the obligation upon

35 Clause 4.1 of the ETSI Guide.
36 Suzuki (2017), 248.
37 *Id.*
38 *Id.*
39 Seoul Central District Court Decision 2011gahap39552 decided on August 24, 2012.
40 Code de la propriété intellectuelle, Article L613–618.

patentees to disclose royalty rates in advance, it may negatively affect the patentees' participation in the standardization process or induce patentees to act in collusion to fix the royalty rate. Given that ETSI's IPR Policy presupposed that a license agreement will be concluded between the patentee and potential licensees upon their negotiations separately after the FRAND declaration made by the patentee to ETSI, the Seoul Central District Court came to the conclusion that it was difficult to recognize any licensing agreement for the benefit of a third party.

Finally, the Seoul Central District Court warned against the possibility of patent holdout[41] if the FRAND declaration was viewed as a contract, or immediately led to a contract, between an SEP holder and an implementer: in cases where an infringer implements an SEP unilaterally and at the same time denies infringement and even the validity of the patent, it is contrary to the policy goal of patent law to assume that there has been a licensing agreement for the benefit of the infringer simply by way of a FRAND declaration made by the patentee. When a malicious infringement is justified by assuming a contract for the benefit of potential licensees, not only is the malicious infringer over-protected, but also the policy goals of fair compensation and appropriate incentives for inventors and patentees are seriously harmed.

3.4 Analysis

In the U.S., courts have defined SEP holders' FRAND commitment with SSOs as a contract with a third-party beneficiary.[42] This approach suggests that SEP holders enter into a binding contractual commitment with SSOs, agreeing to license its SEPs on FRAND terms, and implementers are third-party beneficiary of SEP holders' FRAND commitments to SSOs.[43]

However, the majority view in the civil law countries is different from the contract with third-party beneficiaries approach in the U.S. The judicial practices regarding the legal nature of FRAND in China, Japan and Korea are consistent with a widely accepted understanding that SEP holders' FRAND declaration to an SSO is just a promise to license to other members, rather than licenses themselves, and therefore an SEP holder's FRAND declaration

41 Holdout in the context of FRAND-encumbered SEPs means "an implementer refuses to negotiate in good faith with an [SEP holder] for a license to valid patent(s) that the implementer infringes, and instead forces the [SEP holder] to either undertake significant litigation costs and time delays to extract a licensing payment through a court order, or else to simply drop the matter because the licensing game is no longer worth the candle." *See* Epstein & Noroozi (2017), 1384.

42 *See, e.g.*, *Microsoft Corp. v. Motorola, Inc.*, 696 F.3d 872, 878 (9th Cir. 2012); *Research in Motion Ltd. v. Motorola, Inc.*, 644 F. Supp. 2d 788, 797 (N.D. Tex. 2008); *Ericsson, Inc. v. Samsung Elecs. Co.*, No. 2:06-CV-63, 2007 WL 1202728, at *1 (E.D. Tex. April 20, 2007).

43 Lee (2016), 54.

will constitute neither a licensing agreement nor a contract with third-party beneficiaries because the FRAND declaration was insufficient to spell out the detailed conditions of a license, which should include essential terms, such as license fee, royalty rate, contract duration and so forth.[44] Nor can a FRAND declaration be viewed as an offer of a license. This approach is similar to that of Germany, whose civil law traditionally has a huge influence on those three Asian countries. In Germany, the courts have made it clear that SEP holders' FRAND commitments do not grant other SSO members a right to obtain a license, and the FRAND commitment is nothing but an invitation for third parties to make offers.[45]

The consensus among these three Asian jurisdictions is that the declaration is neither an offer of a license agreement nor a license agreement itself between an SEP holder and an implementer, although none of the courts in these three Asian jurisdictions has clearly defined the legal nature of a FRAND declaration. Moreover, the disputes in these three jurisdictions similarly concerned SEPs originating from the same SSO, namely ETSI. There was, however, a minor difference among these three jurisdictions: the *Huawei* court in China applied Chinese law, whereas Japanese and Korean courts applied French law to determine the legal nature of the FRAND declaration, despite following the same private international law doctrine.

4 The legal effects of a FRAND declaration

Jurisdictions may have quite different approaches to the legal effect of a FRAND declaration.[46] Typically, FRAND declaration leads to both private law and public law effects.[47] In terms of private law effect, in all cases involving FRAND and SEPs, standard implementers need to find an enforcement mechanism to hold SEP holders to their obligation to license their SEPs under FRAND terms.[48] The public law effect, on the other hand, concerns the application of competition law to FRAND-encumbered SEPs and their owners.[49] SEP holders' violation of FRAND declaration may violate competition law as well.[50] This section will explore the legal effect of a FRAND declaration in China, Japan and Korea.

44 Dolmans & Ilan (2012), 7; Kesan & Hayes (2014), 260; Lemley & Shapiro (2013), 1140–1141; Lim (2014), 29.
45 Düsseldorf District Court, Decision of April 24, 2012, 4b O 274/10 – IPCom v Deutsche Telekom and Vodafone; Cotter (2014), 318.
46 Kesan & Hayes (2014), 233.
47 Atik (2019), 952.
48 Lee (2016), 51.
49 Atik (2019), 952.
50 *Id.* at 952–953.

4.1 China

4.1.1 Patent law and civil law

The *Huawei* court ruled that the legal basis for the implementer Huawei to request that the SEP holder InterDigital provide a FRAND rate was the doctrine of fairness and good faith prescribed in the Chinese General Principles of Civil Law and Contract Law.[51] The court also identified three statutes from these two bodies of law as the legal basis for Huawei's FRAND claim against InterDigital:[52]

1 Article 4 of the General Principles of Civil Law: "In civil activities, the principles of voluntariness, fairness, consideration for equal value, and good faith shall be observed".[53]
2 Article 5 of the Contract Law: "The parties shall observe the principle of fairness in defining each other's rights and obligations".[54]
3 Article 6 of the Contract Law: "The parties shall observe the principle of good faith in exercising their rights and fulfilling their obligations".[55]

The *Huawei* court held that InterDigital's FRAND obligation to Huawei could be established by applying the three Articles to construct the scope and effect of InterDigital's FRAND declaration.[56] Although the *Huawei* court did not explain under what circumstances the doctrines of fairness and good faith can be applied to solve FRAND disputes, scholars have explained why such application is not a surprising one in China.

First, as in most civil law countries, the doctrines of fairness and good faith lay out fundamental principles for all civil and commercial activities in China.[57] Chinese scholars and courts have viewed the doctrine of good faith as the "highest guiding principle", "imperial principle" or "royal principle" for the law of obligation.[58] Chinese courts tend to use the doctrine as a catch-all tool to solve civil law and contract-related issues.[59] The doctrine has been used to fill the legislative loopholes in all stages of a potential and actual contractual relationships, including pre-contract formation, performance, modification, termination and post-termination.[60] Therefore, it is natural for the *Huawei* court to apply these

51 2013 Yue Gao Fa Min San Zhong Zi No. 305.
52 *Id.*
53 General Principles of the Civil Law of the People's Republic of China (promulgated by the Nat'l People's Cong., April 12, 1986), art. 4, 1986 P.R.C. Civil and Commercial Laws (China).
54 Contract Law of the People's Republic of China (promulgated by Nat'l People's Cong., March 15, 1999), art. 5, 1999 P.R.C. Contract Law (China).
55 *Id.*
56 2013 Yue Gao Fa Min San Zhong Zi No. 305.
57 Lee (2016), 57.
58 *Id.* at 58.
59 *Id.*
60 *Id.*

two doctrines, especially the doctrine of good faith, to solve challenging issues in the absence of any specific provision.

Second, it is generally accepted in China that parties during the negotiation stage should bear the duties of loyalty, honesty, non-deception, confidentiality and most importantly, of keeping promises.[61] As a result, although the SEP holder's FRAND declaration cannot lead to a contract with SEPs implementers, FRAND declaration and FRAND-compliant negotiation are still promises subject to the doctrine of good faith.

SEP holders, nevertheless, may always argue that based on freedom of contract, they should have freedom to enter into a license agreement, to choose with whom to sign a license agreement and to decide the form and content of such agreement.[62] However, the freedom of contract is limited by the principle of good faith[63] and policy concerns for asymmetric bargaining power or unfair clauses.[64] Additionally, technical standards and FRAND-encumbered SEPs involve not only private interests of both parties but also public interest.[65] The principle of good faith in China was designed precisely to balance the interests of the parties and society.[66] Therefore, a FRAND violation may be an appropriate case for applying the doctrine of good faith.

In addition to the substantive licensing terms, the legal effect of a FRAND declaration also extends to the way in which SEP holders and implementers negotiate with each other. In *Iwncomm v. Sony*, the Beijing High People's Court ruled that SEP holders were obliged to negotiate in good faith with the implementer based on their FRAND declaration.[67] If the implementer seeks a FRAND-compliant license from the patentee, it likewise needs to negotiate with the patentee in good faith.[68] Provided that the SEP holder does not negotiate in good faith with the implementer, the court will not find patent infringement against the implementer.[69] By contrast, if the SEP holder negotiates in good faith with the implementer but the implementer does not likewise negotiate in good faith, the court will order the implementer to stop the implementation of the SEPs.[70] Although the Beijing High People's Court did not explicitly mention its 2017 Guideline on the Determination of Patent Infringements, commentators have indicated that the good faith negotiation framework addressed in *Iwncomm v. Sony* was based

61 *Id.* at 58–59.
62 *Id.* at 60–61.
63 Ling (2002), 49–50.
64 Lee (2016), 61.
65 *Id.* at 42–43, 61.
66 Ling (2002), 53–54.
67 Xian Xidian Jietong Wuxian Wanglao Tongxin Gufen Youxian Gongsi Su Suoni Yidong Tongxin Chanpin (Zhongguo) Youxian Gongsi (西安西电捷通无线网络通信股份有限公司诉索尼移动通信产品(中国)有限公司) [*Iwncomm v. Sony*], 2017 Jing Min Zhong No. 45 (Beijing High People's Ct. 2018).
68 *Id.*
69 *Id.*
70 *Id.*

on this 2017 Guideline.[71] The obligation of good faith negotiation on both SEP holders and implementers has been again confirmed by recent FRAND litigations between Huawei and Samsung.[72]

4.1.2 Competition law

Competition law issues regarding SEPs have drawn attention from academia, judiciaries, and competition authorities in China, especially the competition law effect of FRAND declaration under the country's Anti-Monopoly Law.

4.1.2.1 SAIC'S PROVISIONS ON PROHIBITING THE ABUSE OF INTELLECTUAL PROPERTY RIGHTS

The State Administration for Industry and Commerce (SAIC) in China, which has been renamed as the State Administration for Market Regulation, issued the *Provisions of the State Administration for Industry and Commerce on Prohibiting the Abuse of Intellectual Property Rights to Preclude or Restrict Competition* (关于禁止滥用知识产权排除、限制竞争行为的规定) (*Provisions*) on April 7, 2015, which came into effect on August 1 in the same year.[73] Article 13(3) of the *Provisions* defines an SEP as a "patent which is essential to the implementation of such standard". More importantly, Article 13(2) may become a legal basis for standard implementers to claim FRAND terms against SEP holders in the future:

> Businesses with dominant market position shall not, without justification, engage in the acts below to exclude or restrict competition in the process of setting and implementing standards:
>
> 1 . . .
> 2 once the subject patent becomes a standard-essential patent, [the patent holder] will violate the fair, reasonable and non-discriminatory (FRAND) principle, by precluding or restricting competition, such

71 Liyang Hou and Mengchi Tian, Chapter 11 of the present book.

72 Huawei Jishu Youxian Gongsi Su Sanxing (Zhongguo) Touzi Youxian Gongsi Deng (华为技术有限公司诉三星(中国)投资有限公司等), 2016 Yue 03 Min Chu No. 816 (Shenzhen Intermediate People's Ct. 2018); Huawei Jishu Youxian Gongsi Su Sanxing (Zhongguo) Touzi Youxian Gongsi Deng (华为技术有限公司诉三星(中国)投资有限公司等), 2016 Yue 03 Min Chu No. 840 (Shenzhen Intermediate People's Ct. 2018).

73 Provisions on Prohibiting the Abuse of Intellectual Property Rights to Preclude or Restrict Competition (promulgated by the State Administration for Industry and Commerce, April 7, 2015, August 1, 2015), available at www.kangxin.com/en/index.php?optionid=927&auto_id=726 [https://perma.cc/JC2N-Y8XJ] (China).

as refusal to license, tying products, or imposing other unreasonable terms.[74]

It should be noted that, because the *Provisions* are designed according to Anti-monopoly Law,[75] they are primarily based on antitrust and competition law concerns. Only businesses with "dominant market position" will be charged with FRAND obligations. The context of Article 13 of the *Provisions* differs from normal FRAND disputes, where SEP holders have made FRAND declaration to the SSO concerned. Under the circumstances stipulated by Article 13, a FRAND licensing duty is imposed on SEP holders even if they have not previously made any FRAND declaration.[76] Moreover, the examples of FRAND violations provided in the *Provisions*, such as refusal to deal or tying arrangement conducted by businesses with dominant market positions, are also typical antitrust violations.

4.1.2.2 *HUAWEI V. INTERDIGITAL* (II)

In *Huawei v. InterDigital* (II), the Guangdong High People's Court held that the SEP holder IDC had violated its FRAND declaration and abused its dominant market position by seeking injunction against the implementer Huawei during their license negotiation.[77] The court explained that although Huawei negotiated in good faith with InterDigital, the latter did not likewise negotiate in good faith,[78] and instead forced the former to agree on the excessive licensing terms via threats of injunction and litigation.[79] As a result, InterDigital had violated the Anti-monopoly Law in China.[80] In other words, the legal effect of FRAND declaration under Anti-monopoly Law is that a FRAND-encumbered SEP holder is obliged to negotiate with the implementer in good faith. Accordingly, the SEP holder may violate Anti- monopoly Law by seeking injunction or initiating litigation against the implementer during the negotiation. It should be noted that the decision has not yet been enforced because the Supreme People's Court has decided in December 2018 to hear this case.

74 *Id.*

75 "In order to protect fair market competition, encourage innovation, and stop operators from abusing intellectual property rights to exclude or restrict competition, the Provisions on the Prohibition of the Abuse of Intellectual Property Rights to Exclude or Restrict Competition are formulated in accordance with the Anti-monopoly Law of the People's Republic of China." Provisions, art. 1.

76 Provisions, art. 13.

77 Huawei Jishu Youxian Gongsi Su Jiaohu Shuzi Tongxin Youxian Gongsi (华为技术有限公司诉交互数字通信有限公司) [*Huawei Tech. Co. v. InterDigital Communications, Inc.* (*Huawei v. InterDigital* (II))], 2013 Yue Gao Fa Min San Zhong Zi No. 306 (Guangdong High People's Ct. 2013) (China).

78 *Id.*

79 *Id.*

80 *Id.*

4.1.2.3 THE *QUALCOMM* CASE

Sometimes an SEP holder may violate Anti-monopoly Law but such violation is not directly relevant to the FRAND declaration.[81] For example, on February 10, 2015, the National Development and Reform Commission (NDRC), one of the three competition law authorities in China until March 21, 2018, fined Qualcomm RMB 6.08 billion for abuse of its dominant market position by charging royalty for expired patents, demanding free grant-back licenses, charging excessive royalty rate based on the net wholesale prices of devices, and bundling SEPs with non SEPs.[82] However, the NDRC did not mention Qualcomm's FRAND declaration at all in its decision. In other words, even if the SEP holder or its predecessor did not make any FRAND declaration, it can still violate Anti-monopoly Law by unfair licensing practices against the implementers or potential implementers.

4.2 Japan

4.2.1 Patent law and civil law

FRAND declaration affects SEP holders' rights to claim damages and seek injunctions against the implementers in Japan. In *Samsung v. Apple*, the Tokyo District Court and the IP High Court held that the enforcement of FRAND-encumbered patents were subject to the doctrine of abuse of right under the Japanese Civil Code Article 1(3),[83] a general provision applying to all types of assertion of private rights.[84] However, the Tokyo District Court and the IP High Court had different approaches to the determination of abuse of right associated with FRAND-encumbered SEPs. The Tokyo District Court emphasized more the SEP holders' good faith in negotiating a FRAND license with implementers,[85] whereas the IP High Court's focus was more on the amount of damages and injunctive relief sought by the SEP holders. Nonetheless, when deciding the issues of damages and injunctive relief, the IP High Court still ruled that the SEP holder was obliged to negotiate in good faith with the implementer according to the doctrine of good faith under the Civil Code of Japan.[86] Professor Masabumi Suzuki, a prominent Japanese IP scholar, is of the viewpoint that while Tokyo District Court's approach to doctrine of abuse of right was very case

81 *See also* Hovenkamp (2017), 122 ("[f]irst, a plaintiff probably cannot rely on FRAND breach as a theory of anticompetitive conduct, because a breach of contract generally does not create an antitrust violation. Second, as a result of the first point, the plaintiff must show that the defendant's conduct violates the antitrust laws on its own terms, and not only because it happens to violate a FRAND pledge.")

82 NDRC, Administrative Sanction Decision No. 1 (2015), February 9, 2015.

83 Suzuki (2017), 256–257.

84 Nagakoshi & Tamai (2016), 247.

85 Nakayama & Tamura (2015), 285–286.

86 Masabumi Suzuki, Chapter 9 of the present book.

specific, considering details of negotiations in each case, the IP High Court has provided a more predictable and clear standard to determine the abuse of right in the context of FRAND-encumbered SEPs.[87] In other words, the IP High Court's has provided a more general standard for the determination of abuse of right in the context of FRAND-encumbered SEPs.[88]

The IP High Court held that the SEP holder Samsung had abused its patent right by either filing an injunction or claiming an excessive amount of damages against the standard implementer Apple. In terms of damages, the IP High Court ruled that SEP holders could still claim damages for patent infringement against the implementers within the amount of FRAND terms.[89] Nevertheless, Samsung had abused its patent rights by claiming damages exceeding the FRAND rates.[90] The IP High Court further reasoned that standard implementers ordinarily relied on the SEP holders' FRAND declarations and thus expected FRAND licenses would be available for FRAND-encumbered SEPs.[91] Such reliance should be protected by the law, especially because SEP holders themselves benefited from it as well.[92] Without implementers' reliance on SEP holders' FRAND declaration, SEP holders would not be able to profit from the widespread adoption of the subject standards.[93] However, if the SEP holders could seek damages more than the FRAND terms, such claims would be detrimental to the implementers' aforementioned reliance and thus constitute abuse of patent rights.[94] Consequently, the implementers could legally refuse to pay the amount exceeding the FRAND terms if they proved that SEP holders had made the FRAND declaration.[95]

For the same reason, the IP High Court ruled that unconditionally allowing the SEP holders to seek injunctions against the implementers would be similarly detrimental to the latter's reliance on the former's FRAND declaration, and that such reliance should be protected by the law as well.[96] After all, the implementer had invested significantly to develop its products based on the belief that it would secure a FRAND license from the SEP holder.[97] Moreover, SEP holders' injunctive relief against the implementers was in clear conflict with SSOs' policy goal of widespread standard dissemination and adoption, a goal ultimately aiming to benefit the public in general.[98] Therefore, the IP High Court explained that allowing the SEP holder's injunctive relief would harm not only the implementer's reliance on the FRAND declaration but also the patent law's policy goal of

87 Suzuki (2017), 248–250.
88 Masabumi Suzuki, Chapter 9 of the present book.
89 Suzuki (2017), 248–250.
90 *Id.* at 248–249.
91 *Id.*
92 *Id.* at 249.
93 *Id.*
94 *Id.*
95 *Id.*
96 *Id.* at 251.
97 Nagakoshi & Tamai (2016), 248.
98 Suzuki (2017), 251.

industrial development.[99] As a result, the IP High Court held that an SEP holder would abuse its patent rights if it sought injunctions against an implementer who was a willing FRAND licensee.[100] IP High Court's viewpoint in *Apple v. Samsung* was later adopted by the Tokyo District Court in *Imation v. One Blue*, a case concerning FRAND-encumbered SEPs in Blu-ray disc products.[101]

4.2.2 Competition law

More than a decade ago, the Fair Trade Commission of Japan (JFTC) issued a cease-and-desist order against Qualcomm's abusive and opportunistic behavior in violation of the Antimonopoly Act (AMA) of Japan.[102] To respond to violation of FRAND declaration more efficiently, the JFTC revised the "Antitrust Law Guidelines on the Use of Intellectual Property" in January 2016.[103] According to the revised guidelines, refusing to grant a license to a willing licensee who wishes to implement a standard essential patent under FRAND terms or filing a lawsuit to prevent a willing licensee may be a violation of the AMA when it hinders business activities of a person who researches, develops, produces or sells a product implementing the standard technology, excludes trading opportunities, or degrades competitive order in the market.[104] Whether or not a specific company is regarded as a willing licensee is to be judged by taking into consideration the concrete actions taken by the two companies during the course of their negotiations. Even if the actions by standard essential patent holders do not constitute an abuse of market dominance prohibiting competition in the relevant market, they may still be regarded as "unfair trade practices" under the AMA.[105]

4.3 Korea

4.3.1 Patent law and civil law

In the patent lawsuit between Samsung and Apple, the defendant Apple raised in defence the principle of estoppel and argued that the plaintiff Samsung had

99 Nagakoshi & Tamai (2016), 254–255.

100 *Id.* at 247; Suzuki (2017), 254.

101 Nagakoshi & Tamai (2016), 275–280; Masabumi Suzuki, Chapter 9 of the present book.

102 JFTC Decision on September 30, 2009, available at www.jftc.go.jp/en/pressreleases/yearly-2009/sep/individual-000038.html. However, Tokyo IP High Court stayed the enforcement of the order issued on February 12, 2010. The JFTC has thus far held hearings on 37 different dates according to Qualcomm 2017 Annual Report, available at https://investor.qualcomm.com/static-files/3bee5a52-757b-4ac6-9468-b0102bdc4418, at F31.

103 Antitrust Law Guidelines on the Use of Intellectual Property (知的財産の利用に関する独占禁止法上の指針; amended by JFTC on January 21, 2016).

104 Guidelines for the Use of Intellectual Property under the Antimonopoly Act, Part 3 (Viewpoints from Private Monopolization and Unreasonable Restraint of Trade), (1) (Viewpoints from Private Monopolization).

105 Guidelines for the Use of Intellectual Property under the Antimonopoly Act, section 4 (Viewpoints from Unfair Trade Practices), subsection 2 (Inhibiting the Use of Technology.

already abandoned its right to injunctions. The Seoul Central District Court found that, according to the governing law, the French Civil Code, it was unclear whether the exercise of the right to injunctions was contrary to the principle of estoppel. Given the fact that a FRAND declaration was not a binding contract but a mere willingness to grant a license for a third party, the court held that a FRAND-committed patentee did not waive its right to injunctions.[106] In particular, the court pointed out that given that the defendant Apple had implemented the standard patent technology and yet denied infringement, it was not against the principle of estoppel for the patentee to claim an injunction.

While patentees are normally entitled to injunctions against patent infringements, it may be an abuse of patent rights when a FRAND-committed patentee brings a lawsuit or applies for injunction to prevent infringement without any sincere effort to negotiate to license patents under FRAND terms.[107] The Seoul Central District Court recognized that injunctions to prevent alleged infringers from implementing SEP technologies may violate the policy and function of the standardization system, disrupt the fair competition and fair trade, and violate the principle of good faith in the relationship with implementers and the consumer. It therefore held that it was an abuse of patent right for a FRAND-committed patentee to claim injunctions against alleged infringements without good faith negotiation with the alleged infringer who was a willing licensee.[108] The court found that Samsung's effort to offer a FRAND term license was not in violation of the good faith principle or contrary to the policy of technology standardization; that by contrast there was a failure of a good faith negotiation on the part of Apple. Eventually, the court concluded that given the behavior of both parties, it was difficult to recognize an abuse of patent rights. And, yet, the court made it clear that a FRAND declaration by an SEP holder might restrict patent remedies such as injunctions.

Worth pointing out is that although there are no statutory provisions on the abuse of rights in the Patent Act of Korea, recently there have been an increasing number of cases in which the court has found the exercise of certain types of claims to be contrary to the policy goal of the law and therefore abuse of patent rights – for example, when a patentee brings a lawsuit to prevent infringement of a patent which is highly likely to be invalidated.[109]

4.3.2 Competition law

Korea has dealt with antitrust issues relating to violation of FRAND declaration by Qualcomm's business practices for more than a decade. After a lengthy investigation, Korea Fair Trade Commission (KFTC) concluded in 2009 that Qualcomm had abused its dominant position by discriminatory patent licensing,

106 Seoul Central District Court Decision 2011gahap39552 decided on August 24, 2012.
107 *Id.*
108 *Id.*
109 Supreme Court Decision 2010da95390 decided on January 19, 2012.

among others, despite its FRAND declaration.[110] The KFTC highlighted that the FRAND declaration is a critical measure to prevent the abuse of monopoly power gained by virtue of standardization.[111] On appeal by Qualcomm, the Supreme Court of Korea has recently affirmed the KFTC's findings and remedial orders for the most part[112]

Since the KFTC decision on Qualcomm, there have been hot debates on the effect of FRAND violation on competition law in Korea. As was the case in Europe, there have been views in Korea as well that a FRAND declaration by a patentee would lead to a reasonable expectation for potential implementers, including competitors, to get licenses on FRAND terms.[113]

Nine years later, the KFTC again found that Qualcomm abused its dominant position again by refusing to honor its commitment to license SEPs under FRAND terms and fined Qualcomm USD 912.34 million.[114] Like the Court of Justice of the European Union (CJEU), the KFTC relied partly on the fact that Qualcomm's FRAND declaration caused potential implementers' reasonable expectations to access FRAND-encumbered technologies. According to the finding of the KFTC, it was reasonable for modem chipset manufacturers to expect that an SEP holder who made a FRAND commitment, such as Qualcomm, would have allowed manufacturers to implement the patented technology under FRAND terms.[115] Given the legitimate expectations from a FRAND declaration in the industry, the KFTC came to the conclusion that Qualcomm's violation of its FRAND declaration would highly likely inflict anti-competitive harm on the industry and the consumer welfare as well.[116]

4.4 *Analysis*

4.4.1 *Enforcing FRAND declaration based on general doctrines*

Patent remedies available to a FRAND-committed patentee depend on the legal nature of the FRAND declaration. If the FRAND declaration is viewed as a license agreement of which the implementer is a party, it would be almost impossible for a patentee to claim injunctions against the implementer who has been granted a licence, and the patentee arguably has waived its right to claim injunctions. By contrast, if a FRAND declaration is not viewed as a valid licensing agreement, the implementer will need to substantiate a claim to enforce the patentee's FRAND declaration and to limit patent remedies. Like most countries, courts in China, Japan and Korea have ruled out the possibility that FRAND declaration can form

110 KFTC Decision and Order No. 2009–281, 2009JiSik0329, December 30, 2009.

111 For further detailed analysis of this case, *see* Kim (2017), 187–193.

112 Supreme Court Decision 2013du14726 decided on January 31, 2019.

113 Oh (2016), 64; Park (2018), 172.

114 Korea Fair Trade Commission Decision and Order No. 2017-025, Case No. 2015sigam2118, January 20, 2017, on the Abuse of Market Dominance by Qualcomm.

115 *Id.* para. 235.

116 Jinyul Ju, Chapter 10 of the present book.

a license agreement between an SEP holder and an implementer. Therefore, there has been a common challenge for these courts, namely to find a legal basis to enforce the FRAND declaration or to limit patent remedies in the absence of a contract between the SEP holder and the implementer. The courts need a general provision or doctrine in the law which can be applied to parties without any contractual relations.

The Chinese court applied the doctrine of fairness and good faith, the Japanese court applied the doctrine of abuse of right, and the Korean court applied the doctrine of estoppel as legal bases to enforce the FRAND declaration and to limit SEP holders' patent right against implementers. These doctrines are conceptually overlapping when applied. For example, the good faith doctrine in China has been applied to curb the abuse of legal right.[117] Therefore, abuse of right is sometimes viewed as a part of the good faith doctrine. Moreover, both the good faith doctrine in China and abuse of right doctrine in Japan are applied when the court needs to decide certain issues not specifically stipulated by the law or contractual terms.[118] Some Japanese scholars have even argued that the court should have applied the doctrine of good faith,[119] instead of the doctrine of abuse of right, in deciding whether to approve SEP holders' injunctions against implementers.[120] Beside, Chinese courts sometimes apply the good faith doctrine to require parties keep their promises even in the absence of a contract, which is similar to the doctrine of estoppel. In *Samsung v. Apple*, the Seoul Central District Court constantly used the concepts of abuse of right and good faith to explain how the doctrine of estoppel was applied in the case.[121] The overlapping and interchangeable use of these three doctrines, namely good faith, abuse of right and estoppel, represents a common challenge faced by the courts dealing with FRAND disputes.

4.4.2 *Protectable reliance of the implementers*

In *Samsung v. Apple*, the IP High Court in Japan ruled that Apple, as an implementer, had relied on Samsung's FRAND declaration and such reliance should be protected by the law.[122] Similarly, the KFTC ruled against Qualcomm partly because Qualcomm's FRAND declaration had caused reasonable expectation from the implementers.[123] Although the IP High Court in Japan applied the Japanese Patent Act and Civil Code, and the KFTC decided according to the

117 Ling (2002), 50.

118 *See supra* subsection 4.1.1. The IP High Court in Japan applied abuse of right doctrine to restrict the SEP holder's injunctive relief and damages claim because "there were no other adequate means available at the time to balance the interests of the SEP owners and the implementers." Nagakoshi & Tamai (2016), 251.

119 Japanese Civil Code Art. 1(2): "[t]he exercise of rights and performance of duties must be done in good faith."

120 Nagakoshi & Tamai (2016), 258–259.

121 *See supra* subsection 4.3.1.

122 *See supra* subsection 4.2.1.

123 *See supra* subsection 4.3.2.

Korean Monopoly Regulation and Fair Trade Act, they both pointed out that FRAND declaration creates reliance or expectation from an unspecified number of implementers and such reliance or expectation triggers the SEP holder's obligation under patent and competition laws.[124]

These developments have echoed the "market reliance theory" for FRAND declaration developed by Professor Jorge L. Contreras, which was derived from the equitable doctrine of promissory estoppel[125] and avoids the need to search for a contractual basis for FRAND claims.[126] The purpose of this theory is closely relevant to courts' aforementioned endeavors in looking for a general doctrine to enforce the FRAND obligation.[127] From a comparative law perspective, the CJEU ruling has also confirmed that the market reliance and expectations created by the FRAND declaration can serve as the basis for activating competition law.[128]

4.4.3 FRAND negotiation

FRAND not only refers to licensing terms but also represents the process in which parties negotiate for such terms.[129] Therefore, FRAND declaration is relevant to not only the substantive licensing terms but also the negotiation between SEP holders and implementers. Courts in China, Japan and Korea likewise held that FRAND-encumbered SEP holders were obliged to negotiate with implementers in good faith. The courts in China and Korea further indicated that implementers aiming to obtain FRAND licenses should also negotiate in good faith with SEP holders, and that FRAND declaration may entail mutual good faith obligation in FRAND negotiations.

One specific issue regarding FRAND negotiation is whether SEP holders can seek injunction against implementers. The availability of injunction would significantly affect the bargaining power of the SEP holder and the implementer during their FRAND negotiation. The SEP holder would be placed in a favorable position against the implementer if the injunction is available, and vice versa.[130] Therefore, it is crucial to explore whether SEP holders' right to seek injunctions would be limited by their prior FRAND declaration. The Beijing IP Court developed a standard for good faith FRAND negotiation for both SEP holders and standard implementers:[131] an SEP holder can only sue or seek injunction against an implementer if he has negotiated in good faith but the implementer has not. Similarly, the IP High Court in Japan held that an SEP holder would

124 Oh (2016), 64.

125 Contreras (2015), 517–523.

126 *Id.* at 503–519.

127 *See supra* subsection 4.4.1.

128 *Huawei Technology Co. Ltd v. ZTE Corp., ZTE Deutschland GmbH*, EU Court of Justice, Case C-170/13 Decision of July 16, 2015, paras. 49–53.

129 Cross & Strath (2017), 113.

130 Ko (2014), 210, 213.

131 *See supra* subsection 4.3.1.

abuse its patent right if it sought injunctions against a willing FRAND licensee.[132] The Seoul Central District Court likewise ruled that a FRAND-committed SEP holder would have abused its right if it sought injunctive relief against a willing licensee that is willing to negotiate in good faith.[133]

FRAND traditionally refers to the substantive licensing terms. However, when courts and competition authorities enforce the FRAND declaration, they inevitably need to scrutinize whether the SEP holder and the implementer negotiate for a FRAND license in good faith. Therefore, the implementation of FRAND declaration has procedural implications for licensing negotiation as well. In terms of FRAND negotiation and the availability of injunction for SEP holders, we have seen the convergence of viewpoints between China, Japan and Korea, which represents an East Asian perspective on this issue.

4.4.4 Competition law viewpoint of FRAND declaration

Although SEPs usually trigger competition law concerns, the competition law effect of FRAND declaration is not yet clear. SEP holders may violate competition law even if they have not made any FRAND declaration. The *Qualcomm* case in China is an example in point. The NDRC held that Qualcomm, as an SEP holder, has violated the Anti-monopoly Law, although it did not consider Qualcomm's previous FRAND declaration at all.[134] By contrast, in *Huawei v. InterDigital* (II), the Guangdong High Court opined that InterDigital's violation of its FRAND declaration was a violation of Anti-monopoly Law as well.[135] In Japan, according to the Antitrust Guidelines on the Use of Intellectual Property, a FRAND-committed SEP holder may violate the AMA by refusing to license to or filing an infringement lawsuit against a willing licensee.[136]

KFTC's approach to FRAND declaration is slightly different from those of China and Japan. First, the KFTC has pointed out that FRAND declaration per se can prevent the abuse of market power.[137] Indeed, facing a charge of competition law violation, an SEP holder could use a FRAND undertaking as a defense.[138] This was the case in *Unwired Planet v. Huawei* in the United Kingdom, where the SEP holder argued that it did not have market dominance because, among other things, the FRAND undertaking necessarily weakened its market position.[139] Moreover, the KFTC also considered the fact that FRAND declaration had caused reasonable expectation from implementers, which had certain competition law implications.[140]

132 *See supra* subsection 4.2.1.
133 *See supra* subsection 4.3.1.
134 *See supra* subsection 4.1.2.3.
135 *See supra* subsection 4.1.2.2.
136 *See supra* subsection 4.2.2.
137 *See supra* subsection 4.3.2.
138 Turner (2015), 127–128.
139 *Unwired Planet v. Huawei* [2017] EWHC 711 (Pat) ¶ 650.
140 *See supra* subsection 4.3.2.

5 Conclusion

Most FRAND disputes originate from the FRAND declaration made by the SEP holders. Therefore, it is crucial to understand the legal nature of this declaration. This chapter examines the judicial and competition law authorities' approaches to FRAND declaration in three major Asian civil law jurisdictions: China, Japan and Korea. While courts in these three countries have not recognized that a license agreement can be formed by FRAND declaration, they have applied different but similar legal doctrines to enforce this declaration. Moreover, courts in these three jurisdictions have developed similar approaches to FRAND negotiation and SEP holders' applications for injunction against standard implementers. Lastly, while there is no doubt that SEP holders may violate competition law by abusing their dominant market position, competition policies on FRAND declaration are comparatively unclear in these three countries.

References

Atik, J. 2019. The FRAND ceremony and the engagement of article 102 TFEU in the licensing of standard essential patents. *Fordham International Law Journal*, 42, 949–965.

Carlton, D.W. & Shampine, A.L. 2013. An economic interpretation of FRAND. *Journal of Competition Law and Economics*, 9(3), 531–552.

Contreras, J.L. 2013. Fixing FRAND: a pseudo-pool approach to standards-based patent licensing. *Antitrust Law Journal*, 79, 47–95.

Contreras, J.L. 2015. A market reliance theory for FRAND commitments and other patent pledges. *Utah Law Review*, 2015(2), 479–558.

Contreras, J.L. 2017. From private ordering to public law: the legal frameworks governing standard-essential patents. *Harvard Journal of Law and Technology*, 30, 211–231.

Cotter, T.F. 2014. Comparative law and economics of standard-essential patents and FRAND royalties. *Texas Intellectual Property Law Journal*, 22, 311–363.

Cross, J. & Strath, J. 2017. Fair, reasonable, and non-discriminatory (FRAND) terms: can the court set a FRAND rate? *Computers and Telecommunications Law Review*, 23(5), 112–115

Cui, G. 2014. Standard-essential patents and injunctive relief, in S. Luginbuehl and P. Ganea (Eds.), *Patent Law in Greater China*, 340–362. Edward Elgar, Cheltenham.

Dolmans, M. & Ilan, D. 2012. European antitrust and patent acquisitions: trolls in the patent thickets. *Competition Law International*, 2, 7–18.

Epstein, R.A. & Noroozi, K.B. 2017. Why incentives for "patent holdout" threaten to dismantle FRAND, and why it matters. *Berkeley Technology Law Journal*, 32, 1381–1431.

Kesan, J.P. & Hayes, C.M. 2014. FRAND's forever: standards, patent transfers, and licensing commitments. *Indiana Law Journal*, 89, 231–314.

Kim, R. 2017. Anti-competitive patent licensing practice: Qualcomm's abuse of market dominance, in K-C. Liu (Ed.), *Annotated Leading Patent Cases in Major Asian Jurisdictions*, 184–193. City University of Hong Kong Press, Hong Kong.

Ko, H. 2014. Facilitating negotiation for licensing standard-essential patents in the shadow of injunctive relief possibilities. *Texas Intellectual Property Law Journal*, 22, 209–221.

Hou, L. & Tian, M. 2019. Chapter 11. IPR protection and antitrust regulation of SEPs in China, in K-C. Liu & R.M. Hilty (Eds.), *SEPs, SSO and FRAND – Asian and Global Perspectives on Fostering Innovation in Interconnectivity*. Routledge, London.

Hovenkamp, E. 2017. Tying, exclusivity, and standard-essential patents. *Columbia Science and Technology Law Review*, 19, 79–135.

Ju, J. 2019. Chapter 10. Korea, in K-C. Liu & R.M. Hilty (Eds.), *SEPs, SSO and FRAND – Asian and Global Perspectives on Fostering Innovation in Interconnectivity*. Routledge, London.

Lee, J-A. 2016. Implementing the FRAND standard in China. *Vanderbilt Journal of Entertainment and Technology Law*, 19(1), 37–85.

Lee, J-A. 2017. The determination of FRAND rate for SEPs: Huawei v. InterDigital, in K-C. Liu (Ed.), *Annotated Leading Patent Cases in Major Asian Jurisdictions*, 194–205. City University of Hong Kong Press, Hong Kong.

Lemley, M.A. & Shapiro, C. 2013. A simple approach to setting reasonable royalties for standard-essential patents. *Berkeley Technology Law Journal*, 28, 1135–1166.

Li, J. & Lin, X. 2017. Anti-monopoly case against Qualcomm's patent licensing practice, in K-C. Liu (Ed.), *Annotated Leading Patent Cases in Major Asian Jurisdictions*, 215–229. City University of Hong Kong Press, Hong Kong.

Li, Y. 2017. NDRC's antitrust remedies against Qualcomm's SEP package licensing, in K-C. Liu (Ed.), *Annotated Leading Patent Cases in Major Asian Jurisdictions*, 230–240. City University of Hong Kong Press, Hong Kong.

Lim, D. 2014. Standard essential patents, trolls, and the smartphone wars: triangulating the end game. *Penn State Law Review*, 119, 1–91.

Ling, B. 2002. *Contract Law in China*. Sweet & Maxwell Asia, Hong Kong.

Melamed, A.D. & Shapiro, C. 2018. How antitrust law can make FRAND declaration more effective. *Yale Law Journal*, 127(7), 2110–2140.

Michaels, A.C. 2018. Patent transfer and the bundle of rights. *Brooklyn Law Review*, 83, 933–981.

Nagakoshi, Y. & Tamai, K. 2016. Japan without FRANDs? Recent developments on injunctions and FRAND-encumbered patents in Japan. *AIPLA Quarterly Journal*, 44(2), 243–294.

Nakayama, I. & Tamura, Y. 2015. Denial of injunctive relief on grounds of equity: situation in the U.S. and Japan, in R.M. Hilty & K-C. Liu (Eds.), *Compulsory Licensing: Practical Experiences and Ways Forward*, 267–290. Springer, Berlin, Heidelberg.

Oh, S.H. 2016. How to find unreasonableness of royalties in violation of FRAND declaration. *IP Research Journal*, 11(3), 59–94.

Park, J.S. 2013. Problems of standard patents. *Seoul National University Law Review*, 54(4), 109–178.

Park, Y.S. 2018. A brief analysis of legal issues relating to standard essential patent litigations. *Justice*, 165, 155–183.

Pentheroudakis, C. & Baron, J.A. 2017. *Licensing Terms of Standard Essential Patents: A Comprehensive Analysis of Cases*. European Union.

Ratliff, J. & Rubinfeld, D.L. 2013. The use and threat of injunctions in the RAND context. *Journal of Competition Law and Economics*, 9(1), 1–22.

Richter, H. & Slowinski, P.R. 2019. The data sharing economy: on the emergence of new intermediaries. *IIC – International Review of Intellectual Property and Competition Law*, 1(50), 4–29.

Schellekens, M. 2015. Horizon 2020 and fair and reasonable licenses. *Computer and Telecommunications Law Review*, 21(8), 234–244.

Sidak, J.G. 2016. International trade commission exclusion orders for the infringement of standard-essential patents. *Cornell Journal of Law and Public Policy*, 26, 125–169.

Suzuki, M. 2017. Enforcement of FRAND-encumbered SEPs, in K-C. Liu (Ed.), *Annotated Leading Patent Cases in Major Asian Jurisdictions*, 241–267. City University of Hong Kong Press, Hong Kong.

Suzuki, M. 2019. Chapter 9. Japan, in K-C. Liu & R.M. Hilty (Eds.), *SEPs, SSO and FRAND – Asian and Global Perspectives on Fostering Innovation in Interconnectivity*. Routledge, London.

Turner, J.D.C. 2015. *Intellectual Property and EU Competition Law*. Oxford University Press, Oxford.

Wang, L. 1999. An inquiry into several difficult problems in enacting China's uniform contract law. *Pacific Rim Law and Policy Journal*, 8(2), 351–392.

7 UK perspective

Peter Damerell and Tess Waldron

1 Background

1.1 FRAND declarations

As described previously in this book, where a patent is declared as essential to a standardized technology, the standard setting organization (SSO) in question will typically require the IPR holder to commit to license that patent on reasonable and non-discriminatory (RAND) or fair, reasonable and non-discriminatory (FRAND) terms. Although the wording of these obligations may not be exactly the same, to date no substantive difference of principle between the two requirements has been identified. When the question of enforcement is considered, however, there may well be differences depending on the SSO in question. In particular, the relationship between each SSO and its members and/or third parties will be governed by (1) the rules/codes of practice of the SSO itself, in particular, the precise wording of the undertaking required by that SSO; and (2) the law which governs those documents.

By way of illustration, the European Telecommunications Standards Institute (ETSI), the SSO which has to date received the most judicial attention in the courts of England and Wales, is based in France and was established under French law. Equally, its Rules of Procedure, Policy and Guide are governed by French law and, when a FRAND licensing undertaking is given in an ETSI-approved form, that undertaking is also governed by French law. It follows, therefore, that the enforceability of the ETSI FRAND undertaking by third-party implementers, including those which are not themselves ETSI members, falls to be decided as a matter of French law. By contrast, a FRAND undertaking given to the Indian Telecommunications Standards Development Society (TSDSI), while largely similar to the ETSI FRAND undertaking as a matter of language, is governed by the laws of India, the application of which to the TSDSI FRAND undertaking could result in that undertaking having a different legal effect to one given to ETSI.

Further, although (F)RAND commitments are required by all seven members of the 3GPP (ETSI, the Association of Radio Industries and Businesses [ARIB], the Alliance for Telecommunications Industry Solutions [ATIS], the Chinese Communications Standards Association [CCSA], the Telecommunication Technology

Committee [TTC], the Telecommunications Technology Association [TTA] and the TSDSI), the language of the various undertakings is not uniform. This is also the case for the (F)RAND commitments requested by the American National Standards Institute (ANSI), the Institute of Electrical and Electronics Engineers (IEEE), the International Electrotechnical Commission (IEC), the International Organization for Standardization (ISO), the International Telecommunication Union (ITU), the Telecommunications Industry Association (TIA) and various other SSOs.

As such, although the legal basis and effect of the ETSI FRAND undertaking has been considered in some detail by the courts of England and Wales, it cannot be assumed that the analysis contained in the relevant cases would necessarily apply were the undertaking being considered that of a different SSO. This will in particular be the case if the question of enforcement is considered as a purely contractual issue rather than as a matter of European competition law.

1.2 FRAND in UK proceedings

FRAND issues usually arise in the UK in the context of SEP infringement proceedings where the relief to which an IPR holder may be entitled will be heavily influenced by the relevant FRAND undertaking, on which the defendant will typically rely. A consideration of FRAND will almost inevitably also be important in the assessment as to the merits of any competition law defence advanced by the defendant.

Although, to date, the courts of England and Wales have largely considered FRAND in the context of SEP infringement proceedings, given (1) the court's inherent jurisdiction to grant declaratory relief, described further later; and (2) the confirmation, following the decision in *Unwired Planet*, that at least the ETSI FRAND undertaking takes effect as a contract between ETSI and the IPR holder, which can be enforced by a third party outside of and independently from European competition law, there exists the opportunity for implementers to commence proceedings in the UK seeking to enforce an IPR holder's FRAND undertaking and/or requesting that the court determine FRAND terms for that IPR holder's SEP portfolio. Indeed, in UK proceedings between Apple and Qualcomm, Apple's only claim against one of the Qualcomm defendant companies was for breach of contract based on the ETSI FRAND undertaking.[1]

2 Nature of the FRAND undertaking

The nature of the ETSI FRAND undertaking has only relatively recently been considered in any detail by the courts of England and Wales. While earlier cases

1 In the event, as described further later, this claim failed at an interim stage for jurisdictional reasons and because Apple were unable to demonstrate that the UK defendant (a non-patent-owning entity) had assumed any FRAND licensing obligation (see *Apple Retail UK Limited & Ors v Qualcomm (UK) Limited & Anor* [2018] EWHC 1188 (Pat)).

suggested that the UK would mirror the approach taken in the U.S. and view the ETSI FRAND undertaking as "a contract between the declarant and ETSI to the benefit of third parties",[2] the legal basis for this conclusion was not substantively addressed until the 2017 *Unwired Planet* decision.

In *Unwired Planet* itself, there was actually no dispute between the parties that, as a practical matter, Unwired Planet was bound to license its patents on FRAND terms. Indeed, Unwired Planet's positive case was that the FRAND declaration it had made was directly enforceable by third parties, including the defendants, and Huawei relied on Unwired Planet's FRAND declaration in its defence against the grant of an injunction. The point was initially considered by both the High Court and the Court of Appeal in the context of an interim application brought by Ericsson where the Court of Appeal found that (1) although Unwired Planet was not a member of ETSI, it was "just as constrained by the FRAND undertaking it has given as it would be if it were such a member"; and (2) "as a practical matter, any third party may require UP [Unwired Planet] to grant it a licence under the SEPs on FRAND terms".[3] However, at this interim stage of the proceedings and in light of the particular facts of the case, the legal basis for the Court of Appeal's conclusions, and whether they were of general applicability, was not explored fully.

When it came to the FRAND trial, there remained a dispute about the enforceability of the ETSI FRAND undertaking as a matter of principle under French law. This arose in the context of its effect on the analysis as to whether a SEP holder enjoys a dominant position for the purposes of alleged breaches of Article 102 of the Treaty on the Function of the European Union (TFEU), which prohibits undertakings that are, in fact, dominant from behaving in a manner that restricts competition. In the *Unwired Planet* proceedings it was alleged that Unwired Planet's licensing practices were incompatible with this aspect of European competition law and Unwired Planet relied on the nature of the FRAND undertaking in arguing that it was not in a dominant position.

Against this background, and having conducted a detailed analysis of the parties' written evidence as to French law (under English procedural rules, expert evidence as to foreign law is admissible in respect of the principles that should be applied to the construction of a document governed by that law), the English High Court reached the following conclusions:

1 The completion and filing of an ETSI IPR Declaration Form gives rise to a contract between ETSI and the IPR holder on the terms set out in the Declaration Form;
2 Such a contact can be enforced by third parties under the French law doctrine of *stipulation pour autrui* (broadly speaking, a French law principle that permits the formation of a contract for the benefit of a third party).

2 *Nokia GmbH v IPCom GmbH & Co. KG* [2009] EWHC 2742 (Pat) at para. 26.
3 *Samsung Electronics Co Ltd v Telefonaktiebolaget LM Ericsson* [2016] 5 CMLR 11 at para. 38.

As to the nature of the obligation that can be enforced against an IPR holder, the High Court accepted that a FRAND declaration is not specifically enforceable per se (i.e. the court cannot compel an IPR holder – or an implementer – to enter into a licensing agreement). However, the High Court went on to decide that this would not rob the FRAND undertaking of substantive legal effect because of the interaction between (1) the obligation arising as a result of the IPR holder's declaration, (2) the underlying rights subject to that obligation and (3) the relief available for any infringement of those rights.

In the view of the High Court, an IPR holder that refused to enter into a FRAND licence could not be forced to enter into that licence but, equally, would not normally be entitled to any other relief for patent infringement. As discussed further later, the practical effect of this decision is that, although as a pure matter of contract law neither an implementer nor an IPR holder can rely on the ETSI FRAND undertaking to compel the appropriate counterparty to enter into a licence, the undertaking can have the same indirect effect in circumstances where (1) an IPR holder which has established infringement of a valid SEP faces a choice between entering into a FRAND licence or being prevented from obtaining any form of relief for patent infringement; and (2) an implementer which has been found to infringe must either take a FRAND licence or face an injunction.

3 UK enforcement of the FRAND undertaking by a third-party implementer

3.1 Declaratory relief

As a common law system, English law provides the courts of England and Wales with a significant degree of flexibility and discretion. Of most relevance in the FRAND context is the availability of discretionary declaratory relief under the inherent jurisdiction set out in Civil Procedural Rule 40.20 ("the court may make binding declarations whether or not any other remedy is claimed"), which can provide a party with the means to seek a determination as to the terms of a FRAND licence, either to its own portfolio or to a portfolio that it wishes to license. Where SEPs are in issue other declarations can also be sought including declarations of (1) non-infringement (a statutory right under the Patents Act 1977), (2) validity/invalidity and (3) essentiality/non-essentiality.

Although discretionary declarations of this sort are only available if they will serve a useful purpose (and the courts of England and Wales will not grant declaratory relief that relates only to purely hypothetical issues), where there is a real commercial issue between the parties a declaration can be sought even if there is no existing legal dispute. This provides a potential opportunity for an implementer that wishes to commence proceedings in order to resolve a dispute over the terms that would be FRAND for a given portfolio, in particular an implementer that perceives the courts of England and Wales as a favorable forum for deciding the issue and wishes to ensure that, subject to jurisdiction, those courts are seized of FRAND matters.

Of course, from a theoretical point of view, a FRAND declaration as to terms which the court cannot compel either party to enter into could be viewed as hypothetical. However, not only does the FRAND determination demarcate the relief available to an IPR holder for patent infringement in the manner described further later, but it can also assist in resolving other issues between the parties, including whether the IPR holder's licensing behavior is compatible with competition law, and assist in a commercial resolution of the underlying dispute. As such, and as occurred in *Unwired Planet*, the courts of England and Wales will be prepared to make these sorts of declarations in appropriate cases.

The ability and preparedness to grant declaratory relief in this manner means that the courts of England and Wales can offer a highly effective forum for the resolution of FRAND licensing disputes. While, to date, *Unwired Planet* remains the only case in which the High Court has actually proceeded to set FRAND terms, a number of other FRAND determinations are currently pending, including in *Conversant v Huawei & ZTE* (subject to an ongoing jurisdictional challenge). Other cases in which FRAND issues were raised, including *Vringo v ZTE* and *Nokia v IPCom*, settled before the substantive licensing/FRAND issues were heard.

It is also worth noting that the courts of England and Wales will not necessarily require a finding of SEP infringement before determining FRAND issues. First, as discussed earlier, it may be possible for an implementer to commence proceedings seeking a declaration as to the appropriate FRAND terms for a given portfolio in the absence of *any* dispute as to SEP infringement/essentiality and validity, in which case substantive patent issues may not arise in any event. Second, even when the proceedings are framed more traditionally (i.e. as a SEP infringement action with a FRAND declaration either requested by the SEP owner – usually in the form of a request for endorsement of licensing offers made before the commencement of proceedings – or raised as part of the defence), the courts of England and Wales may, as a matter of case management, determine FRAND questions at an early stage.

As considered further later in the context of jurisdiction, where proceedings are started by the IPR holder, questions of patent infringement are likely to form part of the proceedings because it may be the easiest way for the jurisdiction of the courts of England and Wales to be established. In such circumstances, if the parties were to agree that a FRAND licence is required but were unable to agree its terms, the courts would be likely, in accordance with the discretion afforded them in terms of case management issues, to grant any request to settle terms before adjudging technical patent issues.

However, even where there remains a genuine dispute as to validity and infringement/essentiality, the courts of England and Wales may be receptive to requests from either party to deal with FRAND issues first, on the basis that (particularly where the relevant portfolio is over a certain size and/or there is a consensus as to the appropriate geographical scope of the licence in question) licensing terms represent the heart of the commercial dispute.[4]

3.2 Breach of contract

While declaratory relief can be a very useful tool in resolving FRAND disputes, especially where both parties wish to enter into a licence but cannot agree its terms, the *Unwired Planet* decision also provides an opportunity for an implementer to bring a similar action framed as a claim for breach of contract. Such a claim would be based on (1) the contract that is formed between ETSI and an IPR holder once that IPR holder has made a FRAND declaration; and (2) the enforceability of that contract by third-party beneficiaries in the manner described in *Unwired Planet*.

In some circumstances, these two claims may well be mirror images of each other. For example, an implementer who succeeds in a claim for breach of contract on the grounds that an IPR holder has failed to comply with its obligations under the ETSI FRAND undertaking (in particular its obligation to "be prepared to grant a licence on FRAND terms") will, in most cases, likely also be entitled to a declaration that the IPR holder has failed to offer FRAND terms. However, the two claims can also act in a complementary manner. For example, a finding that an IPR holder is in breach of its obligations under the ETSI FRAND undertaking coupled with a declaration as to the terms, or range of terms, that would be FRAND for a licence to the relevant SEP portfolio provides the basis for a commercial resolution to the dispute: not only is it clear what licensing behavior is not FRAND, but the parties are presented with the terms of a FRAND licence. Of course, the same result could be obtained with two separate declarations, but an advantage of bringing a breach of contract claim as an alternative to (or as well as) proceedings seeking declaratory relief is that the former can found a damages claim, thereby potentially exerting additional commercial pressure on the IPR holder alongside the reputational issues that may be at stake were the courts of England and Wales to decide that its licensing practices were incompatible with its FRAND obligations.

As noted earlier, only the ETSI FRAND undertaking has to date been considered in any detail by the courts of England and Wales and, to the extent that other (F)RAND declarations are worded differently and/or governed by different laws, the conclusions in terms of their enforceability in the UK as a matter of contract law remains uncertain. In particular, a key element of the French law analysis in *Unwired Planet*, without which the High Court would not have been able to decide as it did, was the applicability of the French law doctrine

4 See, for example, the comments of Mr. Justice Henry Carr in *TQ Delta, LLC v Zyxel Communications* [2017] EWHC 3305 (Pat).

of *stipulation pour autrui*, which permits third parties to enforce contractual obligations in certain limited circumstances. Such a principle is recognized in English law and enshrined in the Contracts (Rights of Third Parties) Act 1999. Similarly, the U.S. (another common law jurisdiction) has considered allegations as to the breach of a FRAND commitment as a matter of contract law in, for example, *Microsoft v Motorola*.[5] However, in circumstances where the law applicable to a given (F)RAND undertaking may not recognize third-party rights arising under contracts, a breach of contract claim might not be straightforward, particularly where the third-party implementer is not a member of the SSO in question.

That said, given the pragmatic approach of the courts of England and Wales, the potential difficulty outlined earlier may be purely theoretical. In particular, where it is possible to make a declaration to any of the organizations that make up the 3GPP, it would seem undesirable if the effect of making a declaration to, for example, ATIS, were different from making one to ETSI. In terms of how this potential issue could be addressed, it is worth noting the comment made by the CJEU in *Huawei v ZTE* that an "undertaking to grant licences on FRAND terms creates legitimate expectations on the part of third parties that the proprietor of the SEP will in fact grant licences on such terms".[6] While this observation was made in the context of Article 102 TFEU (such that the CJEU went on to state that "a refusal by the proprietor of the SEP to grant a licence on those terms may, in principle, constitute an abuse within the meaning of Article 102 TFEU"), it could be argued that the "legitimate expectation" created once a (F)RAND declaration is made should be enforceable outside of competition law as a matter of contract.

Further, to the extent that SSO policies contain provisions similar to Clause 6.1*bis* of the ETSI IPR Policy, which was introduced to address concerns raised by the European Commission and which (1) provides that FRAND licensing undertakings should be interpreted as encumbrances that bind successors in interest and (2) requires that IPR holders divesting SEPs include appropriate terms in the relevant transactional documents to ensure that the FRAND undertaking is, in fact, binding on the transferee (and any subsequent transferees), it is at least arguable that the relevant (F)RAND commitment is intended to act as a contractual restriction, directly enforceable by third parties.

Of course, and as discussed further later, the distinction between the enforcement of (F)RAND as a matter of contract law and as a matter of competition law is one without a difference unless so-called competition law FRAND and ETSI (or SSO) FRAND are different concepts in the manner set out in *Unwired Planet*.

5 C10–1823JLR, 2013 U.S. Dist LEXIS 60233 (W.D. Wash., April 25, 2013).
6 Case C-170/13, para. 53.

3.3 Enforcement as a matter of European competition law

3.3.1 Interaction between FRAND and competition law

ETSI was established in 1988, and its IPR Policy was developed in the early 1990s in close coordination with the European Commission. The history of the ETSI FRAND undertaking makes its original purpose clear. In particular, the development of the ETSI IPR Policy reflected and responded to concerns expressed inter alia by the European Commission regarding the potential anti-competitive effects of mobile telephony standardization under GSM and, then, UMTS. It was thought that potential anti-competitive effects might arise in the following two ways:

1 First, an agreement to create and comply with a technical standard may breach Article 101(1) TFEU, which prohibits "all agreements between undertakings . . . which may affect trade between Member States and which have as their object or effect the prevention, restriction or distortion of competition within the internal market", for example because the standardization process may create opportunities for the exchange of competitively sensitive information or for restrictive practices relating to quantities, prices, customer and territory sharing, or because it may foreclose the market to undertakings which do not have access to the technology included in the standard.
2 Second, the ownership of a SEP may give rise to a dominant position on a market for the supply or licensing of the technology governed by that SEP, which may be abused by the holder of the SEP, contrary to Article 102 TFEU, by its refusing to license that SEP and/or by its demanding excessive and unreasonable terms for such a licence (i.e. engaging in what has become known as "patent holdup"). Further, if there are a number of holders of SEPs, each of which is demanding terms and royalties which cumulatively impose an excessive burden on users of the technology (i.e. "royalty stacking"), then effective access to the standard is further inhibited.

It is clear, therefore, that there is a close relationship between the ETSI FRAND undertaking and European competition law in that the former is designed to ensure that the standardization process is not anti-competitive and that widespread adoption of the relevant standards is encouraged, to the benefit of consumers. In this framework, the interests of IPR holders in obtaining "adequate" and "fair" remuneration for their technology is also an important factor, albeit one that must be balanced against "the needs of standardisation for public use in the field of telecommunications".[7]

It can be understood from the CJEU's decision in *Huawei v ZTE* that a failure by a SEP owner to comply with its FRAND undertaking may, in principle,

7 See Clauses 3.1 and 3.2 of the ETSI IPR Policy.

constitute an abuse of dominance under Article 102 TFEU.[8] It has also been settled since Case COMP/38.636 – *Rambus* that a SEP owner cannot evade its obligation to grant licences on FRAND terms by failing to give notice of essential IPR to the relevant SSO at the time the standard was set (and consequently failing to give a FRAND declaration). In such circumstances, proceeding to claim royalties that would not have been obtainable had a FRAND undertaking been given is incompatible with Article 102 TFEU.

As to SEPs that may have been acquired subsequent to the standardization process, the acquirer of a SEP that fails to give a FRAND undertaking and behaves in a non-FRAND manner is unlikely to successfully evade potential liability under Article 102 TFEU. This is because of (1) the concerns expressed by the Commission in relation to the transfer of the FRAND undertaking to entities acquiring SEPs; (2) the subsequent introduction of Clause 6.1*bis* into the ETSI IPR Policy, which characterizes a FRAND undertaking as an encumbrance, binding on a successor-in-title (and requires a transferee to ensure, insofar as possible, that the same is achieved by the inclusion of appropriate provisions in the transfer documentation); and (3) the acceptance by the Commission in Case No COMP/M.6381 – *Google/Motorola Mobility* and Case No COMP/M.7202 – *Lenovo/Motorola Mobility* that no competition law concerns arose when the transferee of a SEP portfolio had undertaken to be bound by the FRAND commitment of the transferor. It is more probable that such a failure, at least when coupled with a refusal or failure to licence on FRAND terms, would be incompatible with Article 102 TFEU (as was the case in *Rambus*).

Finally, from a practical, strategic and reputational point of view, it appears unlikely that any SEP owner would wish to disavow FRAND in this way, not only because of the high risk of being found to have behaved in a manner incompatible with European competition law but also because, at least in the UK as a result of *Unwired Planet* and likely across the European Union following the reasoning in *Huawei v ZTE*, injunctive relief (and, therefore, the ability to ensure that an infringing implementer enters into a licence) will only be available in circumstances where the SEP owner has complied with its FRAND obligation, and the implementer has failed to behave in the manner of a willing licensee.

It follows from the foregoing that FRAND and Article 102 TFEU are closely related. However, they remain two distinct potential constraints on the behavior of IPR holders and it does not necessarily follow that a breach of one will automatically amount to a breach of the other.

3.3.2 Breach of Article 102 TFEU

As explained earlier, Article 102 TFEU prohibits an undertaking in a dominant position from abusing that dominant position such that trade between Member States is, or may be, affected. Of relevance in the SEP licensing context, abuses

8 See, in particular, paras. 52 to 54 of Case C-170/13.

may consist of (1) directly or indirectly imposing unfair purchase or selling prices or other unfair trading conditions contrary to Article 102(a) TFEU; (2) applying dissimilar conditions to equivalent transactions with other trading parties, thereby placing them at a competitive disadvantage in a manner prohibited by Article 102(c) TFEU; and/or (3) making the conclusion of contracts subject to acceptance by the other parties of supplementary obligations which, by their nature or according to commercial usage, have no connection with the subject of such contracts in breach of Article 102(d) TFEU.

Broadly speaking, it could be said that that Article 102(a) TFEU (and potentially Article 102(d) TFEU) oblige SEP owners to offer fair and reasonable (FR) licensing terms while Article 102(c) TFEU (and potentially 102(d) TFEU) require that such terms must also be non-discriminatory (ND). The question then arises as to whether failing to offer FRAND terms would automatically be considered abusive under Article 102 TFEU, an issue that was considered by the High Court in *Unwired Planet*.

In *Unwired Planet*, the High Court found that none of the rates in the licensing offers made by Unwired Planet to Huawei were FRAND. However, this failure to offer FRAND terms was not sufficient for a finding of abuse under Article 102(a) TFEU because, in the view of the High Court, only an offer "which is so far above FRAND as to act to disrupt or prejudice the negotiations themselves . . . will fall foul of Article 102(a) TFEU".[9] This finding is consistent with the High Court's view that the FRAND commitment was intended to be different from and stricter than competition law.[10]

The High Court further decided that FRAND should not be understood as comprising separate "fair and reasonable" and "non-discriminatory" limbs because the determination of a FRAND benchmark rate based on comparable licences should be inherently non-discriminatory.[11] However, in case that interpretation was later held to be wrong, the High Court nevertheless went on to consider what the nature of a stand-alone non-discrimination obligation would be and whether the party alleging a breach of this element of the FRAND obligation would need to establish that the behavior complained of had the actual or potential effect of distorting competition.

9 See para. 765 of [2017] EWHC 2988 (Pat).

10 See, for example, paras. 153 and 757 of [2017] EWHC 2988 (Pat): (1) "Art 102 TFEU only condemns excessive pricing . . . a royalty rate can be at least somewhat higher than the true FRAND rate and still not be contrary to competition law. Therefore, as a matter of principle, the boundary between what is and is not a true FRAND rate as defined by the ETSI undertaking is not and cannot be necessarily co-extensive with competition law . . . for competition law to be engaged it will be necessary but not sufficient for a rate not to be the true FRAND rate"; (2) "I hold as a matter of law that the boundary of what is and is not a FRAND rate is different from the boundary of what is and is not an unfair price contrary to Article 102(a). If the rate imposed is FRAND then it cannot be abusive. But a rate can be higher than the FRAND rate without being abusive too".

11 See para. 502 of [2017] EWHC 2988 (Pat).

Of note, and in contrast to the approach taken when Article 102(a) TFEU abuses were considered, the High Court determined that a stand-alone non-discrimination obligation capable of compelling a licensor to offer the same sub-benchmark rate previously granted to a similarly situated licensee *would* include a competitive distortion requirement.[12] In short, the non-discrimination limb of FRAND would effectively be the same as the obligation under Article 102(c) TFEU and a breach of the former constitute an abuse under the latter. This finding was upheld by the Court of Appeal. At the time of writing, a decision from the Supreme Court on this issue was pending.

Of course, another factor that falls to be assessed under Article 102 TFEU is the seeking of injunctive relief. In *Huawei v ZTE*, the CJEU concluded that a SEP owner will not abuse a dominant position if, prior to commencing proceedings seeking injunctive relief, the alleged infringer has been alerted to the claimed infringement and, having confirmed its willingness to enter into a licence on FRAND terms, been presented with such a licensing offer.[13]

In *Unwired Planet*, although Unwired Planet had (1) started proceedings seeking injunctive relief without making any offer to Huawei and (2) failed to make a FRAND offer at any point before trial, the High Court decided that its conduct did not amount to an abuse under Article 102 TFEU. This finding was based, to a large extent, on the High Court's understanding that, in *Huawei v ZTE*, the CJEU was setting out a safe harbor such that compliance with the judgment would ensure that no Article 102 TFEU breach occurred. However, it did not conclude that a failure to follow the *Huawei v ZTE* steps would result in a finding of abuse. Instead, in such cases it would be for the relevant court to assess whether or not an abuse had occurred. The High Court further noted that the CJEU's judgment did not take into account the ability of an implementer to enforce FRAND as a matter of contract law rather than competition law, which meant that an implementer that has failed to establish a breach of Article 102 TFEU can still require a SEP owner to grant a FRAND licence.[14] In its decision in October 2018, the Court of Appeal agreed with the High Court's interpretation of the CJEU's decision in *Huawei v ZTE*.[15] A further appeal before the Supreme Court was heard in October 2019, but at the time of writing the Supreme Court's decision was still awaited.

In summary, the Unwired Planet case provides authority for the proposition that licensing behaviors which are abusive under Article 102 TFEU are certain to be non-FRAND but that the reverse does not necessarily apply – the court must go on to assess whether the practices complained of were capable of "disrupting" or "prejudicing" negotiations or whether, in all of the circumstances, the licensor's behavior (including the seeking of injunctive relief) is sufficient to amount

12 See para. 503 of [2017] EWHC 2988 (Pat).
13 See for example, para. 71 of [2017] EWHC 2988 (Pat).
14 See paras. 713 to 746 of [2017] EWHC 2988 (Pat).
15 [2018] EWCA Civ 2344.

to a refusal to licence. In relation to this analysis, one criticism that could be made is that, as the vast majority of SEP licensing negotiations are carried out between well-resourced and experienced commercial entities used to litigating SEP and licensing issues, the approach of the licensor would need to be truly unusual/obstructive to be considered abusive by the courts of England and Wales for the purposes of Article 102 TFEU.

3.3.3 FRAND rate/FRAND range

The distinction made by the High Court in *Unwired Planet* between an abuse of dominance under Article 102 TFEU and a breach of FRAND commitment and the arguable divergence from the approach taken by the CJEU in *Huawei v ZTE* can, to a certain extent, be understood as a result of a different approach to the nature of FRAND commitment itself.

In particular, while the High Court accepted that the FRAND commitment was a process as well as a characteristic of certain licensing terms,[16] it concluded that in the final analysis between any two parties there could only be one FRAND licence (i.e. that there was a single set of terms that could be correctly characterized as FRAND for a licence to a particular licensee in respect of a particular portfolio of SEPs). In the view of the High Court, were this not the case it would be difficult for the FRAND obligation to be enforced, especially in circumstances where both licensee and licensor had made FRAND licensing proposals and a tribunal would need to determine which set of terms to prefer.[17] Once this position is established, the notion that a failure to make exactly the licensing offer that the court, having conducted a detailed FRAND determination, decides as the appropriate FRAND licence would mean that the SEP owner had abused a dominant position is unattractive, and it is unsurprising that the High Court made the distinction it did.

By contrast, it is inherent in the scheme set out by the CJEU, which requires an exchange of FRAND offers between licensor and potential licensee, that a range of FRAND rates/terms is envisaged. Once this flexibility is introduced into the analysis, the possibility that a failure to make a FRAND offer could equate to an abuse of dominance appears less severe. Even so, outside of situations where injunctive relief is sought, it seems likely that there is a margin of error within which a licensor that has failed to make an offer inside the FRAND range will not necessarily be guilty of an abuse.

The Court of Appeal in *Unwired Planet* came to a different conclusion from the High Court on the question of whether there can be only one set of FRAND terms for any given set of circumstances. They considered instead that in reality a number of sets of terms may all be fair and reasonable in a given set of

16 See paras. 162 to 163 of [2017] EWHC 2988 (Pat).

17 The so-called *Vringo* problem, named after a previous judgment of Mr. Justice Birss and discussed at paras. 556–557 of [2017] EWHC 2988 (Pat).

circumstances. In relation to the *Vringo* problem, they considered this to be more of a theoretical problem than a real one. If two different sets of terms are each found to be FRAND, then they considered the SEP owner would satisfy its obligation to ETSI if it offered either one of them. Essentially, their position was that the SEP owner could choose the terms most favorable to it. The Court of Appeal did not need to consider whether a failure to make a FRAND offer amounted to an abuse of dominance under Article 102 TFEU (as that issue was not raised on appeal), so did not address the issue of whether there is a difference between a non-FRAND offer and an offer that is abusive.

3.3.4 Other SSOs

As discussed earlier, the enforceability of a (F)RAND undertaking as a matter of contract law may depend on the particular undertaking in question and the law by which it is governed. In the event that the conclusion reached by the High Court in *Unwired Planet* in relation to the ETSI FRAND undertaking cannot be applied to a different obligation, competition law will continue to provide implementers with protection against any abuse, by a SEP owner, of its dominant position.

Once again, however, the distinction may make little practical difference. In any allegation of abuse of dominance, an assessment as to whether licensing behavior is FRAND will likely be relied upon as a defence and, therefore, central to proceedings. Further, as described earlier, it would be unusual for an IPR holder to deny either an underlying obligation to licence on (F)RAND terms, or that such obligation can be directly enforced by third-party implementers. As such, and particularly in light of the pragmatic approach taken by the Court of Appeal in *Samsung v Ericsson* (where the panel was content to accept that Unwired Planet's FRAND undertaking could be relied upon by the defendants without conducting an analysis of the legal basis for this conclusion),[18] it would be an unusual case where only Article 102 was in issue.

3.4 Enforcement – conclusion

By way of summary, there are three potential distinct but interrelated ways in which a third-party implementer can enforce a SEP owner's FRAND obligation: by seeking declaratory relief, by alleging breach of contract and/or by relying on competition law. Of course, this enforcement only goes so far because (1) the courts of England and Wales will not usually compel a party to enter into any contract, including a FRAND licence; and (2) with the exception of declaratory relief, the causes of action available typically demarcate what is not FRAND rather than what is (i.e. provide an implementer with a non-technical defence in SEP infringement proceedings). To look at it another way, the remedies which

18 [2016] 5 CMLR 11.

can be sought by an implementer simply provide a framework which can either enable the parties to freely enter into a FRAND licence or restrict the relief to which the SEP owner is entitled following a finding of infringement, effectively compelling the SEP owner to choose between no relief or the FRAND terms settled by the court.

4 UK enforcement of the FRAND undertaking by a SEP owner

In a similar manner, a SEP owner can only indirectly compel an implementer to enter into a FRAND licence following a finding of infringement by leaving the implementer with a choice between an injunction or taking the terms on offer.

In this regard the courts of England and Wales represent an excellent potential forum for SEP owners because of the possibility that exists in the wake of the *Unwired Planet* proceedings of making an infringing implementer choose between an injunction in the UK or a global portfolio licence. In *Unwired Planet* itself, having decided that, to be enforceable by implementers, "ETSI FRAND" could only mean a single set of terms in a given circumstance, the High Court went on to decide that, where an implementer's operations were (broadly speaking) global, and the SEP owner had a portfolio over which it was impractical to litigate patent by patent or country by country, the FRAND licence would be global in scope. It followed that, after a finding of infringement, the set of FRAND terms on which the SEP owner was entitled to insist were for a global portfolio licence. If the implementer refused to take that licence, it would face an injunction in the UK. As described earlier, the Court of Appeal in *Unwired Planet* disagreed with the High Court in relation to whether there is only a single set of FRAND terms in any given circumstance. They agreed, however, that Unwired Planet was entitled to insist on a global licence and that if Huawei refused to take the licence it should face an injunction. This issue was debated before the Supreme Court in October 2019 and its decision is likely to be very significant for future FRAND disputes in the UK.

Unlike in *Unwired Planet*, where Mr. Justice Birss granted a FRAND injunction,[19] which was stayed pending appeal upon Huawei undertaking to abide by the terms of the FRAND licence until the parties' dispute was finally resolved,[20] in *TQ Delta v ZyXEL*,[21] an injunction was granted against the defendant even before the RAND issues in the proceedings were determined. Mr. Justice Henry Carr found that ZyXEL was not entitled to benefit from the RAND undertaking given by TQ Delta in circumstances where it was not clearly prepared to accept the RAND licence set by the English court. This was so even though ZyXEL (1) relied on a point which may be considered by the Supreme

19 An injunction that would cease to have effect once Huawei entered into a FRAND licence settled by the English court.

20 [2017] EWHC 1304 (Pat).

21 [2019] EWHC 745 (Pat).

Court in the context of the *Unwired Planet* litigation (specifically, the scope of the licence on which a SEP owner is entitled to insist); and (2) raised an argument yet to be considered by the English court as to whether a RAND licence can be determined for an entity (ZyXEL's parent) that is not party to the proceedings. ZyXEL's reluctance was no doubt influenced by the fact that the patent it had been found to infringe would expire before the RAND trial was heard. However, its position was viewed by the judge as "holdout" and the injunction requested by TQ Delta awarded.

5 Other issues

5.1 Jurisdictional considerations

As noted earlier, FRAND issues can be raised by either IPR holders or implementers. However, before commencing proceedings in the UK, the jurisdiction of the courts of England and Wales to adjudicate on the claim in question must be considered. This is a complicated area of law, a full explanation of which is outside the scope of this chapter. At a high level, however (and at the time of writing), questions of jurisdiction will fall to be determined under either the European regime or the relevant common law rules. Of the two systems, the European regime will take precedence where it applies.

5.1.1 The European regime

For the purposes of establishing that the courts of England and Wales have jurisdiction over FRAND issues, the most relevant of the European rules are likely to be the following:

1. Under Article 4(1) of Regulation (EU) No 1215/2012 on jurisdiction and the recognition and enforcement of judgments in civil and commercial matters (recast) (the "Brussels Regulation"), persons domiciled in a Member State shall (subject to certain exceptions, including those contained in Articles 7 and 24) be sued in the courts of that Member State. *Therefore, companies incorporated in England and Wales should usually be sued in the courts of England and Wales.*
2. Under Article 6(1) of the Brussels Regulation (and subject to certain exceptions, including Article 24), if a defendant is not domiciled in a Member State then the jurisdiction of the courts of each Member State shall be determined by the laws of that Member State. *This means that, where a potential defendant is not domiciled within the European Union, the question as to whether the courts of England and Wales have jurisdiction will be determined in accordance with English law.*
3. Under Article 7(2) of the Brussels Regulation, in matters relating to tort (including patent infringement), a person domiciled in a Member State may be sued in the courts of the jurisdiction in which the harmful event occurred. *In other words, the courts of England and Wales have non-exclusive jurisdiction*

in proceedings concerning the infringement (and non-infringement) of UK patents.

4 Under Article 24(4) of the Brussels Regulation, the courts of each Member State have exclusive jurisdiction in proceedings concerning the validity of patents granted in that Member State. *As such, claims concerning the validity of a UK SEP will be within the exclusive jurisdiction of the courts of England and Wales irrespective of the place of domicile of the patentee, and including situations where the patentee is domiciled outside of the European Union.*

The European regime will continue to apply to proceedings brought in the courts of England and Wales at least until the UK leaves the European Union. The rules which apply after this will depend on the arrangements that are eventually agreed between the UK and the European Union. Although, at the time of writing, there is little clarity as to what those rules might be, the UK government has recognized the importance of agreeing reciprocal rules with the European Union, closely mirroring the current system, to support cross-border trade after Brexit.

5.1.2 The common law rules

As explained earlier, where (1) a potential defendant is not domiciled within Europe and (2) the proceedings do not concern the validity of a UK SEP, then jurisdiction will be determined in accordance with English common law rules. In practice this means that jurisdiction will be founded either on English rules of service (within or outside the jurisdiction), or the defendant's submission to the jurisdiction of the English court.

In terms of service, if a defendant is within the jurisdiction of the courts of England and Wales (that is physically present which, in the case of a foreign company, requires that company to be carrying out business at a place within the jurisdiction) and is validly served with proceedings then jurisdiction is established. However, it is possible to challenge jurisdiction assumed in this manner, including on the basis that there is a more appropriate forum in which the case should be heard (a forum conveniens objection).

If the defendant is not within England and Wales and jurisdiction is not established under the European regime then the permission of the court is required before proceedings can be served overseas. To obtain permission it must be established that (1) the claim falls within the categories – the jurisdictional gateways[22] – set out in the relevant provisions of the Civil Procedural Rules (specifically Practice Direction 6B.3.1); (2) the claim has a reasonable prospect of success (reasonable meaning 'real' rather than 'fanciful'); and (3) England is the proper place (forum conveniens) to bring the claim. In effect, the objective of these three limbs is to permit the courts of England and Wales to exercise jurisdiction over

22 Each gateway represents a type of claim over which the English court will accept jurisdiction and, as a consequence, for which permission will be granted to serve the potential defendant outside of the jurisdiction.

foreign defendants where the claim in question has sufficient connection with the territory.

For the purposes of establishing that the courts of England and Wales have jurisdiction over FRAND issues, the most relevant of the jurisdictional gateways are likely to be the following:

1 Gateway 3: the defendant is a necessary and proper party to a claim over which the courts of England and Wales have jurisdiction (other than under one of the jurisdictional gateways);
2 Gateway 9: a claim is made in tort where damage was (or will be) sustained within the jurisdiction;
3 Gateway 11: the subject matter of the claim relates wholly or principally to property (including intellectual property) within the jurisdiction; and/or
4 Gateway 4A: a claim is made against the defendant in reliance on a jurisdictional gateway (e.g. a claim in tort as described in (2)) and a further claim is made against the same defendant which arises out of the same or closely connected facts.

5.1.3 Relevant jurisprudence

Questions as to the jurisdiction of the courts of England & Wales to determine FRAND issues have recently been considered in *Conversant v Huawei & ZTE*[23], *Apple v Qualcomm and Vestel v HEVC Advance & Philips.*[24,25] Similar issues were also raised in the *Unwired Planet* proceedings, albeit in the context of the scope of relief to which Unwired Planet was entitled.

In *Conversant*, the claimant brought proceedings in the High Court for the infringement of four SEPs and also sought declarations that (1) the licensing offers which had been made to Huawei and ZTE were FRAND or, in the alternative, a determination as to the licensing terms that would be FRAND; and (2) the defendants had failed to comply with their own FRAND obligations. Of note, the defendants to the action were Huawei Technologies Co., Limited and ZTE Corporation ("Huawei China" and ZTE China"), both companies incorporated in China, and their respective wholly-owned UK subsidiaries ("Huawei UK" and "ZTE UK"). Both Huawei and ZTE challenged the jurisdiction of the High Court to determine Conversant's claim, arguing that:

1 The declaratory relief sought by Conversant in relation to its global portfolio was the commercial core of the dispute and was, in substance, a claim for the infringement of foreign patents the validity of which was disputed and, as such, the courts of England and Wales did not have jurisdiction to decide the claim; and

23 [2018] EWHC 808 (Pat) and [2019] EWCA Civ 38.
24 [2018] EWHC 1188 (Pat) and [2018] EWHC 2711 (Ch).
25 [2019] EWHC 2766 (Ch).

2 Even if the courts of England and Wales did have jurisdiction, they should decline to exercise it because China (and not England) was the proper or appropriate forum (the forum conveniens).

Huawei and ZTE's jurisdiction challenges were rejected by the High Court and subsequently by the Court of Appeal.

As to (1), the High Court found that it did have jurisdiction to decide the proceedings. First, it held that there could be no dispute that the courts of England and Wales had jurisdiction to determine the SEP infringement claims brought by Conversant against all of the defendants: Conversant's pleaded case was that all of the defendants had carried out infringing acts within the jurisdiction or, in the alternative, that the two Chinese entities were, together with their respective UK subsidiaries, jointly and severally liable for any infringing acts carried out in the UK. Second, the natural consequence of the defendants' position was that no court would be able to determine FRAND terms for a global portfolio absent the consent of the putative licensee, which would need to refrain from raising arguments as to the validity of foreign patents in order for such a claim to be justiciable in any single court. Third, the High Court saw no reason to depart from the analysis set out in *Unwired Planet* (see further later) in which it was decided that there was no conflict between questions as to the validity of foreign patents (in respect of which foreign courts have exclusive jurisdiction) and requiring an implementer to take a worldwide licence, if that licence is FRAND. In this context it was notable that both sets of defendants had commenced proceedings in China challenging the validity of all of the Chinese patents in Conversant's portfolio, and also a determination as to the FRAND royalty for any valid and infringed Conversant Chinese SEP. The High Court noted that such proceedings were expected to conclude before any UK FRAND determination and, therefore, could be incorporated into any FRAND licence settled by the English court.

On appeal, Huawei and ZTE accepted that, in light of the Court of Appeal's decision in the *Unwired Planet* case, its jurisdiction arguments were no longer arguable at the Court of Appeal level. Huawei and ZTE reserved their rights to raise such arguments on any appeal to the Supreme Court. That appeal was heard by the Supreme Court in October 2019 together with the *Unwired Planet* case.

As to (2), given that the High Court had already determined that any global FRAND determination would not concern the validity of foreign patents, it followed that a forum conveniens argument was of no relevance to the position of Huawei UK and ZTE UK, European-domiciled entities to which Article 4(1) of the Brussels Regulation (requiring that persons domiciled in a Member State be sued in that Member State) applied.

The High Court then proceeded to reject the forum conveniens argument as it related to Huawei China and ZTE China, chiefly because it was unclear on the evidence in front of the court whether China would, in fact, provide an alternative forum for resolving the dispute at all. In particular, the evidence relied upon by the parties did not establish that the Chinese courts would either conduct a global FRAND determination of the sort requested by Conversant or assess questions of infringement in relation to the asserted UK SEPs. In this context, Huawei and ZTE's characterization of Conversant's claim as "worldwide royalty claims" or "foreign portfolio claims" was rejected. In the view of the High Court the claims were, in substance, claims for UK SEP infringement and the appropriate relief in relation to any infringement established in respect of which the courts of England and Wales were clearly the appropriate forum.

On appeal, the forum conveniens arguments turned on the manner in which the dispute was characterized. The High Court had characterized the dispute as relating to UK patents as a matter of substance and not just form. The Court of Appeal agreed with this characterization and held, therefore, that the UK was clearly the most appropriate forum, indeed the only possible forum, for the dispute to be tried.

As noted earlier, in reaching their decisions in *Conversant*, the High Court and the Court of Appeal placed significant weight on the analysis conducted in *Unwired Planet*, in which Huawei had relied upon jurisdictional points to argue that a global licence was not FRAND. Of relevance, Unwired Planet had also sued Huawei for SEP infringement in Germany and, at the time of the FRAND trial, failed to establish that any of the asserted German SEPs were both valid and infringed. There were also ongoing proceedings in China where Huawei had sought to revoke certain Unwired Planet patents. Huawei's position was that requiring it to take a global licence (or face a UK injunction) effectively usurped the jurisdiction of the German and Chinese courts to determine the patent proceedings in front of them (including questions as to validity) and was, therefore, at least in relation to the German action, incompatible with the jurisdictional rules set out in the Brussels Regulation.

This argument was rejected by the High Court which decided that the FRAND terms of a licence could be divorced entirely from such jurisdictional questions. In the view of the High Court, where a worldwide licence is FRAND, requiring an implementer to take it does not involve determining questions of validity that fall within the jurisdiction of foreign courts and, in cases where foreign courts are considering issues of validity and infringement, the FRAND licence can include a mechanism to take their findings into account.

The question of whether an implementer which has been found to infringe a national SEP should be required to take a global licence or face a territorial injunction was one of the issues considered by the Court of Appeal in May 2018. As explained earlier, the Court of Appeal agreed with the High Court's findings on that issue. The Supreme Court's decision on this issue is awaited.

Questions of jurisdiction also arose in *Apple v Qualcomm*, in which Apple sought to bring a breach of contract claim alleging that Qualcomm had failed to comply with its obligations to ETSI (on which Apple was entitled to rely). For the reasons discussed in more detail later, the High Court decided that the FRAND claim against the UK-domiciled defendant, Qualcomm (UK) Limited ("Qualcomm UK"), could not proceed. The court also held that it lacked jurisdiction to decide a similar claim against Qualcomm Incorporated ("Qualcomm U.S.") for the following reasons:

1 Gateway 3 could not apply as there was no claim against Qualcomm UK to which Qualcomm U.S. could be a necessary and proper party;
2 Although claims relating to patent validity and essentiality had been validly served on Qualcomm U.S. within the jurisdiction: (a) those claims did not themselves depend on a jurisdictional gateway; and (b) the FRAND claim did not arise out of the same or closely connected facts so gateway 4A was not relevant;
3 The claim for breach of the ETSI declaration by Qualcomm U.S. was not a claim in tort to which gateway 9 could apply; and
4 As Qualcomm U.S. was not domiciled within Europe and the FRAND claim did not concern the validity of a UK SEP, the European regime was not relevant to the question of jurisdiction.

Vestel v HEVC Advance & Philips, was the first 'reverse' FRAND case brought in the courts of England & Wales. Instead of anchoring the claim to the courts of England & Wales by means of a patent action (as was the case in Apple v Qualcomm and Conversant v ZTE & Huawei), the action was framed as an allegation that the defendants (a patent pool and representative pool licensor) had abused their dominant positions. Vestel (an implementer) also sought declarations as to the FRAND terms of a pool licence, as well as a wide-ranging declaration that any injunction sought by the defendants in any jurisdiction would be a breach of Article 102 TFEU.

At the jurisdiction stage, the High Court held that it did not have jurisdiction over the claim, chiefly because Vestel had advanced no plausible case as to how damage would be sustained within the jurisdiction and, therefore, why gateway 9 applied (as against HEVC Advance) and Article 7(2) applied (as against Philips). In particular, having pleaded a case on the loss that would be suffered if it were forced to enter into a non-FRAND licence, Vestel had failed to demonstrate how it could, in fact, be compelled to take such a licence. The court accepted the argument made by the defendants that: (i) absent an injunction, Vestel's alleged contingent loss would never crystallise; and (ii) no court would grant an injunction unless a FRAND offer had been made - in effect, Vestel's case would require a court to facilitate an Article 102 abuse.

The High Court also held that gateway 11 did not apply to the FRAND declarations sought as against HEVC Advance because a global portfolio FRAND determination could not be said to relate to property wholly or principally within the jurisdiction and noted that the broad declaration sought by Vestel in relation to injunctive relief appeared designed to have effect outside of the jurisdiction and so would not have been allowed to proceed even had Vestel succeeded in founding jurisdiction over the remainder of the claim.

It is, therefore, clear that although the courts of England and Wales are both able and willing to conduct FRAND determinations, questions of jurisdiction must be considered before declaratory proceedings are started. Where a FRAND determination is sought as a remedy for infringement of UK SEPs then the English court will certainly have jurisdiction to decide the issue.

5.2 FRAND and corporate groups

As part of the jurisdiction challenge brought by Qualcomm in the *Apple v Qualcomm* proceedings discussed in the preceding section, the reach of the ETSI FRAND undertaking within corporate groups was considered by the High Court. This issue arose because Apple had brought a breach of contract claim against Qualcomm UK alleging that Qualcomm UK had failed to comply with the ETSI FRAND undertaking. Qualcomm sought reverse summary judgment on this aspect of Apple's case (i.e. sought an order under Civil Procedural Rules 24.2 that, as the claim had no real prospect of success, and there was no compelling reason for it to proceed to trial, it should be summarily dismissed) on the basis that Qualcomm UK was bound neither by Clause 6.1 of the ESTI IPR Policy nor the FRAND declarations made by Qualcomm U.S. (the contractual terms alleged to have been breached).

It was not in dispute that Qualcomm UK was a member of ETSI and, as such, obliged in principle to comply with the ETSI IPR Policy. However, in relation to Apple's claim that Qualcomm UK had an obligation under Clause 6.1 of the Policy (under which the Director General of ETSI may request an "owner" of Essential IPR to give a FRAND undertaking) the High Court decided that an "owner" could only be the owner of the relevant essential IPR and that a non-owner (such as Qualcomm UK which had never owned any of the patents relevant to Apple's claim, or been asked by the director general to make a FRAND declaration) simply could not undertake to grant a licence. It followed that Qualcomm UK was not in breach of any obligation under Clause 6.1.

In the alternative, Apple had argued that Qualcomm UK had assumed a FRAND licensing obligation on the basis of the FRAND declarations made by Qualcomm U.S. In particular, Qualcomm U.S. had declared that it and its "Affiliates" were prepared to grant licences to relevant IPR on FRAND terms. An "Affiliate" is defined broadly in the ETSI IPR Policy as "any other legal entity: . . . under the same direct or indirect ownership or control as the first legal entity, or directly or indirectly controlled by the first legal entity", and Qualcomm UK (as well as a substantial number – said to be many hundreds – of other companies within the Qualcomm corporate group) fell within this definition for the purposes of the FRAND declarations made by Qualcomm U.S.

The High Court directed itself to asking, as a matter of interpretation of the FRAND undertaking given by Qualcomm U.S., whether the phrase "the Declarant and/or its Affiliates" should be taken to mean (1) "Qualcomm Incorporated and the First Defendant [Qualcomm UK] and many hundreds of other companies"; or (2) "Qualcomm Incorporated and any Affiliate which is the owner of an IPR which is the subject of the declaration". In this regard, the High Court noted that the phrase "the Declarant and/or its Affiliates" appeared twice in the

FRAND declaration made by Qualcomm U.S., and that in the second place the phrase was used, "the Declarant and/or its Affiliates" stated that they were prepared to grant licences to the relevant IPRs. Given that Qualcomm UK did not own any relevant IPR and there could, therefore, be no question of it granting a licence to that IPR, the High Court reached the conclusion that the reference to "Affiliates" in the FRAND declaration made by Qualcomm U.S. should be understood to include only those Affiliates owning IPR which was the subject of the declaration. On this analysis, Qualcomm UK had not assumed any obligation by virtue of the FRAND declaration made by Qualcomm U.S.

Given the finding of the High Court that Qualcomm UK had not taken on any relevant obligation under either Clause 6.1 of the ETSI IPR Policy or the FRAND declarations made by Qualcomm U.S., it followed that Apple had failed to establish an arguable case that Qualcomm UK was in breach of contract and Qualcomm's summary judgment application was granted. This decision had a significant effect on the jurisdiction of the courts of England and Wales to determine whether Qualcomm U.S. had breached its FRAND obligations. In particular, as noted earlier, had such a case been permitted to continue against Qualcomm UK then Apple would likely have been given permission to serve Qualcomm U.S. outside of the jurisdiction under gateway 3 (on the basis that Qualcomm U.S. was a necessary and proper party to the FRAND claim against Qualcomm UK).

Part III

Asian case law and global experiences

8 Unprepared, unable and unwilling to deal with FRAND licensing of SEPs in Taiwan

Kung-Chung Liu

1 Introduction

The usage of FRAND licensing of SEP first appeared in the European Commission's (EC) "Communication on Intellectual Property Rights and Standardisation" on October 27, 1992, and in the U.S. court decisions and scholarly works in 2003 at the latest.[1] Due to its unique position in the global ICT value chain as a key component supplier and OEM, Taiwan (Republic of China) has long been the battlefield for foreign patentees (IBM, Intel, Microsoft, etc.) to litigate against local patent licensees or manufacturers of ICT devices. In 2001, the Taiwan Fair Trade Commission (TFTC) found that Philips, Sony and Taiyo Yuden were violating the anti-monopoly provisions of the Taiwan Fair Trade Act (TFTA) by abusing their joint monopolistic position in CD-R[2] in their acts of refusing to negotiate reduction of royalty despite freefall of prices of CD-R, refusing to supply patent lists to their licensees and imposing no challenge of patent validity clauses in their licensing agreements. Philips et al. published the technical standards for CD-R in a Red Book, Yellow Book and Orange Book series and formed a patent pool and a joint licensing agreement (JLA) in 1992 with one royalty formula: 3% of the net sales price and not lower than JPY 10. As the pooled patents were essential to the CD-R standard, and constituted standard

1 Thibault Schrepel, "Frand": Statistical Comparison Between Cases and Research Papers, available at https://leconcurrentialiste.com/2014/01/27/frand-statistical-comparison-between-cases-and-research-papers/

2 A compact disc (CD) is an optical disc used to store digital data, originally developed for storing digital audio. The CD, available on the market since October 1982, was jointly developed by Philips and Sony. The technology was later adapted and expanded following the standards set by Philips and Sony in a Red Book, Yellow Book and Orange Book series to include data storage CD-ROM (read-only memory), write-once audio and data storage CD-R (recordable), rewritable media CD-RW, Video Compact Discs (VCD), Super Video Compact Discs (SVCD), PhotoCD, PictureCD, CD-i, and Enhanced CD. The dye materials developed by Taiyo Yuden made it possible for CD-R discs to be compatible with audio CD and CD-ROM discs; see https://en.wikipedia.org/wiki/CD-R. CD-R has phased out of the market with the rise of thumb drives (USB), which have been largely replaced by streaming.

essential patents (SEP), this is the beginning of the TFTC's dealing with the issue of licensing of SEPs.[3]

Noteworthy is that the TFTC back then completely lacked awareness of the antitrust issues of SEPs and the importance of licensing SEPs on fair, reasonable and non-discriminatory (FRAND) terms. Despite being the first in Asia to deal with licensing of SEPs, Taiwan has in the subsequent two decades failed to lead and even failed to gradually catch up with the international trend of tackling FRAND licensing of SEPs for two reasons: the "contracting out" of many cases to arbitration and the discord within the TFTC. The TFTC set itself apart from the mainstream in a stunning decision to settle with the biggest SEP owner in the information and communications technology (ICT) sector, Qualcomm, after first condemning its anticompetitive behaviour. This chapter argues that Taiwan's version of the "FRAND licensing of SEPs" story is about how the TFTC has wasted opportunities and time, and how it is now running on a wrong track. In this chapter, section 2 will retrieve the history about the TFTC's unpreparedness in dealing with the licensing of de facto CD-R SEPs. Section 3 will piece together some of the unreported cases in which Taiwan was prevented from handling these issues. Section 4 will examine the TFTC's decision to fine Qualcomm and its deficiency. Section 5 will take a hard look at the surprising settlement between the TFTC and Qualcomm. The chapter ends in section 6 with some suggestions on how the TFTC can improve its handling of this important topic for the ICT sector.

2 Unprepared to deal with the licensing of de facto CD-R SEPs in 2001

2.1 Abuse of joint monopolistic position found and confirmed by the administrative courts

In 2000, Princo et al., Taiwanese CD-R manufacturers, accused Philips et al. of abusing their monopoly power in the CD-R market through patent pooling and JLA demanding excessive royalties, of engaging in cartels by bundling patents and by licensing in packages, of tying in patents that have already expired, and of obscuring information about the patents to be licensed. On January 20, 2001, the TFTC found that Philips et al. had joint monopoly power in the CD-R patent licensing technology market worldwide and abused it (Philips I). Philips et al. appealed the Philips I decision to the Executive Yuan (the

3 Kung-Chung Liu, The Taiwanese "Philips" CD-R Cases: Abuses of a Monopolistic Position, Cartel and Compulsory Patent Licensing, chapter 6 in Christopher Heath & Anselm Sanders (eds.), *Landmark Intellectual Property Cases and Their Legacy* (The Netherlands: Aspen Publisher, 2010), pp. 12, 83–104; Kung-Chung Liu, Compulsory Licensing of CD-R Patents Owned by Philips, in Kung-Chung Liu (ed.), *Annotated Leading Patent Cases in Major Asian Jurisdictions* (City University of Hong Kong Press, Hong Kong, 2017), pp. 148–161.

Cabinet),[4] which was not convinced by the TFTC's determination of the relevant product market and vacated the Philips I decision, remanding it back to the TFTC. The TFTC reached a decision on April 25, 2002 (Philips II), with the same conclusions. Philips II was appealed to and upheld by the Executive Yuan. Philips et al. appealed the case to the Taipei Administrative High Court. On August 11, 2005, the Taipei Administrative High Court concurred with the TFTC on its finding of an abuse of joint monopolistic market power, which was further upheld by the Supreme Administrative Court in 2007. Both Philips I and II found that Philips et al. violated Article 9(ii) of the TFTA by engaging in two cartel activities, namely designating Philips as the sole contact for JLA and agreeing to only one method of calculating royalty. As mentioned in the introduction, the TFTC's decision was upheld by the Taipei Administrative High Court. However, the fine that the TFTC imposed on Philips, Sony and Taiyo-Yuden has been reduced again and again after 14 years of litigation to TWD 1.8 million, TWD 1 million and TWD 0.5 million, respectively, which is not even enough to recover the administrative costs of the TFTC, not to mention having any deterrent effects on the violators.

2.2 *Full royalty allowed by civil courts despite abuse of dominance – ignorant of FRAND licensing of SEPs from other jurisdictions*

Philips terminated the licensing agreement with Princo in 2000 and filed suit for royalty payment. The Shinju District Court suspended the trial due to the then pending antitrust cases brought by Princo against Philips. The Shinju District Court resumed the trial when the Supreme Administrative Court rejected the TFTC's appeal in April 2007, and came to a decision in August 2008 awarding Philips the full royalty as agreed in the licensing agreement, calculated by 10 times the amount of CD-Rs produced by Princo with a monthly interest of 2% (an annual interest of 24%), despite Philips being found to have abused its dominance.

The Taiwan IP Court (TIPC), acting as court of second instance, decided in a three-judge panel decision, which not only concurred with the district court but also criticized the TFTC's view about patent right and monopoly. Upon appeal, the Supreme Court rescinded the case and remanded it back to the TIPC over the choice of law issue, asserting that Dutch courts should have jurisdiction over

4 The TFTC was structured to be under the Executive Yuan as its subordinate agency since its creation, and its decisions were subject to the latter's review. However, beginning from February 6, 2012, the TFTC became an "independent agency" as Article 3 No. 2 of the Basic Code Governing Central Administrative Agencies Organizations defines ("'Independent agency' means a commission-type collegial organization that exercises its powers and functions independently without the supervision of other agencies, and operates autonomously unless otherwise stipulated."), and its decisions are directly appealable to the Taipei Administrative High Court.

the dispute. The second panel of the IP Court in retrial applied Dutch law and agreed with the previous panel to large extent with only one exception, namely confirming the applicability of the doctrine of frustration of purpose (Wegfall der Geschäftsgrundlage). It reduced the royalty to be paid to Philips to JPY 3 per disc and allowed an annual interest rate of 20%.

The Supreme Court rescinded the decision again because it, in applying the doctrine of frustration of purpose, failed to consider the loss that the one party would suffer, the gain that the other would acquire, and other actual circumstances as a result of frustration of purpose to determine the appropriate amount to be reduced. The third panel of the TIPC, presided over by the same judge who wrote for the first panel, not surprisingly came to the same conclusion. Princo appealed the decision to the Supreme Court, which refused to hear the case.[5] The case became final after 14 years of legal limbo. The parties, the TFTC and courts in Taiwan were completely ignorant of the development of law on FRAND licensing of SEP in other jurisdictions. As a result, the SEP licensee in Taiwan, despite winning its antitrust case against the SEP owner, lost completely in the royalty payment dispute, creating a legal schizophrenia.

3 Unable to deal with SEP licensing issues: licensees' civil law suits in Taiwan preempted by arbitration clause and settlement

There are at least a number of unreported cases in which Taiwanese ICT companies have tried to sue SEP patentees for abusing dominance by violating their respective FRAND commitments. However, reliable information can only be gathered from publicly listed companies, such as the major SEP patentees like InterDigital and Qualcomm, as they are legally required to disclose legal proceedings in their annual reports. Therefore, this section examines the annual reports of InterDigital, excluding Qualcomm's, as the TFTC has a settlement agreement with it (*see infra* section 5), rendering its annual reports less relevant. This section finds that the Taiwanese licensees' civil law suits in Taiwan and the U.S. have been often preempted by arbitration clause of the patent licensing agreement (PLA) and settlement reached with InterDigital.

3.1 Arima v. InterDigital: dismissed by settlement

Arima[6] brought civil law suits against InterDigital in 2014 in Taiwan and PRC, alleging that InterDigital abused its dominant position by forcing Arima to sign a

5 2014 Tai-Shang-Zi 1957 (September 24, 2014).

6 According to Reuters, ARIMA is a Taiwan-based company principally engaged in the design, manufacture, maintenance and distribution of mobile phones. The company provides original design manufacturing (ODM), original equipment manufacturing (OEM) and joint design manufacturing (JDM) services of mobile phones. Its products include multimedia mobile phones, third generation (3G) and 3.5G mobile phones and smartphones, with functions

patent license agreement with InterDigital in 2005, setting an unreasonably high and discriminatory royalty rate, and including other abusive and discriminatory provisions in the license agreement, in violation of the TFTA and Antimonopoly Law of the PRC.[7] However, the two parties entered into a settlement agreement in the second quarter 2015, which maintains the existing patent license agreement and resolves all pending payment disputes between the companies. In addition, the agreement resulted in the dismissal of all current litigations and arbitrations between the companies in all jurisdictions.[8]

3.2 Pegatron v. InterDigital: dismissed by settlement

On May 26, 2015, InterDigital received the civil complaint filed by Pegatron with the TIPC, alleging that InterDigital abused its market power by improperly setting, maintaining or changing the royalties that Pegatron is required to pay and engaging in unreasonable discriminatory treatment and other unfair competition activities. InterDigital filed a complaint in the Northern District Court of California, seeking injunction against Pegatron prohibiting Pegatron from prosecuting Pegatron's action in Taiwan. On June 29, 2015, the court granted InterDigital's motion for a temporary restraining order and preliminary injunction requiring Pegatron to take immediate steps to dismiss the action in Taiwan. On July 1, 2015, InterDigital was informed that Pegatron had withdrawn its complaint from the TIPC.

On August 3, 2015, Pegatron filed an answer and counterclaims to InterDigital's complaint filed in the Northern District Court of California, accused InterDigital of violating multiple sections of the TFTA, section 2 of the Sherman Act, and breaching ETSI, IEEE, and ITU contracts. Pegatron sought a declaration regarding the appropriate FRAND terms and conditions for InterDigital's "declared essential patents", a declaration that InterDigital's SEPs are unenforceable due to patent misuse, and damages in the amount of allegedly excessive non-FRAND royalties Pegatron paid, plus interest and treble damages. On August 7, 2015, Pegatron responded to InterDigital's arbitration demand, disputing the arbitrability of Pegatron's claims. On September 24, 2015, InterDigital moved to compel arbitration and dismiss Pegatron's counterclaims. The court granted InterDigital's motion to compel arbitration of Pegatron's counterclaims and to stay the counterclaims pending the arbitrators' determination of their arbitrability. On January 27, 2016, the parties agreed to stay all remaining aspects of the case in the Northern District Court of California pending such an arbitrability determination. On the same day, the court granted the stay and administratively

---

such as touch panels, QWERTY keyboards, music players, digital cameras, mobile TVs, global positioning systems, push e-mails, Bluetooth, Wi-Fi internet access and others.

7 InterDigital 2014 Annual Report, available at http://ir.interdigital.com/Cache/1500085258.PDF?O=PDF&T=&Y=&D=&FID=1500085258&iid=4103938, at 47.

8 InterDigital 2015 Annual Report, available at http://ir.interdigital.com/Cache/1500086581.PDF?O=PDF&T=&Y=&D=&FID=1500086581&iid=4103938 at 47

closed the case. In January 2018, InterDigital entered into an amended patent license agreement and settlement agreement with Pegatron, dismissed all outstanding litigation and other proceedings among them and also terminated the arbitration.[9]

3.3 *Asustek v. InterDigital: delayed by arbitration for more than four years*

On April 15, 2015, Asustek filed a complaint in the Northern District Court of California against InterDigital, alleging that InterDigital breached its FRAND commitment. Asus sought a judgment that the 2008 Asus PLA is void or unenforceable, damages in the amount of excess royalties Asus paid plus interest, a judgment setting the proper FRAND terms and conditions for InterDigital's patent portfolio, an order requiring InterDigital to grant Asus a license on FRAND terms and conditions, and punitive damages and other relief. In response, on May 30, 2015, InterDigital filed an arbitration demand with the American Arbitration Association's International Center for Dispute Resolution (ICDR). InterDigital filed a motion in the Northern District Court of California to compel arbitration on each of Asus's claims. On August 25, 2015, the court granted InterDigital's motion and ruled that the issue of arbitrability should be decided by an arbitrator, and stayed the proceedings pending that determination. On December 16, 2016, the court set a case schedule that includes a May 2019 trial date.[10]

4 Unwilling to deal with FRAND licensing of SEP

4.1 *The TFTC imposed heavy fine, cease and desist order and corrective measures on Qualcomm in October 2017 for three conducts*

According to Qualcomm 2016 Annual Report,[11] on December 4, 2015, the TFTC notified Qualcomm that it was conducting an investigation into whether Qualcomm's patent licensing arrangements violated the TFTA; on April 27, 2016, the TFTC specified that the allegations under investigation included whether Qualcomm (1) jointly licensed its patents rather than separately licensing standard-essential patents and non-standard-essential patents; (2) charged unreasonable royalties; (3) unreasonably required licensees to grant it cross-licenses; (4) failed to provide lists of licensed patents to licensees; (5) violated a FRAND licensing

9 InterDigital 2017 Annual Report, available at www.snl.com/interactive/newlookandfeel/4103938/2017AnnualReportandNoticeof2018ASMandProxy%20Statement.pdf at 32.
10 InterDigital 2017 Annual Report, at 33.
11 Qualcomm 2016 Annual Report available at https://investor.qualcomm.com/staticfiles/82885245-09c9-489e-92f2-55e02d90a25f, at F-27.

commitment by declining to grant licenses to chipset makers; (6) declined to sell chipsets to unlicensed potential customers; and (7) provided royalty rebates to certain companies in exchange for their exclusive use of Qualcomm's chipsets.

On October 20, 2017, TFTC decided to impose a fine of TWD 23.4 billion (about USD 700 million) on Qualcomm for abusing its dominance, a violation of Article 9(1) of the TFTA, in the standard baseband chips market for CDMA, WCDMA, and LTE by conducting the following: (1) refusal to license SEPs to competing chips makers and demanding restrictive clauses, (2) maintenance of a "no (signing of) licensing agreement, no (supply of) chips" policy, and (3) maintenance of exclusive deals with a specific company [namely Apple – added by the author], and offering rebate. The finding by and large corroborates USFTC's charges filed in January 2017 against Qualcomm for violating section 5 of the Fair Trade Commission Act ("unfair methods of competition are prohibited").[12]

The TFTC also ordered that Qualcomm cease to (1) apply contractual clauses with competing chips makers that demand the latter provide sensitive sales info, such as prices, customers, or volume; (2) apply "no signing of licensing agreement, no supply of chips" clauses with hand phone manufacturers; and (3) apply "exclusive dealing clauses with rebates" with "parties that are related to this

12 In January 2017 the USFTC charged Qualcomm with violating section 5 of the FTC Act with the District Court for the Northern District of California, as Qualcomm maintains a "no license, no chips" policy under which it will supply its baseband processors only on the condition that cell phone manufacturers agree to Qualcomm's preferred license terms. This tactic forces cell phone manufacturers to pay elevated royalties to Qualcomm on products that use a competitor's baseband processors. This is an anticompetitive tax on the use of rivals' processors. "No license, no chips" is a condition that other suppliers of semiconductor devices do not impose. The risk of losing access to Qualcomm baseband processors is too great for a cell phone manufacturer to bear because it would preclude the manufacturer from selling phones for use on important cellular networks. Despite its commitment to license SEPs on FRAND terms, Qualcomm has consistently refused to license those patents to competing suppliers of baseband processor, and extracted exclusive contract from Apple in exchange for reduced patent royalties. Qualcomm precluded Apple from sourcing baseband processors from Qualcomm's competitors from 2011 to 2016. Qualcomm recognized that any competitor that won Apple's business would become stronger, and used exclusivity to prevent Apple from working with and improving the effectiveness of Qualcomm's competitors. The FTC is seeking a court order to undo and prevent Qualcomm's unfair methods of competition in violation of the FTC Act. The Federal Trade Commission v. Qualcomm Incorporated, case number 5:17-cv-00220, Document 1, Filed January 17, 2017. Qualcomm filed a motion to dismiss the FTC complaint for failure to state a claim under Rule 12(b)(6) in April 2017, which was denied by Judge Lucy Koh in June 2017. Judge Koh found that the FTC adequately alleged a FRAND violation by alleging that Qualcomm's royalty rate stayed constant over time despite (a) an increasing royalty base due to the introduction of additional technology in high-end smartphones apart from Qualcomm's SEPs and (b) the decreasing number of Qualcomm SEPs relative to the total SEPs necessary to make a wireless device. Judge Koh suggested that the FTC may be able to prove a violation of FRAND without the need for complicated technical valuation evidence of Qualcomm's SEPs. The trial between the FTC and Qualcomm ended on January 29, 2019. It is up to Judge Lucy Koh to render the verdict.

case". Further, the TFTC imposed on Qualcomm an obligation to (1) notify in writing its chip competitors and hand phone manufacturers to make offer for the revision or conclusion of new patent licensing agreements; (2) negotiate in good will and good faith after receiving the offers; (3) report to the TFTC every six months about the progress of the negotiation; and (4) report the newly revised or concluded contracts to the FTTC within 30 days.[13] Noteworthy is that the TFTC reached the decision in a 4–3 split vote, with three commissioners writing dissenting opinions.[14] The Ministry of Economic Affairs has openly criticized the TFTC's decision in a press release and expressed "deep concerns", stating that it hopes in the future "to work towards the continual cooperation between ICT in Taiwan and Qualcomm in 5G, IOT and future global market based on the principle of equality and reciprocity, in order to maintain a win-win partnership relationship".[15]

4.2 Problems with the TFTC's decision

Objectively speaking, the TFTC's decision in question is flawed in many aspects, which was quite bewildering for the competition community in Taiwan. Only in retrospect, after taking into account that the decision was later revoked and replaced by a settlement between the TFTC and Qualcomm (*see infra* section 5), did people realize that the poor quality of the decision might be attributable to the fact that it was made under an internal split and did not get a chance to be properly developed.

13 TFTC,Gong-Chu-Zi106094(October20,2017),availableatwww.ftc.gov.tw/uploadDecision/561633e4-42bd-4a4f-a679-c5ae5226966b.pdf.

14 The three dissenting commissioners are Shu-Jen Guo, Hsin-fang Wei, and Tsai-Lung Hong.

15 The press release states: "Qualcomm has always been an indispensable cooperation partner for the ICT and semi-conductor industries in Taiwan, covering the whole ecosystem of mobile communications (including mobile phones, pads, notebook computers, infrastructure, network communication, network operation and testing). According to statistics by the Market Intelligence & Consulting Institute under the Institute for Information Industry, Qualcomm has placed orders of NT$155.7 billion to the Taiwanese semiconductor and packaging and testing industry in 2016, which has triggered a value of NT$314.7 billion in the related network and communication industries, which is projected to grow to NT$432.4 in 2017. The TFTC's decision failed to take into consideration Qualcomm's contribution to the industries and business opportunities for future cooperation, and might negatively affect foreign investment in Taiwan. Given that 5G and the Internet of Things have huge potential in the application markets, and Taiwanese companies enjoy technological and cost advantages in the global value chains, and their cooperation with international leading companies would be supplementary, the Ministry of Economic Affairs hopes in the future to work towards the continual cooperation between ICT in Taiwan and Qualcomm in 5G, IOT and future global market based on the principle of equality and reciprocity, in order to maintain a win-win partnership relationship," available at: www.moea.gov.tw/Mns/populace/news/News.aspx?kind=1&menu_id=40&news_id=74079.

4.2.1 Not dealing with FRAND licensing of SEPs

Surprisingly, the TFTC's decision did not touch upon allegations (1)–(4) that were brought against Qualcomm by the TFTC (*see supra* subsection 4.1), which are typical SEP-related issues. By finding that Qualcomm had refused to license SEPs to competing chips makers, maintained a "no licensing agreement, no chips" policy, and maintained exclusive dealing clauses with rebate with Apple, the TFTC's decision was solely focusing on the issue of abuse of dominance, and again most unfortunately missed the chance to deal with FRAND licensing of SEP issues.

4.2.2 Not dealing with double-dipping issue

Even in the context of dealing with the issue of abuse of dominance, the TFTC failed to question the issue of double charging (double dipping, or skinning the same cow twice) by Qualcomm's "no licensing agreement, no chips" clauses with Taiwanese mobile phone manufacturers, which forced the latter to pay "royalty" again for SEPs that are already incorporated in the chips, for which the latter have already paid a sales price. As a result, Qualcomm has collected TWD 400 billion (about USD 13.3 billion) in royalties from Taiwanese licensees in addition to USD 30 billion worth of chips sold to Taiwanese manufacturers.

4.2.3 Coarse calculation of fine

The decision uses less than one page to come to the conclusion that a fine of TWD 23.4 billion is to be imposed on Qualcomm. The decision itself does not mention at all "the violation period", "total product or service sales achieved" or "the previous fiscal year's total sales income" of Qualcomm.[16]

4.2.4 Unclear whether the TFTC adopts the CJEU's procedural demand on SEP patentee in Huawei v. ZTE

The decision refers to Point 4 (3)(iv) of the Fair Trade Commission Disposal Directions (Guidelines) on Technology Licensing Arrangements: "In reviewing technology licensing arrangements, in addition to the reasonableness of the provisions of such arrangements, the Commission shall consider the following factors: International or industry precedents applicable to the relevant market" and goes on to cite the *Huawei v. ZTE* decision of the Court of Justice of the European Union (CJEU).[17] The citation was followed by a sentence which says, "Accordingly, if SEP patentees fail to abide by the above-mentioned procedure,

16 TFTC, Gong-Chu-Zi 106094 (October 20, 2017), p. 68.
17 Case C-170/13, for more details see Matthias Leistner, Chapter 15 of the present book.

then there is abuse of dominance".[18] This sentence does not appear in the *Huawei v. ZTE* decision itself and could only be the work of the TFTC. However, it is indeed unusual and even inappropriate for the TFTC to come to a conclusion of such magnitude without any reasoning of its own.

4.2.5 Deviation from no bundling of SEPs with non-SEPs (per se illegal) stance adopted in Philips CD-R case

The decision deviates from the TFTC's "no bundling of SEPs with non-SEPs" stance adopted in Guidelines on Technology Licensing Agreements,[19] a stance also followed by the Korean Fair Trade Commission (KFTC) and the Chinese National Development and Reform Commission (NDRC).[20] The decision brushed away its previous position by simply mentioning: "It is still difficult to come to conclusion about the positive and negative effects of the bundling licensing of SEPs with Non-SEPs". [21]

4.2.6 Deviation from previous "yes to provisioning of patent list" stance adopted in Philips CD-R Case

The decision deviates from the TFTC's previous "yes to patentee's provisioning of patent list" stance adopted in the Philips CD-R case, and simply says that (such non-provisioning) "probably lacks reprehensibility".[22]

4.2.7 Taking rule-of-reason approach towards SEP patentee's "free cross-licensing" demand

With regards to the legality of the SEP patentee's demand of "royalty-free cross-licensing" from the licensee, the decision seems to suggest that the TFTC takes a rule of reason approach, as it says: "However, since the legitimacy and reasonableness of such clauses (royalty based on the whole devices and royalty-free cross-licensing) are full of controversy, they should be left to the equal negotiation (of the parties) or third-party arbitration or court litigation, to ensure the equality of contract negotiation".[23] In contrast, in the PRC the NDRC treated Qualcomm's demand of royalty-free cross-licensing as abuse of its dominant position

18 TFTC, Gong-Chu-Zi 106094 (October 20, 2017), p. 54.

19 The TFTC Guidelines on Technology Licensing Agreements (last amended in 2016) blacklists "the compelling of the licensing to purchase, accept or use patents or technical know-how that he does not need" (6.6).

20 For more details on the KFTC Qualcomm II case in Korea, see Jinyul Ju, Chapter 10 of the present book. For more details on the NDRC Qualcomm case in the PRC, see Liyang Hou and Mengchi Tian, Chapter 11 of the present book.

21 TFTC, Gong-Chu-Zi 106094 (October 20, 2017), p. 61.

22 *Id.*

23 *Id.*

in the wireless communication SEP licensing market and the baseband chip sale market.[24] Given the technical supremacy of SEP patentees, their overwhelming bargaining power to unilaterally impose such clauses on licensees and the fact they do not provide know-how transfer assistance to the licensees, such royalty-free cross-licensing clauses deserve greater scrutiny.

5 The U-turn that makes TFTC a black sheep among Asian competition authorities

To everyone's surprise, on August 9, 2018, the TFTC settled with Qualcomm during the appeal the latter brought up before the TIPC under the auspices of the TIPC, after Qualcomm made commitments to the satisfaction of the TFTC.[25]

5.1 Qualcomm made commitments

5.1.1 To relinquish the anti-competitive doubts and concerns of the TFTC

Qualcomm agrees to comply and enforce the promise to license to Taiwanese mobile phone manufacturers SEPs in mobile communication, and *intends* to provide licenses to Taiwanese chip suppliers, which is sufficient to dissolve the anti-competitive concerns over Qualcomm's SEP licensing practice that the TFTC's original decision has shown:

1. *To renegotiate licensing terms in good faith*: If Taiwanese mobile phone manufacturers are of the opinion that they have been forced to accept unreasonable licensing terms in their patent licensing agreements with Qualcomm, Qualcomm promises to renegotiate licensing terms in good faith and to solve disputes arising from the renegotiated terms through court or neutral dispute settlement mechanism of arbitration.
2. *Not to suspend the supply of chips during negotiation*: Qualcomm agrees not to suspend or threaten to suspend chips for mobile communications to Taiwanese mobile phone manufacturers, provided that the latter continue to fulfil their obligations under "supply and licensing" contracts during the renegotiation or dispute settlement period and renegotiate in good faith.
3. *To provide non-discriminatory treatment in the licensing of mobile communication SEPs*: Qualcomm promises to provide to Taiwanese mobile phone manufacturers that are of equivalent conditions to non-Taiwanese mobile phone manufacturers non-discriminatory treatment in Qualcomm's licensing schemes for mobile communication SEPs.

24 For more details on the NDRC Qualcomm case in the PRC, see Liyang Hou and Mengchi Tian, Chapter 11 of the present book.

25 The TFTC's press release on August 10, 2018, available at www.ftc.gov.tw/internet/main/doc/docDetail.aspx?uid=126&docid=15551.

4 *To provide Taiwanese chip suppliers a licensing agreement with FRAND terms*: Qualcomm agrees to provide a licensing agreement upon the request of Taiwanese chip suppliers, which would stipulate that Qualcomm shall not bring any law suit against Taiwanese chip suppliers based on the patent claims of its mobile communication SEPs if it has not already offered Taiwanese chip suppliers fair, reasonable and non-discriminatory (FRAND) licensing terms for the patent claims of its mobile communication SEPs in advance.

5 *No more exclusive deal with rebate*: Qualcomm promises that it will no longer conclude any chip supply contract with its chip customers that conditions the provision of royalty rebate on the latter's agreement to exclusively purchase chips from Qualcomm, or which conditions the provision of royalty discount or rebate on a certain percentage of its chip customers' total chip purchase coming from Qualcomm.

6 *To report to the TFTC periodically about the implementation*: Qualcomm promises to report to the TFTC every six months in the next five years on implementation of its promises, and to report to the TFTC the revised or new licensing agreements it has concluded with Taiwanese mobile phone manufacturers or chip suppliers within 30 days from the signing of the agreements.

5.1.2 To invest in Taiwan

Qualcomm agrees not to claim back the TWD 2.73 billion fine it has already paid in instalment, and promises to invest in Taiwan through a five-year scheme, which includes cooperation in 5G, the development of new markets, cooperation with start-up companies and universities, and the establishment of an operation and manufacturing center in Taiwan. Qualcomm will work closely with the TFTC, the Ministry of Economic Affairs and Ministry of Science and Technology to implement the aforementioned projects and investment.

The TFTC is of the opinion that the said investment projects and committed engagement will enhance the macroeconomic interests and public interests by enhancing the semiconductor industry, mobile communications and 5G technology in Taiwan.

Qualcomm issued a press release on the same day that the TFTC announced the settlement, however, with very concise information. As a result, the whole TFTC decision is replaced by the settlement terms and the decision shall be deemed revoked ab initio (from the beginning) and Qualcomm's litigation filed in the Taiwan Intellectual Property Court is closed. As part of the resolution, Qualcomm has agreed to certain process-related commitments confirming principles of mutual good faith and fairness in the negotiation of agreements with handset licensees on Qualcomm's cellular standard essential patents (SEPs). The resolution does not require component-level licensing or set specific financial terms; instead it is focused on commitments that ensure good faith negotiations for the benefit of licensees and SEP owners. As part of the settlement, the parties agreed that the TWD 2.73 billion (about USD 93 million) Qualcomm paid towards the monetary fine through the end of July will be retained by the TFTC and no other amounts will be due. In addition, Qualcomm will drive certain commercial initiatives in Taiwan over the next five years for the benefit of the mobile and semiconductor ecosystem, SMEs and consumers, including 5G collaborations, new market expansion, start-up and university collaborations and the development of a Taiwanese center for operations and manufacturing engineering. Qualcomm will work with the TFTC and sister agencies within the Taiwanese government to implement these initiatives and investments.[26]

5.2 Criticisms

5.2.1 On the TFTC

It is first to be pointed out that the settlement is a glaring contrast to EC's recent decision in January 2018 to fine Qualcomm for its exclusive deal with Apple that provided Apple billions of dollars to shut out rivals from the market for LTE baseband chipsets for over five years.[27] Second, to date, this is the first and only settlement that the TFTC has entered in its 27-year history after it has already found serious violation of the TFTA. As for the reason for such change of mind, some clue could be found from the fact that the two commissioners who were supportive of the decision to sanction Qualcomm were absent from the 1396th TFTC's commissioners meeting, in which the settlement was accepted. These two commissioners later resigned out of protest to the settlement.[28] Deducting the five commissioners who have been consistent in the two decisions (three commissioners who have dissented on the sanction decision and subsequently supported the settlement, and the two who agreed to the sanction and subsequently protested the settlement), clearly it was the chairperson and the vice chairperson who have changed their mind.[29] The chairperson as a political appointee should be obliged to state her reasons for making this decision, otherwise the independence of the TFTC as an independent agency could be undermined. As a matter

26 See www.qualcomm.com/news/releases/2018/08/09/qualcomm-and-taiwan-fair-trade-commission-reach-settlement.

27 See EC press release, available at: http://europa.eu/rapid/press-release_IP-18-421_en.htm.

28 The minutes of the 1396th TFTC's commissioners meeting are available at www.ftc.gov.tw/upload/8df77a16-b65e-47f5-a4f6-4a134e91685e.pdf. The two commissioners are Ting-Dong Yan and Hao-Hong Chang.

29 They are Mei-Ying Huang and Shaw-Jiin Perng. According to Article 4(1) of the Organic Act of the Fair Trade Commission, "The FTC shall consist of seven full-time commissioners to be appointed by nomination by the premier and approval of the Legislative Yuan for a four-year term and the commissioners may be reappointed when their term expires. When making the appointment, the premier shall designate one of the commissioners as the chairperson and another as the vice chairperson. The chairperson, a special appointee, shall represent the FTC in external functions; the vice chairperson shall have the status equivalent to that of Grade-14 senior executive officers; the remaining commissioners shall have the status equivalent to that of Grade-13 senior executive officers."

of fact, she did not provide any explanation. The TFTC thereby runs the risk of fundamentally departing from its role of a mostly ex post and quasi-judicial enforcement agency to an administrative agency that proactively makes ex ante measures to ensure that Qualcomm will implement its promised projects and investment to the extent that the semiconductor industry, mobile communications and 5G technology in Taiwan will be enhanced as a result. This is a regrettable and unwise development for the TFTC.

The formal settlement agreement has not been published by the TFTC or Qualcomm. Presumably there must be a non-disclosure agreement (NDA) between the TFTC and Qualcomm. It is however questionable whether administrative settlement agreement of such magnitude should be kept in the dark.

5.2.2 Putting similar investigations by TFTC on hold

In addition, once the TFTC starts to base its enforcement decision on whether the alleged violators can contribute to Taiwanese industries, it will find it more difficult to bring its years-long investigation against InterDigital to fruition: based on InterDigital's 2014 Annual Report,[30] the TFTC started an investigation on December 6, 2013, against InterDigital's alleged "anti-competitive behaviour under TFTA". According to InterDigital's 2016 Annual Report, during the second quarter of 2016, InterDigital was informed by its local counsel that the staff of the TFTC has completed its investigation and forwarded its recommendations to the TFTC.[31] However, InterDigital's 2017 Annual Report did not mention the subsequent development of the case. As of this writing, the result of the case remains unclear.

5.2.3 Making private enforcement cases difficult

On April 18, 2017, Apple and one of its Taiwanese subsidiaries filed a complaint against Qualcomm in the TIPC alleging that Qualcomm has abused a dominant market position in licensing wireless SEPs and selling baseband chipsets, including improper pricing, refusal to deal, exclusive dealing, tying, imposing unreasonable trade terms and discriminatory treatment. The complaint seeks rulings that Qualcomm not use the sales price of the terminal device as the royalty base for SEPs; not leverage its cellular SEPs to obtain licenses of its non-SEPs or demand cross-licenses without proper compensation; not refuse, reduce, delay or take any other action to limit the supply of its baseband chipsets to non-licensees; that Qualcomm must license its SEPs on FRAND terms; and that Qualcomm shall not seek injunctions based on SEPs. The complaint also seeks damages of TWD 10 million (about USD 0.3 million).[32] The TIPC and Apple would understand-

30 InterDigital 2014 Annual Report, at 47.

31 InterDigital 2016 Annual Report, at 34.

32 Qualcomm 2017 Annual Report, available at https://investor.qualcomm.com/static-files/3bee5a52-757b-4ac6-9468-b0102bdc4418, at F29.

ably be quite troubled by the settlement between the TFTC and Qualcomm, as the TFTC has indicated that all the anti-competitive effects of Qualcomm's licensing practices can be remedied procedurally, mostly through good faith renegotiation, and do not warrant administrative sanction, which can be an insurmountable barrier for the TIPC to cross.

5.2.4 An inexplicable huge contrast between two sides of the Taiwan Strait

Qualcomm's fate in the PRC is very different. In 2015 the then competition authority, NDRC, found that that Qualcomm had abused its dominant position in the wireless communication SEP licensing market and the baseband chip sale market in violation of the PRC's Anti-Monopoly Law and imposed a fine of RMB 6.088 billion (about USD 975 million), which is 8% of Qualcomm's revenue in 2013 in the PRC. As a response, Qualcomm offered not only a rectification plan, which was accepted by the NDRC, but also not to pursue legal action to contest the NDRC's findings.[33] The inexplicable huge contrast between the two sides of the Taiwan Strait in an antitrust case could only give rise to speculation that it is perhaps due to a worsening political relationship, which further deepens people's questioning about the independence of the TFTC.

5.2.5 Creating discriminatory treatment between Taiwanese and non-Taiwanese undertakings

As a globalized conglomerate and dominant SEP patentee which has made FRAND commitment to various standard setting organizations (SSOs), Qualcomm's hands are already tied in its treatment of licensees. If national competition authorities around the world compete to induce Qualcomm to provide extra commitments, such as the rectification plan Qualcomm offered to the NDRC in the PRC,[34] or at least a most favored nation clause to their respective national

33 For more details, see Liyang Hou and Mengchi Tian, Chapter 11 of the present book.

34 According to the rectification plan, Qualcomm agrees to (1) offer licenses to its current 3G and 4G essential Chinese patents separately from its other patents and provide patent lists during negotiation; (2) negotiate with license seekers in good faith and provide fair consideration if it seeks cross-licensing; (3) not condition the sale of baseband chips upon the buyer's signing a patent license agreement with unreasonable terms and agreeing not to challenge unreasonable terms in patent license agreements. For licenses of Qualcomm's 3G and 4G essential Chinese patents for branded devices sold for use in the PRC, Qualcomm will charge royalties of 5% for 3G devices (including multimode 3G/4G devices) and 3.5% for 4G devices (including 3-mode LTE-TDD devices) that do not implement CDMA or WCDMA (the three wireless operators in China all operate 2G, 3G and 4G networks simultaneously, which demands multimode cellphones. Since China Union requires 4-mode devices, China Mobile requires 5-mode devices and China Telecom requires 6- to 7-mode devices, a reduced rate for 3-mode 4G LTE-TDD devices is of little significance); (4) to use 65% of the net selling prices of the device as royalty base.

industries, such as the TFTC seems to be striving to achieve in the settlement in question, extra layers of burden would be imposed on Qualcomm, which could only lead to Balkanization or fragmentation of the licensing of SEPs, namely discriminatory treatment between local and non-local undertakings.

6 Looking forward

6.1 Facing and dealing with FRAND licensing of SEP issues

In the last two decades, the TFTC has had many chances to decide on FRAND licensing of SEP issues. The TFTC could use these decisions to regulate or readjust the ecosystem of SEP licensing, in which Taiwanese hand phone industries and chip suppliers mostly play the role of SEP implementers. Its decisions could well serve as a guiding post or benchmark for its Asian neighbours, which have a similar industrial dependence on SEPs. Some Asian standards for FRAND licensing of SEPs could have been formed. The TFTC should return and reassume its role as an enforcer of competition law, and observe the Asian and even international trend of curbing the monopolistic licensing practice of giant SEP patentees.[35]

6.2 Enhancing transparency

The TFTC's sweeping secrecy about its settlement with Qualcomm over its anti-competitive behavior, although a common practice internationally, is very frustrating for the academics and the public. Understandably, Qualcomm would resist the disclosure with the pretext of protecting its trade secrets. However, elements that constituted violation of Article 9(ii) of the TFTA should not be protected as trade secrets. Without knowing the necessary terms and conditions, there will be no creditable oversight and crowdsourcing for ideas of how the TFTC can reach better judgment in the future. Moreover, the decision of the TFTC is a valuable source for public knowledge about the industry involved, the dissemination of which will help to demystify SEP licensing issues. Compared to the TFTC's previous decisions on abuse of dominance by de facto CD-R standard patentees, namely Philips et al., the present decision has been overly protective of the description about Qualcomm's anti-competitive behavior. Such description about the indispensable element of the violation of the TFTA could hardly be trade secrets and should be disclosed as much as possible.

The TFTC has not set up any formal mechanism for informing the public about its initiation of and ongoing investigation, such as the "statement of objection"

35 For example, in Korea in December 2017 the KFTC again imposed on Qualcomm various sanctions for breach of its FRAND commitment, abuse of dominance, and unfair trade practice (Qualcomm II, USD 854 million fine), eight years after Qualcomm I (about USD 229 million fine). For more details see Jinyul Ju, Chapter 10 of the present book.

adopted in the EU. Therefore, until the TFTC has reached a decision and publicized it, there is no knowing whether there has been any investigation against a company and the scope of such investigation. Therefore, the proper way for the TFTC to enhance its operational transparency in its handling of antitrust cases is to set up a mechanism to inform the public about ongoing cases. One other measure towards enhancing transparency is for the TFTC to release the court document recording the settlement reached under the auspices of the TIPC and even the settlement agreement itself if it is not under NDA.

6.3 *Using the alternative original royalty rate as proxy for a FRAND-compliant rate*

One of the thorny issues in the context of FRAND licensing of SEPs is how to decide the reasonable royalty rate for SEPs. One plausible way is to benchmark against comparable licensing agreements. Again, what constitutes comparable licensing agreements is yet another tough question. One possible solution, although its application scope might be limited, is to revisit the original licensing terms offered by the SEP patentees. For example, in the Philips CD-R case, the original rate offered by the three de facto patentees was 3% of the net sales price. In this case, the three patentees anticipated the sales price would drop with the increase of production volume which is bound to happen with the issue of license, and came up with a scheme to secure and perpetuate its profit margin: to offer a fixed, absolute and floor royalty figure of JPY 10, which was derived by calculating 3% of the sales price of a CD-R at that time, which was about JPY 300. Therefore, when the absolute figure of JPY 10 became abusively high, then the TFTC could resort to 3% of the current net sales price and use it as a proxy for a FRAND-compliant rate and impose the burden of proving this percentage as not on the SEP patentees.

6.4 *The TFTC is advised to demand SEP licensors revise arbitration clause*

Even if Taiwanese SEP licensees were right in all their antitrust complaints in Taiwan or elsewhere, they would probably not get to the stage where competition authorities or courts can render substantive decisions, as SEP patentees routinely implant an arbitration clause in the PLAs, which will compel licensees to arbitrate, rather than to litigate. The result of such arbitration tends to take a formalistic and pure contract law approach to the interpretation of PLA and ignore the dominant market power possessed by SEP licensors and its abuse, as arbitrators would not upset these SEP patentees, who are an important source of income for them.

For example, the American Arbitration Association's ICDR issued a final award on April 17, 2013, in a proceeding InterDigital initiated to resolve a dispute surrounding its 2008 PLA with Pegatron and required Pegatron to pay Qualcomm USD 29.9 million, including USD 23.5 million for past patent royalties through

June 30, 2012, and USD 6.2 million in interest, and additional amounts for certain arbitration costs and expenses.[36] ICDR further issued a final award on May 13, 2014, in a dispute between Arima and InterDigital regarding Arima's PLA with InterDigital and awarded InterDigital unpaid patent license fees of USD 14.5 million plus USD 9.1 million of interest and related fees and costs.[37] Although the details of the cases are not available, their constellation in essence should not be very different from the cases in which Qualcomm has been found abusing its dominance via the PLAs.

However, the TFTC seems to take a naïve view about arbitration in the decision against Qualcomm: "However, since the legitimacy and reasonableness of such clauses (royalty based on the whole devices and royalty-free cross-licensing) are full of controversy, they should be left to the equal negotiation (of the parties) or third party arbitration or court litigation, to ensure the equality of contract negotiation". That is neglecting the fact that there is no room for equal negotiation for local smartphone manufacturers not to agree to an arbitration clause dictated by Qualcomm, which would inevitably favor Qualcomm. Therefore, the TFTC is advised to act via promulgating some guidelines to demand that SEP licensors revise the arbitration clause to limit its application scope to pure contractual disputes, and exclude antitrust-related ones from arbitration. Ironically, the settlement agreement between the TFTC and Qualcomm, not published presumably due to non-disclosure agreement with Qualcomm, must have an arbitration clause that will compel the TFTC to arbitrate in the U.S. the differences it has concerning the interpretation and enforcement of the settlement agreement. Perhaps only when the TFTC is one day forced to conduct a long-distance arbitration will it realize the powerlessness of Taiwanese mobile phone manufacturers in not taking on arbitration clauses and not conducting arbitration effectively.

36 InterDigital 2013 Annual Report, available at http://ir.interdigital.com/Cache/1500085256.PDF?O=PDF&T=&Y=&D=&FID=1500085256&iid=4103938 Annual Report, at 39.

37 InterDigital 2014 Annual Report, at 46.

9 Japan

Masabumi Suzuki

1 Introduction

This chapter discusses Japanese court cases related to standard essential patents (SEPs). In 2014, the Special Division of the Japanese Intellectual Property High Court (IPHC) presented a framework for judging the enforcement of SEPs with fair, reasonable and non-discriminatory (FRAND) declarations in the cases of *Apple v. Samsung*. This chapter mainly introduces and analyzes the IPHC's decisions in *Apple v. Samsung*. A subsequent court decision will also be briefly introduced.

In addition, this chapter presents a succinct explanation about other trends concerning SEPs in Japan, including the treatment under the Anti-monopoly Act (specifically, guidelines issued by the Japanese Fair Trade Commission) and the "Guides" on licensing negotiations issued by the Japan Patent Office (JPO).

2 General legal framework on the enforcement of patents in Japan

As a prerequisite for the following discussion, this section presents the general legal framework for the enforcement of patents in Japan. Patent protection is provided mainly under the Patent Act and the Civil Code of Japan.

First, the effect of the patent right is provided in Article 68 of the Patent Act, which states: "A patentee shall have the exclusive right to work the patented invention as a business".[1] Therefore, the act of working the patented invention as a business without legitimate grounds constitutes direct infringement of patent rights. In addition, Article 101 of the Patent Act provides a list of conducts that constitute indirect infringement of patent rights.[2]

1 An English translation of the Patent Act is available on a website provided by the Japanese government at www.japaneselawtranslation.go.jp/law/detail/?vm=04&re=01&id=42. Unfortunately, the translation has not been updated in a timely manner.

2 For example, acts of producing, assigning, importing or offering for assignment, etc. any product to be used exclusively for the production of the patented product as a business constitute indirect infringement of patents [Article 101 (1) of the Patent Act].

Second, as to remedies against patent infringement, Article 100 (1) of the Patent Act provides for injunctions.[3] In Japanese court practice, while injunctions are not available for general torts in principle under the Civil Code, they are granted almost automatically for both direct and indirect infringement of patents as long as the court finds a likelihood of infringement in the near future. In this manner, the Japanese practice of granting injunctions is different from the U.S. practice after the *eBay* decision by the U.S. Supreme Court.[4] As for damages, the remedy is available for intentional or negligent acts of patent infringement under Article 709 of the Civil Code, which is a provision for general torts. Negligence is presumed for patent infringers as per Article 103 of the Patent Act. Article 102 of the Patent Act further prescribes special methods for calculation of damages, the aim of which is to make it easier for patentees to prove the amount of damages.

Third, when infringement of a valid patent is affirmed, the doctrine of abuse of right, which is stipulated in Article 1 (3) of the Civil Code, is practically the only ground available in denying liability for the infringement. However, courts have applied this doctrine in patent infringement cases in a restrictive way.[5]

3 *Apple v. Samsung*

3.1 Introduction

The cases between Apple Inc. (Apple)[6] and Samsung Electronics Co., Ltd. (Samsung) which started in 2011 dealt with the admissibility of the enforcement of FRAND-encumbered SEPs. The IPHC stated that to seek injunctions and damages exceeding the amount of the FRAND royalty based on FRAND-encumbered SEPs constitutes an abuse of right, as long as the implementer of the standard is willing to get a license under FRAND terms. The court also determined the amount of the FRAND royalty.

3 Article 100 (1) states: "[a] patentee or exclusive licensee may demand that a person who infringes or is likely to infringe the patent right or exclusive license stop or prevent such infringement."

4 *eBay Inc. v. MercExchange*, LLC, 547 U.S. 388 (2006).

5 An exceptional scenario where enforcement of patent rights has been regarded as an abuse of right is the cases involving patents which were found invalid by courts. See the decision of the Japanese Supreme Court, 1998 (O) 364 (April 11, 2000) – *Kilby case*. Article 104–3 was introduced to the Patent Act in 2004 as a basis for the defense of invalidity, and currently such a defense is usually raised on the basis of this article, rather than the general doctrine of abuse of right. Incidentally, in Japan, the doctrine of abuse of right is more often used and adopted in cases concerning infringement of trademark rights. *See, e.g.*, the decision of the Japanese Supreme Court, 1985 (O) 1576 (July 20, 1990) – *Popeye Muffler* case, the decision of the Tokyo District Court, 1997 (Wa) 16468 (April 28, 1999) – *Virusbuster* case, and the decision of the Japanese Supreme Court, 2015 (Ju) 1876 (February 28, 2017) – *Eemax* case.

6 Precisely speaking, the plaintiff in *FRAND Case I* and the defendant (obligor) in *FRAND Case II* and *Case III* was the Japanese subsidiary of Apple Inc.

3.2 Facts[7]

3.2.1 Background

The cases concern disputes over Apple's alleged infringement of Samsung's SEPs. Apple's products at issue (the "Products") conform to the standard of the Universal Mobile Telecommunications System (UMTS), which is the telecommunications standard developed by the Third Generation Partnership Project (3GPP). 3GPP is a private organization established for the purposes of disseminating the third-generation mobile telecommunication system or mobile telephone system (3G), as well as international standardization of related specifications. The European Telecommunications Standards Institute (ETSI), one of the standard setting organizations (SSOs) which established 3GPP, provides the "Intellectual Property Rights Policy" (IPR Policy) as guidelines for the treatment of IPRs.

Samsung holds patent No. 4642898 (the '898 patent) for the invention titled "method and apparatus for transmitting/receiving packet data using a predefined length indicator in a mobile communication system", which contains several patent claims. On August 7, 2007, Samsung, in accordance with ETSI's IPR Policy, notified ETSI that its IPRs including the '898 patent were or were highly likely to be essential IPRs for the UMTS standard, with a declaration that it was prepared to grant an irrevocable license on FRAND terms and conditions.

3.2.2 Case I

In this case, Apple alleged that its production, assignment, import or other acts in relation to the Products did not constitute an act of infringement of the '898 patent, and sought a declaratory judgment to confirm that Samsung was not entitled to seek damages. The Tokyo District Court upheld all of Apple's claims, holding that Apple's Products 1 and 3 did not fall within the technical scope of the '898 patent, and that Samsung's exercise of the right to seek damages based on the '898 Patent for Products 2 and 4 constituted an abuse of right in spite of the fact that these products fell within the technical scope of the '898 patent.[8] Samsung filed an appeal against the judgment.

3.2.3 Case II and Case III

In these cases, Samsung alleged that Apple's production, assignment, import or other acts in relation to the Products[9] constituted infringement of the '898

7 The following "Facts" and "Reasoning of the IPHC" are based on the English translation of the IPHC's decisions provided by the court, available at www.ip.courts.go.jp/eng/hanrei/g_panel/index.html.

8 The decision of the Tokyo District Court, 2011 (Wa) 38969 (February 28, 2013). Products at issue were as follows: 1 = iPhone 3GS, 2 = iPhone 4, 3 = iPad WiFi+3G model, and 4 = iPad 2 WiFi+3G model.

9 The products at issue in *Case II* were iPhone 4 and iPad 2 WiFi+3G model (Product 2 and Product 4 in *Case I*, respectively) while *Case III* covered iPhone 4S (which was not covered in *Case I*).

patent, and petitioned for a provisional disposition order for injunction against Apple and for custody of the infringing products by a court execution officer. The Tokyo District Court held that the Products fell within the technical scope of the '898 patent; however, the court dismissed Samsung's petition by holding that its exercise of right to seek an injunction based on the '898 patent constituted an abuse of right.[10] Samsung filed an appeal against the decisions.

3.3 Decisions by the IPHC

3.3.1 Case I: claims for damages[11]

3.3.1.1 ON THE INFRINGEMENT OF THE '898 PATENT AND A DEFENSE OF PATENT EXHAUSTION

On the issue of whether the Products fell within the technical scope of the '898 patent, the IPHC determined that the Products 1 and 3 did not fall within the technical scope of the patent, whereas Products 2 and 4 did. As to the defense of invalidity of the patent raised by Apple, the IPHC rejected all five grounds for invalidation of the patent.[12]

The IPHC also rejected the allegation of patent exhaustion raised by Apple that Samsung had granted Intel Corporation (Intel) a distribution license for the baseband chip and therefore the patent was exhausted at the time of the sale of the baseband chip by Intel (the essential processes of the patented invention were implemented by the baseband chip which Apple purchased from Intel and installed in the alleged Products).[13] Specifically, the IPHC found that the license between Samsung and Intel had been terminated, and that the baseband chip would not be covered by the license even if it were still in force. In addition, the IPHC explained as a general interpretation of law that when a patentee (or an exclusive licensee) put on the market an item (such as a component for an assembled product) which would be used for the production of a patented product, a third party who bought the item and produced a patented product using the item would not be able to avoid patent infringement by the doctrine of patent exhaustion. However, the court admitted that the third party might be able to justify its conduct by arguing that an implied license for the production of a patented product had been given by the patentee through its sale of the item.

10 The decisions of the Tokyo District Court, 2011 (Yo) 22027 (February 28, 2013) and 2011 (Yo) 22098 (February 28, 2013).

11 The IPHC decision of *Case I* is the longest and most detailed among the three decisions for the three cases because *Case I* was brought to the court as a case on the merits, while the other two cases were procedures for provisional injunctions. Therefore, this chapter focuses on the decision in *Case I*.

12 The IPHC decision of *Case I*, 66–101 (the pages refer to those of the English translation of the decision, *available at* www.ip.courts.go.jp/eng/vcms_lf/25ne10043full.pdf).

13 *Id.* at 101–111.

3.3.1.2 ON THE FORMATION OF A LICENSE AGREEMENT AS A RESULT OF THE FRAND DECLARATION

Before interpreting the legal nature of Samsung's FRAND declaration, the IPHC held that the applicable law was French law.[14] The reasons are threefold. First, Article 7 of the Japanese Act on General Rules for Application of Laws provides that the formation and effect of a juridical act shall be governed by the law of the place chosen by the parties at the time of the act. Second, the IPR Policy of ETSI stated that the policy shall be governed by French law and the FRAND declaration also contained a statement that issues including its validity shall be governed by French law. Third, both of the parties in this dispute agreed on choosing French law as an applicable law.

The IPHC then held that the FRAND declaration could not be considered as an offer to enter into a contract under French law. The court also refused to recognize the formation of a contract for third beneficiaries (*stipulation pour autrui*) between Samsung and ETSI. In conclusion, the court found that no license agreement for the '898 patent was formed as a result of the FRAND declaration, rejecting Apple's allegation.[15]

3.3.1.3 ON WHETHER THE EXERCISE OF THE PATENT RIGHT CONSTITUTES AN ABUSE OF RIGHT

The IPHC then went on to decide whether Samsung's claim for damages constituted an abuse of right and thus should be denied. The court distinguished the claim for damages exceeding the amount of the FRAND royalty from the claim for damages not exceeding the amount of the FRAND royalty, and concluded that the former was an abuse of right while the latter was not.

At the outset, the IPHC discussed the governing law.[16] The court recognized that the legal nature of claims for damages for patent infringement was a tort, and based on Article 17 of the Japanese Act on General Rules for Application of Laws,[17] Japanese law should govern this case with respect to the claim for damages because "the place where the result of the wrongful act occurred" was Japan.

Next, the court analyzed the effects of a FRAND declaration on claims for damages by an SEP holder in a general manner.[18] The court stressed that a FRAND declaration would generate trust in the availability of a license on a FRAND basis on the side of standard implementers, and allowing an SEP holder to claim for

14 *Id.* at 111–112.
15 *Id.* at 112–115.
16 *Id.* at 115.
17 Article 17 of the Japanese Act on General Rules for Application of Laws states: "[t]he formation and effect of a claim arising from a tort shall be governed by the law of the place where the result of the wrongful act occurred; provided, however, that if the occurrence of the result at said place was ordinarily unforeseeable, the law of the place where the wrongful act was committed shall govern."
18 The IPHC decision of *Case I*, 115–125.

damages exceeding the FRAND royalty would be detrimental to such reasonable trust. Specifically, the court stated as follows:

> (A) In the case of a claim for damages based on the essential patent for which a FRAND declaration is made, allowing a claim for damages exceeding the amount of the FRAND royalty may run counter to the trust[19] of the prospective users of the standard, and may also result in the excessive protection of a patented invention. Allowing the patentee such claim is unreasonable as it has various detrimental effects, for example, discouraging the general public from using the technologies of the patented invention, and may hinder the "development of industry", which is the purpose of the Patent Act (Article 1 of the Patent Act). Any party intending to manufacture or sell a standard-compliant product would first look to the IPR guidelines of the relevant standardization body and confirm the availability of a FRAND license for the essential patent, such as the members' obligation of a FRAND declaration for an essential patent, before it makes an investment or commences the manufacturing and sale of such products. If the patentee is later allowed to claim for damages exceeding the FRAND royalty for the standard essential patent, it would be detrimental to the reasonable trust of a party who made an investment for the manufacture or sales of the standard-compliant product in anticipation of availability of a FRAND license. Considering that a standard essential patent owner voluntarily makes a FRAND licensing declaration on the premises that such patent would be made available to the standard implementers, and that the patent forming a part of the standard makes it possible for the owner to attract a wide range of potential licensees, allowing the owner a claim for damages exceeding the amount of the FRAND royalty would result in the excessive protection of such owner, discouraging the dissemination of the technologies of the patented invention, and consequently hinder the "development of industry", which is the purpose of the Patent Act (Article 1 of the Patent Act).[20]

The IPHC at the same time admitted that standard implementers should be ready to pay a FRAND royalty and affirmed that such a royalty to the SEP holder is necessary as a reward for public disclosure of the invention. The court also mentioned that a claim for an injunction should be restricted for SEP holders who had made a FRAND declaration.

> (B) Meanwhile, as long as a claim for damages based on a Standard Essential Patent is within the scope of the amount of the FRAND royalty, a restriction of its exercise would be unreasonable, as such restriction would discourage

19 The English translation provided by the IPHC uses the term "reliance on use" for this part, but the original expression in the decision does not contain words corresponding to "on use" and translating the part to "trust" would be more appropriate.

20 The IPHC decision of *Case I*, 121–122.

> inventors, have a negative impact on the promotion of standardization of technologies, and have a risk of hindering the "development of industry", which is the purpose of the Patent Act (Article 1 of the Patent Act). As a party intending to manufacture or sell a standard-compliant product is presumed to anticipate the payment of the amount of the FRAND royalty, the payment of the damages claimed by the patentee within the scope of the amount of the FRAND royalty is not an unexpected consequence for such party. In addition, in light of the purpose and intention of the FRAND declaration, a patentee who made the declaration should be restricted from exercising the right to seek an injunction against the party willing to enter into a FRAND license agreement. . . . Considering the abovementioned restriction on the patentee who made a FRAND declaration for the exercise of the right to seek an injunction, allowing the patentee to claim for the damages not exceeding the amount of the FRAND royalty has a material significance as the reward for public disclosure of the invention. Therefore, a careful consideration shall be given to the restriction of such right to seek damages.[21]

Based on the analysis explained earlier, the IPHC presented a basic framework for judging claims for damages, which include four considerations. First, if an SEP holder claims for damages exceeding the FRAND royalty against a standard implementer, the latter should be entitled to refuse the payment to the extent that exceeds the amount of the FRAND royalty, as long as the implementer successfully alleges and proves the fact of the patentee's FRAND declaration.[22]

Second, however, if the patentee successfully alleges and proves the fact of the existence of special circumstances, such as that the implementer has no intention of receiving a FRAND license, the patentee should be allowed to claim damages exceeding the amount of the FRAND royalty.[23] The court added that "before allowing the patentee to claim damages exceeding the amount of the FRAND royalty, strict scrutiny shall be made to determine the existence of special circumstances in which the implementer has no intention of receiving a FRAND license".[24]

Third, as for a claim for damages not exceeding the FRAND royalty, the patentee should not be restricted from asserting such a claim even when the patent is an SEP with a FRAND declaration.[25]

Fourth, however, if the standard implementer

> successfully alleges and proves the existence of special circumstances, such as that, after discussing various circumstances in the process of the FRAND

21 *Id.* at 122.
22 *Id.* at 123.
23 *Id.* at 123–124.
24 *Id.* at 124.
25 *Id.*

> declaration and licensing negotiation, it is considered extremely unfair to permit the patentee to claim for damages not exceeding the FRAND royalty, even considering the significance of the right to seek damages as a compensation for the public disclosure of an invention, the possibility cannot be precluded that such patentee's claim is restricted as an abuse of right.[26]

Following the aforementioned basic framework for judging claims for damages, the IPHC proceeded to discuss the factual situation in this particular case.[27] Specifically, the court confirmed that Samsung was claiming for damages exceeding the amount of the FRAND royalty, and examined whether "special circumstances" that would allow the SEP holder to make such a claim existed or not. The court also examined the existence of "special circumstances" that would preclude Samsung from claiming even for damages not exceeding the FRAND royalty.

As to the "special circumstances" of the second kind (for precluding a claim for damages not exceeding the FRAND royalty), the court recognized two specific obligations on Samsung: first, "an obligation to have a good faith negotiation with the appellee [Apple] for the execution of a FRAND license agreement, at least based on the principle of good faith under the Civil Code of Japan", and second, the obligation to disclose IPRs in a timely manner under the IPR Policy of ETSI. Based on the factual situation of the case, the court found that Samsung did not violate these two obligations.[28] The IPHC then explained that the fact that Samsung had filed petitions for provisional dispositions to seek injunctions against Apple would not preclude Samsung from exercising the right to seek damages within the FRAND royalty. The court also discussed Apple's allegation about a violation of the Japanese Antimonopoly Act by Samsung's "series of acts", and stated: "the entire evidence submitted before the court is not sufficient to prove that the claim for damages not exceeding the FRAND royalty constitutes a breach of the Antimonopoly Act".[29] The court concluded that there was no evidence to prove the existence of special circumstances to restrict Samsung from claiming for damages not exceeding the amount of the FRAND royalty. Later in this chapter we will return to two of the issues the IPHC discussed here: the good faith negotiation obligation and the consistency with the Antimonopoly Act.

Next the IPHC examined the "special circumstances" of the first kind (to allow a claim for damages exceeding the FRAND royalty).[30] The court found that Apple could be considered to have had continuous negotiations with an intention

26 *Id.*
27 *Id.* at 125–126.
28 *Id.* at 126–128.
29 *Id.* at 128.
30 *Id.* at 129–130.

to enter into a license agreement with Samsung, and concluded that there were no special circumstances, such as the lack of Apple's intention to receive a FRAND license. The court also stressed that "in light of the purpose and significance of the development of the standards, strict scrutiny shall be made before determining that the prospective licensee has no intention to enter into a license agreement". It is noteworthy that the court did not specifically mention whether Apple's offers of possible royalties were at (or within the range of) the rate of the FRAND royalty.

In conclusion, the IPHC affirmed Apple's allegation that Samsung's claim for damages constituted an abuse of right to the extent that the amount of damages exceeded the FRAND royalty, while rejecting the allegation in respect of the amount of damages not exceeding the FRAND royalty.[31] The court then turned to discuss the amount of damages by estimating the FRAND royalty for Samsung's SEP at issue.

3.3.1.4 ON THE AMOUNT OF DAMAGES AND THE FRAND ROYALTY

The IPHC determined that the amount of the FRAND royalty should be calculated in the following way: (i) multiplying the sales turnover of the infringing products by the ratio which the compliance with the UMTS standard has contributed to the sales turnover, (ii) multiplying the amount obtained in (i) by the royalty rate cap of 5%,[32] which was derived "from the standpoint of preventing the aggregate amount of royalty from being unreasonably high"; and (iii) dividing the amount obtained in (ii) by 529 (the total number of SEPs for the UMTS standard).[33] While the exact figures of the turnover and the contribution ratio are not disclosed in the published version of the IPHC decision, the calculated royalties are JPY 9,239,308 for Product 2 (iPhone 4) and JPY 716,546 for Product 4 (iPad 2 WiFi+3G model).[34]

Recently, the question on whether FRAND royalties should be determined on a global or local basis was raised and discussed in the U.K. case *Unwired Planet v. Huawei* and has attracted much attention among scholars and practitioners. On this point, the IPHC in *Case I* seems to have taken it for granted that the prospective license between the parties would cover only Japan.

31 *Id.* at 130.

32 As to the grounds for the 5% royalty cap, the IPHC referred to Nokia's statement that "the industry-wide aggregate royalty rates for the IPRs for the WCDMA should not exceed 5%", and the practices by the UMTS-related SEPs owners as well as the W-CDMA patent platform limiting the aggregate royalty to not more than 5%.

33 The IPHC decision of *Case I*, 132–138.

34 About USD 81,764 and USD 6,341, respectively, according to the exchange rate as of November 24, 2018 (JPY 113 = USD 1).

3.3.2 Case II and Case III: claims for injunctions

3.3.2.1 ON THE INFRINGEMENT OF THE '898 PATENT

The IPHC found that the Products[35] fell within the technical scope of the '898 patent.[36]

3.3.2.2 ON WHETHER THE EXERCISE OF THE PATENT RIGHT CONSTITUTES ABUSE OF RIGHT

Apple rebutted Samsung's claims by arguing that Samsung's exercise of the patent right to seek preliminary injunctions constituted an abuse of right. The IPHC affirmed this defense and rejected Samsung's claims.

First, the IPHC discussed the governing law applicable to the dispute. Referring to a Supreme Court decision,[37] the court stated that "a claim for an injunction based on a patent right is determined in accordance with the laws of the country where such patent right is registered" and therefore this case should be governed by Japanese law.[38]

Second, the IPHC discussed the relationship between Samsung's FRAND declaration and its claims for injunctions.[39] After reviewing the factual background of the FRAND declaration, the court explained that a FRAND declaration would generate trust in the availability of a license on a FRAND basis on the side of standard implementers, and granting an SEP holder an injunction would be detrimental to the reasonable trust. The court then argued as follows and declared that it was not appropriate to grant an SEP holder who made a FRAND declaration an injunction against a party willing to obtain a license under the FRAND terms.

> A party intending to engage in the manufacturing, sale, etc. of a UMTS standard-compliant product would recognize that, among the patent rights essential for the manufacturing, sale, etc. of such product, at least those owned by ETSI members require the timely disclosure in accordance with ETSI IPR Policy Clause 4.1 and the FRAND licensing declaration under ETSI IPR Policy Clause 6.1. Such party would trust in the availability of a FRAND license through an appropriate negotiation with the patentee. Such

35 For the identification of the Products, *see* (n 9).

36 The IPHC decision of *Case II*, 10–17 (the pages refer to those of the English translation of the decision available at www.ip.courts.go.jp/eng/vcms_lf/25_ra_10007zenbun.pdf. The IPHC's decision of *Case III* is essentially same as that of *Case II*.).

37 The decision of the Japanese Supreme Court, 2000 (Ju) 580 (September 26, 2002) – *Card Reader* case. The Japanese Act on General Rules for Application of Laws does not have a provision concerning the choice of law for litigation on injunctive relief for the infringement of intellectual property.

38 The IPHC decision of *Case II*, 17.

39 *Id.* at 17–25.

trust is worth protecting. Accordingly, in connection with the '898 patent subject to Samsung's FRAND declaration, allowing the unconditional exercise of the right to seek an injunction would be detrimental to the trust of parties who manufacture or sell the UMTS standard-compliant product based on the availability of such license.

Owing to such anticipation of UMTS standard implementers, the patent rights incorporated into the UMTS standard can be widely disseminated among a large number of business enterprises in all part of the world. As a result, an owner of an SEP can benefit from royalty income, which would be unavailable if the patent were not adopted as part of the UMTS standard. In addition, a party which makes a FRAND declaration as required by the ETSI IPR Policy declares on a voluntary basis that it is prepared to grant an irrevocable license under the FRAND terms. So, it is considered that such a patentee does not anticipate the exercise of the right to seek an injunction to maintain its monopoly in the market, so long as it can obtain consideration on the FRAND terms. For such a patentee, it is not so necessary to allow the exercise of the right to seek an injunction to protect its monopoly in the market.

Whenever parties intending to engage in the manufacturing, sale, etc. of any product complying with the UMTS standard implement the UMTS standard, there is no choice but to work the '898 patent, and it is impossible for them to adopt alternative technology or to change the product design. Therefore, if the patentee is unconditionally allowed to exercise the right to seek an injunction based on the '898 patent, the standard implementers may be put into a situation where they are forced to pay a high royalty or to agree to extremely unfavorable license conditions which are not FRAND terms, or to abandon the business project itself, so as to avoid the damage that may arise from such injunction. In addition, the UMTS standard contains a large number of patents owned by different owners (1800 or more patent families are declared as essential by 50 or more patentees). It is considered extremely difficult for a standard user to obtain the licenses in advance, after confirming whether each of such large number of patents is essential or not. Therefore, if the patentee is unconditionally allowed to seek an injunction based on the SEPs, the adoption of the UMTS standard would become practically impossible. Such situation would have a negative impact on the dissemination of the UMTS standard and run counter to the purpose of the ETSI IPR Policy aimed at the harmonization and dissemination of the communication standards. Further, if such situation arises, the general public would be unable to enjoy a variety of benefits which would be available if the harmonization and dissemination of communication standards were achieved.

On the other hand, the court said that an injunction should be granted against a standard implementer who did not intend to obtain a FRAND license, adding that "strict scrutiny shall be made before determining that the implementer has no intention of receiving a FRAND license". The court summarized the standard to judge on the availability of injunctive relief as follows:

> Considering the totality of the above-mentioned circumstances, the exercise of the right to seek an injunction based on the 886 Patent by Samsung would constitute an abuse of right (Article 1 (3) of the Civil Code) and therefore is not allowed, if Apple successfully alleges and proves the fact of Samsung having made the FRAND declaration and Apple's intention of receiving a FRAND license.

The court then examined the facts relating to the negotiation between the parties.[40] While there was "persistent and material discrepancy in the opinions between the parties" as to the royalty rate, the court found Apple's proposals to be

> fairly reasonable, considering the fact that the parties [were] by nature in a conflict-of-interest situation as the prospective licensor and licensee, and that the royalty to be considered appropriate [might] vary depending on the different assessment of the essential nature or significance of individual patent in terms of the UMTS standard, as there [were] no definite criteria for determining the FRAND royalty.

The court concluded that Apple had the intention of receiving a FRAND license.

Based on the foregoing premises, the IPHC concluded that Samsung's petitions for injunctions should be dismissed.

3.3.3 Development after the decisions

These cases were parts of the legal disputes raised in many countries between Apple and Samsung, two giants in the ITC sector. But soon after these decisions, both parties agreed to withdraw the lawsuits including the present ones, except for the pending cases in the U.S. They eventually settled the last case in the U.S. in June 2018.[41]

3.4 Analysis[42]

3.4.1 Legal significance of the decisions

The aforementioned judgments, including the decisions at first instance, have great significance in the development of Japanese law on patent infringement.

40 *Id.* at 25–27.

41 *See, e.g.*, Apple and Samsung End Smartphone Patent Wars, *New York Times*, available at www.nytimes.com/2018/06/27/technology/apple-samsung-smartphone-patent.html (last accessed December 17, 2018).

42 This section is partly based on Masabumi Suzuki, Enforcement of FRAND-encumbered SEPs, in Kung-Chung Liu (ed.), *Annotated Leading Patent Cases in Major Asian Jurisdictions* (City University of Hong Kong Press, Hong Kong, 2017), pp. 241–261.

First, they are the first and so far the only judicial decisions which squarely dealt with the possibility of the enforcement of FRAND-encumbered SEPs in Japan. The decisions by the IPHC are particularly important; they were decided by its Special Division (Grand Panel),[43] which has prescribed clear criteria as to the admissibility of the enforcement of SEPs and determined the exact amount of damages that would correspond to the FRAND royalty. As such, they not only have a precedential meaning in Japan but also are of reference value for other countries faced with disputes involving SEPs.

Second, although the decisions' discussions on the limitation of patent rights are made in the context of FRAND-encumbered SEPs, their implications for the broader question of limiting patent rights in general may be deduced. As already mentioned, the Japanese practice in litigation on patent infringement is to grant injunctive relief automatically whenever the likelihood of infringement is affirmed. These decisions are thus unique in the history of patent litigation in Japan, as they have restricted injunctive relief based on consideration of its effects on related parties.[44]

Third, the IPHC undertook a procedure for public consultation (the so-called Japanese version of the amicus curie process) for the first time in Japan.[45] In this sense, the court procedure for these cases was extraordinary in the Japanese legal history. The procedural aspects seem to reflect the IPHC's acknowledgement of the needs of industry. In addition to the formation of the Special Division and the first-ever adoption of the public consultation procedure, the IPHC issued the decisions promptly (within 15 months after the first instance decisions) in spite of the complicated nature of the cases. Such treatment may be understood as the IPHC's willingness to meet the actual needs of the business community or users of the court's system.[46]

3.4.2 *Problems recognized by the IPHC with respect to FRAND-encumbered SEPs*

The IPHC specifically mentioned the holdup problem by saying that granting an injunction and awarding damages exceeding the amount of the FRAND royalty

43 The Special Division (Grand Panel), which consists of five judges, is set up when a case contains important issues and it is appropriate to provide unified opinions of the IPHC on the issues without delay. *See* Article 310*bis*, the Code of Civil Procedure in Japan.

44 Masabumi Suzuki, Injunctive Relief for Patent Infringement: A New Trend in Japan? in Alexander Bruns & Masabumi Suzuki (eds.), *Preventive Instruments of Social Governance* (Tübingen, Germany: Mohr Siebeck, 2017), pp. 111–118.

45 There is no mechanism like the amicus curie process in Japanese civil litigation. In *Apple v. Samsung*, the IPHC directly requested opinions from the public by way of expert opinions for the parties. The decision for *FRAND Case I* at the end (pp. 139–141) explains the result of the consultation.

46 Chief Judge Masaaki Iimura chaired the Special Division which wrote these decisions. Judge Iimura played a great role in intellectual property litigation in Japan for the past 30 years, and these decisions were issued just before his retirement at the end of May 2015. Therefore, many IP practitioners and scholars in Japan attach a special status to these decisions.

to a holder of FRAND-encumbered SEPs against standard implementers who are willing to accept a license on FRAND terms would result in "excessive protection" of the SEP holder. In *Case I*, the court also discussed the royalty stacking problem; it stated that in order to achieve the goal of ETSI's IPR Policy, "it is reasonable to understand that, not only the amount of royalty for each of the individual essential patents, but also the aggregate of such royalty (aggregate royalty) should be limited within the economically reasonable range" and applied 5% as the "reasonable cap for the aggregate royalty" in the estimation of the FRAND royalty.

On the other hand, the IPHC did not express serious concerns about the holdout problem. Although the court admitted that an SEP holder should be granted an injunction and damages exceeding the amount of the FRAND royalty when the standard implementer was not willing to obtain a license on FRAND terms, it stressed that "strict scrutiny" should be given before finding unwillingness on the side of the implementer.[47] In this aspect, the IPHC's attitude seems to be favorable to standard implementers in finding them to be willing licensees.

3.4.3 Legal ground for the restriction of the enforcement of SEPs: the doctrine of abuse of right

The IPHC stated in essence that given the fact that the SEP holder had made a FRAND declaration, exercising the right based on SEPs to seek injunction as well as damages exceeding the FRAND royalties against willing licensees constitutes an abuse of right, and should be rejected. In this way, the IPHC adopted the doctrine of abuse of right, which had been rather rarely used for restricting the enforcement of patent rights in Japan.[48]

It should be noted, however, that the reasons for finding an abuse of right were very different between the decisions of the Tokyo District Court and the IPHC. Specifically, the Tokyo District Court did not present a general framework for judging on an abuse of right in cases involving FRAND-encumbered SEPs. Instead, the Tokyo District Court pointed to detailed facts concerning the negotiation between the two parties, found that Samsung breached its obligation for good faith negotiation (particularly by not disclosing information necessary for Apple to determine the rate of the FRAND royalty and by not presenting Samsung's own proposal for the FRAND royalty), and affirmed an abuse of right. The application of the doctrine of abuse of right by the District Court was very case specific and based on the finding of a breach of good faith obligation.[49] In contrast, the IPHC presented a general framework for applying the doctrine as

47 *See* subsections 3.3.1.3 and 3.3.2.2.

48 *See* section 2.

49 As explained in subsection 3.2.2, the Tokyo District Court refused to award any damages to Samsung. It is not clear yet whether the court would have still recognized an abuse of right even if Samsung had not been found breaching the good faith negotiation obligation, as did the IPHC.

explained earlier. The IPHC's approach is much clearer and more desirable from the viewpoint of predictability and legal stability. In addition, the IPHC in *Case I* found that Samsung did not violate its obligation for good faith negotiation.

In the application of the doctrine of abuse of right, the IPHC explained that a FRAND declaration would generate "trust" in the availability of a license on the FRAND terms, and granting injunctions and damages exceeding the amount of the FRAND royalty would harm such trust. The court also mentioned the good faith negotiation obligation in *Case I*. In this way, the court based its application of the doctrine of abuse of right on the special relationship between the parties toward a licensing agreement. Thus, although the court denied the existence of a contract between the parties, its approach to limiting the exercise of SEPs can be seen as a contractual approach in a broad sense.

3.4.4 "Willing licensee" requirement

The IPHC found that Apple was a willing licensee and therefore rejected Samsung's claims for injunctions and damages exceeding the amount of the FRAND royalty. A "willing licensee" refers to an entity that has an intention to enter into a license agreement under the FRAND terms. The requirement to be found as a "willing licensee" will significantly affect the actual practice of negotiations on FRAND-encumbered SEPs.

As to this requirement, first, the IPHC distinguished the burden of proof for injunctions from that of damages. In the context of injunction claims, the alleged infringer (standard implementer) bears the burden of proving that he/she is a willing licensee in order to rebut the claims, while the patentee bears the burden to prove that the alleged infringer is an unwilling licensee in order to claim damages exceeding the FRAND royalties. The reason for such a distinction was not clarified. It might reflect the IPHC's perception that the default rule was to grant an injunction to patentees against infringers, while the amount of damages based on the royalties must be proved by the patentee.[50]

Second, the IPHC did not present a general framework for judging whether a party should be regarded as a willing (or an unwilling) licensee. It merely examined the facts of these cases, and affirmed that Apple was a willing licensee. While the court found that there was "persistent and material discrepancy in the opinions between the parties" as to the royalty rate, it still concluded that Apple's proposals could be considered "fairly reasonable" and that Apple had the intention of receiving a FRAND license.[51] It should also be noted that the IPHC explicitly stated that "strict scrutiny shall be made to determine the existence of special circumstances in which the prospective licensee has no intention of

50 Article 102 (3) of the Japanese Patent Act provides that the patentee may regard the amount of licensing royalty as the amount of damages. Under this provision, the burden of proving the amount of royalty is on the patentee.

51 *See* subsections 3.3.1.3 and 3.3.2.2.

receiving a FRAND license". Although it is not very clear what the IPHC means by this statement, it should be interpreted as a caution against applying the willing licensee requirement in a harsh way for standard implementers. For example, as shown in these decisions themselves, implementers' challenge on the validity, essentiality for the standard, or infringement of the patent should not by itself be a reason to deny their willingness, because such a challenge is quite natural for prospective licensees.

3.4.5 Legal effects of the FRAND declaration

The FRAND declaration is, in principle, a contract between SSOs and SEP holders. However, there are different views regarding the contractual effects on standard implementers. There are court decisions in the U.S. and U.K. which recognized contractual relationship between the patentee and implementer, and treated the latter as a third-party beneficiary.[52] In Japan, there is a similar view taken by some scholars,[53] but the majority view among practitioners and scholars including this author is to deny contractual relationship that is directly established by the FRAND declaration.

The IPHC in these cases sided with the majority view, saying that no license agreement was formed as a result of Samsung's FRAND declaration, because such a declaration could not be regarded as an offer for a license agreement. This position seems to be reasonable, at least as an interpretation of the FRAND declaration under the ETSI IPR policy.[54]

However, as mentioned in subsection 3.4.3, it should be noted that the IPHC stressed that Apple and Samsung in these cases were the parties in the process of negotiating toward a licensing agreement, and recognized an abuse of right by Samsung due to the need for the protection of trust in the availability of a license on the side of Apple, which was caused by Samsung's FRAND declaration. The court even explicitly affirmed the good faith negotiation obligation for Samsung in *Case I*.[55] In this way, despite the denial of an established contract, the court's understanding of the relationship between the parties was not very different from the view of recognizing a third-party beneficiary in standard implementers.

52 *See, e.g.*, *Microsoft Corp. v. Motorola, Inc.*, 864 F. Supp. 2d 1023 (W.D. Wash. 2012); *Unwired Planet Int'l Ltd. v. Huawei Techs. Co.* [2018] EWCA Civ 2344.

53 *E.g.*, Yoshiyuki Tamura, *Standardization and Patent Rights: Legal Issues concerning Measures by RAND Provisions*, 90 IPI Forum 18, 23 (2012) (in Japanese).

54 However, the UK courts in *Unwired Planet v. Huawei* took a different view, finding the implementer to be a third-party beneficiary, with regard to the same IPR policy of ETSI and under the same French law as those in the decisions of the IPHC. *Unwired Planet Int'l Ltd. v. Huawei Techs. Co.*, [2017] EWHC 711 (Pat); *Unwired Planet Int'l Ltd. v. Huawei Techs. Co.* [2018] EWCA Civ 2344.

55 The IPHC discussed the good faith negotiation obligation in the context of examining the existence of "special circumstances" for denying damages not exceeding the FRAND royalty. Therefore, the Court did not mention this obligation in *Case II and Case III*.

3.4.6 Damages claims

The Tokyo District Court rejected Samsung's claim for any damages as an abuse of right, even though Apple actually practiced Samsung's patented invention and acknowledged that it would be willing to pay the FRAND royalties. The decision's conclusion was criticized by commentators.[56]

On the other hand, the IPHC rightly affirmed that claiming for damages not exceeding the amount of the FRAND royalty did not constitute an abuse of right, as the patentee should not be restricted from exercising such claim even where the patent was an SEP.

3.4.7 Calculation of the FRAND royalty

The calculation of the FRAND royalty may be the most controversial part of the IPHC's decision in *Case I*. In fact, some commentators criticized the calculated amount of the FRAND royalty as too low.[57]

First, the method of calculation is the so-called top-down approach.[58] In general, "[s]uch top-down mechanisms begin by determining the aggregate royalty burden associated with a standard when considering the royalties owed to any particular patent holder" and "[o]nce an aggregate royalty is determined, various methodologies can then be used to allocate that total among individual SEP holders".[59] This approach is considered to be one of the most promising methods[60] and has been used by courts in other jurisdictions.[61]

Second, it may be debatable, however, whether the calculation method used by the IPHC is suitable for damages. Damages are awarded only after the validity and infringement of the patent are confirmed, and therefore, generally speaking, the royalty rate applied for the calculation of damages should be higher than that for the calculation of actual license fees.

Third, whether damages should be calculated by multiplying both the "contribution ratio of the compliance with the UMTS standard" by the products and the "royalty rate cap" (5%) may also be debatable. The public version decision did not reveal the "contribution ratio". One commentator estimates the ratio to be about 30% and criticizes that "it must be a mistake for the court to apply such a low contribution ratio in addition to the royalty rate cap".[62]

56 *See, e.g.*, Masabumi Suzuki, *Case Review*, 1458 Jurist 17 (2013) (in Japanese).

57 *See, e.g.*, Hisashi Kato, *Apple v. Samsung (iPhone) Case – FRAND*, 1475 Jurist 50 (2015) (in Japanese).

58 *See, e.g.*, Jorge L. Contreras et al., *The Effect of FRAND Commitments on Patent Remedies*, 17 (2018), available at https://ssrn.com/abstract=3248726.

59 *Id.* at 17–18.

60 *Id.* at 17.

61 *In re Innovatio IP Ventures, LLC Patent Litigation* (N.D. Ill. 2013); *Unwired Planet Int'l Ltd. v. Huawei Techs. Co.*, [2017] EWHC 711 (Pat).

62 Kato (n 57) at 55.

3.4.8 Evaluation under the Antimonopoly Act

Apple alleged that Samsung's conduct concerning the SEPs was in violation of the Antimonopoly Act. This argument was made as one of the grounds for the allegation of an abuse of right. In *Case I*, the IPHC responded to it in denial just briefly, while the Court did not discuss it at all in *Case II* and *Case III*. That means that the issue concerning competition law was discussed only in the context of claims for damages, and not in that of claims for injunction. The reason for the omission of any discussion on competition law in the latter cases by the IPHC (and probably by Apple) would have been that Samsung's claims in *Case II* and *Case III* were for provisional disposition order for injunction, and thus the proceedings of these cases were simpler.

The IPHC's rather indifferent response is also understandable because, first, the analysis of the issue under the Antimonopoly Act had not been discussed much even among competition law specialists, and second, the court already had legal grounds to adopt the abuse of right doctrine and did not need to rely on another legal reason related to the Antimonopoly Act. The situation is changing, however. In January 2016, the Japan Fair Trade Commission (JFTC) amended the "Guidelines for the Use of Intellectual Property under the Antimonopoly Act" in order to add evaluation criteria for the illegality of injunction claim by the patentee of FRAND-encumbered SEPs.[63]

3.4.9 Reception of the IPHC's decisions

After the issuance of these decisions, some commentators showed concerns about the negative impact these decisions have on standardization in general due to the IPHC's limitation of injunctions by SEPs and calculation of FRAND royalties,[64] while others expressed more positive views about the decisions' impact on standardization and commercial activities.[65]

4 *Imation v. One Blue*

4.1 Facts

In the 2015 case *Imation v. One Blue*, the Tokyo District Court issued a decision on the exercise of SEPs.[66] In this case, the defendant managed and operated a patent pool of FRAND-encumbered SEPs for standards related to Blu-ray

63 *See* www.jftc.go.jp/en/legislation_gls/imonopoly_guidelines_files/IPGL_Frand.pdf. Part 3 (1)(i)(e) and Part 4 (2)(iv) of the Guidelines discuss acts of holders of FRAND-encumbered SEPs.

64 *E.g.*, Kato (n 57).

65 *E.g.*, Suzuki (n 56); Yoshiyuki Tamura, *Case Review (1) – (5)*, 1028 NBL 27, 1029 NBL 95, 1031 NBL 58, 1032 NBL 34, 1033 NBL 36 (2014) (in Japanese).

66 The decision of the Tokyo District Court, 2015 (Wa) 21383 (February 18, 2015).

disc (BD) products. The defendant sent a notice of patent infringement to business partners of the plaintiff. The notice stated that the plaintiff's BD products infringed the patents in the defendant's patent pool, and the patentees had rights to injunctive relief against the plaintiff. The plaintiff sued the defendant, claiming that the latter's act of sending the notice constituted an act of damaging credit of a competitor under Article 2(1)(xiv)[67] of the Unfair Competition Prevention Act or an act of unfair trade practice under Article 19 of the Antimonopoly Act, and sought an injunction and damages.

4.2 The decision by the Tokyo District Court

The court affirmed that the defendant's conduct constituted an act of unfair competition by damaging reputation of the plaintiff, and granted an injunction against the defendant while rejecting the plaintiff's claim for damages because the defendant lacked intent or negligence.[68] The court acknowledged that a claim for an injunction by the holders of the patent right in defendant's patent pool against standard implementers willing to get a license on FRAND basis should be rejected as an abuse of right. The plaintiff was found as having been willing to obtain a license under FRAND terms, and therefore the defendant's act of notification was determined to be an act of unfair competition.

The reasons why the plaintiff was found to be a willing licensee were facts between the parties, including the defendant's initial presentation of the royalty for a prospective license, the plaintiff's explicit statement of its intention to "pay a fair and reasonable royalty", its rejection of the royalty proposed by the defendant as being not fair nor reasonable, the plaintiff's presentation of a substitute royalty, and its demand to the defendant for disclosure of the basis of the defendant's royalty. With respect to a significant gap between the plaintiff and the defendant in terms of the appropriate royalty, the court gave a statement almost the same as that of the IPHC in *Case I* of *Apple v. Samsung*, concluding that "even if there was a large gap between the two companies for a long period of time, it should not be immediately prevented from finding that the plaintiff had the intention to conclude a licensing agreement on FRAND terms".

4.3 Analysis

This decision completely followed the framework given by the IPHC in *Apple v. Samsung* as to a refusal of claims for injunctions bases on FRAND-encumbered SEPs, and found the standard implementer (the plaintiff) to be a willing licensee.

67 The provision has become Article 2(1)(xv) after the amendment of the Act in 2015.

68 In denying the defendant's intent and negligence, the court took into account that the defendant's conduct at issue had been done before the decisions of the IPHC in *Apple v. Samsung* were issued.

In this way, the decision was the first example of a judgment as to a willing licensee following the framework of the IPHC's decisions.

Whereas the Tokyo District Court affirmed that the defendant's act constituted an act of unfair competition under the Unfair Competition Prevention Act, it did not decide on the applicability of the Antimonopoly Act. Although the legal standards for illegality under the two acts are very different, given the court's recognition of the plaintiff as a willing licensee and the framework shown in the Guidelines by the JFTC,[69] it is very likely that the court would have affirmed an act of unfair trade practice under the Antimonopoly Act in this case.[70]

5 Recent developments and remaining issues

As for the recent developments in Japan after the decisions explained earlier, there has been no court decision which dealt squarely with the enforcement of FRAND-encumbered SEPs and was made public. However, the interest in this issue continues to attract much attention in industry.

The Japan Patent Office (JPO) appears eager to play a role in resolving disputes involving SEPs. In April 2018, the JPO made it possible for users of the advisory system (Article 71 of the Patent Act) to request opinions as to essentiality of patents for standards. In June 2018, the JPO published the "Guide to Licensing Negotiations Involving Standard Essential Patents" (the "Guide").[71] The Guide is said "to enhance transparency and predictability, facilitate negotiations between rights holders and implementers, and help prevent or quickly resolve disputes concerning the licensing of standard essential patents ('SEPs'), which are the patents essential in implementing standards in the field of wireless communications and the like".[72]

While the JPO's Guide shows the trend of global discussion, particularly by courts, about the desirable negotiation process between SEP holders and standard implementers, there have not been any judicial decisions or guidelines that have carefully examined the way of such negotiations in detail under the Japanese law.

Another example of the remaining issues is the treatment of FRAND commitments when SEPs are transferred to third parties. Even if the IPR policy of the SSO stipulates that assignees should also be bound by the FRAND declaration by the assignor (the former patentee) when an SEP is transferred, it seems difficult to construe that the subsequent assignee assumes obligations under the FRAND commitment directly and naturally under Japanese law, because the obligation

69 *See* (n 63) and accompanying text.

70 One commentator suggests that this case should have been decided (positively) under the Antimonopoly Act rather than the Unfair Competition Prevention Act. Akihiko Moridaira, *Case Review*, 1489 Jurist 106 (2016) (in Japanese).

71 The English version is available at www.jpo.go.jp/shiryou/kijun/kijun2/files/seps-tebiki/guide-seps-en.pdf.

72 JPO, Guide, 1.

in the IPR policy does not necessarily extend to the assignee, particularly when the latter is not a member of the SSO. A prima facie theory under Japanese law may be that the legal effect of a contract or the doctrine of good faith should be acknowledged on the basis of the recognizability of the FRAND commitment for the assignee. That is, the assignee should generally be aware of the fact that the patent is an SEP and the assignor had given a FRAND declaration, and thus the FRAND declaration should bind the assignee as an effect of an assignment contract of the SEP or on the basis of the doctrine of good faith and fair dealing. However, it should be kept in mind that the preceding explanations are inevitably subject to the factual relationship of each case.[73]

73 For a discussion on the relationship between the assignment of patent rights and the transfer of status as a party to license agreements under Japanese law, *see* Emiko Maruyama, The Assertion of Use and Profit Rights in the Assignment of Property and the Transfer of Status as a Party to a Contract: License, Rental Rights, and Servitude, 276 *Nagoya U.J.L. & Politics* 33 (2018) (in Japanese).

10 Korea

Jinyul Ju

1 Introduction

There is little doubt that technology standards developed through standard determining organizations (SDOs) are vital to enhance economic efficiency. On the other hand, patents that are essential to complying with a standard, commonly referred to as standard essential patents (SEPs), are to be duly protected in order to promote technology innovation. It is hard to find any reason that SEPs should be less protected than patents that are not essential to complying with a standard (non-SEPs). Indeed, the Korean Patent Act does not discriminate between SEPs and non-SEPs. In regard to SEPs, however, some have raised concerns about the possibility of so-called patent holdup, especially in information technology (IT) industries.[1] As this term means an SEP holder's opportunistic use of "standard" to obtain an unreasonably high royalty,[2] a more accurate term would be "standard holdup".[3] To mitigate the possibility of a standard holdup, not all but most SDOs have required participants, the would-be SEPs owners, to grant SEPs licenses on fair, reasonable and non-discriminatory (FRAND) terms before adopting standards. But others have argued that "patent holdup" is just theoretical, and not found empirically in the real world.[4]

1 See Carl Shapiro, Navigating the Patent Thicket: Cross Licenses, Patent Pools, and Standard Setting, in Adam B. Jaffe et al. (eds.), *International and the Economy*, Vol. 1 (Cambridge, MA: MIT Press, 2001), p. 127.

2 *Id.* at 136 ("If the standard becomes popular, each such patent can confer significant market power on its owner, and the standard itself is subject to holdup if these patent holders are not somehow obligated to license their patents on reasonable terms.")

3 Obviously this is different from an SEP holder's legitimate exercise of its exclusionary rights conferred by patent laws.

4 See Einer Elhauge, Do Patent Holdup and Royalty Stacking Lead to Systematically Excessive Royalties? 4 *J. Comp. L. & Econ.* 535 (2008); Damien Geradin, Moving Away from High-Level Theories: A Market-Driven Analysis of FRAND, 59 *Antitrust Bull.* 327 (2014); Alexander Galetovic & Stephen Haber, The Fallacies of Patent-holdup Theory, 13(1) *J. Comp. L. Econ.* 1 (2017).

On the other hand, the inherent ambiguity of FRAND[5] has raised different concerns about the possibility of so-called reverse patent holdup or patent holdout.[6] Since these terms refer to an implementer's opportunistic use of FRAND commitments to get more generous licensing conditions, a better term would be "FRAND holdup". In addition, by arguing that a breach of FRAND commitment constitutes a violation of competition law, implementers may opportunistically use competition law, thereby pressuring SEP holders to offer more generous licensing terms. To put it differently, there is the potential "misuse of antitrust law or competition law, purportedly motivated by the fear of so-called patent hold-up".[7] It can be called "antitrust holdup".

Where SEP holders and implementers dispute licensing terms, which one – standard holdup or FRAND holdup – is the real problem? Do we have a tool kit for solving the problem precisely? Some might believe that the courts may use modified *Georgia-Pacific* factors[8] to estimate FRAND royalty in the same way

5 See U.S. Department of Justice and Federal Trade Commission, *Antitrust Enforcement and Intellectual Property Rights: Promoting Innovation and Competition* (2007), at p. 47, footnotes 74–75: "[S]ince reasonable is so vague, it doesn't amount to anything."; "RAND [is] an empty term"; "[T]he people who are negotiating for the establishment . . . of a standard don't know what [RAND] mean[s]."; "[T]here has not been much in the way of judicial explication of [RAND licensing terms] so far."

6 See Damien Geradin, *Reverse Hold-Ups: The (Often Ignored) Risks Faced by Innovators in Standardized Areas* (November 12, 2010), available at https://ssrn.com/abstract=1711744; Richard A. Epstein & Kayvan B. Norooz, Why Incentives for Patent Holdout Threaten to Dismantle FRAND, and Why It Matters, 32 *Berkeley Tech. L.J.* 1381 (2017); Ashish Bharadwaj, A Note on the Neglected Issue of Reverse Patent Holdup, 13 *J. of Intellectual Prop. L. & Pract.* 553 (2018); Bowman Heiden & Nicolas Petit, Patent Trespass and the Royalty Gap: Exploring the Nature and Impact of Patent Holdout, 34 *Santa Clara High Tech. L.J.* 179 (2017).

7 Makan Delrahim, U.S. Department of Justice Assistant Attorney General for Antitrust Division, *Take It to the Limit: Respecting Innovation Incentives in the Application of Antitrust Law* (remarks at USC Gould School of Law, November 10, 2017) at 7, available at www.justice.gov/opa/speech/file/1010746/download. As examples of "misuse of antitrust law" in the U.S., he listed three cases before the Federal Trade Commission: Complaint, *In re Negotiated Data Solutions LLC*, No. C-4234, FTC File No. 051-0094 (F.T.C. September 22, 2008), available at www.ftc.gov/sites/default/files/documents/cases/2008/09/080923ndscomplaint.pdf; Complaint, *In re Robert Bosch GmbH*, No. C-4377, FTC File No. 121-0081, 2012 WL 5944820 (F.T.C. November 21, 2012); Complaint, *In re Motorola Mobility LLC & Google Inc.*, No. C-4410, FTC File No. 121-0120 (F.T.C. July 23, 2013), available at www.ftc.gov/sites/default/files/documents/cases/2013/07/130724 googlemotorolacmpt.pdf. *Id.* at 7, footnote 17.

8 Fifteen factors listed by the U.S. district court, in estimating reasonable royalty damages based on a method of hypothetical negotiation between willing licensor and willing licensee at the time the infringement of patent happened, in *Georgia-Pacific Corp. v. U.S. Plywood Corp.*, 318 F. Supp. 1116 (S.D.N.Y. 1970), mod. and aff'd, 446 F.2d 295 (2d Cir. 1971), cert. denied, 404 U.S. 870 (1971).

the U.S. court did in *Microsoft v. Motorola*.[9] But hypothetical negotiation methods are hardly a proper tool to estimate FRAND royalty when an SEP holder and an implementer have actually failed to negotiate. If judges try to determine "reasonable royalty" – which can hardly be estimated precisely – with hypothetical models, they will sail on a sea of doubt.

Besides the problem of holdup or holdout, patents – without regard to SEPs or non-SEPs – have raised antitrust concern about abuse of monopolistic power. For instance, when the patent holder misuses its monopolistic power in order to monopolize the market for unpatented products, it raises an antitrust issue about abuse of dominance. Although jurisprudence concerning abuse of dominance is different from country to country, it can be largely said that the mere exercise of monopolistic power lawfully conferred on the patent holder does not constitute abuse of dominance. It also should be noted that an infringement of FRAND commitment is not the same as antitrust offence because the commitment is not found in competition law. When an SEP holder breaches its FRAND commitment, there is little room for antitrust intervention. But public choice theory[10] suggests that the government may have incentive to maintain and strength its regulatory power on IT industries by intervening in FRAND issue.

Like other some countries, Korea is facing problems concerning the intersection of FRAND-encumbered SEPs and competition law. This chapter aims to briefly introduce and make a comment on four Korean FRAND/SEP-related cases in which patent, contract and antitrust issues are entangled.

2 Overview of FRAND/SEPs cases and Korean antitrust law

2.1 Four cases

There have been four cases in which FRAND-committed SEPs mattered in the antitrust sense in Korea. In December 2009, the Korea Fair Trade Commission (KFTC) imposed administrative sanctions on Qualcomm for alleged abuse of dominance and unfair trade practice under the Monopoly Regulation and Fair Trade Act (MRA) (*Qualcomm I*).[11] In this case, the KFTC inferred Qualcomm's anticompetitive intent from alleged breach of its FRAND commitment. In

9 *Microsoft Corp. v. Motorola Inc.*, 854 F. Supp. 2d 993 (W.D. Wash. 2012), aff'd, 696 F.3d 872 (9th Cir. 2012).

10 For a detailed discussion of public choice theory and competition policy, see Fred S. McChesney & William F. Shughart II (eds.), *The Causes and Consequences of Antitrust: The Public-Choice Perspective* (Chicago: University of Chicago Press, 1995).

11 KFTC No. 2009-281 decision, December 30, 2009. In June 2013, the Seoul High Court confirmed the KFTC's decision on *Qualcomm I* (Seoul High Court 2000Nu3921 decision, June 19, 2013). In January 2019, however, the Supreme Court partially confirmed the Seoul High Court's decision (Supreme Court 2013Du14726, January 2019).

August 2012, the Seoul Central District Court in *Samsung Electronics v. Apple*[12] dismissed Apple's antitrust counterclaim that Samsung Electronics' alleged breach of its FRAND commitment amounts to abuse of dominance and unfair trade practice. In 2015, the KFTC raised antitrust concern about SEPs arising from the merger of Microsoft and Nokia. Eventually Microsoft and the KFTC agreed to settle the case under MRA (*Microsoft/Nokia*).[13] In December 2017, eight years after *Qualcomm I*, the KFTC again imposed on Qualcomm various sanctions for alleged breach of its FRAND commitment, abuse of dominance and unfair trade practice (*Qualcomm II*). [14]

2.2 Korean antitrust law

Korean antitrust law is notorious for its complex pyramid structure as well as shoddily drafted phrases and sentences – full of ambiguity and tautology. The law forms the pyramid structure of the Monopoly Regulation and Fair Trade Act (MRA), the Presidential Enforcement Decree of MRA (Decree), and some provisions – promulgated by delegations of MRA or Decree – of the KFTC's by-law guidelines.[15] Under the pyramid structure, one type of unlawful conduct in MRA can be divided into two, three or more types of unlawful conduct in Decree. Again one type of unlawful conduct in Decree can be divided into two, three or more types of unlawful conduct in a specific by-law guideline. In this way, for instance, abuse of dominance contains more than 20 types of unilateral conducts, and unfair trade practice contain more than 30 types of unilateral conducts.[16] With regard to unilateral conduct of a dominant undertaking, the KFTC may challenge the same conduct at issue as abuse of dominance under Art. 3–2 (1) and also unfair trade practice under Art. 23 (1) at the same time, but imposing administrative sanctions only for abuse of dominance.[17]

First, MRA Art. 3–2 (1) makes it unlawful for dominant undertakings to engage in six types of "undue" conduct as abuse of dominance.[18] By delegation of MRA Art. 3–2 (2), Decree Art. 5 stipulates more than 10 types of "undue" conduct as abuse of dominance. By delegation of Decree, chapter IV of the KFTC's

12 Seoul Central District Court 2011Gahap39552 decision, August 24, 2012.

13 KFTC No. 2015-316 decision, August 24, 2015.

14 KFTC No. 2017-025 decision, January 20, 2017. As of March 2019, the *Qualcomm II* case is pending in the Seoul High Court.

15 Although the by-law guideline itself has no legally binding force, MRA and Decree may delegate the KFTC to specify prohibited conducts more in detail in its by-law guidelines.

16 While abuse of dominance can only be committed by a dominant undertaking, unfair trade practice can be committed by any undertakings regardless of market dominance position.

17 Abuse of dominance and unfair trade practice can be also criminal offenses when the KFTC refers them for criminal prosecution to the Office of Public Prosecution.

18 Abuse of dominance includes: (1) undue pricing, (2) undue control of suppling goods or services, (3) undue hindrance of others' business, (4) undue hindrance of a new competitor's market entrance, (5) undue exclusive dealing, and (6) undue significant harms to consumers' benefit.

Guideline of Review on Abuse of Dominance (AD Guideline) stipulates more than 20 types of abuse of dominance. Because of this pyramid structure of the law concerning abuse of dominance, before deciding whether the behavior at issue is unlawful, it should be determined in advance which specific type of conduct as described in Decree and/or AD Guideline is relevant.

MRA Art. 23 (1) makes it unlawful for undertakings to engage in eight types of "undue" conduct as unfair trade practice.[19] By the pyramid structure, more than 20 types of unlawful conduct are described in Decree Art. 36 and its [Annex Table 1–2] as well as chapter V of the KFTC's Guideline of Review on Unfair Trade Practices (UTP Guideline). Some specific types of unfair trade practice (e.g. refusal to deal, exclusive dealing) overlaps those of abuse of dominance.

Considering the pyramid structure, the KFTC has referred to various types of prohibited conduct – described in Decree Art. 5, AD Guideline IV, Decree [Annex Table 1–2] and/or UTP Guideline – as many as possible. In MRA Art. 3–2 (1) cases, the KFTC has spent time and effort in order to divide the same single type of conduct at issue into two, three or even more prohibited conduct types. This practice makes the KFTC's decisions unnecessarily complicated and hardly readable even for experienced lawyers and judges. Anyway all types of prohibited conduct in Decree Art. 5 as well as AD Guideline IV are the subcategories of "undue" conducts in MRA Art. 3–2 (1). In determining whether the conduct at issue is unlawful, therefore, the final question is always whether the conduct is "undue". Unfortunately, the aforementioned undesirable practice of the KFTC has occasionally led the courts to misunderstand the real antitrust issue.

2.3 *Jurisprudence of abuse of dominance*

To understand the issue of abuse of dominance in the Korean FRAND-encumbered SEP cases, it is necessary to grasp the point of the Supreme Court's jurisprudence. The starting point for this should be *POSCO v. KFTC* (2007),[20] the most important and famous antitrust case in the history of Korean antitrust law. In this case, the Supreme Court reversed and remanded the Seoul High Court's decision that had affirmed the KFTC's decision: POSCO's refusal to deal with HYSCO constitutes "undue hindrance of any other undertaking's business" in MRA Art. 3–2 (1) (iii).

Denying the KFTC's per se illegal approach to abuse of dominance, the *POSCO* court opined for the first time that "undue hindrance of any other undertaking's business" means "anticompetitive conduct" which causes objective probability

19 Unfair trade practice includes (1) undue refusal to deal, (2) undue discrimination, (3) undue exclusion of competitors, (4) undue inducement to deal with competitor's customer, (5) undue coercion to deal with a competitor's customer, (6) abuse of superior bargaining position, (7) undue deal with terms and conditions restricting others' business, (8) undue hindrance of others' business, (9) undue support for other firms, and (10) other conducts that may harm fair trade.

20 Supreme Court 2002Du8023 full bench decision, November 22, 2007.

of "anticompetitive effect" (i.e. "increase in price, decrease in output, harm to innovation, decrease in the number of influential competitors, and decrease in diversity")[21] in the relevant market with "intent to monopolize the market or restrain competition in the market". According to the *POSCO* test, a mere hindrance of another undertaking's business without causing an anticompetitive effect cannot constitute abuse of dominance. The court reasoned that the purpose of MRA is to protect competition, not competitors.

Then how can "objective probability" and "intent" be proved? The court explained that anticompetitive intent would be inferred from actual anticompetitive effect. Accordingly, the KFTC is required to prove that the conduct at issue caused actual anticompetitive effect, then anticompetitive intent would be inferred. To be sure, anticompetitive intent cannot be inferred from a mere hindrance of another undertaking. Indeed the court did not separately examine POSCO's subjective intent in refusing to deal with HYSCO. In *KFTC v. KIA Motor*,[22] the court also did not examine KIA Motor's subjective intent, instead just finding that the KFTC failed to prove actual anticompetitive effect. In *KFTC* v. *SK Telecom*,[23] on the other hand, the Court opined that anticompetitive intent can be justified by a legitimate business reason such as the need to protect patents. These cases indicate that (1) anticompetitive intent is not a subjective or psychological element but an objective one that can be inferred only from observable anticompetitive effect; (2) a mere description of theoretical possibility or conjecture cannot be proof of anticompetitive effect; and (3) legitimate business justification can be used as a defense to argue for the absence of anticompetitive intent despite the existence of actual anticompetitive effect.

On the other hand, the *POSCO* court also mentioned that refusal to deal by a vertically integrated dominant firm in the upstream market may cause anticompetitive effect in the downstream market. As POSCO manufactured "hot coil" as well as "cold rolled steel sheet", the critical question was whether POSCO's refusal to deal in the former market caused anticompetitive effect in the second market. Finally, the Court concluded that POSCO did not violate MRA Art. 3–2 (1) (iii), because the KFTC failed to prove actual anticompetitive effect in the secondary market. In the cases of *T-broad Cable Television v. KFTC*,[24] *KFTC v. SK Telecom*,[25] and *KFTC v. NHN (Naver)*,[26] the Supreme Court concluded that the KFTC's claim of monopoly leveraging cannot be accepted because it did not prove actual anticompetitive effect in the secondary market.

21 Conduct causing "decrease in the number of influential competitors" itself cannot be considered anticompetitive conduct, because competitive conduct may also cause the same effect.
22 Supreme Court 2008Du17707 decision, April 8, 2010.
23 Supreme Court 2008Du1832 decision, October 13, 2011.
24 Supreme Court 2007Du25183 decision, December 11, 2008.
25 Supreme Court 2008Du1832 decision, October 13, 2011.
26 Supreme Court 2009Du20366 decision, November 13, 2014.

2.4 Patents and antitrust issue

Like other countries, the Korean Patent Act also confers on a patentee, without regard to SEP or non-SEP, the rights to exclude others. Accordingly, exclusionary conduct – including seeking injunctive relief – of a patentee is obviously lawful. When there are no alternative technologies, a patentee may legitimately charge monopoly price in order to maximize its profit.[27] Indeed it is well established that seeking monopoly profit itself is not unlawful. That is how the Patent Act rewards innovators. Even though such legitimate conduct inevitably cause anticompetitive effect such as monopoly pricing by excluding competitors, it cannot be an antitrust offence under MRA. If that conduct were condemned as a violation of MRA, the Patent Act simply could not exist. This is why MRA Art. 59 stipulates: "This Act is not applied to the conduct which is deemed a legitimate exercise of rights under the Copyright Act, the Patent Act, the Model Utility Act, the Design Protection Act, or the Trademark Act". Art. 59 provides absolute immunity to the legitimate exercise of exclusionary rights – which fall within the scope of patents and the aims of the Patent Act – even when it restrains competition in the relevant market. Unless the conduct at issue amounts to patent misuse (i.e. patent ambush, sham litigation, or tying patented and unpatented products), the patentee would be immune from antitrust liability under MRA Art. 59. To be sure, according to the *POSCO* test, when patent misuse does not cause anticompetitive effects, it cannot be condemned as abuse of dominance. According to both the *POSCO* test and MRA Art. 59, only when an exercise of SEPs amounts to patent misuse and thereby causes an anticompetitive effect can it be considered abuse of dominance.

In regard to Art. 59, the KFTC issued its Guideline on Unfair Exercise of Intellectual Property Rights (IPR Guideline) in 2009.[28] In 2016 the KFTC amended its IPR Guideline to deal with the issues of FRAND-encumbered SEPs.[29] First,

27 See Phillip Areeda, Louis Kaplow, & Aaron Edlin, *Antitrust Analysis* (New York: Aspen, 2004) at 103 ("The patent guarantees the inventor a monopoly of its invention, and the resulting prospect of monopoly profit stimulates both additional inventive efforts and the investments required to put such inventions rapidly into use.").

28 Because IPR Guideline was promulgated without delegations of either MRA or Decree, it does not have legal binding force. For this reason, the IPR Guideline declares that whether or not an exercise of patent amounts to a violation of MRA should be determined by articles of MRA and Decree.

29 IPR Guideline defines SEPs as "patents for which a party must acquire a license when the party produces products or provides services that implement the standard technologies claimed by the patents, where voluntary commitment is required that the license will be granted on the Fair, Reasonable And Non-Discriminatory (FRAND) conditions to the employing party." (I.3.(6)). But this definition is not right because not all SEP holders are necessarily required to declare FRAND commitments.

paragraph III.5.A of the 2016 IPR Guideline[30] provides six types of unfair exercise of SEPs as follows:

1 [Conduct] of unfairly agreeing to [restrict] price, volume, regions, [trading party], and technology improvement, in the process of discussion [on adopting a technology standard];
2 [Conduct] of unfairly [avoiding patent disclosure] in order to increase the possibility of being [adopted] as a [technology standard] or to avoid prior consultations on the [terms and conditions for] licenses;
3 [Conduct] of [avoiding FRAND commitments] to strengthen market dominance or to exclude competitors;
4 [Conduct] of unfairly [refusing to grant SEPs license];
5 [Conduct] of unfairly imposing discriminatory conditions when licensing [SEPs] or [imposing an unreasonably high] level of royalty;
6 [Conduct of] unfairly restricting the exercise of [a would-be licensee's] patent rights or [unfairly requiring cross-license with regards to a would-be licensee's non-SEPs].

With regard to "unfairly" in paragraph III.5.A, it is not certain whether the KFTC used the term in order to indicate abuse of dominance, unfair trade practice, patent misuse, or all of them. As paragraph III.5.A just abstractly describes six types of conduct, rather than providing clear criteria, it is not very helpful to identify unlawful exercise of SEPs under MRA.

Second, paragraph III.5.B of IPR Guideline particularly mentions seeking injunctions by an SEP holder as follows:

> [An] SEP holder can file an injunction or claim damages to prevent its patent rights from being infringed and to recover damage from the infringement. Among the two, the filing of injunction is a stronger tool for the holder to secure its right than the claim for damages, as an injunction seeks [the prohibition] of production, use, sales, or import of products using infringed technologies, not just seeking simple monetary compensations. However *when an injunction is filed limitlessly, patent hold up*[,] which refers to a situation where an SEP owner requires the payment of excessive royalty from willing licensees or filing an injunction to impose unfair conditions when licensing all with an intention to exclude competitors or obstruct the competitors' business activities[,] *can occur. Thereby an act of filing an injunction* against willing licensees by an SEP holder who promised to license its SEP on FRAND terms *can be determined [to be] a behavior that restricts*

30 English version of the 2016 IPR Guideline is downloadable at the KFTC's website: www.ftc.go.kr/solution/skin/doc.html?fn=d9bdb40caec1ba67c4f1070fc2849ad02db9e5fe2a8ee233bb6bb517ab275e3f&rs=/fileupload/data/result/BBSMSTR_000000002411.

> *competition* in the relevant market, [*because*] *it exceeds the* [*legitimate scope of the*] *exercise of patent right.*
>
> (emphasis added)
>
> [Note 1] SEP holders' [conduct] of filing an injunction while not performing negotiation obligation are highly likely to be determined [to be] an unfair behavior.
>
> (emphasis added)
>
> [Note 2] [*W*]*hen SEP holders' filing of an injunction* against unwilling licensees *is not allowed, reverse hold-up*[,] which refers to a situation where willing licensees do not engage in negotiation in good faith or delay or avoid payment of royalty[,] *can occur.* Also in certain cases, *injunction could be the only way of protecting rights of SEP holders.*
>
> (emphasis added)

Though paragraph III.5.B considers "patent holdup" and "reverse patent holdup" as well, it can be summarized that seeking injunction – without the SEP holder's good faith negotiation – amounts to patent misuse, therefore it constitutes unlawful (anticompetitive) conduct under MRA. But this does not make a sense at all. Among other things, since Art. 126 (1) of the Korean Patent Act confers upon a patentee – without regard to SEPs or non-SEPs – the right to seek preliminary and permanent injunctions, there is no doubt that an SEP holder may request that the courts issue injunctions. When the courts decide to issue an injunction, and even if the injunctions actually restrain competition, the conduct of seeking injunctions is immune from antitrust liability under Art. 59 of MRA. In contrast, what if the courts accept the defense of patent misuse by the implementer, and reject the petition for injunctions? Because of the courts' rejection, seeking injunction itself cannot restrict competition. As previously mentioned, only patent misuse which harms competition can be condemned as abuse of dominance. Therefore it is not possible to condemn seeking injunction under MRA. When the courts reject a request for injunctions by reason of patent misuse, it just implies that the FRAND-committed SEP holder is only allowed to seek monetary damages.

3 *Samsung Electronics v. Apple*

3.1 Overview

Samsung Electronics (Samsung) declared its FRAND commitment to the European Telecommunication Standard Institute (ESTI), and owned some 3G SEPs for cellular handsets. Samsung offered Apple the 2.4% royalty rate of the selling price of its end products. But Apple refused to pay the royalty rate of 2.4% and then unilaterally implemented Samsung's SEPs. In 2000, Samsung filed a patent infringement lawsuit against Apple in the Seoul Central District Court for alleged infringement of its SEPs, seeking injunctive relief against Apple's importation and sale of the i-Phone in Korea. Apple defended by arguing that it had not infringed Samsung's SEPs because the combination of (1) Samsung's FRAND commitment and (2) Apple's unilateral implementation of SEPs already had created a licensing agreement. In addition Apple asserted various counterclaims including an antitrust one. Among other things, Apple argued that Samsung's conduct infringed its FRAND commitment, and constituted a violation of MRA.

In 2012 the court concluded that Apple had infringed Samsung' SEPs, and Samsung's conduct was neither a breach of its FRAND commitment nor a violation of MRA (Seoul Central District Court 2011Gahap39552 decision, August 24, 2012). As Apple withdrew its appeal, the court's decision was finally confirmed.

3.2 *Summary of decision on FRAND-encumbered SEP and antitrust issues*

3.2.1 *Abuse of rights under civil law and patent misuse under the Patent Act*

According to the ESTI's intellectual property rights policy and Samsung's FRAND document submitted to the ESTI, the applicable law for its FRAND commitment is French law. According to French contract law, (1) the FRAND commitment at issue is an agreement between Samsung and the ESTI; (2) the legal status of Apple is a third-party beneficiary; (3) Samsung's FRAND commitment is not a license agreement with Apple; and (4) the combination of Samsung's FRAND commitment and Apple's unilateral implementation of SEPs cannot create a direct and explicit licensing agreement (pp. 174–181).

A FRAND commitment does not include waiving an SEP holder's right to bring a patent infringement lawsuit. Thus Samsung's lawsuit does not constitute a breach of estoppel (pp. 181–182).

Not only an SEP holder but also a potential licensee has the duty to negotiate in good faith for a licensing agreement. When a potential licensee explicitly or implicitly refuses to negotiate and unilaterally implement SEP, the patentee may bring a patent infringement lawsuit – including injunction – under the Patent Act. Because Apple has not negotiated with Samsung in good faith, Samsung may bring this lawsuit against Apple (pp. 183–186).

Considering (1) the rate and range for the 4G Long-Term Evolution (LTE) mobile communication SEPs of 0.8% to 3.25%; (2) the starting rate and range for negotiations regarding Wideband Code Division Multiple Access (WCDMA) SEPs of 1% to 2.75%; and (3) other SEP holders' practices, the rate is not unreasonably high. Accordingly, the rate of 2.4% is not a breach of Samsung's FRAND commitment (pp. 186–191).

Korean civil law prohibits abuse of rights. Samsung's lawsuit was not intended only to cause harassment and harm to Apple. Thus it does not constitute abuse of rights (pp. 189–192).

Patent misuse is not permissible under the Patent Act (Supreme Court 2005Da67223 decision, January 25, 2007). Samsung's lawsuit was not intended to exclude Apple from the relevant market, or to restrain competition. Rather it deems that Apple has not negotiated in good faith. Accordingly Samsung's lawsuit does not constitute patent misuse (pp. 191–196).

3.2.2 Abuse of dominance and unfair trade practice under MRA

Samsung has dominance in the market for 3G mobile telecommunication devices. Samsung's SEPs at issue are deemed an "essential factor" in Decree Art. 5 (3) (iii) (pp. 202–203).

First, Samsung's lawsuit does not constitute "undue denial of access to a factor which is essential for any other undertaking's business" in Decree Art. 5 (3) (iii) for the following reasons:

1 According to the *POSCO* decision, "undue hindrance" means anticompetitive conduct consisting of the objective probability of anticompetitive effects and anticompetitive intent. The intent would be inferred from actual anticompetitive effect (pp. 201–203). There is no evidence that Samsung's lawsuit constitutes anticompetitive conduct (pp. 205–206).
2 There is no evidence that the 2.4% royalty rate is unreasonably high. Even supposing that the rate is unreasonably high, thereby hindering Apple's business, Samsung's anticompetitive intent cannot be inferred from it (p. 206).

Second, Samsung's SEPs royalty does not constitute "undue discrimination of price or terms of trade, which is not consistent with ordinary trade practices" in AD Guideline IV. 3. Ra. (2), or "undue price discrimination" in Decree [Annex Table 1–2] No. 2. Ga, for the following reasons:

1 Samsung did not discriminate against Apple, because there is no evidence that the 2.4% royalty rate is unreasonably high or that Samsung coerced Apple to accept it (p. 208).
2 Even supposing that Samsung discriminated against Apple, there is no evidence of anticompetitive effects (*Id.*)

Third, Samsung did not "[make] any other undertaking hard, by undue methods, to implement a procedure which is needed to continue its business" in AD Guideline IV. 3. Ra. (5), nor did it "unduly seduce customers" in Decree [Annex Table 1–2] No. 4. Na, for the following reasons:

1 Samsung did not breach its duty to disclosure its patents to the ESTI in a timely manner (pp. 210–211).
2 Samsung did not commit any deceptive conduct including patent ambush (pp. 211, 213).

3 Samsung did not deceive the ESTI into adopting its patented technology as a standard. Even supposing that Samsung breached its duty to promptly disclosure its patent, it does not constitute "hindrance of another undertaking's business" [in MRA Art. 3–2 (1) (iii)] or "harm to fair trade" [in MRA Art. 23 (1)] (pp. 212, 214).

3.3 Comment

As the Seoul Central District Court pointed out, a FRAND commitment itself is neither a licensing contract nor a compulsory license. At most FRAND commitments can be a contractual term that may impose on not only an SEP holder but also a potential licensee the duty to negotiate in good faith for a particular licensing agreement. If the good faith bargaining failed because of the potential licensee's bad faith, there are no ways to grant SEP license. This should not be confused with refusal to deal or denial of access to essential facilities in the context of competition law. Notably, the court found that a potential licensee is obliged to negotiate in good faith. If a potential licensee negotiates in bad faith, an SEP holder may seek infringement lawsuit including injunctive relief under the Patent Act. By pointing out that Apple seemed intent on avoiding Samsung's lawsuit by arguing a breach of its FRAND commitment, and paying royalty only by judicial decision rather than by good faith bargaining (p. 186), the court indicates "patent holdout" by Apple.

Without estimating Samsung's SEP royalty rate, the court decided that the 2.4 % royalty rate is not unreasonably high compared to other similar SEP royalty rates. What if the royalty rate of 2.4 % were a monopoly price? Would it be a breach of Samsung's FRAND commitment? It is important to note that the FRAND-encumbered SEP holders are entitled to charge monopoly price – not including extra value due to the standard – because FRAND aims to restrain the standard holdup. Charging royalty rates including only monopolistic prices due to patents – but excluding extra value due to the standards – cannot be a breach of FRAND commitment and/or MRA. Of course, charging extra value due to the standard can be a breach of FRAND commitment. But a breach of FRAND commitment does not constitute a violation of MRA, because FRAND commitments are not an antitrust duty but a contractual obligation. Therefore, when the willing licensee argues that the SEP holder breached its FRAND commitment for the reason that the royalty rate is unreasonably high, it should seek civil remedies in the civil courts.

As the court found, Apple did not prove anticompetitive effects. Instead Apple just described many kinds of prohibited conducts under MRA, Decree, and Guidelines. For this reason, Apple's antitrust counterclaim seemed to be antitrust holdup. Although the court erred in deciding the relevant market,[31] this error is harmless because the court's conclusion is confirmed with the *POSCO* test.

31 According to the Supreme Court's jurisprudence, it is Apple that has to define the relevant market. Because Apple did not define the relevant market, the Seoul Central District Court should have asked Apple to define the market first.

4 *Qualcomm I* case

4.1 Overview

Qualcomm declared its FRAND commitment to the Telecommunication Technology Association of Korea and other SDOs, and owned some SEPs for 2G Code Division Multiple Access (CDMA) mobile telecommunication technologies. Responding to three Korean handset makers' requests for discounts (Samsung, LG Electronics, and PANTECH & CURITEL), Qualcomm provided to them loyalty discounts: (1) discounts on SEPs licensing royalty rate conditioned upon the purchase of its modem chips, (2) discounts on modem chips conditioned upon the amount of purchase of these and RF chips, and (3) discounts on RF chips conditioned upon the amount of purchase of them.

In 2009 the KFTC decided that Qualcomm's conditional discounts constitute abuse of dominance and unfair trade practice (the KFTC No. 2009–281 decision, December 30, 2009). In June 2013 the Seoul High Court found that there were no errors in the KFTC's decision.[32] In January 2019, after more than five years since the Seoul High Court's decision, the Supreme Court delivered its decision that partially confirmed the decision.[33]

4.2 Summary of the KFTC's decision

While Qualcomm has dominant power in the Korean domestic market for CDMA technology, it abused its dominance in the domestic market for CDMA modem chip (pp. 32–37). Qualcomm is a dominant undertaking in the domestic markets for modem chip as well as RF chip (pp. 73–79, 133–139).

First, Qualcomm's conditional discounts on SEPs royalty rate (pp. 28–32) constitute "undue discrimination of price or terms of trade, which is not consistent with ordinary trade practices" in AD Guideline IV. 3. Ra. (2), "undue price discrimination" in Decree [Annex Table 1–2] No. 2. Ga, and "undue hindrance of any other undertaking's business" in MRA Art. 3–2 (1) (iii) for the following reasons:

1. SDOs require participants to declare FRAND commitment in order to restrain its dominant power conferred by SEPs. Because FRAND commitment is a tool to prevent abuse of dominance by an SEP holder, an infringement of FRAND commitment itself causes potential anticompetitive effects. Because Qualcomm is a vertically integrated firm, a breach of its FRAND commitment causes the dangerous probability of a foreclosure effect in the CDMA modem chips market (pp. 18, 42–54).
2. UTP Guideline V. 2 describes "undue discrimination" as unfair trade practice in detail. Accordingly, it can be used to define "undue discrimination"

32 Seoul High Court 2000Nu3921 decision, June 19, 2013.

33 Supreme Court 2013Du14726, January 2019.

as abuse of dominance. UTP Guideline V. 2. Ga. (4) explains one of the exemplary cases about "price discrimination" like this: "when an undertaking, selling two or more kinds of products or services, set different price terms on the condition whether a buyer purchases two or more products or service at the same time". Because Qualcomm sold two different things, a service (license) and product (chip), at the same time, conditional discount itself constitutes price discrimination (p. 38). Therefore Qualcomm's conditional discounts – price discrimination – breached its FRAND commitment (p. 41).

3 Because Qualcomm was aware that its FRAND commitment was needed to prevent harm to competition in the chipsets market, its anticompetitive intent is inferred from the infringement of its FRAND commitment (pp. 40–41, 65).
4 With conditional rebate on modem chips, conditional discounts on SEPs royalty caused actual anticompetitive effects: excluding rival chip makers, decreasing diversity of handsets, and decreasing handset consumer's opportunity to choose in the modem chip market (pp. 54–63, 66).

Second, Qualcomm's conditional rebates on modem chip (pp. 67–73) as well as RF chip (pp. 130–132) constitute "undue exclusive dealing" in Decree Art. 5 (5) (ii) and "undue exclusion of a competitor" in MRA Art. 3–2 (1) (v) for the following reasons:

1 Qualcomm had enough power to exclude its competitors. Accordingly, its conditional rebates have the same effect as exclusive dealing (pp. 82–83, 139–141).
2 Qualcomm provided conditional rebate in order to exclude its competitors. From this, Qualcomm's anticompetitive intent is inferred (pp. 84–95, 141–147). With discounts on SEP royalty, conditional rebate on modem chips caused the dangerous possibility of foreclosure effect in the modem chips market (pp. 95–119). With conditional rebate on the modem chips, conditional rebate on RF chips caused the dangerous possibility of foreclosure effect in the RF chips market (pp. 147–157).
3 Conditional rebate on modem chips as well as RF chips caused actual anticompetitive effects: exclusion of rivals, harm to innovation, and restrain of handset makers' and consumers' rights to choose chips. The price-cost tests – to identify whether conditional rebate-adjusted prices are higher than average costs – are not needed in this case (pp. 123–130, 157–171).

4.3 Comment

Before courts, the KFTC argued that Qualcomm's conditional discounts on SEP royalty rate (SEP discounts) offered to "the same buyer" constitutes price discrimination, and therefore the breach of its FRAND commitment. But price discrimination in the context of MRA means charging different prices to "two or more" different buyers for the same quality and quantity of product or service. Accordingly, a conditional discount offered to the same buyer is neither price discrimination for the purpose of MRA nor a breach of FRAND commitment. The Supreme Court indicated that the KFTC and the Seoul High Court did make errors in deciding that Qualcomm's SEP discount constitutes price discrimination (p. 17). Although the Supreme Court did not explicitly mention whether Qualcomm's SEP discounts constitute a breach of its FRAND commitment or not, considering the KFTC's logic that SEP discount constitutes price discrimination and therefore a breach of FRAND commitment, it can be said that the *Qualcomm I* court did not consider Qualcomm's SEP discounts to be a breach of its FRAND commitment.

However, the Supreme Court decided that the KFTC's injunction against Qualcomm's SEP discounts can be justified on the grounds that SEP discounts were conditioned upon the amount of purchase of its modem chip, and conditional discounts on modem chips (modem discounts) caused a foreclosure effect in the modem chip market,[34] even though SEP discounts does not constitute price discrimination (pp. 15–17).

According to the *Qualcomm I* court's logic, conditional discounts should be treated differently from unconditional discounts. But unconditional discounts have the same exclusionary effect as conditional discounts. In the antitrust sense, there is no practical way to distinguish conditional discounts from unconditional discounts if they have the same effect of price discounts. But the court failed to consider that price competition also has a foreclosure or exclusionary effect against rivals. Because the very nature of price competition is to exclude competitors to some degree, it cannot be said that price competition is anticompetitive conduct due to its exclusionary effect. Unless conditional discounts amount to predatory pricing, they should be treated as legitimate price competition, which MRA was designed to protect. The *Qualcomm I* court missed this point.

5 *Microsoft/Nokia* case

5.1 Overview

MRA Art. 7 (1) prohibits mergers and acquisitions (M&A) which may substantially restrain competition. In 2013 Microsoft concluded a contract to acquire the control of Nokia devices and services business except Nokia's patents, and then filed the merger notification with the KFTC. SEPs at issue were Microsoft's 76 patents needed to run the operation system of Android handsets. Samsung expressed its concern that Microsoft might raise its SEPs royalty. After defining two relevant markets (the SEPs licensing market and the mobile handset market), the KFTC

34 However, in regard to Qualcomm's modem discount offered to LG Electronics during some periods, the Supreme Court found that the KFTC had erred in estimating the foreclosure effect, and reversed the Seoul High Court's decision.

suspected that Microsoft – a vertically integrated firm – might expand its dominance in the SEPs licensing market into in the handset market. The antitrust concern of the KFTC was a "potential" foreclosure effect in the handset market.

In 2014 Microsoft submitted its voluntary corrective proposal to the KFTC in order to seek "consent decision", a settlement with the KFTC. Under MRA Art. 51–2, the KFTC may issue consent decision only when two requirements are satisfied: (1) an undertaking's voluntary corrective proposal amounts to the KFTC's corrective measures that would be imposed if the conducts at issue constitutes a violation of MRA; and (2) the proposal is expected to restore fair and free competition or fair trade, or to protect consumers and/or any other undertaking. Deciding that Microsoft's proposal was consistent with the two requirements, the KFTC conditionally approved the Microsoft/Nokia merger (the KFTC No. 2015–316 decision, August 24, 2015).

5.2 *Summary of consent decision on SEPs*

Microsoft must implement its voluntary corrective proposal (p. 1) as below:

1 Microsoft will grant its SEPs on FRAND terms (p. 21).
2 By reason of an infringement of its SEPs, Microsoft will not seek injunctive relief against manufacturers whose headquarters are located in Korea (*Id.*)
3 When granting its SEPs license, Microsoft will not require royalty-free cross licenses (*Id.*)
4 Microsoft will sell its SEPs to a buyer only when the buyer agrees that it will grant the SEPs licenses on FRAND terms, and also it may resell SEPs to a third party only when the third party agrees to grant SEPs license on FRAND terms (*Id.*)

5.3 *Comment*

The KFTC's concern about a potential foreclosure effect was based on monopoly leveraging theory. But the KFTC did not prove any cognizable probability of anticompetitive effects in the handset market. It seems that the KFTC actually placed great weight upon Samsung's concern. Considering that a voluntary corrective proposal should amounts to the KFTC's corrective measures that would be imposed if the conduct at issue constitutes a violation of MRA (Art. 51–2), the KFTC seems to have regarded some conduct of the SEP holder – breaching a FRAND commitment, seeking injunctive relief, or asking for royalty-free cross-license – as anticompetitive conduct.

6 *Qualcomm II* case

6.1 *Overview*

Qualcomm owned some SEPs for 2G-CDMA, 3G-WCDMA, and 4G-LTE mobile telecommunication technologies which were subject to FRAND commitments as well as other non-SEPs for cellular handsets, and manufactured, sold and serviced modem chipsets. As Qualcomm's patented technologies were designed to be implemented at the level of handsets, its chipset product did not contain its license. Accordingly, purchasers of chipsets, manufactured by either Qualcomm or others, were required to obtain licenses from Qualcomm. With handset makers, Qualcomm concluded the licensing agreements for cellular SEPs and other patents. SEPs royalty rate was based on the net selling price of handsets. According to the contract for supplying chipsets to handset makers, Qualcomm held the right to cease supplying chipsets if a handset maker infringes the licensing agreement. On the other hand, Qualcomm concluded covenants not to sue with chipset makers.

In 2017, the KFTC imposed various sanctions, including an administrative fine of approximately USD 854 million, on Qualcomm for alleged breach of FRAND commitment which allegedly amounts to abuse of dominance as well as unfair trade practice (the KFTC No. 2017–025 decision, January 20, 2017).[35] As of March 2019, Qualcomm's appeal case is pending in the Seoul High Court.

6.2 *Summary of the KFTC's decision*

6.2.1 *Abuse of dominance*

A breach of FRAND commitment by a vertically integrated dominant firm holding SEPs in the field of mobile telecommunication industry constitutes abuse of dominance for the following reasons:

1. A FRAND commitment is the only method to control SEP holders' abuse of dominance. A breach of FRAND commitment itself destroys the only method to prohibit anticompetitive conduct, because there exists no alternative technology (pp. 20–21).
2. A breach of FRAND commitment in the field of mobile communication standards directly raises manufacturing costs of both chipsets and handsets. These raised costs would cause anticompetitive effects such as harm to technology innovation, and a decrease in consumer welfare. In addition, a breach of FRAND commitment distorts competition for a technology standard (p. 22).
3. A breach of the FRAND commitment by a vertically integrated firm directly eliminates its competitors in the downstream markets (p. 23).

The relevant market of SEP at issue is defined as Qualcomm's own global market for SEPs license. Qualcomm has monopoly power with 100% market share in its own three global licensing markets for 2G-CDMA SEPs, 3G-WCDMA SEPs and 4G-LTE SEPs. In addition, Qualcomm has dominant power, with around 50% market share, in each of the three global chipset markets. Thus, Qualcomm

35 In this case, Samsung and other implementers had submitted amicus briefs against Qualcomm.

is a vertically integrated dominant firm in the global markets for SEPs as well as chipsets (pp. 92–96).

Qualcomm's business model consists of three categories of conduct as follows:

1 Conduct 1: Refusal to license, covenants not to sue with chipset makers (pp. 41–65).
2 Conduct 2: Requiring handset makers to conclude the license agreements first as a precondition to concluding the contracts for supplying chipsets, and holding the right to cease supplying chipsets if a handset maker breaches the license agreement (pp. 66–72).
3 Conduct 3: Granting portfolio license for cellular SEPs and non-SEPs for cellular handsets, determining SEPs royalty based on the net selling price of handsets, and asking for royalty-free cross-licensing agreements (pp. 72–81).

Because Conducts 1, 2 and 3 constitute one business model, these conducts are organically related to and strengthened by each other. By Conduct 1, Qualcomm has done Conduct 2; by Conduct 2, Qualcomm has done Conduct 3 (pp. 39–40). Therefore, each of the anticompetitive effects caused by each conduct is also organically related and amplified through each of three adjacent markets: the market for SEPs license, market for chipsets and market for handsets. By circulation and amplification of the conduct at issue, their anticompetitive effects are also circulated and amplified in all relevant markets (p. 184).

6.2.2 Unfair trade practice

Conducts 2 and 3 also constitute "abuse of superior bargaining position" in MRA Art. 23 (1) (iv), "giving disadvantageous conditions of trade to the other party" in Decree [Annex Table 1–2] No. 6. Ra, for the following reasons:

1 Qualcomm has a superior bargaining position which substantially influence handset makers' businesses, because of its dominance in the chipsets market (pp. 186–7, 9).
2 Because Conducts 2 and 3 are "unduly coercing any other undertaking to do disadvantageous trade or conduct" as abuse of dominance, they also amount to "giving disadvantageous conditions of trade to the other party" (pp. 187–191).

6.3 Comment

The KFTC's decision is hardly understandable because it relies on too much conjecture rather than sound evidence. First, the KFTC's decision does not seem to satisfy the *POSCO* test for the following reasons:

1 The KFTC just described imaginary risks of anticompetitive effects with conjecture. The KFTC did not actually prove anticompetitive effects: increase of

quality-adjusted prices, decrease of output, harm to innovation, or decrease of diversity in any relevant market.

2 The KFTC confused FRAND commitments with antitrust duty under MRA Art. 3–2 (1). The KFTC wrongly presumed that a breach of FRAND commitment constitutes abuse of dominance, a violation of MRA Art. 3–2 (1). Anticompetitive effects and intent cannot be inferred from a breach of FRAND commitment.

3 The KFTC's decision was based on its own theory of circulation and amplification of anticompetitive conducts. According to this, Conduct 1 (with other anticompetitive Conducts 2 and 3) caused anticompetitive effects, Conduct 2 (with other anticompetitive Conducts 1 and 3) caused anticompetitive effects, and Conduct 3 (with other anticompetitive Conducts 1 and 2) caused anticompetitive effects. This circular logic cannot be acceptable under the *POSCO* test. The fact that Qualcomm's share in all three markets of CDMA, WCDMA, and LTE chipsets had decreased from 2013 through 2015 (p. 94, Table 46) also shows that the KFTC's conjectures were wrong.

As to the FRAND issue, the KFTC is not a civil court. The KFTC lacks a legitimate jurisdiction to decide whether the conduct at issue is a breach of contract. Because FRAND commitment is at most a contractual term, the KFTC lacks the legitimate power to decide whether Qualcomm's conduct is an infringement of its FRAND commitment. Nevertheless, the KFTC did it with a wrong presumption that a breach of FRAND commitment is the same as abuse of dominance. Moreover, because covenants not to sue allowed chipset makers to access Qualcomm's SEPs, Conduct 1 is hardly to be treated as a breach of FRAND commitment. Moreover, SEPs royalty based on the end products, covenants not to sue, and portfolio "fully paid-up royalty free" cross-licensing agreements have been widely accepted in IT industries. It is hard to accept the KFTC's decision that those practices constitute a breach of FRAND commitment.

Lastly, there is the issue of the reach of MRA. The KFTC applied MRA to not only Qualcomm's domestic conducts but also its extraterritorial conducts. MRA Art. 2–2 stipulates: "This Act applies to the extraterritorial conduct when it affects the domestic market". As to the meaning of "affect" in Art. 2–2, considering other countries' sovereignty, the Supreme Court in the international hard core cartel case[36] opined that extraterritorial application of MRA is allowed only when extraterritorial conduct has "direct, substantial, and reasonably foreseeable [antitrust] effect on the domestic market". In other words, even when extraterritorial conduct caused anticompetitive effect in Korea's domestic market, if the effect is indirect, non-substantial, or unforeseeable, MRA cannot be extraterritorially applied. The KFTC did not prove that Qualcomm's extraterritorial conducts each caused "direct, substantial, and reasonably foreseeable anticompetitive effects" in the Korean domestic market. The KFTC simply described it with one

36 Supreme Court Decision 2012Du13689, May 16, 2014.

sentence: Conducts 1, 2, and 3 have direct, substantial, and reasonably foreseeable effects on the domestic market (p. 192).

7 Conclusion

While some worry about "standard holdup", others are concerned about "FRAND holdup" and/or "antitrust holdup". The explosive growth of global IT markets shows that the possibility of standard holdup is quite theoretical. It is undeniable that thanks to SEPs, implementers could concentrate on competition in the secondary markets. Apple's antitrust counterclaim in *Samsung Electronics v. Apple* can be illustrative of FRAND holdup and antitrust holdup. Surprisingly, in the *Qualcomm I* and *II* cases, the KFTC just presumed that an infringement of FRAND commitment constitutes abuse of dominance under MRA. This presumption cannot satisfy the *POSCO* test.

It is important to note that SDOs' FRAND policies cannot alter or change domestic patent laws because they are not international treaty. Therefore, the courts should apply the same legal standards to patents without regard to SEPs or non-SEPs. It is hard to believe that FRAND policy or commitment may restrain an SEP holders' legitimate rights permissible under domestic patent laws. Where FRAND commitments are mistaken for antitrust duty, just like the KFTC has done in two Qualcomm cases, an erroneous antirust intervention is inevitable. The KFTC and courts should be aware that false-positive interventions unduly restrain SEP holders' legitimate rights, thereby retarding the innovation that both the Patent Act and MRA are designed to protect.

11 IPR protection and antitrust regulation of SEPs in China

Liyang Hou and Mengchi Tian

1 Introduction

It is commonly accepted that antitrust law and intellectual property rights (IPRs) law share a common objective: protecting innovation and competition.[1] Although the two are complementary in nature, they nonetheless do conflict with each other. This disharmony comes from the different focus of the two legal mechanisms. Antitrust law[2] sets its focus on the loss of total social welfare, and concerns itself little with individual gains or suffering. As a comparison, IPR law grants individuals exclusive rights to use a property-equivalent right, such as copyright, patent, trade secret or trademark, and cares less about the social interest as a whole. It thus transpires that certain usages of IPRs might not be good for the whole society, or in antitrust terms "relevant markets", and then should be prohibited by the latter. This is particularly true for standard essential patents (SEPs), thus establishing an arena for the interplay between public interest and private interest. While the interests of patent holders should be protected, the presence of SEP holdup, including abusing injunctions and charging excessive royalty fees, triggers a debate over whether an unlimited use of SEP may not only damage the interest of the patentees but also negatively affect the production and sales of SEP-implementing products in the downstream market, thus ultimately impairing consumer welfare and public interests. Therefore, whether the licensing of SEPs should be regulated in a way different from other patents has become a thorny issue.

The underlying legal concerns are mainly twofold. First, a limit put on the use of IPRs hinders innovation to a greater or lesser extent. IPRs are only temporarily exclusive and will enter the public domain in the end. They are not like tangible property to which private ownership is protected without time limit. It hence might not be worth enforcing competition law in particular when focus is given to the temporary nature of IPRs' anti-competitive effects,

1 Rita Coco, Antitrust Liability for Refusal to License Intellectual Property: A Comparative Analysis and the International Setting, 12 *Marquette Intellectual Prop. L. Rev.* 3–47 (2008).

2 Within this chapter, competition law, antitrust law and anti-monopoly law are used synonymously.

if any. Second, there is no clear borderline between public interest and private interest. Antitrust intervention aims at protecting public interest, while IPRs focus on private interest protection. The private interest of IPR owners must be adversely affected by antitrust intervention. However, it is uncertain whether antitrust intervention may increase public interest at a scale similar to or bigger than the affected private interest. Consequently, antitrust intervention can be justified only if it offers added value to IP laws. In addition, all the long-standing antitrust principles have been built on enforcement against tangible property. Consequently, a different analytical framework should be established when moving to IPRs.[3]

It goes without saying that the balance between antitrust law and IPR law is achieved in divergent ways across jurisdictions. This chapter aims to shed some light on the relevant practice on SEPs in the People's Republic of China (China). Section 2 explores SEP-related patent infringement cases from three aspects, namely non-infringement defense, counter-injunction defense and compensation for damages. The following two sections focus on the antitrust regulation of SEPs, with section 3 exploring related practice of abuse of dominance and section 4 reviewing cases of merger control. Section 5 concludes.

2 SEP-related patent infringements

Patent infringement lawsuits play an important role in patent protection. Patentees can protect their private right by claiming tort liabilities. SEP is no exception. From this perspective, SEP infringements do not bear too much distinctiveness compared with ordinary patents in terms of the application of a certain defense or civil liability. This has been observed throughout the judicial practice in China. However, differences still remain. The Chinese judiciary has also made some development in determining the amount of reasonable compensation.

2.1 Non-infringement defense

As far as SEP infringement cases are concerned, the first question to be clarified is whether disputed patents involving a technical standard justify a non-infringement defense – in other words, whether a license granted by patentees is a precondition to use SEPs. In this regard, the laws and regulations in China have not stated an answer expressly yet, and the judicial practice has been changing over the past years and is still vague for the time being.

In 2008, China's Supreme People's Court took on this question and held that, if the patentee participates in the formulation of a standard and agrees to incorporate its patents into the national, industrial or local standard, it will be deemed

3 Liyang Hou, The Essential Facilities Doctrine – What Was Wrong in Microsoft? 43(4) *Int'l J. Intellectual Prop. & Competition L.* 251–271 (2012).

that the patentee has permitted others to use its patents after the standard takes effect; and the subsequent use by others does not constitute patent infringements stipulated in Article 11 of the Patent Law.[4, 5] Consequently, the fact that disputed patents have been incorporated into standards constitutes a non-infringement defense. In addition, the Supreme People's Court also made a comment on the royalty fee in this reply. It stated that while the patentees are indeed allowed to charge the implementers a certain royalty fee, the amount should be significantly lower than the normal license fees. If the patentee has promised to waive the royalties during the standard setting process, he/she may not renounce this promise later.

However, the precedential effect of this reply was challenged quickly afterwards. One year later in the *Zhang Jingting v. Ziya River* case, the plaintiff, Mr. Zhang Jingting, was the owner of the disputed patent which was incorporated into the Construction Design Standard of Hebei Province. The defendant, Ziya River Company (Ziya), was the constructor who used the disputed patent without obtaining permission from Mr. Zhang during the construction of a residential building. Mr. Zhang claimed that Ziya violated his patent right and therefore should cease the infringement and compensate for his losses. The court of first instance held that patents involving technical standards could be used on the condition of prior license. Hence, Ziya shall be liable for the infringing conduct.[6] However, the court of appeal cited the aforementioned reply of the Supreme People's Court, and reversed the first judgment based on the fact that, since the disputed patent has been incorporated into a local standard and the patentee participated in the formulation process, it shall be deemed that Mr. Zhang has permitted others to use his patent; consequently Ziya did not violate the Patent Law.[7] Afterwards, Mr. Zhang applied for retrial to the Supreme People's Court. The Supreme People's Court held that the fact that the patentee agreed to incorporate their patents into the local standard does not mean that they are obliged to grant free licenses to anyone implementing this standard. Instead, SEPs shall be exploited on the condition of a prior license with a settled royalty fee in accordance with the principle of FRAND (fair, reasonable and non-discriminatory). Accordingly, patentees were held to be entitled to seek remedies through the judiciary in the case of a patent infringement.[8] Since then, it has become ambiguous as to whether implementers are required to obtain a prior license for SEPs before using them.

4 Patent Law of the People's Republic of China (2008 Amendment), [2008] Presidential Order No. 8, December 27, 2008, Article 11.

5 The Supreme People's Court, A Reply, July 8, 2008, [2008] Min San Ta Zi No. 4.

6 Shijiazhuang Intermediate People's Court, *Zhang Jingting v. Ziya River*, [2009] Shi Min Wu Chu Zi No. 163.

7 Hebei High People's Court, *Zhang Jingting v. Ziya River*, March 27, 2011, [2011] Ji Min San Zhong Zi No. 15.

8 Supreme People's Court, *Zhang Jingting v. Ziya River*, January 12, 2014, [2012] Min Ti Zi No. 125.

Three years later, courts in Beijing trying the *Iwncomm v. Sony* case had to answer this question again.[9] The plaintiff, Iwncomm, was the patentee whose technologies had become a widely adopted standard in the local wireless industry in China. It was claimed by Iwncomm that Sony violated its patent rights by using the patents in question for a long time without acquiring a license from Iwncomm or paying any royalty fees. The judgment of the first instance followed the logic of the Supreme Court's judgment in the *Zhang Jingting v. Ziya River* case, and maintained that the constitutive requirement of patent infringement will not be changed due to the standardization. Using even an SEP without permission still amounts to a patent infringement. Furthermore, the court of first instance also held that the FRAND statement made by the patentee during the standardization process is a unilateral act, and does not formulate a license agreement. However, the second instance judgment made by the Beijing High People's Court reached the same conclusion, but with different reasoning. The court of appeal distinguished mandatory standards from recommended standards, and held that SEPs within mandatory standards are obligatory, and hence can be used directly without permission. In contrast, SEPs within recommended standards are not eligible for a non-infringement defense. According to Article 24.1 of Interpretation (II) of the Supreme People's Court on Several Issues concerning the Application of Law in the Trial of Patent Infringement Dispute Cases, with regard to any recommended national, industrial or local standard where SEPs are involved, the defense that it does not infringe the patent right due to the implementation of such standard shall not be accepted by the courts.[10] In this case, since the patent in question was incorporated into a national mandatory standard, a prior license should then not have been necessary. However, the appeal court took a further look at the effectiveness of this mandatory standard, concluded that the standard involved should be regarded as a recommended standard in nature, and consequently dismissed the non-infringement defense.

To conclude, the re-trial judgment of *Zhang Jingting v. Ziya River* reversed the previous view of the Supreme People's Court, and rejected the statement that the fact that a patent has been incorporated into a standard suggests that the patentee permits anyone else who implements the standard to use its patents without a prior license. Furthermore, the first-instance judgment of *Iwncomm v. Sony* clarified that whether the patents in question are essential in a technical standard is not relevant to the analysis of patent infringement, and that it cannot be inferred from the FRAND statement that a licensing agreement has been concluded after SEPs are incorporated into a standard. Subsequently, the Beijing High People's Court made a distinction between mandatory standards

9 Beijing Intellectual Property Court, *Iwncomm v. Sony*, March 22, 2017, [2015] Jing Zhi Min Chu Zi No. 1194; and Beijing High People's Court, *Iwncomm v. Sony*, March 28, 2018, [2017] Jing Min Zhong No. 454.

10 Interpretation (II) of the Supreme People's Court on Several Issues concerning the Application of Law in the Trial of Patent Infringement Dispute Cases [2016] Judicial Interpretation No. 1, March 21, 2016.

and recommended standards. In case of mandatory standards, a prior license is not necessary before using such patents, which was consistent with the opinion of the first-instance court. In comparison, prior permission becomes necessary where recommended standards are involved. Unfortunately, the appeal court did not explain the reason behind such a distinction. There is still uncertainty, since the appeal court judgment is not in tune with the Supreme Court's opinion in *Zhang Jingting v. Ziya River*.

2.2 *Counter-injunction defense*

In addition to the difference in the requirement for prior permission, the factors to evaluate whether an injunction should be granted are also different between ordinary patent infringement cases and SEP infringement ones. This was particularly provided for in the Guideline to the Determination of Patent Infringements [2017] ("the Beijing Guideline"), published by the Beijing High People's Court in 2017. Later, the Beijing Guideline played an important role in *Iwncomm v. Sony*, reviewed by the Beijing High People's Court.[11]

The provisions concerning counter-injunction defense in the Beijing Guideline roughly cover four aspects: (1) the definition and scope of SEPs; (2) the basic obligations of the negotiating parties; (3) the analytical framework to determine the imposition of injunctions; and (4) the factors to assess the fault of the parties.

2.2.1 *The definition and scope of SEPs*

First, the Beijing Guideline defines SEP as "a patent that must be used in implementing a technical standard". The term "must" emphasizes the irreplaceable nature of the patent in meeting the relevant technical standards. As for the denotation of SEPs, the Beijing Guideline first clarifies the scope of the "technical standards", including, for example, (1) recommended national, industrial or local standards and (2) standards established by the International Organization for Standardization (ISO) or other standard organizations, where the patentee has made a FRAND commitment. Moreover, the Beijing Guideline defines the SEP as patents that are expressly involved in and essential to the aforementioned standards. The "expressly" herein shall be evaluated in accordance with industry practices and policies of standard organizations.[12]

2.2.2 *The basic obligations of the negotiating parties*

Subsequently, the Beijing Guideline imposes the basic obligations upon parties in the SEP licensing negotiations. Adherence to the principle of good faith remains

11 Beijing High People's Court, *Iwncomm v. Sony*, March 28, 2018, [2017] Jing Min Zhong No. 454.

12 The Beijing Guideline, Article 149.

the primary obligation of both parties. Besides, the patentees who have been subject to the FRAND obligations shall comply with the obligations all the time, and bear the burden to prove the specific contents of the obligations where these are subject to dispute.[13]

2.2.3 *The analytical framework to determine the imposition of injunction*

Next, regarding injunctions, the key in the analytical framework of the Beijing Guideline is to evaluate and compare the degree of fault of both parties. Specifically, if the patentee violates the obligations under its commitment intentionally, while the alleged infringer is not at fault, the accused infringer would not be subject to an injunction.[14] A cease and desist order would normally not be granted if both parties are not at fault, and the defendant without delay submits to the courts the claimed royalty fee or a guarantee no less than the amount of the claimed royalty fee.[15] If both parties are at fault, the court should analyze and compare the degree of fault of both parties, determine which party assumes the primary responsibility for hindering the licensing negotiation, and finally conclude whether the alleged infringer shall be subject to an injunction.[16] As for the circumstance where only the alleged infringer is at fault, although the Beijing Guideline does not specifically elaborate on this, it can be inferred from the aforementioned analytical framework that the alleged infringer shall be injuncted from using the disputed patents.

2.2.4 *The factors to assess the fault of the parties*

Lastly, the Beijing Guideline provides several specific factors to assess the degree of fault of both parties, including but not limited to (1) prior notice of infringement; (2) initiation and facilitation of licensing negotiations; and (3) other behaviors with obvious faults. To be more specific, before initiating the lawsuit the patentee shall notify the alleged infringer of the infringement in writing, and specify the scope and the method of the infringement act. The alleged infringer should respond within a reasonable time after receiving the notice. The party who fails to comply with these obligations shall be deemed at fault. In terms of the initiation and facilitation of licensing negotiations, the Beijing Guideline specifies that, after the alleged infringer expresses its willingness to participate in the licensing negotiation, the patentee should provide the information on patents, put forward licensing conditions and come up with a reasonable time limit for the subsequent reply in accordance with business practices and trading habits.

13 *Id.* Article 150–151.
14 *Id.* Article 149.
15 *Id.* Article 152.
16 *Id.* Article 153.

The alleged infringer shall reply within a reasonable time indicating whether it accepts the licensing conditions proposed by the patentee; if not, it shall put forward a new proposal about the licensing conditions. In addition, it shall be deemed as behavior with obvious fault where any party obstructs, delays, interrupts or refuses to participate in the licensing negotiations without justification, and/or insists on unreasonable trading conditions which account for the breakdown in negotiation.[17]

2.2.5 *Comments*

Based on the aforementioned provisions, there are both similarities and divergences between the infringement disputes involved SEPs and those of ordinary patents in terms of the imposition of injunctions. On the one hand, SEPs and ordinary patents share the common nature of private rights. Thus, the possibility of injunctions shall not be excluded completely in disputes, even if involving SEPs. If the alleged infringer fails to negotiate with the patentee in good faith while using the patents concerned without paying royalty fees, civil liability must be imposed to stop such infringement. Therefore, the Beijing Guideline maintains the possibility of imposing injunctions when the alleged infringer is obviously responsible for the discontinuance of the licensing negotiation. On the other hand, since it is impossible to avoid the use of SEPs when implementing technical standards before obtaining the license, the patentee may thus be able to force the alleged infringer to accept excessively high royalty fees or other unreasonable conditions by means of litigation. If there is no limit on the granting of injunctions, the patentee might be overprotected to the detriment of the implementers, and thus may grab excessive profits that exceed a reasonable return on its innovation. Therefore, the Beijing Guideline imposes strict conditions on the application of such remedy. Especially where both parties are at fault, the courts shall not order the alleged infringer to refrain from using the disputed patents so long as it submits a reasonable amount of royalty fee or provides a guarantee no less than that amount to the court. The fundamental arrangement for SEPs is to make them accessible to all potential licensees. In other words, as long as the alleged infringer has no intention of infringement or holdout, or expresses its willingness to negotiate by submitting royalty fee or providing guarantee in a reasonable amount (the reasonable amount is to be decided by courts and not by the infringer), the use of SEPs in question, even without prior permission, shall not be prohibited.

Injunctions shall not be granted in SEP infringement disputes, unless the fault of the alleged infringer is more serious than that of the patentee. Therefore, how to assess the degree of fault between both parties becomes the key issue. In *Iwncomm v. Sony*, where Iwncomm applied to the court for ordering Sony to stop using disputed patents, the judgment made by Beijing High People's Court followed the analytical framework established in the Beijing Guideline and identified

17 *Id*. Article 152–153.

misdeed mainly on the basis of the parties' performance during the licensing negotiation. The matters obstructing their negotiation were that Sony requested that Iwncomm provide the claim charts, and that Iwncomm insisted that Sony sign a non-disclosure agreement. The Beijing High People's Court held that claim charts were not essential to the negotiation. Since Iwncomm had submitted patent lists and expressed its willingness to provide any reasonable assistance, Sony should have been able to identify whether it used the disputed patents in the process of production without claim charts. Therefore, it was not reasonable for Sony to ask Iwncomm for the claim charts. In addition, Sony delayed the negotiation deliberately, failed to submit royalty fee or provide guarantee to the court, and therefore shall be deemed at obvious fault. With regard to the request to sign non-disclosure agreements, the court held that this was a common practice before providing claim charts, since claim charts usually involve core secrets of the patentee. Consequently, Iwncomm's requirement of non-disclosure agreements was reasonable. Besides, Iwncomm had fulfilled its obligations as a patentee by explaining the technologies related to WAPI, providing the patent lists and clarifying the licensing conditions. Therefore, Iwncomm was not the party to blame. In the end, the court held that Sony was responsible for the breakdown in licensing negotiation, and consequently imposed an injunction on Sony.

2.3 Compensation for damages

2.3.1 Comparable royalties versus the gains which the infringer has obtained from the infringement

According to Article 65 of the Patent Law, in order to determine the amount of compensation, the court shall choose the subsequent methods in the following order: (1) the actual losses incurred by the patentee; (2) if it is not possible to calculate the loss, the gains which the infringer has obtained from the infringement; (3) where both the loss and the gains cannot be confirmed, certain times of the royalties for licensing the patents; and (4) when all the previous methods cannot work, statutory damages between RMB 10,000 and RMB 1 million. Since it is in principle difficult to determine the loss incurred by the patentee as well as the gains obtained by the infringer, and the amount of money involved in SEPs infringement disputes is often huge, the courts often refer to the approach of determining compensation based on a certain multiplier of licensing royalties to other licensees, obviously exceeding RMB 1 million.[18]

In *Iwncomm v. Sony*,[19] the patentee Iwncomm submitted four license agreements signed with others who were not related to the case. Subsequently, the

18 For example, the damages decided by Beijing Intellectual Property Court in case *Iwncomm v. Sony* amounted to RMB 8,629,173 yuan.

19 Beijing Intellectual Property Court, *Iwncomm v. Sony*, March 22, 2017, [2015] Jing Zhi Min Chu Zi No. 1194; and Beijing High People's Court, *Iwncomm v. Sony*, March 28, 2018, [2017] Jing Min Zhong No. 454.

court assessed the geographical scope, time scope and core patents involved in the four agreements, and concluded that these agreements were comparable with the license contract in question. Therefore, the court held that the reasonable royalty fee shall be RMB 1 yuan per unit as stipulated in the aforementioned agreements, and the amount of compensation shall be three times this royalty fee.

In *Huawei v. InterDigital*,[20] since compensation for tort damage was not the key issue in this case, the courts in Guangdong had first established that the determination of royalty fee should be compatible with the FRAND principle, and then the following factors should be considered: (1) the contribution of the disputed SEPs to the technical innovation concerned; (2) the ratio between the amount of royalty fee and the sales profits of the products; (3) the added value after being incorporated into the standard; (4) other relevant factors. Subsequently, when considering the requirement of non-discrimination, the court adopted the comparable license method as aforementioned. In this regard, the court referred to the licensing fees between InterDigital and Apple, Samsung and others. Since the licensing rates between InterDigital and Samsung were concluded under litigation, while those of Apple were the result of equal and voluntary negotiation, the court held that the licensing rate of 0.0187% between InterDigital and Apple was more comparable in this case. Finally, taking into consideration the different scope of licensing and the accumulation of royalties and other relevant factors, the court in the end determined the FRAND licensing rate to be 0.019%.

The reasoning for the decisions in *Huawei v. Samsung* rendered by the court in Fujian[21] was different from the preceding case. When determining the amount of compensation, the main method adopted by the court was to estimate the gains which the infringer has obtained from the infringement rather than calculating the normal royalty fees. First, the court evaluated the sales volume and profit of the products in question based on the evidence submitted by the parties, and then inferred that the earnings of the defendant fell into the range of RMB 2.65 billion to RMB 10.11 billion. Thereafter, the court made a qualitative assessment on the value contribution of the disputed patents to the final product. The court held that the disputed patents were core patents of the graphics operations page, which contributed substantially to the profit of intelligent mobile devices. In addition, although the disputed patents were not SEPs, they had been widely used by the final products and gained popular acceptance from consumers. After taking all the above into consideration, the court supported the compensation claim of RMB 80 million submitted by the patentee.

20 Shenzhen Intermediate People's Court, *Huawei v. InterDigital*, February 4, 2013, [2011] Shen Zhong Fa Zhi Min Chu Zi No. 857; and Guangdong High People's Court, *Huawei v. InterDigital*, October 16, 2013, [2013] Yue Gao Fa Min San Zhong Zi No. 305.

21 Quanzhou Intermediate People's Court, *Huawei v. Samsung*, March 29, 2017, [2016] Min 05 Min Chu No. 725; and Fujian High People's Court, *Huawei v. Samsung*, December 22, 2017, [2017] Min Zhong No. 501.

2.3.2 Comments

It can be observed from the preceding three cases that there are two major methods to determine the amount of compensation for cases involving SEPs or SEP-like patents in the judicial practice of China. One is to calculate the normal royalties of disputed patents plus damages, and the other is to estimate the gains which the infringer had obtained from the infringement. The former involves the judicial determination of the SEP license fee by mainly referencing comparable licenses. However, the method of comparable license may not work effectively due to poor comparability of referenced agreements. In reality, the differences between licensing transactions can be significant due to the number of patents, the method of payment, the scope of licensing and so on. For instance, in *Huawei v. InterDigital*, although the contract between InterDigital and Apple was reached on an equal and voluntary basis, and thus should be more comparable than others, the agreement featured a lump sum of royalty fee in 2007 when the expected sales of Apple's products was quite uncertain. Therefore, the court held that it was not favorable for the patentee to take this agreement as a reference to determine the licensing rate.

The second method of estimating the profits obtained from the infringement is generally equal to evaluating the contribution of the disputed patents to the profits of the final products. There is hence a common point between the calculation method in *Huawei v. Samsung* and the top-down method for determining SEP license fee.[22] Both of them first require the estimation of the total sales profit of products in question, and then analyze the value contribution of disputed patents to this profit. However, the difference between them is also crucial. The top-down method requires accurately figuring out the proportion of total patent fees in the profit, and the value of disputed SEPs in the total patent fees. For example, in *In re Innovatio*,[23] the court first calculated the profit of the patented products, and then identified the contribution by dividing the number of Innovatio patents by the total number of SEPs. By contrast, in *Huawei v. Samsung*, the court only provided a qualitative description of the value contribution, which although it avoids the difficulty and infeasibility of quantitative analysis, adds ambiguity and uncertainty to the determination of the amount of compensation. In sum, both methods have their own advantages and disadvantages. Which one to choose depends on the context of specific cases, and further clarification is needed from the judicial practice in the future.

22 Jorge L. Contreras & Mengchi Tian, Global Standard War: Patent and Competition Disputes in North America, Europe and Asia, 1 *Competition L. Policy Rev.* 101–130 (2018).

23 U.S. District Court for the Northern District of Illinois, Eastern Division, *In re Innovatio IP Ventures, LLC*, September 27, 2013, No. 11 C 9308.

3 SEP-related abuse

The antitrust enforcement in China has been developed much more quickly since the Anti-monopoly Law (AML) was adopted in 2008 than most jurisdictions where antitrust enforcement was almost dormant in the initial years. The antitrust enforcement related to SEP can be divided into two categories, one of abuse of dominant market power and the other of merger control. With regard to the first category, there is a regulation issued by the State Administration for Industry and Commerce (SAIC),[24] a former competition agency in China,[25] a case of private enforcement and another of public enforcement, and a guideline published by the Guangdong High People's Court. The SAIC and the court's guideline offer some specific guidance on abusive conduct regarding SEPs. The *Huawei v. InterDigital* cases[26] adjudicated by the Guangdong courts in 2013, and the Qualcomm case decided by the National Development of Reform Commission (NDRC), another former competition agency in China, in 2015, dealt with price-related abusive conduct. The second category contains a body of merger reviews conducted by the Ministry of Commerce (MOFCOM), also a former Chinese competition authority. It will be discussed in a subsequent section.

3.1 SAIC Regulation

The SAIC Regulation comprises 19 articles and may be divided into five parts: (a) goals and principles; (b) analytical approach; (c) safe harbors; (d) abuse of dominance; and (e) investigation procedures. It is promulgated with the purpose of clarifying the uncertainties left by Article 55 of the AML, which contains a very general principle that prohibits "abuses of IPRs" which eliminate or restrict competition, while the use of IPRs is exempted from the AML. It starts by pointing out that the AML and IPR laws have the shared goals of promoting innovation and competition, improving efficiency, and safeguarding the interests of consumers and the public interest.[27]

24 SAIC, "Regulation on the Prohibition of Abusing Intellectual Property Rights to Eliminate or Restrict Competition" (SAIC Regulation), SAIC Order Nr 74 [2015].

25 There were three competition agencies in China before 2018, namely the National Development and Reform Commission, the State Administration for Industry and Commerce, and the Ministry of Commerce. In the governmental reconstruction in 2018, all three competition agencies were integrated into the new State Administration for Market Regulation directly under the State Council.

26 Shenzhen Intermediate People's Court, *Huawei v. InterDigital*, February 4, 2013, [2011] Shen Zhong Fa Zhi Min Chu Zi No. 857; and No. 858; and Guangdong High People's Court, *Huawei v. InterDigital*, October 16, 2013, [2013] Yue Gao Fa Min San Zhong Zi No. 305 and Guangdong High People's Court, *Huawei v. InterDigital*, October 21, 2013, [2013] Yue Gao Fa Min San Zhong Zi No. 306.

27 SAIC Regulation (n 24), Article 2.

The SAIC Regulation puts forward a five-step analysis.[28] When investigating, the SAIC needs to identify the characteristics and form of the conduct and the type of relationship (i.e. horizontal or vertical) between the companies involved, to define the relevant market, and to examine the market positions of the parties concerned. As the fifth and last step, the SAIC needs to appraise the impact of the conduct on competition in the relevant market. Factors to assess the impact on competition include (1) the companies' market position vis-à-vis trading partners; (2) the degree of market concentration; (3) entry barriers; (4) industry practices and the level of development; (5) the duration and scope of restraints to competition; (6) the impact on innovation and technology dissemination; and (7) the innovation capacity and dynamics of technological change.

The SAIC Regulation contains provisions which prevent dominant undertakings from refusing to license patents after they have become essential utilities,[29] from issuing exclusive licensing,[30] tying-in,[31] attaching unreasonable trading conditions[32] or practicing discriminatory strategies.[33] In addition, Article 13 deals specifically with the interaction between the exercise of IPRs and standards. It first sets out the general principle that undertakings may not adopt conduct to exclude or restrict competition during the process of setting and implementing standards, including mandatory demands of national technical requirements, while exercising IPRs (paragraph 1). It then provides two specific prohibitions, unless justifications can be provided (paragraph 2). The first one concerns patent assertion after the patent has been included in the standard despite having deliberately failed to disclose information and/or expressly "giving up" the right to assert the patent during the standard setting process. The second prohibition takes aim at conduct that excludes or restricts competition by violating the FRAND principle after its patent has become SEP, such as refusing to license, tying in other products, or licensing under unfair conditions. However, the SIAC has never applied the Regulation in any cases since its adoption. The NDRC has thus far not adopted any guideline, but applied AML on one SEP patentee. Similarly, in 2018 the Guangdong High People's Court has issued Guidelines on Adjudicating Cases of Disputes Over Standard-Essential Patents.

3.2 Huawei v. InterDigital

This case was one of many lawsuits filed by Huawei against InterDigital around the globe.[34] InterDigital's main business was to license patents on mobile

28 *Id.* Article 15.
29 *Id.* Article 7.
30 *Id.* Article 8.
31 *Id.* Article 9.
32 *Id.* Article 10.
33 *Id.* Article 11.
34 Alison Jones, Standard-Essential Patents: FRAND Commitments, Injunctions and the Smartphone Wars, 10 *Eur. Competition J.* (2014).

communications standards, including both SEPs and non-SEPs. Huawei, while also owning SEPs on mobile communications, is mainly a communication equipment producer. Huawei sued InterDigital on two accounts based on the Patent Law and the AML, respectively.[35] With its antitrust claims, Huawei submitted that InterDigital (1) set unreasonably high royalty rates for its patents; (2) applied unreasonable discriminatory royalty rates; (3) required free cross-licensing of Huawei's patents; (4) tied SEPs with non-SEPs; and (5) refused to license its patents by filing injunction applications with relevant U.S. authorities. Huawei's claims, except the fifth one, were supported by both the court of first instance and the court of appeal in Guangdong Province, China.

The courts first defined the relevant markets based on demand-side and supply-side substitution. The relevant markets were defined as every SEP owned by InterDigital in relation to mobile communications standards. The courts held that there were no actual or potential substitutes for SEPs. Without those SEPs, Huawei could not produce the related products. Consequently, every SEP was unique, and could not be substituted. Furthermore, from the perspective of supply-side substitution, InterDigital was the only supplier on the relevant market. There was no possibility for Huawei to switch to other competitors.

After having defined the relevant markets as every SEP, the determination of InterDigital's dominant market position was of no surprise. As the only supplier in every relevant market, there were no actual or potential competitors for InterDigital; therefore, the courts made a quick conclusion that InterDigital was dominant in all the relevant markets.

The last step was to evaluate whether InterDigital abused its dominant position. The courts first examined the issue of unreasonably high royalty rates. Their analysis was mainly based on a comparison with the royalty rates given to other firms, such as Apple, Samsung, RIM and HTC. The courts found that the rates proposed to Huawei were at least seven times higher than the ones offered to other firms. InterDigital did not provide any evidence to justify the higher rates proposed to Huawei with cost reasons. Consequently, the courts ruled that the proposed high royalty rates constituted unreasonably high prices under the AML.

With regards to tying, the courts first looked at the tying of SEPs with non-SEPs, which fell into the scope of tying under Article 17 of the AML, and opined that non-SEPs were possible substitutes. Its tying with non-SEPs may allow InterDigital to leverage its market power in the market for SEPs to non-SEPs market. Subsequently, the courts examined Huawei's claim that it was also tying under the AML to license the SPEs on a global basis, as Huawei has asked for licensing agreement only for China and the U.S. The courts affirmed that such a global license could decrease transaction costs for international firms, and remains a common practice in the industry, and is therefore not an antitrust violation.

In the end, the courts required InterDigital to cease its conduct regarding unreasonably high rates and tying. It is interesting to note that the courts set a

35 See (n 20).

specific FRAND rate. The applicable royalty rate for the licensing of the standard essential Chinese patents was determined at 0.019%, down significantly from the royalty rate initially required by InterDigital.[36]

3.3 NDRC against Qualcomm

The *Qualcomm* case was handled by the NDRC, and also related to SEPs of mobile communications standards.[37] Qualcomm is a firm with much stronger market power regarding mobile communication SEPs than InterDigital. Different from InterDigital, Qualcomm is also an active player for baseband chips. The NDRC held Qualcomm liable for its abusive behavior, and imposed a fine of RMB 6.088 billion, a record for antitrust fines in China until now.

Without having reference to *Huawei v. InterDigital*, the NDRC defined the relevant market for mobile communication SEPs in the same manner and based on the same logic as *Huawei v. InterDigital*: every SEP owned by Qualcomm is a relevant market. The relevant geographic market was defined as national (including both China and the U.S.) because IPR regulations were national. Such a market definition resulted in an inevitable conclusion that Qualcomm was dominant in the relevant markets by reason of its 100% market shares, its ability to control the market, no countervailing buying power and high entry barriers.

Due to Qualcomm's prominent presence in the baseband chips market, the NDRC also defined a relevant market for baseband chips, and designated Qualcomm as the dominant firm there. The major reasons were the following. First, Qualcomm's market share was well above 50%, consistently much higher than the second biggest player, MTK, which had only 15.5% market share. Second, Qualcomm enjoyed competitive advantages in technologies, product performance and strong brand name. All of these made it an unavoidable firm for mobile equipment producers on the downstream market. Finally, entry barriers to this market proved extremely high. No potential competitors could enter the market in the short term. The geographic market was defined as worldwide. Although the conclusion on the geographic market in this case seemed different from *Huawei v. InterDigital*, the reasoning in the two cases was the same. Due to the restraints of IPR regulations, both cases acknowledged that the geographic market should be national. However, in *Huawei v. InterDigital* the disputed conduct took place only in China and the U.S., and thus the geographic market was defined in accordance with the claims. In the current case, since the NDRC investigated Qualcomm's behavior across the world, the geographic market was then defined as the aggregation of all the national markets, hence worldwide.

36 NDRC also made an investigation against InterDigital, which however ended in a settlement, as InterDigital has put forward commitments (NDRC 214).

37 Case *Qualcomm*, NDRC [2015] Nr.1, February 9, 2015.

Subsequently, the NDRC investigated three types of abusive behavior, unreasonably high royalty rates, tying SEPs with non-SEPs, and attaching unreasonable trading conditions respectively.

With regard to unreasonably high royalty rates, the NDRC did not examine whether the royalty rates imposed by Qualcomm were excessively high per se, or discriminatory as the courts did in *Huawei v. InterDigital*. Rather, the NDRC specifically reviewed two issues. First, Qualcomm, when licensing its patents, did not offer a list of patents to its trading partners, and forced its partners to pay royalty fees for expired patents, dismissing Qualcomm's claim that new patents were frequently added into the patent portfolio, as those new patents were not of similar value to the invalid patents. The NDRC ruled that it was illegal to require trading partners to pay royalty fees for expired patents. Second, when licensing its patents Qualcomm constantly required free cross-license from its trading partners. Since cross-license should not be free but paid on a competitive market setting, Qualcomm request was an abuse of its dominance. The NDRC concluded that Qualcomm's pricing strategy fell under the scope of unreasonably high prices within the AML.

Similar to the conduct analyzed in the previous paragraph, the second type of abusive conduct concerned tying SEPs with non-SEPs, which was also one of Qualcomm's long-time business strategies. The NDRC identified the anti-competitive effects of such a tying-in from two aspects. First, it limited the licensees' freedom of choice, and forced them to pay more than they might actually need. Second, it could foreclose the market of non-SEPs against actual and potential competitors.

3.4 Guangdong Guideline

In order to handle SEP-related disputes involving mobile communications, the Guangdong High People's Court in 2018 issued the Guideline on Adjudicating Disputes on Standard Essential Patents ("the Guangdong Guideline").[38] This Guideline consists of four parts: (a) fundamental issues, (b) injunctions, (c) royalty rates and (d) monopolistic disputes involving SEPs.

3.4.1 Fundamental issues

First and foremost, the term SEP is defined as "a patent that must be used in implementing a technical standard",[39] which is the same as the definition maintained by the Beijing Guideline. The Guangdong Guideline then provides that the principle of good faith, the FRAND commitments made by the patent holders and the IPR policies implemented by the standards organizations are most

38 Guangdong High People's Court, The Guideline on Adjudicating Disputes on Standard Essential Patents (Trial), available at www.gaohangip.com/article/3187.html.

39 The Guangdong Guideline, Article 1.

relevant to evaluating cases involving SEPs.[40] It is also stipulated that, if the patent holders are changed due to inheritance, transfer and so forth, the FRAND commitments made by the original patent holders shall be binding also on the successor and/or assignee.[41] In addition, the laws or regulations where the courts are located and where the protection is claimed shall be applicable in general when interpreting the FRAND commitments, defining the scope of the rights and determining the nature of the disputed conducts.[42]

3.4.2 Injunctions

The Guangdong Guideline sets four conditions for SEP-related injunctions. First, the court should identify the specific content of the standard in question, and then determine whether the disputed patents are SEPs. Second, if there is evidence that the alleged infringing products meet the standard involving the disputed SEPs, it can be presumed that the products in question fall into the scope of the SEP claims. Third, if the alleged infringer denies that the products in question fall into the scope of the SEP claims, he/she shall provide evidence to prove that the disputed SEPs have not been implemented.[43] Fourth, the patent holders' and the implementers' conduct should be assessed to see if they are compatible with the FRAND principle and common commercial practice. Moreover, the methods and considerations listed within the Guangdong Guideline are similar to the Beijing Guideline.[44]

3.4.3 Royalty rates

The Guangdong Guideline also sheds some light on how to calculate FRAND royalty rates. The subsequent methods are specified: (1) to refer to a comparable licensing agreement; (2) to analyze the market value of the disputed SEPs; (3) to refer to the licensing information in a comparable patent pool; and (4) other methods.[45] Furthermore, the guideline also specifies factors that should employed to evaluate every method. Comparable licensing agreements should be evaluated by referring to factors such as the parties concerned, subject matters, patents involved in the royalty rates and so forth.[46] The comparison with other patent pools should allow for reasonable differences between the licensing agreements concerned and other ones.[47] The market value of a patent within a standard should be calculated based on the total value of the standard and the

40 *Id.* Article 2–3, 5–7.
41 *Id.* Article 4.
42 *Id.* Article 8.
43 *Id.* Article 9.
44 *Id.* Article 10–14.
45 *Id.* Article 18.
46 *Id.* Article 20.
47 *Id.* Article 21–22.

contribution of the patent concerned within the standard.[48] In addition, within circumstance where the licensed geographical scope of the disputed SEPs goes beyond the court's jurisdiction, the court enjoys the discretion of determining the royalty rate only within its own jurisdiction, unless the other party raises a reasonable objection.[49]

3.4.4 Monopolistic disputes involving SEPs

The Guangdong Guideline also specifies the analytical framework for competition assessment in disputes involving SEPs.[50] In particular, the substitutability of the licensed objects and the geographical nature of IPRs shall be considered when defining the relevant markets.[51] Moreover, when determining whether the patent holders possess dominant positions in the relevant markets, the guideline offers several important factors in addition to market shares, including the binding force of the FRAND commitments, the restraints of the disputed patents regarding trading conditions, the dependence and countervailing power of implementers and so forth.[52] In addition, the Guangdong Guideline also stipulates that it is not per se illegal under the AML when the patent holders have violated the FRAND commitments or applied for injunctions. The effect of excluding or restricting competition must be further analyzed based on the specific circumstances of the case.[53] Similarly, when determining whether the royalty rates requested by patent holder are high and unfair under the AML, factors to be taken into account include the previous licensing agreements, the deviation of the requested royalty rates from the market price, the total royalty rates involving in the negotiation as a whole and others.[54]

4 SEPs-related mergers

Although the MOFCOM has not defined SEPs in any guideline on SEP-related mergers, it did give a definition in two decisions.[55] The MOFCOM's definition of SEPs is exactly the same as the SAIC, but gives a more specific definition to standards, namely binding documents that are adopted by standard setting organizations (SSOs) or alliances and are commonly and repeatedly applicable. Different from the definition of the SAIC that might cover de facto standards, the MOFCOM includes only standards set by SSOs. The

48 *Id.* Article 23.
49 *Id.* Article 16.
50 *Id.* Article 25.
51 *Id.* Article 26.
52 *Id.* Article 27.
53 *Id.* Article 28–29.
54 *Id.* Article 30–31.
55 Case *Microsoft/Nokia*, Mofcom [2014] Nr. 24, April 8, 2014; and Case *Nokia/Alcatel Lucent*, Mofcom [2015] Nr. 44, October 19, 2015.

following three cases show how the MOFCOM has specifically analyzed SEPs and may affect competition.

4.1 Cases

The earliest case was the *Google/Motorola* case in 2012.[56] The relevant product markets concerned comprised mobile operating systems, mobile smartphones, and SEPs for mobile communications. At that time, Google's Android OS occupied 73.99% market share on the market for mobile operating systems, far beyond its competitors, such as Symbian's 12.53% and iOS's 10.67%. While Motorola was not a strong competitor anymore on the market for mobile smartphones, it did own many SEPs for mobile communications. The MOFCOM observed that the entry barriers for mobile operating systems and mobile communication standards were too high. Consequently, the post-merger competition concerns were raised from two perspectives. First, Google might reserve the latest version of its Android OS only for Motorola, thus handicapping other producers of mobile smartphones. Second, after the merger Google, when licensing its patents related to mobile communication standards, might attach unreasonable conditions, thereby harming competition and impairing consumer interests.

Microsoft's acquisition of Nokia came as the second case.[57] This was similar to the case *Google/Motorola*. The involved products included mobile operating systems, mobile smartphones, and SEPs for mobile communications. The major problem was still about SEPs of mobile communications on the one hand and Google's Android OS, to which Microsoft owned SEPs on the other. Similar to the previous case, the MOFCOM was concerned that Microsoft might increase the royalty fees or refuse to license its SEPs in relation to mobile communications and Android OS.

The last case was a horizontal merger between Nokia and Alcatel Lucent.[58] This case was different from the previous two. Nokia and Alcatel Lucent were direct competitors in many aspects, such as radio access network devices, core network system devices, network infrastructure devices and SEP licensing. Regarding the first three products, the merged entity was confronted with fierce competition. Their combined market shares were squeezed to a small level, and would not limit or restrain competition. However, the major concern of the MOFCOM was still about SEP licensing, the same as the previous two cases.

4.2 Relevant markets for SEPs

Until now, the only industrial sector reviewed by the MOFCOM with concerns over SEPs is the standards for mobile communications, as presented by the

56 Case *Google/Motorola*, Mofcom [2012] Nr. 25, May 19, 2012.
57 Case *Microsoft/Nokia*, Mofcom [2014] Nr. 24, April 8, 2014.
58 Case *Nokia/Alcatel Lucent*, Mofcom [2015] Nr. 44, October 19, 2015.

preceding three cases. As far as market definition for SEPs is concerned, there are discrepancies between the MOFCOM and other authorities. The latter maintain that relevant markets should be defined as containing every SEP of mobile communications standards. In comparison, the MOFCOM seems not to endorse such an approach. While in *Google/Motorola* the MOFCOM did not touch upon the relevant markets and market power of Motorola with regard to SEPs, it did make some endeavor in furthering its analyses in the other two cases. It first indicated that all the SEPs for mobile communications standards might be defined into sub-markets from demand-side substitution based on different standards, such as 2G, 3G and 4G. In the end, the MOFCOM defined a separate market containing all SEPs. The exact boundaries of the relevant markets were not specified, since a narrower market definition would affect the final results.

4.3 Assessing market power

When subsequently proceeding to the evaluation of market power, other authorities came to a quick conclusion that every SEP holder has dominance for the reason of no actual or potential competition. As a comparison, the MOFCOM nonetheless took a different approach, in particular in the case *Nokia/Alcatel Lucent*. Within this horizontal-merger case, the MOFCOM assessed whether after the merger the entity would acquire or strengthen its ability, incentive or possibility to limit market competition.[59] Factors examined included concentration ratio, countervailing buying power and indispensability of these SEPs to others. There is little doubt that SEPs for mobile communications standards can easily fulfill the second and the third requirements. With regard to the first, the MOFCOM specially looked at market shares of Nokia and Alcatel Lucent. Their combined market shares would be increased from 25%–35% to 35%–45% for 2G and 3G, and jump from the second place to the first place for 4G. The conclusion was drawn afterwards that this merger indeed limits competition.

Such an evaluation first implies that the MOFCOM probably sees relevant markets for SEPs as comprised of three markets (i.e. SEPs for 2G, 3G and 4G). Second, it also suggests that the MOFCOM takes market shares as an important factor to evaluate market power. However, since after the merger the entity would become the biggest company in the relevant market, the question remains whether SEP holders whose market shares are not significant can be considered to possess market power.

4.4 Remedies

The merits of the three cases might be different, as *Google/Motorola* and *Microsoft/Nokia* were vertical mergers, while *Nokia/Alcatel Lucent* was a horizontal

59 Interim Measures of Competition Assessment for Concentrations, Mofcom [2011] Nr. 55, 29 August 2011, Article 4.

merger. However, the competition concern was exactly the same. In all three cases, the MOFCOM raised the same issue, that the merged entity would attach unreasonable conditions when licensing SEPs. This might partly address the concern raised in the previous section, that SEP holders, even when their market shares are not the largest in the relevant market, might enjoy market power. Moreover, the remedies imposed by the MOFCOM in all three cases give a clear trend of going from general to specific.

First, in all the cases, the principal remedy was that the merged entity must continue to respect the FRAND obligations that they have undertaken through participation in the relevant SSOs. This remedy might not be innovative, because all those companies must respect their commitments to the SSOs. In *Microsoft/Nokia* and *Nokia/Alcatel Lucent*, the FRAND requirements went further. The MOFCOM required the merged entities to accept that a license under FRAND should not be conditioned on licensees accepting that the merged entities were not bound by the FRAND obligations promised to the relevant SSOs. Moreover, the merged entities must maintain that third parties who acquire those SEPs shall also respect the same set of obligations.

Second, the MOFCOM in *Microsoft/Nokia* and *Nokia/Alcatel Lucent* set some limits on the charging of royalty fees. When setting royalty fees, the merged entities should take into account the subsequent factors, including but not limited to, SEPs or SEP combinations included, licensing period, licensing products, business models related to retail and distribution, standards covered, acceptance by the market of the standardized function, structure of licensing agreements, value of grant-back and other non-monetary compensation, payment methods and applicable industries. After merger, the merged entities should not deviate from the commonly applicable royalty charge at present, unless the aforementioned factors are different.

Finally, the MOFCOM put limitations on seeking injunctions in addition to the FRAND obligation in *Microsoft/Nokia* and *Nokia/Alcatel Lucent*, echoing the European Commission's practice in *Samsung*.[60] Most importantly, the MOFCOM specified the conditions where the merged entity shall not seek injunctions. Injunctions can only be sought where SEP holders have made offers compatible with the FRAND obligations and the potential licensees nevertheless do not accept and respect the offers in good faith. Moreover, the subsequent situations may be considered unsuitable for injunctions where the potential licensees, without undue delay, agree to file the disputes with the merged entities on the disrespect of the FRAND obligations to an independent authority, and promise to be bound by the decision of that authority, to sign licensing agreements based on the decision, and to pay royalty fees and damages based on the decision.

60 European Commission, "Commission accepts legally binding commitments by Samsung Electronics on standard essential patent injunctions", IP-14-490, April 29, 2014.

4.5 De facto standards

The preceding three cases showcase the MOFCOM's approach to mergers related to SEPs concerning standards set by SSOs. This part will discuss the MOFCOM's handling of IPR issues concerning de facto standards in mergers. De facto standards are standards not set by SSOs, but developed by companies by themselves. They are not as compulsory as SEPs. However, due to the strong market power of the companies concerned, they may produce anti-competitive effects similar to those of SEPs. The MOFCOM has delivered its opinion on de facto standards in three subsequent cases.

In the first case, General Electric (GE) and Shenhua Group, China's largest coal producer, proposed to set up a 50–50 gasification joint venture to specialize in converting coal into a synthesis gas.[61] This was a vertical merger. GE owned the technology for such a conversion, while Shenhua Group, an SOE, produced and supplied coal, electricity and heating. The MOFCOM discovered that the upstream market for the technology licensing was highly concentrated, with only three competitors, as well as high entry barriers. GE was the one with the highest market share. In the downstream market, Shenhua Group was the biggest supplier of coal for synthesis gas in China. The MOFCOM was concerned that after the merger the joint venture would not be restrained by competitors, thus possibly limiting competition in the upstream market. In the end, the merged entity promised not to leverage its market power in the licensing market. Moreover, it was specifically prohibited from conditioning the supply of coal on the use of GE's technology by other companies, or increasing the costs to use competing technologies.

The second case involved a joint venture (JV) established by ARM Limited (ARM), Giesecke & Devrient GmbH (G&D) and Gemalto N.V. (Gemalto).[62] The purpose of the JV was to develop and market a TEE (trusted execution environment) solution. The key participant in this JV was ARM, whose main business was to license semiconductor intellectual property for application processors. Although the MOFCOM did not provide any data, it concluded that ARM had relatively strong market power there. The JV's activities (i.e. developing and marketing TEE) were downstream to ARM's business and dependent on ARM's TrustZone technology. The MOFCOM was concerned that ARM might discriminate against other developers of TEE when licensing its technologies, or might downgrade the performance of other developers of TEE by manipulating its own IPRs in certain ways. These two concerns were exactly what the commitments targeted. Within the commitments, ARM promised to publish the necessary information to develop TEE based on its TrustZone in a non-discriminatory and timely manner, and not to design its patent ecology in such a way as to downgrade the performance of third-party TEEs.

61 *General Electronics/Shenhua Group*, Mofcom [2011] Nr. 74, November 10, 2010.
62 *ARM/G&D/Gemalto*, Mofcom [2012] Nr. 87, December 6, 2012.

The last case was the acquisition of Merck KGaA (Merck) over AZ Electronics.[63] The two relevant markets defined included liquid display crystals and photoresists, which are widely used in the manufacture of flat panel displays. Merck had more than 70% market share in the Chinese market of liquid crystal displays, and AZ Electronics had more than 50% market share in the Chinese market of photoresistors. Due to the strong market power of the two entities, MOFCOM became concerned with the strengthened market position after the merger, based on the possibility of cross-subsidy between the two markets, thereby further limiting the already limited competition. Previous experience suggests a structural remedy under similar situations because of the tremendous market shares of the participants of the merger. Possibly in order to trade for a non-divestiture commitment, Merck mainly vowed (1) not to bundle the two products and (2) to license its patents for liquid display crystals based on non-exclusive, reasonable and non-discriminatory terms.

It has been widely acknowledged that SEPs are in most cases substitutable with market power.[64] It is doubtless that the MOFCOM maintains a rather strict approach on mergers involving SEPs. When dealing with non-SEPs, it is observed that the MOFCOM becomes more tolerant. The three cases discussed in this section exhibited a common feature of de facto standards, and there were no SSOs as the cases of SEPs. Strictly speaking, they are not standards according to the definition of SEPs made by the MOFCOM. However, the merged entities nevertheless held a very strong market position, even though the MOFCOM did not make this clear in the decisions. Due to their strong market presence, de facto standards could allow those merged entities to control the market in a way similar to SEP owners. In all the cases, the MOFCOM expressed its concerns that the merged entities might artificially increase the costs of other operators which switch to a substitutable technology. As a result, the commitments were imposed in the same way as those in an SEP-related merger (i.e. the FRAND obligations). Special attention might be paid to the Merck/AZ Electronics case, where the MOFCOM imposed FRAND remedies without a proper market definition of IPR licensing. However, the commitments in this case might have been self-proposed by Merck in order to avoid a structural remedy.

5 Conclusion

Access to technology and development of domestic and indigenous technology are key factors in China's development strategy. Often technology is protected by IPRs, and hence IPR policy can play an important role in implementing the strategy. In addition to the IPR protection, in Chinese government circles, antitrust law is increasingly viewed as an instrument to tackle perceived "monopolistic"

63 *Merck/AZ Electronics*, Mofcom [2014] Nr. 30, April 30, 2014.

64 Thomas F. Cotter, Comparative Law and Economics of Standard-Essential Patents and FRAND Royalties, 22 *Texas Intell. Prop. L.J.* (2014).

strangleholds in technology development and transfer. In the realm of SEPs, which raise a different issue than other types of IPRs, since they are strengthened by standards, ultimately the Chinese authorities have to strike a delicate balance between the private interest of the SEP holders and the public interest in standardization. This process is far from completion.

Chinese competition agencies and courts have been actively shaping the implementation of SEPs in the Chinese market. With regards to IPR protection, the courts have paid much attention to patent infringement cases involving SEPs. The key issues that concerned the courts were non-infringement defense, counter-injunction defense and the determination of compensation. With regard to antitrust regulation, the NDRC, the MOFCOM and the courts mainly focused on price-related and merger-related abuse of SEPs. The MOFCOM was concerned with the SEPs holders' ability to leverage their market power in adjacent markets, and was thus inclined to impose a FRAND obligation on those firms. The NDRC and the courts focused on high royalty fees and tying of SPEs with non-SEPs. However, their current approach might be too harsh on SEP holders. Although this might benefit Chinese mobile equipment makers in the short term, it could also be used against Chinese firms in the middle to long term. Time will tell how the new balance will be struck.

12 Standard essential patents and FRAND licensing

A view from India

Biswajit Dhar and Reji K. Joseph

1 Introduction

Technical standards have assumed significance in every facet of our existence. They serve the interests of the consumers by addressing the problems arising from the inefficiencies of the standard markets. Producers benefit from standardization since transactions costs can be reduced. Standards are therefore important for enhancing efficiency of the production systems, the dividends of which accrue to the consumers.[1]

In the international markets, standards play a critical role in spurring the growth of value chains across goods and services. The use of standards helps in achieving economies of scale and scope, both within and across countries. Standards have become a vital trigger for innovation and growth.

Standards enable products developed by different companies to operate and communicate with each other. Such interoperability of standards gives rise to beneficial network effects, which, in turn, contribute to efficiencies. Interoperability standards are important in many industries but are mostly relevant in those that are dependent on the information and communication technologies (ICT). However, with the advent of artificial intelligence (AI) in virtually all sectors, interoperability standards are now poised to expand in an unprecedented manner.

Over the past couple of decades, most interoperable standards have been developed by groups of market participants who have collaborated within voluntary associations known as standard setting organizations (SSOs). SSOs often establish new standards through a collective action of their members.

Standards themselves are usually not patentable, but products manufactured in accordance with the protocols and parameters specified by standards can satisfy the statutory requirements for patent protection. Once patented technologies are incorporated in the standards, these technologies are beneficial to the standards for they improve the performance of the systems and/or are helpful in getting better match with other design requirements, thereby giving rise to standard essential patents (SEPs).

1 National Research Council 2013, 121–140.

Incorporation of a patented technology into a standard considerably enhances the market power of the patent holder. This situation brings with it tensions between the holders and the users of SEP patentees, arising mostly from the anti-competitive practices of the SEP holders, such as by demanding high rents for licensing the technology embedded in the patent. These tensions are higher when the SEPs find widespread acceptance.

For nearly two decades, patent abuses involving SEPs have been addressed through active interventions of the SSOs, competition authorities and the courts. Through these interventions prospective licensees have been able to obtain licences on SEPs on fair, reasonable and non-discriminatory (FRAND) terms.

This chapter has two substantive parts. In the first, the chapter explores the conceptual bases of licensing of SEPs, especially FRAND licensing. While this form of licensing has been well accepted in practice, both in the way the SSOs manage SEPs and more recently, through the interventions by the courts, there seems to be less conceptual clarity as to what would constitute a "fair" royalty rate and "non-discriminatory" licensing practice. The response of the SEP holders to the FRAND licensing authorized by the courts has also emerged as contentious issue. Section 3 of the chapter analyzes cases of FRAND licensing in India, where courts have adjudicated cases resulting in the grant of licences on FRAND terms. There are several questions that these cases have given rise to, especially the terms on which the licences were granted.

2 Licensing of standard essential patents

2.1 *Anti-competitive effects of the market power of SEP: lock-in, holdup and royalty stacking*

Economists have provided the justification for the patent system in terms of the incentives that inventor can enjoy in the exercise of her/his patent rights.[2] But while the conditions for exploitation of a patent are laid down by the monopoly rights over the invention, the rents start flowing in only after the patentee has successfully commercialized the patent. Inclusion of a patent in a standard, or, in other words, transformation of a patent into a SEP, holds the key to successful commercialization of a patent.

In the absence of to a patent becoming a SEP, the ability of the patent holder to earn from licensing of the technology was limited due to the competition from alternate technologies. Once a patented technology is incorporated into a standard, alternate technologies that are not part of the standard lose their significance and are therefore unable to compete with the technology represented by the SEP.[3] For a potential user of a patented technology prior to the patent becoming a SEP, negotiating licensing terms would be much simpler as they would need

2 Arrow 1962.

3 Carlton and Shampine 2013, 3.

to pay for the incremental value which the patented technology in consideration offers as compared to the next best available alternative. However, once a patent becomes a SEP, possibility of negotiations based on the incremental value shuts down and the bargaining power of the SEP holder is enhanced considerably.

There are two related sets of challenges for market competition caused by the functioning of the SEPs. The first is lock-in, which implies that patented technologies that do not have ready substitutes must be relied on for the products to work. Lock-in arises as it is difficult to switch to a different technology once the standard is adopted. The second is holdup, where holders that are part of the SEP, seek royalties substantially in excess of the value a technology had prior to its inclusion in a standard. A third challenge a potential user of SEPs faces a third problem is royalty stacking. This situation can arise when one or several SEP holders demand royalties on each of their patents resulting in considerable increase in the payments for technologies.

Patent holdup occurs when SEP holders hold up a manufacturers after the adoption of a standard by refusing to license SEPs or extracting very high royalty or by forcing the manufacturers to accept onerous licensing terms through threat of injunction or other means. The manufacturers could find themselves in a vulnerable situation after committing their investments for adapting to the new standard. The SEP holders, on the other hand, point out the issue of patent holdout where a potential licensee may refuse to pay a "reasonable" royalty rate for using a SEP in a standards-compliant product.[4] As the economic justification for the patent system goes, free riding on innovative ideas should be checked in order to incentivize innovation. Given the enhanced market power an SEP holder would have, measures adopted by it to assert its right to exclude others through infringement suits are likely to have public interest considerations.

2.2 *What are FRAND terms?*

2.2.1 *Fair, reasonable and non-discriminatory in general*

In order to address the anti-competitive effects of the market power of SEP holders, many SSOs require its members to license SEPs to potential licensors on FRAND terms. The European Telecommunications Standard Institute (ETSI), an SSO set up to lay down standards for the telecommunication industry, particularly 2G (GSM, GPRS and EDGE), 3G (UMTS, WCDMA and HSPA) and 4G (LTE), requires its members to make an irrevocable undertaking that they would license their patents on FRAND terms and conditions. Clause 6.1 of the ETSI Intellectual Property Rights Policy states that

> when an essential IPR relating to a particular standard or technical specification is brought to the attention of ETSI, the Director-General of ETSI shall

4 Contreras 2017, 16.

> immediately request the owner to give within three months an irrevocable undertaking in writing that it is prepared to grant irrevocable licences on fair, reasonable and non-discriminatory ("FRAND") terms and conditions under such IPR to at least the following extent:
>
> - manufacture, including the right to make or have made customized components and sub-systems to the licensee's own design for use in manufacture;
> - sell, lease, or otherwise dispose of equipment so manufactured;
> - repair, use, or operate equipment; and
> - use methods.[5]

However, even those SSOs which require the SEP holders to license their patents on FRAND terms do not provide a holistic definition of what constitute FRAND terms, which are then left to the interpretation of courts and regulators. Most of the discussions on the meaning of FRAND have been focused on "reasonableness" and to a lesser extent on "non-discrimination". The principles of "fairness" in FRAND have not received adequate attention, which may have led many scholars and even the courts (particularly in the U.S.) to use the term RAND instead of FRAND.

Carlton and Shampine have provided a yardstick on "reasonable royalty", meaning royalty that does not include any holdup value.[6] This royalty would be same as the one that would have been charged when the patent had not become a SEP and the licensee had no sunken costs. In such a situation, the royalty would be based on the incremental value the patent offers to the licensee as compared to the next best alternative. Carlton and Shampine point out that this is the widely agreed upon, though not universally, meaning of "reasonable royalty". However, there is no widely agreed upon understanding on non-discriminatory principle of FRAND. For some, it means that there is no discrimination in the royalty (i.e. SEP holder charges the same royalty from all licensees). For some others, non-discrimination means that all those firms that implement the standard should be able to secure a license, there is no obligation on the licensor to charge same royalty from all the licensees, and royalty would be determined on the basis of the negotiation between the licensor and licensee. Yet another view is that non-discrimination means that all implementers of a standard are able to obtain a license for SEPs and all similarly situated firms pay the same rate of royalty.[7] A report of European Commission interprets the meaning of FRAND terms as

> holders of essential patents are bound to license their SEPs for the manufacture, sale, and use of standard-compliant products, on terms that do not

5 ETSI Intellectual Property Rights Policy (n 63).
6 Carlton and Shampine 2013, 9.
7 *Id.* at 10.

differ from those applied to another licensee in similar conditions. The licensing terms and the royalty rates charged for essential patents must adequately and fairly reward SEP owners for the value of their innovation. In other words, the licensing terms should appropriately reward the patent holder for investing in the development of his innovation and making it available.[8]

2.2.2 The calculation of reasonable royalty rates in particular

There is also no agreement on the criteria to be used for calculating reasonable royalty rates. According to Lemley, "without some idea of what those terms are, reasonable and non-discriminatory licensing loses much of its meaning".[9] The difficulty in arriving at "reasonable royalty" was reflected on by Swanson and Baumol (2005), who were among the first to provide a criterion for RAND licensing. Their argument was that the term "reasonable" in the context of what they called "RAND licensing" "must be defined and implemented by reference to *ex-ante* competition, i.e., competition in advance of standard selection".[10]

Farrell et al. developed the concept of "incremental value", suggesting that the "FRAND royalties should be capped at the added value a SEP contributes to products implementing the standard".[11] Competition authorities of U.S. and EU support the "ex ante incremental value" approach (i.e. incremental value of a patented invention over the next best available alternative at the time of establishing the standard). This approach to FRAND aims at addressing "the hold-up problem by isolating the intrinsic value of the technology from the ex-post value of practising the standard".[12] But there are practical issues while implementing this approach in the determination of royalty rate for substituting patents in a standard is not easy and, furthermore, any such substitution would change the performance and the value of the standard in several ways. The other approach to the calculation of royalty rate involves the *Georgia-Pacific* factors,[13] which are based on a hypothetical negotiation between the licensor and licensee. What makes the *Georgia-Pacific* factors different from the ex ante incremental value approach is that it assumes the implementer has already sunk costs and started using the SEP and the negotiation begins when infringement takes place.

8 European Commission 2015, 10.
9 Lemley 2002, 1964.
10 Swanson & Baumol 2005, 10–11. Swanson and Baumol refer to the interpretation of the term "reasonable" provided by Shapiro and Varian: "Reasonable should mean the royalties that the patent holder could obtain in open, up-front competition with other technologies, not the royalties that the patent holder can extract once other participants are effectively locked in to use technology covered by the patent".
11 Layne-Farrar 2016, 8.
12 European Commission 2015, 17.
13 This method was put forward by a U.S. court in the judgment of *Georgia-Pacific Corp. v. U.S. Plywood Corp.*, 318 F. Supp. 1116 (S.D.N.Y. 1970); see also William Hubbard, Chapter 5 of the present book.

The bases of working out the royalty rates have been quite contentious. The issue of contention is whether the royalty rates should be based on the sale prices of the equipment or the prices of the components that use patented technologies. Courts have adopted divergent approaches in deciding the bases for royalty rates. In *Lucent v. Gateway*, the U.S. Court of Appeals for the Federal Circuit clarified that base for calculation of royalty "can always be the value of the entire commercial embodiment . . . *even when the patented invention is a small component of a much larger commercial product, awarding a reasonable royalty based on either sale price or number of units sold can be economically justified*".[14] This approach, however, has been contested: by basing royalty rates on the sale price of the end product, the SEP holders would be unduly benefiting from the contributions other inventors have made in the product. In some cases, courts have taken a contrary view that determination of royalty should be based on the "smallest saleable patent-practicing unit" (SSPPU). The SSPPU principle means that claims of SEP holder "must be limited to the most "upstream' product that both practices the patent's claims and is capable of being transacted in the market".[15] The principle of SSPPU was first applied in 2009 by Randall Rader, the then chief judge of the Federal Circuit Court, in *Cornell University v. Hewlett-Packard.*

However, the determination of FRAND/RAND terms, especially FRAND/RAND royalty rate continued to be an unresolved issue until *Microsoft v. Motorola*, in which the court provided a methodology for determining RAND royalty rate.[16] This dispute was on Motorola's SEPs in two standards which the Microsoft was using: the wireless local area network (WLAN) standard, known as the "802.11 Standard", and the advanced video coding technology standard, known as the "H.264 Standard". Motorola demanded a royalty of 2.25% of the sale price of end products for its SEPs in each of the two standards. Microsoft alleged that Motorola has breached its RAND commitments by demanding unreasonable royalty. According to Microsoft, the royalty should be based on the incremental value of the invention and not on the sale price of end products. While deliberating on the charges made by both parties, the court observed that it would not be possible to find out whether Motorola had breached its RAND commitments without having a clear understating of the meaning of RAND. The court laid down a set of basic principles to be used for assessing RAND terms. They were[17]:

1 "Widespread adoption of their standards".
2 "In the context of a dispute concerning whether or not a given royalty is RAND, a proper methodology used to determine a RAND royalty should

14 *Lucent Technologies, Inc. v. Gateway, Inc.*, 580 F.3d 1301, 1336 (Fed. Cir. 2009), http://legacy.alixpartners.com/en/Publications/AllArticles/tabid/635/articleType/ArticleView/articleId/374/Uniloc-and-Its-Impact-on-the-Entire-Market-Value-Rule.aspx#sthash.8UgxqIlU.dpbs; see also William Hubbard, Chapter 5 of the present book.

15 Putnam and Williams 2016, 5.

16 U.S. District Court 2013.

17 *Id.* ORDER-25.

therefore recognize and seek to mitigate the risk of patent hold-up that RAND commitments are intended to avoid".

3 "Likewise, a proper methodology for determining a RAND royalty should address the risk of royalty stacking by considering the aggregate royalties that would apply if other SEP holders made royalty demands of the implementer".
4 "At the same time, a RAND royalty should be set with the understanding that SSOs include technology intended to create valuable standards. To induce the creation of valuable standards, the RAND commitment must guarantee that holders of valuable intellectual property will receive reasonable royalties on that property".
5 "From an economic perspective, a RAND commitment should be interpreted to limit a patent holder to a reasonable royalty on the economic value of its patented technology itself, apart from the value associated with incorporation of the patented technology into the standard".

The court also used a modified version of the *Georgia-Pacific* factors to recreate a hypothetical negotiation between the two parties. Using the aforementioned principles and the *Georgia-Pacific* factors, the court worked out the upper and lower bounds of RAND royalty for Motorola's patents in both the standards and determined the RAND royalty that Microsoft needs to pay as follows:

1 Motorola's SEPs in H.264 standard: Lower bound – 0.555 cents per unit; Upper bound – 16.389 cents per unit; RAND royalty Microsoft needs to pay – 0.555 cents per unit;
2 Motorola's SEPs in 802.11 standard: Lower bound – 0.8 cents per unit; Upper bound – 19.5 cents per unit; RAND royalty Microsoft needs to pay – 3.471 cents per unit.

The court rejected the argument of Microsoft that RAND royalty needs to be based on the incremental value of the invention due to the difficulties in finding out the incremental value of a SEP in a standard. In the evolution of FRAND jurisprudence, the judgment on *Microsoft v. Motorola* has made a landmark contribution. This has been in evidence in the disputes adjudicated in India, which will be elaborated in the following section.

2.2.3 To issue injunctive relief or not?

The SEP holders seek injunctive relief when their patents are infringed or patent holdout takes place. Most patent statutes recognize that injunctions in favour of patentee are available as remedies for infringement. Several jurisdictions interpreted the meaning of right to exclude as nothing other than right to injunctive relief.[18] There are instances when the courts have not been able to tailor the injunctive relief

18 Pai 2014.

in proportion to the actual harm caused by an infringement: "a properly tailored injunction may sometimes contain terms that go beyond the plaintiff's rightful position to avoid falling short of it".[19] An injunctive relief in favour of the patentee, which is not proportionate to the actual harm, can further enhance the market power of the SEP holder. Failure of the patentee to license on FRAND terms will be addressed by agencies dealing with anti-competition practices.

The notion of injunctive relief as a default remedy was overturned by the court in *eBay v. MercExchange*. The court held that granting of injunctive relief should be based on the assessment of certain factors. The court opined:

> according to well-established principles of equity, a plaintiff seeking a permanent injunction must satisfy a four-factor test before a Court may grant such relief. A plaintiff must demonstrate: (1) that it has suffered an irreparable injury; (2) that remedies available at law, such as monetary damages, are inadequate to compensate for that injury; (3) that, considering the balance of hardships between the plaintiff and defendant, a remedy in equity is warranted; and (4) that the public interest would not be disserved by a permanent injunction. . . . These familiar principles apply with equal force to disputes arising under the Patent Act.[20]

The court also observed that the threat of injunctive relief can be used by the SEP holder as a bargaining tool to charge very high royalty from potential licensees. According to the court:

> an industry has developed in which firms use patents not as a basis for producing and selling goods but, instead, primarily for obtaining licensing fees. . . . For these firms, an injunction, and the potentially serious sanctions arising from its violation, can be employed as a bargaining tool to charge exorbitant fees to companies that seek to buy licenses to practice the patent.[21]

3 FRAND disputes in India

Disputes on SEP licensing on FRAND terms are relatively new to India. As per the available information, there have been 10 disputes thus far; eight of these disputes involve eight patents of Ericsson, which are part of three technologies used in 2G and 3G devices (see summary of disputes in the Appendix).

Ericsson's disputes began in 2011 when the company brought a case against Kingtech Electronics (India) Pvt. Ltd for infringing Ericsson's SEPs on Adaptive Multi-Rate Speech Codec (AMR) technology and demanded banning of imports by Kingtech of products incorporating AMR technology.[22]

19 Schoenbrod 1988, 671.
20 Supreme Court of the United States 2006, 1.
21 *Id.* at 4.
22 Kingtech Electronics (India) Pvt. Ltd and Anr V. Union of India and Ors. 2011.

In 2013, Ericsson filed a case against an Indian company, Micromax Informatics Limited, alleging that the latter was importing handsets that incorporated eight of its patents that were registered in India and were valid. Almost concurrently, Intex Technologies Limited, an Indian smartphone manufacturer, filed a complaint before the Competition Commission of India (CCI) arguing that Ericsson was guilty of abuse of dominant position.

In 2013, Vringo Infrastructure filed a civil suit against ZTE, its CEO Xu Dejun, and its Indian subsidiary ZTE Telecom India for infringement of its patent, IN 243980, which according to Vringo is a SEP for the CDMA 2000 family of standards. This dispute was settled in 2014 with the defendant agreeing to a licensing arrangement with the patent holder.

The most recent and currently ongoing dispute is between Dolby International AB, a major manufacturer of sound devices and two Chinese companies, namely, Oppo Mobiles India Private Limited and Vivo Mobiles India Private Limited, which was initiated in 2016.

In the following discussion, we will dwell on the key issues raised in the three sets of disputes.

3.1 *Ericsson's disputes*

The eight Ericsson patents that were the subject matter of its disputes covered three technologies used in 2G and 3G devices 3G. These three technologies are (1) AMR, which conserves the use of bandwidth and enhances speech quality; (2) 3G, which enables a single mobile station to handle multi-services; and (3) Enhanced Data rates for GSM Evolution (EDGE), which enables improved data transmission. Following table gives the details of Ericsson's eight patents relevant for the three technologies.

Among the FRAND disputes in India, Ericsson's disputes with Micromax, Intex and CCI are very significant as they have addressed some critical issues that emerge in the context of the interaction between patent law and competition law.

3.1.1 *Obligations on the part of licensee to enter into meaningful negotiation*

In the interim order pertaining to the dispute between Ericsson and Intex, the court made following observations to characterize Intex as an "unwilling licensee":

1 Ericsson, in view of its FRAND commitment, offered a FRAND license to Intex.
2 Intex appeared to avoid a meaningful negotiation by not stating the royalty it could offer.

At one point of the negotiation, on May 23, 2013, Intex expressed that the revised rates offered by Ericsson may be acceptable to it; but later it made a

Table 12.1 Ericsson's patents which are the subject matter of FRAND disputes in India

Technology	*Indian Patent No.*	*Specification*
AMR	IN203034	Linear Predictive Analysis by synthesis encoding method and encoder
	IN203036	Apparatus for producing from an original speech signal a plurality of parameters
	IN234157	A method of encoding/decoding multi-codebook fixed bitrate CELP signal block
	IN203686	Method and system for alternating transmission of codec mode information
	IN213723	Method and apparatus for generating comfort noise in a speech decoder
3G	IN229632	Multi service handling by a single mobile station
	IN240471	A mobile radio for use in a mobile radio communication system
EDGE	IN241747	A transceiving omit unit for block automatic retransmission request

Source: Compiled by authors from interim judgment of High Court of Delhi in *Ericsson v. Intex*, issued on March 13, 2015.

petition with the Intellectual Property Appellate Board (IPAB), challenging the validity of Ericsson's patents, and filed a complaint with CCI alleging abuse of dominant position by Ericsson. During the hearing of interim application, Intex was not making any reasonable and fruitful offer in terms of royalty payment except that it would pay royalty based on the cost of chip.

3 Intex's complaint with CCI was "solely with the view to prolong litigation by avoiding paying the royalty".[23]
4 Intex was not serious in its negotiations with Ericsson. It had entered into negotiation with Ericsson on FRAND licensing agreement and later it decided to challenge the validity of the patents on which the negotiations were held. The court raised the question whether Intex would have challenged the validity of patents had there been FRAND agreement executed? And the answer was obvious to the Court: "No".[24]

The aforementioned observations of the court raise a few questions. What is the meaning of FRAND terms? Is a potential licensee obliged to make a counter offer when the patent holder offers a non-FRAND license terms? Should a licensee waive off its right to challenge the validity patents, which is otherwise

23 *Telefonaktiebolaget Lm Ericsson v. Intex Technologies (India) Ltd.* 2013, para. 137.
24 *Id.* para. 149.

guaranteed in sections 25.2 and 140.1(d) of Patents Act, in order to execute a FRAND license agreement?

The Court did not provide any interpretation of the meaning of the term FRAND. It seems that the Court has taken a view of FRAND terms as non-discrimination among firms that implement the standard in issuing licenses; but the licensor may charge different royalty from the implementers. This may be the reason for Court's observation that despite the FRAND offer of Ericsson, Intex did not make a counter offer. However, in *Ericsson v. Competition Commission of India*, the judgment shows that Intex had indeed made counter offers; but it is not clear if it had specified the rate of royalty it could offer. The judgment mentions that

> Ericsson provided its commercial terms for a PLA to Intex on 23rd April 2013 and the same were discussed between the parties at a meeting held on 23rd May 2013, wherein Ericsson agreed to provide the revised terms. These were provided by Ericsson to Intex on 30th May 2013. Intex made a counter-offer on 19th June 2013, which, according to Ericsson was unfeasible.[25]

In negotiations on licensing agreement, FRAND royalty is only one aspect of the terms of the agreement. If other terms of the agreement are onerous, as Intex and Micromax had pointed out in their complaints to CCI, is the potential licensee still obliged to make a counter offer on royalty and leave aside other terms? In *Microsoft v. Motorola*, the court held that "initial offers do not have to be on RAND terms so long as a RAND license eventually issues". This may imply that negotiations should be in good faith so that a dialogue takes place between the parties which ultimately leads to FRAND terms. In such situations, the licensee is expected to enter into a meaningful dialogue. But if the negotiations are not in good faith or threats have been made to yield a favourable outcome, there may not be any obligation on the licensee to make counter offers. In the dispute *Ericsson v. Competition Commission of India*, the High Court of Delhi clarified that in some cases, threats by a SEP holder who is already in a dominant position could amount to abuse of dominant position. If such threats are directed to persuade the implementer to accept non-FRAND terms, it is clearly an abuse of dominant position. The court refused to accept the argument of Ericsson that Micromax and Intex were "unwilling licensees" by clarifying that "willing licensee" means "a potential licensee who is willing to accept licence of valid patents on FRAND terms".[26] Thus, the court proceedings in India have established that the negotiations on FRAND licensing should take place in good faith and that SEP holders should not abuse their position of dominance in the negotiation process.

25 *Telefonaktiebolaget LM Ericsson v. Competition Commission of India and Another 2016*, para. 13.4.

26 *Id.* para. 205.

In the interim order of *Ericsson v. Intex*, the court took the position that a FRAND licensee should not challenge the validity of the patents for which the agreement was executed. In other words, the licensee should waive off its right to challenge the validity of patents. Such presumptions go against section 25.2 of the Patents Act of India, which provides for challenging a patent, even after its grant. This section states: "at any time after the grant of patent but before the expiry of a period of one year from the date of publication of grant of a patent, any person interested may give notice of opposition to the Controller in the prescribed manner". Section 140.1(d) of Patents Act clarifies that any clause in the contract in relation to sale, lease or licensing for manufacture of a patented article that prevents the licensee from challenging the validity of a patent, is unlawful. It states:

> it shall not be lawful to insert in any contract for or in relation to the sale or lease of a patented article or an article made by a patented process; or in licence to manufacture or use a patented article; or in a licence to work any process protected by a patent, a condition the effect of which may be to provide exclusive grant back, prevention to challenges to validity of Patent and coercive package licensing and any such condition shall be void.

In *Ericsson v. Competition Commission of India*, the court clarified that a person who has entered into a licensing agreement still has the right to challenge the validity of the patent.

3.1.2 Appropriate forum for adjudication

In *Ericsson v. Competition Commission of India*, Ericsson argued that Patents Act, being a special act, would prevail over the Competition Act; therefore, issues regarding abuse of patent rights including abuse of dominant position are required to be addressed under the provisions of the Patents Act and not under provisions of the Competition Act. Ericsson also argued that CCI does not have the jurisdiction to entertain complaints on rate of royalty related to SEPs. The court rejected the arguments of Ericsson by pointing out that the objective of Parliament in establishing the Competition Act was not to encroach upon other acts but to complement them. Competition Act is directed to curtail certain anti-competitive agreements, abuse of dominant position and formation of combinations which are likely to adversely impact competition. The court clarified that CCI is the appropriate forum to adjudicate issues of abuse of dominant position, even if they are occurring while one is exercising his/her patent rights. It also clarified that CCI is the competent authority to determine the rate of royalty as the subject matter of the issue was abuse of dominant position.

3.1.3 Basis for calculation of royalty rate

In *Ericsson v. Intex*, the court took the view that determination of royalty should be based on the sale price of the end product and not on the chipset. The interim judgment stated, "the argument that defendant has to pay the royalty on the chipset value cannot be accepted in view of plaintiff's practice of charging royalty on the device price is non-discriminatory (FRAND)".[27] The CCI, however, seems to hold the view during the preliminary investigation that royalty based on sale price of end product is non-FRAND. The position of CCI would be clear when the final report of the investigation is prepared.

3.2 *Vringo v. ZTE*

Vringo had filed two suits against ZTE pertaining to patents IN243980 and IN200572 which according to it were SEPs. Patent IN243980 is a SEP for CDMA standards and IN200572 is a SEP for base station controller of 2G and 3G infrastructure. In both cases, the court granted immediate injunctive relief to Vringo. In the latter dispute, the injunction was lifted later and on the condition that ZTE would deposited INR 178.5 million in the court towards payment of royalty. But in 2015, ZTE entered into a confidential deal with Vringo which granted ZTE and its affiliates a "non-exclusive, non-transferable, worldwide perpetual license" of certain patents owned by Vringo.[28]

Vringo had FRAND disputes with ZTE in different countries. All the disputes have been related to the portfolio of 500 patents which Vringo had purchased from Nokia. In the UK, Vringo filed a suit against ZTE alleging that the latter did not accept its FRAND offer. ZTE held that Vringo's offer is on a portfolio of patents all of which it did not require and that Vringo's patents were not valid. Vringo argued that the preliminary trial should first establish whether it had made FRAND offer and then address the infringement issue. The Court refused to accept the Vringo's argument and held that when the defendant is willing to take license to valid patents the Court could not force it to accept the license without determining the validity of patents.[29] The confidential agreement between the companies have arrived and ended all the disputes that were going in different countries.

3.3 *Dolby v. Oppo and Vivo*

The most recent case of FRAND licensing is the dispute between Dolby International AB and two Chinese companies, Oppo Mobiles India Private Limited (Oppo) and Vivo Mobiles India Private Limited (Vivo). Dolby brought five cases against the two companies before the High Court of Delhi in 2016, claiming that cell phones, tablets and televisions being manufactured by Oppo and Vivo produce sound of high quality, which is possible only by using Dolby's technology that were covered by four patents, namely, IN 230121, IN 242206, IN 264129

27 *Telefonaktiebolaget LM Ericsson v. Intex Technologies (India) Ltd.* 2015, para. 158.
28 Vringo Infrastructure Inc and Xu Dejun & Ors 2013.
29 Foster 2015.

and IN 224775. Dolby further claimed that whenever the aforementioned products manufactured or sold by Oppo and Vivo are ISO/IEC 14496–3:2009(E) compliant, they use HE-AAC v1 technology (also known as aacPlus v1, eAAC, AAC+ or CT-aacPlus) and High Efficiency Advanced Audio Coding v2 technology (also known as aacPlus v2, eAAC+, AAC++ or Enhanced AAC+), and infringe Dolby's patents. These patents were in force and were SEPs.

In the first instance, the Judge issued an order restraining Oppo and Vivo from manufacturing, assembling, importing, selling or offering for sale cell phones, tablets and televisions that were ISO/IEC 14496–3:2009(E) compliant and which used Dolby's patented technologies.

In their response, the defendants, Oppo and Vivo, submitted to the court that they should be allowed to continue manufacturing and selling the products that were embedded with Dolby's technology and that they were ready and willing to deposit in the court appropriate royalty with immediate effect. The two companies offered to deposit royalty at the rate of INR 32 for every machine that they would manufacture, sell or import. They were thus willing to recognize Dolby's claim over the four patents.[30]

However, Dolby's contention was that the two prospective licensees should pay royalty at the highest rate, which would work out to about INR 38 for every machine manufactured, sold or imported. The court adjudicated that Dolby's royalty should be fixed at INR 34 for every machine manufactured, sold or imported as an interim royalty before the final disposal of the case. This was, therefore, the FRAND licensing rate determined by the court. The earlier order of the court was modified and the Indian entities were permitted to continue manufacturing, selling and importing the products.

In a subsequent development, one of the defendants in the case, namely Oppo, brought before the court evidence of royalty stacking by Dolby. Oppo argued that while Dolby had filed the initial suit complaining about the infringement of its four patents, the FRAND rates, which were being charged as per the court order, were for the entire family of 600 patents. Oppo pointed out that Dolby held only eight valid patents in India and that under no circumstances could Dolby demand royalty payments at the FRAND rates for its entire family of patents.

The Court observed that the defendants, even by way of an interim arrangement, should not be made to pay the rates which Dolby had demanded for a family of as many as 600 patents, especially when the dispute that they had brought before the Court was for enforcing rights in case of only four patents. The Court addressed the issue of royalty stacking by Dolby by revising downwards the FRAND rate in its revised order. In its order of November 23, 2016, the court directed the defendants to deposit an amount calculated at the rate of INR 20 for every machine manufactured, sold or imported instead of INR 34 it had ordered earlier. The lower FRAND rate was made applicable, subject to the

30 Dolby International AB & Anr v. GDN Enterprises Private Limited & Ors and Dolby International AB & Anr v. Das Telecom Private Limited & Ors. 2016a.

defendants paying the balance amount due to Dolby, if any, in accordance with the earlier order.[31]

4 Concluding comments

This chapter provided a perspective on the licensing of SEPs, analyzing, in particular, the ways in which the terms "non-discrimination" and "reasonable" have been discussed in the academic literature in the context of FRAND licensing. The discussion pointed to the fact that at the conceptual level, the yardsticks on which the two key concepts, namely, "fair" royalty rates and "non-discrimination" in the grant of licences, are still at best works in progress. Injunctive relief has frequently been used to remedy the situation of patent infringement, but questions remain as to whether the remedies are in proportion to the infringement of SEPs.

The chapter discussed the important disputes arising from the exercise of their rights by the holders of SEPs, which have been adjudicated in India by the courts and the Competition Commission of India. The courts have written a number of important decisions granting FRAND licences, which can be the basis for the development of some interesting norms for the grant of FRAND licences. More generally, these decisions can potentially set new yardsticks for patent licensing in the country, the import of which would be clear in later years.

References

Arrow, K. 1962. Economic welfare and the allocation of resources for invention, in *The Rate and Direction of Inventive Activity: Economic and Social Factors*. Universities-National Bureau Committee for Economic Research, Committee on Economic Growth of the Social Science Research Council. Princeton University Press for National Bureau Committee for Economic Research.

Best IT World (India) Private Limited (iBall) v. Telefonaktiebolaget L M Ericsson (Publ) and Ericsson India Private Limited. Competition Commission of India. Case No. 04 of 2015. Available at: www.cci.gov.in/sites/default/files/042015_0.pdf [Accessed on 25 September 2017].

Carlton, Dennis W. & Shampine, Allan L. 2013. An economic interpretation of FRAND. *Journal of Law and Economics*, 9(3), 531–552.

Contreras, Jorge L. 2017. *Technical Standards, Standards-Setting Organizations and Intellectual Property: A Survey of the Literature (with an Emphasis on Empirical Approaches)*. Utah Law Faculty Scholarship 11. Available at: http://dc.law.utah.edu/scholarship/11 [Accessed on 30 August 2017].

Dolby International AB & Anr v. GDN Enterprises Private Limited & Ors and Dolby International AB & Anr v. Das Telecom Private Limited & Ors. and Dolby International AB & Anr v. Mitashi Edutainment Pvt. Ltd and Dolby International AB & Anr v. Shreejee Tradelinks & Anr and Dolby International AB & Anr and Universal

31 Dolby International AB & Anr v. GDN Enterprises Private Limited & Ors. 2016b.

Digital Connect Limited & Ors. 2016. CS(COMM) 1425/2016, CS(COMM) 1426/2016, CS(COMM)1427/2016, CS(COMM) 1428/2016 & CS(COMM) 1429/2016. Order issued by the High Court of Delhi on 20.10.2016. Available at: http://delhihighcourt.nic.in/dhcqrydisp_o.asp?ctype=CS(COMM)&cno=1425&cyear=2016&orderdt=20-oct-2016&judge1=rse [Accessed on 29 September 2017].

Dolby International AB & Anr v. GDN Enterprises Private Limited & Ors and Dolby International AB & Anr v. Das Telecom Private Limited & Ors. 2016. CS(COMM) 1425/2016 & CS(COMM) 1426/2016. Order issued by the High Court of Delhi on 27.10.2016. Available at: http://delhihighcourt.nic.in/dhcqrydisp_o.asp?pn=208102&yr=2016 [Accessed on 29 September 2017].

Dolby International AB & Anr v. GDN Enterprises Private Limited & Ors. 2016. 1426/2016. Order issued by the High Court of Delhi on 23.11.2016. Available at: http://delhihighcourt.nic.in/dhcqrydisp_o.asp?ctype=CS(COMM)&cno=1425&cyear=2016&orderdt=23-nov-2016&judge1=rse [Accessed on 29 Septembe 2017].

European Commission. 2015. Fair, reasonable and non-discriminatory (FRAND) licensing terms. *JRC Science and Policy Report*. Available at: http://publications.jrc.ec.europa.eu/repository/bitstream/JRC96258/jrc96258.pdf [Accessed on 15 September 2017].

Foster, Tom. 2015. *Vringo V. ZTE: FRAND Terms and Injunctive Relief for Infringement of Standards Essential Patents*. Available at: https://gowlingwlg.com/en/global/insights-resources/vringo-v-zte-frand-terms-and-injunctive-relief-for-infringement-of-standards-essential-patents [Accessed on 2 September 2017].

Kingtech Electronics (India) Pvt. Ltd. and Anr v. Union of India and Ors, W.P.(C) 6878/2011 and C.M. No. 15811/2011, Order issued by the High Court of Delhi on 19 December 2011. Available at: http://delhihighcourt.nic.in/dhcqrydisp_o.asp?pn=263209&yr=2011 [Accessed on: 20 August 2017].

Layne-Farrar, Anne. 2016. The economics of FRAND, in D. Sokol (Ed.), *Antitrust Intellectual Property & High Tech Handbook*. University of Cambridge Press, Cambridge. Available at: www.researchgate.net/publication/292604780_The_economics_of_FRAND.

Lemley, Mark A. 2002. Intellectual property rights and standard-setting organizations, *California Law Review*, 90(6), 1889–1980.

National Research Council. 2013. *Patent Challenges for Standard-Setting in the Global Economy: Lessons from Information and Communications Technology*. The National Academies Press, Washington, DC. Available at: https://doi.org/10.17226/18510 [Accessed on 27 August 2017].

Pai, Yogesh. 2014. The rationale basis for FRANDly courts denying injunctive relief for SEPs infringement. *Journal of Intellectual Property Rights*, 19, March, 146–156.

Press Information Bureau. 2017. Commerce and Industry Minister Smt. Nirmala Sitharaman has said that India should take lead in making quality products available to world at an affordable price, Ministry of Commerce & Industry. Government of India. Ministry of Commerce and Industry. May 1. Available at: http://pib.nic.in/newsite/PrintRelease.aspx?relid=161429 [Accessed on 15 September 2017].

Putnam, Jonathan D. & Williams, Tim A. 2016. *The Smallest Saleable Patent-Practicing Unit: Theory and Evidence*. Available at: http://ssrn.com/abstract=2835617.

Schoenbrod, David S. 1988. The measure of an injunction; A principle to replace balancing the equities and tailoring the remedy. *Minnesota Law Review*, 72, 627–690.

Shapiro, Carl and Varian, Hal R. 1999. *Information Rules: A Strategic Guide to the Network Economy*. Harvard Business School Press, Boston, MA.

Supreme Court of the United States. 2006. EBAY INC., V. MERCEXCHANGE, L.L.C., 547 (2006), Opinion of the Court. Available at: https://supreme.justia.com/cases/federal/us/547/388/ [Accessed on 30 August 2017].

Swanson, Daniel G. & Baumol, William J. 2005. Reasonable and nondiscriminatory (RAND) royalties, standards selection and control of market power. *Antitrust Law Journal*, 73(1), 1–58.

Telefonaktiebolaget LM Ericsson V. Competition Commission of India and Another. 2014. CM Nos.911/2014 & 915/2014 and W.P.(C) 1006/2014 & CM Nos.2037/2014 & 2040/2014, judgement delivered on 30 March 2016. Available at: http://lobis.nic.in/ddir/dhc/VIB/judgement/30-03-2016/VIB30032016CW4642014.pdf [Accessed on 10 September 2017].

Telefonaktiebolaget LM Ericsson V. Competition Commission of India and Another. 2016. W.P.(C) 464/2014 & CM Nos.911/2014 & 915/2014 and W.P.(C) 1006/2014 & CM Nos.2037/2014 & 2040/2014, judgement delivered on 30 March 2016. Available at: http://lobis.nic.in/ddir/dhc/VIB/judgement/30-03-2016/VIB30032016CW4642014.pdf [Accessed on 30 August 2017].

Telefonaktiebolaget LM Ericsson V. Gionee Communication Equipment Co. Ltd. and Anr. 2013. CS (OS) No. 2010 of 2013, judgement delivered on 31 October 2013. Available at: http://delhihighcourt.nic.in/dhcqrydisp_o.asp?pn=211053&yr=2013 [Accessed on 25 September 2017].

Telefonaktiebolaget LM Ericsson V. Intex Technologies (India) Ltd. 2013. IA No. 6735/2014 in CS (OS) No. 1045/2014, judgement delivered by High Court of Delhi on 13 March 2015. Available at: http://lobis.nic.in/ddir/dhc/MAN/judgement/16-03-2015/MAN13032015S10452014.pdf [Accessed on 30 August 2017].

Telefonktiebolaget LM Ericsson V. Lava International Ltd. 2016. CS(OS) 764/2015, judgment pronounced on 1 March 2016. Available at: https://indiankanoon.org/doc/181502352/ [Accessed on 15 September 2017].

Telefonaktiebolaget LM Ericsson V. Mercury Electronics and Anr. 2014. CS(OS) 442/2013, judgement delivered on 12 November 2014. Available at: https://indiankanoon.org/doc/156863327/ [Accessed on 25 September 2017].

Telefonaktiebolaget LM Ericsson V. Union of India and Ors. 2011. LPA 1104/2011, judgement delivered on 13 July 2012. Available at: https://indiankanoon.org/doc/170144590/ [Accessed on 25 August 2017].

Telefonaktiebolaget LM Ericsson V. Xiaomi Technology and Ors. 2015. IA 3074/2015 in CS(OS) 3775/2014, judgement delivered on 22 April 2016. Available at: http://lobis.nic.in/ddir/dhc/VKR/judgement/23-04-2016/VKR22042016S377522014.pdf [Accessed on 10 September 2017].

Telefonaktiebolaget LM V. Kingtech Electronics (India) and Ors. 2012. CS(OS) 68/2012, judgement delivered on 28 August 2013. Available at: http://delhihighcourt.nic.in/dhcqrydisp_o.asp?pn=163228&yr=2013 [Accessed on 25 August 2017].

U.S. District Court. 2013. Western District of Washington at Seattle, Microsoft Corporation V. Motorola INC, et al., Case No. C10–1823JLR, Judgement delivered on 25 April 2013. Available at: www.essentialpatentblog.com/wp-content/uploads/sites/64/2013/04/2013.04.25-D.E.-681-Findings-of-Fact-and-Conclusions-of-Law-setting-RAND-royalty1.pdf [Accessed on 1 September 2017].

Vringo Infrastructure Inc and Anr V. Xu Dejun and Ors. 2013. CS(OS) 2168/2013, judgment delivered on 8 November 2013. Available at: http://delhihighcourt.nic.in/dhcqrydisp_o.asp?pn=221627&yr=2013 [Accessed on 1 September 2017].

Vringo Infrastructure Inc. & Anr. v. Indiamart Intermesh Ltd. & Ors. 2014. I.A. No. 2112/2014 in C.S. (OS) No. 314 of 2014, Judgement delivered on 5 August 2014. Available at: http://lobis.nic.in/ddir/dhc/VKS/judgement/07-08-2014/VKS05082014S3142014.pdf [Accessed on 27 September 2017].

Vringo Settles with ZTE. 2015. China IPR. December 14. Available at: https://chinaipr.com/2015/12/14/vringo-settles-with-zte/ [Accessed on 25 October 2017].

Xiaomi Technology and ANR v Telefonaktiebolaget LM Ericsson (PUBL) and ANR. 2014. FAO(OS). 522/2014. Available at: www.delhidistrictcourts.nic.in/DEC14/Xiaomi%20Technology%20Vs.%20Telefonaktiesola%20a%20get%20L%20M%20Ericsson.pdf [Accessed on 10 September 2017].

Appendix: Summary of SEP FRAND disputes in India

Litigants	*Year of Dispute(s)*	*Grievance Redressal Body/Bodies*	*Dispute(s) and Decision(s) of Grievance Redressal Body/Bodies*
Ericsson v. Kingtech Electronics (India) Pvt. Ltd.	2011	Commissioner of Customs	Ericsson filed a complaint alleging infringement of its SEPs on AMR technology by Kingtech and demanded banning of imports by Kingtech of products incorporating AMR technology. Consignments imported by Kingtech were detained by customs authorities.
	2011	High Court of Delhi	Kingtech filed a writ petition in High Court of Delhi alleging that customs authorities had confiscated its imports without giving adequate reasons. The court stayed the impugned order. Ericsson filed an appeal challenging this order.
	2012	High Court of Delhi	Directed the commissioner of customs to pass a fresh order, showing the reason to believe that infringement has taken place.
	2013	High Court of Delhi	Court granted injunctive relief to Ericsson by restricting Kingtech from importing mobile phones incorporating Ericsson's AMR technology patents. In case of any import of consignment, Kingtech was supposed to intimate Ericsson and objections raised by Ericsson had to be entertained.

Litigants	*Year of Dispute(s)*	*Grievance Redressal Body/Bodies*	*Dispute(s) and Decision(s) of Grievance Redressal Body/Bodies*
Ericsson v. Micromax	2013	High Court of Delhi	Ericsson filed a civil suit against Micromax alleging infringement of its eight SEPs related to 2G/AMR, 3G and EDGE technologies. In the court, both the parties agreed to negotiate a license agreement on FRAND terms. Till the final determination of royalty rate, Micromax was to pay royalty at interim rate: Phones/devices capable of GSM:1.25% of sales price, GPRS+GSM:1.75%, EDGE+GPRS+GSM:2%, and WCDMA/HSPA:2%. Dongles/ Data cards at $2.50 per unit.
	2013	Competition Commission of India	Micromax filed a complaint alleging abuse of dominant position by Ericsson. Main allegations: (1) royalty rate demanded by Ericsson was unfair and did not reflect the Indian realities; (2) royalty demanded by Ericsson would make the business unviable. Ericsson resorted to threats of interim injunctions and custom seizures to force acceptance of its terms. Ericsson also threatened to file intimation with SEBI to block Initial Public Offer of Micromax. These actions of Ericsson amounted to abuse of its dominant position. CCI found merit in the allegation of Micromax and directed the Director General to investigate the alleged violation of provisions of Competition Act.

Litigants	*Year of Dispute(s)*	*Grievance Redressal Body/Bodies*	*Dispute(s) and Decision(s) of Grievance Redressal Body/Bodies*
	2014		Micromax disputed the rate of royalty of the interim order issued on March 19, 2013. Ericsson produced before the court, 26 licensing agreements it had entered into with other Indian parties. Based on the assessment

Litigants	*Year of Dispute(s)*	*Grievance Redressal Body/Bodies*	*Dispute(s) and Decision(s) of Grievance Redressal Body/Bodies*
Ericsson v. Micromax		High Court of Delhi	of these agreements, the Court revised the rate of royalty (till the dispute was finally settled): *From the date of filing of the complaint to November 12, 2015* (a) GSM phones/devices: 0.8% of net selling price (b) GPRS + GSM phones/devices: 0.8% of net selling price (c) EDGE + GPRS + GSM phones/devices: 1% of net selling price (d) WCDMA/HSPA phones/devices, calling tablets: 1% of the net selling price. *From November 13, 2015 to November 12, 2016* (a) GSM phones/ devices: 0.8% of net selling price (b) GPRS + GSM phones/devices: 0.8% of net selling price (c) EDGE + GPRS + GSM phones/devices: 1.1% of net selling price (d) WCDMA/HSPA phones/devices, calling tablets: 1.1% of the net selling price *From November 13, 2016 to November 12, 2020* (a) GSM phones/ devices: 0.8% of net selling price (b) GPRS + GSM phones/devices: 1% of net selling price (c) EDGE + GPRS + GSM phones/devices: 1.3% of net selling price (d) WCDMA/HSPA phones/devices, calling tablets: 1.3% of the net selling price
Ericsson v. Gionee	2013	High Court of Delhi	Material facts of this dispute are the same as that of *Ericsson v. Micromax*. The court ordered an interim royalty payment arrangement as in the case of *Ericsson v. Micromax* in 2013. In 2014, both parties informed the court about their intention to appoint a mediator to settle the licensing terms. But the mediation failed and the court has ordered the matter to be listed for framing of issues.

Litigants	*Year of Dispute(s)*	*Grievance Redressal Body/Bodies*	*Dispute(s) and Decision(s) of Grievance Redressal Body/Bodies*
Ericsson v. Intex	2013	Competition Commission of India (CCI)	Intex complained against abuse of dominant position by Ericsson. Basis of complaint: (a) Ericsson insisted that Intex obtained licenses without disclosing the patents which were alleged to be infringed. The terms of agreement were "grossly onerous, oppressive, unfair, unreasonable and discriminatory". (b) Ericsson insisted on a non-disclosure agreement (NDA) for disclosing the patents allegedly infringed by Intex. NDA contained onerous clauses, imposing huge legal costs on Intex. (c) Exorbitant royalty demanded by Ericsson, based on the final value of the product and not on the components using patented technologies. (d) Ericsson used discriminatory licensing practices, treating SEP holding companies differently from all others. This altered conditions for competition in the market. (e) Ericsson offered the entire pool of patents as a bouquet though Intex did not want all of them. It also refused to offer specific royalty rate to each SEP. CCI found merit in Intex's complaint and directed its director general to investigate possible violation of Competition Act.
	2014	High Court of Delhi	Ericsson sued Intex, seeking permanent injunction, for infringing its eight SEPs. Intex challenged the essentiality of Ericsson's patents to the standard and the validity of patents. The court upheld the essentiality of the patents as well as their validity. As an interim arrangement, the court directed Intex to pay royalty to Ericsson. The court also gave an option to Intex to continue to import and sell the products incorporating Ericsson's patented technologies on payment of interim royalty as in the case of Micromax.

Litigants	Year of Dispute(s)	Grievance Redressal Body/Bodies	Dispute(s) and Decision(s) of Grievance Redressal Body/Bodies
	2016	High Court of Delhi	The court considered the two writ petitions (by Ericsson against Micromax and Intex in response to the order of CCI) together. It dismissed the petitions observing that SEP grants its holder dominant position and significant bargaining power. Licensing SEP on FRAND terms was important. The court concluded that when abuse of market dominance was the subject matter, the CCI was the competent authority to adjudicate. Determination of rates of royalty was also under the purview of CCI.
Ericsson v. Lava	2016	High Court of Delhi	Ericsson filed infringement suit against Lava on its eight SEPs. Efforts of both the parties to agree on a FRAND licensing agreement failed. The court granted injunctive relief to Ericsson. It restricted Lava from manufacturing, importing, selling and offering for sale any device incorporating the patented technology of Ericsson. Interim injunction to stop production, import, export and sale. Lava was directed to pay interim royalty to Ericsson for the period from the filing of suit until June 20, 2016, at the rate which was prescribed to Micromax. Unlike in *Ericsson v. Micromax*, where the court allowed Micromax to continue manufacturing, importing and selling the devices on payment of interim royalty, the court did not allow Lava ruled otherwise.

Litigants	Year of Dispute(s)	Grievance Redressal Body/Bodies	Dispute(s) and Decision(s) of Grievance Redressal Body/Bodies
Ericsson v. Xiaomi	2014	High Court of Delhi	Ericsson sued Xiaomi for infringing its eight SEPs. Xiaomi challenged the injunction arguing that it was using chipsets provided by Qualcomm, which had licensing agreement with Ericsson. The court allowed Xiaomi to import and sell in India subject to the condition that it would sell only devices containing Qualcomm chips and deposit INR 100 towards royalty for every infringing device imported into India.

Litigants	*Year of Dispute(s)*	*Grievance Redressal Body/Bodies*	*Dispute(s) and Decision(s) of Grievance Redressal Body/Bodies*
	2016	High Court of Delhi	The court vacated the earlier interim order in two of the eight patents, as Ericsson was found to have concealed information on its "multi-product license agreement" with Qualcomm for the two patents. This agreement which was already in force when Ericsson sued Xiaomi for infringing charges allows Qualcomm to make, use, sell and import chipsets and devices containing Ericsson's relevant patented technologies. The court ruled that Xiaomi bought chipsets from Qualcomm and did not infringe Ericsson's patents.
Ericsson v. iBall	2015	Competition Commission of India	Ericsson issued a letter to iBall stating that latter's mobile device infringed Ericsson's patents and offered a FRAND global patent license agreement (GPLA). Ericsson insisted that details of the agreement would be disclosed only after signing of NDA. iBall filed a complaint before the CCI against abuse of dominant position by Ericsson. Basis of the complaint: (1) terms of NDA were onerous; (2) royalty rate was high; (3) Ericsson tied and bundled patents not required by iBall; and (4) royalty rates based on the sale price of the product and not on the cost of the technology used. CCI found evidence of abuse of dominant position by Ericsson and directed its director general to conduct an enquiry. Ericsson moved Delhi High Court against CCI; the court directed CCI, not to proceed with the investigation. Ericsson and iBall entered into a GPLA and settled the matter out of court.
Vringo v. ZTE	2013	High Court of Delhi	Vringo Infrastructure filed a civil suit against ZTE and its Indian subsidiary ZTE Telecom India for infringement of its patent, which Vringo claimed, was a SEP for CDMA2000 family of standards. The court issued an injunction order against defendants, their officers, directors, agents, employees, distributors, customers etc.

Litigants	*Year of Dispute(s)*	*Grievance Redressal Body/Bodies*	*Dispute(s) and Decision(s) of Grievance Redressal Body/Bodies*
			"from manufacturing, assembling, importing, selling or offering for sale or advertising on their products or any other similar devices that include the 3G technology CDMA2000, which may amount to the infringement of the plaintiff's patent".
	2014	High Court of Delhi	Vringo filed an infringement suit against ZTE, ZTE Telecom India and Indiamart, a distributor of ZTE products. According to Vringo, this patent was part of a standard related to base station controller of 2G and 3G infrastructure. In February 2014, the court granted an interim injunction restraining ZTE from importing, selling, advertising, installing or operating devices that incorporate the infringing technology. In August 2014, the injunction was lifted on the condition that ZTE would deposit INR 178.5 million in the court. In December 2015, Vringo entered into a "confidential settlement and licensing agreement" with ZTE and its affiliates. Under this agreement, ZTE was granted a "non-exclusive, non-transferable, worldwide perpetual license" of certain patents owned by Vringo. ZTE agreed to pay a lump sum amount of USD 21.5 million to Vringo.

Litigants	*Year of Dispute(s)*	*Grievance Redressal Body/Bodies*	*Dispute(s) and Decision(s) of Grievance Redressal Body/Bodies*
	2016		Dolby International AB claimed that cell phones, tablets and televisions manufactured by Oppo and Vivo produce sound of high quality, which is possible only by using Dolby's technology, covered by four patents. The judge issued an order restraining Oppo and Vivo from manufacturing/assembling/importing/selling/offering for sale, cell phones, tablets and televisions that used Dolby's patents.

Litigants	Year of Dispute(s)	Grievance Redressal Body/Bodies	Dispute(s) and Decision(s) of Grievance Redressal Body/Bodies
Dolby v. Oppo and Vivo		High Court of Delhi	Oppo and Vivo submitted that they should be enabled to continue manufacturing and selling the products that used Dolby's technology since they were willing to deposit appropriate royalty in the court. The court determined that Dolby's royalty should be INR 34 for every machine manufactured/sold/imported as an interim royalty. The earlier order of the court was modified and Oppo/Vivo were permitted to manufacture/sell/import the products. In a subsequent development, one of the defendants in the case, brought before the court evidence of royalty stacking by Dolby arguing that the FRAND rates were being charged for the entire family of 600 patents instead of the four patents. Taking cognisance, the court directed Oppo/Vivo to deposit INR 20 for every machine manufactured/sold/imported instead of INR 34 ordered earlier.

Source: Compiled by authors from various sources.

13 The paradox of relief

Reconciling remedies in patent law and competition law for FRAND cases in India

Feroz Ali

1 Introduction

Like too many choices, having too many reliefs may not be a good thing.[1] This is especially true for FRAND (fair, reasonable and non-discriminatory) licensing of SEPs (standard essential patents), where having multiple remedies with different fora to agitate them could lead to instances where the existence of reliefs in one domain can be cited to vitiate the reliefs available in another. A typical case involving FRAND licensing of SEPs encompasses a barrage of reliefs for the SEP holder and the standard implementer. When the SEP holder files a patent infringement suit, the primary reliefs include injunction and damages or an account of profits.[2] The SEP holder may also claim ancillary reliefs such as seizure, forfeiture or destruction of infringing goods.[3] The defendant, usually the standard implementer, will have the option of claiming the following relief: a declaration of non-infringement,[4] counter-claiming that the patent is invalid by raising the various grounds of revocation[5] and seeking a declaration with regard to essentiality of the SEP.[6] The defendant in an infringement suit involving an SEP can also claim as a defence that in a contract with the SEP holder there was a restrictive condition declared void by the Act.[7] Though not a relief that directly flows out of a patent infringement suit, the defendant could also file an application for compulsory licence under the various grounds available under the Act.[8] Apart from the reliefs under the Patents Act, the defendant may approach the Competition Commission of India (CCI) for reliefs including discontinuation of an anti-competitive agreement or abuse of dominant position and modification

1 *Cf.* Barry Schwartz, *The Paradox of Choice: Why More Is Less* (New York: Harper Perennial, 2004) (arguing that having more choices may not be beneficial and cutting down the number of choices may lead to better decision making).
2 Patent Act, 1970, § 108(1).
3 *Id.* at § 108(2).
4 *Id.* at § 105.
5 *Id.* at § 107(1).
6 Specific Relief Act, 1963, § 34.
7 Patent Act, 1970, (n 3) at § 140(3).
8 *Id.* at §§ 84 and 91.

of existing agreements.[9] Thus, the standard implementer is enriched with reliefs both under Patents Act and the Competition Act.

However, the plethora of reliefs available to the standard implementer, rather than resulting in quicker resolution of disputes protracts settlement and creates a paradox: the availability of reliefs under one domain is often cited to deny reliefs in another domain. The paradox arises in a FRAND licensing situation when the relief of applying for a compulsory licence under the Patents Act is cited to oust the jurisdiction under the Competition Act to modify existing licensing agreements. This was illustrated lucidly in the *Ericsson* cases, where Indian mobile phone manufacturers, Micromax Informatics Ltd and Intex Technologies (India) Ltd, filed complaints before the CCI against Ericsson alleging violations under the Competition Act, 2002.[10] While Ericsson (the SEP holder) has approached the courts with patent infringement suits seeking injunctive reliefs, Micromax and Intex (the standard implementers) approached the CCI alleging anti-competitive practices. The striking feature of FRAND cases in India is ouster of jurisdiction argument that SEP holders make against the power of the CCI to decide cases involving FRAND licenses. By questioning the jurisdiction of the CCI, the SEP holders not only circumscribe the available reliefs under competition laws but also attenuate the recourse those affected by stronger IP rights have (i.e. to seek a response in competition law).[11] Raising arguments on ouster of jurisdiction of the CCI is not a new issue. There have been many cases where the jurisdiction of the CCI was questioned before, especially in cases involving intellectual property (IP) rights.[12]

But what sets the FRAND cases apart is the manner in which the ouster of jurisdiction of the CCI is argued: ouster arguments are usually raised upon an understanding that the authority does not have the requisite power to decide an issue and concomitantly, the power vests with a different authority. More importantly, since the core issue to be settled in a FRAND case involves the royalty terms, ouster arguments citing the power of a different forum to determine the royalty may implicitly indicate the willingness to submit to royalty determination by a third-party. Ouster arguments bring out the difference between the concepts of "patent abuse" and "anti-competitive practices", that is whether the act complained of before the CCI involved abuse of IP or abuse of dominance, both of which can be redressed by a third-party determination of royalty rates. If the

9 Competition Act, 2002, § 27.

10 *See Micromax Informatics Limited v. Telefonaktiebolaget LM Ericsson (PUBL)*, 2013 SCC OnLine CCI 78; *Intex Technologies (India) Ltd v. Telefonaktiebolaget LM Ericsson*, 2014 SCC OnLine CCI 8 [hereinafter "Ericsson cases"].

11 Mark A. Lemley, A New Balance Between IP and Antitrust, 13 *Sw. J.L. Trade Am.* 237 (2006) (arguing for countering stronger IP rights with stronger antitrust enforcements).

12 *See Aamir Khan Productions v. Union of India*, 2010 (112) Bom L R 3778. *See also Kingfisher Airlines Limited v. Competition Commission of India*, (2010) 4 *Comp L.J.* 557 (Bom), *Manju Bharadwaj v. Zee Telefilms Ltd*, (1996) 20 *CLA* 229, *Vallal Peruman v. Godfrey Phillips (India) Ltd*, (1995) 16 *CLA* 201.

courts have a clear understanding of these two concepts, which have traditionally emerged as different concepts throughout history, it becomes easier for the courts to decide not only the issue of jurisdiction but also how royalty rates are determined.

This conceptual confusion is not confined to cases involving FRAND licences of SEPs. The pattern of raising jurisdictional objections against the CCI was witnessed in cases involving FRAND-like licences. Recently in the *Monsanto* cases,[13] Monsanto argued the ouster of jurisdiction of the CCI in a case involving its patents over GM (genetically modified) seeds stating that "the CCI had no jurisdiction in respect of any matter relating to IP rights including the rights pertaining to licensing of patents and trademarks, which fall within the exclusive jurisdiction of the authority/civil courts as provided under the Patents Act, 1970 and the Trade Marks Act, 1999".[14] The ouster of jurisdiction argument also proceeds on the different relief a party to the dispute is entitled to make at different fora.

The *Ericsson* and *Monsanto* cases show that conflicting arguments relating to IP and competition law raised in tandem had in common the manner in which the technology is commercialized, that is the business model involving the implementation of the technology by downstream implementers for the payment of royalty before it reaches the ultimate user. Naturally, the mode of relationship between the patent holder and the technology user was one of licensor and licensee. The business model in both the cases were focused on allowing use and obtaining royalty from the user, which is at variance to the business model usually followed by pharmaceutical patent holders where the focus is to injunct the user and attain market exclusively.[15] The *Ericsson* and *Monsanto* cases demonstrate that courts should factor the business model and the manner of implementation of technology in determining the reliefs that the parties claim.

With this introduction, this chapter moves forward to analyze the underlying reasons for why parties to FRAND licence of SEPs opt for different fora claiming reliefs under IP laws and competition laws and explaining how the misunderstanding surrounding the related concepts of "patent abuse" and "anti-competitive practice" have led to questioning the jurisdiction of CCI in both

13 *Ministry of Agriculture and Farmers Welfare v. Mahyco Monsanto Biotech (India) Ltd* 2016 SCC OnLine CCI 14 : [2016] CCI 6; *Ministry of Agriculture and Farmers Welfare v. Mahyco Monsanto Biotech (India) Ltd* 2016 SCC OnLine CCI 40; *Nuziveedu Seeds Ltd v. Mahyco Monsanto Biotech India Ltd* 2016 SCC OnLine CCI 48; *Ministry of Agriculture and Farmers Welfare v. Mahyco Monsanto Biotech (India) Ltd* 2016 SCC OnLine CCI 93; *Monsanto Technology LLC v. Nuziveedu Seeds Ltd* 2017 SCC OnLine Del 7652; *Nuziveedu Seeds Ltd v. Monsanto Technology LLC* 2018 SCC OnLine Del 8326; *Monsanto Technology LLC v. Nuziveedu Seeds Ltd* 2019 SCC OnLine SC 25.

14 *Mahyco Monsanto Biotech (India) Private Ltd v. Competition Commission of India* 2018 SCC OnLine Del 12991.

15 Richard A. Epstein & F. Scott Kieff, Questioning the Frequency and Wisdom of Compulsory Licensing for Pharmaceutical Patents Symposium: The Licensing of Intellectual Property, 78 *U. Chi. L. Rev.* 71–94 (2011) (noting that large pharmaceutical companies are never non-practising trolls and are not interested in licensing arrangement as a revenue model).

the *Ericsson* and *Monsanto* cases. Section 2 looks at the evolution of the issue in the context of FRAND licences in the *Ericsson* cases and the similar arguments raised in the context of FRAND-like cases (i.e. the *Monsanto* cases) and explains the common themes in technology and business models in the *Ericsson* and *Monsanto* cases. The unique nature of technology in both the cases which allows patent holders to collect royalties from downstream implementers aligns both set of cases on common ground. Section 3 discusses the ouster of jurisdiction argument raised before the CCI in the context of different IP laws, clarifies the misconceptions involving "patent abuse" and "anti-competitive practices" under Indian law and proffers a way forward in determining such disputes. Section 4 concludes the chapter.

2 The Ericsson and Monsanto cases

Despite falling under diverse fields of technology, both the *Ericsson* and *Monsanto* cases follow the model of allowing others to use their IP with the intent of collecting royalty, as opposed to exclusively exploiting the IP by restraining users, a model that is common in the pharmaceutical sector. Both the cases, covering FRAND licences, had the following traits in common: (1) technology covered by the patents was licensed to downstream implementers for royalty payments; (2) downstream implementers found the licensing terms onerous and approached the CCI for reliefs; and (3) the existence of remedies in patent law was cited to exclude the jurisdiction of competition law.

2.1 FRAND licences involving Ericsson

Telefonaktiebolaget LM Ericsson ("Ericsson") owned a large portfolio of SEPs used in mobile handsets and network stations. SEPs cover technologies that have been uniformly accepted and implemented across various countries to ensure uniformity and compatibility for seamless transmission of data and call around the world.[16] Ericsson, as a member of the European Telecommunication Standard Institute (ETSI), the European Standard Setting Organisation (SSO) which lays down standards for the telecommunication industry with particular reference to the 2G (GSM, GPRS, EDGE), 3G (UMTS, WCDMA, HSPA) and 4G (LTE) standards, had patents covering technology adopted as a part of a standard.[17]

Clause 6.1 of the ETSI Intellectual Property Rights Policy provides for a FRAND licenses.[18] It states that when an essential IPR relating to a particular standard or technical specification is brought to the ETSI's notice, it shall request

16 *Telefonaktiebolaget LM Ericsson (PUBL) v. Competition Commission of India and Another* 2016 SCC OnLine Del 1951 para. 8.

17 *Id.* at para. 9.

18 See, ETSI IPR Policy, ETSI – IPR, Intellectual Property Rights, FRAND, www.etsi.org/intellectual-property-rights (last visited March 23, 2019).

the owner to give an irrevocable undertaking in writing that it is prepared to grant irrevocable licenses on FRAND terms. Ericsson had undertaken to offer its SEPs on FRAND terms.[19]

2.1.1 Dispute with regard to royalty payments

Ericsson tried to negotiate with the Indian mobile companies to make them enter into Ericsson's global patent license agreement (GPLA) while insisting that the companies sign a non-disclosure agreement (NDA) as a pre-condition for letting the companies know about their infringement. Additionally, Ericsson refused to state the license rates meted out to other licensees in light of NDAs signed by the parties.[20] Ericsson had been contacting Indian mobile phone companies, including Micromax and Intex, which were using these SEPs without a license.

When Micromax refused to sign the GPLA and the NDA, Ericsson filed a suit in the Delhi High Court.[21] The single judge passed an ex parte order stating that Ericsson had made out a prima facie case, and that it would suffer irreparable harm if the injunction was not granted. The court also authorized the search and report of any consignments imported by Micromax, as well as a search of its office premises. Following which, both the parties approached the court stating that they had decided to work towards a FRAND licence agreement. The interim royalty rates were also decided to be at the range of 1.25%–2% of the sale price.[22] Additionally Micromax had to pay the interim royalty amount within five days of its intimation of arrival of the consignment by customs. The court had indicated that Ericsson could inspect the customs and if Ericsson found no objections, the consignment could be handed over to Micromax. The parties had the option of resorting to mediation on the failure to arrive at FRAND terms pursuant to negotiations.[23]

In the patent infringement cases filed by Ericsson with respect to FRAND licensing, the court had made provisions for the payment of royalty, half of which was to be paid directly and the remaining to be furnished by way of a bank guarantee.[24] The court also stated that for a future period arising every six months, the same terms would apply until the pendency of the suit.[25] The court clearly stated that the order was a mere interim arrangement and was not a determination of FRAND rates.[26] The court also stated that the defendants in each case could not

19 *Telefonaktiebolaget LM Ericsson (PUBL) v. Competition Commission of India and Another* 2016 SCC OnLine Del 1951, (n 18) at 10.

20 *Id.* at 12.

21 *Telefonaktiebolaget LM Ericsson v Mercury Electronics* 2013 SCC OnLine Del 4934: (2014) 206 DLT 423.

22 *Id.*

23 *Id.* at 3.

24 *Telefonaktiebolaget LM Ericsson v Intex Technologies (India)* 2015 SCC OnLine Del 8229.

25 *Id.*

26 *Id.*

rely upon the rates mentioned, before any competition authority or any other similar fora as the decision was not final.[27] The court held that the argument of Intex of being charged based on the price of the chipsets could not be taken as that would not be in compliance with Ericsson's licenses based on FRAND terms made with other parties.[28] The court also stated that if a FRAND agreement was not signed and the royalty was not paid, then this would impact other licences of Ericsson.

2.1.2 Downstream implementers approach the CCI

After the failure of the efforts to mediate, Micromax filed information under section 19(1)(a) of the Competition Act, before the CCI, accusing Ericsson, inter alia, of abusing its position of dominance in the relevant market.[29] Micromax and Intex, being downstream implementers of the technology who were now restrained from using the technology by an order of the court, filed individual complaints before the CCI.[30] Micromax alleged that Ericsson was demanding unfair, discriminatory and exorbitant royalty for its patents.[31] The CCI had in both the cases held that Ericsson was in abuse of its dominant position and assigned the Director General to investigate.[32] The Commission noted Micromax's contention that Ericsson was abusing its dominant position as it was the owner of the essential patents.[33] The Commission also noted that the charging of royalty based on the products was unfair.[34] The Commission assigned the director general to conduct investigation stating clearly that this was not based on FRAND terms.[35]

The reasoning of the CCI was that Micromax had in its complaint stated that Ericsson was abusing its dominant position as the sole possessor of these essential patents by imposing exorbitant royalty rates.[36] These royalty rates were based on the sale price of the phone and which meant that Micromax had to pay the royalty based on each phone instead of royalty based on the patents used.[37] Due to this, royalty for use of same chipset in a smartphone amounted to more than 10 times the royalty for ordinary phone.[38] Micromax also stated that this method of

27 *Telefonaktiebolaget LM Ericsson v Intex Technologies (India)* 2015 SCC OnLine Del 8229 (n 28) at 160.

28 *Id.* at 158.

29 *Micromax Informatics Limited v. Telefonaktiebolaget LM Ericsson (PUBL)* 2013 SCC OnLine CCI 78 (n 11).

30 *Intex Technologies (India) Ltd v. Telefonaktiebolaget LM Ericsson* 2014 SCC OnLine CCI 8, (n 11); *Micromax Informatics Limited v. Telefonaktiebolaget LM Ericsson (PUBL)* 2013 SCC OnLine CCI 78 (n 11).

31 *Id.* at 2.

32 *Id.*

33 *Id.*

34 *Id.* at 8.

35 *Id.* at 9.

36 *Id.* at 3.

37 *Id.*

38 *Id.* at 4.

payment would be affecting the end consumer as the price of the phone would be significantly increased.[39] Micromax also alleged that imposing the NDA prevented it from discussing or comparing the rates offered to other parties. Ericsson in its defence stated that Micromax had taken a different stand before the High Court, when it started making royalty payments in furtherance of the interim arrangement.[40] In its defence, Ericsson had also stated that as the case was of a civil and commercial nature the Commission had no authority to grant rates.[41] Ericsson also stated that the seeking of injunction would not amount to abuse of dominance.[42]

The Commission in its decision outlined the position of Ericsson as a member of a SSO[43] and threw light on the ETSI's role as an SSO respectively. The Commission also stated the importance of the FRAND terms to prevent patent holdup and royalty stacking.[44] The Commission observed that as Ericsson was the owner of the eight SEPs that were approved by the Department of Telecommunication, Government of India, it was in a dominant position.[45] The Commission also held that the granting of royalty rates that were in no way related to the products acted as an abuse of FRAND terms as well as dominant position.[46] The Commission held that charging "two different license fees per unit phone for use of the same technology prima facie is discriminatory and also reflects excessive pricing vis-a-vis high cost phones".[47] A similar case was made out by Intex based on similar grounds and both the CCI as well as the court held the same opinion as held in the Micromax case. The CCI made observations on the issue of abuse of dominant position by Ericsson. The Commission not only looked at the fact that these patents were essential but also looked at the unfair jurisdictional terms of the GPLA and the NDA. In both the patent infringement cases before the High Court, it was decided that the patents were valid and the companies had to pay royalties to Ericsson and enter into FRAND negotiations.[48]

2.1.3 CCI order challenged before High Court

Aggrieved by the order of the CCI, Ericsson filed a petition before the Delhi High Court for judicial review of the order passed by the CCI.[49] This was the first time, questions were raised on SEP licensing, FRAND terms and jurisdictional authority of the CCI. Ericsson argued that the remedy of compulsory licensing

39 *Id.*
40 *Id.*
41 *Id.*
42 *Id.*
43 *Id.* at 5.
44 *Id.* at 6.
45 *Id.*
46 *Id.* at 7.
47 *Id.*
48 *Telefonaktiebolaget LM Ericsson v Intex Technologies (India)* 2015 SCC OnLine Del 8229 (n 28).
49 *Telefonaktiebolaget LM Ericsson (PUBL) v. Competition Commission of India and Another* 2016 SCC OnLine Del 1951 (n 18).

provided in the Indian Patents Act would override the remedies provided under the Competition Act, and also that the orders passed by the CCI were without jurisdiction.[50] Ericsson questioned the jurisdictional powers of the CCI, stating that it did not possess the authority to decide cases on patent royalty. It was argued by Ericsson that the Patents Act provided enough mechanisms to deal with the abuse of dominant position and hence there was no need to seek recourse to the Competition Act. Ericsson stated that the Patents Act had various provisions in the Act itself for the redressal of the grievances of any person with respect to the non-availability of the rights to use a patent. Citing the provisions of compulsory licensing, it stated that in the presence of such a provision, a need to seek recourse under the Competition Act was unnecessary.[51] The High Court held that the CCI had the jurisdiction to hear the case, stating also that the remedies for abuse of dominant position provided under the Patent Act and the Competition Act were different and not conflicting.[52]

Micromax and Intex also stated that Ericsson had in its FRAND negotiations acted in an “opaque, non-transparent and a high handed manner”, using threats of infringement cases to coerce the companies to sign the GPLA. Ericsson had also threatened to file a complaint to the Securities Exchange SEBI, to curb Micromax’s entry into the stock market.[53] Additionally Intex stated that Ericsson had indulged in the process of “bundling and tying licensing”,[54] which Intex alleged was anti-competitive. The High Court held that it was evident that Ericsson was in a position to dominate and the mobile phone companies would have had to adhere to the rates in order to use the technology.[55] Ericsson, it was observed, was a member of the ETSI and hence was bound to offer its SEPs on FRAND terms.[56] The court analyzed the question citing examples from various cases including the recent judgment in the *Huawei Technologies Co. Ltd v. ZTE Corp.*,[57] and drew similarities between the TFEU (Treaty on the Functioning of the European Union) and the Competition Act.[58] The court held that in certain cases the seeking of injunction by an SEP holder would amount to abuse of dominance. Stating that the threat of injunction would coerce the

50 *Id.* Patent Act, 1970 (n 3) at § 84. Compulsory Licensing as defined under the Indian Patents Act provides that after three years of a grant of a patent any person could seek for a grant of compulsory license for that patent on grounds such as the failure to meet reasonable requirement of the public, unaffordability, and non-working in India. Hence under section 84 of the Indian Patents Act any person could seek a compulsory license with respect to a patent, if it fulfils any of three grounds mentioned.

51 *Id.* at para. 109.

52 *Id.* at para. 215.

53 *Telefonaktiebolaget LM Ericsson (PUBL) v. Competition Commission of India and Another* 2016 SCC OnLine Del 1951 (n 18) at 181.

54 *Id.* at 135.

55 *Id.*

56 *Id.*

57 *Id.* at 144.

58 *Id.*

companies to adhere to the license agreement in order to prevent their business from being stalled.[59] The court also observed that an owner of an SEP had a different standing compared to that of the owner of a non-SEP patent. The SEPs were essential without which the implementing companies could not adhere to a standard. Hence there was an apparent dominant position by virtue of the type of patent which made it possible to force a licensee into agreeing to a non-FRAND license.[60]

The court compared and defined the Patents Act as well as the Competition Act stating that while one was for the promotion of inventiveness the other was devised to ensure fair competition in the market. Stating also that the Patents Act was in generally designed to give monopolistic power to the owner of the patents whereas the Competition Act dealt with the prevention of monopolistic anticompetitive practices.[61] The court then analyzed in detail the various provisions of both the acts including the history of the provisions dealing with anticompetitive practices. It looked at the various remedies provided by the acts in dealing with the subject issue. The court held that the remedies provided under section 27 of the Competition Act were dissimilar and not mutually exclusive to the provisions of the section 84 of the Patents Act.[62] It observed that the provisions of section 84 of the Patents Act provided for a specific remedy for individuals whereas the provisions of the Competition Act provided for a remedy against the whole world, adding that the scope of the enactments were different.[63] The court held that although the Patents Act did provide remedies through compulsory licensing there was no express remedy against breach of FRAND obligations.[64] Hence the court held that "there is no irreconcilable repugnancy or conflict between the Competition Act and the Patents Act" and where there is no irreconcilable conflict between the two acts, "the jurisdiction of CCI to entertain complaints for abuse of dominance in respect of patent rights cannot be ousted".[65]

2.2 FRAND licences involving Monsanto

Monsanto's case involved FRAND licences for the patent covering transgenic Bt. cotton seeds which it offered to downstream implementers, the domestic seed companies.[66] Monsanto had entered into sub-license agreements with several domestic seed companies. The seed companies like Nuziveedu received 50 grams

59 *Id.* at 152.
60 *Id.* at 153.
61 *Telefonaktiebolaget LM Ericsson (PUBL) v. Competition Commission of India and Another* 2016 SCC OnLine Del 1951 (n 18) at 110.
62 *Id.* at 162.
63 *Id.* at 169.
64 *Id.* at 137.
65 *Id.* at 174.
66 Indian Patent No. 214436 for "Methods for Transforming Plants to Express *Bacillus thuringiensis delta-endotoxins*".

of transgenic Bt. cotton varietal seeds in consideration of an upfront payment of INR 5 million. The sub-license agreement contains stipulations including the obligation of the seed companies to pay the "trait value".[67]

2.2.1 Dispute with regard to royalty payments

Monsanto filed a patent infringement suit before the Delhi High Court claiming that the defendants continued to "market and sell" genetically modified hybrid cotton planting seeds despite of termination of the sub-license agreements including trademark sub-license agreements. Monsanto alleged violation of their registered patent (IN 214436) and trademarks BOLLGARD and BOLLGARD II. The defendants, Monsanto alleged, engaged in acts that amounted to infringement or passing off "illegally" manufactured products sold or offered to be sold in such packing or under labels (BOLLGARD) bearing such marks as are identical or deceptively or confusingly similar to its rights.

Similar to the *Ericsson* cases, the parties claimed an array of reliefs: Monsanto prayed for permanent prohibitory injunction against such infringement of registered patent and trademarks, or passing off, mandatory injunction for requisite disclosures, recall of infringing products or material and delivering up in addition to rendition of accounts, leading to award of damages (including penal) and so forth;[68] and Nuziveedu, the defendant, made two counter-claims, one praying for a declaration that the sub-licensing agreements executed by Monsanto in their favour were valid, binding and in force and the other praying for revocation of the Monsanto's patent No. 214436.[69]

A set of earlier sub-license agreements entered into by the parties in 2004 ran into some dispute with regard to the "trait value", which came up before the Monopolies and Restrictive Trade Practices Commission (MRTPC).[70] The parties, however, settled the dispute. A similar pattern of issuing notices of termination for non-payment of trait value was followed by Monsanto earlier, but the matter was resolved between the two parties.[71]

Disputes arose when the Central Government, in terms of Cotton Seeds Price (Control) Order, 2015, declared the maximum selling price of Bt. cotton seed packets which affected the royalty payments of Monsanto.[72] The FRAND nature of the licensing was brought out by the Guidelines issued by the Government

67 *Monsanto Technology LLC v. Nuziveedu Seeds Ltd* 2017 SCC OnLine Del 7652 (n 14) at 21.
68 *Id.* at 21.
69 *Id.* at 4.
70 The Monopolies and Restrictive Trade Practices Act, 1969 was the precursor to the Competition Act, 2002. In 1999, the Government of India constituted a High Level Committee to examine the then existing provisions of the Monopolies and Restrictive Trade Practices Act, 1969 for shifting the focus of the law from curbing monopolies to promoting competition. The Committee recommended a modern competition law in line with the international developments to suit Indian conditions. *See Telefonaktiebolaget LM Ericsson (PUBL) v. Competition Commission of India and Another* 2016 SCC OnLine Del 1951 (n 18) at 112.
71 *Monsanto Technology LLC v. Nuziveedu Seeds Ltd* 2017 SCC OnLine Del 7652 (n 14) at 22.
72 *Id.* at 53.

of India, "Licensing and Formats for GM Technology Agreement Guidelines, 2016", which obliges the licensor and licensees to ensure that all agreements executed by them are non-discriminative to encourage competition and availability of GM cotton seeds to cotton farmers at fair and reasonable prices.[73] In the light of the government fixing the prices, Nuziveedu informed Monsanto that the 2015 sub-license agreements stood statutorily modified and required Monsanto to charge the revised trait value. Monsanto turned down the request and approached the Bombay High Court for reliefs under section 9 of the Arbitration and Conciliation Act, 1996, citing the arbitration clause in the sub-license agreement and seeking direction on Nuziveedu to deposit the amounts representing the trait value payable to Monsanto as per the agreement.[74] Monsanto terminated the sub-license agreements and sued for patent and trademark infringement before the Delhi High Court.[75]

2.2.2 Downstream implementers approach the CCI

Monsanto's action triggered a set of cases filed before the CCI by various parties,[76] against Monsanto and its subsidiaries, alleging contravention of sections 3 and 4 of the Competition Act, 2002.[77] The Department of Agriculture, Cooperation and Farmers Welfare in the Ministry of Agriculture and Farmers Welfare, Government of India (MOA&FW) registered a reference case against Monsanto before the CCI, whereas Nuziveedu and other entities filed information on similar lines.[78] The CCI held, by a majority decision, that a prima facie case of contravention of sections 3(4) and 4 of the Competition Act, 2002 was made out and ordered investigation into the matter.[79]

Monsanto sued for patent infringement before the single judge of the Delhi High Court.[80] The order of the single judge in the patent infringement case was challenged by Nuziveedu and the same was reversed by the Division Bench of the Delhi High Court.[81] Monsanto appealed against the order to the Supreme Court. The Supreme Court reversed the order of the Division Bench and remanded the matter back to the single judge.[82]

73 *Id.* at 55. These are, in effect, FRAND licences as the Guidelines require the licences to non-discriminatory and the prices (royalty) to be fair and reasonable.
74 *Id.* at 57.
75 *Monsanto Technology LLC v. Nuziveedu Seeds Ltd* 2017 SCC OnLine Del 7652 (n 14).
76 The parties include Department of Agriculture, Cooperation and Farmers Welfare, Ministry of Agriculture and Farmer's Welfare, Government of India, Nuziveedu Seeds Ltd, Prabhat Agri Biotech and Pravardhan Seeds Pvt. Ltd. *See Ministry of Agriculture and Farmers Welfare v. Mahyco Monsanto Biotech (India) Ltd*, Reference Case No. 2/2015 and 107/2015, 1–3 (2016).
77 *Id.* ¶¶ 2–3.
78 *Monsanto Technology LLC v. Nuziveedu Seeds Ltd* 2017 SCC OnLine Del 7652 (n 14) at 65.
79 *Department of Agriculture v. Mahyco Monsanto Biotech* 2017 SCC OnLine Del 7652.
80 *Monsanto Technology LLC v. Nuziveedu Seeds Ltd* 2017 SCC OnLine Del 7652 (n 14).
81 *Nuziveedu Seeds Ltd v. Monsanto Technology LLC* 2018 SCC OnLine Del 8326 (n 14).
82 *Monsanto Technology LLC v. Nuziveedu Seeds Ltd* 2019 SCC OnLine SC 25 (n 14).

2.2.3 CCI order challenged before High Court

Monsanto questioned the order of the CCI directing investigation by invoking the writ jurisdiction of the Delhi High Court and the matter is still pending consideration,[83] questioning the jurisdiction of the CCI to decide matters involving its patents.[84] Monsanto argued that ouster of jurisdiction of the CCI on matters relating to IP rights including the rights pertaining to licensing of patents and trademarks, and stated that matters concerning IP would fall exclusively within the jurisdiction of civil courts.[85]

3 The jurisdiction of CCI: between patent abuse and anti-competitive practices

3.1 Ouster arguments

Since the establishment of the CCI, and even during the existence of its predecessor, the MRTPC, parties have been raising ouster arguments to divest the jurisdiction of the Commission. Though the lack of jurisdiction argument can be raised on its own, stating that the CCI does not have powers to look into a particular matter,[86] many a times the jurisdiction argument is raised under the pretext that some other authority has the power to look into the matter and hence the CCI should be divested of its powers to look into the same. Though competition law operated in tandem with other laws, the scheme of the Competition Act, 2002 makes it abundantly clear that the powers of CCI cannot be divested by other authorities or laws. The Competition Act has overriding effect over other laws.[87] It also provides for exclusion of jurisdiction of civil courts in respect of matters which the Commission or the Appellate Tribunal is empowered to determine under the act.[88] Further, the powers under the act are in addition to and not in derogation of the provisions of any other law.[89] The courts have consistently affirmed these principles.[90]

83 *Mahyco Monsanto Biotech (India) Private Ltd v. Competition Commission of India* 2018 SCC OnLine Del 12991 (n 16).
84 *Id.*
85 *Id.*
86 *Kingfisher Airlines Limited v. Competition Commission of India* (2010) 4 *Comp L.J.* 557 (Bom) (n 13).
87 Competition Act, 2002 (n 10) at 60.
88 *Id.* at 61.
89 *Id.* at 62.
90 *See, e.g., Telefonaktiebolaget LM Ericsson (PUBL) v. Competition Commission of India and Another* 2016 SCC OnLine Del 1951, 144 (holding that the Competition Act and Patents Act are special acts operating in their respective fields).

In the *Aamir Khan Productions* case,[91] the petitioners challenged the show cause notices issued by the CCI stating that the proceedings in respect of films would be covered under the Copyright Act, 1957. The director general had concluded that the persons named in the report of the director general had acted in concert by forming a cartel with a view of extracting higher revenue for the supply of films to the multiplexes and, for achieving the objects, had indulged in limiting/controlling the supply of films in the market by refusing to release films to multiplexes for exhibition thereby succeeding in raising the revenue sharing ratio. This was a violation under section 3(3) of the Competition Act, 2002. In response, the petitioners challenged the show cause notice and argued before the Bombay High Court that the exhibition of a feature film was a subject matter of Copyright Act and was specifically excluded under section 3(5) of the Competition Act, 2002. The petitioners argued that the only remedy available to the multiplex owners was to approach the Copyright Board under section 31 of the Copyright Act, 1957. It was argued that the scheme of the Copyright Act, in particular, sections 14, 30 and 31, is subject only to the right of the others to obtain compulsory licence and also the terms on which such licence can be granted.[92]

The issue that arose in the *Ericsson* cases as well as the *Monsanto* cases was whether the remedies provided under section 84 of the Patent Act, 1970 for certain acts pertaining to patented inventions will bar the jurisdiction of Competition Commission under the Competition Act, 2002. The object of the Patents Act, 1970 is to consolidate the laws relating to patents. The Patents Act not only deals with provisions for application, prosecution, grant, revocation and surrender of patents,[93] it also contains special provisions where the patents granted under the said Act are abused. Chapter XVI of the Patents Act, which covers "Working of Patents, Compulsory Licences and Revocation", deals with instances where the grant of patents could lead to abuse or misuse like non-working and so forth.[94] The Competition Act, 2002 seeks to ensure fair competition in India by prohibiting trade practices which cause appreciable adverse effect to competition in markets within India and to curb negative aspects of competition through the medium of CCI.[95] The main objective of competition law is to promote economic efficiency using competition as one of the means of assisting the creation of market that is responsive to consumer preferences.[96]

91 *Aamir Khan Productions v. Union of India*, 2010 (112) Bom LR 3778 (n 13).
92 Relying on *Entertainment Network India Limited v. Super Cassette Industries Limited* 2008 13 SCC 30.
93 Patent Act, 1970 (n 3) at Chapters III, IV, VIII and XII.
94 *Id.* at § 83(f).
95 Competition Act, 2002 (n 10), Statement of Objects and Reasons.
96 Competition Commission of India v. SAIL, (2010) 10 SCC 744, 755.

3.1.1 Patent abuse

Patent abuse refers to the unjustified use of the acquired patent rights. Section 83(f) of the Patents Act states that

> the patent right is not abused by the patentee or person deriving title or interest on patent from the patentee, and the patentee or a person deriving title or interest on patent from the patentee does not resort to practices which unreasonably restrain trade or adversely affect the international transfer of technology.[97]

Section 84 mentions the specific cases of patent abuse and provides for remedies by way of compulsory licence. Patent abuse is understood as abuse of patent rights through non-working and importation and abuse of patent rights to extend monopoly through insertion of conditions for sale, lease or license of the patented processes/products.[98] These abuses are addressed by sections 84 and 140 of the Patents Act. The Competition Act prohibits anti-competitive practices. Specific prohibited practices include agreements that prevent, restrict or distort competition and abuse of dominance.[99]

Patent abuse as a concept is distinct from anti-competitive practices. The scope of patent right granted under the Patents Act should be ascertained first before analyzing the terms "patent abuse" and "anti-competitive practices". The rights of the patentee granted by and under section 48 of the Patent Act, 1970 is not absolute and is "subject to other provisions" of the Patent Act. Chapter XVI of the Patent Act, which provides for grant of compulsory licences under various circumstances, is subject to conditions spelt out therein. The different types of conditions that may result in patent abuse can be remedied by the grant of the compulsory licence under section 84. Thus, when the reasonable requirement of the public is not satisfied, the invention is not available to the public at an affordable price or the invention is not worked in India, the Patents Act regards the act as an abuse resulting from the granted patent.

3.1.2 Anti-competitive practices

The Patents Act expressly excludes anti-competitive practices and does not have the power to deal with anti-competitive practices that come under the Competition Act, 2002. This is provided for in the proviso to section 84(6)(iv), which states that the clause shall not be applicable to anti-competitive practices,[100]

97 Patent Act, 1970 (n 3) at § 83(f).

98 Justice N. Rajagopala Ayyangar, Report on the Revision of the Patents Law 191 (1959).

99 Competition Act, 2002 (n 10) at §§ 3 and 4.

100 Patent Act, 1970, 84(6)(iv) (stating that as to whether the applicant has made efforts to obtain a licence from the patentee on reasonable terms and conditions and such efforts have not been successful within a reasonable period as the Controller may deem fit: Provided

specifically excluding "establishment of a ground of anti-competitive practices" from the scope of granting compulsory licence.[101] The reference to obtain a licence is only with regard to the three instances covered by section 84 (i.e. reasonable requirement of the public is not satisfied), the invention is not available to the public at an affordable price or the invention is not worked in India. The anti-competitive practices enumerated in section 84 are explained further in section 90(1)(ix), wherein it is stated:

> (ix) that in case the licence is granted to remedy a practice determined after judicial or administrative process to be anti-competitive, the licensee shall be permitted to export the patented product, if need be.

It is important to note that the aforementioned provisions of Chapter XVI only go so far to state that in granting a compulsory licences, the Controller shall have regard to anti-competitive practices resorted by the patentee and may grant license to remedy the same. However, none of the provisions specify as to who has the power to adjudicate and conclude that a certain practice of a patentee is anti-competitive or amounts to abuse of the patentee's position of dominance. Section 90(1)(ix) of the Patents Act, which was amended in 2005, envisages the grant of a compulsory licences to remedy a practice determined "after judicial or administrative process" to be anti-competitive.[102] Hence, the Patents Act acknowledges the jurisdiction of the Competition Act, 2002 by referring to "a practice determined after judicial or administrative process to be anti-competitive". The determination of anti-competitive practice by administrative process refers to the powers of the CCI.

Anti-competitive agreements under the Competition Act, 2002 includes arrangements, understandings or even action in concert.[103]

3.2 *Legislative intent to keep concepts separate*

The legislative intent, in the creation of the Patents Act and the Competition Act, was clear in keeping "patent abuse" and "anti-competitive practices" separate. Such an interpretation would also be consistent with the recommendations of Justice N. Rajagopala Ayyangar in the Report on the Revision of the Patents Law submitted in 1959 (popularly known as the "Ayyangar Committee Report"),

---

that this clause shall not be applicable in case of national emergency or other circumstances of extreme urgency or in case of public non-commercial use or on establishment of a ground of anti-competitive practices adopted by the patentee, but shall not be required to take into account matters subsequent to the making of the application).

101 *Id.* at 84.

102 *Id.* at 90(1)(ix).

103 *CCI v. Coordination Committee of Artistes & Technicians of W.B. Film & Television* (2017) 5 SCC 17, 39.

which forms the basis of the Patents Act, 1970 and repealed the Monopolies and Restrictive Trade Practices Act, 1969.

3.2.1 Ayyangar Committee Report

The Ayyangar Committee identified three types of abuses: (1) through non-working and importation; (2) extending monopoly through insertion of conditions for sale, lease or license of the patented processes/products; and (3) use of patents or a group of patents to form monopolistic cartels and combinations to control production and distribution.[104] The grant of compulsory licences has been identified as the measure to counter the first type of abuse. To deal with the second type of abuse, a provision on the lines of section 140 of the Patents Act was recommended.[105] However, the third type, referred to as use of patents to form cartels, was recognized as resulting from excessive concentration of economic

104 Justice N. Rajagopala Ayyangar (n 139) at 191.

105 Section140. Avoidance of certain restrictive conditions

(1) It shall not be lawful to insert –

(i) in any contract for or in relation to the sale or lease of a patented article or an article made by a patented process; or

(ii) in a licence to manufacture or use a patented article; or

(iii) in a licence to work any process protected by a patent, a condition the effect of which may be –

(a) to require the purchaser, lessee, or licensee to acquire from the vendor, lessor, or licensor, or his nominees, or to prohibit him from acquiring or to restrict in any manner or to any extent his right to acquire from any person or to prohibit him from acquiring except from the vendor, lessor, or licensor or his nominees, any article other than the patented article or an article other than that made by the patented process; or

(b) to prohibit the purchaser, lessee or licensee from using, or to restrict in any manner or to any extent the right of the purchaser, lessee or licensee, to use an article other than the patented article or an article other than that made by the patented process, which is not supplied by the vendor, lessor or licensor or his nominee; or

(c) to prohibit the purchaser, lessee or licensee from using or to restrict in any manner or to any extent the right of the purchaser, lessee or licensee to use any process other than the patented process, or

(d) to provide exclusive grant back, prevention to challenges to validity of patent and coercive package licensing, and any such condition shall be void.

(2) A condition of the nature referred to in clause (a) or clause (b) or clause (c) of sub-section (1) shall not cease to be a condition falling within that subsection merely by reason of the fact that the agreement containing it has been entered into separately, whether before or after the contract relating to the sale, lease or licence of the patented article or process.

(3) In proceedings against any person for the infringement of a patent, it shall be a defence to prove that at the time of the infringement there was in force a contract relating to the patent and containing a condition declared unlawful by this section:

power, and would also include abuse of dominant position using patents. Justice Ayyangar recommended the creation of a separate legislation and constitution of a separate commission.[106] Extracted next are the relevant portions of the Report:

> 201. I am however, not dealing with this matter in any detail for two reasons; first, though patents might sometimes form a convenient nuclei on which monopolistic combinations (and restrictive practices which are the concomitant of combinations and to effectuate which the combination might come into existence) are based, the problem cannot be solved by any amendment of the Patents law but only by dealing with it comprehensively so as to touch the manifold forms which these combinations might assume and in which they could operate. This has been the manner in which legislation in other countries has tackled the problem and with reason. There are no materials available on the basis of which this information could be gathered. It does not need any argument to establish, that without an evaluation of the evil, its nature and extent, the remedy to counter it cannot be devised.[107]
>
> . . .
>
> 203. I would therefore recommend the appointment of a commission to enquire into its existence of monopolies in the country in the sense in which the term is understood in this field of the law and the prevalence of restrictive trade practices which are detrimental to the interests of the public generally and to suggest measures to remedy the evil if found to exist. In the context of large scale industrialisation of the country that is proceeding apace, I consider that such an enquiry would be found to yield fruitful results and constitute an assurance to the general public that the economic advantages resulting from the country's advance are being diverted to individual aggrandisement.[108]

Provided that this sub-section shall not apply if the plaintiff is not a party to the contract and proves to the satisfaction of the court that the restrictive condition was inserted in the contract without his knowledge and consent, express or implied.

(4) Nothing in this section shall –

(a) affect a condition in a contract by which a person is prohibited from selling goods other than those of a particular person;
(b) validate a contract which, but for this section, would be invalid;
(c) affect a condition in a contract for the lease of, or licence to use, a patented article, by which the lessor or licensor reserves to himself or his nominee the right to supply such new parts of the patented article as may be required or to put or keep it in repair.

106 *Id.* at 200.
107 *Id.* at 201.
108 *Id.* at 203.

These observations and recommendations of the Ayyangar Committee reveal that the Patents Act was never meant to deal with market distortion since the nature of the enquiry is beyond the scope of the Act. The Ayyangar Committee struck a distinction between "abuse of patent rights by non-working" and "use of economic power" accrued by virtue of holding of a patent or group of patents. While the former is dealt with by the provisions of compulsory licences and the latter was meant to be looked into by a separate commission having the necessary mandate and wherewithal to deal with anticompetitive behaviour, which clearly points to the CCI. The Monopolies and Restrictive Trade Practices Act, 1969 (the precursor to the Competition Act, 2002) was enacted and existed even before the Patents Act, 1970 and the legislative intent was to keep the domains of both the Acts separate and distinct.

Section 3(5) of the Competition Act, 2002 permits action taken by a patentee to restrain infringement of its right, or "reasonable conditions" imposed by the patentee which are necessary for protection of any of its bundle of rights which comprise the patent right.[109] The term "reasonable conditions" imposed in connection with protection of patent rights states that there must be a real and reasonable nexus between the condition imposed on a third party by a patentee and the object of preventing infringement of the patent right. Therefore, should the condition fail to be reasonable, it would run afoul of the proscription under section 3, and would therefore fall under the jurisdiction of the Competition Commission.

3.2.2 Raghavan Committee Report

The Report of the High Level Committee on Competition Policy and Law published in the year 2000 also makes the distinction between IP rights and competition law and states that during the exercise of an IP right, if any anti-competitive trade practice or conduct is visible to the detriment of consumer interest or public interest, it would be the subject matter of the competition law.[110]

Section 3(5) embodies this recommendation since it strikes a balance between protection of IP and prevention of anti-competitive practices employed under the garb of IP protection. This position was reiterated in the erstwhile Planning Commission's Report of the Working Group on Competition Policy published in the year 2007, wherein it observed that while the IPR laws in India have provisions to take care of these potential IPR related competition abuses, including the provision for compulsory licensing, the Competition Act, 2002 does have a specific provision to deal with anticompetitive behavior arising out of unreasonable restraint imposed by a holder of IP which could also be a factor to be considered while determining "dominance of an enterprise" attained under a statute in the relevant market.[111] Under section 27(d) of the Competition Act, 2002 the CCI

109 Competition Act, 2002 (n 10) at 3(5).

110 S.V.S. Raghavan, Report on Competition Policy and Law (2000).

111 Vinod Dhall, Report of the Working Group on Competition Policy 4.1.13 (2007).

may by order direct that the agreements shall stand modified to the extent and in the manner as may be specified in the order by the Commission. The grant of compulsory license amounts to a statutory arrangement created by the law whereas the power to modify an existing agreements is only vested with the CCI.

4 Conclusion

Under Indian law, there is a clear demarcation of rights under the IP laws and the competition laws. Patent law provides for limited instances of "patent abuse" which can be remedied under section 84, whereas "anti-competitive practices" are specifically excluded under the Patents Act. Though the Controller of Patents has the power to grant compulsory licences involving patents, there has to be a determination of a practice as anti-competitive by a judicial or administrative authority, as the Controller does not have the power to make a determination on an anti-competitive practice. The administrative process referred to in section 90 of the Patents Act for determining an anti-competitive practice is the investigation directed by the CCI. Though grant of compulsory license amounts to a statutory arrangement created by the law, the power to modify an existing agreement is only vested with the CCI.

The remedies under Patents Act and Competition Act are different. The scope of the compulsory licences is limited, whereby any person interested may make an application to the Controller for grant of compulsory license on patent, at any time after the expiration of three years from the date of grant of a patent on specific grounds such as, reasonable requirements of public with respect to patented invention have not been satisfied, patented invention is not available to public at reasonably affordable price, or the patented invention is not worked in the territory of India. On the other hand, there is no limitation for seeking remedy under the Competition Act, 2002. The locus of a person seeking a remedy under the Patents Act for a compulsory licence and an order by the CCI pursuant to investigation is also different.

When patent holders raise jurisdictional arguments, albeit for the limited purpose of taking the case away from the purview of the competition law, they implicitly concede to the principle that a third-party settlement of royalty rates when they are unable to decide mutually what the royalties would be. Every time the argument is made that the existence of remedies in the form of compulsory licences for patents and copyright, the right holders indicate the possibility of a third-party settlement to the issues pending between them. It does not, in principle, matter whether the compulsory licence is granted by the Patent Office or by the CCI. The power of the CCI to modify agreements will be critical in deciding cases of covering FRAND terms regardless of the domain of technology.

The disputes involving Ericsson's patents, as observed by the Delhi High Court, relate to a demand for royalty in respect of SEPs held by Ericsson.[112]

112 *Telefonaktiebolaget LM Ericsson (PUBL) v. Competition Commission of India and Another* 2016 SCC OnLine Del 1951 (n 18) at 3.

Similarly, the disputes around Monsanto's patents revolved around a demand for payment of trait value.[113] Courts and authorities faced with the task of deciding essentially royalty based on technology used by downstream implementers should look at the business model involved in monetizing the IP. Understanding the transactional objective, i.e., the business model in monetizing the IP, can lay down the conditions that any authority, be it the high court deciding an infringement case or the CCI deciding violation complaints, shall consider when the patent covers a particular field of technology designed for downstream implementers and factor the objectives of the parties in crafting the relief.

113 *Monsanto Technology LLC v. Nuziveedu Seeds Ltd* 2017 SCC OnLine Del 7652 (n 14) at 21.

14 FRAND as a legal concept at the intersection between competition law and intellectual property law

The road ahead for Singapore?

Burton Ong

1 Introduction

Disputes involving the licensing of standard essential patents (SEP) have not reached the shores of Singapore, largely because of the small size of the jurisdiction and the absence of significant market players in the relevant high-technology manufacturing sectors operating within this jurisdiction. Unlike other Asian jurisdictions, Singapore does not have national champions in the mobile telecommunications industry who need access to SEP-protected technologies in order to manufacture standard-compliant products. However, Singapore does have aspirations to be an international center for dispute resolution, and it is conceivable that such disputes may be addressed in Singapore litigation, arbitration or regulatory proceedings in future. This chapter seeks to explore the question: if confronted by an SEP-related dispute, how might our local legal institutions respond to allegations (which invariably arise in these sorts of cases) that one party has not licensed its SEPs on fair, reasonable and non-discriminatory (FRAND) terms? How should a Singapore tribunal decide if the royalty rates or licensing fees charged by an SEP holder are FRAND? What lessons can be drawn from the experiences of the more developed antitrust jurisdictions?

2 FRAND-related licensing issues arising from SEP disputes

SEP disputes raise distinctive issues not encountered in traditional legal disputes involving patent holders and patent licensees, or prospective licensees. The obvious difference lies in the nature of the patented subject matter: SEPs involve technologies that have been adopted and incorporated into a technological standard, frequently the result of a standard setting process carried out by standard setting organizations (SSOs), while the inventions protected by regular patents do not go through such selection processes. In exchange for including their patented technologies into technology standards formulated by SSOs, SEP owners are required to make a series of commitments relating to their future patent licensing practices – these will vary depending on the framework of rules and policies that SSOs have chosen to adopt. One of the central features of such frameworks is the patent owner's commitment to grant future licences of their patented technologies on FRAND terms.[1] FRAND commitments of this nature aim to facilitate access to SEPs by implementers after the patented technology is designated one of the component technologies of a prescribed standard. Implementers have no choice but to use the SEP-protected invention if they wish to produce standard-compliant products, thereby placing SEP holders in positions of market power. The FRAND commitment or undertaking given by the SEP holder militates against its freedom to exercise that market power by demanding prohibitively high royalty rates – the so-called patent holdup problem – which could result in a less widespread adoption of the technological standard and limit the benefits reaped from the standard setting process.

The exact nature of the legal "obligation" assumed by the SEP holder to grant future licences of its patent on FRAND terms is not entirely clear. On the one hand, it appears contractual in nature because the commitment or undertaking given by the SEP holder is found in the policies adopted by SSOs, which presumably comprise the terms of a contract between the SEP holder, the SSOs and possibly all the participants in the standard setting process. On the other hand, one might also regard the SEP holder's obligation to licence the SEP on FRAND terms to be derived from its "special responsibility" as a dominant undertaking under Anglo-European competition law principles, where it is obliged not to allow its conduct to impair genuine undistorted competition[2] in the downstream market for standard-compliant products that have no choice but to implement the patented technology. The legal nature of the obligation – whether it is primarily a private law obligation or if it should take on the quasi-public law character associated with competition law principles – plays an important role in determining how FRAND-related licensing disputes between SEP holders and prospective licensees or patent infringers ought to be resolved. The appropriate forum for resolving such FRAND-related licensing disputes, and the kinds of

1 For example, the *Common Patent Policy* for the International Telecommunication Union, International Organization for Standardization and International Electrotechnical Commission states that SSO participants who have disclosed their ownership of patents over technologies being considered for inclusion in a technology standard should be "willing to negotiate licences with other parties on a non-discriminatory basis on reasonable terms and conditions". See www.itu.int/en/ITU-T/ipr/Pages/policy.aspx. Similarly the Institute of Electrical Electronics Engineers (IEEE) is an SSO with policies requiring participants to disclose their ownership of SEPs and declare that they "will make available a license for [their SEPs] to an unrestricted number of Applicants on a worldwide basis without compensation or under Reasonable Rates, with other reasonable terms and conditions . . . [and that] . . . such a statement signifies that reasonable terms and conditions . . . are sufficient compensation for a license to use those [SEPs] and precludes seeking, or seeking to enforce, [injunctive relief against standard implementers]." See [6.2] of the IEEE-SA Standards Board Bylaws, available at https://standards.ieee.org/about/policies/bylaws/sect6-7.html. In the same vein, the European Telecommunications Standards Institute (ETSI) has an IPR policy which, at [6.1], requires SSO members who have declared ownership of SEPs to "grant irrevocable licences on fair, reasonable and non-discriminatory ('FRAND') terms and conditions" to standard-implementers. See ETSI Intellectual Property Rights Policy (n 63).

2 Case 322/81 *Michelin v Commission* (1983) at [57].

remedies that may be pursued, may also depend on how this obligation is defined and understood.

When SEP-related disputes subsequently occur, the measures taken by the parties to advance their respective positions may play out in the following manner. When technology implementers who need to utilize the patented technology to produce products that comply with technology standards are unable to secure SEP licences from SEP holders on mutually agreed terms, SEP holders then have to decide which legal route(s) they should take to vindicate their patent rights. Litigation before the courts may be an obvious choice for proceedings commenced by the SEP holder, where such disputes are likely to be framed as patent infringement suits with SEP-related issues being raised in defence by the alleged infringer. Arbitration and other alternative dispute resolution mechanisms may be another route taken where the parties want to keep the dispute out of the public eye and focus their efforts on working out a private settlement between themselves. Complaints by the prospective SEP licensee to a national competition authority may also be initiated as an alternative, or in addition, to the legal proceedings simultaneously pursued elsewhere. This might be part of a strategy to place additional pressure on the SEP holder to restrain itself from engaging in conduct (such as seeking injunctive relief in its patent enforcement proceedings) that might be construed by the competition authority as abusive of the SEP holder's dominant position.

Regardless of where these disputes end up being resolved, they will all invariably have to address a common issue: whether or not the SEP holder's conduct towards the alleged infringer or prospective licensee is consistent with the former's "obligation" to licence the SEP on FRAND terms. This line of inquiry would invariably require the tribunal or authority to scrutinize the royalty rates that the SEP holder has charged, or proposed to charge, the prospective licensee: are these patent licensing fees fair (towards the patent holder/licensor, insofar as it appropriately rewards them for the value created by the patented invention), reasonable (from the licensee's perspective, insofar as it makes the patented invention accessible to anyone seeking to implement it into standard-compliant products) and non-discriminatory (as between the prospective licensee and other similarly situated licensees, such that downstream competition between licensees is not distorted by the divergent licensing fees charged by the licensor? Is the royalty rate sought by the SEP holder consistent with the SEP holder's FRAND-licensing obligations? At this juncture, interesting questions arise as to whether and how the tribunal or authority ought to evaluate the royalty-calculation methodology adopted by the SEP holder. Are patent royalty rates a purely commercial matter that should be left entirely to the operation of market forces? Or is there a basis for legal intervention in light of the possible harms to competition and consumers arising from potential market failures?

3 The concept of FRAND licence terms and royalties in Singapore

Even though there are no laws, regulations or official guidelines in Singapore dealing specifically with the question of how the courts or competition authorities ought to approach the question of whether licence royalty rates are FRAND or not, this is not an entirely unfamiliar question within our legal landscape. Similar principles related to the "fairness" or "reasonableness" of the fees payable by licensees can be found scattered across different parts of Singapore's intellectual property and competition law frameworks.

3.1 Copyright law and patent law

Under the Copyright Act, for instance, statutory licences are available to permit educational institutions to make copies, or to communicate via electronic means, of copyright protected subject matter for educational purposes.[3] Records of the copying or communications made by the educational institution have to be kept, setting out such particulars as may be prescribed by the regulations.[4] This allows copyright owners to subsequently seek payment of "an amount by way of equitable remuneration" from such institutions as agreed upon between the parties or, in default of agreement, an amount as determined by the Copyright Tribunal.[5] The concept of "equitable remuneration" being paid to copyright owners for statutory copyright licences prescribed by the Act is also applied to a number of contexts. These include the reproduction of works for the purpose of broadcasting,[6] the copying of works for the benefit of persons with reading disabilities and assisting intellectually handicapped readers,[7] the making of cinematograph films solely for the purpose of including copyright works in a television broadcast or cable programme,[8] the making of a copy of sound recordings for broadcasting purposes[9] and to determine how much should be paid to the copyright owner when sound recordings or cinematograph films of the work, or an adaptation of the work, are made.[10] How the Copyright Tribunal determines the "equitable remuneration" to be paid to the copyright owner for the use of the copyright work will necessarily involve striking a balance between competing interests, including the proprietary nature of the copyright subject matter, as well as the interests of copyright users and the broader public interest objectives associated which each of these activities.

Within the framework of the Patents Act, the Singapore courts are empowered to grant compulsory licences of a patent on the ground that the licence is necessary to remedy an anti-competitive practice.[11] This provision has not been invoked by would-be patent licensees since 2004, when it was introduced into

3 Copyright Act section 52.
4 Copyright Act section 52(7).
5 Copyright Act sections 52(11) and 158.
6 Copyright Act section 43.
7 Copyright Act sections 54 and 54A, and 158.
8 Copyright Act section 68(3).
9 Copyright Act section 107(3).
10 Copyright Act section 156A.
11 Patents Act, section 55(1).

the statute, but it is safe to assume that what constitutes an "anti-competitive practice" will be interpreted in a manner consistent with the statutory provisions of the Singapore Competition Act, which was enacted during the same time period. However, it is worth noting that section 55(2) of the Act stipulates the circumstances in which the grant of a patent licence is necessary to remedy an anti-competitive practice as including situations where:

(a) there is a market for the patented invention in Singapore;
(b) that market –
   (i) is not being supplied; or
   (ii) is not being supplied on reasonable terms; and
(c) the court is of the view that the proprietor of the patent has no valid reason for failing to supply that market with the patented invention, whether directly or through a licensee, on reasonable terms.

Should this provision in the Act be deployed by an applicant against the patent proprietor, the court will have to decide if the market for the patented invention is being "supplied on reasonable terms" and whether the patent proprietor had a justification for not doing so. Furthermore, the grant of a compulsory licence under section 55 of the Patents Act requires the applicant to pay remuneration to the patentee "as may be agreed" by the parties or "in default of agreement, as . . . determined by the court on the application of the person or the patentee", with the courts statutorily required to ensure that the patentee receives "reasonable remuneration having regard to the economic value of the patentee".[12] If a judge had to hear such a patent dispute in Singapore, the court would have to determine the "reasonable" market value of a licence for the patented invention, as this would be relevant to the question of whether the market for the invention had been supplied on reasonable terms, as well as the question of how much remuneration ought to be due to the patent proprietor as payment for the compulsory licence.

3.2 Competition law

Under Singapore's Competition Act, one of the remedial powers given to the Competition and Consumer Commission of Singapore (CCCS) is the discretion to accept commitments from the parties under investigation for infringing one of the three main prohibitions of the Act. This is expressed in the statute as the power to "accept . . . as [the CCCS] thinks appropriate, a commitment to take or refrain from taking such action as [the CCCS] considers appropriate for the purpose of remedying, mitigating or preventing" the harms to competition which

12 Patents Act, sections 55(6) and 55(7).

may be expected to result from the conduct of the parties.[13] Such commitments given to the CCCS, which are notionally voluntary in nature, are alternatives to directions that the CCCS may order, which may include requiring the infringing parties to take specified actions "to remedy, mitigate or eliminate any adverse effects of such infringement . . . and to prevent the recurrence of such infringement or circumstances".[14]

Unlike the more general FRAND undertakings typically given to SSOs (to grant SEP licences to all interested licencees on FRAND terms), the FRAND commitments that are given to the competition authority are more specific in nature. Such commitments are given by parties to the competition authority while their conduct is being scrutinized by the competition authority for contravening the competition rules. These FRAND commitments are thus quasi-remedial in nature, insofar as they involve promises to behave in specific ways that address the competition concerns of the competition authority, in exchange for the competition authority discontinuing its investigations or giving clearance for a proposed merger. While technically "voluntary" in nature, the precise scope and contours of such commitments are worked out by the parties after going back and forth with the competition authority, who must be satisfied that they appropriately address the competition issues raised before the commitments are accepted.

Cases in which FRAND commitments have been given to a competition authority, which do not involve SEPs, involve broadly similar circumstances as those surrounding the SEPs and the standard setting process. Two parallels can be drawn between SEP and non-SEP cases which illustrate why the FRAND concept has been applied in these contexts.

First, an event occurs which results in a party acquiring significant market power. In the context of SEPs, it is the adoption of patent-protected technology into a standard set by an SSO, making it essential for a licence to be obtained from the SEP holder by those who wish to produce standard-compliant products. In the non-SEP context, infrastructural investments into a particular brand of lifts resulted in a captive aftermarket for lift maintenance service providers who had access to the corresponding brand of spare parts (*see infra* subsection 3.2.1), while a merger which gave a vertically integrated market player exclusive distribution rights over a large portfolio of highly popular book titles raised concerns about whether competing downstream retailers might face price discrimination in the post-merger landscape (*see infra* subsection 3.2.2). The underlying goal of the FRAND commitment in both SEP and non-SEP cases is similar – to facilitate third-party access to that which the market-power wielding party has exclusive rights over, thereby facilitating competition in a downstream market.

13 Competition Act, sections 60A(1) (the section 54 prohibition – mergers), 60A(1A) (the section 34 prohibition – anti-competitive agreements) and 60A(1B) (the section 47 prohibition – abuse of dominance).

14 Competition Act, section 69.

Second, FRAND commitments in both SEP and non-SEP cases attempt to balance the countervailing interests of the relevant parties in a flexible way. The giver of the FRAND undertaking or commitment deserves to be fairly compensated for the value of his assets, including any investments made in innovation, while the beneficiary of the FRAND undertaking or commitment must not have to pay excessive fees that are commercially unviable, including royalties that amount to "patent holdup", thereby preventing effective competition in the downstream market. Parties also need to have some latitude to reach agreements which take into consideration their respective commercial interests, and all surrounding market circumstances, when implementing their FRAND commitments or undertakings.

While FRAND undertakings given to SSOs have been regarded as contractual in nature, giving third-party potential licensees legal entitlements against the SEP holder, it is not entirely clear if FRAND commitments to the competition authority entail the same legal ramifications. An SEP holder's failure to grant an SEP licence to third parties who are willing licensees may be regarded as a breach of contract and result in the court's denial of injunctive relief for patent infringement. In contrast, the consequences of non-adherence to a FRAND commitment given to the competition authority leads to the revocation of the authority's non-infringement decision and the recommencement or continuation of its investigations against the parties.[15]

3.2.1 Lift spare parts

Among the commitments which the CCCS has extracted from undertakings in Singapore are those which have required dominant undertakings to supply their products to competitors at FRAND rates. Investigations by the CCCS into the supply of lift spare parts in Housing and Development Board (HDB) estates revealed restrictive trade practices that could have amounted to refusals by a dominant or sole supplier to supply essential products, that cannot be otherwise obtained, that were potentially in breach of the section 47 prohibition against abuse of dominance. Third-party lift maintenance contractors faced difficulties obtaining lift spare parts for the different lift brands from the original lift installers, making it difficult for these maintenance contractors to compete in tenders for lift maintenance projects called by town councils, where multiple brands of lifts are installed in each HDB estate. Acting on a complaint it received, the CCCS investigated several companies for refusing to supply lift spare parts for the maintenance of lifts in HDB estates but did not reach an infringement decision. Instead, three suppliers of particular brands of lift spare parts provided commitments to the CCCS to supply these products to third-party maintenance contractors in Singapore to enable the latter to more effectively compete for lift maintenance contracts. This also allowed town councils to choose to call for a

15 Competition Act, section 60B(2).

Table 14.1 FRAND commitments given to the CCCS (lift spare parts)

Name of Supplier	*Lift Brand*	*Nature of Supply Commitments given*
E M Services (July 14, 2016)	BLT (manufactured by Shenyang Yuanda Intellectual Industry Group Co. Ltd)	Sale of spare parts to purchaser "based on terms and conditions (e.g. on pricing, quantity, delivery time and warranty period) reasonably similar to those provided by the relevant lift spare parts manufacturer"
BNF Engineering (March 28, 2018)	BNF	Sale to purchaser of spare parts "on a fair, reasonable and non-discriminatory basis"
C&W Services Operations (March 28, 2018)	Ulift	Sale to purchaser of spare parts "on a fair, reasonable and non-discriminatory basis"

single tender for lift maintenance services that covered a range of different lift brands, rather than having to contract with multiple parties representing the different lift brands.[16]

The commitments made by these suppliers to sell lift spare parts to third-party lift maintenance contractors are qualified by the following conditions:

- The purchaser is registered with the Building and Construction Authority to perform lift installation and lift contractor services;
- The purchaser provides documentary proof that the owner has appointed the purchaser to carry out maintenance of the relevant brand of lift;
- The spare parts supplied do not need to come from the supplier's own inventory stock, with the supplier required to send out orders for the parts from the manufacturer within seven working days from the date or receipt of the purchasers request as long as the manufacturer is still producing these parts;
- The purchaser agrees to indemnify the supplier if the purchaser's negligence causes a lift breakdown, injury, death or any loss whatsoever;[17]
- The purchaser undertakes not to reverse engineer or otherwise modify the purchased lift spare parts;

16 CCCS Media Release, "CCS Investigates Restrictive Industry Practices in the Supply of Lift Spare Parts in HDB Estates", July 14, 2016.

17 This condition was adopted by E M Services and BNF Engineering, but not C&W Services. In C&W's commitments, the condition attached to the supply of lift spare parts required the purchaser to "defend, indemnify and hold harmless CWO from and against any and all liabilities, damages, judgments, costs, expenses and fees resulting from any claims, litigation or actions arising out of or relating to CWO's sale of the ULift Spare Parts to the purchaser, except where such losses are caused by defective ULift Spare Parts supplied by CWO, or CWO's gross negligence or willful default".

- The purchaser only uses the purchase lift spare parts for the relevant brand of lift intended by the manufacturer and agrees that the supplier shall not be liable if these purchased parts are incompatible with the relevant lift to be repaired and/or are obsolete;
- The purchaser acknowledges that supplier holds various proprietary trade marks, service marks, certification marks, logos and other images, recognizing that the sale of spare parts does not transfer any of these intellectual property rights; none of these marks may be used by the purchaser in any way without the written permission of the supplier, regardless of whether such uses would otherwise be considered legally permissible or fair use;[18]
- The purchaser is bound by an alternative dispute resolution clause in the supply contract (which may, for instance, require disputes arising from their dealings with the supplier to be resolved by negotiation and mediation).

Several observations can be made about these voluntary commitments, which were accepted by the CCCS and regarded as sufficient to fully address its competition concerns arising from the supply of these brands of lift spare parts.

First, the 2018 commitments accepted by the CCCS appear less certain than those that were given in 2016. While reference was made to the FRAND concept in the 2018 commitments accepted by the CCCS – where both suppliers had committed themselves to selling lift spare parts to their competitors in the lift maintenance contractor market "on a fair, reasonable and non-discriminatory basis" – the CCCS gave no guidance as to the substantive meaning of this concept or how it might be interpreted. In comparison, there appears to be marginally more clarity in language used by the supplier in the commitment given in 2016 to sell spare parts to third-party lift maintenance contractors "based on terms . . . reasonably similar to those provided by the relevant lift spare parts manufacturer". The 2016 commitment uses the contract terms between the Singapore-based supplier of lift spare parts and the manufacturer from whom these spare parts originate as a fixed benchmark against which the "fairness" and "reasonableness" of terms of the supply contract for these spare parts to third-party maintenance contractors can be evaluated.

Second, the list of conditions that qualify the FRAND-supply commitment given by these lift spare parts suppliers are not uniform, allowing for the inclusion of specific contractual terms that may be regarded as potentially onerous towards the purchasers of the spare parts. The commitment given by C&W Services, for instance, is qualified by an expansive condition where the purchaser

> agrees to defend, indemnify and hold harmless [the supplier] from and against any and all liabilities, damages, judgments, costs, expenses and fees

18 This condition was adopted by E M Services and BNF Engineering, but not C&W Services. In C&W's commitments, the condition attached to the supply of lift spare parts simply required the purchaser to agree that the supplier owned all of the intellectual property rights in the ULift Spare Parts, and that the purchaser agreed not to claim "any right, title or interest in any of the intellectual property rights in the ULift Spare Parts".

> resulting from any claims, litigation or actions arising out of or relating to [the supplier's] sale of the [lift spare parts] to the purchaser, except where such losses are caused by [defective spare parts], or [the lift supplier's] gross negligence or willful default.

It would seem that this clause operates as a blanket exclusion of any liability in contract or tort incurred by the lift supplier towards the purchaser, potentially depriving the purchaser of any legal recourse under his supply contract against the supplier unless his grievance involves defective products, gross negligence or willful default.[19] Assuming that this clause becomes incorporated into C&W's standard terms of business, it may end up being invalidated by section 3 of the *Unfair Contract Terms Act* to the extent that it fails to satisfy that statute's test of "reasonableness".[20]

Third, the FRAND nature of the supply commitment given by the lift spare part suppliers may be compromised to some extent by restrictions on the purchaser's ability to communicate the brand names of the lifts whose spare parts the purchaser has acquired. One of the conditions that qualify the FRAND commitment is that the purchaser is not allowed to use marks, logos and images in respect of which the supplier holds intellectual property rights, even where such use would have been permitted by statute because it falls within a legislatively prescribed exception to the exclusive rights conferred upon the intellectual property owner. Without the written permission of the lift spare parts supplier, the purchaser would not be able to use the brand names of the lift spare parts that he has acquired when advertising his lift maintenance services, even though this would have been permissible under Singapore's trade mark laws.[21]

3.2.2 TPL-Penguin merger

The other context in which the Singapore competition authority has accepted FRAND commitments involves a merger that raised competition concerns, but

19 If this contractual clause operates to protect the supplier in his supply contracts with the purchaser, the purchaser may not, for instance, take legal action against the supplier for delayed shipments, damaged goods or other instances of defective performance that would have, ordinarily, entitled the purchaser to recover damages for breach of contract.

20 One of the main factors identified in the Second Schedule of the Unfair Contract Terms Act, which contains guidelines for the application of the reasonableness test, is "the strength of the bargaining positions of the parties relative to each other, taking into account (among other things) alternative means by which the customer's requirements could have been met".

21 Section 28(1)(b) and (c) of the Trade Marks Act provide that a person does not infringe a registered trade mark when "(b) he uses a sign to indicate (i) the kind, quality, quantity, intended purpose, value, geographical origin or other characteristic of goods or services . . . or (c) he uses the trade mark to indicate the intended purpose of goods (in particular as accessories or spare parts) or services, and such use is in accordance with honest practices in industrial or commercial matters."

which was allowed to proceed after such merging parties offered such commitments to the CCCS.[22] The acquiring party (TPL) was a vertically integrated book publishing, distribution, marketing and retailing business, while the target (the Penguin Group of Companies) was the local distribution and marketing arm of an international publishing conglomerate, the Penguin Random House (PRH) group. The CCCS had competition concerns arising from an exclusive distributorship arrangement that would be implemented with the completion of the merger, where the merged entity would be appointed the sole distributor of English language book titles from book publishers (Penguin Books Ltd, The Random House Group Ltd, Dorling Kindersley Ltd) that belong to the PRH group (See Figure 14.1). The merged entity had a market share of 40%–50% of the market for the marketing and distribution of English-language-only print trade books, more than double of the market share of the next largest market player, with the post-merger concentration ratio of the three largest post-merger market players (CR3) somewhere between 60%–70%. In the CCCS assessment, the merged entity would have a degree of market power arising from the high barriers to market entry and insufficient countervailing power from retailers, including indirect competitive pressures faced by the merged entity from the

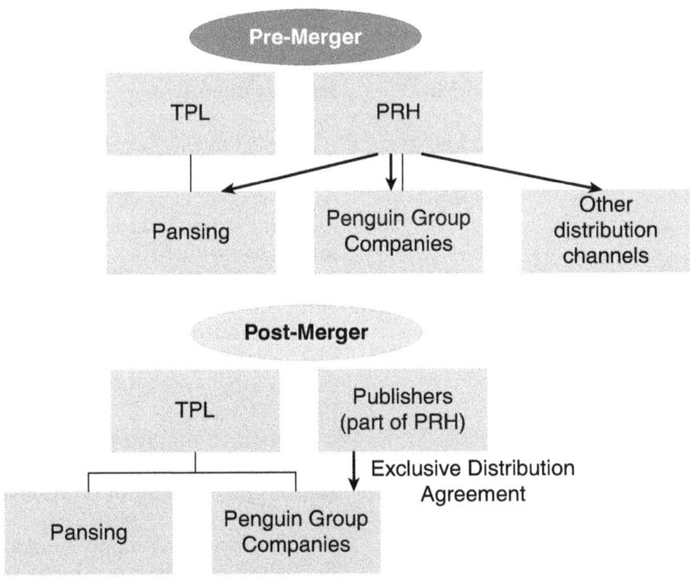

Figure 14.1 Acquisition of Penguin Group of Companies by TPL

22 Case No. CCS 400/001/17, Grounds of Decision, Acquisition by Times Publishing Limited of Penguin Random House Pte Ltd and Penguin Books Malaysia Sdn Bhd (September 25, 2017). ("*Times Publishing Limited – Penguin*")

online book retail platforms. Given that the merged entity would have exclusive distribution rights to a "substantial list of book titles", while also being affiliated to the downstream retailer that was part of the TPL group, the CCCS also took the view "there may be incentive for the merged entity to foreclose third party retailers",[23] as well as "the incentive . . . to discriminate against third party retailers such as through price discrimination which might render third party retailers commercially unviable".[24] These vertical effects thus raised competition concerns in the retail market for English language books which made the CCCS unable to clear the merger at the end of its Phase 1 review. In lieu of proceeding to a Phase 2 review of the merger, which would have entailed a more detailed and comprehensive review of the likely effects of the merger, TPL offered a set of commitments to the CCCS to address the competition authority's competition concerns (See Table 14.2).

The CCCS concluded that, subject to the implementation of and compliance with the Commitments, the acquisition of the Penguin Group of Companies by TPL would not infringe the section 54 prohibition (against mergers that substantially lessen competition) of the Competition Act. Three observations can

Table 14.2 FRAND commitments given to the CCCS (TPL-Penguin merger)[25]

Potential Competition Concerns	*Commitments*
1 The merged entity may refuse to supply or restrict supply to third-party retailers	TPL undertakes to supply third-party retailers the full range of Publishers' books.
2 The merged entity may discriminate by increasing price or offering unfavorable supply terms to third-party retailers.	With regard to pricing, TPL undertakes to supply the Publishers' books to third-party retailers at pricing which is non-discriminatory, including to apply the same Distributor Recommended Retail Price to all retailers. The Commitments allow TPL to apply varying discounts to the Distributor Recommended Retail Price based on a set of objective discount criteria *only if* the criteria are applied in a FRAND manner. With regard to supply terms, TPL undertakes to ensure that their adjustments to trading terms are FRAND towards third-party retailers.
3 The merged entity may raise prices at the distribution level for all retailers to foreclose competition at the retail level.	The commitment to supply books by the Publishers to third-party retailers at prices which are fair and reasonable.

23 *Times Publishing Limited – Penguin*, at [134(a)] and [134(b)].
24 *Id.* at [137].
25 *Id.* at [162].

be made about the FRAND commitments that were given by the parties to the CCCS in this case.

First, the necessity of these commitments may be called into question because no conclusive analysis was made by the CCCS of the effects of the merger, and the accompanying exclusive distribution agreement, on the post-merger landscape. These FRAND commitments were probably motivated by a desire from the parties to expedite the regulatory approval process rather than to respond to actually predicted anti-competitive outcomes arising from the merger. There may not, in fact, have been actual need for these measures to be promised by the merged entity if a full economic analysis of the competitive landscape had been carried out.

Second, it is unclear whether such commitments were justifiable restrictions on the commercial freedom of the parties even if the possible future conduct of the merged entity towards its rivals – refusals to supply and discriminatory pricing – had actually materialized. It is unclear that such conduct would have actually infringed the section 47 prohibition against abuses of a dominant position even if they had been actually carried out, given the high legal threshold that would have had to be established and the potential availability of objective justification defences.

Third, even if these commitments were called for to address real competition concerns associated with this transaction, they were crafted in such a way as to give the merged entity very wide latitude to apply "varying discounts to the Distributor Recommended Retail Price based on . . . objective criteria" set out by the parties, which include factors such as the credit performance of the retailers, location and rental costs of the retailers, as well as the potential for business development with the retailers. The parties were required to appoint an independent Monitoring Trustee to monitor compliance with the commitments and to provide the CCCS with an annual written report, as well as a written assessment of all complaints made regarding potential breaches of the commitments. It remains to be seen how the Monitoring Trustee will interpret the content and breadth of the commitments given by TPL to the CCCS – what benchmarks will it use to determine the merits of the complaints made by retailers, who would not have access to the terms of the different retail distribution agreements entered into by the merged entity with different retail outlets? How would the Monitoring Trustee (or the CCCS, for that matter) determine whether these commitments have been breached, given that there does not seem to be any objective standard against which to measure the merged entity's compliance with its commitment to supply books from PRH's publishers to book retailers on a FRAND basis, to apply its "objective discount criteria" in a FRAND manner, or to make adjustments to any of its trading terms that are FRAND toward third-party retailers?

4 Learning from the experiences of other jurisdictions

Given the extremely limited experience that Singapore has had with the interpretation, application and implementation of FRAND as a legal concept, in both IP and non-IP related contexts, how this area of jurisprudence evolves going forward will be speculative at best. It is likely that courts, tribunals and adjudicators in Singapore will pay close attention to the experiences of more developed jurisdictions in dealing with FRAND-related legal disputes. In particular, the case law from the United Kingdom and the U.S., which have broadly similar common law legal frameworks, patent law systems and antitrust rules, are likely to be regarded as persuasive authorities in Singapore. Before distilling a set of broad principles that might be applied in Singapore, it may be fruitful to summarize some of the landmark decisions involving FRAND-related legal pronouncements from these jurisdictions.

4.1 U.S.

4.1.1 Microsoft v Motorola (I)[26]

One of the seminal cases in which a court has tried to decipher the meaning of FRAND, this decision by Judge Robart has been regularly used as a reference point in later judicial decisions where disputes have arisen as to whether the patent royalty rates or licensing terms offered by the parties are FRAND-compliant or not. The issue in this case was whether Motorola had breached a contractual obligation, arising from a commitment it had given to two SSOs – IEEE and ITU – to license its SEPs at a reasonable and non-discriminatory rate (RAND),[27] by issuing patent licence offer letters to Microsoft which regarded as excessive. Earlier decisions taken by the court in relation to this dispute had interpreted the RAND commitment given by Motorola as creating enforceable contractual rights in favour of third-party beneficiaries who use the standards that incorporate the SEPs, and that the SEP holder was obliged to make offers to licence their patents in good faith – initial offers made by Motorola did not have to be on RAND terms so long as the licensor was prepared to eventually issue a RAND licence.[28] In order to determine if the SEP holder's opening offers were in good faith, it was necessary to "compare [these offered rates] with a reasonable RAND royalty rate and, because more than one rate could conceivably be RAND, a reasonable RAND royalty range", so the bench trial was held to determine a RAND royalty range for Motorola's SEPs and a specific RAND royalty rate for Motorola's SEPs to enable the fact finder at a later trial to determine whether Motorola had breached its RAND obligation to offer licences for its patents in good faith.[29]

This case developed a framework for assessing RAND royalty rates that was premised on a list of factors articulated by an earlier U.S. District Court decision

26 *Microsoft Corporation v Motorola* Inc. No C10–1823JLR, U.S. District Court W.D. Washington at Seattle (April 25, 2013) (Decision of James L. Robart, District Judge).

27 "RAND" has been interpreted by subsequent courts as having essentially the same meaning as "FRAND". See *Unwired Planet v Huawei* (n 53 below) at [89].

28 *Microsoft v Motorola* (n 26 above) at [2].

29 *Id.* at [3].

involving the calculation of compensatory damages for patent infringement, based on the hypothetical licensing fees which the patent holder could have charged the infringing party if the latter had been prepared to negotiate patent licence.[30] In essence, this framework involved determining what reasonable royalty rates the parties could have arrived at had they engaged in a hypothetical negotiation between themselves, taking into consideration the specific nature of the SEPs by "looking at the importance of the SEPs to the standard and the importance of the standard and the SEPs to the products at issue" and applying a modified version of the *Georgia-Pacific* factors. The court recognized that the hypothetical negotiation they had to conduct in the SEP context was different from the typical *Georgia-Pacific* analysis previously conducted by the courts in other patent infringement cases because of two key factors: first, that the owner of the SEP was under an obligation to licence on RAND terms; and second, that the implementer of the standard would understand that it had to take a license from many SEP owners, rather than just one, such that the overall licensing situation had to be considered rather than the specific SEP licence(s) being negotiated for.[31]

Applying this framework, the court recognized that the purpose of the RAND commitment was to encourage widespread adoption of the technological standard, prevent patent "holdup" (where the SEP holder was able to demand more than the value of its patented technology and attempt to capture some of the value of the standard itself) and address "royalty stacking" concerns (where achieving standard-compliance required the standard implementer to obtain multiple patent licences for the numerous SEPs covering the many technologies incorporated into a standard, such that the payment of excessive royalties to individual SEP owners might result in cumulative royalty payments that undermine the commercial viability of the standard).[32] The court also emphasized the importance of focusing the analysis on the value of the patented technology apart from the value associated with its incorporation into the standard, where a reasonable royalty would not take into account the value to the licensee created by the existence of the standard itself but would instead consider "the contribution of the patent to the technical capabilities of the standard and also the contribution of those relevant technological capabilities to the implementer and the implementer's products".[33]

After reviewing an extensive volume of evidence, including numerous patent licence royalty rates suggested by the parties to be comparable licences and expert evidence, Justice Robart eventually worked out both specific RAND royalty rates, as well as upper and lower royalty rates that demarcated the range of RAND royalty rates, for each of the two technology standards in issue in this

30 See *Georgia-Pacific Corp v U.S. Plywood Corp*, 318 F. Supp. 1116 (S.D.N.Y. 1970) ("*Georgia-Pacific*").

31 *Microsoft v Motorola* (n 24 above) at [92] and [67].

32 *Id.* at [51]–[66] and, in relation to patent-stacking in particular, see [455]–[460].

33 *Id.* at [103]–[104].

case. Care was taken, when scrutinizing the purported comparable licences, to determine both the importance of the SEP to the standard (e.g. whether the patent provided technical value to the standard, whether it was directed to a core feature of the standard and what alternatives were available to the parties that may have provided similar technical value) and the importance of the SEP to the implementer's products in terms of its contribution and centrality to the overall product functionality.[34] Examples of royalty rates from other SEP licences were only considered reliable indicators of RAND royalty rates for Motorola's SEP portfolios if they were not arrived at under the threat of a potential patent infringement lawsuit,[35] if they were capable of being unpacked (from non-standard essential patents, for example) or disaggregated (in cross-licensing, for example) to make them comparable to the SEP licence offers being analyzed,[36] and if proper account was given to the value received by the licensor in granting the patent licence, apart from the royalties received, such as the access he may get to other patents within a patent pool when he consents to licence his patent via a patent pool licence.[37]

It is worth noting that the court considered that, under certain circumstances, patent pool licence rates to be "a strong indicator of a RAND royalty rate" for a similar SEP portfolio over the same technologies that have been included in a standard because patent pools have characteristics which are closely aligned with the purposes of the RAND commitment, where the patent pool tries to "strike a balance between setting a royalty high enough to motivate a significant number of patent holders to contribute their patents to the pool and low enough to ensure that licensees would implement . . . [the standard incorporates the technologies in the patent pool] rather than use alternatives" since "[t]his practice nicely aligns with two cornerstones of the RAND obligation: (1) SSOs seek to include advanced technology to create valuable standards, while at the same time, (2) ensuring widespread adoption".[38]

4.1.2 In re Innovatio[39]

Shortly after the *Microsoft v Motorola (I)* decision, another U.S. District Court had the opportunity to apply Justice Robart's framework of principles for calculating RAND royalty rates for SEP holders. The context of this decision was, however, different insofar as it involved an attempt to assess the potential damages that Innovatio could claim against various defendant manufacturers of electronic

34 *Id.* at, for example, [256], [259], [289] and [301].

35 *Id.* at [415], [443].

36 *Id.* at [426]–[427].

37 *Id.* at [502]–[507].

38 *Id.* at [510]–[514].

39 *In re Innovatio IP Ventures, LLC Patent Litigation*, Case No. 11 C 9308, U.S. District Court, N.D. Illinois, Eastern Division (September 27, 2013) (Decision of James F. Holderman, District Judge).

devices for infringing Innovatio's SEPs over wireless internet access technologies, albeit before the court made determinations on questions of patent validity and infringement. The hypothetical bilateral negotiation model, using the modified *Georgia-Pacific* factors, developed in the earlier *Microsoft v Motorola (I)* decision, was applied in the *Innovatio* case by Justice Holderman subject to a few modifications.[40] First, a single RAND rate, rather than a range of RAND rates, had to be determined in this case because the purpose of the trial was to calculate the potential damages payable to the SEP holder. Second, the patents in this case had also been previously found to be essential in an earlier trial, removing any uncertainty that the parties would have had on this issue in an ex ante hypothetical negotiation, thereby making it inappropriate to make downward adjustments (as were made by Judge Robart in *Microsoft v Motorola (I)*) to RAND rates calculated in a pre-litigation context. Third, the court in this case found that the appropriate royalty base for calculating RAND royalty rates was the average price of a Wi-Fi chip, the small module that provided wireless connectivity to electronic devices in which it was inserted, rather than the final manufactured product.[41]

The court in *In re Innovatio* concluded that the SEPs owned by Innovatio were of "moderate to high importance" to the technological standard, a finding which played a significant role in identifying which proposed comparable licences suggested by the parties were appropriate indicators of RAND royalty rates. The proposed comparable licences suggested by the SEP holder were regarded as inappropriate because they were either regarded as not accurately market-determined rates because they were arrived at in the context of litigation settlement, involved large numbers of patents that were numerically incomparable to the SEP portfolio in question or involved technology standards that were different from the subject matter of this case. The proposed comparable licences suggested by the manufacturer-defendants, particularly licences under a patent pool, were regarded by the court as inappropriate benchmarks for RAND royalty rates because of the low number of licensors who participated in the pool, suggesting that the prices were too low to give patent holders a reasonable return on their technology. The evidence also suggested that the patents in this patent pool were low-value patents, while the patents in this case had been determined to be of moderate to high importance to the technology standard.

Justice Holderman rejected the "bottom-up" approach presented by the defendant's expert witness, which essentially involved determining the cost of implementing reasonable alternatives to the SEPs that could have been adopted

40 *In re Innovatio IP Ventures* (n 39 above) at 6–7.

41 The court accepted the defendant's arguments that patent royalties should be calculated based on the "smallest saleable patent-practising unit", endorsing the position taken in earlier non-RAND cases, particularly *LaserDynamics, Inc v Quanta Computer*, 694 F.3d at 67, quoting *Cornell Univ. v. Hewlett-Packard Co.*, 609 F. Supp. 2d 279, 287 (N.D.N.Y. 2009), because Innovatio had not provided a legally sound or factually credible method to apportion the price of the defendants' end products to the value of only Innovatio's patented features.

into the standard – based on the theory that a hypothetical negotiation between the parties would have resulted in the licensee not willing to pay more for the SEPs than the amount necessary to adopt alternative technologies. This approach was regarded as unsatisfactory because there were no alternatives to Innovatio's patents and an accurate analysis was too complicated for the courts to perform because substituting one technology for another within the context of a standard which incorporates many different technologies would entail multiple consequential changes being made simultaneously, given that "the performance of the standard is multi-dimensional".[42]

On the other hand, Justice Holderman accepted another approach proposed by the defendant's expert witness – the "top-down" approach, which involved calculating the average profit made on each Wi-Fi chip, "thereby isolating the portion of income from the sale of the chip available to the chipmaker to pay royalties on intellectual property", from which the RAND rate is calculated by multiplying the available profit on a chip by a fraction based on the number of SEPs in question over the total number of SEPs covered by the standard.[43] The court also accepted economic analysis which posited that "the top 10% of all electronics patents account for 84% of the value in all electronic patents", which led it to multiply the profit margin on a Wi-Fi chip by 84% to determine the total value attributable to the top 10% of the SEPs that covered the technology standard (which included Innovatio's patents, which were of moderate to high value) before calculating a fraction of this value as the RAND royalty rate (using the number of SEPs held by Innovatio as the numerator and 10% of the estimated total number of SEPs as the denominator).

The "top-down" approach was also acknowledged by the court as advantageous in two ways. First, it addressed concerns about royalty stacking because the overall profit margin from the sale of each chip was taken as a starting point, thereby ensuring that the overall aggregate SEP royalty burden on the licensee is not cumulatively excessive. Second, it was regarded as an appropriate method because it was premised on the average profit earned by chip manufacturers on each chip, rather than the profit margins of each manufacturer on their respective products, thereby preventing the SEP holder from discriminating between licensees by charging royalty rates based on their market positions. [44]

42 *In re Innovatio IP Ventures* (n 39 above) at 37, citing Justice Robart in *Microsoft v Motorola* (n 26 above) at 13.

43 *In re Innovatio IP Ventures* (n 39 above) at 37–39, with Justice Holderman noting that "[a]lthough the Top Down approach is not perfect, no approach for calculating a RAND rate is in light of the inherent uncertainty in calculating a reasonable royalty" before concluding that "the Top Down approach best approximates the RAND rate that the parties to a hypothetical ex ante negotiation most likely would have agreed upon . . . before Innovatio's patents were adopted into the standard".

44 *In re Innovatio IP Ventures* (n 39 above) at 38–40. Justice Holderman went on to observe that there were "few available comparable licences that were negotiated in the RAND context" and that "[u]ntil more RAND licences are available, courts and litigants must look

4.1.3 TCL v Ericsson[45]

The parties to this dispute had been embroiled in a multi-jurisdictional legal proceedings after Ericsson, the owner of a portfolio of SEPs covering the 4G mobile telecommunications standard, was unable to conclude a FRAND licensing with TCL, a mobile telephone manufacturer who implemented this standard in its products. This case involved a consolidation of several lawsuits under which TCL agreed to be bound by the court's determination of FRAND terms for a worldwide SEP portfolio licence. Ericsson was ordered by the court to file "FRAND contentions" – alternative option of licensing offers made to TCL on terms which it contended were FRAND in nature – for the court to assess. Justice Selna held that while neither of these offers made consisted of FRAND rates, Ericsson had negotiated in good faith. Instead, the court derived a FRAND royalty rate of its own after identifying six licensees that were "similarly situated" to TCL and engaging in a comparable licensing analysis. It "unpacked" the royalty rates charged in each comparable licences – to account for cross-licensing, lump-sum payments, pass-through rights and other issues – in order to derive one-way royalty rates expressed as percentage royalties without caps or floors.

As a starting point, the court focused on deciphering the scope of the FRAND undertaking given by Ericsson to the ETSI, the 4G mobile standard SSO, on the basis that TCL was entitled to enforce this contractual undertaking as a third-party beneficiary under French law, the governing law of the IPR declarations given by ETSI's members. In the court's view, ETSI's IPR Policy was formulated with several concerns in mind, including addressing the problem of holdup, as well as preventing price-discrimination between licensees – even though "the precise contours of the FRAND obligation were never crystallized in a definitive formulation" – and in the absence of definitive guidance in assessing whether Ericsson's offers were "non-discriminatory", the court agreed with TCL that it had to "turn to law, logic and economics" to make this determination.[46]

In deciding whether Ericsson's SEP licensing offers were "fair and reasonable" for the purposes of compliance with its FRAND undertaking, the court was presented with two choices – a "top-down" approach advanced by TCL, under which a reasonable total aggregate royalty for all SEPs was first determined before being apportioned between all SEP owners based on the relative value of their portfolios against the total value of all SEPs in the standard, and an "ex-Standard" approach proposed by Ericsson, under which ex ante value of the SEPs is assessed, independently of any value arising from their incorporation into a standard, by reference to their specific technical contributions as compared to

---

to other methods for calculating a RAND royalty, such as [the expert witness'] Top Down proposal".

45 *TCL Communications Technology Holdings v Telefonaktiebolaget LM Ericsson*, Case No, SACV 14-341 JVS (DFMx), U.S. District Court, C.D. California (August 11, 2017) (Decision of James V. Selna, District Judge).

46 *TCL v Ericsson* (n 45 above) at 7–8.

the best available alternative technologies that could have been selected for inclusion in the standard instead. Justice Selna rejected the latter approach because of methodological flaws in the expert witness' calculations that led him to conclude that it "lacked fundamental credibility". Instead, the judge adopted the "top down" approach because it prevented royalty stacking and patent holdup, as the method started with the "maximum aggregate royalty burden and works down to a fair and reasonable rate"; this approach "examined the essentiality, importance and contribution of Ericsson's patents for each standard and provided a method to account for the value of expired and acquired patents, as well as regional differences in Ericsson's patent portfolio".[47]

The merits of the top-down approach, in the eyes of the court, included the fact that it relied on public statements made by Ericsson and other SEP holders to induce people to adopt and invest in each standard, where such statements were made before the standard was adopted, "providing SEP owners with incentive to be reasonable with their overall expectations and greatly reducing the risk of hold-up and royalty stacking".[48] After determining the total aggregate royalty as a percentage of handset prices, the court then calculated Ericsson's proportional share of this number by expressing the total number of Ericsson's SEPs (the numerator) as a fraction of the total number of SEPs for the standard in question (the denominator), with appropriate adjustments made to these numbers to account for over-declarations of essentiality and to account for differences in patent portfolio strength in different countries.[49] Different combinations of values were thus used for Ericsson's 2G, 3G and 4G SEP portfolios, and plugged into

47 *TCL v Ericsson* (n 45 above) at 9, while caveating with a "central observation that "[t]he search for precision and absolute certainty is a doomed undertaking" and that the Court's effort was to determine "whether each expert's work has a reasonable level reliability and convincing force that allows the Court to make a judgment whether to accept the ultimate conclusions advanced".

48 *TCL v Ericsson* (n 45 above) at 14.

49 *Id.* at 24–25. Given that Ericsson had fewer SEPs in other jurisdictions compared to its SEP portfolio in the U.S., it was appropriate to calculate separate FRAND royalty rates for these non-U.S. regions to reflect the fact that some of its inventions which have not been patented outside of the U.S. are in the public domain. While recognizing that "as a matter of commercial reality, firms regularly adopt a single world-wide rate", Justice Selna thought a global patent rate that did not account for differences in national patent strength provided the SEP owner "a royalty based on features that are unpatented in many jurisdictions". For the sake of avoiding "complications that disproportionately increase the complexity and difficulty in understanding and enforcing any final judgment", given that "the parties have requested a global adjudication", the court chose to divide the world into three patent portfolio regions, assigning regional strength ratios (derived from the weaker value shares of patent portfolios in regions outside of the U.S. as a percentage of the value of Ericsson's U.S. SEP portfolio) – the U.S. SEP portfolio (100%), the European SEP portfolio and the rest of the world (using China's SEP portfolio as floor because TCL manufactured its products in China for export around the world, meaning that "the strength of Ericsson's SEP portfolio in China will therefore determine the lowest FRAND rate for any product TCL sells globally").

$$\text{Total Aggregate Royalty} \times \frac{\text{Number of unexpired SEPs owned by Licensor}}{\text{Total Number of SEPs in the Standard}} \times \text{Regional Strenth Ratio}$$

Figure 14.2 FRAND calculation formula used in *TCL v Ericsson*

the following formula to determine the FRAND royalty rate for each portfolio in each geographic region.

To determine whether Ericsson's SEP licensing offers were non-discriminatory, Justice Selna decided that it was necessary to apply a "market-based approach that considers comparable licenses". For the SEP holder under a FRAND obligation, this meant that "like, or close to, like rates must be offered to firms which are similarly situated", where the court took the view that it had to identify licensee firms that were "similarly situated to TCL" in that they were "well-established firms in the global market", disregarding factors such as the firms' "overall financial success or risk, brand recognition, the operating system of their devices, or the existence of retail stores".[50] Having identified these similarly situated firms, their licences with the SEP holder had to be unpacked, converting cross-licences and lump-sum payments into comparable one-way royalty rates, before they could be used as FRAND benchmarks to assess if the rates offered to TCL were discriminatory or not. Based on the drafting history of the ETSI IPR Policy, the court rejected the application of the "most favoured nation" or "most favoured licensee" principle (where the licensor had to offer every licensee the lowest royalty rate it charged any single licensee) as part of the SEP holder's FRAND obligation, holding that lower licensing rates offered to other licensees could be used as benchmarks for reasonableness comparisons "but not as absolute standards which must be met" and rejecting Ericsson's contention that there had to be competitive harm (an effect of impairing the development or adoption of standards) before different rates charged to different licensees could be considered discriminatory.[51]

Applying the framework described earlier, the court reached the conclusion that neither licensing offers made by Ericsson were consistent with their FRAND obligation when viewed against the rates derived from its top down analysis; nor were Ericsson's royalty rates non-discriminatory because they were "radically divergent from the rates which Ericsson agreed to accept from licensees similarly situated to TCL".[52] The court ultimately declined to resolve the legal question of

50 *TCL v Ericsson* (n 45 above) at 30–31.

51 *Id.* at 49–50, noting that there was no basis to "engraft into the FRAND analysis the distinction which American antitrust law makes between harm to competition, which is actionable, and mere harm to a competitor which is not", and that "[t]he Sherman Act and its long history provide no guide to understanding ETSI's non discrimination under FRAND."

52 *TCL v Ericsson* (n 45 above) at 26 and 50.

whether the FRAND duty requires the licensor to actually offer rates which are in fact FRAND, since no claim for damages for breach of contract would have been available in this case, with TCL only entitled to a declaration that the SEP licensing offers made by Ericsson to TCL were not FRAND rates because they were "not fair and reasonable, and are discriminatory" since Ericsson had – at the time it made its offers to TCL – already entered into licences with licensees similarly situated to TCL, at rates that were substantially lower than its "FRAND contentions".

4.2 UK – Unwired Planet v Huawei[53]

This was a long-running case involved an SEP licensing dispute between Unwired Planet, an SEP-owning patent assertion entity, and Huawei, a standard-implementing manufacturer of mobile communication devices. The parties were unable to agree on the licensing terms for Unwired Planet's SEPs over 2G, 3G and 4G technologies, with Unwired Planet prepared to offer either a worldwide or UK-only licence of its SEP portfolio while Huawei only willing to take on a UK-only licence. Unwired Planet commenced legal proceedings for patent infringement in the English courts and sought a patent injunction against Huawei, on the basis that Unwired Planet was prepared to licence its SEPs to Huawei in accordance with the former's FRAND undertaking to ETSI, which had been rejected by Huawei.

In its defence, Huawei argued that injunctive relief should be denied to Unwired Planet because the SEP holder had breached its FRAND undertaking, and had also infringed Article 102 of the Treaty for the Functioning of Europe (TFEU) by seeking a patent injunction in contravention of the framework set out by the Court of Justice in *Huawei Technologies v ZTE Corp*.[54] In earlier proceedings, the court had found that Huawei had infringed the SEPs, which were valid UK patents. The patent injunction sought by Unwired Planet was granted because Huawei was not willing to take up a worldwide licence, which the court had found to be FRAND, and since Unwired Planet had not breached any competition laws by seeking injunctive relief against Huawei. Even though the royalty rates offered by Unwired Planet were, ultimately, found by the court to be higher than what was FRAND, Unwired Planet had indicated that it was prepared to accept whatever rates and terms were set by the court, whereas Huawei took the position that only a UK-specific portfolio licence would be FRAND.[55]

Interpreting the meaning and scope of Unwired Planet's FRAND undertaking in respect of its SEPs, the English court recognized that "a proper analysis

53 *Unwired Planet International Ltd v Huawei Technologies*, [2017] EWHC 711 (Pat) (Decision of J. Birss), affirmed on appeal in *Unwired Planet International v Huawei Technologies*, [2018] EWCA Civ 2344.

54 Case C-170/13 (July 16, 2015).

55 *Unwired Planet v Huawei* (n 53 above) at [23].

of the full legal situation needs to have regard to the intellectual property rights which the FRAND undertaking relates to as well as the contractual position. It also needs to take into account competition law".[56] The purpose of making a judicial determination of an appropriate FRAND royalty rate for Unwired Planet's SEPs was to enable the court to decide if the SEP holder seeking injunctive relief had fulfilled his FRAND obligation, where the court's equitable discretion as to whether or not to grant the patent injunction sought would depend on whether the SEP holder was prepared to accept FRAND terms.[57] In other words, the analysis of the FRAND commitment, the compliance with which was approached as a matter of contract law,[58] was carried out to determine the availability of patent injunctions against the defendant.

As far as competition law was concerned, the court took the position that a royalty rate that was not FRAND was not necessarily one that gave rise to a competition law infringement (such as excessive pricing under Article 102 TFEU), and that while competition law considerations "may well indicate why a rate is not FRAND but in general and as a matter of principle, for competition law to be engaged, it will be necessary but not sufficient for a rate not to be the true FRAND rate".[59] Recognizing that the courts "cannot craft a set of FRAND terms out of thin air", the main approach advocated by Justice Birss was to pursue the comparable licence analysis, which is used in other dispute resolution settings such as in the Copyright Tribunal, to assess a reasonable royalty rate for the intellectual property owner – these real-life comparable licences provide evidence of what real parties in real negotiations have agreed upon to determine what would be fair, reasonable and non-discriminatory.[60] In identifying whether or not a licence was comparable, it was relevant to consider the identity of the licensor and how recently the licence was entered into, rather than whether the licensee was a big or small market player.[61] After comparable licences have been identified, it was necessary for the court to "unpack" their royalty rates to the extent where direct comparisons

56 *Id.* at [142].

57 *Id.* at [166] ("I think an English court would at least refuse to grant a patentee an injunction if it refused to accept FRAND terms. That would be a proper exercise of the court's equitable jurisdiction to grant or refuse an injunction").

58 *Unwired Planet v Huawei* (n 53 above) at [99]. The court analyzed the FRAND commitment as a contractual obligation arising for the benefit of third parties under French law, the governing law for the SSO's (ETSI) IPR Policy.

59 *Unwired Planet v Huawei* (n 53 above) at [153], noting that "as a matter of principle, the boundary between what is and is not a true FRAND rate as defined by the ETSI principles is not and cannot be co-extensive with competition law."

60 *Unwired Planet v Huawei* (n 53 above) at [169]–[170].

61 *Id.* at [175], nothing that it "would not be FRAND for a small new entrant to the market to have to pay a higher royalty rate than an established large entity", such that "the FRAND rate ought to be generally non-discriminatory in that it is determined primarily by reference to the value of the patents being licensed and has the result that all licensees who need the same kind of licence will be charged the same kind of rate".

can be drawn.[62] Once a comparable royalty rate had been isolated from a comparable licence, it would then be necessary to measure the relative value of Unwired Planet's SEP portfolio against the patent portfolio in the comparable licence and work out the FRAND benchmark royalty rate for Unwired Planet.

A "patent counting" approach was unavoidable given the sheer number of SEPs involved for each standard, making it necessary to analyze the value of SEPs in broad categories rather than weighing individual patents against one another.[63] The proportion of the SEP holder's patent portfolio for a particular standard could then be determined, using the number of SEPs in that portfolio as the numerator and the total number of SEPs covering the standard as the denominator. With this ratio between the number of SEPs to be licensed by Unwired Planet and all the SEPs that licensees would have to licence in order to implement the standard, it would then be possible to perform a cross-check on the FRAND benchmark royalty rate derived from comparable licences to calculate the implied total aggregate royalty burden imposed on licensees – using the "top-down" approach – to see if this figure was consistent with the industry's understanding of what was a commercially appropriate overall royalty rate for licensing such patents.

The "comparable licence" approach utilized by Justice Birss as the main method for calculating an appropriate FRAND royalty rate for Unwired Planet's SEPs, and the "top-down" approach that was used as a cross-check on the commercial sensibility of the benchmark rate derived, is summarized below.

Comparable Licence Approach:

E → *Royalty rate from comparable licence*
R → *Strength ratio of SEP holder's portfolio relative to SEP portfolio in comparable licence*
Benchmark royality = $E \times R$

Top-down approach (as a cross-check):

S → *SEP holder's proportionate share of all relevant SEPs in a particular standard*
T → *Implied total aggregate royalty burden for that particular standard*

$$\frac{\textit{Benchmark royalty rate}}{S} = T$$

Figure 14.3 FRAND calculation formulae used in *Unwired Planet v Huawei*

62 *Unwired Planet v Huawei* (n 53 above) at [187], noting that comparable licences may have very different fee structures because they are cross-licences or lump-sum royalties, covering different regions or possessing other complications.
63 *Unwired Planet v Huawei* (n 53 above) at [183].

5 Conclusion

It is too early to tell how Singapore courts, or the Singapore competition authority, will define the exact nature or scope of FRAND undertakings or commitments, as legal concepts, given that actual SEP disputes have yet to reach our shores. The non-SEP contexts in which FRAND commitments have been given to the Competition and Consumer Commission of Singapore have also emerged only very recently, with insufficient details as to how disputes arising from them are likely to be resolved. However, it is probably safe to assume that the case law from other developed jurisdictions, particularly the U.S. and the UK, will be looked upon as persuasive authorities should our decision-making bodies be faced with similar issues relating to the FRAND concept in future. It might thus be worth summarizing the key guiding principles (Table 14.3) and methodologies (Table 14.4) that have been applied by the U.S. and English courts as a starting point for predicting how the FRAND concept will be analyzed in Singapore.

Table 14.3 Guiding principles applied to the interpretation of the meaning of "FRAND"

Guiding Principles	*FRAND royalty rates aim to promote widespread adoption of the standard*	*FRAND royalty rates should mitigate the risk of patent holdup*	*FRAND royalty rates should address the risk of royalty stacking*	*FRAND royalty rates should ensure SEP holders receive reasonable compensation*	*FRAND royalty rates should be limited to the economic value of the patented technology itself*	*FRAND royalty rates do not have be equal to the lowest royalty rate offered to a specific licensee*
Microsoft v Motorola (I)	✓ [70]	✓ [71], [111]	✓ [72], [112]	"to induce the creation of valuable standards" [73], [113]	✓ "apart from the value associated with the incorporation of the patented technology into the standard" [74], [103]–[104] [80], [106] (comparison with ex ante alternatives available)	
In Re Innovatio	✓ "the court will consider whether the overall royalty of all standard-essential patents would prohibit widespread adoption of the standard"	✓ "If hold-up occurs, implementing the standard becomes excessively expensive for consumers, undermining the standard setting process and jeopardizing further adoption of the standard"	✓ "concern of royalty stacking requires that the court, to . . . evaluate a proposed RAND rate in the light of the total royalties an implementer would have to pay to practice the standard"	"RAND rate must be set high enough to ensure that innovators in the future have an appropriate incentive to invest in future developments and to contribute their inventions to the standard setting process" Reverse patent holdup (holdout) was not recognized as a significant concern in general as it was not unique to SEPs	✓ (though recognizing "the difficulty of distinguishing between the intrinsic value of the technology and the value of standardization")	

TCL v Ericsson	Ex ante statements made by SEP holder about appropriate total aggregate royalty burdens provide insight and incentive to encourage other companies to invest in the standard				Citing *Ericsson v D-Link*,[64] *CSIRO*[65] and *In re Innovatio*	Drafters of ETSI IPR Policy did not intend "non-discriminatory" to ensure exactly the same treatment or identical license terms for all licensees of the same patent portfolio
Unwired Planet v Huawei	✓ [83] "As a society we want the best, most up to date technology to be incorporated into the latest standards".	✓ [92]–[93] Agreed with summary from Guangdong High Court, China	✓ Prepared to use top-down approach, by determining the patentee's share of the total number of SEPs that comprise the standard, to determine the total aggregate royalty for the standard as a cross-check for the benchmark rate arrived at	[92] "to secure a proper reward for innovation" [95]–[96] potential for "hold out" by patent licensee recognized	[97] Accepted evidence from economists that patentee "it is not necessary to deprive the patentee of its fair share of" the value associated with "the inclusion of his technology into the standard and the value of the products that are using those standards", recognizing that this position differed from that taken by the U.S. court in *In re Innovatio*.	✓ [502] ETSI FRAND undertaking should not be interpreted as introducing a "hard-edged non-discrimination obligation" unless other competition law principles relating to discriminatory pricing (i.e. the need to show distortion to competition) were adopted as well. Endorsed on appeal by the UKCA at [194]–[205]

64 *Ericsson v D-Link*, 773 F.3d at 1232–1233.
65 *Commonwealth Scientific & Indus. Research Organization v Cisco Systems, Inc*, 809 F.3d 1295 (Fed. Cir. 2015).

Table 14.4 Methodologies for calculation of FRAND royalty rates

Methodology	*Hypothetical Bilateral Negotiations*	*Real-world references: Comparable Licences*	*Taking average of reliable indicators*	*"Top-down" approach*
Microsoft v Motorola (I)	✓ [83], [95]–[115]	✓ [84], [108]	✓ [616] "process of averaging is common in business negotiations"	
In Re Innovatio	✓	✓		✓ [38]–[39]
TCL v Ericsson	Acknowledged that *Georgia-Pacific* framework established a multi-faceted test for establishing a reasonable royalty in patent infringement cases, but declined to carry out full-blown *Georgia-Pacific* analysis "in the unique context of a FRAND dispute"	✓ Market-based approach which considers comparable licenses needed to evaluate "non-discrimination" element of FRAND Similarly situated firms to be identified and their licences with SEP holder unpacked for comparison Actual licences to the patented technology at issue are probative as to what constitutes a fair and reasonable royalty since they reflect the economic value of the patented technology in the market place		✓ Prevents royalty stacking and holdup Relied on previous public statements made by SEP holder on what a fair cumulative royalty rate for the industry should be
Unwired Planet v Huawei		✓ [170], [179] "The real question is what would be fair, reasonable and non-discriminatory. Asking what a willing licensor and a willing licensee in the relevant circumstances acting without holding out or holding up would agree upon is likely to help decide that question"		✓ [263]–[268] Useful only as a cross-check to support benchmark rates calculated using comparable licences because of "conceptual difficulty" of selecting the total royalty burden to start with.

15 European experiences

EU and Germany

*Matthias Leistner**

1 Introduction

Before the influential Huawei/ZTE judgment of the CJEU[1] in 2015, the situation in regard to standard essential patents (SEPs) in Germany and Europe was substantially influenced by the Orange Book Standard judgment of the German Federal Court of Justice (*Bundesgerichtshof, BGH*).[2] The Orange Book Standard judgment of 2009, however, did not concern a patent, subject to a FRAND licensing commitment or a legal standard, but a mere de facto standard in regard to a broadly licensed patent pool.[3] Nonetheless, it also governed the discussion about the treatment of injunctions based on SEPs, which are subject to FRAND commitments. At least with regard to such SEPs, it was criticized by many legal authors as too harsh on the standard implementers.[4]

* Professor and GRUR Chair for Civil Law and Intellectual Property Law with Information Law and IT-Law at Ludwig Maximilian University (LMU), Munich. The author thanks his Research Assistant, Ms. Viola Pless, for valuable help in collecting and structuring the case law and literature references for this chapter.

1 CJEU, July 16, 2015, C-170/13, ECLI:EU:C:2015:477 – *Huawei Technology Co. Ltd v ZTE Corp.*

2 Federal Court of Justice (*Bundesgerichtshof*), May 6, 2009, KZR 39/06, GRUR 2009, 694 (=BeckRS 2009, 13174) – Orange-Book-Standard.

3 P. Picht, The ECJ Rules on Standard-essential Patents: Thoughts and Issues Post-Huawei, 37(9) *ECLR* 365, 367 (2016); W. Kellenter & A. Verhauwen, Systematik und Anwendung des kartellrechtlichen Zwangslizenzeinwandes nach "Huawei/ZTE" und "Orange-Book", *GRUR* 761, 762 (2018) (in German).

4 Picht, The ECJ Rules on Standard-essential Patents at 365, 367 with further references; H. Ullrich, Patents and Standards – A Comment on the German Federal Supreme Court Decision Orange Book Standard, *IIC* 337, 343 (2010) et seq.; P. Maume, *Huawei/ZTE*, or, how the CJEU Closed the Orange Book, 6(2) *QMJIP* 207, 216 (2016); further P. Picht, Standardsetzung und Patentmissbrauch – Schlagkraft und Entwicklungsbedarf des europäischen Kartellrechts, *GRUR Int.* 1, 14 (2014) (in German) and P. Maume & C. Tapia, Der Zwangslizenzeinwand ein Jahr nach dem Orange Book Standard – mehr Fragen als Antworten, *GRUR Int.* 923, 923 (2010) (in German) with further references; nonetheless, part of the German legal literature approved the Orange Book Standard judgment, see e.g. D. Jestaedt, Der Lizenzerteilungsanspruch nach der BGH-Entscheidung Orange-Book-Standard, *GRUR* 801, 805 (2009); T. Nägele & S. Jacobs, Zwangslizenzen im Patentrecht – unter besonderer Berücksichtigung des kartellrechtlichen Zwangslizenzeinwands im Patentverletzungsprozess, *WRP* 1062, 1073 (2009) (in German).

Accordingly, for SEPs subject to a FRAND declaration, the European Commission in 2014 in its Motorola and Samsung Decisions[5] developed a 'willing licensee' test based on competition theory, which placed materially fewer obligations on the implementers of FRAND-encumbered SEPs than the Orange Book Standard judgment.[6] The CJEU has established a middle way in its 2015 Huawei/ZTE judgment, based less on competition theory and more on general fundamental rights and civil law considerations, to identify the willingness to license of both parties by way of a procedural 'ping pong'-like step-by-step approach (*see infra* section 2).

Considering that the questions in Huawei/ZTE had been referred to the CJEU by the Düsseldorf Regional Court (*Landgericht Düsseldorf*), it is not surprising that a considerable number of SEP proceedings in Germany,[7] which had been brought to the German courts before or during the CJEU preliminary reference proceedings, were stayed to await the pending CJEU judgment. Consequently, shortly after the CJEU's judgment, there has already emerged a rather broad post-Huawei court practice in Germany, which has (at least partly) answered some of the detailed questions left open by the CJEU, and which at the same time shows that the CJEU's approach does indeed work in practice (*see infra* section 3).

Nonetheless, at the same time a lot of the more fundamental implications and questions raised by the CJEU's judgment still remain open. Also, while the CJEU's approach undoubtedly does help to select out the non-willing licensor or licensee (i.e. the holdup[8] or holdout[9] cases), problems remain with regard

5 European Commission, April 29, 2004, AT.39985 – Motorola; European Commission, April 29, 2014, AT.39939 – Samsung.

6 M. Rato & M. English, An Assessment of Injunctions, Patents, and Standards Following the Court of Justice's *Huawei/ZTE Ruling*, 7(2) *JECLAP* 103, 103 (2016).

7 The court practice in the U.K. after Huawei/ZTE is outlined in Chapter 7. See also S. Lawrance & F. Brooks, *Unwired Planet v Huawei*: The First UK FRAND Determination, *JECLAP* 170 (2018); J. Cross & J. Strath, Unwired Planet v Huawei – the FRAND Injunction, *CTLR* 178 (2017); P. Picht, *Unwired Planet v. Huawei*: A Seminal SEP/FRAND decision from the UK, 12(10) *JIPLP* 867 (2017); P. Treacy & M. Hunt, Litigating a 'FRAND' Patent Licence: The *Unwired Planet v Huawei* Judgment, 124 *JIPLP* (2018).

8 See further on patent holdup in regard to SEPs J. Farrel et al., Standard Setting, Patents, and Hold-up, 74 *Antitrust L.J.* 603 (2007) et seq.; M. Lemley, Intellectual Property Rights and Standard-Setting Organizations, 90 *Cal. L. Rev.* 1889 (2002); M. Lemley & C. Shapiro, Patent Holdup and Royalty Stacking, 85 *Tex. L. Rev.* 1991 (2007); see also (under a more general, historical perspective) R. Merges, The Trouble with Trolls: Innovation, Rent-seeking, and Patent Law Reform, 24 *Berkeley Tech. L.J.* 1583 (2009). More recent contributions from Europe include V. Angweny, Hold-up, Hold-out and F/Rand: The Quest for Balance, *GRUR Int.* 105, 107 (2017) et seq.; Picht, The ECJ Rules on Standard-Essential Patents at 365, each with comprehensive further references. However, other authors have argued that patent holdup is a mere catchword, which does not describe an empirically warranted problematic situation in the markets, cf. e.g. Rato & English (n 6) 103, 105 et seq.

9 For the concept of patent holdout in regard to SEP patents see Angweny (n 8) 105, 110 et seq.; C. Chien, *Holding Up and Holding Out*, 21 *Mich. Telecomm. Tech. L. Rev.* 1 (2014), available at https://repository.law.umich.edu/mttlr/vol21/iss1/1 (last accessed October 15, 2018); Picht, The ECJ Rules on Standard-Essential Patents at 365; Rato & English (n 6) 103, 105 et seq., D. Geradin & M. Rato, Can Standard-Setting Lead to Exploitive

to royalty stacking and the appropriate adjustment of royalty rates also between generally willing licensing parties (in particular for smaller players). Hence, some essential questions remain open and possibly new regulatory perspectives, in particular for procedural and institutional approaches to SEP licensing, have to be developed (*see infra* section 4).

2 The CJEU's Huawei/ZTE judgment – a major step ahead

2.1 The facts of the case and the scope of the Huawei/ZTE doctrine

The facts and reference questions in Huawei/ZTE are broadly known and have been described in many case comments.[10] This shall not be repeated here. Suffice it to say that Huawei/ZTE concerned a mobile phone SEP subject to a FRAND commitment with the European Telecommunications Standards Institute (ETSI), for which no standard licensing program was established and published, so that the parties of the dispute engaged in unsuccessful licensing negotiations (namely on a possible cross-license which was rejected by the patent holder).[11]

Against that background it has been argued in part of the German literature that the ratio decidendi of Huawei/ZTE does not extend to mere de facto industry standards without FRAND declaration (such as at issue in the Orange Book Standard judgment) and does not apply to SEPs with an established and published licensing program either. Furthermore, it has even been argued that for all such cases, the Orange Book Standard principles remain good law.[12]

However, such a strict qualification and distinction of the Huawei/ZTE judgment is not justified. This is because, first, an *industry SEP* can undoubtedly lead to a market dominant position of the patent holder; depending on the circumstances of the case, a situation might result in which the unwillingness to license does consequently lead to the prevention of a new product or service

---

Abuse? A Dissonant View on Patent Hold-Up, Royalty Stacking and Meaning of FRAND, 3(1) *ECJ* 101, 125 (2007) et seq.

10 H. Tsilikas, *Huawei v. ZTE* in Context – EU Competition Policy and Collaborative Standardization in Wireless Telecommunications, *IIC* 151, 169 (2017) et seq.; P. Batista & G. Mazutti, Comment on "Huawei Technologies" (C-170/13): Standard Essential Patents and Competition Law – How Far Does the CJEU Go? *IIC* 244 (2016); Maume (n 4) 207, 221; Rato & English (n 6) 103, 104; T. McIver, A. Pomana, & J. Schmidt, Between Patent Protection and Abuse of Dominance: Highest EU Court Issues Landmark Decision on Standard-essential Patents, 36(12) *ECLR* 533 (2015); M. Jakobs & F. Hübener, SEP or no SEP? Open Questions after Huawei/ZTE, 37(1) *ECLR* 33, 34 (2016); D. Wilson, A. Moir, N. Ruesink-Brown, & K. Fountoukakos, CJEU Permits Standard Essential Patent (SEP) Injunctions Against Infringers Who Engage in Delaying Tactics or Do Not Respond Diligently with a Good Faith Counter-Offer, 37(11) *E.I.P.R.* 741, 742 (2015).

11 CJEU, July 16, 2015, C-170/13, ECLI:EU:C:2015:477 – *Huawei Technology Co. Ltd v ZTE Corp.*

12 Kellenter & Verhauwen (n 3) 761, 762 et seq.

emerging in the secondary market, which can then be regarded as exceptional circumstances that trigger compulsory licenses and thus also the respective defence against injunctions under Art. 102 TFEU.[13] Hence, the question what Huawei/ZTE means for such situations rather comes down to the issue of market dominance on which, however, Huawei/ZTE is mute, as market dominance for the patent had been established by the national court and was not disputed in the proceedings.[14] Second, it has to be emphasized that Huawei/ZTE is not exclusively rooted in competition theory and Art. 102 TFEU doctrine anyway. This has been outlined (and partly criticized) by some authors already.[15] Indeed, the judgment also essentially relies on a fundamental rights analysis[16] and on general civil law doctrines, such as 'good faith' or 'recognized commercial practices'.[17] This even raises the question for the future of whether the ratio of the judgment would have to be applied to certain situations of patent holdup, where market dominance cannot be established (*see* on this perspective subsection 4.1). At present, at least this clearly shows that Huawei/ZTE can certainly not be discarded for mere industry de facto standards, as it contains a broadly based doctrine and procedural test, which has at least the general potential to be applied beyond the scope of SEPs with a FRAND declaration by the patent holder.

Third, as for *SEPs with an established and published licensing program*, one might indeed argue that in such cases leniency with regard to the details of the individual licensing offer of the patent holder might be warranted, as it is easier for the implementer to get information on the general licensing practice of the right holder. However, while this might require nuanced and flexible application of the Huawei/ZTE criteria on the facts of such a case, it certainly does not justify a principled conclusion that Huawei/ZTE is not applicable at all and instead Orange Book Standard would apply.[18] This is also because the necessity of the initial notification step and the details of the further steps of the 'ping pong' procedure, established by Huawei/ZTE, such as necessities of timely reaction on both sides, the requirements

13 Cf. already M. Leistner, Intellectual Property and Competition Law: The European Development from Magill to IMS Health Compared to Recent German and US Case Law, *ZWER* 138, 150 (2005) et seq. (also on the meanwhile relatively low threshold of the 'new product' test).

14 CJEU, July 16, 2015, C-170/13, ECLI:EU:C:2015:477, note 43 – *Huawei Technology Co. Ltd v ZTE Corp.*

15 Picht, The ECJ Rules on Standard-Essential Patents at 365, 370.

16 CJEU, July 16, 2015, C-170/13, ECLI:EU:C:2015:477, notes 32, 42 et seq. – *Huawei Technology Co. Ltd v ZTE Corp.*

17 CJEU, July 16, 2015, C-170/13, ECLI:EU:C:2015:477, notes 65, 71 – *Huawei Technology Co. Ltd v ZTE Corp.*

18 Indeed, the CJEU's judgment rather implies the opposite, i.e. an applicability of Huawei/ZTE also to SEPs with an established and published licensing program of the SEP owner. This is because in C-170/13, ECLI:EU:C:2015:477, note 64 – *Huawei Technology Co. Ltd v ZTE Corp.*, the CJEU mainly derives the duty to make an initial FRAND offer from the FRAND declaration by the SEP owner and then, only as an additional argument ('Furthermore . . .') refers to the information asymmetry with regard to SEPs where no licensing program is established and published.

and time for security to be provided by the implementer etc. are equally applicable to SEPs with an established and published licensing program.

It is important, though, that the Huawei/ZTE judgment, which addresses possible abusive behavior consisting in unduly threatening implementers by actions for injunctive relief, is only concerned with abusive claims for an *injunction* by the SEP holder. Thus, its effects on possible *damages claims* and respective accessory actions for accounting and other information to calculate the damages are at best indirect (*see infra* subsection 3.4 on the German courts' case law on such still considerable indirect effects).

2.2 The Huawei/ZTE "test"

Compared to Orange Book Standard, CJEU's Huawei/ZTE judgment establishes an abuse test which effectively turns the Orange Book Standard ratio upside down. By contrast to Orange Book Standard, it *puts the burden of initiative* from the very first step *on the SEP holder* in what develops into a multiple-step or ('ping pong') test, which attempts to establish minimum guideposts for a reasonable basic licensing negotiation structure of respectively willing licensing parties.[19]

The often-described test[20] shall only briefly be outlined here (as many of the more intricate details will be discussed infra in subsection 3.2):

1 The SEP holder has to 'alert the alleged infringer of the infringement complained about by designating th[e] SEP and specifying the way in which it has been infringed';[21]
2 The alleged infringer has to express 'its willingness to conclude a licensing agreement on FRAND terms';[22]
3 Then 'it is for the . . . [SEP holder] to present to that alleged infringer a specific, written[23] offer for a license on FRAND terms, in accordance with the

19 G. Colangelo & V. Torti, Filing Huawei's Gaps: The Recent German Case Law on Standard Essential Patents, 38(12) *ECLR* 538, 541 (2017); Tsilikas (n 10) 151; 170 et seq.; Batista & Mazutti (n 10) 244, 247 et seq.; Jakobs & Hübener (n 10) 33, 37. Further, see also P. Picht, "FRAND wars 2.0" – Rechtsprechung im Anschluss an die Huawei/ZTE-Entscheidung des EuGH (Teil 1), *WuW* 234 (2018) and (Teil 2), *WuW* 300 (2018) (in German).

20 Batista & Mazutti, (n 10) 244, 245 et seq.; Tsilikas (n 10) 151, 169 et seq.; Wilson, Moir, Ruesink-Brown, & Fountoukakos (n 10) 741, 742; Picht, The ECJ Rules on Standard-essential Patents at 365, 367 et seq.; Rato & English (n 6) 103, 107 et seq.

21 CJEU, July16, 2015, C-170/13, ECLI:EU:C:2015:47, note 61 – *Huawei Technology Co. Ltd v ZTE Corp.*

22 CJEU, July 16, 2015, C-170/13, ECLI:EU:C:2015:477, note 63 – *Huawei Technology Co. Ltd v ZTE Corp.*

23 Düsseldorf Higher Regional Court (*Oberlandesgericht, OLG Düsseldorf*) has explained in its judgment March 30, 2017, I-15 U 66/15, GRUR 2017, 1219, note 169 (=BeckRS 2017, 124408, note 170) – Mobiles Kommunikationssystem that the requirement of written form is also met by communications via telefax or e-mail, which practically corresponds to the so-called text form in German law (see Sec. 126b German Civil Code (*Bürgerliches Gesetzbuch*)), referring to T. Kühnen, Handbuch der Patentverletzung (Heymanns Verlag, Köln, 2018), Chap. E, note 323.

undertaking given to the standardization body, specifying, in particular, the amount of the royalty and the way in which that royalty is to be calculated';[24]

4 Upon which 'it is for the alleged infringer diligently to respond to that offer, in accordance with recognized commercial practices in the field and in good faith, a point which must be established on the basis of objective factors and which implies, in particular, that there are no delaying tactics';

5 If the alleged infringer is already using the SEP before a licensing agreement has been concluded, from the point at which his counter-offer is rejected, the burden is on the alleged infringer to 'provide appropriate security, in accordance with recognized commercial practices in the field, for example by providing a bank guarantee or by placing the amounts necessary on deposit. The calculation of that security must include, inter alia, the number of the past acts of use of the SEP, and the alleged infringer must be able to render an account in respect of those acts of use'.

6 Ultimately, 'where no agreement is reached on the details of the FRAND terms . . ., the parties may, by common agreement, request that the amount of the royalty be determined by an independent third party, by decision without delay'.

In addition, and possibly also in reaction to the German Federal Court of Justice's different ruling in Orange Book Standard,[25] the CJEU clarifies that 'an alleged infringer cannot be criticized either for challenging, in parallel to the negotiations relating to the grant of licenses, the validity of . . . [the] patents and/or the essential nature of . . . [the] patents to the standard in which they are included and/or their actual use, or for reserving the right to do so in the future'.[26]

2.3 Reactions in legal literature

Apart from further considerations on the fundamental underpinnings and general implications of the judgment,[27] as regards the multiple-step or 'ping pong' test, most reactions in legal literature have been generally positive.[28]

24 CJEU, July 16, 2015, C-170/13, ECLI:EU:C:2015:477, note 63 – *Huawei Technology Co. Ltd v ZTE Corp.*

25 Which required an 'unconditional' license offer (Federal Court of Justice, May 6, 2009, KZR 39/06, GRUR 2009, 694, note 29 (=BeckRS 2009, 13174, note 29) – Orange-Book-Standard); *see, e.g.*, the justified criticism by Ullrich, IIC 2010, 337, 343 et seq.; for further references *see supra* footnote 4.

26 CJEU, July 16, 2015, C-170/13, ECLI:EU:C:2015:477, note 69 – *Huawei Technology Co. Ltd v ZTE Corp.*

27 These aspects will be treated infra at section 4.

28 *See, e.g.*, Batista & Mazutti, (n 10) 244, 247 et seq.; Wilson, Moir, Ruesink-Brown, & Fountoukakos (n 10) 741, 742; McIver, Pomana, & Schmidt (n 10) 533, 535; Jakobs & Hübener (n 10) 33, 34, 39; R. Jacob & A. Milner, Lessons from *Huawei v. ZTE*, October 2016, available at www.4ipcouncil.com/news/latest-research-4ip-council-lessons-huawei-v-zte, 1, 1 et seq. (last accessed October 1, 2018).

However, partly, the judgment has been criticized as not being genuinely justified by existing case law and competition law theory.[29] Furthermore, the envisaged step-by-step structure for the licensing negotiations has been characterized and criticized as being stylized, formalistic and thus artificial.[30] However, this criticism overlooks that the step-by-step structure established by the court was hardly ever meant to be an authentic replicate of normal 'real life' licensing negotiations. Instead, the structure aims to establish appropriate guideposts which willing licensing parties *can hold to* in order to establish a *legally secure* licensing process in the specific situation where an SEP is concerned and 'normal' licensing negotiations are about to fail. In Europe, these situations hitherto were characterized by considerable legal uncertainty and have resulted in leeway for patent holdup or holdout. Thus, a critique based on the artificial structure of the CJEU's test is misguided. It fails to acknowledge that this new clear and simplified sequential structure allows patent holders and implementers to reasonably foresee which necessary steps they have to take in order to avoid being charged with abusive behavior or (vice versa) in order not to jeopardize their right to a FRAND licensing process. This more structured process, as a necessary interim step in order to establish minimum good faith, might then reach the ultimate goal of the parties in engaging in a successful negotiation process.

At the same time, the Court's test contains many open-ended terms and does not really specify and detail the step-by-step requirements on the European level.[31] Also, it remains partly unclear which consequences violations of the duties on the different steps of the process will have for the respective duties on the subsequent steps.[32] Hence, many fundamental[33] as well as detailed questions have undoubtedly been left open by the Court's judgment. Some of the more detailed issues, however, have now already been addressed by the Member States' courts in the aftermath of the Huawei/ZTE judgment. The two most important jurisdictions in that regard have been the U.K. and Germany. While case law in the U.K. is covered in Chapter 7, the German case law will be comprehensively discussed in what follows.

29 Rato & English (n 6) 103 et seq.; Picht, The ECJ Rules on Standard-essential Patents at 370 et seq.; D. Geradin, European Union Competition Law, Intellectual Property Law and Standardization, available at https://ssrn.com/abstract=2907632 (last accessed October 15, 2018), 20 et seq.; Tsilikas (n 10) 151, 171 et seq.; Colangelo & Torti (n 19) 538 et seq. with further references.

30 Rato & English (n 6) 103, 110 et seq.

31 Batista & Mazutti (n 10) 47, 244, 249 et seq.; Wilson, Moir, Ruesink-Brown, & Fountoukakos, (n 10) 741, 743; Geradin (n 29); Maume (n 4) 207, 224; Jacob & Milner (n 28).

32 Colangelo & Torti (n 19) 538, 541 et seq.; Tsilikas (n 10) 151, 172; Picht, 'FRAND wars 2.0' – Rechtsprechung im Anschluss at 234, 236 et seq.

33 On some of the more fundamental questions and implications of the judgment, *see infra* section 4.

3 The subsequent German case law – getting into the details

3.1 Introduction: the legal framework in German law

Considering that contract law and general doctrines, such as 'good faith', are still mainly rooted in national law of the Member States, it is not surprising that the *legal interface* between precedent abusive behavior of the SEP holder according to Art. 102 TFEU (*abuse*) and the negation of the claim for an injunction (*defence*) remained rather unclear in the Huawei/ZTE judgment.[34] This might also have contributed to the intermingling of legal concepts in the judgment, which in describing the several steps of the multiple step licensing process also referred to *'good faith'* and *'recognized commercial practices'*.

In German law, the interface is based on Sec. 242 German Civil Code, which refers to good faith and has been further specified in case law and legal doctrine. Thus, filing an action for an injunction is contrary to good faith, if the right holder abusively denied a license before and would therefore immediately be required to grant a license under competition law anyway. In this framework, German courts have decided a rather large number of cases in the period before Huawei/ZTE.[35] By contrast, since Huawei/ZTE the analysis of the German courts has centered on the open questions and leeway for specification left open by the CJEU's judgment.

3.2 Filling the gaps

Among the most influential patent courts in Germany, that is the Regional and Higher Regional Courts in Düsseldorf, Mannheim/Karlsruhe and Munich,[36] only the Düsseldorf and the Mannheim/Karlsruhe courts have ruled on SEP-related issues in a number of cases after Huawei/ZTE.

3.2.1 Dominant position of the SEP holder

As a dominant position was a given in Huawei/ZTE, the CJEU did not further elaborate on the *concept of dominance* with regard to SEP holders.[37] Most

34 Rato & English (n 6) 103, 110 et seq.; Geradin (n 29) 1, 19 et seq.; Colangelo, 538 et seq.

35 Karlsruhe Higher Regional Court (*Oberlandesgericht, OLG Karlsruhe*), February 27, 2012, 6 U 136/11, GRUR 2012, 736 (=BeckRS 2012, 05121) – GPRS-Zwangslizenz II; Düsseldorf Higher Regional Court, January 20, 2011, 2 U 9210, WuW 2011, 401 (=LSK 2011, 140463); January 28, 2011, 2 U 129/08, BeckRS 2010, 16641.

36 While perfectly understanding and interpreting the *substance* of German case law, with regard to the denomination of the different courts Lord Kitchin got it wrong in a technical detail in [2018] EWCA Civ 2344, note 63 and note 64 – Unwired Planet/Huawei, when speaking of the 'Regional Court' of Mannheim and the Düsseldorf 'District Court', respectively. In fact, both courts are Regional Courts (*Landgerichte*).

37 Differently GA *Wathelet,* who had emphasized (insofar correctly) that an SEP holder does not automatically have a dominant position but had at the same time (incorrectly) assumed

German courts since Huawei/ZTE have also avoided the question and more or less immediately engaged in a Huawei/ZTE step-by-step analysis. Alternatively, some courts continue to consider to use Sec. 242 German Civil Act (good faith and prohibition of self-contradictory behavior) to derive the requirement of compliance with the Huawei/ZTE steps from the SEP holders' FRAND declarations in relation to ETSI.[38]

However, the condition of market dominance is certainly relevant for the competence of the CJEU and the scope of the ratio decidendi of Huawei/ZTE. In that regard, it has to be acknowledged that the inclusion of a patent in a standard does not as such indicate market dominance as the Düsseldorf Courts have correctly emphasized in two recent judgments.[39] Instead, market dominance has to be established *in the follow-up market for the products and services*, which shall be offered on the basis of using the patent.[40] In that regard, standards contain not only essential patents in the strict sense which are *indispensable* for the product to be in compliance with the standard and to achieve interoperability, but also many *add-on patents* which offer *certain* further functionalities and improvements not indispensable to the functioning of the standard in the strict sense. Hence, where SEPs are not part of the *indispensable* core of a standard, further analysis of market dominance is essential in many cases. Also the question of how to deal with situations where the SEP holder is not in a dominant position in the sense of Art. 102 TFEU[41] has to be answered.

For those patents which are not part of the indispensable core of a standard, according to the Düsseldorf courts, it is inevitably necessary to objectively

---

that ownership of an SEP established a rebuttable presumption of market dominance, cf. GA *Wathelet*, Opinion, 20. November 2014, Case C-170/13, ECLI:EU:C:2014:2391, note 57 et seq. – *Huawei Technology Co. Ltd v ZTE Corp.* Justifiably against such a presumption Düsseldorf Higher Regional Court, March 30, 2017, I-15 U 66/15, GRUR 2017, 1219, note 129 (=BeckRS 2017, 124408, note 130) – Mobiles Kommunikationssystem.

38 Mannheim Regional Court (*LG Mannheim*), November 27, 2015, 2 O 106/14, GRUR-RS 2015, 2007, note 133, (considered as a possible obiter, which was not relevant for the case since there was no abusive behavior anyway); similarly in result Düsseldorf Higher Regional Court, March 30, 2017, I-15 U 66/15, GRUR 2017, 1219, note 176 (=BeckRS 2017, 124408, note 177), – Mobiles Kommunikationssystem for discrimination cases, where the obligation not to unjustifiably discriminate, shall follow from the FRAND declaration itself in conjunction with Art. 102c TFEU to which the FRAND declaration relates.

39 Düsseldorf Higher Regional Court, March 30, 2017, I-15 U 66/15, GRUR 2017, 1219, notes 125 et seq. (=BeckRS 2017, 124408, notes 126 et seq.) – Mobiles Kommunikationssystem; Düsseldorf Regional Court, January 19, 2016, 4b O 120/14, GRUR-RS 2016, 08288, notes 268 et seq. – Kommunikationssystem.

40 See generally Düsseldorf Higher Regional Court, March 30, 2017, I-15 U 66/15, GRUR 2017, 1219, note 129 (=BeckRS 2017, 124408, note 130), – Mobiles Kommunikationssystem. In that regard, however, the attitude of the English courts seems to be different; see the overall conclusion of the High Court, EWHC, April 5, 2017, 711 (Pat), note 741 – Unwired Planet/Huawei; endorsed by the Court of Appeals in [2018] EWCA Civ 2344, note 213 et seq. – Unwired Planet/Huawei.

41 For some thoughts on the latter point, *see infra* subsection 4.1.

analyze all the facts of the case in hand with regard to the situation in the product or service market in order to establish a dominant position.[42] On that basis, in particular for substitutable technical features, the crucial question must be whether without using the patented technology a competitive offer would not be possible in the secondary product or process market. For this analysis, the fact that the technological feature in question has already broadly penetrated the market can play an important role as an indicator of market dominance. By contrast, if the patent concerns a minor technical feature, which is neither necessary for achieving interoperability nor essentially important for the functioning of the product or service from the viewpoint of the customers, SEP ownership does not automatically establish a dominant position of the SEP holder.

As mentioned earlier, German courts since Huawei/ZTE have also considered whether the Huawei/ZTE requirements should not *apply notwithstanding market dominance* just because the SEP holder notified its patent for inclusion in the standard and thereby declared his willingness to license the patent under FRAND conditions. Hitherto, the courts tend to continue to apply Sec. 242 German Civil Code in such cases. The result is that a refusal to comply with the requirements of the CJEU for the FRAND licensing of SEPs might *as such* amount to a prohibited self-contradictory behavior of the patent holder and thus trigger a Huawei/ZTE defence.[43]

3.2.2 *Essentiality of the SEP*

An interesting and important follow-up question concerns the issue of how to deal with situations where an SEP was included in the standard by the standard setting organisation (SSO) even though it was *not at all essential to the standard in the first place*. This situation is quite frequent in practice, as no strict analysis is carried out by the SSOs as to whether a notified patent is really essential to the standard in question. One might consider treating these cases along the lines of the aforementioned case law on patent holders who declared their FRAND licensing willingness but are not dominant undertakings. Hence, the patent holder would nonetheless be obliged to comply with the Huawei/ZTE requirements if he himself notified his patents to the SSOs for the standard, since non-compliance might possibly be regarded as impermissible self-contradictory behavior under Sec. 242 German Civil Code.

3.2.3 *Catching up on the Huawei/ZTE requirements during the court proceedings?*

As many cases had been stayed pending the European judgment, the first question for the German courts to answer was whether the necessary notification (first

42 Düsseldorf Higher Regional Court, March 30, 2017, I-15 U 66/15, GRUR 2017, 1219, notes 125 et seq. (=BeckRS 2017, 124408, notes 126 et seq.) – Mobiles Kommunikationssystem; Düsseldorf Regional Court, January 19, 2016, 4b O 120/14, GRUR-RS 2016, 08288, note 268 – Kommunikationssystem.

43 See references in footnote 38.

step) and also the FRAND offer by the SEP holder could still be declared ***during the court proceedings***. For *'old' cases*, which were filed before Huawei/ZTE, after some initial uncertainty, German courts accept that the infringement alert and the initial FRAND offer by the SEP holder can also be declared during the court proceedings.[44]

As for *new cases*, the situation in the German courts initially was less clear.[45] Meanwhile, the clear majority opinion in case law requires that the notification to the infringer be made *before* the start of the court proceedings.[46] Partly the courts also distinguish between situations where the alleged infringer is willing to take a license and a belated notification shall not suffice, as the ongoing court proceedings would put undue pressure on the alleged infringer, and situations where the alleged infringer shows unwillingness to accept a license and more leniency is warranted for belated notifications.[47]

Further, for new cases the German courts tend to require that *the initial FRAND offer* by the patent holder also be made *before* the filing of a court action against the alleged infringer.[48] Otherwise, the negotiations would take place under the *Damocles' sword* of the pending action for an injunction and would thus not be sufficiently free on the side of the implementer. From this author's viewpoint, the assumption that pending court proceedings could lead to undue pressure on alleged infringers of SEPs seems hardly realistic.[49] Even the smaller players in the field are certainly aware of patent issues and have access to respective legal advice. Under these circumstances, ongoing court proceedings might even help to initiate and structure the Huawei/ZTE step-by-step procedure. Also, in case of a belated FRAND offer the courts can easily hold the proceedings

44 Düsseldorf Higher Regional Court, May 9, 2016, I-15 U 35/16, GRUR-RS 2016, 09322, notes 17 et seq. – Saint Lawrence/Vodafone; I-15 U 36/16, May 9, 2016, GRUR-RS 2016, 09323 (=BeckRS 2016, 9323), notes 18 et seq. – Zwangslizenzeinwand; see also Karlsruhe Higher Regional Court, May 31, 2016, 6 U 55/16, GRUR-RS 2016, 10660, notes 19 et seq. (=BeckRS 2016, 10660, notes 19 et seq.); for detailed analyses see Picht, 'FRAND Wars 2.0' – Rechtsprechung im Anschluss at 234, 235 et seq.

45 Kellenter & Verhauwen (n 3) 761, 766 et seq.; Picht, 'FRAND Wars 2.0' – Rechtsprechung im Anschluss at 234, 235 et seq.

46 Düsseldorf Regional Court, March 31, 2016, 4a O 126/14, GRUR-RS 2016, 8040, notes 127 et seq. – Saint Lawrence/Vodafone; March 31, 2016, 4a O 73/14, BeckRS 2016, 131580, notes 154 et seq. (=juris, notes 215 et seq.) – Saint Lawrence/Vodafone; Karlsruhe Higher Regional Court, August 29, 2016, 6 U 57/16, GRUR-RS 2016, 16061, note 25 (=BeckRS 2016, 16061, note 25).

47 *See also infra* subsection 3.2.4 on the related question of whether an overall analysis of the parties' conduct is applied by the German courts or rather a strict step-by-step approach.

48 See e.g. Düsseldorf Regional Court, July 13, 2017, 4a O 27/16, GRUR-RS 2017, 130336, notes 186 et seq. (=BeckRS 2017, 130336, notes 186 et seq.); Düsseldorf Higher Regional Court, March 30, 2017, I-15 U 66/15, GRUR 2017, 1219, note 168 (=BeckRS 2017, 124408, note 169) – Mobiles Kommunikationssystem.

49 Similarly also Kellenter & Verhauwen (n 3) 761, 767 et seq., who also point out that in the CJEU's judgment, which was concerned with the specific reference questions of the Düsseldorf Regional Court, the issue of pressure on the implementer because of pending court proceedings has not been addressed expressly.

until the Huawei/ZTE procedure has been carried out (or possibly even moderate this procedure). If one takes into account that at the same time it is accepted in German law that a right holder who did not fulfil the necessary Huawei/ZTE requirements can withdraw his pending action for an injunction in order to file a new action after fulfilling the requirements,[50] it would seem unduly formalistic not to accept belated FRAND offers even during court procedures. Hence, *belated FRAND offers* during ongoing court proceedings should be permitted; the proceedings should be stayed in such a case pending the outcome of the Huawei/ZTE communications between the parties.[51] Incidentally, this would also align German case law with the attitude of the English courts in *Unwired Planet/Huawei*.[52]

3.2.4 A strict step-by-step procedure or an overall analysis of the parties' conduct?

Considering that the whole Huawei/ZTE doctrine might be regarded as a procedural approach to identify the genuine willingness of the parties to conclude a license, it is a fundamentally important question whether the individual Huawei/ZTE steps have to be *strictly separately* assessed by the courts (ping-pong or step-by-step approach) or whether the subsequent reaction of the other side can also be taken into account in assessing precedent steps (*overall analysis approach*). The UK High Court tends to apply an overall analysis in order to procedurally assess the willingness of the parties to engage in serious licensing negotiations.[53]

Thus far in German court practice, the issue comes down to the practically immensely relevant question whether an initially insufficient (i.e. more or less obviously non-FRAND) licensing offer by the right holder can nonetheless trigger reaction requirements for a FRAND counter-offer on the side of the

50 Düsseldorf Higher Regional Court, May 9, 2016, I-15 U 35/16, GRUR-RS 2016, 09322, note 20 – Saint Lawrence/Vodafone; I-15 U 36/16, GRUR-RS 2016, 09323, note 20 – Zwangslizenzeinwand.

51 See on all this Kellenter & Verhauwen (n 3) 761, 764 and 766 et seq.

52 See EWHC (*High Court of Justice*), April 5, 2017, 711 (Pat), note 741 – Unwired Planet/Huawei. Expressly endorsed by the Court of Appeal; although Lord Kitchin accepted in its appeal judgment that under Huawei/ZTE there are specific requirements for the patent holders before bringing action for injunctive relief, it endorsed the result and approach of Birss J., since patent holders' failure to comply with these requirements did not undermine the English overall approach and understanding of the Huawei/ZTE framework adopted by the judge as a matter of principle; see [2018] EWCA Civ 2344, note 95 and further in note 269 et seq. – Unwired Planet/Huawei.

53 Birss J is very clear that according to his understanding the CJEU did not 's[eek] . . . to set out a series of rigid predefined rules, compliance with which is never abusive whereas deviation from which is always abusive, all regardless of the circumstances'. Further, he underlines that circumstances of the case can vary. See EWHC, April 5, 2017, 711 (Pat), note 741 – Unwired Planet/Huawei. This general approach and understanding of Huawei/ZTE was in essence endorsed by the Court of Appeals in [2018] EWCA Civ 2344, note 95 and further in note 230 et seq. – Unwired Planet/Huawei.

implementer. Or, vice versa, whether an initial non-FRAND offer is fatal for the right holder even when the alleged infringer does not react at all. Initially, there were some split decisions in that regard, with the Mannheim Regional Court granting more leniency to the SEP holder than the Düsseldorf courts.[54] Meanwhile, the Karlsruhe Higher Regional Court has quite clearly corrected the more lenient attitude of the Mannheim court, clarifying that any duty to react on the side of the implementer is dependent on an initial FRAND offer on the side of the SEP holder. This is in line with the consistent case law of both the Düsseldorf Regional and Higher Regional Courts, which have insisted that an initial FRAND offer is unconditionally required from the SEP holder to trigger any further reaction duties on the side of the alleged infringer and which thus from the very beginning have applied a *strict step-by-step approach*.[55]

Hence, at the moment it can be summarized that a strict step-by-step approach is applied by the German courts. Only an initial FRAND offer by the SEP holder triggers further reaction duties, in particular the duty to react with a FRAND counter-offer, on the side of the alleged infringer.[56] As a consequence, even if there is no adequate reaction by the alleged infringer, the court will have to assess whether the initial offer by the right holder was within the FRAND range (on the assumption that FRAND indeed is a range and on the hitherto attempts of the German courts to further specify their assessment of FRAND offers, *see infra* subsection 4.2).

While this case law on principle is convincing for genuine SEPs, since given the FRAND commitment in such cases, the right holder should indeed be under an unconditional obligation to initially make a FRAND offer, one might of course discuss the details. Hence it seems worth considering whether there should be more leniency if on the one hand the initial offer was not obviously non-FRAND

54 See e.g. Mannheim Regional Court, November 27, 2015, 2 O 106/14, GRUR-RS 2015, 20077, note 140 where the court considered it sufficient when the alert of the alleged infringement was made after the submission of the claim (in German *Anhängigkeit*) but before the beginning of the proceedings (in German *Rechtshängigkeit*) in case the unwillingness to license by the alleged infringer would become obvious in the further court proceedings; see also Mannheim Regional Court, January 29, 2016, 7 O 66/15, GRUR-RS 2016, 4228, note 49; March 4, 2016, 7 O 96/14, GRUR-RS 2016, 06527, note 53 – Pioneer/Acer; July 1, 2016, 7 O 209/15, GRUR-RS 2016, 18389, note 61, where formal requirements with regard to the SEP holder's FRAND licensing offer are emphasized. See for a comprehensive analysis also Picht, 'FRAND Wars 2.0' – Rechtsprechung im Anschluss at 234, 237.

55 Düsseldorf Higher Regional Court, January 13, 2016, I-15 U 65/15, GRUR-RS 2016, 1679, notes 19 et seq. (=BeckRS 2016, 1679, notes 19 et seq.); Karlsruhe Higher Regional Court, May 31, 2016, 6 U 55/16, GRUR-RS 2016, 10660, notes 27 et seq. (=BeckRS 2016, 10660, notes 27 et seq.) – Pioneer/Acer; initially different in first instance by Düsseldorf Regional Court, November 3, 2015, 4a O 144/14, GRUR-RS 2015, 19564, notes 91 et seq. (=BeckRS 2015, 19564, notes 91 et seq.); but now also applying the strict step-by-step approach, see e.g. Düsseldorf Regional Court, July 13, 2017, 4a O 27/16, GRUR-RS 2017, 130336, notes 175 et seq. (=BeckRS 2017, 130336, notes 174 et seq.).

56 *Id.*

and, on the other hand, the alleged infringer does not at all react to this. Under such circumstances, reasons of administrative efficiency as well as the overall character of the Huawei/ZTE procedure as a test to identify the genuine willingness to license on the side of both parties might argue in the direction of a more overall assessment of the parties' pre-court behavior along the general lines of the UK High Court in Unwired Planet/Huawei.[57]

3.2.5 Alert of the alleged infringement

After having outlined and briefly discussed the more general issues of timing and sequence of the major Huawei/ZTE steps, in the following the *specific requirements* which German courts have developed *for each of these steps* shall be outlined in detail.

As for the *initial alert*, in line with the CJEU's judgment, German courts have required that the SEP holder specify the allegedly infringed patent by providing the *patent number* and clarify by which *product or service* and specifically by which *action* of the implementer the patent shall be infringed.[58] At this stage, a reference to the specific standard in question[59] or the usual presentation of *claim charts* is sufficient;[60] by contrast, no specific and detailed explanation as to why the alleged practice of the infringer falls under the patent claims and infringes the patent will be required. In particular, the stricter requirements of an infringement action do not have to be fulfilled.[61]

Concerning the practically important question of *to whom* an infringement alert has to be addressed, the German courts have accepted that the SEP holder addresses the *holding company* when faced with infringement by a daughter company in a group of companies, in particular if he is justified in ultimately offering a worldwide-license anyway.[62]

57 Although Mannheim Regional Court meanwhile, according to the general line set out by Karlsruhe Higher Regional Court, has somewhat changed its line and applies a step-by-step approach as well, it still obviously tries to adhere to a rather overall assessment when indicating that the meaning of the CJEU concept was to set requirements for a fair procedure in order to reach settlement about the licensing conditions on the whole and that the courts ultimately need to evaluate the overall behavior on both sides. See more recently Mannheim Regional Court, November 10, 2017, 7 O 28/16, GRUR-RR 2018, 273, note 82 (=BeckRS 2017, 146786, note 81) – Funkstation. For a detailed analysis and in favor of the overall assessment approach see Kellenter & Verhauwen (n 3) 761, 769.

58 Mannheim Regional Court, March 4, 2016, 7 O 96/14, GRUR-RS 2016, 06527, note 52 – Pioneer/Acer; November 25, 2016, 7 O 44/6, BeckRs 2016, 127663, note 65; November 17, 2016, 7 O 19/16, BeckRS 2016, 108197, note 501; July 1, 2016, 7 O 209/15, GRUR-RS 2016, 18389, note 60; August 19, 2016, 7 O 19/16, GRUR-RS 2016, 19467, note 51.

59 See e.g. Düsseldorf Higher Regional Court, March 30, 2017, I-15 U 66/15, GRUR 2017, 1219, note 143 (=BeckRS 2017, 124408, note 144) – Mobiles Kommunikationssystem.

60 *Id.*

61 *Id.*

62 Düsseldorf Regional Court, November 3, 2015, 4a O 144/14, GRUR-RS 2015, 19564, notes 96 et seq. (=BeckRS 2015, 19564, notes 96 et seq.); Mannheim Regional Court,

3.2.6 Declaration of willingness to license by the alleged infringer

As for the content of the principled *declaration of willingness to license* by the alleged infringer, recent German courts' judgments generally have *not imposed strict requirements* on the alleged infringer. An informal and even rather general declaration of the alleged infringer which clearly implies his willingness to take a license is regarded as sufficient.[63]

Against this background, it seems consistent that German courts have been rather strict with regard to the *time period* within which the alleged infringer has to react to the notification of infringement. The Mannheim courts tend to establish very strict deadlines and have regarded a reaction time of more than three months as insufficient.[64] The Düsseldorf courts have emphasized that the reaction period might depend on an overall assessment of the facts of the case, in particular the complexity of the notification of infringement and consequently the complexity of the assessments necessary on the side of the alleged infringer, but have nonetheless applied a rule of thumb of a reaction period of *a maximum of five months* after the infringement alert.[65] While parts of the German literature suggest requiring even stricter periods,[66] we tend to agree with a reaction period of five months maximum, as this seems to be consistent with the hitherto

---

November 10, 2017, 7 O 28/16, GRUR-RR 2018, 273, note 83 (=BeckRS 2017, 146786, note 82); Düsseldorf Higher Regional Court, March 30, 2017, I-15 U 66/15, GRUR 2017, 1219, note 145 (=BeckRS 2017, 124408, note 146) – Mobiles Kommunikationssystem. The related question of whether companies on different levels of the production, distribution and service chain can also be addressed by the SEP holder will not be treated here, as it is inextricably linked to the substantive question of whom the right holder can address with regard to infringement actions and thus has mainly to be answered on the basis of substantive patent law.

63 Düsseldorf Higher Regional Court, March 30, 2017, I-15 U 66/15, GRUR 2017, 1219, notes 151 et seq. (=BeckRS 2017, 124408, note 152) – Mobiles Kommunikationssystem. According to the court, a declaration of willingness does not have to be expressed, but can also be implied from the behavior of the implementer depending on the case in hand (note 152). But the general declaration of willingness to license by the alleged infringer must not be made subject to the condition of a non-appealable ruling and/or the validity of the SEP (note 163). Further, the court develops specific criteria according to which additional conditions or qualifications of the general willingness to license can ultimately be understood as an unwillingness to license for which it is necessary that the implementer seriously and unambiguously refuse to license (in the sense of an 'ultimate word').

64 Mannheim Regional Court, November 27, 2015, 2 O 106/14, GRUR-RS 2015, 20077, note 146.

65 Düsseldorf Higher Regional Court, May 9, 2016, I-15 U 35/16, GRUR-RS 2016, 09322, note 27 – Saint Lawrence/Vodafone; March 30, 2017, I-15 U 66/15, GRUR 2017, 1219, note 151 (=BeckRS 2017, 124408, note 152) – Mobiles Kommunikationssystem; Düsseldorf Regional Court, March 31, 2016, 4a O 126/14, GRUR-RS 2016, 8040, note 152 – Saint Lawrence/Vodafone.

66 Kühnen (n 23), Chap. E, note 334 where two months are considered to be the maximum time limit, which can only be exceeded under particular circumstances with regard to the case at hand.

rather lenient substantive requirements for this first reaction by the implementer in German case law.

3.2.7 FRAND licensing offer by the SEP holder

As for the *obligatory content of the licensing offer by the SEP holder*, three main characteristics can be identified in German case law. First, the courts try to orientate themselves along the lines of the *actual business practice* in the respective field (i.e. the recognized commercial practices play a central role for the assessment). Essentially, the precedent licensing practice of the respective SEP holder will be taken into account to assess an actual offer. Second, the courts focus on certain *structural elements* which have to be contained, can be contained or (vice versa) must not be contained in FRAND offers, while shying away from positively specifying FRAND terms, in particular the actual percentage of license fees. Third, the German courts tend to assume that FRAND defines a certain *range for possible offers* by the parties, and not a definite set of licensing terms and royalties.[67]

For several reasons, the concept of *FRAND as a range* seems in fact to be without alternative.[68] Hence, there is a certain leeway for possible FRAND offers if they at least comply with certain essential structural requirements and precedent business practice.[69] In that regard, as has been said, German courts try to orientate themselves along the lines of *actual business practice in the field*. First, the German courts require that FRAND offers contain all the necessary essential elements of a licensing contract, plus objective criteria which allow the implementer to assess why the SEP holder regards his own offer as FRAND.[70] More specifically, the Higher Regional Court in Düsseldorf has required that a FRAND offer indicate the royalty or license fee, the connecting factors, upon which the

67 Picht, The ECJ Rules on Standard-essential Patents at 365, 372; Colangelo & Torti (n 19) 538, 543 et seq.

68 For convincing argumentation in favor of understanding FRAND as a range see Picht, The ECJ Rules on Standard-essential Patents at 365, 372 and Colangelo & Torti (n 19) 538, 543 et seq. In fact, it seems that not even a single unitary method to determine FRAND can be determined in advance, since the selection and combination of multiple methodical approaches to determine the FRAND range will necessarily also depend on the particular facts of the case, cf. Colangelo & Torti (n 19) 538, 543; Geradin (n 29) 1, 11. Of a different opinion was Birss J, when stating that only one single set of licensing terms would be 'the rate which the parties in a given set of circumstances would converge upon and agree to' and therefore would be workable (EWHC, April 5, 2017, 711 (Pat), notes 148 and 156 – Unwired Planet/Huawei), which is however now corrected in [2018] EWCA Civ 2344, note 121 et seq. – Unwired Planet/Huawei. *See also infra* subsection 4.2.

69 This obviously raises the problem of how to deal with situations where both offers, i.e. the initial offer by the SEP holder as well as the counter-offer by the implementer, are accepted as FRAND. *See* on this problem subsection 3.3.

70 Mannheim Regional Court, March 4, 2016, 7 O 96/14, GRUR-RS 2016, 06527, note 53 – Pioneer/Acer; January 29, 2016, 7 O 66/15, GRUR-RS 2016, 4228, note 49; Düsseldorf Higher Regional Court, March 30, 2017, I-15 U 66/15, GRUR 2017, 1219, note 169 (=BeckRS 2017, 124408, note 170) – Mobiles Kommunikationssystem;

calculation of the royalty or license fee is based, substantive regulation with regard to all questions which are usually part of a licensing agreement in the respective field, as well as substantive information on the reasons why the SEP holder regards his own offer as FRAND.[71]

In particular, when licenses have been granted to third parties before, while German courts accept that there might be many legitimate reasons for different treatment of different parties and consequently a broad leeway for differentiated terms in IP licensing, they will not accept obvious, 'evident' differences without justification in the realm of SEP licensing.[72] As there might loom an information asymmetry disadvantaging the implementer here, the German courts require the SEP holder to deliver *information on comparable licenses* in order to define and justify the differentiated treatment.[73] Indeed, this accessory information burden on the SEP holder is essential when information on already concluded licensing agreements is not public, as the implementer would obviously not be in a position to acquire further information on these precedent licenses.

Practically, the *comparison with pre-existing licensing agreements* of the patent holder will thus play an essential role in assessing the offered license.[74] Also, industry practice in the respective field plays an important role. Most importantly, from this follows that worldwide licenses (and also group-wide licenses for a group of companies) can be offered where this is in line with practice in the respective field under the specific circumstances of the case (e.g. because the standard-based product is distributed globally).[75] As for the offered *patent portfolio*, actual precedent licensing practices as well as public licensing programs of the SEP holder are important indicators for the legitimacy of the offered portfolio.[76] In line with actual practice in the IT-industry, Mannheim Regional Court allows the SEP holder to name a selection of particularly important patents from

71 Düsseldorf Higher Regional Court, March 30, 2017, I-15 U 66/15, GRUR 2017, 1219, note 169 (=BeckRS 2017, 124408, note 170) – Mobiles Kommunikationssystem.

72 On the basis of Art. 102 s. 2 lit. c TFEU Düsseldorf Higher Regional Court, March 30, 2017, I-15 U 66/15, GRUR 2017, 1219, notes 171 et seq. (=BeckRS 2017, 124408, notes 172 et seq.) – Mobiles Kommunikationssystem.

73 Düsseldorf Higher Regional Court, March 30, 2017, I-15 U 66/15, GRUR 2017, 1219, note 177 (=BeckRS 2017, 124408, note 178) – Mobiles Kommunikationssystem.

74 This is in line with Düsseldorf Regional Court, March 31, 2016, 4a O 73/14, juris, notes 225 et seq. (=BeckRS 2016, 131580, notes 164 et seq.); March 31, 2016, 4a O 126/14, GRUR-RS 2016, 8040, notes 159 et seq./164 et seq.

75 Mannheim Regional Court, March 4, 2016, 7 O 96/14, GRUR-RS 2016, 06527, note 92/97 – Pioneer/Acer; Düsseldorf Regional Court, July 13, 2017, 4a O 27/16, GRUR-RS 2017, 130336, note 225 (=BeckRS 2017, 130336, note 223); March 31, 2016, 4a O 126/14, GRUR-RS 2016, 8040, notes 160 et seq. – Saint Lawrence/Vodafone; March 31, 2016, 4a O 73/14, juris, notes 226 et seq. (=BeckRS 2016, 131580, notes 165 et seq.) – Saint Lawrence/Vodafone. Further, see also M. Königs, Patentpools (2014), notes 114 et seq. (in German but with further references in English) with detailed examination of the criteria of FRAND commitments in the light of patent portfolio licenses.

76 Mannheim Regional Court, March 4, 2016, 7 O 96/14, GRUR-RS 2016, 06527, note 97 – Pioneer/Acer.

the portfolio ('*beauty list*') to illustrate the essentiality of the patent portfolio for the standard in question by way of claim charts.[77] However, bundling of essential with non-essential patents within one licensing portfolio will not be permitted.[78]

As for possible *connecting factors to calculate the license fees*, in line with actual practice, a royalty per piece of product (e.g. a mobile phone) produced or sold in a protection country will be accepted.[79] As for the actual calculation of the per-piece royalty (as well as the question of what the permissible largest saleable unit should be or whether licensing rates should always be connected to the smallest saleable units) German courts have hitherto not genuinely engaged in specifying such factors or fees. However, a *proportional comparison with pool-licenses for patent pools* which also comprise the SEPs of the SEP holder in question shall be a legitimate indicator:[80] a calculation based on the quantitative share of the patents of the SEP holder compared to the overall number of patents in a respective pool has been accepted by the Mannheim Regional Court.[81] Further, it is remarkable that the German courts have begun to take into account *royalty stacking* aspects as well as the inevitably dynamic character of any SEP licensing contract. The Düsseldorf Regional Court has emphasized (albeit hitherto only explicitly for the case of portfolio splits) that a single licensing fee will only be FRAND when – taken together with all the other necessary licenses – it does not lead to an unduly high licensing burden on the implementer.[82] Also, from this author's viewpoint, a worldwide license should include *provisions on a future decrease* of the licensing

77 *Id*, note 94 – Pioneer/Acer.

78 Düsseldorf Regional Court, March 31, 2016, 4a O 126/14, GRUR-RS 2016, 8040, note 162 – Saint Lawrence/Vodafone; March 31, 2016, 4a O 73/14, juris, note 228 (=BeckRS 2016, 131580, note 167) – Saint Lawrence/Vodafone.

79 Düsseldorf Regional Court, March 31, 2016, 4a O 73/14, juris, note 230 (=BeckRS 2016, 131580, note 169); March 31, 2016, 4a O 126/14, GRUR-RS 2016, 8040, note 164 – Saint Lawrence/Vodafone; Mannheim Regional Court, January 29, 2016, 7 O 66/15, GRUR-RS 2016, 4228, note 51.

80 Düsseldorf Regional Court, March 31, 2016, 4a O 73/14, juris, notes 243 et seq. (=BeckRS 2016, 131580, notes 182 et seq.). But the court illustrates that price development for per-piece royalty rates is not always proportional. Especially a larger number of licensed patents in total and portfolios owned by various undertakings can lead to a significantly lower per-patent royalty rate (in the portfolio or pool), which makes certain differentiations necessary when singular patents are licensed. See for further analysis also Picht, "FRAND wars 2.0" – Rechtsprechung im Anschluss at 300, 303.

81 Mannheim Regional Court, January 29, 2016, 7 O 66/15, GRUR-RS 2016, 4228, notes 51 et seq.; March 4, 2016, 7 O 96/14, GRUR-RS 2016, 06527, notes 120 et seq. – Pioneer/Acer. See with a similar interpretation of the court's judgment Picht, "FRAND wars 2.0" – Rechtsprechung im Anschluss at 300, 303.

82 See expressly Düsseldorf Regional Court, January 19, 2016, 4b O 120/14, GRUR-RS 2016, 08288, notes 164 – Kommunikationssystem. On the facts, however, the court accepts the portfolio split, where the previous royalty rate is so far below the FRAND range or at least so clearly in the lower range of possible FRAND conditions that a subsequently possible increase would still be FRAND compliant anyway. See for further discussion of royalty stacking against the background of German case law Picht, "FRAND wars 2.0" – Rechtsprechung im Anschluss at 300, 307 et seq.

fee if parts of the included patents successively expire entirely or in parts of the licensing area.[83]

Finally, in the aftermath of the Orange Book Standard judgment, which assessed this differently for a non-FRAND patent, it is particularly important to point out that *no challenge clauses* (regarding the validity or the standard essentiality of the patent, or the alleged infringement by the implementer) will no longer be accepted by the German courts in FRAND licensing offers for SEPs.[84]

3.2.8 Counter-offer and provision of appropriate security by the alleged infringer

The *counter-offer of the alleged infringer* has to be specific and consequently must contain a *concrete royalty or license fee*. The offer to leave the specification of the royalty or license fee to a third party is not sufficient.[85] Also, a worldwide license

83 Doubtfully, Mannheim Regional Court, in its judgment of March 4, 2016, 7 O 96/14, GRUR-RS 2016, 06527, note 106 – Pioneer/Acer, is of the (counter-)opinion that the lack of such a provision does *not* lead to the conclusion of *obvious* non-FRAND conformity of the offer in the framework of an overall analysis, also taking into account the behavior of the implementer. By contrast, similar to the approach, proposed here, Court of Appeals in [2018] EWCA Civ 2344, note 82 – Unwired Planet/Huawei; High Court, EWHC, April 5, 2017, 711 (Pat), note 567 (and cf. also note 532 on possible adaptation clauses in worldwide licenses) – Unwired Planet/Huawei: FRAND license should have provisions for sales in non-patent countries – hence it seems, that if patents were rendered invalid afterwards, leading to new patent-free territory, this should accordingly lead to an adaptation of the license fees under Justice Birss' approach.

84 By contrast, according to the Düsseldorf Higher Regional Court, March 30, 2017, I-15 U 66/15, GRUR 2017, 1219, notes 163 et seq. (=BeckRS 2017, 124408, notes 164 et seq.) – Mobiles Kommunikationssystem, the implementer must not, *in its initial reaction* to the notification, make already its *general* willingness to take a license dependent on the validity or standard-essentiality of the patent. Where such conditions are, indeed, the 'ultimate word' of the implementer and not just a first step in order to identify the scope of necessary licenses etc., such a reaction will not be sufficient for indicating the willingness to license on the side of the implementer. Thus, while conditions or termination clauses with regard to the validity or essentiality of the alleged SEP in the licensing counter-offer by the implementer are permissible (Mannheim Regional Court, November 27, 2015, 2 O 106/14, GRUR-RS 2015, 20077, note 146; Düsseldorf Regional Court, March 31, 2016, 4a O 73/14, juris, notes 164, 188 (=BeckRS 2016, 131580, notes 127, 103) – Saint Lawrence/Vodafone; March 31, 2016, 4a O 126/14, GRUR-RS 2016, 8040, notes 122, 197 – Saint Lawrence/Vodafone.), it is not permissible to condition the general willingness to license as such on the validity or essentiality of the patent. See for the latter point also footnote 63.

85 Düsseldorf Regional Court, March 31, 2016, 4a O 73/14, juris, notes 292 et seq. (=BeckRS 2016, 131580, notes 231 et seq.) – Saint Lawrence/Vodafone; March 31, 2016, 4a O 126/14, GRUR-RS 2016, 8040, note 226 – Saint Lawrence/Vodafone; Mannheim Regional Court, November 27, 2015, 2 O 106/14, GRUR-RS 2015, 20077, note 164. With reference to CJEU, July 16, 2015, C-170/13, ECLI:EU:C:2015:477, notes 67, 68 – Huawei Technology Co. Ltd v ZTE Corp., the courts emphasize that the determination of licensing conditions by a third party can only take place after rejection of the counter-offer and on the ground of mutual consent of both parties. See for detailed analysis of various

has to be offered if the implementer or a member of the group of companies of the implementer uses the patented invention in third countries where patent protection exists.[86] Furthermore, the existence and publication of a license program with standard licensing fees by the SEP holder also plays a role to specify the requirements for a FRAND counter-offer. If the counter-offer is far below such standard license fees, it will not be regarded as FRAND, since this would discriminate against other already existing licensees.[87]

If the counter-offer of the alleged infringer is declined by the SEP holder, according to Huawei/ZTE, the implementer has to provide *security* for the pending licensing fees, calculated on the basis of his own counter-offer and actual use.[88] This applies *retroactively* for all uses since the beginning of the alleged infringement.[89]

3.3 Situation after the exchange of offers: some implications of recent German case law and open questions

It is a consequence of the concept of *FRAND as a range* that *two FRAND compliant offers might be in existence.*[90] Hence, different situations have to be distinguished.

3.3.1 If the original offer of the patent holder was non-FRAND

Due to the step-by-step character of the CJEU's and the German courts' approach, if the original offer of the patent holder was non-FRAND, his action for an injunction has to be denied. Possible exceptions to this rule, if at all, have only been considered by the German courts if the non-FRAND character was not

---

further aspects with regard to the counter-offer also Picht, "FRAND wars 2.0" – Rechtsprechung im Anschluss at 300, 304 et seq.

86 Düsseldorf Regional Court, March 31, 2016, 4a O 73/14, juris, note 294 (=BeckRS 2016, 131580, note 233) – Saint Lawrence/Vodafone; March 31, 2016, 4a O 126/14, GRUR-RS 2016, 8040, note 228 – Saint Lawrence/Vodafone; Mannheim Regional Court, March 4, 2016, 7 O 96/14, GRUR-RS 2016, 06527, note 110 – Pioneer/Acer.

87 Düsseldorf Regional Court, March 31, 2016, 4a O 73/14, juris, note 298 (=BeckRS 2016, 131580, note 237) – Saint Lawrence/Vodafone; March 31, 2016, 4a O 126/14, GRUR-RS 2016, 8040, note 232 – Saint Lawrence/Vodafone.

88 See e.g. Mannheim Regional Court, November 27, 2015, 2 O 106/14, GRUR-RS 2015, 20077, notes 167 et seq.; Düsseldorf Regional Court, November 3, 2015, 4a O 144/14, GRUR-RS 2015, 19564, notes 94 et seq.; March 31, 2016, 4a O 73/14, juris, notes 300 et seq. (=BeckRS 2016, 131580, notes 239 et seq.) – Saint Lawrence/Vodafone; March 31, 2016, 4a O 126/14, GRUR-RS 2016, 8040, note 201 – Saint Lawrence/Vodafone.

89 *Id.*

90 See on this issue already Birss J. in [2013] EWHC 1591 (Pat) and [2015] EWHC 214 (Pat) – Vringo/ZTE; the Court of Appeals, [2018] EWCA Civ 2344, note 121 et seq. – Unwired Planet/Huawei, now proposes to solve the issue by leaving the patent holder the choice between the two FRAND licensing proposals, effectively leading to the implementation of the patent holder's offer in most cases.

obvious and if the infringer did not adequately react at all; but even these older judgments seem to be overruled in the meanwhile.[91]

3.3.2 *If the original offer of the patent holder was FRAND and the infringer's offer is non-FRAND*

If the original offer of the patent holder was FRAND and the infringer's offer is non-FRAND, an injunction can be granted if the general substantive and formal conditions are met.

3.3.3 *If both offers are FRAND, but alleged infringer has not provided security in a timely manner*

If both offers are FRAND, but alleged infringer has not provided security in a timely manner, an injunction can be granted.[92]

3.3.4 *If both offers are FRAND and the alleged infringer has complied with his duty to provide security*

The situation is open when both offers are FRAND and the alleged infringer has adequately provided security; the CJEU's judgment offers little guidance in that regard. Actually, it only opens the possibility, if both parties agree, to request that the amount of the royalty be *determined by an independent third party*. But what if the parties do not agree on that procedure or if they cannot find an independent third party on whom they both agree? The German literature is split on the *approach to such situations*. Parts of the literature argue that the patent holder has fulfilled his duties under the FRAND declaration and that he does not have to agree with an additional mediation procedure. Therefore, according to this opinion, his initial offer should have precedence; if the implementer thus rejected this initial offer, an injunction should be granted.[93] However, at least with regard to genuine SEPs, and if they vest a dominant market position in the person of the right holder, this opinion does not sufficiently consider that with regard to such patents the indispensable relevance for the standard leads as such to considerable additional welfare gains which should not be completely internalized on the side of the patent holder even if this was in conformity with and the result of market practice.[94]

91 See on the details above 3.2.4.

92 Thus, an injunction certainly can be granted if the implementer did not provide security for several months and only reacts in the court proceedings. See judgments cited in footnote 88 with differences in detail due to the particularities of the respective cases. For further details, see also Picht, "FRAND wars 2.0" – Rechtsprechung im Anschluss at 300, 304 et seq.

93 Kellenter & Verhauwen (n 3) 761, 771. Similarly, now Court of Appeals [2018] EWCA Civ 2344, note 121 et seq. – Unwired Planet/Huawei: patent holder has the choice between the offers.

94 Similarly Picht, The ECJ Rules on Standard-essential Patents at 365, 372.

Thus, we think that *settlement negotiations arbitrated by the court*, which can indicate certain structural guideposts for fixing FRAND terms to the parties, should be the first choice in such situations. In a second step, it might be considered that *the court proposes an independent third party* to specify a proposal for FRAND terms.[95] If the parties cannot agree on this, in a third step it should be *up to the courts to balance the involved interests and determine FRAND terms* (i.e. to make the choice between the competing offers or even to develop a middle way) with regard to SEPs, where the right holder is indeed in a dominant market position.[96]

Where this latter condition is not met, however, it seems difficult to justify the obtrusion of such a 'compromise' license upon the right holder. *Absent a dominant market position of the right holder*, and under the mere obligation of the FRAND commitment, it seems that *the right holder's offer*, if it was FRAND, *should take precedence* over the counter-offer of the implementer.[97]

3.4 Consequences of Huawei/ZTE for damages claims: outline of German case law

Naturally, as the essential holdup problem relates to *injunctions*, the Huawei/ZTE principles as such *do not directly influence actions for damages*. However, an *indirect impact is possible*, as non-compliance with Huawei/ZTE duties on the side of the patent holder combined with compliance on the side of the implementer should typically lead to a damages cap. According to prevailing (and justified)[98] German case law, in such cases damages should only be calculated on the basis of the *fictitious royalty*, thus effectively equaling the damages claim with a FRAND license, excluding the alternative calculation methods.[99]

95 *See* on proposals for procedural and institutional improvements in subsection 4.3.

96 But differently now Court of Appeals [2018] EWCA Civ 2344, note 121 et seq. – Unwired Planet/Huawei.

97 This is also effectively the solution applied by the Court of Appeals [2018] EWCA Civ 2344, note 121 et seq. – Unwired Planet/Huawei: patent holder has the choice. Similarly, though going further, Jacob & Milner (n 28). The authors propose to grant an injunction if the implementer refuses the patent holder's FRAND offer, as the key question would be whether the SEP holder's offer was FRAND.

98 Kühnen (n 23), Chap. E, note 387 et seq.

99 Correctly Düsseldorf Regional Court, January 19, 2016, 4b O 120/14, GRUR-RS 2016, 08288, notes 280 et seq. – Kommunikationssystem; Düsseldorf Higher Regional Court, March 30, 2017, I-15 U 66/15, GRUR 2017, 1219, notes 228 et seq. (in particular note 238 with further references) (=BeckRS 2017, 124408, notes 228 et seq., in particular note 236 with further references) – Mobiles Kommunikationssystem. By contrast Mannheim Regional Court, November 10, 2017, 7 O 28/16, GRUR-RR 2018, 273, notes 71 et seq. (=BeckRS 2017, 146786, notes 70 et seq.) – Funkstations. Although in the case at hand Mannheim Regional Court leaves the question ultimately open, it regards a material restriction of the claims for information and accounting and capping of the claims for damages not justified, as the enforceability of those claims is independent from compliance with the Huawei/ZTE requirement according to the court. Karlsruhe Higher Regional Court, August 29, 2016, 6 U 57/16, GRUR-RS 2016, 16061, notes 31 et seq. (=BeckRS 2016, 16061, notes 31 et seq.) remains skeptical but is in line with Mannheim Regional Court

Further, in Huawei/ZTE, the CJEU (because of the specific reference questions but also because of its limited jurisdiction in the field) did not have to answer the question of whether violations of the Huawei/ZTE requirements on the side of the SEP holder can give rise to a ***damages claim by the implementer***. This links up to the general issue of whether unjustified threats or claims can give rise to damages claims by their addressees. As a general problem, this important issue is unresolved on the European level, since the Enforcement Directive[100] does not contain provisions in that regard. However, in many Member States' laws, actions are possible on the grounds of general civil law doctrines. As for SEPs and Huawei/ZTE settings, importantly, the Düsseldorf Regional Court has decided that a violation of the Huawei/ZTE requirements by a market dominant undertaking as a violation of competition law rules ***gives rise to a damages claim of the implementer*** under Sec. 33 German Competition Act in conjunction with Art. 102 TFEU (or Secs. 19, 20 German Competition Act, which regulate abusive practices of dominant undertakings in German law).[101]

4 Perspectives

As the summary of case law in this chapter shows, many of the detailed questions left open by the Huawei/ZTE judgment have been addressed actively by German case law, and the CJEU's general principles are apt to provide ***valuable and legally certain guideposts*** for further specification in Member States' case law. However, particularly important ***differences between the attitude of the German courts and the High Court's Unwired Planet/Huawei judgment*** were hinted at in this chapter (which can be compared with Chapter 7 on U.K. law).[102] In fact, these differences highlight some of the main open questions[103] after Huawei/

when stating that information about the restriction of those claims cannot be drawn from the CJEU judgment in Huawei/ZTE. Further, it finds the judgment arguable due to the fact that a judgment of the Federal Court of Justice does not exist so far and that in the German legal basis of patent damages claims (i.e. § 139 Sec. 1 PatG (German Patent Act)) such a restriction is not expressly provided. For further details, see also Picht, "FRAND wars 2.0" – Rechtsprechung im Anschluss at 300, 304 et seq.

100 Directive 2004/48/EC of the European Parliament and of the Council of April 29, 2004 on the enforcement of intellectual property rights (OJL 157 of April 30, 2004).

101 Düsseldorf Regional Court, January 19, 2016, 4b O 120/14, GRUR-RS 2016, 08288, notes 290 et seq. – Kommunikationssystem.

102 S. Lawrance & F. Brooks, Unwired Planet v Huawei: The First UK FRAND Determination, *JECLAP* 2018, 170; J. Cross & J. Strath, Unwired Planet v Huawei – the FRAND Injunction, *CTLR* 178 (2017); Picht, *Unwired Planet v. Huawei* at 867; Treacy & Hunt (n 7) 124.

103 Of course, some other issues, less related to the Huawei/ZTE setting, are also not yet entirely clarified at least in German practice, such as a possibly differentiated treatment of pure Patent Assertion Entities (PAEs), the characterization and specification of the FRAND commitment in private international law and national contract law (which, by contrast to the situation in the UK, has not yet been addressed by the German courts), and the possibility of NDAs between the patent holder and the implementer.

ZTE which will have to be answered in the future, possibly also by another reference to the CJEU.

Apart from these more practical open questions, some *fundamental implications and problems* of the CJEU's judgment shall be briefly mentioned and discussed in this section.

4.1 Market dominance and possible generalization of the CJEU's doctrine for all FRAND-incumbent SEPs

First, it has already been pointed out that neither the CJEU's judgment nor most of the post-Huawei/ZTE case law in Germany substantively addressed the *condition of market dominance*. Some guideposts with regard to the actual assessment of market dominance in regard to SEPs have been outlined in subsection 3.2.1. Generally, both the CJEU's Huawei/ZTE judgment as well as the follow-up case law by the German courts seem to reflect a certain *'emancipation' from competition law.*[104]

While a neat and clean competition-law-based theory is missing, the Huawei/ZTE judgment takes recourse to more general concepts: a balancing of the involved *fundamental rights* and the *general civil law doctrines*, such as good faith and recognized commercial practices, for the specification of the procedural requirements.[105]

In fact, this is well in line with the EJCU's attitude in *other areas of IP*. Particularly, the analysis of the involved fundamental rights and the objective of balancing these rights in accordance with the general principle of proportionality plays an essential role in many of the Court's copyright law judgments.[106] Furthermore, recent copyright law judgments, such as FAPL/Murphy[107] or Oracle/UsedSoft,[108] the primary EU-law-based concept of the *'specific subject matter' of the intellectual property right* in question has been utilized to curb licensing practices, which would have allowed the right holders to achieve more than an appropriate remuneration for the use of their works. This case law has addressed not only practices of artificially partitioning the unitary market (it has a long tradition in doing so),

104 Picht, The ECJ Rules on Standard-essential Patents at 370; Rato & English (n 6) 103, 109 et seq.

105 CJEU, July 16, 2015, C-170/13, ECLI:EU:C:2015:477, notes 42, 45 et seq., 65 – Huawei Technology Co. Ltd v ZTE Corp. See also Picht, The ECJ Rules on Standard-essential Patents at 365, 370.

106 See for a comprehensive summary M. Leistner/V. Roder, Die Rechtsprechung des EuGH zum Unionsurheberrecht aus methodischer Sicht – zugleich ein Beitrag zur Fortentwicklung des europäischen Privatrechts im Mehrebenensystem, ZfPW 2016, 129, 147 et seq. (in German); for selective examples of the trend see also M. Leistner, Europe's Copyright Law Decade: Recent Case Law of the European Court of Justice and Policy Perspectives, *CMLR* 559, 592 (2014) et seq.

107 CJEU, February 3, 2011, C-429/08, ECLI:EU:C:2011:43 – FAPL/Murphy.

108 CJEU, July 3, 2012, C-128/11, ECLI:EU:C:2012:407 – Oracle/UsedSoft.

but also practices by which the right holders attempted to *monopolize secondary markets*, such as the market of trade in second-hand software.

Against this general background it would at least be possible, and in fact not too surprising, if the court in the future *extends* the Huawei/ZTE principles beyond situations of actual market dominance to cover all patents for which the owner is bound by a FRAND declaration, on the basis of primary law (specific subject matter of patent rights) and a fundamental right analysis. Anyway, the ground has already been laid for such a development in Huawei/ZTE.

4.2 FRAND as a range

Second, it should be emphasized that FRAND inevitably has to be regarded as a *range of possible licensing conditions* instead of as a specifically defined set of license terms.[109] This raises the issue of how to further specify FRAND if two or multiple conflicting offers of the parties could be regarded as FRAND.[110]

In fact, undoubtedly, the Huawei/ZTE doctrine can only help to identify non-willing potential licensors or licensees in holdup or holdout situations and can thus help to distinguish the different case groups. However, for cases where both parties are indeed genuinely willing to negotiate a reasonable license and complying with the Huawei/ZTE guideposts, but cannot come to terms, the judgment ultimately cannot help substantively with fixing reasonable license fees. Indeed, it represents a procedural approach and necessarily cannot be of help with respect to the substantive issue of narrowing down definite FRAND terms.[111]

4.3 Alternative mechanisms to determine FRAND: specifying the responsibilities of the SSOs and some other ideas for the future

As far as possible, the attempt to define FRAND terms should be avoided anyway, as any administrative or judicial engagement in price finding in such complex areas is ultimately bound to fail.[112] Thus, *alternative mechanisms* to approach the task of defining FRAND terms will have to be considered.

From this author's viewpoint the most promising way ahead would be to *require the SSOs* to take licensing practice into account from the very beginning

109 Just as Picht, The ECJ Rules on Standard-essential Patents at 365, 372; Colangelo & Torti (n 19) 538, 543 et seq.; N. Petit, HUAWEI v ZTE: Judicial Conservatism at the Patent-Antitrust Intersection, *CPI Antitrust Chronicle*, October 2015 (2), available at http://ssrn.com/abstract=2681377, 1, 7 (last accessed October 15, 2018). Differing view EWHC, April 5, 2017, 711 (Pat), notes 148 and 156 – Unwired Planet/Huawei, now corrected by [2018] EWCA Civ 2344, note 121 et seq. – Unwired Planet/Huawei.

110 See above 3.3. See also on that problem Birss J. in [2013] EWHC 1591 (Pat) and [2015] EWHC 214 (Pat) – Vringo/ZTE; further [2018] EWCA Civ 2344, note 121 et seq. – Unwired Planet/Huawei.

111 See on that issue above 3.3.

112 Similarly Picht, The ECJ Rules on Standard-essential Patents at 365, 374.

and to include such considerations, including aspects of royalty stacking, in their policies and in the procedural framework for inclusion of new patents in certain standards. Although this of course bears the danger that cost considerations could lead to a second-best technical solution being adopted in the standard, many proposals have been made in academic discussion which would allow minimizing this danger.

If reasonable approaches are not achieved upon the initiative of the SSOs, further initiatives for incentivizing and regulating respective self-regulation of the SSOs should be contemplated.[113] To tackle the issue at this early stage would also have the advantage that licensing issues would be taken into account before certain of the patents in the standard turn out to be particularly valuable. This might help to reduce the danger of distorted determination of FRAND licensing terms with hindsight[114] after implementation has already taken place on a broader scale. All this, however, is far beyond the reach of this chapter and partly dealt with in Chapter 17.

Apart from attempts to tackle the issue on the level of the SSOs, more or less specific and different proposals for new ***procedural and institutional approaches*** to help define possible FRAND terms and solve the issues of SEP licensing have been made in literature.[115] Specifically, the introduction of new copyright-like collecting societies has been suggested in the German literature.[116] This suggestion certainly deserves attention. However, for the time being, the problems in SEP licensing are very different from the typical copyright licensing problems which were solved by the emergence of collecting societies in the markets. Thus, the problem of atomistic multiple ownership is not really present to the same extent in the SEP markets as in copyright. Against this background, it seems hardly conceivable how SEP holders should be incentivized to take part in any such collecting society. The more recent experience of different pool administrators when trying to set up broad telecommunications standard pools in fact is rather disheartening in that regard.

All in all, we believe that any attempt and research to improve conditions for further *procedures* to help negotiate a viable FRAND determination between the parties, such as new information rights or other tools in civil procedure,[117] should

113 Thus, e.g. competition law exemptions could be made dependent on the SSO's adoption of respective policies.

114 This danger is mentioned in Picht, The ECJ Rules on Standard-essential Patents at 365, 374.

115 Picht, The ECJ Rules on Standard-essential Patents at 365, 375 (2016); M. Schaefer & C. Czychowski, Wer bestimmt, was FRAND ist? Ein Blick über den patentrechtlichen Tellerrand, *GRUR* 582 (2018) (in German).

116 Schaefer & Czychowski (n 115) 582.

117 See e.g. S. Dorn, Technische Standardisierung im Spannungsfeld von Immaterialgüterrecht, *Kartellrecht und Innovation* 167 (2014) et seq. (in German, but including further references in English), for alternative concepts and instruments to help and urge the workable

be met with approval and also be encouraged. However, with SSOs in existence, and a number of patent pool administrators more or rather less successfully trying to enter the SEP licensing markets, it is doubtful whether thinking about *new institutions* will help a lot.[118]

4.4 Conflicting FRAND judgments in the global arena?

A series of new, intriguing research questions are emerging. To mention just one obvious issue which has already been contemplated in the aftermath of the High Court's Unwired Planet/Huawei judgment:[119] if different influential national courts, such as the Western District Court of Washington in Microsoft/Motorola,[120] the High Court in Unwired Planet/Huawei,[121] the Shenzhen Intermediate People's Court[122] and others, now engage in the legal assessment of worldwide (or national) FRAND licensing terms, which of these legally approved and enforceable licenses will prevail? If in the overall context of a decreasing willingness to promote free trade in the global arena, SEPs increasingly become the object of trade policy, this might lead to a vicious circle of conflicting judgments on the ground, follow-up anti-suit injunctions, and thus considerable new

---

negotiation of FRAND licensing terms; for further possibilities in German procedural law *id.* at 373 et seq.

118 Differently Picht, The ECJ Rules on Standard-essential Patents at 365, 374 et seq.

119 The High Court's approach was endorsed by the Court of Appeals, [2018] EWCA Civ 2344, note 100 et seq. – Unwired Planet/Huawei, because the Court of Appeals was of the opinion that it does not overextend the jurisdiction of the English courts and does not lead to relevant practical problems. Doctrinally, this approach seems convincing. Also, it has to be admitted that depending on the circumstances of the case, global portfolio licenses will often be in line with actual licensing practice in the respective technological field and can be structured in a way which provides for adaptation if material change occurs with regard to the right's situation in a significant part of the geographical licensing area. However, the ongoing proceedings in China and the issue of subsequent anti-suit injunctions in England (on this and on other cases in the U.S., see in the subsequent footnotes) already show that the English courts' approach is not immune from creating considerable practical difficulties on a global scale since (possibly also as a matter of trade policy) it is by no means self-evident that the FRAND terms, set by English, German or U.S. courts will be accepted in other economically and strategically important jurisdictions. Whether the resulting practical problems are larger than those in usual patent licensing and enforcement remains to be seen.

120 W.D. Wash, April 5, 2013, C10–1823JLR, notes 509 et seq. – Microsoft/Motorola.

121 EWHC, April 5, 2017, 711 (Pat), notes 524 et seq. – Unwired Planet/Huawei.

122 Shenzhen Intermediate People's Court, Case Nos. 816 of 2016 and 840 of 2016, Judgment of January 11, 2018; meanwhile, this judgment is the object of an anti-suit injunction of the U.S. District Court for the Northern District of California, Case No. 3:16-cv-02787-WHO, Order of April 13, 2018 – Huawei/Samsung. Cf. more limited on the specific circumstances of a different case (only national licenses required) the Guangdong High People's Court in Huawei v InterDigital (2013) Guangdong High Ct. Civ. Third Instance No 305: national license for U.S. and China.

inefficiencies in global licensing and enforcement of SEPs. Against this background, the increasing anti-free-trade tendencies in major world economies and the inevitably resulting trend to make IP rights the object of trade wars, looming on the horizon, are emphatically regretted here.

On the other hand, practically, this and many other problems might also be slightly overestimated, considering that these cases only concern on principle willing licensing parties. Hence presumably, with increasing legal certainty about the procedure, it might be hoped that the parties will prospectively settle more often than in the past.

5 Conclusion

In fact, the judgment in Huawei/ZTE has already substantively helped to structure and solve at least some of the ongoing FRAND conflicts in Europe. As the analysis of the German case law in this chapter shows, it has undoubtedly helped to smooth out the hitherto rather choppy waters by providing for a generally applicable procedural framework. This now allows us to turn to a discussion of more specific legal aspects in the courts.

References

Angweny, V. 2017. Hold-up, hold-out and F/Rand: the quest for balance. *GRUR International*, 105–114.

Batista, P., Mazutti, G. 2016. Comment on "Huawei Technologies" (C-170/13): standard essential patents and competition law – how far does the CJEU go? *IIC*, 244–252.

Chien, C. 2014. Holding up and holding out. *Michigan Telecommunications & Technology Law Review*, 21, 1–41.

Colangelo, G. & Torti, V. 2017. Filing Huawei's gaps: the recent German case law on standard essential patents. *ECLR*, 38(12), 538–546.

Cross, J. & Strath, J. 2017. Unwired Planet v Huawei – the FRAND Injunction. *CTLR*, 178–180.

Dorn, S. 2014. *Technische Standardisierung im Spannungsfeld von Immaterialgüterrecht, Kartellrecht und Innovation.* Kovac, Hamburg.

Farrel, J., Hayes, J., Shapiro, C. & Sullivan, T. 2007. Standard setting, patents, and hold-up. *Antitrust Law Journal*, 74, 603–670.

Geradin, D. 2017. *European Union Competition Law, Intellectual Property Law and Standardization.* Available at: https://ssrn.com/abstract=2907632.

Geradin, D. & Rato, M. 2007. Can standard-setting lead to exploitive abuse? A dissonant view on patent hold-up, royalty stacking and meaning of FRAND. *ECJ*, 3(1), 101–161.

Jacob, R. & Milner, A. 2016. *Lessons from Huawei v. ZTE*, 1–18. Available at: www.4ipcouncil.com/news/latest-research-4ip-council-lessons-huawei-v-zte.

Jakobs, M. & Hübener, F. 2016. SEP or no SEP? Open questions after Huawei/ZTE. *ECLR*, 37(1), 33–39.

Jestaedt, D. 2009. Der Lizenzerteilungsanspruch nach der BGH-Entscheidung "Orange-Book-Standard". *GRUR*, 801–805.

Kellenter, W. & Verhauwen, A. 2018. Systematik und Anwendung des kartellrechtlichen Zwangslizenzeinwandes nach “Huawei/ZTE” und “Orange-Book”. *GRUR*, 761–771.

Königs, M. 2014. *Patentpools*. Nomos, Baden-Baden.

Kühnen, T. 2018. *Handbuch der Patentverletzung*. Heymanns Verlag, Köln.

Lawrance, S. & Brooks, F. 2018. Unwired Planet v Huawei: the first UK FRAND determination. *JECLAP*, 170–175.

Leistner, M. 2014. Europe’s copyright law decade: recent case law of the European Court of Justice and policy perspectives. *CMLR*, 559–600.

Leistner, M. & Roder, V. 2016. Die Rechtsprechung des EuGH zum Unionsurheberrecht aus methodischer Sicht – zugleich ein Beitrag zur Fortentwicklung des europäischen Privatrechts im Mehrebenensystem. *ZfPW*, 129–172.

Lemley, M. 2002. Intellectual property rights and standard-setting organizations. *California Law Review*, 90, 1889–1980.

Lemley, M. & Shapiro, C. 2007. Patent holdup and royalty stacking. *Texas Law Review*, 85, 1991–2050.

Maume, P. 2016. *Huawei/ZTE*, or, how the CJEU closed the Orange Book. *QMJIP*, 6(2), 207–226.

Maume, P. & Tapia, C. 2010. Der Zwangslizenzeinwand ein Jahr nach dem Orange Book Standard – mehr Fragen als Antworten. *GRUR International*, 923–930.

McIver, T., Pomana, A. & Schmidt, J. 2015. Between patent protection and abuse of dominance: highest EU court issues landmark decision on standard-essential patents. *ECLR*, 36(12), 533–535.

Merges, R. 2009. The trouble with trolls: innovation, rent-seeking, and patent law reform. *Berkeley Technology Law Journal*, 24, 1583–1614.

Nägele, T. & Jacobs, S. 2009. Zwangslizenzen im Patentrecht – unter besonderer Berücksichtigung des kartellrechtlichen Zwangslizenzeinwands im Patentverletzungsprozess. *WRP*, 1062–1075.

Petit, N. 2015. HUAWEI v ZTE: judicial conservatism at the patent-antitrust intersection. *CPI*, 2–8.

Picht, P. 2014. Standardsetzung und Patentmissbrauch – Schlagkraft und Entwicklungsbedarf des europäischen Kartellrechts. *GRUR International*, 1–17.

Picht, P. 2016. The ECJ rules on standard-essential patents: thoughts and issues post-Huawei. *ECLR*, 37(9), 365–375.

Picht, P. 2017. *Unwired Planet v. Huawei*: a seminal SEP/FRAND decision from the UK. *JIPLP*, 12(10), 867–880.

Picht, P. 2018a. “FRAND wars 2.0” – Rechtsprechung im Anschluss an die Huawei/ZTE-Entscheidung des EuGH (Teil 1). *WuW*, 234–241.

Picht, P. 2018b. “FRAND wars 2.0” – Rechtsprechung im Anschluss an die Huawei/ZTE-Entscheidung des EuGH (Teil 2). *WuW*, 300–309.

Rato, M. & English, M. 2016. An assessment of injunctions, patents, and standards following the Court of Justice’s *Huawei/ZTE ruling*. *JECLAP*, 7(2), 103–112.

Schaefer, M. & Czychowski, C. 2018. Wer bestimmt, was FRAND ist? Ein Blick über den patentrechtlichen Tellerrand. *GRUR*, 582–585.

Treacy, P. & Hunt, M. 2018. Litigating a ‘FRAND’ patent licence: the *Unwired Planet v Huawei* judgment. *JIPLP*, 124–131.

Tsilikas, H. 2017. Huawei v. ZTE in context – EU competition policy and collaborative standardization in wireless telecommunications. *IIC*, 151–178.

Ullrich, H. 2010. Patents and standards – a comment on the German Federal Supreme Court decision Orange Book standard. *IIC*, 337–351.

Wilson, D., Moir, A., Ruesink-Brown, N. & Fountoukakos, K. 2015. CJEU permits standard essential patent (SEP) injunctions against infringers who engage in delaying tactics or do not respond diligently with a good faith counter-offer. *E.I.P.R.*, 37(11), 741–743.

Part IV

Regulated self-regulation

16 Stakeholders' views on policy concerns and regulatory framework for self-regulation by SSOs

Fair Standards Alliance[1]

1 Background – why FRAND matters

In today's connected ecosystems, different products made by different companies must be able to work together. Without standards creating that interoperability, the ability of companies to provide meaningful innovative products to consumers is limited. Standards provide common, interoperable platforms which companies can use as the basis for competitive differentiation. Such platforms not only generate competitive mass markets, but also enable the supply chain efficiencies needed for industry to provide leading-edge innovation to consumers at affordable prices.

Successful standards provide market players with the confidence required to invest in implementing those standards (e.g. by making the necessary investments in developing, manufacturing and marketing standard-implementing products) and to add their own unique, product-differentiating technologies to standardized features. Consumers benefit from the availability of such distinctive, yet interoperable, products at reasonable costs.

Policy makers have long recognized the importance of standards for innovation and competitiveness and have put regulatory and legislative frameworks in place to foster successful standardization. The European Commission's Communication on standard essential patents published in November 2017 emphasizes the importance of a strategic approach to standardization for boosting the

1 The Fair Standards Alliance is a European based association that has been incorporated to promote in the European Union and beyond a number of Key Principles regarding the licensing of standards-essential patents (SEPs) on a fair and reasonable, and non-discriminatory (FRAND) basis. The Fair Standards Alliance (FSA) has 40+ members, ranging from SMEs to large multinationals, and dispersed through a variety of industries. Our members include car makers, TV broadcasters, telecommunication network operators, cellular handset makers, chip designers, module developers, Wi-Fi companies and many more. We innovate at all levels of the supply chain and throughout industry segments. Innovation is crucial to our members; together, we invest over EUR 100 billion to R&D globally every year, and we have more than 300,000 patents that are either granted or pending. Our members all contribute significantly to the European economy, which benefits businesses and consumers with the commitment to drive innovation, jobs and growth for decades to come.

European Union's further economic growth, and elevates the recognition of the importance of standards to a matter of primary concern.

However, it is equally broadly recognized that only fair standards practices can deliver on the potential for enabling innovation and growth. There are a number of aspects that make a standard fair. The majority of successful standard setting organizations today have adopted such fair standards in their by-laws. However, common adherence to one important attribute of fairness in standards has failed to keep pace with developments in competitive market ecosystems – namely fairness in the licensing of standards-essential patents.

Because the core objective of standardization is the wide-spread adoption of the technologies it describes, participants in most standards-setting organizations voluntarily agree to grant licenses to their SEPs on "fair, reasonable and non-discriminatory" (FRAND) terms. These FRAND commitments accomplish two goals: first, implementers of a standard can feel secure that they can get licenses on fair and reasonable terms; and second, the SEP holders can receive appropriate remuneration for their patented inventions.

2 Key principles for FRAND licensing

2.1 FRAND should mean fair and reasonable and non-discriminatory to all

Many standards setting organizations provide in their intellectual property rights policy (IPR Policy) that SEPs shall be available for license by any company wanting to manufacture and sell equipment.

However, some SEP holders say they will only grant licenses at the end-product level, presumably in the hope that they can tax a much larger royalty base than just the price of the component supplying the patented functionality. Some SEP holders even seek royalties from users of such end products; this has gone as far as demanding royalties from coffee shops, restaurants, or hotels that offer Wi-Fi-based wireless connectivity to their customers. When inappropriately seeking royalties only from parties at the higher end of the value chain, SEP owners are potentially rewarded for innovations that have nothing to do with their SEPs.

The SEP holder seeking FRAND compensation for its valid and infringed SEPs should receive the same royalty regardless of where it licenses in the supply chain. For example, if the SEP's value is X euros, that value remains the same even if the component incorporating the SEP is bundled in a complex multifunction device or if applied in an end-user application.

The Alliance believes that SEP holders breach their FRAND commitment when they refuse to license implementers simply because of their position in the product supply chain. Such refusals violate the basic commitment to license on a non-discriminatory basis. Tolerating discriminatory refusals to license threatens to undermine incentives for a wide variety of standard setting participants, who will be prevented from licensing the standard they helped to develop.

Therefore, we believe that holders of FRAND-encumbered SEPs should offer licenses on fair and reasonable and non-discriminatory terms to all companies, organizations, and individuals at all levels of the supply chain of an end product who implement, or wish to implement, the relevant standard, in accordance with the terms of the applicable IPR Policy of the relevant standards setting organization.

2.2 *Injunctions should be available only in limited circumstances*

Nobody can implement a standard without implementing the SEPs associated with that standard. If a product is to meet the requirements of the standard, it is not possible to design around it, the implementer therefore being 'locked in'. This puts SEP holders in powerful positions because, if the patent is valid and infringed, the SEP holder has the right under patent law to apply at Court for an injunction to stop the product being sold.

The ability of a SEP holder to threaten a good faith implementer with an injunction distorts licensing negotiations to the detriment of that implementer. A rational implementer can be coerced into accepting to pay higher than reasonable royalties just to avoid the risk of being barred from selling its product.

An owner of a SEP who has voluntarily committed to provide licenses to its SEP is acting unfairly, and is reneging on its FRAND commitment, when threatening such an implementer with an injunction, or when seizing goods at customs without a court decision of infringement. Good faith implementers who are willing to license the SEP they use should not be faced with that risk. Simply asserting defences, questioning the validity or essentiality of SEPs, or asserting counterclaims should not mean that a potential licensee is acting in bad faith or is an 'unwilling' licensee.

2.3 *Enhanced transparency regarding FRAND-encumbered SEP licensing*

Many SEP holders operate their licensing programs under cloaks of secrecy, requiring potential licensees to enter into confidentiality agreements. These confidentiality agreements prevent companies from discussing the proposed or existing financial terms of the licenses (such as upfront payments or royalty rates) with any other companies. At the same time, during negotiations of licenses, SEP holders represent to potential licensees that other companies have accepted the financial terms of the proposed license. Because of the confidentiality restrictions imposed on the prospective licensee (and other licensees) the prospective licensee is unable to verify if what the SEP holder has represented is true.

By making SEP licensing information transparently available, a level playing field will be created and companies will benefit from enhanced cost predictability for their products, irrespective of size or negotiating power, and end users will be able to make more informed purchase choices.

We encourage SEP holders to be open and transparent regarding, amongst other things, which companies in the supply chain are licensed, the FRAND royalties that are charged, how they are calculated and other licensing conditions.

2.4 *A FRAND promise should extend to a transferee if the SEP is sold*

In recent years a practice has developed where some SEP holders divide up or 'fragment' their portfolios of patents. Transferring ownership of SEPs in principle should not present a problem in the context of SEP and FRAND licensing, and parties generally should be free to transfer patents as they see fit – provided the recipient respects the previously committed licensing obligations.

Problems can arise if SEPs are transferred to new owners that do not abide by the FRAND commitments made by the former owner. If the licensing commitments do not transfer with SEPs, SEP acquirers may refuse to offer FRAND terms to implementers of the relevant standards. Furthermore, the diffusion of SEP portfolios over more and more independent owners can exacerbate the problem of royalty stacking – namely that the royalties independently demanded by multiple holders of SEPs on the same standard do not account for the presence of other SEPs on the same standard and thereby lead to an inappropriately high overall royalty.

We believe that if a FRAND-encumbered SEP is transferred, the initial transferee and all subsequent transferees must remain bound by the FRAND commitment. We would like standards-setting organizations, policy makers and regulators to remain vigilant in addressing such circumstances, and to ensure that patent assertion entities are not utilized as mere proxies to obscure behaviour that seeks to get around FRAND commitments and that would be more obviously abusive if pursued directly.

3 No patent tying – only relevant patents should be required to be licensed

Portfolio licensing (whether for SEPs to a particular standard, all patents relevant to a particular type of device, or to a company's entire patent portfolio) can be an attractive choice for companies because it can reduce costs and administrative burdens. Rather than having to license patents piecemeal, a portfolio-wide license can provide stability and predictability and can promote "patent peace" between companies for a number of years.

However, these business incentives for entering into portfolio licenses should not mean that a licensee must be required to license a SEP holder's entire patent portfolio if it does not practice all of the inventions.

It is important to maintain the right of a potential licensee to only license the patents it needs from a SEP holder, including taking a license to less than a full portfolio. For example, a provider of cellular phones or components likely will have no need for a license for network infrastructure SEPs. Likewise, a company that operates only in a particular country or geographic region should not be required to pay for worldwide rights that it does not need.

While some parties may voluntarily and mutually agree to broader licenses, a holder of a FRAND-encumbered SEP should not be able, as a condition of granting a FRAND license to the SEP, to require implementers to (1) take licenses to patents that are not essential to the standard, or that are invalid or not infringed by the implementer; or (2) grant a license to the implementer's patents that are not essential to the standard.

4 Fair and reasonable royalties

The calculation of a FRAND royalty in any specific case can be complex and may reflect many case-specific factors. Nevertheless, there are also many generic factors that should always be considered when determining what constitutes a fair and reasonable royalty or licensing fee. Taking such generic factors into account will aid the efficiency of licensing negotiations between SEP licensors and licensees, and could reduce the need for parties to resort to litigation to establish a FRAND royalty.

Owners of SEPs should receive fair and reasonable compensation for the contributions they make to innovation by making their inventions available to a standard. However, they should not receive compensation based on anything beyond the inventive value of the patented invention itself.

Royalty rates for SEPs that do not take into account the value of innovation and investment added by implementers of standards unjustly enrich SEP owners based on the contributions made by others. This artificial burden on innovation will ultimately stifle industry's ability to offer value for money to consumers.

In order to implement this principle, the following (non-exhaustive) list of considerations should be taken into account, and appropriately applied to each specific case.

4.1 *Must not tax features of a product that are unrelated to the patented invention*

Some SEP holders suggest that licensing rates should be based on downstream uses of standardized technology. Licensing polices that seek to charge such rates are unfair – they violate the FRAND commitment because they seek compensation for unpatented technologies or technologies that the patent holder did not invent or create. For example, when a smartphone has an innovative user interface that helps drive consumer demand for that device, the owner of a patent essential to a cellular standard should not be permitted to use that patent to appropriate any portion of the value of the user interface. Instead, in most circumstances, FRAND licensing rates should be determined with reference to the device, or the part of the device, that implements the patented invention; this ensures that the patent holder obtains fair compensation for what it actually invented, and not compensation for the value of others' work or contributions. In other words, the price of a brick should be independent of whether that brick is used for building a garage or a mansion – and the royalty for a SEP associated with a standard that enables an internet of things (IoT) device to be wirelessly connected to other IoT devices (or the cloud) should be independent of whether that first IoT device is a smart watch, a refrigerator or a car.

That is why it is so important to not blindly base royalty rates for SEPs on the overall value of an end device that makes use of the SEP's invention, but to rather carefully consider the actual value that the SEP contributes to that end device. Often, that assessment can greatly be aided by considering the smallest component that actually implements the patented invention. When that part can be isolated as a separately saleable unit (a brick for building various types of buildings), a fair royalty rate will typically bear a relation to the price of that unit.

4.2 *Must not exploit the fact that the standard cannot be implemented without licensing the SEP*

FRAND royalty must reflect only the value of the SEP, not the additional value conferred on it by its inclusion in the standard. The value of the standard reflects contributions from the entire community that developed the standard, and from the ecosystem having adopted the standard, rather than by the SEP holder alone.

Standards have inherent value attributable to the common agreement for all to use the same technology to ensure interoperability between manufacturers' products. SEP owners greatly benefit from having their patents included in a standard because adoption of their invention is no longer driven only by the merit of that invention in itself, but by the commercial imperative for market players to make their products interoperate with the ecosystem of all other products using the same standard. Market players will therefore implement the SEP, even when it only covers a small detail of the standard's functionality that does not present a significant technical challenge, but where the technical specification simply required choosing one of several possible solutions for completeness. Standardization can transform the potential licensing revenue of a patent dramatically if each and every device complying with the standard will necessarily use it.

Standardization can also significantly lower the patent holder's cost involved in finding out who is using their patent and can be approached for compensation.

In choosing to make a FRAND commitment, a SEP holder willingly makes a trade-off in return for these benefits. Unlike the more general patent holder, the SEP holder has voluntarily accepted as part of the quid pro quo of standardization that the per-unit royalties it may earn will be constrained by the "fair, reasonable, and non-discriminatory" commitment.

A FRAND license must not reward SEP holders for the value associated with the standard itself but for only the technical contribution of the SEP to the standard. Seeking value attributable to standardization would be unjust and an attempt to co-opt the work of others and of the standardization process.

4.3 *Must take into account the actual and potential aggregate royalty demands for other SEPs*

A FRAND rate must consider royalties for other patents required to implement the standard. The goal of widespread adoption of a standard cannot be achieved if these aggregate demands are not considered when determining a FRAND rate, or else a 'royalty stack' will be created that makes implementing the standard uneconomical.

Some SEP licensors have suggested that royalty stacking is merely theoretical. But as a practical matter, no rational SEP licensee views a single SEP licensing negotiation in isolation; rather, the licensee necessarily views the current negotiation in the context of past and future negotiations for all SEPs needed to practice the standard (or at least those for which it is reasonably foreseeable that will be demanded).

Accordingly, the rational willing licensee will not agree to pay royalties for a single license that would make it uneconomical to sell a product that implements the standard. It follows that the licensee necessarily will need to take into account the potential royalty stack, even in its first negotiation.

Moreover, taking action to address royalty stacking only after a prohibitively expensive royalty stack has been created necessarily will not prevent harmful effects from royalty stacking. If the first royalty is not set in light of the potential aggregate demands to come, a disproportionate share of royalties would go to those SEP holders first in line, without regard to the relative value of their SEP, simply because they acted quickly and aggressively to demand higher than appropriate royalties.

4.4 *Must take into account the fact that prices come down over time and that SEP holders may be remunerated for use of their technology in other parts of the value chain*

Many licensors seek to charge fixed prices per unit, or provide fixed monetary caps or minimums, as part of their licensing programmes. These programmes often do not sufficiently take into account the fact that the prices of products reduce over time.

Similarly, SEP licensing programmes should take account of the fact that the SEP holder may also be financially benefiting in other parts of the eco-system and value chain from use of standardized technology.

17 How FRAND harmony is ensured within SSOs – Comparing ETSI and IEEE

*Shengtao Hu**

1 Introduction

Mobile technologies, the most rapidly adopted technologies in human history, have fundamentally and dramatically changed the way we work, learn, travel, consume and communicate with one another. The Information and Communication Technology (ICT) sector has enjoyed unprecedented success due to de jure standards. Through standardization companies share their best technologies derived from massive investments in research and development (R&D) in exchange of a 'fair return on investment'. Through access to the standard under fair, reasonable and non-discriminatory (FRAND) terms, companies that have not invested in R&D can rather easily enter the ICT market at a reasonable cost, as do companies that have developed their own technologies but keep them proprietary (or keep such technologies exclusively to themselves).The rules on the process of developing standards and the IPR policy are the most important governance regime of a standard setting organization (SSO). With this background in mind, the second half of this chapter focuses on the relevant aspects of 3GPP, the most significant SSO alliance for cellular technology development and on the European Telecommunications Standardization Institute (ETSI), which is one of the 3GPP founding organizational partners. It also examines the Institute of Electrical and Electronics Engineers (IEEE), another influential SSO in the ICT sector. The illustration of the working of IPR policies of ETSI and IEEE 2015 is done for the purpose of providing a comparison to show how different approaches adopted by these two SSOs have led to different results. After so doing, we reach some conclusions.

2 Process of standardization within 3GPP: a dynamic competition and collaboration

Since its original scope in late 1990 to develop technical specifications for 3G, 3GPP has evolved considerably. So far, 3GPP has been responsible for the maintenance and evolution of the 2G, 3G and 4G standards, and the forthcoming 5G.

3GPP is both a collaborative and competitive forum, comprised of a large set of individual members, such as manufacturers, chipset vendors, infrastructure

* Director, IPR Policy, Ericsson. All views expressed in this chapter are those of the author and do not necessarily represent the views of Ericsson.

vendors, operators, analytic firms, research institutes, universities and so on. Currently the total number of 3GPP members is close to 700.[1] The membership body is very diverse, bringing together a good mix of players representing diverse perspectives and interests.

The progress of 3GPP standards development work is driven by technical contributions from some major members. However, most members do not take an active role within 3GPP, such as the entities working on analytics of 3GPP or latecomers in the cellular technology sector, just to name a few. Meaningful participation in the 3GPP standards development requires substantial R&D manpower input and huge amount of financial investment, including sending representatives to meetings. Companies gain trust and credibility in 3GPP through long term participation and consistent efforts to develop and contribute the best technical specifications and solutions into the standards.

When an individual member company believes that it possesses a valuable technical solution to a problem that needs solving in order to achieve the agreed performance requirements for the standard being developed, it can submit its solution to the standard through a formal proposal. Then intensive group discussions and analysis will be conducted on that proposal, usually leading to competing solutions proposed by different members. All the proposals are under the close scrutiny by leading global experts, including those from the entities that often are fierce competitors in the marketplace, and thus may have an interest in undermining each other's submissions. Within 3GPP whether the proposed contributions would be accepted is subject to the decision based on consensus and technical merit.[2] Successful contributors must convince fellow 3GPP working group participants, including competitors, that their contribution offers the best solution to address that certain technical problem. That is to say, during the standards development process, each member company has the freedom to submit cutting-edge technical proposals that, as such, may contain patentable subject matter, but only those with highest quality can make it through to being accepted into the standard. In a consensus-based competitive process of a project involving hundreds of companies from over 40 countries, this is not an easy task.[3] Take the development of the 4G standards as an example, according to an independent Signals Report, the members of the Radio Access Network (RAN) groups submitted 23,235 (!) technical proposals when developing their part of 4G technology, from which only 15.9% were approved and accepted into the LTE standard.[4]

1 See https://webapp.etsi.org/3gppmembership/Results.asp?Member=ALL_PARTNERS&SortMember=Name&DirMember=ASC&SortPartner=Name&DirPartner=ASC.

2 See more about 3GPP Working Procedures at www.3gpp.org/ftp/Information/Working_Procedures/3GPP_WP.pdf.

3 See more about 3GPP at www.3gpp.org/about-3gpp.

4 See Signals Research Group, The Essentials of Intellectual Property, 2010, available at: www.ericsson.com/assets/local/news/2015/1/101220_lte_contribution_whitepaper.pdf. On the value of standardization, see also C. Tapia, Securing a Competitive Future, *Patent Lawyer*, January/February 2016.

Collaboration within 3GPP has promoted a highly competitive level playing field, where smaller members are awarded the same opportunity as others to influence the standard development process. Needless to say, work in 3GPP is carried out in strict compliance with applicable competition laws.[5]

3 FRAND assurances and consensus in decision-making process: lessons from ETSI vs IEEE 2015

3.1 Rationale of IPR policy

SSOs, serve as a platform for joint development of performance and interoperability standards and bring together both contributors and users of standard essential patents (SEPs), inherently bear the inner tension of conflicting interest between the holders and users of SEPs. The linkage between SEPs and SSOs can be traced at least as far back to 1932, when American Standards Association (ASA), the predecessor of American National Standards Institute (ANSI), recommended that 'if a patentee be willing to grant such rights as will avoid monopolistic tendencies, favorable consideration to the inclusion of such patented designs in a standard might be given'.[6]

Since then, SSOs have promoted widespread dissemination of standardized technologies through adopting IPR policies that provide a balance between the rights of SEP holders to be adequately rewarded and the rights of users to access essential technology where a FRAND assurance is provided. This is typically achieved generally through one or both of the following obligations on SEP holders: (1) an obligation to disclose the relevant potential SEPs to the extent they are aware of them, and/or (2) an obligation to disclose whether, or not, the patent holder is willing to commit to grant licenses to such patents on certain terms and conditions. Obviously, the extent of the obligations imposed on the patent holders may have significant influence on the willingness and readiness of the potential members when determining whether to join a certain SSO, or whether to make contributions to a certain standardization project within a given SSO. According to the relevant studies, technology contributors respond more favorably to SSOs with IPR policies that adequately reward the IPR holder for the use of its IPR, resulting in higher quality standards.[7]

5 Seewww.3gpp.org/about-3gpp/legal-matters/21-3gpp-calendar/1616-statement-of-antitrust-compliance.

6 *See* Am. Standards Ass'n, Minutes of Meeting of Standards Council (November 30, 1932) cited from footnote 17 from Jorge Contreras, A Brief History of FRAND: Analyzing Current Debates in Standard Setting and Antitrust Through A Historical Lens, available at www.researchgate.net/publication/272302053_A_Brief_History_of_FRAND_Analyzing_Current_Debates_in_Standard_Setting_and_Antitrust_Through_a_Historical_Lens.

7 Joshua D. Wright, SSOs, FRAND, and Antitrust: Lessons from the Economics of Incomplete Contracts 2013, available at www.ftc.gov/sites/default/files/documents/public_statements/ssos-frand-and-antitrust-lessons-economics-incomplete-contracts/130912cpip.pdf.

It should be noted that there is no obligation for the patentees to give licensing commitments. Most SSOs have adopted the rules requesting the SEP holders to indicate whether they are willing to commit to license their SEPs under FRAND terms.[8] These commitments are meant to provide the technology users access to the SEPs while ensuring that patent holders receive an adequate compensation for their investments in research and development. In other words, a FRAND commitment is a two-way street applied to both SEP holders and technology users, where both the patent holder and the potential licensee should engage in good faith FRAND negotiations. By its notion, FRAND commitment acts as a well-accepted compromise. However, it should be noted that the commitment is a flexible one, and obtains its exact meaning on a case by case basis. Therefore, it is fair to ask: given the vagueness in the exact meaning of a FRAND commitment, how should one go about figuring out its meaning.

Obviously, regulators and academia may have concerns. They tend to think about the possibility that a regulatory response may be warranted to cure inefficiencies resulting from the ambiguity in SSOs' IPR policies.[9] However, viewing the diversity among different SSOs' IPR policies, which suggests choice and strong competitive forces at work, what a specific IPR policy looks like is ultimately a reflection of what has been anticipated by sophisticated parties who are conscious of the need for contractual flexibility. Vague FRAND commitments are thus a designed feature, rather than an unexpected failure, of the system.[10] Therefore, how to address the relevant issues relating to IPR policy is best left to the specific SSO and its members, rather than any government agencies. And the SSO should follow an open and consensus-building process when launching any initiatives toward their IPR policies.

3.2 ETSI's success story

The ETSI explains in 3.1 of its IPR Policy that:[11]

> In order to further this objective the ETSI IPR POLICY seeks to reduce the risk to ETSI, MEMBERS, and others applying ETSI STANDARDS and TECHNICAL SPECIFICATIONS, that investment in the preparation, adoption and application of STANDARDS could be wasted as a result of an ESSENTIAL IPR for a STANDARD or TECHNICAL SPECIFICATION being unavailable. In achieving this objective, the ETSI IPR POLICY seeks a balance between the needs of standardization for public use in the field of telecommunications and the rights of the owners of IPRs.

8 Footnotes 12, 14 from Contreras (n 7).

9 Wright (n 8).

10 See Daryl Lim, Standard Essential Patents, Trolls, and the Smartphone Wars: Triangulating the End Game, available at www.pennstatelawreview.org/wp-content/uploads/2015/02/1-LIM.pdf; Wright (n 8).

11 ETSI Intellectual Property Rights Policy (n 63).

As mentioned earlier, the terms 'fair', 'reasonable', and 'non-discriminatory' are meant to be used as guidelines, rather than as strict definitions, enabling flexibility in bilateral negotiations. The overwhelming majority of participants to the standardization efforts in 3GPP have made FRAND declarations. Observations reveal that companies remain continuously committed to FRAND.

In practice, consensus is the fundamental principle during the decision making process in the ETSI. Thus, any proposed changes to the IPR policy will need to be endorsed by the membership and finally approved by consensus. A series of meetings of ETSI's IPR Special Committee (IPR SC) were reconvened as a response to the requests from some members by ETSI back to 2012. The key issues for discussion were possible clarification of FRAND, transfer of SEPs and the use of injunctive relief. The IPR SC fairly easily reached consensus on amendments to the IPR Policy and the Guide in respect of patent transfers. In March 2013 the IPR Policy was amended to make clear that FRAND commitments transfer with SEPs when SEPs are transferred to new owners.

However, suggestions relating to the definition of FRAND and possible limitations to the use of injunctive relief proved more contentious.[12] Given the competition authorities' focus at that time on the circumstances in which an SEP holder should be awarded an injunction was thoroughly discussed.

> The European Commission reported on the recent Commission antitrust decisions in the Motorola Mobility and Samsung Electronics cases which provide that, under EU law, injunctions are in principle available for all patent holders including standard essential patent (SEP) holders but can be restricted in exceptional circumstances based on antitrust law, in particular where the SEP holder is facing a willing licensee. The IPR SC also noted the recent U.S. Court of Appeals for the Federal Circuit ruling in the case of Apple versus Motorola Mobility.[13]

Despite of all the heavy involvement by the EC in the lengthy discussions spanning nine IPR SC meetings over a two-year period, consensus could not be reached because of divergences between those who are principal users of cellular standards and those who have been major contributors to ETSI standards. As a result, on the issue of injunctive relief the ETSI IPR policy remains the same as where it has been standing.

12 www.etsi.org/newsroom/news/672-2013-05-etsi-ipr-committee-dialogue?highlight=WyJldHNpIiwiZXRzaSdzIiwiJ2V0c2kiLCJldHNpJ3NkaXJlY3RvciIsIidldHNpJ3MiLDIwMTNd.

13 www.etsi.org/newsroom/news/812-2014-07-news-etsi-ipr-committee-continues-discussions-on-injunctive-relief?highlight=WyJldHNpIiwiZXRzaSdzIiwiJ2V0c2kiLCJldHNpJ3NkaXJlY3RvciIsIidldHNpJ3MiLCJpbmp1bmN0aXZlIl0=.

Noteworthy is that the issue of injunctive relief has now been resolved by courts in the EU and U.S. In the 2015 CJEU *Huawei-ZTE* decision, the court has delineated a safe harbor from competition scrutiny for licensors who follow a delineated good faith negotiation scheme.[14] On the other side of the Atlantic, in its 2014 *Apple v. Motorola* decision, the U.S. Court of Appeals for the Federal Circuit found no reason to create any separate rule or analytical framework for addressing injunctions for FRAND-assured patents, noting that the eBay framework provides ample flexibility for addressing the unique aspects of FRAND-assured patents and industry standards in general.[15] More recently, in December 2018, the U.S. Department of Justice Antitrust Division formally withdrew its assent to the 2013 joint 'Policy Statement on Remedies for Standards-Essential Patents Subject to Voluntary F/RAND Commitments' that contemplated different injunctions rules for SEPs.[16]

Obviously, finding consensus in ETSI can sometimes take time but it is the best way to ensure the delicate balance between the sometimes conflicting interests of its membership. Though ETSI's IPR policy has undergone certain changes over the past 20 years they have all come about through a consensus-based process. ETSI's commitment to find consensus, including for IPR Policy changes, between its very diversified membership explains how it has achieved increasing international success since more than 30 years.

14 Case C-170/13 Huawei Technologies Co. Limited v. ZTE Corp. (Fifth Chamber, July 16, 2015) available at http://curia.europa.eu/juris/document/document.jsf;jsessionid=9ea7d2dc30ddec4f949241db44d296cc9739f41099c5.e34KaxiLc3qMb40Rch0SaxuRa3j0?text=&docid=165911&pageIndex=0&doclang=EN&mode=req&dir=&occ=first&part=1&cid=747013. See also D. Kallay, The ECJ Huawei – ZTE Decision: En Route to Ending Hold-Out? *CPI Antitrust Chronicle*, October 2015 (2), available at www.competitionpolicyinternational.com/briefing/pdfs/The-ECJ-Huawei.pdf.

15 *Apple Inc. v. Motorola Inc.*, 757 F.3d 1286, 1331–1332 (Fed. Cir. 2014), *overruled on other grounds by Williamson v. Citrix Online, LLC*, 792 F.3d 1339 (Fed. Cir. 2015) ("To the extent that the district court applied a per se rule that injunctions are unavailable for SEPs, it erred. . . . [W]e see no reason to create . . . a separate rule or analytical framework for addressing injunctions for FRAND-committed patents. The framework laid out by the Supreme Court in eBay, as interpreted by subsequent decisions of this court, provides ample strength and flexibility for addressing the unique aspects of FRAND committed patents and industry standards in general. 547 U.S. at 391–94. . . . [T]he public has an interest in encouraging participation in standard-setting organizations but also in ensuring that SEPs are not overvalued. While these are important concerns, the district courts are more than capable of considering these factual issues when deciding whether to issue an injunction under the principles in eBay.").

16 Assistant Attorney General Makan Delrahim, "Telegraph Road": Incentivizing Innovation at the Intersection of Patent and Antitrust Law, available at www.justice.gov/opa/speech/assistant-attorney-general-makan-delrahim-delivers-remarks-19th-annual-berkeley-stanford. The announcement noted that "[t]he 2013 statement has not accurately conveyed [the DOJ] position about when and how patent holders should be able to exclude competitors from practicing their technologies."

3.3 IEEE 2015: serious lessons to be learnt

Contrary to all other ICT SSOs, the IEEE has chosen to deviate from the so-called FRAND harmony[17] with its development and adoption of the new and dramatically different IEEE 2015 patent policy. In developing its new patent policy, the IEEE used a closed group and a secret drafting team within itself, in which comments provided on the new IPR policy drafts by technology contributors (SEP owners) were disregarded, and the principles of due process, openness and consensus that generally apply to the development of IEEE standards were missing. The imbalanced new policy[18] was approved in March 2015.

In a nutshell, the new policy include the following elements: (1) a new definition of 'reasonable rate' that significantly devalues SEPs through (a) limiting the value to be based on the value added to the smallest saleable compliant implementation, (b) requiring the value to reflect relative contribution by other patent holders, and (c) effectively eliminating comparable licenses as a benchmark for value;[19] (2) prevention of essential patent holders who are willing to commit to grant RAND licenses under its new policy from seeking an injunction for infringement, regardless of the behavior of the infringer; (3) a newly specified "Compliant Implementation" definition (which shall mean any product, e.g. component, sub-assembly or end-product, or service that conforms to any mandatory or optional portion of a normative clause of an IEEE Standard) resulting in mandatory licensing on the component level.[20] 'IEEE's stated objective was to protect users from patent holdup, which was alleged without substantiation. What it really wants is to undermine standard-essential patent values and the ability of SEP owners to receive adequate compensation from licensing their SEPs'.[21]

17 Ron Katznelson (2015), Perilous Deviations from FRAND Harmony- Operational Pitfalls of the 2015 IEEE Patent Policy, 2015 IEEE 9th International Conference on Standardization and Innovation in Information Technology (SIIT), available at http://ieeexplore.ieee.org/document/7535599/

18 See http://standards.ieee.org/develop/policies/bylaws/approved-changes.pdf.

19 "Reasonable rate" shall mean appropriate compensation to the patent holder for the practice of an Essential Patent Claim excluding the value, if any, resulting from the inclusion of that Essential Patent Claim's technology in the IEEE Standard. In addition, determination of such Reasonable Rates should include, but need not be limited to, the consideration of: • The value that the functionality of the claimed invention or inventive feature within the Essential Patent Claim contributes to the value of the relevant functionality of the smallest saleable Compliant Implementation that practices the Essential Patent Claim. • The value that the Essential Patent Claim contributes to the smallest saleable Compliant Implementation that practices that claim, in light of the value contributed by all Essential Patent Claims for the same IEEE Standard practiced in that Compliant Implementation. • Existing licenses covering use of the Essential Patent Claim, where such licenses were not obtained under the explicit or implicit threat of a Prohibitive Order, and where the circumstances and resulting licenses are otherwise sufficiently comparable to the circumstances of the contemplated license.

20 See redline reflecting policy changes at http://grouper.ieee.org/groups/pp-dialog/drafts_comments/SBBylaws_100614_redline_current.pdf.

21 Keith Mallinson, Development of Innovative New Standards Jeopardized by IEEE Patent Policy (September 2017), available at www.4ipcouncil.com/application/files/6015/0479/2147/Mallinson_IEEE_LOA_report.pdf.

As a matter of fact, the new policy walks away from the efficiencies and industry practices that have focused on providing freedom to operate to manufacturers for the implementation of a standardized technology. As Katznelson puts it: [22]

> IEEE's new departure from de facto industry standard licensing practice will put parties into irreconcilable legal positions: SEP [(Standard Essential Patent)] licenses for new standards may not simultaneously conform to the new FRAND terms mandated by the 2015 IEEE patent policy, and to legacy FRAND terms in the old licenses that necessarily follows legacy technology. This will undermine dynamic efficiencies in innovation where new standards incorporate other legacy standards by reference as 'normative', and where standard amendments are rolled up into new revisions of the standard. Under this new patent policy, IEEE Societies will be handicapped in developing new standards that build on legacy standards.

Negative letters of assurance (LOA) are instances where patent holders decline to provide FRAND assurances to future users of the standard. Statistical studies of negative or missing LOAs[23] after the 2015 policy change have been conducted by scholars.[24] The studies find a sharp increase in negative LOAs submitted by companies that are concerned with the new patent policy. Almost 50% of all LOAs submitted from January 1, 2016, to June 30, 2017, were negative. The presence of so many negative LOAs is highlighting the challenges that the new patent policy is facing. It appears that companies that submitted negative LOAs are innovators whose technology has contributed to the success of many standards. These companies have had committed to licensing under the old patent policy, but are now uncomfortable with the new policy, or simply not in a position to provide assurances under the new policy because that would force them to agree to unfavorable terms which devalue their IP, and render it impossible to enforce altogether.

This evidently creates confusion and uncertainty in the marketplace as to the future of IEEE standards. Thus, implementation of an IEEE standard into a product now carries significant risks that such product could be held from the market or banned by patent owners who have not made positive commitments under the updated patent policy. Even companies that respect intellectual property could face costly litigation or even injunctions brought by the owners of

22 *Id.* at 4.

23 IEEE-SA Standards Board: PatCom: https://standards.ieee.org/about/sasb/patcom/patents.html.

24 Kirti Gupta and Georgios Effraimidis, IEEE Patent Policy Revisions: An Empirical Examination of Impact, Roundtable on Empirical Methods in Intellectual Property, Searle Center on Law, Regulation, and Economic Growth, Northwestern University, 2018, available at www.law.northwestern.edu/research-faculty/searlecenter/events/roundtable/documents/effraimidis_gupta.pdf; Ron Katznelson, The IEEE Controversial Policy on Standard Essential Patents – The Empirical Record Since Adoption, Symposium on Antitrust, Standard Essential Patents, and the Fallacy of the Anticommons Tragedy, Berkeley, CA, 2016, available at http://bit.ly/IEEE-LOAs.

essential patents that are covered by negative LOAs, and hence have not been committed to be licensed under FRAND terms.

Take the 802.11 standard as an example. 802.11 standard covers Wi-Fi, one of the most widespread and relied upon communication technology ever deployed. It is under the risk of being jeopardized by the new policy.[25] Assuming a technology innovator has submitted positive LOAs covering patents relevant to 802.11ac under the old IEEE IPR policy, and is bound by a FRAND commitment based on the previous policy. Assuming now the same innovator has developed a patented technology that is included in the new 802.11ax standard, and submits negative LOAs for essential patents relating to the new improvement under the new policy. As a result, part of the innovator's portfolio will be bound by FRAND assurances under the old policy, and part of the innovator's portfolio will not be bound by FRAND assurances under the new policy. Clearly, most 802.11 compliant products will require a license to the whole portfolio. By submitting negative LOAs resulting from the implicit devaluation of patent value under the new policy, the patent owner will be put in the complex and challenging position of negotiating two very different licenses, potentially with different licensees (the new policy suggests that chip or module manufacturers should also be entitled to take a license). Moreover, existing licensees will inevitably demand the recent, for them more favorable terms, creating chaos in the market.

According to one empirical study in the Wi-Fi standard, about 70% of LOAs submitted from January 1, 2016, and January 1, 2019, were negative. In addition, based on an analysis focusing on 802.11 Project Authorization Requests (PARs) count conducted by Gupta and Effraimidisr,[26] the average count has dropped by 4.2% after the policy update and, if one restricts their analysis to the period 2012–2017, the decline is even much higher (16% decline after 2015).

European SSOs CEN and CENELEC also criticized the IEEE policy change, noting that 'CEN and CENELEC do not support initiatives taken by some SDOs

25 *See, e.g.*, Keith Mallinson, Development of Innovative New Standards Jeopardized by IEEE Patent Policy, 4iP Council, 2017, available at www.4ipcouncil.com/application/files/6015/0479/2147/Mallinson_IEEE_LOA_report.pdf. Matteo Sabattini, Defining Fairness: Promoting Standards Development By Balancing The Interests Of Patent Owners And Implementers, LES Nouvelles, 2016, available at www.lesi.org/les-nouvelles/les-nouvelles-article-of-the-month/les-nouvelles-article-of-the-month-archives/les-nouvelles-article-of-the-month-october-2016; Ron Katznelson, Perilous Deviations from FRAND Harmony- Operational Pitfalls of the 2015 IEEE Patent Policy, 2015 IEEE 9th International Conference on Standardization and Innovation in Information Technology (SIIT), 2015, available at http://ieeexplore.ieee.org/document/7535599/.

26 The IEEE-SA has often rebutted assertions by scholars that the new patent policy has resulted in decreased participation by the industry or challenges for IEEE-SA itself. On the contrary, IEEE-SA claims that recent growth in corporate membership and an overall increase in PARs proves that the institute is thriving, and industry engagement is solid. Nevertheless, activities in R&D-intensive working groups, which are mostly impacted by the patent policy, appear to be stagnating at best.

to provide guidance on, or impose compliance with, FRAND pricing, valuation and rate-setting methodologies. Such initiatives create high risks of antitrust liability under the rules on anticompetitive agreements. They should therefore be avoided'. As a matter of fact, IEEE is now facing a preliminary antitrust inquiry by the U.S. DOJ Antitrust Division over alleged dominance and exclusionary conduct by a Special Interest Group (SIG) called DensiFI. The DOJ is looking into whether DensiFI excluded technologies by some companies that are not members of the SIG. The DOJ's document preservation letters refer to IEEE's certain actions relating to DensiFi, suggesting the agency is interested in the standard group's role in policing alleged abuse of dominance within its ranks.[27]

4 Conclusion

When looking at the process of standards development, the success of 3GPP evidences that openness and balance are fundamental pro-competitive aspect of standardization, and consensus[28] is the cornerstone of decision making therein. A strong commitment to comply with these principles, is a prerequisite for 3GPP's continuous success with the development of future generations of cellular technology standards.

When IP policies of SSOs are reviewed, every SSO should keep it in mind that 'Designing IPR policies that achieve their goal, requires a proper balance between the rights of innovators and implementers, is a necessary requirement for an SDO to be successful'.[29] This premise is true not only for an SSO at the inception of its IPR policy, but also at least equally important for any later revisions and reviews, after sunk costs have been made. To achieve that, SSOs should be cautious when considering changes to their policies. Reviewing procedures in a way that could favor one specific group of stakeholders or implicitly excluding one group of participants in the reviewing process, should be prevented. Instead, special care should be taken by SSOs to encourage broad participation by diverse and balanced stakeholders. Only with the full participation of representatives, could it be possible for an SDO to avoid any biased behaviors of introducing unbalance and, ultimately, avoid any behavior that would harm the sustainable development of standards.

As seen earlier, the differences between ETSI's and IEEE's IPR policies stem not from differences in membership, but rather from differences the governance rules. While both SSOs have large, heterogeneous memberships, with innovator

27 Joshua Sisco & Leah Nylen, DOJ Probes Role of Special Interest Group in New WiFi Standard, MLex, January 26, 2018, available at https://mlexmarketinsight.com/insights-center/editors-picks/antitrust/north-america/doj-probes-role-of-special-interest-group-in-new-wifi-standard

28 ISO defines consensus as "general agreement where there is no sustained opposition to substantial issues by any important part of the concerned interests, in a process that seeks to take into account the views of all parties concerned."

29 *Id.* at 25.

and implementer members of all sizes, geographic locations, and industry niches, their rules for adopting and changing internal policies differ significantly. ETSI has established its governance rules through SSO-wide consensus. In contrast, IEEE has used a small task force structure to determine its governance rules. This structural difference leads to the totally different outcome of the revised IPR policies.

Last but not least, as far as the suggestions that antitrust enforcement should intervene due to the supposed 'vagueness' of FRAND commitments, the remarks by the Assistant Attorney General for Antitrust Division of Department of Justice Makan Delrahim are instructive:

> [E]nforcers should carefully examine and recognize the risk that SSO participants might engage in a form of buyer's cartel, what economists call a monopsony effect.
>
> When implementers act together within a standard-setting organization as the gatekeeper to sales of products including a new technology, they have both the motive and means to impose anticompetitive licensing terms. At the extreme, they can shut down a potential new technology in favor of the status quo, all to the detriment of consumers. The risk of failing to implement a new technology does not fall equally on innovators and implementers. The prospect of hold-out offers implementers a crucial bargaining chip. Unlike the unilateral hold-up problem, implementers can impose this leverage before they make significant investments in new technology.[30]

"When it comes to the test for obtaining injunctive relief against infringement, patent law already strikes a careful balance that optimizes the incentive to innovate, for the benefit of the public".[31] And "Antitrust law should not police FRAND commitments to SSOs".[32]

30 Makan Delrahim, Take It to the Limit: Respecting Innovation Incentives in the Application of Antitrust Law, – Application of Competition Policy to Technology and IP Licensing, November 10, 2017, available at www.justice.gov/opa/speech/file/1010746/download

31 Delrahim (n 31).

32 *Id.* at 25.

18 Propositions for regulated self-regulation of SSOs

Kung-Chung Liu and Haoran Zhang

1 SSOs as subject of antitrust scrutiny

Although collaborative standard setting can produce substantial benefits from many aspects,[1] it also inherently gives rise to antitrust risks as standard setting organizations (SSOs), by their nature, require agreements among competitors. The collaborative standard setting process replaces marketplace competition for selecting technology once one of the competing technologies has been chosen, and competition between technologies is generally diminished due to the high costs of switching to alternatives.[2] In the collaboration, there are risks of excluding alternative technologies due to either combined economic incentives of members to implement the chosen technology or abuse of market power gained by the standard.[3] While the collaboration among competitors is reasonably necessary to promote compatibility and interoperability, it also needs to be conducted with great care under the supervision of the antitrust law, lest it reduce competition beyond what is necessary to achieve greater benefits.[4] Therefore, "any agreement on the part of SSO members is potentially subject to antitrust scrutiny as a contract, combination or conspiracy, in restraint of trade".[5]

1 U.S. DOJ and FTC, Antitrust Enforcement and Intellectual Property Rights: Promoting Innovation and Competition, 2007, 34, available at www.ftc.gov/sites/default/files/documents/reports/antitrust-enforcement-and-intellectual-property-rights-promoting-innovation-and-competition-report.s.department-justice-and-federal-trade-commission/p040101promotinginnovationandcompetitionrpt0704.pdf.

2 John Dubianshy, Competition, Intellectual Property Rights and Collaboratively Set Standards: Federal Trade Commission Advocacy and Enforcement, in Ashish Bharadwaj, Vishwas Devaiah & Indranath Gupta (eds.), *Complications and Quandaries in the ICT SectorStandard Essential Patents and Competition Issues* (Berlin: Springer, 2018), pp. 105–139.

3 Jeffrey Blumenfeld & Robert Lipstein, Antitrust and SSO Developments, 4th Annual Advanced Patent Law Institute at USPTO, available at www.crowell.com/documents/Antitrust-and-SSO-Developments_presentation.pdf.

4 Douglas Melamed & Carl Shapiro, How Antitrust Law Can Make FRAND Commitments More Effective, 127 *Yale L.J.* 2129 (2018).

5 Thomas Cotter, Patent Holdups, Patent Remedies, and Antitrust Responses, 34 *J. Corp. L.* 1200 (2009).

1.1 The U.S.

1.1.1 The FTC: safeguarding against manipulation of standard setting process or improper use of the resultant standard

Early on, the Federal Trade Commission (FTC) was conscious of the competition concerns related to SSOs. In December 1978, initiated a rulemaking procedure to examine the extent of possible FTC Act violations (unfair methods of competition, and unfair or deceptive acts or practices) in standards development and certification, and its Bureau of Consumer Protection completed a report in 1983 which presented the staff's recommendation about FTC enforcement action in this area. The report found "standards are developed by committees composed substantially of representatives of competing firms within the affected industry and others with clear commercial interests without procedural safeguards, particularly a substantive complaint handling process to check upon unreasonable standard decisions. Participants tended to promulgate standards that enhance their own competitive position or exclude competitors out of the market".[6] The FTC has since taken measures against SSOs in at least three cases:[7]

1 *In the Matter of Dell Computer Corporation*, an FTC Administrative Complaint was filed on November 2, 1995. The settlement was also announced on November 2, 1995 (Dell will not enforce patent rights for widely used computer feature). The SSO implicated was VESA (Video Electronics Standards Association).
2 *In the Matter of Rambus*, an FTC Administrative Complaint was filed on June 19, 2002. The FTC published its decision on February 5, 2007, which was later overturned by the District of Columbia Circuit. The SSO implicated was JEDEC (Joint Electron Device Engineering Council), which promulgates standards for the memory chip market, DRAM in particular.
3 *In the Matter of UNOCAL*, an FTC Administrative Complaint was filed March 4, 2003. The FTC issued its decision on August 2, 2005. The SSO implicated was the California Air Resources Board (CARB).

1.1.2 The courts

Recognizing that collaboratively set standards can reduce competition and consumer choice, and have the potential of prescribing the direction for market

6 Federal Trade Commission Bureau of Consumer Protection, FINAL STAFF REPORT: STANDARDS AND CERTIFICATION (1983), 333–334.

7 Anne Layne-Farrar, A Review of IPR Policy Revisions in the Wake of Antitrust Actions, 2–3, available at www.researchgate.net/publication/271547732_A_review_of_IPR_policy_revisions_in_the_wake_of_antitrust_actions.

development,[8] the U.S. courts have been sensitive to antitrust issues that may arise and have found antitrust liability in circumstances involving the manipulation of the standard setting process or the improper use of the resultant standard to gain competitive advantage over rivals. Courts have focused on SSOs' internal policies that self-policed such misconduct and clarified that SSOs were obligated to provide safeguards to ensure competition envisioned by antitrust law.[9] For example, in 1982 the U.S. Supreme Court found in *American Society of Mechanical Engineers, Inc. v. Hydrolevel Corp.* that a scheme by a member company and an officer of the SSO to cause a competitor's product to be wrongfully deemed non-compliant with the standard violated both sections 1 and 2 of the Sherman Act.[10] It is noteworthy that the FTC in its amicus curiae brief suggested the SSOs should be obligated to adopt safeguards to avoid antitrust violation.[11]

In 1988 the Supreme Court clearly established the principle in *Allied Tube & Conduit Corporation v. Indian Head, Inc.* that the SSO and its members should take effective steps to minimize the harm from the monopolies that their collaboration confers upon SEP holders, which must be no more restrictive of competition than reasonably necessary to enable achievement of the legitimate purpose of standard setting.[12] The Supreme Court started off by confirming that SSOs have traditionally been objects of antitrust scrutiny:

> Typically, private standard-setting associations, like the Association in this case, include members having horizontal and vertical business relations. There is no doubt that the members of such associations often have economic incentives to restrain competition and that the product standards set by such associations have a serious potential for anticompetitive harm. Agreement on a product standard is, after all, implicitly an agreement not to manufacture, distribute, or purchase certain types of products. Accordingly, private standard-setting associations have traditionally been objects of antitrust scrutiny.[13]

8 See Federal Trade Commission Bureau of Consumer Protection, STANDARDS AND CERTIFICATION: FINAL STAFF REPORT 28, 34 (1983); Katz & Shapiro, Systems Competition at 105–106; Richard Gilbert, Symposium on Compatibility: Incentives and Market Structure, 40 *J. Indus. Econ.* 1 (1992).

9 *See, e.g.*, *Radiant Burners, Inc. v. Peoples Gas Light & Coke Co.*, 364 U.S. 656 (1961); *American Soc. of Mechanical Engineers v. Hydrolevel Corp.*, 456 U.S. 556 (1982); *Northwest Wholesale Stationers, Inc. v. Pacific Stationery & Printing Co.*, 472 U.S. 284 (1985); *Allied Tube & Conduit Corporation v. Indian Head, Inc.*, 486 U.S. 492 (1988).

10 456 U.S. 556 (1982).

11 Brief for United States as Amici Curiae, *American Soc. of Mechanical Engineers, Inc. v. Hydrolevel Corp.*, 456 U.S. 556 (1981) (No. 80-1765) (joined by Ernest J. Isenstadt, then Acting General Counsel, FTC).

12 Douglas Melamed & Carl Shapiro, How Antitrust Law Can Make FRAND Commitments More Effective, 127 *Yale L.J.* 2130 (2018).

13 *Allied Tube v. Indian Head, Inc.*, 486 U.S. 492 (1988), at 500.

It went on to confirm that collaborative standard setting has significant pro-competitive value, if based on unbiased expert analysis:

> When, however, private associations promulgate safety standards based on the merits of objective expert judgments and through procedures that prevent the standard-setting process from being biased by members with economic interests in stifling product competition, those private standards can have significant [pro-competitive] advantages.[14]

Finally, the court concluded that the SSO cannot validate the anticompetitive activities of its members by adopting rules that fail to provide safeguards *sufficient to prevent the standard setting process from being biased by members with economic interests*.[15] This principle has repeatedly been expressed in lower court decisions and antitrust enforcement agency guidelines.[16] These cases have influenced the antitrust compliance rules and procedures adopted by many SSOs.[17]

1.1.3 Congress: the 2004 Standards Development Organization Advancement Act of 2004 relieves SSOs from certain antitrust concerns

In 2004 the U.S. Congress has determined that the threat of treble damages pressures SSOs to restrict their standards development activities at a great cost to the U.S., and therefore enacted the Standards Development Organization Advancement Act of 2004 (SDOAA), which extends the protections provided by the National Cooperative Research and Production Act of 1993 (NCRPA) to relieve SSOs from certain antitrust concerns and facilitates the development of pro-competitive standards. The NCRPA provides that certain joint ventures will have their antitrust liability assessed under the rule of reason, and that special rules for attorney fees apply in antitrust cases challenging certain joint ventures. In addition, it permits parties participating in joint research, development, and production ventures to limit their possible antitrust damage exposure to actual as opposed to treble damages[18] by filing a notification with DOJ and FTC.[19]

14 *Id.*

15 *Allied Tube v. Indian Head, Inc.*, 486 U.S. 492 (1988), at 509.

16 *See, e.g.*, *Kreuzer v. American Academy of Periodontology*, which concerned the lawfulness of a professional association's rules of practice. The court reasoned as follows: "[A] practice intended to benefit the public may have a collateral adverse effect on competition. If it does, then such a practice must be the least restrictive means of achieving the desired goal and the public benefit rendered must outweigh the adverse effect on competition." *Allied Tube v. Indian Head, Inc.*, 486 U.S. at 509. Also see Douglas Melamed & Carl Shapiro, How Antitrust Law Can Make FRAND Commitments More Effective, 127 *Yale L.J.* 2130 (2018).

17 U.S. DOJ and FTC. Antitrust Enforcement and Intellectual Property Rights: Promoting Innovation and Competition, April 2007, 50.

18 15 U.S.C. 4303(a).

19 Pub. L. No. 108–237, 118 Stat. 661 (2004).

Under SDOAA, activities of SSOs having specified procedures to protect their objectivity and openness[20] are judged under rule of reason.[21]

1.1.4 The DOJ: the rise and fall of the 2013 DOJ-USPTO policy statement on remedies for SEPs subject to voluntary F/RAND commitments

In the 2013 Joint Department of Justice (DOJ) Patent Office (USPTO) "Policy Statement on Remedies for Standards-Essential Patents Subject to Voluntary F/RAND Commitments", it was stated that

> in some circumstances, the remedy of an injunction or exclusion order may be inconsistent with the public interest. This concern is particularly acute in cases where an exclusion order based on a F/RAND-encumbered patent appears to be incompatible with the terms of a patent holder's existing F/RAND licensing commitment to an SDO.[22]

However, since November 2017, the U.S. Assistant Attorney General of DOJ Makan Delrahim has moved the DOJ in a direction that allows SEP owners more freedom to use the exclusionary potential of those patents. The DOJ also has redirected its focus toward the conduct of licensees and the SSOs. On December 7, 2018, Delrahim took another step and withdrew the DOJ's assent to the more balanced 2013 Joint DOJ-USPTO "Policy Statement on Remedies for Standards-Essential Patents Subject to Voluntary F/RAND Commitments".

1.2 The EU

1.2.1 1992 intellectual property rights and standardization communication

In the European Union (EU), given the voluntary nature of standard-making, the European Commission (EC) started to regulate standard-making not directly

20 15 U.S.C. § 4301 a(8) prescribes: The term "standards development organization" means a domestic or international organization that plans, develops, establishes, or coordinates voluntary consensus standards using procedures that incorporate the attributes of openness, balance of interests, due process, an appeals process, and consensus in a manner consistent with the Office of Management and Budget Circular Number A – 119, as revised February 10, 1998. The term "standards development organization" shall not, for purposes of this chapter, include the parties participating in the standards development organization.

21 15 U.S.C. § 4302 provides that: "In any action under the antitrust laws . . . the conduct of (1) any person in making or performing a contract to carry out a joint venture, or (2) a standards development organization while engaged in a standards development activity, shall not be deemed illegal per se; such conduct shall be judged on the basis of its reasonableness, taking into account all relevant factors affecting competition, including, but not limited to, effects on competition in properly defined, relevant research, development, product, process, and service markets."

22 Available at www.justice.gov/atr/page/file/1118381/download, at 5.

by legislative proposals, but first via a communication in 1992: "Intellectual Property Rights and Standardization". The communication sets out a number of principles which the EC believes should form the basis of any internal rules which standards bodies may wish to elaborate. Standards bodies remain free to structure their membership rules and their internal organizational procedures as they wish. The results of their activity, must, however correspond to the standardization needs of the Community and must be made in conformity with the laws of the Community and its international obligations.[23] According to this communication, European standard-making bodies should ensure that:

> 1. all persons wishing to use European standards must be given access to those standards; 2. standards are available for use on fair, reasonable and non-discriminatory terms, but taking into account the circumstances of the use; 3. best efforts are made to identify holders of any intellectual property rights by conducting searches, by publication of adequate information, and, where appropriate, by holding public enquiries, before adopting a standard, work on a particular solution only continuing if all known intellectual property rights can be licensed for use in the standard; 4. fair conditions are provided to the holders of IPRs, especially with regard to the time limits for identifying IPRs and agreeing to their use, and in respect of arbitration mechanisms as to royalty rates.[24]

1.2.2 2011 horizontal guidelines

The EC issued Guidelines on the applicability of Article 81 of the EC Treaty to horizontal cooperation agreements (2001/C 3/02) in 2001, which was expanded and replaced by the 2011 Guidelines on the applicability of Article 101 of the Treaty on the Functioning of the European Union to horizontal cooperation agreements (Horizontal Guidelines). The EC confirms that standardization agreements usually produce significant positive economic effects,[25] but points out that standardization can also be detrimental to competition through three main channels, namely reduction in price competition, foreclosure of innovative technologies, and exclusion of, or discrimination against, certain companies by prevention of effective access to the standard.[26] Standardization agreements which do not restrict competition by object must be analyzed in their legal and economic context with regard to their actual and likely effect on competition. In the absence of market power, a standardization agreement is not capable of producing restrictive effects on competition. Therefore, restrictive effects are most unlikely in a situation where there is effective competition between a number

23 EC, Intellectual Property Rights and Standardization, COM (92) 445 final, October 27, 1992, 1.1.3–1.1.4.

24 EC, Intellectual Property Rights and Standardization, 6.2.1.

25 EC, Horizontal Guidelines (Text with EEA relevance) 2011/C 11/01, para. 263.

26 EC, Horizontal Guidelines para. 264. Born Lundqvist, Standardization under EU Competition Rules and US Antitrust Laws: The Rise and Limits of Self-Regulation. Edward Elgar, 2013, 198.

of voluntary standards.[27] If a standardization agreement constitutes restriction of competition within Article 101(1), yet provides significant efficiency gains[28] that can be passed on to consumers and outweigh the restrictive effects on competition,[29] it can still be exempted according to Article 101(3). In addition, like the immunity created by the Standards Act of the U.S., the 2011 Horizontal Guidelines established a safe harbor for the standard setting activities:

> Where participation in standard-setting is unrestricted and the procedure for adopting the standard in question is transparent, standardization agreements which contain no obligation to comply with the standard and provide access to the standard on fair, reasonable and non-discriminatory terms will normally not restrict competition within the meaning of Article 101(1).[30]

As to IPRs incorporated into the standard, the general assumption is that SSOs and their participants have obligation to ensure effective access to the standard, which should prevent IPR holders from making the implementation of a standard difficult by refusing to license or by requesting unfair or unreasonable fees after the industry has been locked into the standard or by charging discriminatory royalty fees, and FRAND commitment is a clear and balanced policy to achieve this goal.[31] However, in the enforcement of FRAND commitment, the SSOs need to require good faith disclosure and ensure the IPR is bound by the commitment even after transfer of the IPR.[32]

> Compliance with Article 101 by the standard-setting organisation does not require the standard-setting organisation to verify whether licensing terms of participants fulfil the FRAND commitment. Participants will have to assess for themselves whether the licensing terms and in particular the fees they charge fulfil the FRAND commitment. Therefore, when deciding whether to commit to FRAND for a particular IPR, participants will need to anticipate the implications of the FRAND commitment, notably on their ability to freely set the level of their fees.[33]

1.2.3 2012 regulation on European standardization[34]

The 2012 Regulation on European standardization expressly confirms that European standardization organizations (CEN (European Committee for

27 EC, Horizontal Guidelines para. 277.
28 *Id.* para. 308.
29 *Id.* para. 321.
30 *Id.* para. 280.
31 *Id.* paras. 284 and 287.
32 *Id.* paras. 285 and 286.
33 *Id.* para. 288.
34 Regulation (EU) No. 1025/2012 of the European Parliament and Council of October 25, 2012 on European standardization amending Council Directives 89/686/EEC and

Standardization), Cenelec (European Committee for Electrotechnical Standardization) and ETSI (European Telecommunications Standards Institute) are subject to competition law to the extent that they can be considered an undertaking or an association of undertakings within the meaning of Articles 101 and 102 TFEU.[35] Consequently, the standard setting agreements made by these three SSOs can infringe Articles 101 and 102 TFEU.[36]

1.2.4 2017 communication setting out the EU approach to SEPs[37]

In its April 2016 Communication on Standardisation Priorities for the Digital Single Market, the EC identified three main areas where the SEP licensing environment could be improved: opaque information on SEP exposure; unclear valuation of patented technologies reading on standards and the definition of FRAND; and the risk of uncertainty in enforcement of SEPs. In addition, the role of open source communities in the development of standards also should be assessed. The EC therefore issued in 2017 Communication Setting out the EU approach to SEPs to address the urgent need to set out key principles that foster a balanced, smooth and predictable framework for SEPs. These key principles reflect two main objectives: incentivizing the development and inclusion of top technologies in standards, by preserving fair and adequate return for these contributions; and ensuring smooth and wide dissemination of standardized technologies based on fair access conditions.

2 Deficiencies of current FRAND enforcement framework

By and large, the SSOs' FRAND policy system was established before the 1990s, when the main challenges were patent ambush, excessive royalty rates and patent transfer problems.[38] The present enforcement framework of FRAND commitment through negotiation of parties in good faith and under supervision of a third party was formed under that background. However, in the past 30 years,

---

93/15/EEC and Directives 94/9/EC, 94/25/EC, 95/16/EC, 97/23/EC, 98/34/EC, 2004/22/EC, 2007/23/EC, 2009/23/EC and 2009/105/EC of the European Parliament and of the Council and repealing Council Decision 87/95/EEC and Decision No 1673/2006/EC of the European Parliament and of the Council.

35 Preamble (13), Regulation (EU) No. 1025/2012 of the European Parliament and Council of October 25, 2012 on European standardization.

36 TFEU Article 101 prohibits as incompatible with the common market all agreements between undertakings, decisions by associations of undertakings and concerted practices which may affect trade between Member States and which have as their object or effect the prevention, restriction or distortion of competition within the common market. Article 102 prohibits the abuse of dominant market power.

37 Available at https://eur-lex.europa.eu/legal-content/EN/TXT/HTML/?uri=CELEX:52017DC0712&from=EN.

38 Layne-Farrar (n 7) at 6.

the environment surrounding SEPs has greatly changed, the information asymmetry between patentees and implementers has expanded, the transaction costs have increased significantly, and the divergence in legal standards between jurisdictions that are headquarters to SSO and jurisdictions that are home to SEP-implementing manufacturers has further crystalized.

2.1 Over-declaration of SEPs

In the last 30 years, the cumulative number of SEP declarations by SEP holders with various SSOs has drastically increased,[39] whereby a patent thicket is created and manufacturers need to obtain licenses from multiple patentees.[40] For example, according to the 3GPP consortium, the number of SEP holders for 3G and 4G has grown from two in 1994 to 130 in 2013, and the number of declared SEPs rose from fewer than 150 in 1994 to more than 150,000 in 2013.[41] According to empirical research by IPlytics,[42] there are over 200,000 SEPs declared with global major SSOs.[43] However, patent pool licensing is in a minor proportion; only 9% of declared SEPs are pooled, making the transaction costs for securing licenses for SEPs prohibitively high. The increasing number of SEP declarations and SEP holders reflects a combination of factors, such as the growing demand for standards, antitrust scrutiny, the fact that SSOs do not perform any check on essentiality, etc. For example, the Common Patent Policy for ITU-T/ITU-R/ISO/IEC prescribes,

> In order to facilitate both the standards-making process and the application of Recommendations Deliverables, each Organization makes available to the public a Patent Information database . . . The Patent Information databases are not certified to be either accurate or complete, but only reflect the information that has been communicated to the Organizations. As such,

39 Pentheroudakis & Baron (n 8); doi:10.2791/32230, 31.

40 Carl Shapiro, Navigating the Patent Thicket: Cross Licenses, Patent Pools, and Standard-Setting (March 2001), available at https://ssrn.com/abstract=273550.

41 Alexander Galetovic & Kirti Gupta, Royalty Stacking and Standard Essential Patents: Theory and Evidence from the World Mobile Wireless Industry (February 13, 2017), available at https://ssrn.com/abstract=2790347.

42 Tim Pohlmann & Knut Blind, Landscaping Study on Standard Essential Patents (SEPs) 2016, 8 and 53, available at http://ec.europa.eu/DocsRoom/documents/20741/attachments/1/translations/en/renditions/native.

43 Major SSOs include Advanced Television Systems Committee (ATSC), American National Standards Institute (ANSI), BluRay Disc Association, Broadband Forum, DVD Forum, CEN, ETSI, International Electrotechnical Commission (IEC); Institute of Electrical and Electronics Engineers (IEEE), Internet Engineering Taskforce (IETF), International Organization for Standardization (ISO), ITU Telecommunication Standardization Sector, Open Mobile Alliance (OMA), Organization for the Advancement of Structured Information Standards (OASIS), Society of Motion Picture and Television Engineers (SMPTE) and Telecommunications Industry Association (TIA).

> the Patent Information databases may be viewed as simply raising a flag to alert users that they may wish to contact the entities who have communicated Declaration Forms to the Organizations in order to determine if patent licenses must be obtained for use or implementation of a particular Recommendation/Deliverable.[44]

According to ANSI's IPR policy, SSOs are required to record the statement, "no position is taken with respect to the validity of any such claim(s) or of any patent rights in connection therewith". And "provisions involving business relations between buyer and seller such as guarantees, warranties, and other commercial terms and conditions shall not be included in an American National Standard".[45]

In addition, a strategic race to own essential patents,[46] so that SEP holders can license their patents to the whole industry or obtain freedom to operate through cross-licensing agreements, also leads to over-declaration of SEPs. Some industry insiders estimate that only around 30% or less of declared SEPs are really needed for the implementation of a standard.[47] For example, Fairfield Resources International, Inc., the Association of Radio Industries and Businesses of Japan and the Telecommunications Technology Association of South Korea have found out that there are only 529 genuine SEPs in the 1,889 declared SEP families within the 3GPP.[48] In *Huawei v. Samsung*, SEPs Assessment Data from Thomson Reuters indicates that out of 7,077 declared SEPs families in 4G/LTE world over, only 2,535 patents are real SEPs.[49]

2.2 Comparable license terms hidden in black box

Although, under the influence of ANSI, ETSI, ISO, IEC and ITU, FRAND policy has been a global standard for standardization adopted by SSOs,[50] SSOs' FRAND rules are almost always quite vague, and in practice, most SSOs have made almost no effort to enforce their FRAND rules and left enforcement efforts

44 IEC, ISO, ITO, Guidelines for Implementation of the Common Patent Policy for ITU-T/ITU-R/ISO/IEC (November 2, 2018), 6, available at www.itu.int/dms_pub/itu-t/oth/04/04/T04040000010005PDFE.pdf.

45 ANSI Essential Requirements: Due process requirements for American National Standards (January 2019), 3.1.3.

46 Dieter Ernst, Standard-Essential Patents within Global NetworksAn Emerging Economies Perspective (December 2, 2016), available at https://ssrn.com/abstract=2873198.

47 *Id.*

48 See Tokyo IP High Court, 2013 (Ne) 10043 (May 16, 2014), available at www.ip.courts.go.jp/eng/vcms_lf/25ne10043full.pdf, at 132.

49 See *Huawei v. Samsung*, Shenzhen Intermediate People's Court, Judgment of January 11, 2018, (2016) Yue 03 Min Chu 840, 161.

50 Jorge Contreras, Form and Variation in FRAND and other Standards Licensing Commitments, in Jorge Contreras (eds.), *The Cambridge Handbook of Technical Standardization Law* (Cambridge: Cambridge University Press, 2018), p. 172.

to others.[51] In practice, SEP licensing has always been that parties first sign non-disclosure agreements (NDAs) before the commercial and technological negotiation. For example, ETSI's IPR Guide points out that "It is recognized that NDAs may be used to protect the commercial interests of both potential licensor and potential licensee during an essential IPR licensing negotiation, and this general practice is not challenged".[52] In addition, signing an NDA in FRAND licensing is widely regarded as justified by SEP holders' confidentiality interests in some jurisdictions. In UK, a court held that

> publication of the commercial licensing information in issue (subject to a few exceptions) would substantially weaken the position of various companies mentioned in the judgment, particularly as licensors but also as licensees. That interference with the competitive position of the telecommunications market is unwarranted.[53]

In Germany, the court held that SEP holder has "justified confidentiality interests, for instance by entering into an NDA".[54] In the PRC, refusal to sign an NDA is regarded as a sign of unwillingness to obtain license, which could result in injunctive relief.[55]

2.3 *Conflicting legal standards lead to trade protectionism and even legal chauvinism*

Given the international distribution of ICT technologies and products, a FRAND license usually happens on a worldwide basis. However, the current FRAND enforcement framework only allows national courts to settle SEP disputes separately and each in its own way. In case of conflicting legal standards, patentees and implementers choose the preferred jurisdiction to launch a lawsuit, resulting in injunction being granted in one jurisdiction and the license terms being determined in another. In this case, which decision shall prevail? Conflicting rules and decisions make it more complicated and difficult for parties to reach a FRAND

51 Rudi Bekkers & Andrew Updegrove, A Study of IPR Policies and Practices of a Representative Group of Standards Setting Organizations worldwide, 20.

52 ETSI, § 4.4 Guide on Intellectual Property Rights [adopted by Board #94 (September 19, 2013), available at www.etsi.org/images/files/IPR/etsi-guide-on-ipr.pdf], which is intended to help ETSI members and any other party involved in ETSI's standardization activities to understand and implement the ETSI IPR Policy. According to the public statement made by the ETSI, "The ETSI IPR Policy and the IPR Guide texts stand as independent documents in their own right." Available at www.etsi.org/intellectual-property-rights.

53 *Unwired Planet International Ltd v. Huawei Technologies Co. Ltd (UK) Co. Ltd & Anor* [2017] EWHC 3083 (Pat)., November 30, 2017.

54 *Sisvel v ZTE*, District Court Dusseldorf, 4a O 27/16, 13.07.2017; Dusseldorf Appeal Court decision, I-2 U23/17, July 18, 2017.

55 See *Iwncomm v. Sony*, Beijing High People's Court, Judgment of March 28, 2018 (2017) Jing Min Zhong Zi No. 454.

license by negotiation. Parties may engage in opportunism, attempting to achieve "the first strike" advantages in their favored jurisdiction to maximize their commercial interests, rather than negotiating in good faith.

Courts in the U.S. and UK have also begun to use disputes over domestic patent rights as vehicles for shaping the global business arrangements of private parties, absent any violation of national law. They have increasingly sought to define such global contractual arrangements between multinational firms solely on the basis of patents asserted within their jurisdictions, aided by tools such as the anti-suit injunction. Since *Microsoft v. Motorola*,[56] the U.S. courts have applied the antisuit injunction broadly to prohibit litigants from initiating or continuing parallel litigation in another jurisdiction. A UK court also held antisuit injunction to be permissible in *Conversant v. Huawei and ZTE*.[57] Our principal concern is that local action might be largely disposed of by foreign anti-suit injunction.

Originally anti-suit injunction was meant to prevent forum shopping. However, given different legal standards adopted by different jurisdictions based on their positions in the global value chains, prevalent anti-suit injunction runs a high risk of trade protectionism and even legal chauvinism. Evidence already shows that jurisdictions have begun to develop positions favorable to one particular party (patent holders versus product manufacturers) in such disputes. As suggested by one prominent English law firm, the pro-patent Court of Appeal decision in *Conversant v. Huawei and ZTE*[58] "is likely to cement the UK's place as a jurisdiction of choice for SEP owners who are looking to obtain global FRAND determinations".[59] By the same token, jurisdictions renowned for setting low global FRAND rates or otherwise hostile to the claims of patent holders may attract manufacturers seeking to challenge the rates offered by those patent holders. India could be such a jurisdiction, as might China.[60] This might lead to a vicious circle of conflicting judgments on the grounds, follow-up anti-suit injunction and considerable new inefficiencies in global licensing and enforcement of

56 The U.S. District Court for the Western District of Washington granted Microsoft an anti-suit injunction preventing Motorola from enforcing a potential German court injunction in a parallel patent infringement proceeding. See *Microsoft Corp. v. Motorola Inc.*, No. 10-01823-JLR (April 12, 2012) (Order). For other U.S. cases see Kung-Chung Liu, Chapter 1 of the present book, subsection 5.2.

57 In this case, an injunction would have been issued but for ZTE's pre-emptive amendment of its foreign claims; see *Conversant Wireless Licensing S.A.R.L. v. Huawei Techs. Co. Ltd. and ZTE Corp.*, [2018] EWHC 2549 (Ch) at 24 (October 2, 2018).

58 [2019] EWCA Civ 38 (January 30, 2019).

59 L.L.P. Bristows, *Conversant v Huawei & ZTE*: Court of Appeal jurisdiction judgment – Key Points at 3 (January 30, 2019), available at www.bristows.com/news-and-publications/articles/the-unwired-planet-appeal-and-future-issues.

60 Jorge Contreras, The New Extraterritoriality: FRAND Royalties, Anti-Suit Injunctions and the Global Race to The Bottom in Disputes Over Standards-Essential Patents (February 21, 2019), 25 *B.U.J. Sci. Tech. L.* (2019 Forthcoming), available at SSRN: https://ssrn.com/abstract=3339378.

SEPs.[61] These unproductive litigation races distort the processes and motivations behind judicial and administrative rulemaking and incentivize litigation when negotiation or compromise might be more appropriate and efficient. Accordingly, multijurisdictional solutions are needed to address these problems.[62]

3 To overcome the challenges through self-regulation by SSOs[63]

SSOs are a form of industry and competitor collaboration, and the creation and promotion of standards is usually procompetitive and efficiency-enhancing. However, the collective action of SSOs does confer SEP owners ex post monopoly power in the market. Consequently, SSOs should provide safeguards for sufficient implementation of the standards. In addition, SSOs are closest to all participants in the market, have professional knowledge about the standards and their major contributors, are not limited by national boundaries, and therefore are best positioned to tackle the problem from the roots. That said, the current enforcement framework can hardly promote the FRAND licensing of SEPs efficiently. A more effective FRAND policy and enforcement system led by SSOs are needed. Regulatory agency is advised to exercise oversight over SSOs in making sure the latter put in place adequate mechanisms towards that goal.[64]

As an intermediary, in addition to providing arbitration service to SEP owners and implementers as suggested in Chapter 1 (subsection 4.4.4), SSOs can further provide the following self-regulation functions.

3.1 Essentiality check

Inclusion of a patent in a standard and the declaration of its essentiality for the standard can lead to a dominant position of its owner, which could restraint competition. With the problem of over-declaration of SEPs, the declaration and disclosure of SEPs can play a very limited role in reducing the high burden of willing licensees. Furthermore, the over-declaration of SEPs implies that SEP holders pass non-SEPs off as SEPs and ask the licensees to pay for patents that are not essential for implementing the standard. Therefore, the truthfulness of this declared essentiality should not be left unchecked. Conducting essentiality check

61 Matthias Leistner, Chapter 15 of the present book.

62 Contreras (n 60).

63 Kung-Chung Liu, Chapter 1 of the present book.

64 2012 EC Regulation on European standardization prescribes only that public authorities participate in standardization at all stages of the development of standards: "The EC has recognized that "Due to the importance of standardisation as a tool to support Union legislation and policies and in order to avoid ex-post objections to and modifications of harmonised standards, it is important that public authorities participate in standardisation at all stages of the development of those standards where they may be involved and especially in the areas covered by Union harmonisation legislation for products." (Preamble (25)).

would increase the predictability and transparency with regard to whether the disputed patent is essential to the standard and would facilitate licensing negotiations conducted by any other parties. However, most SSOs only ask for ex ante disclosure and do not check the essentiality. For example ETSI, to which over 70% of the worldwide SEP declarations were made,[65] provides

> Information on IPR by ETSI 7.1 Any published STANDARD or TECHNICAL SPECIFICATION shall include information pertaining to ESSENTIAL IPRs which are brought to the attention of ETSI prior to such publication. 7.2 ETSI shall establish appropriate procedures to allow access to information at any time with respect to ESSENTIAL IPRs which have been brought to the attention of ETSI.[66]

Fortunately, the EC "considers that declared SEPs should be subject to reliable scrutiny of their essentiality for a standard, and will launch a pilot project for SEPs in selected technologies with a view to facilitating the introduction of an appropriate scrutiny mechanism".[67] When considering essentiality checks, the EC suggests that "patent offices may well be natural candidates for exploiting synergies and reducing costs", and "will support further analysis of their feasibility to ensure effective and proportionate solutions. Depending on the outcome of this project, an independent European body could be tasked to proceed with SEP essentiality assessment".[68] Japanese Patent Office (JPO) implements the new operation of the advisory opinion system to determine standard essentiality from April 1, 2018, based on Article 71(1) of Japanese Patent Act.[69] However, we argue that considering the cross-border character of SEP disputes, a mechanism to check the essentiality of declared SEPs conducted by SSOs would be the most efficient way. After the finalization of standards, the SSOs should conduct essentiality checks, at least via systematic sampling, and make the results available to the public.

3.2 *FRAND-compliant royalty rates depository*

In order to ascertain whether the royalties that the SEP owners are charging are fair and free of discrimination, comparable licenses are of high reference value.[70]

65 Tim Pohlmann & Knut Blind, Landscaping Study on Standard Essential Patents, 2016, 53, available at http://ec.europa.eu/DocsRoom/documents/20741/attachments/1/translations/en/renditions/native.

66 ETSI Intellectual Property Rights Policy (n 63).

67 EC, 1.2.3. Com/2017/0712 Setting out the EU approach to Standard Essential Patents.

68 *Id.*

69 See JPO, Implementation of the New Operation of Advisory Opinion System to Determine Standard Essentiality and Publication of the 'Manual of "Hantei" (Advisory Opinion) for Essentiality Check', available at www.jpo.go.jp/e/system/trial_appeal/hantei_hyojun.html. Article 71(1) of Japanese Patent Act provides "A request may be made to the Patent Office for its advisory opinion on the technical scope of a patented invention."

70 See e.g. U.S.: *Microsoft Corp. v. Motorola, Inc.*, No. C10-1823JLR, 2013 WL 2111217; Germany: *Saint Lawrence v Vodafone*, Dusseldorf District Court, 4a O 73/14, March 31,

However, as a result of wide use of NDAs, prior license information is seldom disclosed. Parties have to negotiate based on their own, sometimes limited licensing experiences, and asymmetric information. A transparent and competitive licensing market can hardly exist. SEPs licensing negotiation are carried out in a black box, which is the breeding ground for abusive conduct.[71] As to how to guarantee licensing SEPs in a FRAND way, ETSI is only paying lip service, and "expects its members (as well as non-ETSI members) to engage in an impartial and honest essential IPR licensing negotiation process for FRAND terms and conditions".[72] The EC has therefore rightly pointed out that

> there is a need to increase accessibility of experience, expertise and know-how around FRAND determination. Valuable insight has been gained and approaches developed from licensing agreements, mediations, arbitrations and court decisions over many years. Significant resources and efforts have been devoted to clarifying, analysing and valuing patents and technology. As there is no common repository for such expertise, work and research may be unnecessarily duplicated at serious cost to the parties involved. More accessible FRAND-related information could increase predictability for businesses such as IoT players, facilitate the licensing process in general and provide support and benchmarks in dispute settlement.[73]

We advocate that it is worth considering imposing a duty on SSOs to ask SEP owners to deposit the FRAND-compliant royalty rates that they have charged other licensees for the same SEPs and even for different SEPs. The royalty rates can hardly be trade secrets, as they are part of the FRAND commitment that would inevitably be subject to examination. Even if royalty rates were recognized as trade secrets, depositing royalty rates at SSOs will not necessarily compromise their secrecy when necessary protection measures are put in place. The depositing of this information will lead to accumulation of accessibility of experience, expertise and know-how around FRAND determination, which will enable SSOs to provide assistance to courts and competition authorities, and even to mediate FRAND terms and conditions by themselves.

3.3 Concretizing FRAND-compliant terms

SSOs have largely refrained from operationalizing FRAND terms for two important reasons: technical experts are not in a good position to decide on

---

2016; UK: *Unwired Planet v Huawei* judgment ([2017] EWHC 2988 (Pat)); PRC: *Huawei v. InterDigital*, Guangdong Higher People's Court, Judgment of October 16, 2013, (2013) Yue Gao Fa Min San Zhong Zi 305.

71 For example, in its SEPs portfolio licensing agreement, Qualcomm prohibits its licensees from reselling acquired chips to its competitor, which is covered by the NDA. See Kung-Chung Liu, Chapter 1 of the present book.

72 ETSI, § 4.4 Guide on Intellectual Property Rights.

73 EC, 2.4. Com/2017/0712 Setting out the EU approach to Standard Essential Patents.

licensing terms, and SSOs fear antitrust violation for possible price fixing.[74] However, some SSOs have begun to break up the harmonized IPR policy practice and defined FRAND more clearly, making efforts to enforce the FRAND commitment. In 2007, the same year the EC initiated formal proceedings against Qualcomm (though it did not issue a Statement of Objection and eventually dropped the investigation without action), VITA (the organization promulgating VME bus standards) adopted an ex ante royalty disclosure policy that asks their members to declare the maximum royalty rate for their patents with essential claims, as part of its licensing declaration.[75] If a member fails to do so, it has to license its patents on a royalty-free basis. It is voluntary with IEEE and ETSI.[76]

Following an increase in patent litigation over the meaning of F/RAND terms, IEEE has concluded that the ex ante disclosure provision it had included in its patent policy in 2007 had not helped to define RAND as it had anticipated.[77] In 2015, IEEE adopted a dramatically different patent policy, which is regarded as deviation from the so-called FRAND harmony.[78] The new policy includes the following elements: (1) a new definition of "reasonable rate" that significantly devalues SEPs through (a) limiting the value to be based on the value added to the smallest saleable compliant implementation, (b) requiring the value to reflect relative contribution by other patent holders, and (c) effectively eliminating comparable licenses as a benchmark for value;[79] (2) prevention of

74 Yogesh Pai, Private Proprietary Standards and Public Law: Invoking WTO's Competition Dimension to Avoid Global Market Distortion (November 16, 2012), 21, available at https://ssrn.com/abstract=2177064.

75 According to Renata Hesse & Frances Marshall, in practice patentees usually declare a much higher royalty, which helped little to define FRAND; see Renata Hesse & Frances Marshall, U.S. Antitrust Aspects of FRAND Disputes, in Jorge Contreras (ed.), ***The Cambridge Handbook of Technical Standardization Law*** (Cambridge: Cambridge University Press, 2018), p. 269.

76 Layne-Farrar (n 7) at 6.

77 Hesse & Marshall (n 75) 269.

78 Katznelson (n 26).

79 IEEE-SA Standards Board Bylaws § 6.1 provides: "'Reasonable rate' shall mean appropriate compensation to the patent holder for the practice of an Essential Patent Claim excluding the value, if any, resulting from the inclusion of that Essential Patent Claim's technology in the IEEE Standard. In addition, determination of such Reasonable Rates should include, but need not be limited to, the consideration of: •The value that the functionality of the claimed invention or inventive feature within the Essential Patent Claim contributes to the value of the relevant functionality of the smallest saleable Compliant Implementation that practices the Essential Patent Claim. •The value that the Essential Patent Claim contributes to the smallest saleable Compliant Implementation that practices that claim, in light of the value contributed by all Essential Patent Claims for the same IEEE Standard practiced in that Compliant Implementation. •Existing licenses covering use of the Essential Patent Claim, where such licenses were not obtained under the explicit or implicit threat of a Prohibitive Order, and where the circumstances and resulting licenses are otherwise sufficiently comparable to the circumstances of the contemplated license."

essential patent holders who are willing to commit to grant RAND licenses from seeking an injunction for infringement, regardless of the behavior of the infringer;[80] (3) a newly specified "Compliant Implementation" definition which means any product (e.g. component, sub-assembly or end-product) or service that conforms to any mandatory or optional portion of a normative clause of an IEEE standard, resulting in mandatory licensing on the component level; (4) good faith negotiation obligation without unreasonable delay.[81] The new patent policy also explicitly gives parties that issue a Letter of Assurance (LoA) an option to provide (1) a not-to-exceed license fee or rate commitment, (2) a sample license agreement or (3) one or more material licensing terms. Understandably, the IEEE 2015 patent policy led to criticisms from SEP holders for allegedly hurting their innovation incentives.[82] However, "the impact of the IEEE policy update on the governance of standardization is significant".[83] We are therefore of the opinion that IEEE 2015 patent policy could serve as a model for all SSOs to fulfill their mission and purpose.

80 IEEE-SA Standards Board Bylaws § 6.2 provides: "A statement that the Submitter will make available a license for Essential Patent Claims to an unrestricted number of Applicants on a worldwide basis without compensation or under Reasonable Rates, with other reasonable terms and conditions that are demonstrably free of any unfair discrimination to make, have made, use, sell, offer to sell, or import any Compliant Implementation that practices the Essential Patent Claims for use in conforming with the IEEE Standard. An Accepted LOA that contains such a statement signifies that reasonable terms and conditions, including without compensation or under Reasonable Rates, are sufficient compensation for a license to use those Essential Patent Claims and precludes seeking, or seeking to enforce, a Prohibitive Order except as provided in this policy."

"The Submitter of an Accepted LOA who has committed to make available a license for one or more Essential Patent Claims agrees that it shall neither seek nor seek to enforce a Prohibitive Order based on such Essential Patent Claim(s) in a jurisdiction unless the implementer fails to participate in, or to comply with the outcome of, an adjudication, including an affirming first-level appellate review, if sought by any party within applicable deadlines, in that jurisdiction by one or more courts that have the authority to: determine Reasonable Rates and other reasonable terms and conditions; adjudicate patent validity, enforceability, essentiality, and infringement; award monetary damages; and resolve any defenses and counterclaims. In jurisdictions where the failure to request a Prohibitive Order in a pleading waives the right to seek a Prohibitive Order at a later time, a Submitter may conditionally plead the right to seek a Prohibitive Order to preserve its right to do so later, if and when this policy's conditions for seeking, or seeking to enforce, a Prohibitive Order are met."

81 IEEE-SA Standards Board Bylaws § 6.2 provides: "The Submitter and the Applicant should engage in good faith negotiations (if sought by either party) without unreasonable delay or may litigate or, with the parties' mutual agreement, arbitrate: over patent validity, enforceability, essentiality, or infringement; Reasonable Rates or other reasonable licensing terms and conditions; compensation for unpaid past royalties or a future royalty rate; any defenses or counterclaims; or any other related issues."

82 See Fair Standards Alliance and Shengtao Hu, Chapter 16 of the present book.

83 Pentheroudakis & Baron (n 8) 15.

4 To light-handedly regulate self-regulation by SSOs through international cooperation among key competition authorities

Almost all the SSOs are headquartered in the EU and U.S. Therefore, if competition authorities on both sides of the Atlantic can cooperate to regulate SSOs, which should not be too big a problem, as both the USFTC and EC have dealt with SSOs-related issues, that would be a good start. Important and more challenging, though, is how to integrate competition authorities of other jurisdictions. It is only fair and appropriate to include at least competition agencies of Taiwan, South Korea and China, as they have dealt with FRAND licensing of SEPs issues, as the present book sufficiently illustrates, and the three economies are important in the ICT industries (for more details, see Chapter 1 of the present book).[84] The five competition agencies can form a consortium or working group. Among the many reform proposals targeting IPR within standard setting contexts are suggestions that competition agencies either dictate policy rules for SSOs or at least define guidelines that SSOs would then be (strongly) encouraged to follow.[85] We are of the opinion that heavy-handed interventions are unwarranted",[86] and rather, some guidelines from competition agencies in the aforementioned key jurisdictions may be more useful.

As suggested by Chryssoula Pentheroudakis and Justus Baron, policy action should encourage more clarity and flexibility in the definition of FRAND. Articulating a common set of criteria and guidelines for practice – anchored in a clear definition of FRAND – could facilitate private negotiations, enhance due diligence on behalf of the parties, limit the need to seek a third-party determination of a FRAND rate, and, in the case of litigation, help courts set convergent standards while allowing flexibility on a case-by-case basis.[87]

5 Conclusion

Under the perspective of competition law, standard setting is a kind of collaboration which has some restraints on competition, and therefore SSOs should minimize the restraints on competition to the extent reasonably possible. In addition, in the area of standard setting, SSOs have already taking over the role of national states, and should all the more be subject to a certain degree of oversight and regulation. We therefore suggest SSOs should be mandated by a consortium

84 Chryssoula Pentheroudakis & Justus Baron argue that "global advocacy and the ongoing dialogue between European policymakers and their counterparts in the US, China and *the rest of the world* could counteract the potentially distortive effects of domestic policies by exploring *common ground and identifying best practices* that safeguard the interests of society as a whole." "(emphasis added) See Pentheroudakis & Baron (n 8) 16 and 169.

85 Layne-Farrar (n 7) 1.

86 *Id.* at 2.

87 Pentheroudakis & Baron (n 8) 15, 165.

of the aforementioned five key national competition authorities to play a more important role in seeing through the smooth FRAND licensing of SEPs by having to conduct essentiality checks, to be the depository of information on FRAND-compliant royalty rates, to concretize FRAND-compliant terms and to provide FRAND royalty arbitration. "Good governance rules" for SSOs must be developed under competition law.[88]

88 Born Lundqvist, *Standardization under EU Competition Rules and US Antitrust Laws: The Rise and Limits of Self-Regulation* (Cheltenham, UK: Edward Elgar, 2013), p. 336.

Index

For Product Safety Concerns and Information please contact our EU representative GPSR@taylorandfrancis.com
Taylor & Francis Verlag GmbH, Kaufingerstraße 24, 80331 München, Germany

www.ingramcontent.com/pod-product-compliance
Ingram Content Group UK Ltd.
Pitfield, Milton Keynes, MK11 3LW, UK
UKHW022007180926
475701UK00003B/237